Getting there •
Where to stay • Where to eat

GOING PLACES

Alaska and the Yukon for Families

BY
NANCY THALIA REYNOLDS

Co-author of
*Going Places: Family Getaways
in the Pacific Northwest*

Bergman Books
SEATTLE, WASHINGTON

Also available at local bookstores:

Out and About Seattle With Kids

A comprehensive guidebook with all the information needed to plan family activities in one of the Northwest's favorite cities for families. It includes indoor and outdoor active fun, kid culture, spectator sports, excursions and outings, birthday parties and restaurants. Getting to know the Emerald City is an adventure with this family-oriented book at hand.

Out and About Portland With Kids

This guidebook will help you get to know the Rose City with your family. It introduces the reader to Portland's places, providing information specially geared to families. Included is information on active fun, kid culture, excursions, restaurants and much more. Discover Portland and have fun doing it.

Going Places: Family Getaways in the Pacific Northwest

From spectacular natural features, to city adventures—this family travel guide tells you what you need to know when planning a weekend adventure, or week-long vacation in Washington, Oregon, and British Columbia. You'll get terrific suggestions on where to stay, where to eat, and what to see and do. Peppered with sage advice from parent reviewers, *Going Places* gives the reader the low-down on dozens of family-friendly places.

Copyright ©2005 by Bergman Books

All rights reserved. No portion of this book may be reproduced in any form without written permission from the publisher.

Printed in the United States of America

Distributed by Sasquatch Books
Seattle, Washington
www.sasquatchbooks.com
custserv@sasquatchbooks.com

Library of Congress Cataloging-in-Publication Data is available.

10 09 08 07 06 05   6 5 4 3 2 1

ISBN: 1-57061-452-0

Art Direction/Design: Emily Johnson
Cover Illustration: Cary Pillo Lassen
Maps: Kevin Cain

Table of Contents

1 Alaska and the Yukon:
Introduction 5
How to Use This Book 7
Places to Stay 7
Places to Eat 11
What to See and Do 12
When to Visit 12
Preparing for Your Trip 13
Statewide Resources 19

2 Getting There 25
By Air 26
By Land 28
By Sea: Public Ferries 32

3 Alaska Cruises 43
Is Cruising for You? 44
The Cruising Life: A Primer for Families 45
Line by Line 52
Departing from Seattle and Vancouver 61

4 Alaska Panhandle/Inside Passage 69
Ketchikan 75
Sitka 87
Juneau 99
Haines 116
Skagway 124

5 Alaska Highway:
Yukon Territory and British Columbia 135
Getting to the Alaska Highway 140
Trans Canada Highway: Vancouver to Cache Creek 143
Highway 97: Cache Creek to Prince George 144
Alternate Route North: The Cassiar Highway 151
Highway 97: Prince George to Dawson Creek 153
Alaska Highway: Dawson Creek to Yukon Border 157
Yukon Territory 167
Alaska Highway: Yukon Border to Whitehorse 172
Alaska Highway: Whitehorse to the Alaska Border 189
Alaska Highway: Alaska Border to Delta Junction 194
North Klondike Highway: Whitehorse to Dawson City 201
Top of the World and Taylor Highways: Dawson City to Tok 217
Side Trips 219

6 Anchorage and Environs 227
Anchorage 231
Southeast of Anchorage 251
East of Anchorage: Glenn Highway to Glennallen 258

7 Kenai Peninsula 267
Seward 273
Cooper Landing 284
Soldotna 287
Kenai 291
Homer 297
Seldovia 309

8 The Southwest:
Kodiak Island and Dutch Harbor/Unalaska .. 317
Kodiak Island 319
Unalaska Island 335
City of Unalaska/Dutch Harbor 336

9 Talkeetna:
Denali National Park and Environs 347
Talkeetna 354
Denali National Park and Preserve 363

10 Fairbanks and the Interior 377
Fairbanks 383
Chena Hot Springs 403
Richardson Highway: Fairbanks to Valdez 406
Valdez 408

Index 413

Contributors 435

Acknowledgments 439

Feedback Form 443

1 Alaska and the Yukon: Introduction

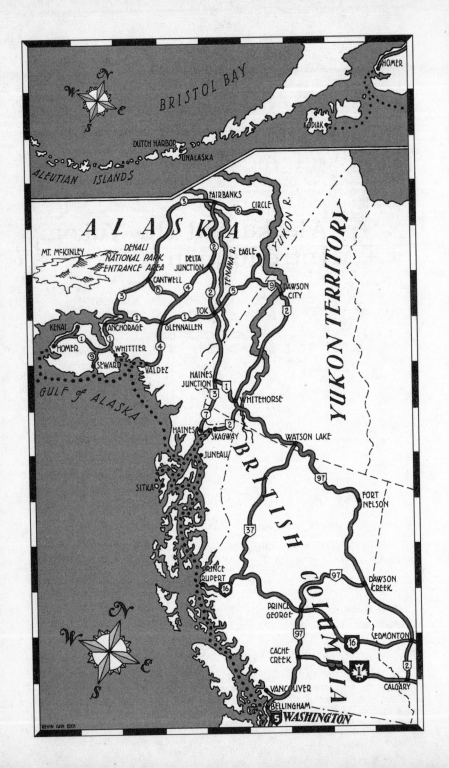

1 Alaska and the Yukon: Introduction

A FAMILY VACATION can be strenuous or relaxing, an adventure or an escape. It can be a journey of discovery or of recognition. A trip to Alaska and the Yukon combines these elements in one unforgettable experience, allowing visitors a rare opportunity to explore one of the last frontiers on our planet. This is where the wide open spaces go on forever. Fjords wind through steep mountains from which enormous glaciers calve into the sea with a noise like distant thunder. Bald eagles line up in the treetops eyeing a rushing river for signs of spawning salmon. A moose daintily picks its way across the highway at sunrise. Far-off mountains seem impossibly close in the clear, unpolluted air. A canopy of stars and an aurora borealis shimmer in the cobalt night sky, unobscured by city lights.

In many ways, visiting this area is more like visiting a foreign country than another state or Canadian province. The culture is different and, given the size and wildness of the state and its distance from the rest of the country, a family vacation here takes careful planning. In *Going Places: Alaska and the Yukon for Families*, we introduce you to some of the best options for a family vacation in Alaska, along with suggestions for how to make the most of your experience.

You'll also find tips tailored to families: how to choose a family-friendly cruise, how to keep the kids entertained on the road, how to manage close encounters with furry, finned, and feathered friends. Along with these are the usual *Going Places* features—parent comments and candid reports on the child-friendliness of popular destinations.

How to Use This Book

For this new *Going Places* title, we've introduced new features and expanded others:

- The presence of a listing in this book, with only a few exceptions, indicates that it has something to offer families. The presence of the ☺ symbol indicates an exceptionally child-friendly establishment or activity.
- Some essays in the book have been provided by parents and children.
- We have included campgrounds as a regular feature under "Places to Stay."
- Expanded resource listings include fun ways for parents and kids to learn more about their destination.

Places to Stay

We have included a range of choices and provided general price information without attempting to give precise dollar figures. Prices are subject to frequent change, so be sure to check when booking to avoid surprises. And remember that there is often enormous variation between high- and off-season prices. If traveling outside of June, July, or August, you can expect to pay as much as one-third less.

Unless otherwise indicated, accommodations described accept credit cards and provide free parking, TVs, and en suite bathrooms. The FYI section lists other important amenities, including kitchen facilities, on-site restaurant, fireplace, swimming pool and exercise facilities, and whether pets are accepted. Unless otherwise specified, cribs and rollaways are assumed to be available on request for a fee; expect to pay about $10 for these extras.

Rate information is for a family of four per night. That usually means a spacious single room with two double or queen beds and/or sofabeds. "Children stay free" means that no charge is made by the hotel for children who sleep in your room with you. If you book a separate room for the kids, you'll have to pay for two rooms. Suites are described, where available. Bear in mind that hotel prices can be higher overall in Alaska than in the "lower 48" and that Yukon Territory prices can be higher than those in British Columbia.

Accommodation rates are classified as follows:

($) indicates rates are $100 or less.

($$) indicates rates are between $100 and $175.

($$$) indicates rates are over $175.

Hotel Chains

Good family accommodation is provided by many hotel chains, whose amenities are generally the same from location to location. A brief description of some chains follows in this section; contact information is included in each section where a chain hotel is available. For example, below you'll find a general description of the Guesthouse Inn chain; in the Anchorage and Fairbanks sections, you'll find contact information for Guesthouse Inns at those locations.

Amenities can vary from site to site. However, if a feature is listed, it is almost certainly going to be available. If a feature is especially important to you, check by phone or Web site before booking.

Choice Hotels: Comfort Inn/Suites, Clarion Suites, Econolodge, Quality Inn

800/4-CHOICE; www3.choicehotels.com
Washington, British Columbia, Alberta, and Alaska locations; children under 19 stay free.

Clarion Inns and Suites ($$-$$$). Spacious rooms with refrigerator and microwave; restaurant; swimming pool and exercise facilities.

Comfort Inns and Comfort Suites ($$-$$$). Large rooms; free continental breakfast; microwave, refrigerator, some kitchens; swimming pool (Anchorage and Fairbanks).

Econolodge ($). Comfortable, but basic; free breakfast.

Quality Inn, Hotel, Suites ($$). Suites with two-room layout; free breakfast; restaurant; swimming pool; exercise facilities. (Fort St. John, B.C.).

Guesthouse Inn/Aspen ($-$$)
800/GUEST4U; www.aspenhotelsak.com
Anchorage, Fairbanks, Juneau, Soldotna, and Valdez locations; refrigerator and microwave; free continental breakfast; exercise room. In Juneau only: family suites with bunk beds and Nintendo. All sites except Valdez: swimming pool.

Hampton Inns, Suites, Hilton Hotels ($$-$$$)
Hampton: 800/426-7866; www.hamptoninn.com; Hilton: 800/774-1500; www.hilton.com
Washington, Alberta, British Columbia, and Anchorage locations.

Hampton Inns and Suites. Free breakfast; Anchorage and Alberta: swimming pool; exercise facilities.

Hilton Hotels. On-site restaurant; swimming pool; exercise facilities.

Holiday Inn, Holiday Inn Express
800/465-4329; www.sixcontinentshotels.com/holiday-inn
Washington, Alberta, British Columbia, and Anchorage locations; family oriented; some allow pets.

Holiday Inn ($-$$). On-site restaurant; kids under 13 eat free; swimming pool, fitness center.

Holiday Inn Express ($-$$). Free breakfast (usually); swimming pool.

Marriott, Courtyard, Residence Inns, Springhill Suites
888/236-2427; www.marriott.com
Washington, British Columbia, Alberta, and Alaska locations. Wide range of amenities and prices: Courtyard and Springhill (low end); Marriott and Residence (high end). At most (except Courtyard) children under 18 stay free. At Courtyard: children under 13 usually stay free.

Courtyard ($-$$ US; $$$ summer Alaska rates). On-site restaurant; swimming pool; exercise room. Service animals only.

Marriott ($-$$$). Restaurant; swimming pool; exercise facilities. Service animals only.

Residence Inn ($$-$$$). Studio to 2-bedroom, 2-bath configuration; kitchen; free breakfast; swimming pool; pets permitted (fee, some sites).

Springhill Suites ($-$$). Refrigerator, microwave; free breakfast; on-site restaurant (some locations). Anchorage and Fairbanks: no restaurant. Swimming pool; exercise facilities.

Ramada Inn, Ramada Inn Limited

888/298-2054; www.the.ramada.com

Washington, British Columbia, Alberta, Anchorage locations. Children under 18 stay free.

Ramada Inn ($$-$$$). Farthest north site is Prince George, BC. Spacious rooms; on-site restaurant; most sites: swimming pool; exercise facilities. Pets usually prohibited, but check.

Ramada Limited ($$-$$$). Central and northern BC, Anchorage. Most: refrigerator, microwave. Some: free breakfast. Quesnel and Fort St. John: swimming pool. Pets allowed some sites; call for details.

Super 8 ($)

800/800/8000; www.super8.com

Central and northern BC; Alaska locations. No swimming pools. Most: children under 13 stay free; free breakfast.

Travelodge ($)

888/515-6375; www.travelodge.com

Washington, BC, Alberta, Alaska locations. Some have refrigerator, microwave, on-site restaurant, hot tub. Juneau: swimming pool. Quesnel, BC and Juneau, AK have "sleepy bear" rooms with VCR, microwave, refrigerator, kid-size furnishings, gift; check Web site for other locations. Pets usually allowed.

Westmark ($-$$)

800/544-0970; www.westmarkhotels.com

Alaska and Yukon locations. Children under 13 stay free. Large properties that cater to tour groups; advance bookings a must. All have restaurants except Totem Square Inn (Sitka) and Denali Sourdough Cabins. Some open May-Sept only.

Forest Service Cabins

The U.S. Forest Service makes cabins available for public use in many western states. Most are located in the nation's two largest national forests, both in Alaska: the Chugach and Tongass National Forests. Cabins are usually, but not always, inaccessible by road, and are accessed on foot or by boat or plane. Expect table and benches, stove, beds and bunks without mattresses, and outhouses. There is no potable water, indoor plumbing, or electricity. Visitors must bring bedding, air mattresses, utensils, water, food, and fuel for the stove. The family dog is welcome, but should be kept on a leash and closely monitored.

These sturdy cabins are usually located in spectacularly beautiful settings overlooking lakes, ocean, or streams, often with panoramic vistas. Families regularly make use of these cabins, which always sleep a minimum of four people and often many more. A-frame cabins contain sleeping lofts. (See "Inside Passage" for a description of one family's visit to a Forest Service cabin, page 84.) Fees vary from $25-45 per night, and permits are required. In summer, consecutive stays

Campgrounds in Alaska and Canada

Campgrounds in Alaska
Going North
www.goingnorthrv.com/parklocator/

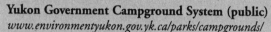

Campgrounds in Canada
Campgrounds in British Columbia (public and private)
www.travel.bc.ca/camping/

Yukon Government Campground System (public)
www.environmentyukon.gov.yk.ca/parks/campgrounds/

Private Campgrounds for RVs
(for owners of recreational vehicles traveling in Canada)
www.gorving.ca/camping/

are limited to three nights in Chugach and seven in Tongass. Reservations can be made up to 180 days in advance. These are immensely popular and the more accessible cabins go fast. For reservations, call the National Recreation Reservation Service (NRRS) at 877/444-6777 or visit the Forest Service Web site at www.fs.fed.us/r10/.

Camping

Public campgrounds in the north offer a predictable range of amenities: Cleared campsites, fireplaces or firepits, clean outhouses and potable water are usually givens. Some have nature trails, beaches and boat-launch facilities, playgrounds, and wheelchair-accessible sites. Researching what they offer (or lack) is easy thanks to helpful Web sites and brochures. The farther afield you go, the less likely you are to encounter flush toilets, electrical hookups, and other features common to campgrounds in more developed areas. In the Yukon especially, you will find rustic public campgrounds amid extraordinarily beautiful surroundings. A selection of state, provincial, and national park campgrounds is described in the text, along with private campgrounds. In Alaska and the Yukon, many hotels, inns, and motels offer RV parking, and some even allow tent camping. They often include handy amenities, from restaurants and gift shops to gas stations. The number of sites may be limited, however, so if you plan to rely on them, be sure to call and book ahead.

Places to Eat

No question, dining can be expensive up north. Where food must be flown or shipped in, as in Sitka or Juneau, prices can strain the family budget. Where deliveries are by road, prices are more comparable to southern Canada and the lower 48, but you should still expect to pay a bit more.

American visitors to British Columbia and the Yukon will find high prices offset by the favorable currency exchange rate.

Northern restaurants tend to be informal and welcoming to families, and in this book you'll find some of the best affordable family-dining options. In bigger towns, you'll notice the usual names in fast food, but outside population centers be prepared for long stretches without a single McDonalds or Burger King. If your kids enjoy fresh salmon or chicken, Alaska's ubiquitous salmon bakes—fixed-price, all-you-can-eat meals, usually served outdoors—are a great option. Expect to pay about $25 per adult, and perhaps half that for kids. The meal includes salad, veggies, and drinks along with a hefty serving of salmon, chicken or ribs, and of course dessert (usually Alaskan blueberry cake). Your kids will find plenty of other youngsters to race around with while you enjoy your meal.

What to See & Do

Alaska and the Yukon are brimming with opportunities for active, outdoor family fun. We include a wide variety of options for all age, fitness, and budget levels. There is plenty to do indoors, too. Museums and science centers offer state-of-the-art exhibits and programs. Alaska Natives and Canadian First Nations operate attractions of historical and cultural interest. Throughout the north, nuggets of living history await exploration, from Gold Rush-era mines to restored riverboats that once plied northern rivers. For attractions, information of interest to parents, such as whether an attraction is suitable for very young children, is included.

When to Visit

Most tourists visit the north in summer. Of course, at this time you'll encounter plenty of other visitors. Alaska's national parks alone accommodate about 2 million visitors annually. If you can, consider making a trip in May, early June, or September. Crowds will be smaller, prices lower, and insects scarcer. As late as mid-September, your youngsters are likely to go to bed before the sun does. In June, there are nearly 19 hours of daylight in Anchorage and Whitehorse, 22 in Fairbanks. But even in mid-summer, if you're willing to rent a car and leave the prime tour destinations behind, you'll find the crowds quickly melt away.

Summer weather is moderate in the panhandle, along the Inside Passage, and around Prince William Sound. Expect temperatures in the 60s to low 70s. In the Yukon and interior of Alaska, temperatures can get very hot on long summer days. You'll find plenty of sun and mosquitoes; see "Things that Bite and Sting," page 18 later in this chapter. If you are going farther afield, to Kodiak or the Aleutian Islands, be prepared for considerably colder temperatures, wind, and rain.

Recent years have brought visitors north in winter, too. Girdwood, 37 miles from Anchorage, has become a major ski resort. Throughout the north, cross-country skiing is available just about everywhere that gets snow. (Remember that much of the panhandle sees little snow in winter.) Snowshoeing and snowmachining are popular across the north. Mushing opportunities are available for all ages and experience levels. Or sit back and watch someone else do it from a ringside seat at the Yukon Quest Dogsled Race between Fairbanks and Whitehorse. In December, Anchorage and Whitehorse experience just five-and-a-half daylight hours, Fairbanks three-and-a-half. While this limits some outdoor options, conditions couldn't be better for viewing the aurora borealis, a growing winter tourist attraction in Alaska.

About Prices

Prices for various attractions are given throughout this book. Consider these as general guidelines, since prices are always subject to change. For Canadian destinations, prices are given in Canadian dollars. For the U.S., prices are in U.S. dollars.

Preparing for Your Trip

What to Bring

Visitors from British Columbia and the Pacific Northwest will be familiar with the injunction to "dress in layers." Some areas are more likely to have cool weather and rain—and others are hotter and dryer—so it's best to be prepared for every eventuality. In general, a T-shirt under a sweatshirt, light sweater, or windbreaker, and shorts under jeans or long pants are the way to go. Zip-off cargo pants that separate into two or three different lengths are handy.

Alaska and the Yukon are known for their large and voracious mosquito population. Bright and dark colors attract these pesky insects. It may seem practical to bring darker colors that hide those chocolate-pudding and grass stains, but it's smarter to go instead for the lightest shades you can find (bugs are less attracted to white or light colors). Fabrics heavy enough to repel Alaska's bugs-on-steroids are the best choice.

Summer
• Lightweight, light-colored summer wear
• Sweatshirt
• Light raingear
• Warm jacket (later than mid-August, nights get chilly; away from the coast, snow can fall in September)
• Light cotton socks
• Warm wool socks
• Hat/sun visor
• Waterproof gloves
• Sneakers/walking shoes
• Hiking boots
• Sturdy, waterproof daypack
• Water bottle
• Sunglasses
• Sunscreen

- Good binoculars (the stronger the better) and/or portable telescope
- Berry and plant identification books
- Insect repellant (brands containing DEET work best, but check with your healthcare provider to get the best protection that's safe for kids)

Winter

Along with summer items, bring layers of clothing for very low temperatures
- Mittens
- Star chart (for stargazing)
- Warm hat that covers ears
- Long underwear (silk is good)
- Extra wool socks

Dressing Your Child for Alaska

This advice is offered by Alaskan Bridjette March who draws on her personal experience growing up, raising a family, and working as a travel agent in Alaska.

It is important to choose appropriate attire for visits to Alaska. No matter where you visit, there is one constant to Alaskan weather—it changes, and it changes rapidly! It's a good idea to visit Web sites that can give you a clue to weather patterns for the period you are visiting. Although it won't give you the variations for each day, the overall temperatures can give you some idea about appropriate clothing. The magic tool for comfort in Alaska is layering. Although each region of the state has unique climatic features, this concept applies to all regions and to all seasons.

In Summer

Southeastern Alaska is similar to the Pacific Northwest. It is glorious and green and almost all the area is on or close to the ocean. Raingear is probably the most useful clothing you can bring. Often, the rain is misty, light, and sporadic, but it can also be a downpour. Any activity near the sea usually means a breeze and cooler temperatures. Underneath the raingear, depending on the weather forecast and season, you might choose anything from shorts and halters to turtlenecks and fleece.

Central Alaska is never too hot. Although shorts and tops and even swimsuits are appropriate on certain days, Anchorage area almost never exceeds 75 F. In the summer, T-shirts, jeans, and windbreakers are adequate. Tennis shoes or light hiking shoes are perfect.

Northern Alaska can get really hot in the summer and equally cold in the winter. Here, shorts and sleeveless tops are comfortable on many days. There are some pesky mosquitoes in summer, so lightweight long-sleeved shirts are helpful too. In Denali National Park and Preserve, be prepared for a wide range of temperatures. In summer, a turtleneck suits on some days; a T-shirt on others. Take a daypack for these types of places and layer: T-shirt, turtleneck, fleece vest and windbreaker/raincoat (GoreTex, if possible). Additionally, for hikers polypropylene-type fabrics are better than natural fabrics. They keep the elements at bay and dry out more easily. I love the pants with zippers that allow them to be turned into shorts. What to wear for fishing? The best thing I ever purchased was a rainsuit made by Helly Hansen in a bright cobalt blue! This gear is also excellent for outdoor football games farther south. Even if you're lucky enough to have a clear day out on the ocean or on one of Alaska's many rivers, there is a lot of water spray and lots of it will end up on you. These suits come in children's sizes, too.

I used to tell my friends from "Outside" that any activity is fun provided you are properly dressed and color-coordinated! This goes for hiking, fishing, and even duck hunting. This raingear will hold you in good stead if you take one of the local sightseeing boat trips. It doesn't always rain; if you bring your gear, it most likely won't!

In Winter

Here, layers need to be serious. There are several thicknesses of fleece designed for harsh conditions. My favorite for winter is "expedition weight." For watching the Idita-bike take off from Wasilla in the winter of 2002, I wore silk long underwear, top and bottom, an expedition-weight turtleneck, a sweater, a fleece vest, a GoreTex windbreaker, fleece headband, and fleece mittens. My great-niece was dressed in her regular clothing—turtleneck and warm winter pants, a fleece-lined snowsuit (one-piece), fleece hat, and fleece mittens with straps to keep them from getting lost. We both had Sorel boots good for -20 degrees F.

A Word About Rain

Odds are, you'll be rained on during your visit. Be sure to bring waterproof raingear, including jacket, pants, and hats for everyone. Gloves are a must and waterproof hiking boots are a good idea. Outfits that allow easy movement and that breathe, like GoreTex, are ideal. Most outdoor activities in the north proceed regardless of rain, so it's unlikely that a long-planned kayak adventure or river-rafting trip will be affected. Planning ahead and preparing your kids (and yourselves) for the wet stuff can help you rise above it and have a terrific time anyway.

Keeping Children Safe

Parenting expert Jan Faull has these suggestions for keeping your children safe while in a rugged environment that can pose different dangers than most families confront on a regular basis.

When traveling with children in Alaska or the Yukon, particularly if you plan to hike, camp, or kayak, keep in mind that you are operating in an environment in which they will need careful parental supervision and instruction. While you are likely to do some reading, ask questions of experts who know the territory, follow the directions of your guide, and read all warning signs, your children can't be expected to do any of these things. Preschool-aged children have minimal self-control and even school-aged kids need supervision, as most will proceed without much planning or forethought.

Here are some steps to take to help keep your children safe:

1. Offer information. For instance, in the case of bears, let your children know that a mother bear becomes angry if a person walks between her and her cubs; that bears will keep away from humans, so it's important not to surprise them; and that bears will run after people who are running. (See "Bear Basics" later in this chapter for more tips.)

2. Create rules relating to that information. For instance: don't get between a mother bear and her cubs; whistle, sing, or talk while you hike to warn the bears that you're in their vicinity; don't run if you see a bear; stand still.

3. Practice the rules, and demonstrate them if possible. Tell a real-life story relating to the topic.

4. Reinforce positive behavior. For instance, when hiking, it's critical to stay on the trail and for children to stay in sight. Say, "I see that Rachel and Monica are right in the middle of the trail. I can see you, and I know you're safe."

5. Help your children "read" the environment by explaining what you're seeing and why you're responding as you are: "See these rocks over here; they're slippery with moss and water on them. If you step on them you'll be in danger because you could slip and slide right down this crevasse."

It's good to give reminders of the safety rules and prompt your children as they encounter this challenging terrain. You walk a fine line: keeping a protective eye on your children while providing safe opportunities for them to test their minds and bodies.

Coping With Seasickness

If you travel to Alaska by cruise ship or ferry—or go on one of the many excursions that take you out on the water—chances are good that someone in your family will get seasick. If you've never taken such a trip before, it's best to be prepared. A child who suffers from other forms of motion sickness is likely to get seasick, too, and overall, children are more subject to seasickness than adults.

Seasickness is more likely if you are on open, unprotected waters, and if you are traveling in a small boat or ferry, rather than on a large cruise ship. Sometimes, just getting outside in the open air will ease nausea. In other cases, you might want to use a motion-sickness remedy. Dramamine, available in the U.S., or Gravol, sold in Canada, both available over the counter, are two possibilities. Whenever you purchase these, check for appropriate child doses. And it's not a bad idea to check with your physician before you leave about options and dosages for adults and children as well as effective prescription remedies, if needed.

Crossing the Border

If it's been awhile since you crossed the border between the U.S. and Canada, you're in for a few surprises. Safety and security concerns have caused both countries to revise their border-crossing procedures. Today, you can expect substantial waits at the most popular crossings, such as the Peace Arch in Blaine, Washington, although waits are often much shorter away from the coast and at crossings in the north between British Columbia and Yukon Territory and Alaska.

American and Canadian visitors, including children, must bring either a valid passport or birth certificate. No matter how you travel—by air, sea, or road—these requirements apply.

If you are traveling with children but without both their parents (for example, if you are taking a neighbor's child on a family vacation or if you are traveling as a single parent), be sure to bring a letter from the child's parent(s), notarized if possible (any bank can do this), that grants you authorization to travel with the child.

Up-to-the-minute information on wait times at the border and other matters (such as changes in procedures) can be obtained from U.S. and Canadian government Web sites. Border wait times are usually given only for the larger border crossings; smaller, less-traveled crossings generally don't have long waits.

For Canadian Government border information check www.ccra-adrc.gc.ca/customs/general/times/. For U.S. Government border information check with www.customs.ustreas.gov/sep11infof/.

Bear Basics

All species of North American bears—black, brown, and polar—thrive in Alaska and the Yukon. But to spot a bear in the wild yourself takes a bit of luck (and in the case of polar bears, your chances are nil outside the Arctic). Bear encounters can be wonderful or terrifying or a bit of both. For families who are unaccustomed to the presence of bears nearby, it is essential that everyone be prepared for such encounters, including small children.

We don't recommend northern backcountry camping for families who are unfamiliar with the north and its wildlife. While it's possible to camp and coexist safely with bears, enforcing all the important safety steps—keeping kids close at all times, rigorously separating food and food-covered clothing from the family campsite at night—can be hard. However, car camping and RV camping work very well for families.

Even families who don't camp out may encounter bears on a hike just about anywhere up north. So every child old enough to hike independently (without holding an adult hand) needs to know what to do when confronted by these large, furry mammals. Here's a primer:

- Get up-to-date information on recent bear sightings before you set out on a hike: check with the local visitor center, tourist information center, park headquarters, or ranger station. This information is often prominently posted on bulletin boards. If not, ask. View videos or attend ranger talks on bear safety offered at park visitor centers, even if you won't be camping out. Also check at the trailhead before setting out on a hike. Sometimes sightings are noted there.
- Don't bring the family dog along on a hike in bear country if you can help it. If you must, make sure the dog is leashed at all times.
- Instruct children in how to handle bear encounters, and review the rules each time you set out on a hike. Kids need to learn not to run out of earshot of other hikers or out of parental sight when hiking in unfamiliar terrain. (See "Keeping Children Safe," page 15.)

- Even the youngest child should know never to approach a bear, especially a cub (mom is bound to be close by and anxious to protect her baby).
- Make noise when hiking. Talk loudly, sing, clap hands and wave your arms. Laugh and tell jokes. Bears have excellent hearing and smell and, if they have time, will generally avoid humans.
- If you encounter a bear, stop and back off slowly, diagonally if possible. Talk to it and wave your arms. The goal is to help the bear identify you as human (and not prey). Pick up small children and hold them close.
- If a bear approaches, stop moving; do not run away (any bear can easily out-run you), but stand your ground. Do not stare at the bear. Talk to it calmly; if it approaches, raise your voice and talk loudly. Use a human voice. Don't growl or squeal.
- If a bear charges (unlikely in the extreme), fall to the ground and play dead. Curl up in a ball facing down (if you're wearing a backpack it can help shield you) with your hands behind your neck and elbows folded in front of your face.
- If you are camping out, even in a large park campground, you'll still need to follow the stringent rules for storing food and disposing of garbage. These rules help keep you and all other humans safe and also protect the bears. Acquiring a taste for human food amounts to a death sentence for a bear.

Things that Bite and Sting

If there is one indispensable item every summer visitor needs to bring on a visit to the northern interior, it's bug juice. Clothing that protects against bugs is another essential. Mosquitoes and their annoying brethren—black, deer, and horse flies—are all plentiful. Fending them off can be annoying for adults and traumatic for kids; a trip to Fairbanks' Creamer's Field in July is likely to be sheer misery if you aren't well protected. What can you do to keep your family as bite-free as possible?

Mosquitoes are drawn to bright colors, so dress in light, neutral tones and cover up as much as possible. Bring along oversized long-sleeved, very light-weight white shirts for everyone that you're willing to dispose of after the trip when they've been stained with sunscreen and insect repellent.

Visit a good recreational equipment store for a variety of ingenious options designed to help you outwit stinging critters. A good bet is a lightweight hat with a mosquito net attached that unfolds to cover the head and shoulders.

Bring a good sunscreen and insect repellent (formulas containing DEET are the most effective) for all family members; but ask your healthcare provider for advice before choosing coverage for children under 12.

When possible, choose cool, windy days for outdoor activities when bugs will be fewer. Remember that swamps and still water attract mosquitoes. And bear in mind that early morning and late evening are the bugs' favorite times to congregate. Before committing to an outdoor tour, find out which insects will be likely to join you on your trip. And ask for advice; outfitters may have good tips on avoiding bites.

A good read about mosquitoes that kids will enjoy is *The Mosquito Book*, by Scott Anderson and Terry Dierckins (Dennoch Press, 1998). In addition to answering every mosquito question a child could think up (such as "Why do mosquitoes like ankles so much?"), it serves up grisly facts kids love to share ("It would take 1,120,000 bites to drain the blood from an adult human being.") along with useful information about bite prevention and treatment.

Not all the insects you'll encounter will be mosquitoes; to help kids learn about others, the National Audubon Society's *First Field Guide to Insects* (Scholastic, 1998) offers an introduction to a wide variety of insects and information about their habits and habitats. For the very youngest scientist, *Amazing Insects*, one of the Eyewitness Juniors Series (Knopf, 1993), is a useful guide.

Kids will enjoy reading the insect-based recipes at www.ent.iastate.edu/misc/insectsasfood/, even if they're not inspired to actually cook them. The Young Entomologists Society Web site (members.aol.com/YESedu/mainmenu/) lists abundant resources to help kids learn about a host of creepy crawlies.

Statewide Resources

At the end of sections, you'll find useful resources for further exploring that region. Here are some helpful statewide resources.

Visitor Information

State of Alaska Visitor Information
www.dced.state.ak.us/tourism/sources/visinfo/

Juneau Office
217 2nd St, Ste 201, Juneau, AK 99801; 907/586-2323;
e-mail: asccjuno@ptialaska.net

Anchorage Regional Office
PO Box 91896, Anchorage, AK 99509; 907/278-2722;
e-mail: asccanch@ptialaska.net

Alaska Department of Fish and Game
PO Box 25526, Juneau, AK 99802-5526; 907/465-4100;
www.state.ak.us/adfg/geninfo/contact/
Information on fishing, hunting, permits and licenses, and wildlife viewing

Alaska Natural History Association
750 W 2nd Ave, Ste 100; Anchorage, AK 99501-2167; 907/274-8440;
www.alaskanha.org
Nonprofit organization that works to conserve public lands in partnership with local and national agencies

Alaska Public Lands Information Centers (APLIC)
www.nps.gov/aplic/center/
These four interagency visitor centers in Ketchikan, Anchorage, Fairbanks, and

Ten Cool Web Sites for Kids

Children can take part in the fun of planning a trip by doing some of their own research. These Web sites offer especially kid-friendly information on northern geology, biology, history, native cultures, and more.

Anchorage Museum of History and Art
(www.anchoragemuseum.org/kids/)
This museum offers a host of excellent programs for children and families. The Kid's Corner page offers a variety of online opportunities to learn about Alaska's heritage.

Brown and Grizzly Bears *(www.bear.org)*
Bears are among the most popular attractions in the north, so visitors of all ages should find this site interesting. Kodiaks, grizzlies, and more are featured here, with photos and fact sheets. Younger kids will enjoy visiting the kids' area.

Earthquakes for Kids & Grownups *(earthquake.usgs.gov/4kids/)*
This young-user-friendly site run by the U.S. Geological Survey has plenty to interest earthquake enthusiasts young and old.

Geophysical Institute of the University of Alaska
(www.gi.alaska.edu)
At this site, check out recent earthquakes in Alaska, discover the latest volcanic hotspots, and view astonishing auroras. There is an aurora forecast, lots of cool weather science, and much more, including links to good kid-science sites.

Tok offer information on parks, camping, fishing, tourism, natural resources, and more. National and state agencies are represented (see "Resources" under those sections). The Web site has valuable information helpful in planning a visit.

Alaska Wilderness Recreation and Tourism Association
2207 Spenard Rd, Ste 201, Anchorage, AK 99503; 907/258-3171;
www.awrta.org
Information on planning a trip to the Alaskan wilderness

National Wildlife Federation
11100 Wildlife Center Dr, Reston, VA 20190-5362; 703/438-6000; www.nwf.org
The largest member-supported conservation association in the United States, the NWF is a good place to research Alaska's wildlife, natural history, and conservation issues. It contains many resources just for kids. To help your young naturalist get up to speed, the NWF also publishes three magazines for children: *Wild Animal Baby* (for the teething and crawling set); *Your Big Backyard* (for ages 3-7); and *Ranger Rick* (for older elementary school-age kids).

U.S. Fish & Wildlife Service (for system of Alaska National Wildlife Refuges)
www.r7.fws.gov

National Audubon Society *(www.audubon.org/bird/watch/kids/)*
Using the ideas offered by the WatchList for Kids can help children become knowledgeable birders.

National Oceanic and Atmospheric Administration
(www.education.noaa.gov/students/; www.education.noaa.gov/coolsites/)
At these sites, kids can explore weather, climate change, and the oceans and coast. Perennial kid favorites like tornadoes, hurricanes, and tsunamis get star treatment; games and activities are provided.

National Snow and Ice Data Center *(nsidc.org)*
This site provides information, activities, and "cold links" to information about the icy wet stuff.

Ultimate Iditarod *(www.ultimateiditarod.com/teachers/)*
One of many sites about mushing, this one covers the sport in general, the Iditarod, and mushing events.

Windows to the Universe *(www.windows.ucar.edu)*
This site, especially good for older kids, is operated by the University Corporation for Atmospheric Research. It contains interactive pages on the aurora, outer space, the weather, and more.

Yukon GenWeb Links for Kids *(www.rootsweb.com/~cangwkid/Yukon/)*
This page contains an assortment of links to kid-friendly topics of interest in the Yukon and Alaska, from Klondike Gold Rush history to First Nations cultures. ▣

Challenge Alaska
888/430-2738; www.challenge.ak.org
Recreational opportunities for people with disabilities in Alaska

ExploreNorth
www.explorenorth.com
This Web site covers and links to sites about the circumpolar north, including Alaska and the Yukon. A good all-purpose site for travel and tourism information.

Yukon Department of Tourism
Box 2703, 1st Floor, 100 Hanson St, Whitehorse, YK Y1A 2C6;
867/667-5036; www.touryukon.com

Books
There are many wonderful books about Alaska and the Yukon for all ages along with excellent field guides to regional flora and fauna.

Armstrong, Robert H. *Guide to the Birds of Alaska.* Alaska Northwest Books, 1980.

Cook, James. *The Journals of Captain James Cook,* Beaglehole, ed. Boydell & Brewer, 1999. Read the fascinating story of the explorer's travels.

Ewing, Susan. *Great Alaska Nature Factbook: A Guide to the State's Remarkable Animals, Plants, & Natural Features.* Alaska Northwest Books, 1996.

Ford, Corey. *Where the Sea Breaks Its Back: The Epic Story of Early Naturalist Georg Steller and the Russian Exploration of Alaska.* Alaska Northwest Books, 1992. This classic tells the exciting story of Steller's journey of discovery with the second Bering expedition to Alaska in 1741.

Lopez, Barry. *Arctic Dreams: Imagination and Desire in an Arctic Landscape.* Bantam Books, 1996. This work is an extraordinary synthesis of natural history, personal reflection, and travel in the far north.

McPhee, John. *Coming into the Country.* Noonday Press, 1991. This vivid account of Alaska's emergence into statehood has become a classic.

Mergler, Wayne, ed. *The Last New Land: Alaska Past and Present,* Alaska Northwest Books, 1996. This comprehensive anthology of writings on Alaska ranges from creation myth to contemporary memoir.

Pedersen, Gunnar. *The Highway Angler. Fishing Alaska Publications,* 1999. In successive editions of this comprehensive guide, readers are shown how and where to fish throughout Alaska.

Ritter, Harry. *Alaska's History: The People, Land, and Events of the North Country.* Alaska Northwest Books, 1993.

Smelcer, John E. *The Raven and the Totem: Traditional Alaska Native Myths and Tales.* Salmon Run Press, 1992. In this collection of 60 tales, imaginative and haunting Alaska Native legends are brought to life.

Wolfe, Art, and Nick Jans. *Alaska.* Sasquatch Books, 2000. Beautiful photos and text introduce the reader to the landscapes and wildlife of the state.

Good Reads for Older Kids

Kaniut, Larry. *Danger Stalks the Land: Alaskan Tales of Death and Survival.* St. Martin's Griffin, 1999. Although a good choice for teens, this collection of thrilling tales could scare younger children.

Krakauer, Jon. *Into the Wild.* Knopf, 1997. This is an unsettling, yet mesmerizing account of a young man whose beliefs led him into the wilderness north of Denali National Park, not far from the Parks Highway, where he lost his life. Mature teens will find it thought-provoking.

Specht, Robert. *Tisha: The Story of a Young Teacher in the Alaska Wilderness.* Bantam Books, 1982. This well-told story has become a classic and will appeal to children middle-school age and older.

Walsh Shepherd, Donna. *Alaska, America the Beautiful.* Children's Press, 1999. A concisely written history of Alaska illustrated with photos, this book is ideal for kids 9-12.

Books for the Whole Family

Alaska Almanac. Alaska Northwest Books. This is an annual compendium of fascinating Alaska facts.

The Unabridged Jack London. Running Press, 1981. This contains all the London classics.

Paulsen, Gary. *Winterdance.* Harcourt, 1994. A popular children's author tells the exciting and hilarious story of his adventures running the Iditarod.

Service, Robert. *The Spell of the Yukon.* Parents will remember these vivid poems, fun to read aloud.

Read-Aloud Titles for Younger Kids

Each of these picture books appeals to young children, with interesting text and vivid northern images.

Aasch, Frank. *Song of the North.* Harcourt, 1999.

Cartwright, Shannon and Charlene Kreeger. *Alaska ABC.* Paws IV, Sasquatch Books.

Gill, Shelley and Shannon Cartwright. *Alaska Mother Goose.* Paws IV, Sasquatch Books, 1992.

Harrison, Ted. *A Northern Alphabet.* Tundra Books, 1989.

Luenn, Nancy. *Nessa's Fish.* Atheneum, 1993.

Murphy, Claire Rudolf. *A Child's Alaska.* Alaska Northwest Books, 1994.

Sabuda, Robert. *The Blizzard's Robe.* Atheneum, 1999.

A Note About Web Site URLs

URLs can change, and frequently do. In this book we give you the full Web address for the page on a given Web site to which we are referring you. If you encounter difficulties navigating to it, try retyping the address into your browser, leaving off the page. That is, if you can't get to www.gorving.ca/camping/, type in www.gorving.ca; once you have reached the Web site, you can search for the page you want.

Tell Us More

We'd love to hear about your own family's experiences in Alaska and the Yukon. Did we leave out a wonderful destination? Is there something you'd like other families to know about a destination covered here? At the end of this book, you'll find a form to fill out to help you share your discoveries with us. *We look forward to hearing from you.*

2 Getting There

2 Getting There

"GETTING THERE IS half the fun!" We've often heard this said but it takes on a new meaning when it comes to Alaska and the Yukon. Unless you fly to Alaska, getting there will take awhile. For many families, this fact is the biggest obstacle to planning a northern vacation. To overcome it, you'll need to embrace the trip itself as an integral part of your getaway.

For a taste of Alaska when time is limited, nothing beats flying. But if you've got the time, don't rule out other options. Every year families drive the Alaska Highway (also known as the AlCan) and live to tell the tale; quite a few even make the round trip! Others fly or take the Alaska ferry or a cruise up the Inside Passage.

By Air

To Alaska

Alaska Airlines (800/252-7522; www.alaskaair.com) serves major Alaska destinations and many smaller ones; Alaska also flies nonstop from west-coast U.S. cities to Juneau and from there to other destinations along the Inside Passage. Continental (800/525-0280, U.S.; 800/231-0856, outside the U.S.; www.continental.com), Delta (800/221-1212; www.delta.com), Northwest (800/225-2525; www.nwa.com), and United Airlines (800/864-8331; www.ual.com) also serve Anchorage. From Anchorage, flights connect with Alaska Airlines flights to Fairbanks, Kodiak, and other points.

To Yukon Territory

Canadian carrier **Air Canada** (888/247-2262; www.aircanada.ca.com) flies between major U.S. cities, Canadian cities, and Whitehorse. Flights require a change of planes in Canada, usually Vancouver. **Air North** (800/764-0407, U.S.; 800/661-0407, Canada; www.flyairnorth.com) flies between Whitehorse and Fairbanks.

In Alaska and the Yukon, there are many small airlines, air charter services, and air taxis. If your destination is not served by a major airline, it is almost certain to be served by a small air service. To locate in-Alaska air carriers, check the State of Alaska Web site: www.dced.state.ak.us/tourism/getting/airwithin/. You'll also find a listing of charters and air taxis at www.outdoorsdirectory.com. For a selection of Yukon Territory regional air services, charters, and taxis, click the Transportation button on the Yukon Web site at http://TourYukon.com.

Coping With the Brave New World of Air Travel

A few extra preparations will make your flight more pleasant and minimize hassles. Bring a passport or birth certificate for all family members if taking an international flight. For domestic flights, you'll need government-issued (federal, state, or local) photo ID for anyone age 16 and older; it's a good idea to have government-issued ID for children, too, such as Social Security cards. Keep these handy at all times. These rules are subject to change, so check with your airline or travel agent when you book.

Pack all sharp or even remotely hazardous objects in checked luggage. Check with your airline about their rules for carry-on luggage. U.S. federal regulations limit each air traveler to one piece of carry-on luggage in addition to one smaller item such as a small backpack or purse. Airlines set the rules for permissible carry-on sizes for their planes; check with your airline for specific sizes. If you don't purchase a separate seat for a small child, that child will not have a carry-on allowance.

Include snacks, books, games, paper and drawing materials, and changes of clothes in carry-on luggage. Airlines continue to downsize food service and other in-flight amenities, so bring extra snacks and pack accordingly.

Hand-carry film through metal detectors. Airport luggage screening can irreparably damage film; the Anchorage airport uses scanning equipment that is almost certain to do so.

When you must change planes at a major airport, call or check its Web site for family-friendly amenities before you travel. At larger airports, you can rent DVD players and movies for in-airport and in-flight use (InMotion Pictures, 877/383-8747; www.inmotionpictures.com.) For $12, you get the player, one movie, headset, batteries, and carrying case; each additional movie is $4. Extra headsets are $3. Other options are available. Rentals can be returned at the destination airport or mailed back.

Resources
Books:
Benjamin, Elizabeth. *My First Plane Ride*. Golden Books, 1999 (infant to preschool)

Civardi, Anne. *Going on a Plane*. EDCP, 1989 (infant to preschool)

Rockwell, Anne F. *Planes*. Penguin Putnam, 1985 (infant to preschool)

Windsor, Natalie. *How to Fly: For Kids*. Corkscrew Press, 1995 (ages 8-12)

Web Sites:
Flying with Kids (www.flyingwith kids.com)

Here you'll find articles, checklists, and ideas for families traveling by air with very young kids, links to travel agents specializing in family travel, and companies that make products of interest to families such as backpacks filled with travel entertainment.

Quick Aid Airport Directory (www.QuickAid.com)

This useful site has detailed information on airports, maps, airport services, parking, and hotels. ◼

Flight times to Anchorage
From Seattle = 3.25 hours
From Los Angeles = 5.25 hours
From Salt Lake City = 4.5 hours
From Chicago = 5.5 hours
From New York City = 8 hours
From Miami = 9 hours
Note: Times do not include stopovers for connecting flights.

By Land

Traveling to Alaska by land means driving on Canadian highways, and the Alaska Highway—most of which is in Canada. This highway bears only a superficial resemblance to the dirt road hastily constructed in 1942 by the U.S. Army to supply northern airbases during World War II. Modern motorists find a paved road, traveled daily by cars, trucks, and buses through some of North America's most scenic landscapes, served by gas stations, restaurants, hotels, and campgrounds. Because much of the area is sparsely populated and not over-traveled, you'll find hotels and campgrounds with plenty of space. Along much of the route, wildlife—caribou, black bears, moose, bald eagles, and more—is abundant and visible from the road. Exceptional roadside attractions range from the fabled Liard Hot Springs in the northern Rocky Mountains to Kluane and Wrangell-St. Elias National Parks. (See Chapter 5 for details on the Alaska Highway and other roads north.)

If your family enjoys road trips and the thrill of discovering unique small communities, learning about First Nations cultures, and experiencing extraordinary wilderness scenery, this is the way to go. Along the route you'll find the world's largest network of connected national parks, Canada's highest mountains, abundant wildlife, great hiking, and stargazing without light pollution. Because the distance from the Washington-BC border to Fairbanks is 2,300 miles, you'll need at least two weeks just to drive one way and still have time to investigate attractions along the way.

Alaska and the Yukon by Bus

Yes, it's possible (if not necessarily desirable) to get where you need to by bus. In Canada, **Greyhound** (250/782-4275, 800/661-8747; www.greyhound.ca) serves Prince George, Fort St. John, Chetwynd, Fort Nelson, Watson Lake, and Whitehorse several times a week, year round. **Alaska Direct Bus Line** (907/277-6652, 800/770-6652; www.tok.alaaska.com/directbus/) provides service between Yukon and Alaska cities.

For something completely different—and we mean *completely*—**Green Tortoise** (415/956-7500, 800/867-8647 [U.S. and Canada]; www.green tortoise.com) runs bus tours from San Francisco to Alaska, stopping to pick up passengers along the way. Children 8 and above are accepted; whether they'll have a good time is another matter. For one parent's take on their child-friendliness, check out the Green Tortoise Web site children's page. Buses lack toilets and showers, but do have sleeping areas. It's BYOSB (bring your own sleeping bag), and passengers pay into a food fund for cuisine that is usually vegetarian. Costs are phenomenally low by comparison with other Alaska tours. Their 29-day Alaska expedition, at $1,750 per person, includes 70 percent of meal costs, park entry fees, a variety of activities, bus trip one way, and one-way airfare between San Francisco or Seattle and Anchorage, with a ferry trip along the Inside Passage thrown in. Add-ons resemble the onshore excursions offered on cruise ships, but at far lower cost.

Travel by Rail

Some families drive one way and fly or take a cruise or ferry on the return trip. If you leave your vehicle at home, you can combine rail travel with road travel north by rental car. **Via Rail** (888/842-7245 [Canada], 800/561-3949; www.viarail.ca) offers year-round service from eastern Canada to the Pacific. The two-day train trip from Jasper through Prince George, where you'll need to spend the night, to Prince Rupert is breathtaking; for one parent contributor's experience, see "To Prince Rupert on the *Skeena*," page 30.

The **Alaska Railroad** (800/544-0552, 907/265-2300; www.akrr.com) runs trains daily in summer between Anchorage and Fairbanks, a 12-hour trip; between Anchorage and Seward, 4.3 hours; and Anchorage and Whittier, on Prince William Sound, a 2.5 hour trip.

Land Travel Resources

Car Rentals

Several agencies rent cars, minivans, SUVs, and RVs to drive one way or round trip to Alaska and the Yukon, crossing the Canadian-U.S. border. You'll pay plenty, but deals are available. Because distances are so great, it's to your advantage to choose a plan that includes unlimited mileage. Agencies include **Alamo** (800/462-5266; www.goalamo.com) and **Hertz** (800/654-3131; www.hertz.com).

Print Materials on Road Travel

Help Along the Way: Emergency Medical Services for Alaska's Travelers. Download this useful pamphlet from the Alaska state Web site (www.dced.state.ak.us/tourism/getting/driving/). It has information on equipping a vehicle for travel in the north, basic first aid, state road-safety laws, and locations of emergency services along the way.

The Milepost. Morris Communications. This comprehensive trip planner, first published in 1949, is updated yearly. It contains detailed, mile-by-mile descriptions of all major roads in Alaska, much of BC and the Yukon, and some in the Northwest Territories and Alberta. Included with *The Milepost* is a trip-planning map and the year's Alaska ferry and train schedules, along with useful information on communities large and small, and many photos. Take the entries on accommodation and dining with a grain of salt; these are paid advertisements (so identified). Descriptions of local attractions and

To Prince Rupert on the Skeena

By Christian Boatsman

Canada's VIA Rail operates daylight train service from Jasper, AB, through Prince George to Prince Rupert, BC. The *Skeena* offers breathtaking views of the Canadian Rockies, glaciers, waterfalls, rivers, and fjords, as it travels 725 miles in two days. Traveling by train is great for families because it allows kids more space to spread out. Unfortunately, trains can be slow, and VIA Rail passenger trains do not have the right-of-way over freight trains, so travel time can be a bit unpredictable due to the number of stops required to allow other trains to pass.

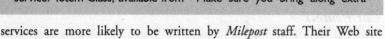

The *Skeena* has two classes of service: Totem Class, available from mid-May to mid-October, is a premium service featuring regional cuisine served at your seat and offering exclusive access to the Park car, with panoramic views from the domed upper deck and lounges on the lower deck. Cost from Jasper to Prince Rupert is $480/adult, $432/ student or senior, and $360/child 2-11 years. Economy Class is available year-round, but passengers are restricted to their own car. Food service (not included in the fare) consists of prepackaged sandwiches, soup, snacks, and drinks, sold whenever the food service attendant is not waiting on Totem Class passengers. Make sure you bring along extra

services are more likely to be written by *Milepost* staff. Their Web site (www.themilepost.com) has useful articles and links.

Books on Rail Travel

Alaska's Railroads. Alaska Geographic, 1992. The history of railroads in Alaska is told in photos.

Clifford, Howard. *Alaska/Yukon Railroads: An Illustrated History.* Oso Publishing, 1999. Great photography accompanied by text.

Cohen, Stan. *Rails Across the Tundra: A Historical Album of the Alaska Railroad.* Missoula, 2001. This is another lyrical, photographic history of Alaskan railroads.

Zahn, Laura and Anita Williams. *Ride Guide to the Historic Alaska Railroad.* TurnAgain Products, 1987

Books for Kids

Pennington, Bonnie. *Tommy's Train Ride on the Alaska Railroad.* Publication Consultants, 1999. A child takes a train ride with his father from Anchorage to Fairbanks with plenty to see along the way.

Siebert, Diane. *Train Song.* Ty Crowell, 1990. This poetic picture book for very young kids echoes the sleepy rhythm of the rails.

food since the food service is spotty. Cost from Jasper to Prince Rupert is $124/adult, $108/student or senior, and $62/child 2-11 years.

East and westbound trains depart only Sunday, Wednesday, and Friday with a mandatory stop for the night in Prince George. Overnight accommodations and transfers are not included in the fare price. Make hotel reservations well in advance since Prince George has a limited number of hotel and guesthouse beds.

The *Skeena* car attendants make announcements in both English and French to keep passengers up to date with arrival times, possible delays, and upcoming sights. Westbound from Jasper, watch for the spectacular view of 12,973-foot Mount Robson on the right side of the train, about 57 miles from Jasper.

Robson is so tall it actually creates its own weather. It's a rare day that the summit isn't shrouded by clouds, which is why Mount Robson is also known as Cloud Cap Mountain.

The terrain the *Skeena* covers varies from the Continental Divide in the high Canadian Rockies to the shores of Chatham Sound near the Pacific Ocean. Watch for occasional wildlife (bears, elk, moose, deer, eagles).

Although the days are long and Economy Class can be a bit confining, families should enjoy a train trip on the *Skeena*. The view from the tracks is spectacular, the countryside is constantly changing, and there's plenty of room to stretch out and relax. If you're not in a hurry, it's a great way to better understand that old adage, "getting there is half the fun." ◙

Thompson, Richard. *Jesse on the Night Train*. Annick Press, 1990. A brave little girl riding the rails in the darkness helps the engineer keep the train running while the passengers sleep.

Road and Weather Conditions

Keeping abreast of road and weather conditions is essential for northern road travel. Major construction and road-improvement projects are an annual certainty. Check state and provincial government Web sites for links to road-construction information. If your route takes you through a construction zone (and most do), be prepared for longer waits and rougher conditions than in the south. Pilot cars guide caravans of motorists through long, gravelly construction sites that sometimes go on for miles. Waits range from a few minutes to half an hour or more. Pack some extra patience, along with water and snacks, and if you're gearing up for a long day of driving, find out whether you'll encounter construction and get wait estimates. Public agencies and tourist information centers often have printed handouts on likely delays.

Alaska

State of Alaska Information Resource Center (www.stateofalaska.com/statelinks/transportation/). This site provides information on Alaska roads, the ferry system, railroads, and airports.

Travel Planning

Planning family vacation activities together is a fun way to get children invested in the adventure that awaits them. Start by helping them explore the region through their interests. If they aren't sure what they want to see, do a little research yourself first and give them a range of options. Paleontology, archeology, and prehistory; gold panning and the Klondike Gold Rush; whale and other sealife; volcanoes, earthquakes, and the Aurora Borealis are popular choices.

Have the kids do some online research and present their case for an activity or focus to the rest of the family. If they're stumped, offer a few tantalizing tidbits of information to whet their interest. For example:

- Alaska is the state farthest north, west, and east in the U.S. (let the kids figure out why).

- Alaska has 17 of the 20 highest peaks in the U.S. and over three million lakes; one of its glaciers is larger than Switzerland. The Yukon River, at 2,200 miles, is the world's fourth longest.

- At least seven varieties of dinosaurs once thrived in Alaska and the Yukon.

- During the Klondike Gold Rush, prospectors used camels as pack animals.

- Because it was so expensive to transport goods to the Klondike, items such as potatoes were worth—literally—their weight in gold.

- Yukon First Nations used to hunt the woolly mammoth (Alaska's State Fossil). A working model of a mammoth trap is on view in the town of Carmacks, YT.

National Weather Service (www.nws.noaa.gov). This federal government site provides detailed short- and long-term weather forecasts.

Canada

Environment Canada (weatheroffice.ec.gc.ca/forecast/maps/yk_e/). This site features Yukon weather conditions.

Provincial Highways Road Reports, Ministry of Transportation (www.th.gov. bc.ca/bchighways/roadreports/roadreports/). Check this site for weather conditions in British Columbia.

Road Condition Report for Yukon Territory (www.gov.yk.ca/depts/cts/highways/report1/). Road conditions in the Yukon are published here.

By Sea: Public Ferries

Forty percent of first-time visitors to Alaska arrive by sea, and that's no surprise. If you're looking for the most relaxing way to go—from no-frills but comfortable ferries to luxurious cruise ships—this is it. You'll be rocked to sleep by gentle waves at night and entranced by orcas and bald eagles by day. Ferry and cruise lines are reaching out to the family-travel market as never before,

- During successive ice ages, a large area of Russia, Alaska, and the Yukon known as Beringia remained ice-free. Giant beavers, ground sloths, and camels flourished; the latter crossed the Beringia land bridge from Asia and are thought to be progenitors of South American llamas.

Resources

Alaska Fast Facts and Trivia (www.50states.com/facts/alaska/). This site contains nuggets of information that should kick-start kid interest in Alaska.

Alaska Science Explained (www.alaskascience.com). This site for kids has intriguing articles, including "The Aurora Explained" and "Let's Make a Rocket"; (materials, parents will be relieved to learn, consist of wood, paper, cardboard and wire).

Alaska Science Forum (www.gi.alaska.edu/ScienceForum/). One of the best all-round, easy-to-use resources for Alaska's natural history, the University of Alaska's Geophysical Institute forum will appeal to kids with an interest in earthquakes, tsunamis, and volcanoes.

Ask a Geologist (earthnet.bio.ns.ca/english/start_geology/). On this site, U.S. or Canadian geologists answer geological queries from older kids.

Facts on the Yukon (www.get2know canada.ca/get2_yk/). You'll get basic facts about Yukon Territory here.

Prehistory of Alaska (National Park Service; www.nps.gov/akso/akarc/). For the young archeologist or anthropologist, this well-organized page offers thumbnail prehistoric sketches of Alaska.◙

and on both you'll find plenty of family fun. This section discusses ferry travel to Alaska. For cruise travel, see the next chapter, "Alaska Cruises."

The government of Alaska operates an extensive ferry system from the northern coast of Washington state up the coast of British Columbia and along the Inside Passage to Alaska. Traveling by ferry is a different experience from cruise-ship travel. You'll have to work a little harder to entertain the kids on ferries, which don't offer the kids' programs that cruise lines provide, but ferry trips are easier on the family budget. Alaska ferries now provide movie theaters, video arcades, and informal dining options; plus, they carry naturalists, artists, and storytellers on summer sailings, and plenty of kids for yours to hang out with. If your plans include exploring Alaska by road, bringing your vehicle avoids the expense of car rental. You can bring the family dog, too. Although comfortable, Alaska ferry accommodation and amenities are not comparable to cruise ship features. Cabins are small and meals are not included in the fare.

Alaska Marine Highway System (AMHS)

Since 1963, Alaska ferries have operated year round in Alaska, connecting the state to Washington and British Columbia. The **Alaska Marine Highway System** (800/642-0066; www.dot.state.ak.us/amhs/) serves 32 communities with nine vessels ranging from small to cruise-ship size. All

Real Deals

One of the best deals in Alaska is the **Alaska Pass** (800/248-7598, overseas: 206/463-6550; www.alaska pass.com), which gives you unlimited travel on the Alaska Marine Ferry System, Alaska Railroad, Alaskon Express Motor-coaches/Grayline, and White Pass and Yukon Railroad (offering service between Skagway and Whitehorse). Pass hold-ers can reach just about every tourist destination in Alaska. Note that airfares are not included in the Alaska Pass. The pass is valid for travel offered between mid-May and mid-September. Fifteen days of con-secutive travel cost $689/adult, $345/child 2-11. Flexible passes are offered from 8-12 days and from 12-21 days. For the shorter period, you can travel for eight days within a 12-day period ($589/adult, $295/child 2-11). For the longer period, you can travel 12 out of 21 days ($699/adult, $350/child 2-11). And if you have more time, there's a pass for 22 consecutive days of travel for $799/adult, $400/child 2-11. With the pass, you receive schedules for all the partic-ipating carriers, a map for planning, and a guidebook with suggested itineraries and supplementary information.◙

carry vehicles and pets. In this section, we look at the ferries that travel between Washington state or British Columbia and Skagway, AK, with stops along the Inside Passage. Other AMHS routes are described elsewhere in this book. Advance bookings are a good idea; if you plan to take a vehicle and/or book a cabin, reserve at least six months in advance.

The Ferry Experience

For adventurous families on a tight budget, the cheapest way to go is to stake a claim in the comfortable lounge seating area, or pitch a tent on deck. This is a long tradition on Alaska's ferries, but it can be noisy. Getting a cabin is defi-nitely worth the price. The cabins are fairly Spartan, but perfectly comfortable.

If you are traveling with the family pet, be aware that access to the car deck is limited when the ship is underway, and the car deck is not heated. Also, if you are traveling in a recreational vehicle, you will not be allowed to stay in it when the ship is underway. You can access your vehicle when the ferry is docked and at one or two 15-minute intervals each day.

You can devise varied vacation scenarios for your family using the Alaska ferry system. However, unless you arrange stopovers in advance (that is, get off the ferry, spend a day or two on shore, then continue on another ferry), you won't have time to see much during the stops en route. With planning, you can craft a trip with overnight stops at Ketchikan, Sitka, or Juneau. This is an affordable and fascinating way to see the Inside Passage. Ferries also stop at smaller communities that lack docking facilities for large cruise ships.

Not only are there interesting things to do in these communities, you'll have fewer crowds to contend with. Reservations are essential; AMHS can help you put together an itinerary that works with their schedules. For tips and details on the coastal communities where the AMHS stops along the Inside Passage (Ketchikan, Juneau, Sitka, Haines, and Skagway), including lodging, dining, and attractions along the ferry routes, see "Inside Passage."

Standard Ferry Amenities

Accommodation   Most ferries have staterooms available. These are two-, three-, or four-berth cabins; most have bathrooms with showers. Many travelers eschew the cost of renting a cabin and instead pitch a tent on deck or lay out a sleeping bag on a reclining deck chair in the solarium, which although partly open to the outside is sheltered and well heated. You'll have to eat in the cafeteria or dining room; using a stove is prohibited. Linens and blankets can be rented on board. All ferries have public showers (most are coin-operated) except the *Bartlett* which has no shower facilities. Only you can determine how well the small fry will take to four nights of this. One popular alternative is to stake out a claim in one of the lounges (those that double as movie theaters are best for the purpose) on a comfortable recliner. Lockers can be rented to stow valuables.

Cost   Children ages 2-11 pay half the adult fare (rounded up to the nearest dollar); kids under 2 ride free. Vehicles are charged according to length. You'll also pay for bicycles or kayaks. Cabin prices depend on size and amenities.

Dining   All ferries have a cafeteria offering plenty of child pleasers. The *Columbia* and *Kennicott* also have a formal dining room with kids' menu. Prices for all dining options are moderate. Ferries also have cocktail lounges (off-limits to anyone under 21).

Entertainment   The larger ferries have lounges that serve as movie theaters some of the time, but don't expect first-run offerings. You're more likely to see a travelogue about Alaska or a family film that's out on video. Ship gift shops stock reading material, toiletries, and other practicalities, along with a few toys and coloring books. In summer several times a day, forest service or national park employees give talks on the region, wildlife, local and natural history. Alaska Natives share fascinating stories about their culture.

Amenities, Ship by Ship

The following ships sail the Inside Passage route (schedules vary depending on season):

M/V Columbia   625 passengers, 134 vehicles; 45 four-berth cabins (some with sitting room), 59 two-berth cabins, 3 wheelchair-accessible cabins; dining room, cafeteria; gift shop, video arcade, forward observation lounge, solarium; Laundromat.

M/V Kennicott   748 passengers, 80 vehicles; 51 four-berth cabins, 34 three-berth cabins, 24 two-berth roomettes, 5 wheelchair-accessible cabins; cafeteria; gift shop, solarium; observation lounges.

☛ **Parent Tip**

If you're traveling on the *Columbia*, ask for a cabin with a sitting room when you book. (You'll need to book early to have a chance at one.) They come with a table and four chairs, plus a bit of welcome leg room. If they're gone, ask for one of the larger cabins amidships. If the wheelchair-accessible cabins are not required by wheelchair users, they are a good bet for families, being a bit roomier. And don't despair if you were too late to reserve a cabin; put your name on the waiting list anyway. There are always no-shows. ◙

M/V Malaspina 500 passengers, 88 vehicles; 46 four-berth cabins, 27 two-berth cabins; cafeteria; gift shop, video arcade, children's play area; solarium, forward observation lounge.

M/V Matanuska 745 passengers, 88 vehicles; 6 four-berth cabins, 82 two-berth cabins, 1 wheelchair-accessible cabin; cafeteria; gift shop, forward observation lounge, solarium; Laundromat.

M/V Taku 450 passengers, 69 vehicles; 6 four-berth cabins, 35 two-berth cabins, 2 wheelchair-accessible cabins; cafeteria; gift shop, solarium, observation lounge.

Bellingham-Based Ferries

The southern terminus of the AMHS is in Bellingham, WA. From here, ferries travel north to Skagway several days a week in summer. If your starting point is Bellingham, your ferry will not stop in Prince Rupert or anywhere else in Canada; the first stop will be Ketchikan.

Some AMHS ferries begin their northward journey in Canada at Prince Rupert, discussed later in this section. The ferry originating in Prince Rupert makes most of the same stops as the ferry from Bellingham.

Getting to the Bellingham Ferry

By Road The Bellingham Cruise Terminal is a two-hour drive north of Seattle on Interstate 5. Parking is available at the terminal (360/676-2500; www.portofbellingham.com; $6/daily, $30/weekly). Frequent daily shuttle service is provided between Seattle-Tacoma International Airport and the Bellingham Cruise Terminal by **Airporter Shuttle** (866/235-5247; 360/380-8800; enjoytheride.com. Cost: $55/adult, roundtrip, $32, one way; $49/seniors, student, round trip, $27, one way; children under 16 ride free with paid adult fare). Operating between Vancouver International Airport, Bellingham Airport, and downtown Seattle and SeaTac is the **Quick Shuttle** (604/244-3744; 800/665-2122; www.quickcoach.com).

By Air Bellingham International Airport is served primarily by Horizon Air (800/547-9308; horizonair.alaskaair.com), a subsidiary of Alaska Airlines. Horizon has multiple daily flights between Seattle and other west-coast cities, and Bellingham.

That Sinking Feeling

Inside Passage seas, for the most part, are remarkably calm. However, there are two places where it is not uncommon to encounter rocky seas: Queen Charlotte Sound and Dixon Entrance. Each is a stretch of water that's unprotected from the west by land. This means that high seas come rolling in from the Pacific, across literally thousands of miles of open ocean.

Queen Charlotte Sound lies between the northern tip of Vancouver Island and the Queen Charlotte Islands. For about an hour, ferries experience a lot of movement here. Farther north, Dixon Entrance, between the northern tip of Graham Island and Prince of Wales Island, is a shorter stretch of open sea that can be rocky as well. Approaching or leaving Sitka, on the west coast of Baranof Island, heavy seas can be encountered. On a cruise ship, it's unlikely you'll feel more than a bit of up-and-down motion, rarely enough to make anyone seasick. But ferries are another matter. They are smaller ships—and also run year round. If you travel off-season, expect rougher seas.

Ferry personnel usually notify passengers about what's coming far enough in advance to take preventive measures to ward off seasickness. For those prone to seasickness—or who might be—try Dramamine or Gravol. Ferry gift shops stock adult-strength Dramamine and an herbal remedy, but don't carry children's dosages, so you'll need to supply those yourself (check with your doctor first). If the worst happens, and someone gets sick, well—they're not alone and ferry staff have seen it all before. Even if kids prove to be great sailors, they may be scared the first time they encounter high seas. And don't underestimate the impact of even mildly rocky seas on small children who've seen the film *Titanic*! As always with kids, if you can prepare them in advance, they're more likely to take the experience in stride. On an Alaska cruise, a parent reviewer's 10-year-old daughter became anxious when the ship went through Dixon Entrance. Unable to convince her child that there was nothing to worry about, the mother finally escorted her to the Purser's office where a friendly young staff member told the girl she needn't be concerned. Just what her mother had told her, but it was more consoling coming from someone in uniform. The girl went back to bed happily and ignored the waves for the rest of the voyage. ▣

By Train Daily train service connecting Bellingham, Seattle, and Vancouver, BC, is provided by **Amtrak** (800/USA-RAIL; www.amtrak.com). The trip between Seattle and Bellingham takes two hours (starting at about $18/adult, one way); between Vancouver and Bellingham, an hour and a half (about $22/adult, one way). Call for details. The Fairhaven Train Station is adjacent to the cruise terminal.

BELLINGHAM

This city of 67,000 makes the most of its scenic waterfront location. Captain George Vancouver found a flourishing Lummi community here when he "discovered" the area in 1792. Lumber mills, coal mining, and the railroad have kept the town humming ever since. The local economy remains diversified, and today Bellingham is one of the state's principal ports.

Places to Stay

Just about every name in hotel chains is represented here. Two options reasonably close to the ferry terminal include **Holiday Inn Express** (4160 Guide Meridian; 360/671-4800; www.sixcontinentshotels.com/hiexpress) and **Quality Inn Baron Suites** (100 E Kellogg Rd; 360/647-8000; www.hometown.aol.com/qibaron). Both have plenty of rooms, heated swimming pools, and allow pets. For more information, see Chapter 1.

The **Fairhaven Village Inn** (1200 10th St; 877/733-1100, 360/733-1311; www.nwcountryinns.com; [$$-$$$]) is two blocks from the ferry terminal. Children under 13 stay free with parents, and there's a free continental breakfast. Rates are moderate to expensive; premises are smoke-free.

What to See & Do

If you have a few hours before your ferry leaves (usually early evening), check out the historic Fairhaven District, with attractive old buildings and interesting shops. Stop by **Village Books** for a browse and a quick meal at the **Colophon Café** (1208 11th St; 360/647-0092. Open Mon-Sat 9am-10pm).

A network of waterfront parks offer great strolling possibilities and the opportunity for little legs to stretch. Adjacent to the terminal, **Marine Park** (200 Harris St) has a covered picnic area and great views.

If the weather drives you indoors, check out the **Whatcom Children's Museum** (227 Prospect St; 360/733-8769; www.whatcommuseum.org/childrens/. Open Sun, Tue-Wed noon-5pm; Thurs-Sat 10am-5pm; closed Mon. Cost: $2.50).

For visitor information, visit the **Bellingham/Whatcom County Convention & Visitor Bureau** at the intersection of Potter & Lincoln. Look for the lighthouse in front (904 Potter St; 360/671-3990; www.bellingham.org. Open daily, 8:30am-5:30pm; closed major holidays).

Prince Rupert-Based Ferries

An alternative to taking the Alaska ferry from Bellingham is to start farther north, from Prince Rupert, BC. Getting here takes a little more time, but the trip to Prince Rupert is lovely. Once you board in Prince Rupert, the schedule is similar to the Bellingham-based ferries, but you'll have shaved a day off your trip.

Getting to the Prince Rupert Ferry

By Air Air Canada's feeder airline, **Air Canada Jazz** (888/247-2262; www.flyjazz.ca), connects Portland and Seattle with Prince Rupert; you'll change planes in Vancouver. **Hawk Air** (866/429-5247, 800/487-1216;

www.hawkair.net) has multiple daily flights between Vancouver and Prince Rupert. The airport is on an island outside of town, a short ferry ride from the town center.

By Train Three times a week, Via Rail's **Skeena** travels between Jasper, AB, and Prince Rupert, a two-day trip with a stopover in Prince George. See "Travel by Rail," page 29.

By Road The Yellowhead (Hwy 16) runs east from Prince Rupert to Prince George and beyond. See "By Land," page 28.

By Boat BC Ferries (250/386-3431, 888/223-3779 [BC only]; www.bc ferries.bc.ca) boats connect Port Hardy, on northern Vancouver Island, to Prince Rupert, a 15-hour trip. Like their Alaska counterparts, BC ferries are family-friendly and visit terrific destinations that are almost impossible to reach any other way. **Pacific Coastal Airlines** (604/273-8666, 800/663-2872; www.pacific-coastal.com) offers daily service between Vancouver and Port Hardy. For information on how to get to Port Hardy and what to do there, contact the **Port Hardy Chamber of Commerce** (P.O. Box 249, Port Hardy, BC. V0N 2P0; 250/949-7622, FAX: 250/949-6653; www.ph-chamber.bc.ca.)

PRINCE RUPERT

This attractive town of 17,500, just 85 miles south of Ketchikan, AK, is worth a look. The AMHS ferry terminal (250/627-1744) is a few miles south of downtown, next to the BC Ferry Terminal (250/624-9627). If you don't have a vehicle, the short taxi ride from downtown will cost about $8.

Places to Stay

The Crest Hotel (222 First Ave W; 250/624-6771, 800/663-8150; www.cresthotel.bc.ca. [$$-$$$]) overlooks the harbor. There's a good fine-dining restaurant here, but a better choice is to head for the Green Apple (301 McBride; 250/627-1666) for great fish and chips. The Crest's fitness facilities are off limits to kids, but overall this is a family-friendly choice. Another good place to roost is the **Eagle Bluff B&B** (201 Cow Bay Rd; 250/627-4955, 800/833-1550. [$]) located in Cow Bay, once an industrial waterfront wasteland, now a distinctive neighborhood of boutiques and coffeehouses. The B&B is perched on a wharf overlooking the harbor and fishing fleet; parent reviewers found it warm and welcoming for families. There are five rooms plus a family suite with a queen bed, double sofabed, bathroom, and a small adjoining room with two single beds; it's popular, so book well in advance.

What to See & Do

In Cow Bay, you'll find the **Visitor Info Centre** (215 Cow Bay Rd, Suite 100; 250/624-5637, 800/667-1994; www.tourismprincerupert.com). A short walk from the Crest hotel is the **Museum of Northern BC** (100 First Ave W; 250/624-5637, 800/667-1994; museumofnorthernbc.com. Hours: Mon-Sat 9am-8pm; Sun 9am-5pm [June-Aug]; Mon-Sat 9am-5pm; closed Sun [rest of year]. Cost: $5/adult, $2/student, $1/child, free/child under 5, $10/family), a superb museum that serves as an excellent introduction to West Coast First

Nations. Check out the totem poles and unusual Argillite carvings. In summer, watch native carvers at work in the carving shed. Allow at least an hour, plus time to explore the excellent, extensive gift shop. The **Kwinitsa Railway Station Museum** is included in price of admission. For a meal, check out **PegLeg's Seaside Grill** (3-101 1st Ave E; 250/624-5667; open daily 11am-9pm [summer]; Sun-Thurs 11:30am-7:30pm; Fri-Sat 11:30am-9pm [rest of year]) with good seafood, a laid-back atmosphere, and kids' menu.

Maritime Travel Resources

Books
Parent Ed
Fredston, Jill. *Rowing to Latitude.* North Point Press, 2001. This is a fascinating account of rowing along wild northern coastlines.

Matsen, Brad and Ray Troll. *Planet Ocean: Dancing to the Fossil Record.* Ten Speed Press, 1995. Wildly and wonderfully illustrated by Ketchikan artist Ray Troll, this book brings the planet's history to life through an examination of the story our oceans tell.

Rennick, Penny, Ed. *Seals, Sea Lions and Sea Otters.* Alaska Geographic, 2000. This book offers a pictorial look at and history of these marine mammals.

Just for Kids
Cole, Janice. *The Magic School Bus on the Ocean Floor.* Scholastic, 1992. Oceanographic science is delivered in digestibly small and funny vignettes.

Day, Trevor. *DK Guide to the Oceans.* Dorling Kindersley, 2002. This is a useful, all-purpose guide.

Kalman, Bobbie. *What Is a Marine Mammal?* Crabtree, 2000. For elementary school-age kids, this book offers a scientific introduction to marine mammals.

Lewis, Paul Owen. *Davy's Dream: A Young Boy's Adventures with Wild Orca Whales.* Tricycle Press, 1988. This is a lushly illustrated classic tale from a Pacific Northwesterner.

Matero, Robert. *The Birth of a Humpback Whale.* Atheneum, 1996. This book teaches elementary school-age kids about humpbacks by telling the life story of one whale.

Page, Debra. *Orcas Around Me: My Alaskan Summer.* Whitman, 1997. This lovely book tells the story of an 8-year-old boy's adventures on a southeast Alaska fishing boat, including encounters with wildlife.

Rockwell, Anne. *Ferryboat Ride!* Crown, 1999. A simple picture book that serves as an introduction to ferry travel for the pre-reading set.

VanCleave, Janice. *Janice VanCleave's Oceans for Every Kid: Easy Activities That Make Learning Science Fun.* John Wiley & Sons, 1996. A variety of activities for kids ages 8-12 teaches them about the oceans; materials and step-by-step instructions are included.

Web Sites

Monterey Bay Aquarium (www.mbayaq.org). This site offers educational resources for adults and kids on the ocean and its residents, including a bibliography and useful links.

Whale Songs (www.whales.ot.com). This site includes cetacean facts and trivia for children.

3 Alaska Cruises

3 Alaska Cruises

FAMILY CRUISING IS now one of the fastest-growing segments of cruise travel. Thanks to vigorous competition, cruise lines today offer fares within the budgets of more families than ever before.

Between May and September, dozens of ships belonging to the six cruise lines profiled in this chapter sail between Vancouver, BC, or Seattle, WA, and points in Alaska. Most cruises run seven days and visit the same five or six destinations: picturesque Inside Passage communities and deep fjords surrounded by glaciers, waterfalls, and mountains. Cruise lines may offer more than one itinerary, but most round-trip cruises include Ketchikan, Juneau, Sitka, Skagway, and either Glacier Bay or Hubbard Glacier. (Glacier Bay National Park has in recent years restricted the number of cruise ships visiting each summer, so there are fewer sailings here than in the past.) Less visited ports include Wrangell, Valdez (on Prince William Sound), and Haines. One-way cruises stop at the same destinations, shuttling Seattle or Vancouver to Seward (on the Kenai Peninsula) and back again.

Is Cruising for You?

The cruise experience can be wonderful, but it's not for everyone. If your priority is to get out into the Alaskan landscape, there are better choices. But if your goal is a relaxing family holiday in which you can explore by day, easily accommodate a wide variety of interests, age groups, and energy levels, and return to your comfortable floating home by night, this could be a great choice.

The price of cruising has remained stable, even dropping in recent years. In 2003, a one-week Alaska cruise on a major cruise line generally cost $700-1,100 per person, with the lowest fare for a seven-day, one-way Inside Passage cruise just under $600. On top of basic fares, discounts may be offered, from free stateroom upgrades to "kids travel free" policies. See "Pricing Cruise Packages" and "Six Ways to Keep Cruising Affordable" later in this chapter.

Cruising is a culture with its own vocabulary, rituals, and traditions and each cruise line has its own take on the culture. Some are formal, elegant, and adult-oriented, others more casual. Some offer trips packed with fascinating classes and workshops on the regions you visit; others place equal emphasis on gambling, Las Vegas-style shows, and socializing. Nowadays, most cruise lines have kids' programs. However, some offer full-day programs in spacious, well-equipped settings while others offer, at best, partial programming. Some cruise lines offer special programs for teens—from teen—only shore excursions to shipboard discos—while others leave kids in this age group to their own devices.

Somewhat ironically, although cruises explore some of Alaska's loveliest scenery and most extraordinary wildlife, cruise travel is not just—or even mostly—about the destination. Cruising culture centers on the life of the ship, not the life on shore. (In fact, some cruisers skip most in-ports and don't even spend a lot of time on deck.)

Another thing to remember is that port time is quite limited. Legal constraints that govern cruise ships prohibit them from docking overnight. On shore excursions, you'll get a taste in small chunks of what Alaska has to offer. You can do a bit of shopping and sightseeing, visit a museum, go on a hike, or take a helicopter tour. But you won't be able to do all those things—on one trip, that is. Maybe that's why so many cruise passengers are return customers!

Taking the time to research options and consider the features most important to your family will help narrow the field of choices and make it more likely that you end up with a trip that lives up to your investment and expectations.

The Cruising Life: A Primer for Families

If you are new to cruising, it's a good idea to familiarize yourself with the overall "cruise culture" before you commit your family to it. Some elements are common to the major cruise lines. How they sit with you will go a long way toward determining your level of enjoyment. Expect to encounter the following on all or most Alaska cruise ships:

Accessibility All the major cruise lines have a limited number of wheelchair-accessible staterooms, usually large and, therefore, among the higher priced. Because many cruisers are elderly folks, ships are designed to help the less able-bodied get around. These features (elevators, wide corridors and doorways, lots of seating in public areas) come in handy for parents juggling toddlers and strollers.

Arrival and Departure Boarding 2,000 passengers and their luggage is a challenge in security-conscious times. Cruise passengers aren't known for traveling light, and it may take awhile before suitcases arrive in the stateroom. In just hours, cruise staff must help passengers disembark, clean and prepare the ship for new guests, and help a new group board. Disembarking at the end of the cruise can be even more taxing. Since passengers usually disembark early in the morning, luggage is collected the night before from staterooms and assembled for customs or transfer. You'll need to stow in carry-on bags everything needed for the next day, as it could be a long time before you see your suitcases. Passengers often make the mistake of trying to be first off the boat. Hallways jammed with people are not pleasant places to hang out, especially for kids lost in the human forest. Find a comfortable spot (your stateroom, if possible) and wait out the crush of departing passengers. When planning your trip, try to arrange transfers so that you won't miss your connection if the cruise is delayed for a few hours.

Baby-sitting In addition to children's programs, cruise lines often provide group baby-sitting while ships are in port so that adults can take a shore

One Child's Alaska Cruise Experience

By Emily Webb

Our ship had everything from a mini mall to swimming pools. (There were two pools. I liked the one outside best.) Downstairs was a beauty salon (well, so I was told; I'm only 10 and I don't need makeovers yet, but I could tell who went in and who went out—in a good way!). There was a movie theater playing everybody's favorite movies, an ice cream bar, shopping areas, a bar for grownups, plus a place just for kids. And kids: if you want, you might get to participate in a live show for everybody on the ship. I was in a Beach Boys number ("Surfing USA"). Anyway, I am going way ahead. You get great treats.

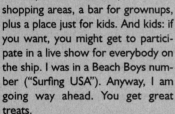

Kids can sign up for really cool adventures. You get to go out on wonderful trips off ship; I went on a kids-only hike. We saw a black bear; he was kind of close, but our guide told us to walk slowly by, and it was OK. That is also good for the parents; you don't have to worry one bit; you can do whatever you want. The library is good if you want a nice quiet area; you can just chill and there are head-to-toe windows so that you can look at the many wonders of wherever you are. I looked up a book that I thought they wouldn't have, and they did.

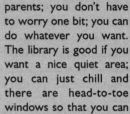

You also get to have your picture taken with the captain. I met a really good friend, Shannon. She is 11 and lives in California. The memories you get are ones you can keep forever. I loved the cruise. ▣

excursion on their own. Some cruise lines provide late-evening baby-sitting in your stateroom. Often, baby-sitters are off-duty children's program staff, who are qualified childcare professionals and known to your kids already through the kids' program.

Booking The complicated world of cruise travel and the many decisions you have to make can be overwhelming. You can book directly through the cruise line or work with a travel agent who specializes in cruise travel and can help you choose between options. It's possible to book online, too. Whichever route you choose, research the options, ask a lot of questions, and weigh choices carefully. Online cruise travel forums in which cruise passengers share information and opinions about cruising can be a helpful resource.

Casinos, Lounges, and Bars One way cruise lines keep prices affordable is by offering onboard casino gambling. Children under 18 are prohibited from gambling, so the presence of casinos is unlikely to affect them. Piano bars and lounges that serve alcohol and permit smoking are off-limits to children as well.

Children's Programs Cruise lines offer children's programs most days at sea (though rarely while the ship is in port). Evening programs include slumber parties or pajama movie nights. Programs range from art projects to organized

---

☛ Parent Tip

Today's cruise ships are floating cities, up to 1,000 feet in length, with 10 to 12 passenger decks. Elevators and escalators help move people around, but expect a very long walk to some locations if your cabin is close to one end of the vessel. If your kids are young enough to fit in an umbrella stroller, bring one along. (Some ships provide these, but generally they have to be reserved in advance; inquire when booking.) Before you book, study the layout of the ship (deck plans are available online and in print brochures) and pick a location handy to the children's center, restaurants, pools, and other amenities. ◉

---

games, learning activities (for example, a naturalist program on sea otters), and more. Unless otherwise indicated, children's programs covered in this book come free with the cruise.

Children's programs are open to all kids, within behavior parameters set by the cruise line. Expectations are that children will follow the rules. Staff will tolerate an infraction or two, but if problems persist, they reserve the right to turn away children. Be sure your children understand what is and is not allowed. Violent or destructive behavior, drug or alcohol use, refusal to follow rules, especially safety rules, can result in expulsion.

Cruise lines usually require that parents sign kids in and out each day; some give parents pagers to use in case a problem arises and the staff needs to contact them. Older kids (13 and above) are given more freedom to come and go without parental or staff supervision. Staff is assigned on the basis of how many kids show up on a particular day in order to ensure a constant ratio of staff to kids.

Computers Today's cruise ships nearly all have Internet lounges or cafés where passengers can check e-mail, play computer games, and surf the Internet. Some lines offer software workshops. Connection fees quickly mount up; you might want to set limits on your children's computer use. An option some cruisers choose for checking e-mail is to visit **Soapy's Station** (see "Inside Passage"), which provides fax, e-mail, and computer services, in Ketchikan and Juneau.

Density Today's cruise ships may carry between 1,200-2,500 passengers along with a sizable crew. Such large ships rarely feel crowded. But if solitude is important to you, cruising may not be your best choice. This is a highly social way of vacationing. Most children take to the density like ducklings to water. Parent reviewers report that their kids quickly found playmates and loved being where the action is (i.e., everywhere but their stateroom).

Dining Cruising today includes many family-friendly dining options. Special diets can be accommodated if arrangements are made in advance. Vegetarian menus are available. At least one large, traditional dining room, with multiple sittings, will provide the gourmet meals that appeal to grown-ups. Cruise lines now offer heart-healthy and vegetarian selections along with the traditional dishes. Early sittings are popular, so to get the kids fed before 9 pm, specify at booking that you want the early sitting. Expect highchairs and booster seats, kid's menu, and staff sensitive to the culinary requirements of picky small fry. However, the ambience and pace of dining is comparable to an elegant restaurant, so if the kids are cranky and starving, the ship's casual-dining option might be a better choice.

You'll find at least one drop-in restaurant or café on board where kids with ketchup-stained T-shirts will fit right in; service will likely be buffet or cafeteria-style. Fast food (hot dogs, burgers, pizza, soft drinks, and ice cream) is usually available throughout the day at several locations.

A shipboard dining trend that's swept the cruise industry in recent years is the so-called "alternative restaurant," much like a pricey land-based restaurant. Reservations are required and a flat fee is levied, between $10 and $30 per person per meal.

Dress Casual vacation and resort wear is standard for daytime cruise events. Evenings are another matter. Although the requirement that cruise passengers appear in tux and evening gown has devolved over time, adult guests are expected to don formal wear for some dinners and shipboard events. In practice, this means suit and tie for men, and cocktail or evening dress for women. For children, a blouse and skirt or dress for girls, slacks and a nice shirt for boys is fine.

Exercise, Sports, Health, and Fitness Along with swimming pools, hot tubs, and saunas, today's cruise ships have gyms, running tracks, sport courts, golf links, rock-climbing walls, tracks for fitness walking, and often a trained staff that can help you devise an onboard fitness regimen. However, many of these features are off-limits to young kids. Some pools and hot tubs may be dedicated to children's use.

Game Rooms and Libraries Here you'll find a selection of board games, jigsaw puzzles, and at least some books for kids along with books for adults. These amenities vary widely among ships.

Healthcare Like planes and schools, a ship can be an incubator for viruses. Although chances are you won't get ill, it's not out of the question to catch a cold or stomach flu. A few high-profile cases of shipboard illness have caused cruise lines to take extra care to maintain good ship hygiene. All cruise lines profiled in this chapter belong to the International Council of Cruise Lines (ICCL) and follow their guidelines for shipboard medical care. These include providing licensed physicians and nurses on call 24 hours a day. The number of passengers determines the number of staff. Dental services usually are not provided. For more information, check the ICCL Web site: www.iccl.org/policies/medical2/.

Laundry In addition to laundry service and dry cleaning, for which all cruise lines charge a fee, many cruise ships offer coin-operated Laundromats, irons, and ironing boards. However, lineups to use these facilities are common. Packing durable, hand-washable clothing can free you from having to hang around the dryer.

Midnight Buffet Once a given on cruise ships, these are disappearing. Most cruise lines offer them occasionally, but attending a late-night buffet can make it hard for kids to stay awake during the next day's activities. As these are fairly adult-oriented, most kids will be satisfied to skip them (unless they showcase dessert).

Minimum Age   Some cruise lines don't allow children under 2 years on cruises; Princess does not accept kids under six months. And expectant moms take note: most cruise lines ban women from traveling after the 24th week of pregnancy, timed from the last day of travel.

Movie Theaters   Most cruise ships have a movie theater showing a variety of films, many rated G or PG. However, some films will be targeted for adult audiences. Stateroom TVs run a selection of movies daily, some rated G or PG.

Night Life   Expect lavish, Las Vegas-style live entertainment nightly. While kids are usually welcome, they might be bored. Cabarets and lounges offer more subdued live music; these usually have bars and allow smoking, so children may be prohibited. A welcome innovation on many ships is the teen disco where teens can dance, hang out, listen to "their" music, and sip on sodas.

Onboard Activities   Cruising blends structured activities with time and opportunities to engage in independent activities. Daytime choices range from aerobics to naturalist talks, along with gambling, shopping, and traditional shipboard pastimes like shuffleboard and Ping Pong. In the evening, options include more gambling, gala shows, live and disco music with dancing. For just about every activity, there is likely to be a workshop or class on how to improve at it—mostly adult oriented.

Onboard Shops   These tend to be less child-oriented than other ship amenities. Art, jewelry, duty-free products, and a selection of toiletries are always available. Don't count on much in the way of disposable diapers and other parenting essentials, though. And while adult clothing stores have a decent selection, kid wear is mostly limited to the fancy (and pricey) T-shirts and apparel grandparents buy as gifts. Expect a few kids' books and toys, along with a coloring book or two, but not much else. See "Inside Passage" for on-shore shopping suggestions.

Paying Onboard   For all onboard financial transactions, passengers are issued special credit cards, usually based on your credit-card imprint. On some ships, these cards also serve as ID, to be presented whenever boarding or leaving the ship. Children are issued their own cards, and generally can use them to play arcade games, use the computer, and make shipboard purchases. Parents can veto use of cards by their children, however. Ask yourself: Can I trust my 6-year-old with a credit card? Then take it from there.

Photos and Videos   Whether it's a blessing or a curse is your call, but cruise lines employ photographers to take photos of passengers engaged in various shipboard activities. These are available for sale during the trip and are usually excellent, but cost as much as $25 a photo. Some cruise lines record each voyage on videotape and sell these to passengers. It can be a thrill for youngsters to see themselves on a professional-quality video, but an expensive thrill.

Positioning Cruise   At least twice a year, Alaska cruise ships move from one part of the world to another. For example, some ships that cruise Alaska waters in summer, cruise Hawaiian waters in winter. The cruise in which the ship travels from Alaska to Hawaii is called a positioning cruise.

Prepaid Soft Drink Card   A popular cruise feature is the prepaid soft drink card. For a set fee, purchasers get a card with which they can obtain unlimited soft drinks during the cruise. Some cruise lines restrict these to children only. Parents might want to carefully weigh the pros and cons of this expenditure.

Pricing Cruise Packages   Comparing prices and packages offered by cruise lines is a challenge. Rates are designed to ensure that as many passenger slots as possible are filled. Deals include reduced or no fee for children in parents' stateroom, reduced rates for the third and fourth passengers in a stateroom, two-for-the-price-of-one specials, free or reduced-price add-ons (such as airfare), free stateroom upgrades, early payment discounts, and much more. The later you book, the more likely prices will come down. But waiting entails some risks: family-size staterooms may all be booked. If you don't enjoy the challenge of finding the best deal out there, ask a cruise-travel specialist for help.

Public Announcements   A not-always-welcome addition to cruising life, frequent public address announcements are made throughout the ship, including staterooms, informing passengers of upcoming shipboard activities. Some announcements are safety-related (such as lifeboat drills), but most are not.

Security Procedures   Since the fall of 2001, cruise lines have tightened security procedures similarly to airlines. All luggage is x-rayed, and all tourists pass through metal detectors and have their ID checked each time they board. These procedures mean that you'll spend more of your cruise standing in line than you might have a few years ago. Leaving the ship a little late and arriving back a little early at ports of call can shorten wait time.

Shipboard Safety   Early in each voyage, a lifeboat drill is held. These can be somewhat chaotic, as a thousand passengers, not yet familiar with the ship's layout, try to find their designated lifeboat stations. The enormous size of cruise ships means that getting lost is a real possibility. Children's programs sometimes offer ship-wide "treasure hunts" whose hidden agenda is to familiarize small fry with the ship. There are plenty of places for kids to get into trouble onboard. Some cruise lines issue or rent pagers or two-way radios to help parents keep track of kids, but there's no substitute for old-fashioned vigilance.

Shore Excursions   At every port, cruise lines provide an assortment of organized on-shore activities. The cost is not included in the cruise package. See "Six Ways to Make Cruising Affordable" for tips on how to keep these costs under control. However you decide to play it, remember that kids have lots to keep them busy onboard and may stay up later than usual. It's easy for young children to become exhausted. Onshore excursions often start early; kids will enjoy them more if they've had enough shut-eye.

Spas   Most cruise ships have full-service spas, provided by independent contractors, offering massage, aromatherapy, facials, manicures, steam baths, and more. Expect a hard sell to purchase spa products. Unless otherwise stated in this text, these facilities are off-limits to kids under 18. In addition to spas, you'll find beauty parlors/hair salons on all cruise ships.

☞ **Parent Tip**

When you've just gotten your preschooler down for a much-needed nap, a blaring announcement over the stateroom PA system can undo all your hard work in a moment. When you board, ask your cabin steward how to turn off or lower the volume of the PA system in your cabin. Most ships allow you to do this for activity announcements, though not for safety announcements. ◙

Staff The ratio of staff to passengers is quite generous, and staff is trained to be courteous and helpful to all ages. Cruise travel has its roots in the old class system. Children who are not accustomed to being waited on may benefit from a few lessons on how to interact with ship staff.

Staterooms Today's ships are configured so that most staterooms are outside (have windows), and many have balconies. (Sometimes views are obstructed; be sure to verify you've got a view when booking. Obstructed view staterooms are less expensive.) Inside cabins are designed and decorated to reduce claustrophobia. Most ships also have a limited number of connecting staterooms and a few family-size suites that can accommodate six or more comfortably. Standard staterooms are configured for two people, with two single beds that can convert to a queen or king-size bed. Larger staterooms have either one or two bunks that unfold from the ceiling (and for which access during the day is limited or impossible) or a sofabed. Larger staterooms can easily accommodate cribs and rollaways, and many cruise lines carry a few of these. (Request one when you book and on boarding.) Bathtubs are fairly scarce; if you'd rather have a tub than a shower, be sure to so specify when booking, and expect to pay more. Satellite phones allow ship-to-shore calls; closed-circuit TVs show films, news, and travelogues about ports of call. Twenty-four-hour room service is common.

Supplementary Fees Cruise lines, like other businesses, are looking for ways to boost profits as they compete for clients with attractively low fares. Along with traditional charges—such as for shipboard photos, alcoholic and soft drinks, and shore excursions—new fees are creeping in. Most lines now include alternative restaurants for which diners pay a flat fee; some have also experimented with charging for previously free activities, such as spa, pool, and gym use, kid pizza parties, or hot chocolate.

Talent Show Most cruises include a guest talent show in their entertainment line-up. Kids are often encouraged to participate, and some children's programs include rehearsals and opportunities to 'star' in the show.

Tenders This term refers to the small boats, usually covered motorboats, that ferry cruise passengers from ship to shore and back again. Owing to limited cruise-dock facilities or ports that are too small to accommodate large vessels, some ships anchor out and get passengers to shore on tenders.

Tipping On most cruise lines, tipping cabin stewards and dining staff is expected. Some cruise lines will bill you a daily fee to cover tips. If not, for a cruise of seven days expect to tip about $10 per day per adult in your family. Cruise lines will provide tipping guidelines.

Staying Well Onboard

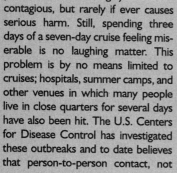

Recent cruise ship outbreaks of Norwalk or Norwalk-like viruses (NLVs), aka "stomach flu," have ruined some vacations and led other travelers to cancel cruise plans. The virus is highly contagious, but rarely if ever causes serious harm. Still, spending three days of a seven-day cruise feeling miserable is no laughing matter. This problem is by no means limited to cruises; hospitals, summer camps, and other venues in which many people live in close quarters for several days have also been hit. The U.S. Centers for Disease Control has investigated these outbreaks and to date believes that person-to-person contact, not ship sanitation practices, is the culprit in most cases. To prevent NLV, cruise ships are doing their best to maintain high sanitation standards. As a passenger, what can you do?

Make sure that everyone washes hands before meals and after toileting. Use hot water and soap, and instruct kids to take at least 20 seconds each time.

Don't allow children in diapers to venture into wading or swimming pools.

If someone in your party gets sick, immediately notify ship personnel and seek medical help. Cruise ship medical staff can help alleviate symptoms and keep a virus from spreading. ◼

Video Arcades   Just about all cruise ships have game arcades; some are exceptionally large. Cruise lines are sensitive to parental concerns about game content, and you can expect at least some staff supervision. Machines are usually identified as to age-appropriateness.

Line by Line

These descriptions provide a general introduction to what each cruise line offers families. Listings include Alaska-bound ships only. Amenities such as casinos, live shows, and bars are not listed. All sailings take place between May and September. Because pricing is so volatile, we've made no effort to indicate prices. Depending on when you book and what kind of deals are being offered, you can expect to pay $600 or more per person for an inside cabin on a seven-day cruise, up to $4,000 or more for premium accommodation on the same cruise.

Carnival Cruise Lines

888/CARNIVAL; www.carnival.com

FYI: 1 ship; large staterooms with ocean views and balconies, some connecting rooms, quads with 2 upper bunks, some suites with bathtubs; 4 restaurants, kids' menu, room service; teen disco (evenings); swimming pools; waterslide, hot tubs, spa and gym; playground equipment and mini-basketball; Fun House dedicated, staffed children's area & programs (ages 2-15, video arcade; movie theater; Internet café; small library; self-service laundry; baby-sitting; reduced rates (ages 2-12) on shore excursions.

This cruise line markets itself to younger travelers and is priced affordably for families, with many family-friendly features. Only one Carnival ship, the *Carnival Spirit*, cruises Alaskan waters; it carries 2,124 passengers. The décor is art deco and lavish. Carnival bills its vessels as 'fun ships,' and it's hard to disagree.

Noise levels can be high. However, since it is very popular with families your kids are certain to find plenty of playmates on board. Dining choices include a formal dining room with reserved sittings, a reservations-only alternative restaurant, and two casual options, one of which serves pizza 24/7. Purchase of a fountain card entitles kids to unlimited sodas for the entire trip (price varies with length of sailing).

Children's Programs and Activities Carnival is one of the few lines to permit children as young as 2 in its kids' program and to allow staff to change diapers. Kids are divided into four age groups: 2-5, 6-8, 9-11, and 12-15. Programs are wellstaffed and run 9am-10pm at the Fun House, a 2,400-square-foot, well-equipped children's center with toys, activities, crafts, video screens for showing films, Macintosh computers with games, and Sony Playstation. There are three interconnected areas: one has arts and crafts, one houses the computer lab, and one is an all-purpose playroom with a video wall. In addition, baby-sitting is offered at the Fun House 10pm-3am while sailing and on port days for younger kids. Some activities include the whole family. Sample activities include karaoke, T-shirt decorating, talent show, slumber party (extra fee), movie night, and Ping Pong.

Kids will also enjoy exploring Pharaoh's Palace, a Las Vegas-style nightclub that spans three decks and is wildly decorated in ancient-Egyptian style. Nearby is the Techno Arcade, an exceptionally large assortment of games organized by content and age-appropriateness. While there is no teen center, a disco is dedicated to evening teen use, and supervised teen shore excursions can be arranged.

Destinations All cruises are seven-day, one-way trips between Vancouver, BC (Canada Place Cruise Terminal), and Seward, AK, with stops at Ketchikan, Sitka, Juneau, and Skagway.

Celebrity Cruises
800/722-5941; www.celebritycruises.com
FYI: 3 ships; large staterooms and suites (some with VCR), good storage; some connecting staterooms, balconies, bathtubs; 3 restaurants, room service, kids' menu; swimming pools; spa, fitness center (17 & older), hot tubs; CD-listening room, movie theater; Fun Factory: dedicated, staffed children's area & programs (ages 3-17); teen club & disco (Mercury, Summit), video arcade; Internet café; library; game rooms; baby-sitting; reduced rates for kids on shore excursions (under 13)

This line has a reputation for elegance and haute cuisine, two things most kids don't include on their wish lists. Celebrity doesn't go out of its way to advertise its kid-friendly features, but there are plenty of them. Although the line has an upmarket reputation, it's not hard to find bargains if you do your homework.

Celebrity's Alaska cruise vessels are the *Mercury* (1,870 passengers) and the newer, somewhat larger sister ships *Infinity* and *Summit* (1,950 passengers each). They each have a large formal dining room, an alternative restaurant, and informal dining options. On all ships, only one of the pools is covered (has a dome), and it's available only to ages 17 and above as it is located in the spa. There is a kids' wading pool. The *Mercury* and *Summit* have dedicated teen facilities.

The shipboard ambience is a tad more elegant than some; dress codes are taken seriously. Extra touches abound, such as Internet access (for a hefty fee) and interactive TV (order meals, purchase shore excursions, gamble) in staterooms. The CD-listening room is an underutilized feature kids will enjoy, though it's not targeted just to them. The two-story library is oriented more toward adults than children.

Children's Programs and Activities   The Fun Factory has computers, Sony Playstation, videos, indoor and outdoor playground equipment, and a closed-circuit TV station. Children must be toilet trained to participate. The program divides kids into Shipmates (ages 3-7), Cadets (7-9), Ensigns (10-12), and Admiral T's (13-17). Activities include arts and crafts, races, exercise workouts and games, a pizza party (while parents attend a formal dinner), Foosball, Ping Pong, and a slumber party. All are free. Kids can participate in TV production, creating their own broadcasts, commercials, and entertainment programming; the shows run on a channel on the ship's closed-circuit TV system. Teens can play basketball, pool games, and tour the ship's professional theater. For a fee, group baby-sitting is available on in-port days and in-cabin in evenings.

Destinations   Cruises are seven days, either one-way or round-trip, between Vancouver (Canada Place Cruise Terminal) and Seward. Ports of call are Ketchikan, Juneau, Sitka, Valdez, and Skagway. In May and September, positioning cruises run between San Francisco and Alaska, with varied itineraries.

Holland America

877/932-4259; www.hollandamerica.com
FYI: 6 ships; large staterooms and suites, some balconies, some connecting rooms (except Statendam), triples & quads, some bathtubs; 2 restaurants, room service, kids' menu; 2 swimming pools, hot tubs, spa, fitness center; gym & sport court (except Statendam); jogging track (Statendam only); Club HAL: staffed children's program (ages 5-17); dedicated children's area (Maasdam only); video arcade; movie theater; Internet café; library and game room; self-service laundry; babysitting; reduced rates for children (under 13) on shore excursions; dedicated children's shore excursions

This cruise line appeals to a somewhat older population, but you'll find plenty of families on its summer Alaska cruises. Alaska vessels include the *Amsterdam* (1,380 passengers), the sister ships *Ryndam*, *Statendam*, and *Veendam* (1,266 each), and the *Volendam* and *Zaandam* (1,440 each). A good choice for a multigenerational family reunion, HAL has excellent, though limited, children's programs and activities designed to appeal to many ages. The décor is handsome and sturdy. The library is large, with an excellent assortment of books for kids as well as adults, and there's plenty of room to sit and read here. The game room has games, cards, and jigsaw puzzles, and plenty of tables to lay them out on.

Staterooms are generously sized, with plenty of storage; affordably priced inside triples and quads are a good bet for families on a budget. So far, the line has resisted the trend toward alternative restaurants. There's a formal dining room and the Lido, a casual buffet-style restaurant with lots of options. Fast food (burgers, tacos, hot dogs) is served on the Lido deck throughout the day, which is also where you'll find the pool, under the retractable dome along with several hot tubs. The other pool is theoretically off limits to kids (although parents report seeing small fry in it).

Children's Programs and Activities All ships offer Club HAL, but only the *Maasdam* has a dedicated children's area. It is looser in structure than other cruise-line programs and doesn't accommodate children under age 5. Kids are divided by age: 5-8, 9-12, and 13-17. Because there's no dedicated kids' area, activities can be somewhat ad hoc. (It's not unusual to find a Club HAL counselor leading a group of kids around the ship in search of a free room in which to do crafts.) Despite this, programming and staff are of high quality. Hours vary, and kids are free to come and go. Programming runs roughly five hours a day, with morning, afternoon, and evening sessions. On in-port days, activities are timed according to when the ship leaves. Activities include arts and crafts, games, naturalist and historical programs, tie-dye, a pajama movie night, and participation in the talent show. Club HAL is weakest in teen choices; there's no club or disco, and the arcade is on the small side. On the other hand, this line offers an excellent assortment of teen shore excursions, including kayaking and canoeing trips, and shore excursions for younger kids to places like Sitka's Raptor Center.

Destinations Round trip and one-way seven-day sailings are offered. Round trips originate in Seattle or Vancouver (Canada Place Cruise Terminal). One-way cruises all run between Vancouver and Seward. Ports of call include Ketchikan, Sitka, Juneau, Skagway, and Haines.

Norwegian Cruise Lines

800/327-7030; www.ncl.com
FYI: 3 ships; small-average staterooms and suites, bathtubs in suites, some refrigerators, balconies, some connecting staterooms; many restaurants, kids' menus, room service; teen clubs (2 ships); swimming pools, kids' pools (2 ships), hot tubs, spa, fitness center, jogging and walking tracks, sport court; Kids' Korner: dedicated, staffed children's area and programs (ages 2-17), video arcade; theaters, Internet café; library; baby-sitting (group only); family shore excursions; reduced rates on shore excursions (under 13), some free for kids under 4 on parent's lap

This cruise line is famous for high-quality entertainment and solid children's programs. Its "freestyle cruising" program in which passengers dine where and when they choose rather than at a specified time and assigned table, adds flexibility to dining options, always a plus for families. The program also makes disembarkation easier. The Alaska fleet includes the *Norwegian Wind* (1,748 passengers), the *Norwegian Sky* (2,002), and the newest, *Norwegian*

Sun, (2,002). If there is a drawback to NCL, it's that staterooms tend to be small with little storage space. For families with two or more kids, connecting rooms are your best bet; or book on the *Sun,* which has bigger staterooms. The *Sky* and *Sun* have refrigerators in every stateroom; the *Wind* does not. Families traveling on the *Wind* and *Sun* take note: the jogging track runs right outside stateroom doors on the Promenade Deck. Other decks are quieter.

All three vessels have at least four restaurants as well as a selection of casual dining options which offer sandwiches, pizza, ice cream, and snacks. Many of the restaurants fall in the "alternative" category and levy charges; all provide kid cuisine as does the room service menu. The ambience is as varied as the cuisine, ranging from formal to intimate to casual, so families should have no difficulty finding something that appeals. The near elimination of dress codes will probably come as a relief to most parents.

Other amenities can be a bit uneven. The entertainment is a cut above the cruise ship norm, and if you like Broadway shows you'll be in heaven. The libraries are on the small side and open for limited hours.

Children's Programs and Activities   Kids' programs at NCL are long established and of high quality. At the Kids' Korner, the center where activities take place, staff provides programming for children grouped into Junior Sailors (2-5), First Mates (6-8), Navigators (9-12), and Teens (13-17). Activities include arts and crafts, T-shirt painting, cooking classes, video-watching, a pajama party, naturalist activities, and a mix of indoor and outdoor sports and games. The *Sky* and *Sun* each have dedicated kid swimming pools and teen clubs. According to NCL, staff is trained in childcare. Kids need not be potty trained but staff will not change diapers. Instead, parents are given beepers and paged when a new diaper is required. The program begins on the first evening, and is offered daily throughout the cruise, including evenings (7-10pm). Group baby-sitting is available for a fee 9am-5pm on in-port days, and every evening 10pm-1am. There's no in-cabin baby-sitting.

Destinations   All sailings are round trip (or nearly). Sailings start in Seattle or Vancouver (Ballantyne Pier Cruise Terminal) and take six or seven days; some cruises start in Seattle and end in Vancouver, and vice versa. Ports of call include Ketchikan, Juneau, Skagway, Wrangell, and Victoria, BC.

Princess

800/PRINCESS; www.princess.com
FYI: 7 ships; small-average staterooms and suites, some connecting suites, triples, &
quads, balconies, bathtubs, refrigerators; restaurants, food court (some ships), room
service; library, game room; Internet café (some); swimming pools, hot tubs, spa, fit-
ness center, sport court, jogging track; Princess Kids: dedicated, staffed children's
area & programs (ages 3-17), some teen clubs, disco, video arcades; movie theater;
self-service laundry (except Pacific); in-cabin baby-sitting only; reduced rates (ages
4-12) on some shore excursions; some excursions free for kids under 4 on parent's lap

Princess has been bringing cruise passengers to Alaska for decades and has developed a network of successful land-based tours to complement its cruises;

it runs lodges throughout Alaska. Vessels have a distinctively boxy shape and lack the graceful, old-fashioned contours of Celebrity or Holland America ships; but these folks have had years to iron out the kinks in their system and they have a winning formula. The Alaska fleet includes the *Coral* (1,970 passengers), *Dawn* (1,950), *Diamond* (2,670), *Island* (1,970), *Pacific* (680), *Star* (2,600), and *Sun* (1,950). Princess runs more ships to Alaska than any other line. (The *Coral, Island,* and *Pacific,* debuting in late 2002 and 2003, are not reviewed here.) Princess bills its approach "Personal Choice Cruising"; as on NCL, this includes flexible dining options, a plus for parents.

Staterooms tend to be small, from the family perspective, although most outside cabins have balconies. (Some cruisers report that, owing to ship design, balconies are stacked closely together.) On the *Sun* and *Pacific,* families with more than two kids will need to book adjacent rooms, as no connecting rooms or large suites are available. Princess follows the trend of blending traditional dining rooms with alternative restaurants. Unlike most other cruise lines, Princess charges for ice cream, except at meal time.

Children's Programs and Activities Kids' programming is a strong suit of this line. Princess Kids divides kids into Pelicans (ages 3-7), Pirateers (8-12), and Off Limits (13-17). Programs and kid amenities vary by ship, but all program hours are 9am-noon, 2-5pm, and 7-10pm on sea days; in port, hours are 9am-5pm. Additionally, teen centers are open 10pm-1am. Group babysitting is available for younger kids from 10pm-1am for a fee. Princess uses a National Wildlife Federation curriculum, offers a Junior Ranger program, fun science-based activities, and the usual arts and crafts, games, and activities. There's a pizza dinner for kids, one night each voyage. Most ships have a kids' pool, and teens have their own facility. Teen activities include dinners, dancing, and sports. Overall, this is one of the best-balanced kids' programs afloat.

Destinations Princess ships sail between Seattle or Vancouver (Canada Place Cruise Terminal) round trip or one-way to Alaska; all cruises are seven days. (Princess also offers 11-day round-trip cruises from San Francisco.) Ports of call include Ketchikan, Juneau, Sitka, Skagway, and Seward.

Royal Caribbean International

800/398-9819; www.royalcaribbean.com
FYI: 3 ships; small-average staterooms and suites, family suites, connecting rooms, triples & quads, bathtubs in suites; some refrigerators, balconies; restaurants, kids' menu, room service; swimming pools, hot tubs, spa, fitness center, sport court, jogging track, rock-climbing wall (Radiance), miniature golf; library, observatory; Adventure Ocean: dedicated, staffed children's program (ages 3-17), teen center, video arcade; Internet café; baby-sitting

Despite its name, RCI is a major player in Alaska cruising, appealing to the same demographic as Carnival, but with a slightly more upscale image. Ships serving Alaska are the *Legend of the Seas* (2,076 passengers), *Radiance of the Seas* (2,501), and *Vision of the Seas* (2,435). Staterooms are on the small side, although the number of balconies is considerable. The newest vessel of the three, *Radiance*

Murder Most Northern

Fans (adults and children) of mystery fiction which evokes a sense of place have a wealth of books to choose from that feature northern settings. A remarkable number of writers have chosen to set their tales of murder and mayhem north of the 60th parallel or in the remote Alaska panhandle; many authors are northern natives who take pride in getting the details right. Curling up with a northern mystery is a fun way to pass the time on an Inside Passage cruise, and what's more, you're not just ingesting empty literary calories; you'll be learning about the world you're going to explore! Here are a few choices:

Adult Fiction

Sue Henry chose Alaska's most distinctive sporting event for her Alex Jensen series debut novel, *Murder on the Iditarod Trail* (William Morrow, 1993), in which musher Jessie Arnold, along with other mushers, must outrun a murderer. State Trooper Jensen and musher Arnold feature in Henry's later novels, which also offer vivid Alaska and Yukon settings.

Christopher Lane has written a police procedural series that features Ray Attla, an Inupiat police officer on Alaska's North Slope. The series starts with *Elements of a Kill: An Inupiat Eskimo Mystery.* (Avon, 1998.)

of the Seas, has larger staterooms, balconies, and more amenities. All ships are large, and public spaces are vast and well designed. Family suites sleep up to eight.

The cuisine is fine, but this is not a cruise line for foodies (although it's likely to please kids). Restaurants on *Vision* and *Legend* are limited to one formal dining room and a casual restaurant. Additionally, *Radiance* has two alternative restaurants. For fitness buffs, on the other hand, RCI has a lot to offer. Internet access is convenient, and entertainment is excellent for those whose tastes run to Broadway shows. Unusual among cruise ships, there's a bookstore cum espresso café on *Radiance.*

Children's Programs and Activities Adventure Ocean, the RCI take on kid cruise culture, divides kids into Aquanauts (3-5), Explorers (6-8), Voyagers (9-12), and Navigators (13-17). Kids must be toilet trained (disposable pull-ups won't cut it). Activities include science and naturalist programs, arts and crafts, computer games, talent show, pajama party, storytelling, T-shirt decorating, and so on. Teens have games, karaoke, a pool party, sports, dancing, a Toga Party and their own facilities. On the *Radiance of the Seas,* there's a kids' pool and waterslide. Program hours are 9am-noon, 2-5pm and 7-10pm on sea days; 9am-noon and 7-10 pm in port. Teen activities are also available 10:30pm-2am nightly. RCI

In White Sky, Black Ice: A Nathan Active Mystery, (Soho Press, 1999), Stan Jones introduced Nathan Active, an Inupiat Alaska State Trooper in the village of Chukchi, the start of another police-procedural series.

Dead Stick (Prime Crime, 1998) begins a mystery series by Megan Mallory Rust featuring Alaska aviator and sleuth Taylor Morgan.

Dana Stabenow began her Kate Shugak mystery series with *A Cold Day for Murder* (Berkley, 1992) and has continued with many more titles. Kate is an Alaska Native working as a private investigator in a variety of vivid Alaska settings. Stabenow's Liam Campbell police-procedural series follows the career of the Alaska State Trooper, starting with *Fire and Ice: A Liam Campbell Mystery* (Dutton, 1998.)

In *The Woman Who Married a Bear* (Soho Press, 1992), John Straley, introduced Cecil Younger, an under-employed private eye who appears in a continuing Alaska PI series.

Canadian journalist Scott Young wrote two acclaimed police procedurals featuring Matteesie Kitologitak, an Inuk Mountie in the Northwest Territories, *Love in a Cold Climate* (Macmillan Canada, 1988) and *The Shaman's Knife* (Viking, 1993).

Children's Fiction

In *Snow Problem: The Case of the Mushing Madness* (Learning Triangle Press, 1998), by Marianne Meyer, the Super Crew help out Arnold Rutabegger, a stuntman on a film shoot in Alaska that's been plagued by mysterious accidents.

In *The Mystery of the Black Raven: Boxcar Children's Special, No. 12*, (Albert Whitman, 1999), by Gertrude Chandler Warner, the boxcar children encounter an intriguing mystery on the way to Skagway. ◼

advertises that its kid program staff holds four-year degrees or better in education, recreation, or a related field. Group baby-sitting is available for a fee from 10pm-1am nightly and on port days from noon through departure; again, kids must be potty trained. In-room baby-sitting can also be arranged, with 24-hour notice.

Destinations RCI sails from Vancouver's Ballantyne Pier Cruise Terminal on seven-day trips, round-trip or one-way. Ports of call include Ketchikan, Juneau, Sitka, Skagway, and Seward.

Resources

Books for Adults

Horwitz, Tony. *Blue Latitudes*. Henry Holt, 2002. Captain James Cook's three 18th century Pacific voyages, including Alaska, are covered in this biography.

Lofgren, Orvar. *On Holiday: A History of Vacationing*. University of California Press, 1999. This book offers an entertaining history of 200 years of tourism.

Miller, William H. *The Liners: A Voyage of Discovery*. Motorbooks International, 1997. The history of the modern ocean liner is laid out, from its origins to the present.

Six Ways to Keep Cruising Affordable

No doubt about it: cruising can be a pricey proposition for a family. While at first it seems that all costs are included in the price of a cruise, shore excursions and activities are a major exception. A two-hour excursion booked through the cruise line can run a family of four anywhere from $120 to $1,000 or more. Other add-on expenses include tips, beverages (such as soft drinks and alcohol) that are not consumed with meals, photos, souvenirs, arcade games, and Internet access. Here are some ways to cushion the costs.

1. Travel early or late in the cruising season (end of May to mid June; late August to early September) when prices are lower.  (But try to avoid taking kids out of school; even if you're OK with that, there will be few, if any, kids for yours to play with.) Thanks to the latitude and climate of the Inside Passage, you can expect long nights and moderate temperatures whenever you go.

2. Book an inside cabin. Savings are huge, and other shipboard amenities are identical wherever you roost. How much time will you spend on your balcony, after all?

3. Before booking, look at prospective itineraries. Study the shore excursions on offer (most of this information, including prices, will be on the cruise line's Web site). Choose carefully. Some excursions are worth the splurge. For instance, a flightseeing trip over the Misty Fjords will cost a bundle, but there's no better way to see this extraordinary wilderness.

4. Be selective when choosing shore excursions which are geared to the needs of older passengers, for whom accessibility is important. Often, what you pay for includes transportation to an activity or attraction within easy walking distance. Why pay $40 each for a walking tour of downtown Ketchikan? We're not talking Manhattan here! Most Inside Passage towns can be explored on foot. Many visitor information centers conduct free guided tours, or you can pick up a walking map at a visitor center and set out to explore on your own.

5. It can cost less to arrange your own shore excursion than to sign on to the cruise line's tour. It will be more work, though. And whether it's practical depends on how long the ship is in port and how far the dock is from town. Most cruise lines offer similar excursions, for which they contract with local outfitters chosen in part because they can accommodate large numbers of cruise passengers at once. Smaller outfitters may offer as good or better service and some of these outfitters meet cruise ships at the dock. You'll see them holding up signs advertising their tours when you arrive. Another possibility is to act as your own outfitter. If you have your heart set on visiting Mendenhall Glacier, outside Juneau, you could rent a vehicle for the day and find the glacier on your own. See "Inside Passage" for more ideas.

6. Last but far from least: **Establish a daily budget** for everyone. Remember that if you do not set limits for your child (and yourself), no one else is going to do it. ◼

Books for Kids

Leigh, Suzanna. *Puzzle Ocean.* EDC Publications, 1996. Small pre-readers hunt for hidden objects on the pages of this book featuring the story of a little girl and a mermaid.

Mandel, Peter. *My Ocean Liner: Across the North Atlantic on the Great Ship Normandie.* Stemmer House, 2000. This picture book, beautifully illustrated by Betsey MacDonald, recounts a child's life on one of the classic steamers sailing from New York to France in 1939.

Tilly, Jim. *Hal's Magical Cruise—Alaska.* Misty Mountain Publishing, 1995. Appropriate for beginning readers, this storybook features a talking boat and a variety of creatures cavorting in the Inside Passage.

Warner, Gertrude Chandler. *The Mystery Cruise* (Boxcar Children Mysteries, 29). Whitman, 1992. In this story from the popular Boxcar Children series, mysterious events occur aboard the *West Wind* cruise ship.

Web Sites

There are a lot of cruise-travel sites and several host online cruising forums in which you can ask questions of seasoned cruisers. But keep an open mind about what you read. Some reviews are hidden ads for the product they are ostensibly critiquing. Others express opinions that are legitimate, but not necessarily reliable. One traveler's wonderful or horrible adventure doesn't mean that your family will have the same experience. Still, reading cruise reviews can help you to identify issues you might not have thought about.

Cruise 411 (www.cruise411.com/info_center/detailed_description/) This site has easy-to-read listings of shipboard statistics and amenities for major cruise lines.

CruiseMates (www.cruisemates.com) Detailed consumer reviews of cruise lines and ships are included at this site.

Departing from Seattle and Vancouver

If your family lives a fair distance from the cruise terminal, consider building in extra time at either end of your cruise, both to allow for delays and to take the opportunity to do a spot of sightseeing.

In this book we cover only cruises that depart from Seattle or Vancouver. However, cruises between California and Alaska are another growing trend. Princess and Crystal offer Alaska cruises from San Francisco; Celebrity has two-week, one-way cruises between San Diego and Alaska, with stops in San Francisco and Victoria, BC. Cruise travel continues to expand, and more options are likely to appear in the future. But think carefully about booking an extra-long cruise with young kids. Not only are these substantially more expensive, but over 14 nights even your nearest and dearest can get on your nerves in a stateroom the size of junior's bedroom. For information and options on cruise travel from California, contact the **Port of San Francisco** (415/274-0507; www.sfport.com/) or **Port of San Diego** (619/686-6200; www.portofsandiego.org/sandiego_maritime/css_main.asp).

Seattle-Based Cruises

Although Vancouver is still the primary port of departure for Alaska cruise ships, Seattle attracts more cruise lines and sailings each year. Americans who sail from the United States can avoid the delays and stresses of going through immigration and customs. The **Seattle Cruise Terminal** (Bell Street Pier Cruise Terminal, Pier 66; 206/615-3900; www.portseattle.org/harbor/cruise/b_info/) is conveniently situated on Elliott Bay in downtown Seattle. It's a busy place and to relieve congestion, the new **Terminal 30 Cruise Facility** (2431 E Marginal Way S; 206/615-3900; e-mail: cruise@portseattle.org) opened on the "SoDo" (south of downtown) waterfront in May of 2003.

By Road Seattle can be reached from north or south via Interstate 5, 180 miles from Portland, OR; from Vancouver, BC, it's 130 miles. Interstate 90 connects Seattle with points east.

By Air Most major US air carriers and many international airlines use Seattle-Tacoma International Airport (SeaTac). A taxi or limousine from the airport to the cruise terminal costs about $30. A variety of shuttle buses and vans run between the airport and other regional cities; check with the **Port of Seattle** for details (206/433-5388; www.portseattle.org/seatac/transport/shuttlebus/). **Airport Express** runs shuttle buses between the airport and many downtown hotels (206/626-6088, 800/426-7505; www.graylineofseattle.com. Cost: $8.50/adult, $6/child 2-12, free/under 2).

By Train You can get to Seattle via **Amtrak** (800/USA-RAIL; www.amtrak.com) from points north, south, and east. The Amtrak *Cascades* runs between Eugene, OR, and Vancouver, BC, with stops in Seattle and other points; the *Coast Starlight* between California and Seattle; the *Empire Builder* between Chicago and Seattle.

SEATTLE

Seattle is a major tourist destination in its own right, so if your cruise departs from here, it makes sense to add a day or two to your trip and investigate. Many family attractions are on or near the waterfront. However, downtown Seattle is short on affordable, comfortable accommodation; the most affordable places to stay are elsewhere in the city (see sidebar). General tourist information is available through the **Seattle-King County Convention & Visitor Bureau** (Washington State Convention and Trade Center, 800 Convention Pl, Galleria Level; 206/461-5840; www.Seeseattle.org open year round).

Places to Stay

Within walking distance is the 200-room **Edgewater** (Pier 67, 2411

Alaskan Way; 206/728-7000, 800/624-0670; www.edgewaterhotel.com. **$$$**) It will cost you, but hey, this is downtown Seattle's only waterfront hotel! Children under 19 stay free with parents. A less pricey option is the pleasant **Pensione Nichols** (1923 1st Ave; 206/441-7125, 800/400-7125; www.seattle-bed-breakfast.com. **$-$$**) This family-friendly B&B has 10 rooms that share four bathrooms. It also has two comfortable suites, each with kitchen and bath, suitable for families. Kids under 10 stay free with parents. In summer, there's a two-night minimum stay on weekends. It's a short taxi ride to the cruise terminal, but you can easily get to downtown Seattle attractions on foot.

South and two blocks east of the waterfront in Pioneer Square, the **Best Western Pioneer Square Hotel** (77 Yesler Way; 206/340-1234, 800/800-5512; www.pioneersquare.com. **$$**) has 75 smallish rooms and suites in a renovated historic building. There's a free continental breakfast, and kids under 12 stay free.

What to See & Do

Seattle's cruise terminal is steps away from some of Seattle's most popular family attractions. The waterfront is lined with old buildings that have been reborn as shops and restaurants, along with working ferry docks, public fishing piers, and parks, and it's all best experienced on foot. But if time is short, you can hop on the **Waterfront Trolley** that runs to Pioneer Square, with stops at Pike Street Market, the aquarium, parks, and shopping, and get to your destination in minutes.

Housed with the cruise terminal at the Bell Street Pier (Pier 66) is the **Odyssey: Maritime Discovery Center** (206/374-4000; www.seattle aquarium.org. Hours: 10am-5pm Tue-Sat, noon-5pm Sun, closed Mon. Cost: $7/adult, $5/child 5-18, $2/child, 2-4, free/under 2). Four galleries introduce visitors to the region's maritime culture: fishing, shipping, trade, and recreation. Combine a visit here with a visit to the **Seattle Aquarium** (Pier 59, 206/386-4320; www.seattleaquarium.org. Open 10am-7pm [summer], 10am-5pm [rest of year] Cost: $9.75/adult, $7/child 6-18, $5/child 3-5, free/under 3), a few piers down. The aquarium features the natural world of the oceans to complement the human world Odyssey displays; there's also an Imax theater. Visitors to both maritime museums can purchase combined tickets at a discount. Also at the Bell Street Pier, you'll find three Anthony's restaurants, which offer various takes on seafood. Try **Anthony's Bell Street Diner** for casual, family-friendly fare, and **Anthony's Fish Bar** for fish and chips (either: 206/448-6688).

With more time to spare, walk south to the **Pike Market Hillclimb** to the **Pike Place Market** (lots of stairs up to the nation's oldest, continuously operating farmer's market), which has—along with geoducks, produce, and crafts for sale—cafés, shops crammed with affordable kid souvenirs, and chaotic activity. It's open daily.

If your cruise takes you to Skagway, AK, be sure to visit the **Klondike**

More Downtown
Seattle and Vancouver Hotels

For detailed descriptions of these hotel chains (including Web sites and toll-free phone numbers), see "Hotel Chains," in the Introduction. Many more options exist. Check with the Visitor Bureau for more choices.

Seattle Chain Hotels

Comfort Suites-
Downtown/Seattle Center
601 Roy St; 206/282-2600. ($$)

Courtyard by Marriott-
Downtown/Lake Union
925 Westlake Ave N; 206/213-0100;
($$-$$$)

Hampton Inn & Suites-
Downtown/Seattle Center
700 5th Ave N; 206/282-7700.
($$-$$$)

Holiday Inn Express-Downtown
226 Aurora Ave N; 206/441-7222.
($-$$)

Residence Inn by Marriott-
Downtown
800 Fairview Ave N; 206/223-8160.
($$$)

Travelodge by the Space Needle
200 6th Ave; 206/441-7878. ($-$$)

Vancouver Chain Hotels

Hampton Inn & Suites-Downtown
Vancouver
111 Robson St; 604/602-1008.
($$-$$$)

Quality Hotel-Inn at False Creek
1335 Howe St; 604/682-0229. ($$)

Ramada Inn & Suites-Downtown
Vancouver
1221 Granville St; 604/685-1111.
($-$$)

Ramada Limited-Downtown
Vancouver
435 Pender St; 604/488-1088.
($$)

Residence Inn by Marriott
Vancouver
1234 Hornby St; 604/688-1234.
($$-$$$)

Travelodge Vancouver Centre
1304 Howe St, 604/682-2767. ($)

Gold Rush National Historical Park in Pioneer Square (117 Main St, 206/553-7220; open 9am-5pm daily; free). Although most of the park is up in Skagway, this is where it all started in 1897, when 10,000 prospectors set sail for Alaska within two years. The park features photos and artifacts of the era, along with videos and, in summer, interpretive programs and gold-panning demos. Just doors from the park is downtown Seattle's flagship independent bookseller, **Elliott Bay Book Company**, at 101 Main Street. In the excellent children's section, kids can stock up on books for the trip. Pioneer Square is also where you'll find **Magic Mouse Toys** (603 1st Ave, 206/682-8097), a two-story, very well stocked emporium. There are plenty of other fun shops to explore along 1st Avenue. If you have young kids, you might want to skip the **Underground Tour**. Despite the alluring name, it is not particularly child-friendly.

☞ Parent Tip: Waiting to Board

There's a good chance that you'll spend a few hours waiting to board your cruise ship, and a few more waiting for your luggage to arrive in your stateroom. If two ships are boarding at the same time and same terminal, there may be 4,000 or more passengers to be processed, along with a third as many cruise ship staff. It can be stressful trying to figure out where to go, which group you belong to (passengers are divided into smaller groups for embarkation), and what you need to do. Here are steps you can take to make the process more manageable:

Research boarding options in advance. Arrive a little earlier than scheduled for embarkation. If early boarding privileges are available to you, take advantage of them.

Pack appropriately; think "long flight." Have on hand a change of underwear for everyone, toiletries, wet wipes, snacks, drinks, and especially, kid entertainment and activities. It's not uncommon to spend an hour or two in line with nowhere to sit and few, if any, services. Books, portable board games, CD player and music, cards, coloring books and crayons are worth their weight in gold.

Prepare the family for the experience. It is easier to manage the chaos if you know what to expect.

Arrive rested. If you have a flight, train ride, or long drive to the port of embarkation, arrange to arrive in town a day or two early. Stay in a hotel nearby and relax. Sleep in, do some sightseeing and shopping, and arrive at the cruise terminal in good shape for whatever awaits you. ▣

Vancouver-Based Cruises

Most Alaska cruises depart from Vancouver, one of the world's loveliest cities, just north of the U.S.-Canada border, set against a breathtaking backdrop of tall mountains and deep fjords.

By Road It's a 130-mile drive north on Interstate 5 from Seattle. Visitors from the east can choose the TransCanada (Hwy 1) or, if coming from up north, take the Yellowhead Highway (Hwy 16) from Edmonton, then either Highway 5 or Highway 97 south to Vancouver. If you're heading to Vancouver from the eastern United States, take Interstate 90 to Seattle and then Interstate 5 north.

Cruise ships depart from one of Vancouver's two terminals. **Canada Place Cruise Ship Terminal** (999 Canada Place, 604/665-9000, 888/767-8826; www.portvancouver.com/cruise/)—large, relatively new, and set in the heart of Vancouver's business district with plenty of shopping and activities close at hand—is the busiest. **Ballantyne Pier Cruise Ship Terminal** (655 Centennial Rd, 604/665-9000, 888/767-8826; www.portvancouver.com/cruise/cruise_terminals_ballantyne/) is smaller, older, and located in an industrial neighborhood with little to see or do in the vicinity.

By Air Many major U.S. and international carriers fly to Vancouver. For a list of airlines serving Vancouver, check the **Vancouver International Airport** Web site (www.yvr.ca/flightinfo/airlines.asp). To get to the cruise terminals, you can take a cab (expect to pay about $26) or a limo (about $34 for six to eight passengers). Or catch the **Airporter** (604/946-8866, 800/668-3141; www.yvrairporter.com; not to be confused with the U.S. Airporter). Shuttles depart at 20-minute intervals and take about 35 minutes to get from the airport to the terminal; family fares are $24 one-way.

If you're flying into Seattle, you can take the train (see below) to Vancouver or the **Quick Shuttle** bus (604/940-4428, 800/665-2122; www.quick coach.com; $44/adult, $24/child 5-12, free/under 5) which runs between Seattle Tacoma International Airport, Bellingham Airport, downtown Seattle and Vancouver destinations, including the cruise terminal.

By Train The Amtrak Cascades (800/USA-RAIL; www.wsdot.wa.gov/amtrak/. Cost: $23/adult; 2-15/half price; free/under 2) runs from Seattle to Vancouver. The remarkably scenic trip follows the Puget Sound coastline on its 3.5-hour journey. The route extends from Eugene, OR to Vancouver, with connections to other U.S. destinations. There's a snack bar and restaurant onboard, and free movies, edited to meet PG standards. Bring your own headphones or purchase them on the train. From Pacific Central Station, you'll need to catch a cab to the cruise terminal (about $8). **VIA Rail** (800/561-8630; www.viarail.ca/) offers service three times a week from points east to Vancouver. Children ages 12 to 17 pay a percent of adult economy fare; ages 2 to 11 pay half fare; under 2 ride free, if not occupying a separate seat. Kids' programming offered by VIA Rail includes movies, activity kits, and—in summer—guides whose duties include entertaining small fry. Train food-service includes kid menus.

VANCOUVER

Many cruise passengers arrange to spend a day or two in Vancouver on one end of their journey. Vancouver is brimming with fun family activities; if you don't have a car, take advantage of Vancouver's excellent public transit (the envy of folks south of the border) to get around.

Places to Stay

Accommodation is plentiful and ranges from low-priced (especially for Americans) to very expensive by any standard. For sheer convenience, nothing beats the **Pan Pacific Hotel** (300-999 Canada Pl; 604/662-8111; 800/937-1515; www.panpacific.com; 504 rooms, 39 suites; restaurants. **$$$**). All rooms have a view and there's a spa with a pool, but weary parents may appreciate most the fact that the cruise terminal is in the same building complex. Kids under 19 stay free in the same room with parents. In summer, promotional rates are offered in combination with cruises.

A more moderately priced option a short walk away is the **Delta Vancouver Suite Hotel** (550 W Hastings; 604/689-8188, 877/814-7706; www.delta hotels.com; 225 suites; restaurant. **$$**), catering to cruise passengers. Suites

---

☛ **Parent Tip:**
Vancouver's Two Cruise Terminals

Neither of Vancouver's cruise terminals offers much in the way of entertainment or seating, especially for kids. Kiosks are more likely to sell cigars than toys, and there is no children's area. If the worst happens and you're stuck at Canada Place with cranky kids, hike across the street, where you'll find a mall, a small park with a bit of green space, and **Schlotzky's Deli** (Waterfront Center, 604/689-2867), which serves up deli fare, pizzas, and box lunches you can carry away with you. If your ship leaves from Ballantyne Pier, though, you're out of luck; it's surrounded only by container-shipping docks. ▣

---

are spacious, but lack kitchens. The fitness center and pool stay open late. Children under 18 stay free with parents. Kids under 7 eat free, and kids 7-12 eat half-price (ordering from the adult menu). Delta's two other Vancouver locations have similar amenities.

What to See & Do

Across the street from the cruise terminal you'll find the **Visitor Info Centre** (200 Burrard; 604/683-2000; www.tourismvancouver.com). Take a walk around the **Promenade at Canada Place** (directly above the terminal), marvel at the views of Burrard Inlet and Grouse Mountain, and check out the ship you'll soon be boarding. For an even better view, visit the Lookout atop the **Harbour Centre Tower**, a few blocks east of the terminal (555 W Hastings; 8:30am-10:30pm daily [summer]; 9am-9pm [winter]. Cost: $10/adult, $7/student, youth 11-17, $4/child 5-10, free/under 5). The glass elevator makes the 40-story climb to the Observation Deck in 50 seconds. Daily guided tours are offered on the hour.

Back at sea level, head up to Cordova Street and head east; stroll through historic **Gastown**, full of touristy shops and sidewalk cafés, where the world's only **steam clock** (Cambie & Water Sts), puffs a breathy tune every 15 minutes. Guided tours are offered in summer (ask at the Visitor Info Centre). If the weather is rainy (and that's possible any time of year), explore the city's network of underground shopping malls. Pick up a map at the Info Centre, and head north. If your legs hold out, you might want to surface from the **Pacific Mall** at Robson Street and check out the **Vancouver Art Gallery,** a block over at 750 Hornby Street. Vancouver's many downtown malls feature food courts offering the usual favorites in kid cuisine.

If you have a vehicle or time to hop a bus, go farther afield: east on Georgia Street to **Stanley Park**, the 400-hectare peninsula that juts north into Burrard Inlet. Bordered by a nine-km seawall promenade, perfect for small legs to dash along, the park has gardens, recreational facilities, and the world-class **Vancouver Aquarium** (604/659-3474; 9:30am-7pm [summer]; 10am-5:30pm [winter]. Cost: $14.95/adult, $11.95/youth 13-18, $8.95/child 4-12, free/under 4). The aquarium's beluga whales are a big draw, along with animal feedings and shows, touch pools, and the Amazon Gallery.

Also worthwhile is a visit to **Science World** (1455 Quebec St; 604/443-7440; 10am-5pm Mon-Fri, until 6pm weekends and holidays. Cost: $12.75/adult, $8.50/child 4-18, free/child under 4, $42.50/family). You can drive here, but why not take the **Sky Train**? Get on at the Waterfront Station and get off at Main Street. You'll be across the street from the Centre's distinctive geodesic dome, where you'll find a zillion small Canadians racing around among the exhibits; no doubt your own offspring will soon be doing likewise.

4 Alaska Panhandle and the Inside Passage

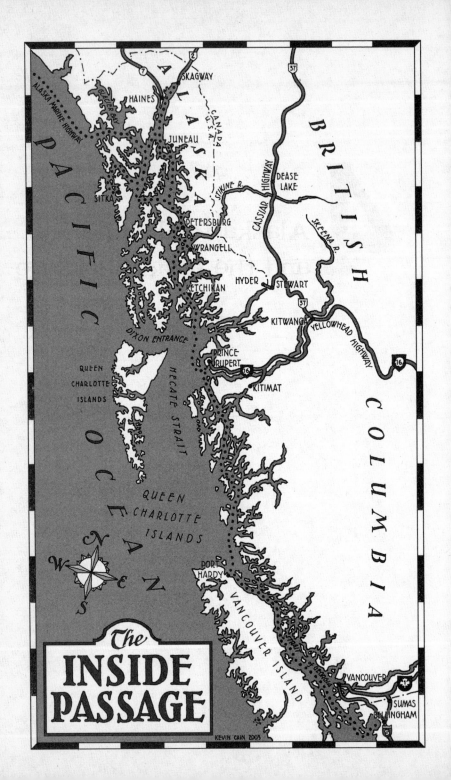

The INSIDE PASSAGE

KEVIN CAIN 2003

4 Alaska Panhandle and the Inside Passage

THE PERENNIALLY POPULAR Alaska panhandle offers a host of family-friendly activities and the mildest climate in the state. While much of this area is accessible only by air or sea, that doesn't deter the 850,000 tourists who visit each year.

There is so much to do that it can be hard to choose among the wildlife cruises, glacier flyovers, hikes, and Native village tours, not to mention the shopping. Do your homework before you arrive and accept that there won't be time to do it all. Tourists dragging huge shopping bags, dashing frantically back to cruise ships on the verge of departure, are a fairly common sight.

The largest town on the coast is Alaska's capital, Juneau. The limited accessibility of the capital to the rest of the state is a perennial subject for debate, but so far, efforts to move the capital to the state's interior have failed. One reason may be the temperate climate; temperatures seldom drop much below freezing in winter. Rain is another story; it can be a near-constant companion, although some towns are sheltered in a kind of rain shadow that keeps them relatively dry; for example, Haines averages 60 inches of rain per year, while Ketchikan gets 160.

Cruise ships arrive May through September, but you can visit any month by ferry or plane. There are always trade-offs: in summer you'll get the longest and driest days—and lots of other tourists. In spring, fall, and winter, days are shorter and colder and many attractions are closed, but you'll have no crowds to contend with. If you can, consider making your trip in early summer or right before school resumes in September. For families visiting the region, opportunities for recreation, education, and exploration abound. Each small town has its own unique history and character, showcased in some of Alaska's best museums. Your chances of encountering whales and sea otters, bald eagles, black and brown bears, and Sitka deer are good. Hike in the lush rainforest, comb tidepools and beaches for treasures, visit a Russian Orthodox cathedral with centuries-old icons, fly over and land on a glacier, kayak in the pristine waters of Misty Fjords—whatever you choose, you'll run out of time before you run out of choices.

History

For thousands of years, the southeast was home to the Tlingit, Tsimshian, and Haida tribes, who lived well off the land and sea. The lush rainforest provided useful plants and berries; cedar trees furnished materials for building houses and canoes, baskets, boxes, clothing, and much more; and the sea provided abundant fish and shellfish. The richness of the environment allowed Native people to evolve high-level cultures with advanced arts, examples of which are on display in museums and Native communities that welcome visitors.

Traders and explorers arrived in the mid-18th century. The search for furs brought the Russians, who made Sitka the capital of their North American territories. Decades later in 1776, the search for a Northwest Passage to Asia led Captain James Cook here. The century of Russian colonization left its mark on Sitka and can be seen in its churches, other buildings, and culture. The Tlingit Natives did not take well to being colonized, but they lost the struggle to defend their lands from Russian encroachment. Diseases brought by European traders, prospectors, and settlers decimated the population. Still, the powerful Tlingit controlled access between the coast and interior (which they had colonized) for generations until the Klondike Gold Rush brought thousands of prospectors into their territory, eventually ending Tlingit control over trade.

Juneau experienced its own gold rush nearly 20 years before the strike in the Klondike; successive gold rushes brought prospectors up the Inside Passage, especially to Haines and Skagway, on their way to the Klondike, and to Fairbanks and Nome. The need to maintain order during the Gold Rush led to the establishment of Alaska's first military base in Haines, which was useful during World War II in building the Haines Highway to connect Haines and the Inside Passage to the new Alaska Highway and the interior. The timber and fishing industries ensured that after the Gold Rush ended, communities continued and thrived. Still, populations here have never been large: The total population from Ketchikan to Skagway and Haines is under 80,000. Today, tourism is gradually eclipsing other industries along the Inside Passage.

Getting to the Inside Passage

By Air Alaska Airlines (800/252-7522; www.alaskair.com) serves Juneau, Ketchikan, Sitka, Petersburg, Wrangell, and Gustavus/Glacier Bay, but not Skagway or Haines; however, both towns are accessible by road. Smaller airlines connect coastal towns to destinations elsewhere in Alaska and the Yukon.

By Sea From mid-May through September, cruise lines visit Ketchikan, Juneau, Sitka, Glacier Bay/Gustavus, and Skagway; a few visit Haines and Wrangell as well (see "Alaska Cruises"). The **Alaska Marine Highway System** (800/642-0066; www.dot.state.ak.us/amhs/) has year-round service between Bellingham or Prince Rupert and Skagway, serving Ketchikan, Wrangell, Petersburg, Sitka, Juneau, and Haines; additional AMHS and private ferries serve smaller southeast communities.

Resources

Regional Tourist Information
Southeast Alaska Tourism Council (www.alaskainfo.org)

Information on Camping, Hiking, and Wilderness Activities
Alaska State Parks
Southeast Area Office, 400 Willoughby, 4th Fl, Juneau, AK 99801, 907/465-4563

Alaska Department of Natural Resources
907/762-2261; www.dnr.state.ak.us/

Bureau of Land Management Alaska
907/474-2250; www.ak.blm.gov

Reading

Books and Publications

Alaskan Southeaster Magazine (907/789-4410, 800/478-3702; www.alaskan southeaster.com). This monthly magazine focuses on the places, people, and lifestyles of southeast Alaska.

Alaska Native Cultures and Art

Bancroft-Hunt, Norman; and Forman, Werner. *People of the Totem: The Indians of the Pacific Northwest.* University of Oklahoma Press, 1979. Illustrated with many photos, this book covers the history, cosmology, and culture of these tribes.

Levi-Strauss, Claude. *The Way of the Masks.* University of Washington Press, 1979. In this classic, a great anthropologist studies extraordinary masks as a means of investigating the cultures that produced them.

Malin, Edward. *A World of Faces: Masks of the Northwest Coast Indians.* Timber Press, 1978. This book describes the masks, their purpose, and how they were made and used.

Reid, Bill. *The Raven Steals the Light.* University of Washington Press, 1984. Haida myths are lavishly illustrated by the great Haida artist and sculptor, Bill Reid.

Samuel, Cheryl. *The Chilkat Dancing Blanket.* University of Oklahoma Press, 1982. This book covers everything you wanted to know about these complex and beautiful blankets, which can take a year to weave.

Nature and Natural History

Eppenbach, Sarah. *Alaska's Southeast: Touring the Inside Passage.* Pacific Search Press, 1983. This book surveys the natural and human history of the region.

Nickerson, Roy. *Sea Otters: A Natural History and Guide.* Chronicle Books, 1984. Black and white photos illustrate this guide to these fascinating, furry ocean dwellers.

O'Clair, Rita, Armstrong, Robert, and Carstensen, Richard. *The Nature of Southeast Alaska.* Alaska Northwest Books, 1997. This comprehensive guide is a good introduction to the region's flora and fauna.

Piggott, Margaret. *Discover Southeast Alaska with Pack and Paddle.* Mountaineers, 1990. This is the second edition of a classic guide to hikes and boat trips from Ketchikan to Skagway.

Ricks, Byron. *Homelands: Kayaking the Inside Passage.* HarperCollins, 1999. This is the account of a five-month kayaking adventure from Glacier Bay to Puget Sound.

Books for Younger Kids

Cameron, Anne. *How the Loon Lost her Voice, How Raven Freed the Moon, Lazy Boy, Loon and Raven Tales, Orca's Song, Raven & Snipe, Raven Goes Berrypicking,* and *Raven Returns the Water.* Harbour Publishing, various dates. Cameron retells Native stories and legends in picture books for young children.

Gill, Shelley. *The Last American Rainforest: Tongass.* Paws IV Publishing, 1997. This charming picture book tells how a Tlingit girl and her aunt hunt for special tree roots with which to make a ceremonial hat.

Paul, Frances Lackey. *Kahtahah: A Tlingit Girl.* Alaska Northwest Books, 1996. More in-depth than many picture books, this one details a young girl's life and culture, and is beautifully illustrated by Rie Muñoz.

Books for Older Kids

Cameron, Anne. *Daughters of Copper Woman, Dzelarhons.* Harbour Publishing, various dates. These are richly detailed retellings of northwest coast myths.

Martin, Nora. *The Eagle's Shadow.* Scholastic, 1997. A 12-year-old girl sent to her mother's relatives in an Alaskan Tlingit village in 1946 discovers the richness and value of her heritage.

Robinson, Gail. *Raven the Trickster.* Chatto & Windus, 1981. This collection contains nine stories of Raven from Native American legends.

Staub, Frank. *Children of the Tlingit.* Carolrhoda Books, 1999. This is an excellent introduction to Tlingit culture for younger kids.

Activity Books and CD-ROMs

Learning About Nature Along the Inside Passage: A Naturalist's Notebook. Alaska Natural History Association, 1997. This excellent resource for kids middle-school age and older, covers regional wildlife, geology, culture, and history.

McNutt, Nan. *The Button Blanket: Northwest Coast Indian Art Activity Book.* Sasquatch, 1997. Written for the 5-9 age group, this book tells the story of a potlatch and supplies designs and instructions for creating a bentwood button blanket.

Smith, A.G. *Northwest Coast Punch-Out Indian Village.* General Publishing, 1994. A complete village, with big house, totem poles, canoes, and people is ready for children to punch out and assemble.

Alaska's Inside Passage. National Geographic. Glacier Bay, Klondike Gold Rush National Historical Park, Sitka National Historical Park, and Tongass National Forest are explored in this CD-ROM. Included are maps, interactive interpretive programs, and more (Windows and Macintosh).

KETCHIKAN

Located on Revillagigedo Island near the northern British Columbia border, Ketchikan is the first stop on northbound Alaska cruises and Alaska ferries starting from Bellingham. Ketchikan is wedged tightly between the steep mountains of the island's west coast and the Tongass Narrows that separate it from Gravina Island. To the east lies 2.2-million-acre Misty Fjords National Monument. Eighty-seven miles to the south is Prince Rupert, BC, and 600 miles farther south is Seattle. There is one north-south artery, Tongass Highway, and only about 35 miles of road on the entire island.

Ketchikan offers a hefty dose of old-world charm, an accessible downtown waterfront, excellent shopping, and gorgeous scenery, so it's not surprising to find a glut of cruise ships here on any day from late May to mid-September. In 2002, over 650,000 cruise ship passengers visited Ketchikan, and that number is expected to grow.

The region is home to Tlingit, Haida, and Tsimshian peoples, whose art gives the city its distinctive character. Ketchikan has a lively frontier history. Although never central to the Klondike Gold Rush, the town benefited from its location in the path of northbound prospectors in need of supplies. Incorporated in 1900, the town had the first paved road in Alaska and by 1930 was the state's largest city (it has since dropped to fourth place). Today, the population of greater Ketchikan is about 14,500.

For families, there is much to see and do in Ketchikan. Native communities, museums, and interesting shops are easily accessible and the neighboring wilderness is stunning. Don't let the weather get in the way of enjoying your visit here. Yes, Ketchikan gets 162 inches of rain per year. But the climate is mild, and hey, it's just water.

Getting to Ketchikan

By Air **Alaska Airlines** (907/225-2145, 800/252-7522; www.alaskair.com) serves Ketchikan year round (see "Getting There" for details). **Taquan Air** (907/225-8800, 800/770-8800; www.taquanair.com) has scheduled service between Ketchikan and nearby communities, including Metlakatla and Hyder; they also arrange charters. **Promech Air** (800/860-3845; www.promech.com) has scheduled service to Prince of Wales Island.

By Sea The **Alaska Marine Ferry System** (907/465-3941, 800/642-0066; www.dot.state.ak.us/amhs/) serves Ketchikan year round, with multiple weekly sailings between May and September. From Bellingham, the ferry trip takes 37 hours; from Juneau, about 24 hours. The Alaska ferry dock is two miles north of town on the Tongass Highway. Smaller Alaska ferries connect Ketchikan to nearby Prince of Wales Island and Metlakatla. The **Inter-Island Ferry Authority** (907/826-4848, 866/308-4848; www.inter islandferry.com) operates year-round car ferries between Ketchikan and Prince of Wales Island.

Getting Around

Ketchikan International Airport is on Gravina Island, requiring a five-minute ferry ride and a drive into town. Shuttle vans meet the ferry on the mainland.

907/225-6800; www.borough.ketchikan.ak.us/transportation/Ferry/ferry_home/. Ferries run every 15 minutes in summer, every 30 minutes the rest of the year. Cost $2.50/adult, $1.50/child 6-11; free/under 6.

The Bus, Ketchikan's public transit system, has two lines: Green and Blue. Both stop at the airport ferry and Alaska ferry docks.

907/225-8726; borough.Ketchikan.ak.us. Every 15 minutes on Tongass Ave, Mon-Sat, reduced hours Sun Green line: $1.50/adult, $1.25/student, child 5-11, free/under 5. Blue Line: $2.25/adult, $2/student, child 5-11, free/under 5.

Alaska Car Rental (907/225-5123, 800/662-0007; www.akcarrental.com) has two locations: one at the airport and one at 2828 Tongass Avenue. **Budget Car Rental** (907/225-6004 [airport], 907/225-8383 [townside], 800/478-2438) is also at the airport, with an in-town location at 4950 N Tongass Highway. For taxi service, try the **SE Alaska Cab Co.** (3950 Tongass Ave, 907/225-2133).

Places to Stay

The Landing (Best Western) ($-$$)

3434 Tongass Ave, 907/225-5166, 800/428-8304; www.landinghotel.com
FYI: 76 rooms & mini-suites, refrigerator/microwave; two restaurants; fitness center; pets OK; courtesy van for in-town destinations.

This comfortable hotel offers good value, and is located across from the ferry terminal. There's a nice view. The location is several miles from downtown.

WestCoast Cape Fox Lodge ($$-$$$)

800 Venetia Way, 907/225-8001, 800/325-4000; www.westcoasthotels.com
FYI: 72 rooms & suites; restaurant.

Perched above the Tongass Narrows, this hotel offers panoramic views and a lovely interior featuring an impressive collection of Tlingit basketry and Native Alaskan arts. Rooms are large; if good weather is predicted, spring for the more expensive view rooms, and keep your fingers crossed. Visitors can reach the lodge from downtown via the funicular on Creek Street (see "What to See & Do").

66 PARENT COMMENTS 99

"The kids loved taking the tram up and down to town. The restaurant was very kid-friendly with an added bonus of a fabulous view."

Super 8 Motel-Ketchikan ($)

2151 Sea Level Dr, 907/225-9088; www.super8.com
FYI: 82 units

> ☛ **Parent Tip**
>
> A ride on each of Ketchikan's two bus lines amounts to a low-priced survey of the city's attractions, plus a look at residents and their neighborhoods that you won't see on a tour. Kids will enjoy going through the tunnel on the way to or from the ferries ◙

Camping & Cabins

There are limited camping facilities near Ketchikan. Your best bet is the **Ward Lake Recreation Area**, accessed from Ward Lake Road (see "Hiking"), with three campgrounds: **Signal Creek Campground** (24 units, water, tables, grates, toilets, garbage cans; open May 1-Sept 30); **Three C's Campground** (4 units, water, grates, tables, toilets; open April 15-Sept 30); and **Last Chance Campground** (19 units, water, tables, grates, toilets, garbage cans, RV sites [no dumping]; open May 29-Sept 30).

Public cabins can be rented in the **Tongass National Forest** (877/444-6777; www.fs.fed.us/r10/tongass/). Cabins are $25-45 per night and can be rented for up to seven nights between May and September and up to 10 nights for the rest of the year. Users must pack in everything, including water. Cabins come with bunks (but no mattresses), table, benches, wood or oil stove, broom, axe, and outhouse.

Places to Eat

Annabelle's Famous Keg and Chowder House

326 Front St, 907/225-6009
Hours: Sun-Thurs 7am-9:30pm; Fri-Sat 7am-10:30pm

Tucked inside the historic Gilmore Hotel, dating from 1927, is this Ketchikan institution with its dark but attractive wood-paneled interior, full of diners and bustling wait staff. Dinners offer fine cuisine at some of Ketchikan's highest prices; breakfast or lunch is a better choice for families. Sourdough pancakes, fish and chips, and a selection of chowders are likely kid-pleasers.

Heen Kahidi Dining Room & Lounge

In the WestCoast Cape Fox Lodge, 800 Venetia Way; 907/225-8001;
www.westcoasthotels.com
Hours: Mon-Sat, 7am-10pm, Sun 7am-9pm (summer); daily 7am-9pm (rest of year)

This restaurant has a great view overlooking the Tongass Narrows, and the food is fine, too. Try fish and chips and other seafood selections. Be sure to leave room for dessert; they do an interesting take on crème bruleé. The kids' menu offers just what you'd expect.

Steamers on the Dock
76 Front St, 907/225-1600
Hours: 11am-11pm daily
For a splurge, try this restaurant perched above the downtown wharf. It specializes in seafood but also offers pasta, chicken, and vegetarian entrées. There's a kids' menu, and one small child reviewer gives the restaurant high marks for its clam chowder. Prices are high, but so is quality.

What to See & Do

Stroll & Browse

Ketchikan has a well-deserved reputation as a great place to shop. World-class artists reside in this small burg, and most sell their work to visitors. Start your exploration with a visit to the **Ketchikan Visitors Bureau** (131 Front St, next to the Cruise Ship Dock; 907/225-6166, 800-770-3300; www.visit ketchikan.com) and pick up a walking map. Explore the shops along Mission Street as you make your way toward Ketchikan Creek. Check out the high-quality Native masks, wood carvings and jewelry, and other works by local artists, at **Eagle Spirit Gallery** (310 Mission St, 907/225-6626). **Scanlon Gallery** (318 Mission St, 907/247-4730) has similar items but a wider range of prices; **Exploration Gallery** (633 Mission St, 907/225-4278) has local soaps and jewelry, plus interesting maps and prints. Venturing up less-traveled side streets can net rewarding finds: The **Blue Heron Gallery** (123 Steadman, 907/225-1982) has local arts and crafts at reasonable prices. Mammoth ivory is a good buy (no, it's not proscribed; it's too late for the mammoth to be endangered!)

Allow time to wander around **Creek Street,** where historic wooden buildings sit on pilings above the creek, connected by a boardwalk. The street is a bit of a tourist trap. **Dolly's House** (24 Creek St, 907/225-6329, open daily; $4) is the restored bordello of Dolly Arthur, a famous sex worker here in what used to be one of Alaska's premiere red-light districts. The house features fairly risqué photos. A better bet for families is **Soho Coho** (Star Bldg, 5 Creek St, 907/225-5954; www.trollart.com), a shop selling work by renowned local artist Ray Troll, whose quirky kid-pleasing depictions of life natural and unnatural adorn T-shirts, coffee mugs, posters, and books. Other local artists are also featured. Upstairs in the same building is **Parnassus Books** (907/225-7690), whose tiny rooms are filled with a rich variety of reading material, especially local history and Native culture, along with a fine kids' section. **Sam McGee's: A Taste of Alaska** (18 Creek St, 907/225-3252) has a variety of Alaskan goodies: fireweed pancake syrup, wild cranberry jelly, smoked salmon, and other northern treats. There are usually samples to try.

When the young ones are fed up with shopping, head to **Ketchikan Creek,** where the water teems with spawning salmon in August and early September. Visitors in late summer are almost certain to encounter salmon in various states of post-spawn decay. It's not a pretty sight, but it is sure to fascinate kids. Given the uncertain status of wild salmon today, this opportunity is

Totem Poles

The great cultures of the Pacific Northwest were fortunate to evolve in a gentle climate with abundant food, and, like other cultures with time on their hands, they flourished artistically, creating massive vertical sculptures. These totem poles serve many functions: They tell community or family stories, commemorate the dead, and sometimes ridicule individuals whose exasperating behavior prompted this nonviolent form of getting even. Totem poles are designed to stand outdoors, be subject to the elements, and deteriorate over time. Photographs of late 19th century coastal communities show villages with rows of big houses fronted by imposing totem poles. As many villages along the coast were devastated by disease and abandoned, their totem poles gradually disintegrated. Some European settlers destroyed totem poles systematically, mistaking them for religious symbols. In the late 1930s, the US Forest Service and Civilian Conservation Corps worked with Native carvers to preserve the remaining totem poles, and the results of their efforts can be seen throughout Southeast Alaska.

Like other Inside Passage towns, Ketchikan's parks and public

buildings are graced with totem poles. In Ketchikan, after you've paid a visit to the Totem Heritage Center, Saxman Native Village, or Totem Bight State Historical Park, encourage the kids to keep a lookout for totem poles in town. At the top of the Creek Street funicular, check out the fine collection in front of the WestCoast Cape Fox Lodge, as well as at the Southeast Alaska Discovery Center, in front of the Tongass Historical Museum library building, and at Eagle Park (close to the tunnel off Front Street). Help children identify the animals on the poles by their signature traits: the beaver's buckteeth and flat tail; the eagle's strong, curved beak; the raven's long sharp beak; the killer whale's dorsal fin and big teeth.

Shearar, Cheryl. *Understanding Northwest Coast Art: A Guide to Crests, Beings, and Symbols.* University of Washington Press, 2000. This is a straightforward guide to the language and symbolism of totem poles.

Stewart, Hillary. *Looking at Totem Poles.* University of Washington Press, 1993. By a noted expert in the field, this work surveys and explains over 100 totem poles. ◙

☛ Parent Tip

If you're here on a weekday morning, take advantage of the story time for young kids, often hosted then by the Ketchikan Public Library, in the same building as the Tongass Historical Museum. ▣

---

increasingly rare. The sight of a huge sparkling fish leaping many feet into the air every few seconds is mesmerizing.

Kids will also enjoy going up the **Cape Fox Hill-Creek Street Funicular** ($1/each way) which rises 211 feet straight up to the WestCoast Cape Fox Lodge. It takes just a few minutes, and it's less scary and far less expensive than the Mount Roberts tram in Juneau. If you have time, instead of taking the funicular down, walk on the "Married Man's Trail" (the alternate route to the backdoors of Ketchikan's old brothels, which were in operation until 1962). Young boating enthusiasts will enjoy a look at the fishing vessels and yachts in the small boat harbor downtown, south of Creek Street just across the Stedman Street Bridge.

If the weather lets you down, escape indoors to the **Salmon Landing Market**, south of the cruise ship dock, the closest thing to a mall downtown. Here's where you'll find local teens—and inexpensive, fast food. You can dry off, sip coffee, and watch the kids devour hot dogs (an endangered species in cruise-ship oriented downtown Ketchikan). When you've recharged your batteries, investigate the **Dockside Gallery** (5 Salmon Landing, Ste 12, 907/225-2858) upstairs. Young crafters might enjoy the adjoining **Bead Shoppe**, with beading supplies and books.

Parks

Close to the Totem Heritage Center (601 Deermount St), you'll find a kids' playground with swings, climbing equipment, and slide; the **City Park** across the creek has picnic tables. **Harborview Park** (521 Water St), on the far side of the tunnel, has great views and picnic tables.

Museums

Southwest Alaska Discovery Center ☺ A short stroll from the cruise ship dock, this attractive museum is operated by the Alaska Public Lands Information Center (APLIC), which offers trip-planning services as well as exhibits on natural history and information on visiting the Tongass National Forest, Misty Fjords National Monument, and other nearby national parks. The museum also showcases local Native cultures (Tlingit, Haida, and Tsimshian), the local ecosystem, and human impact on this rich, yet fragile, environment. There are hands-on exhibits for youngsters. A small theater shows films on the region. There is an excellent store—stock up on any maps you need.
50 Main St, 907/228-6220; www.fs.fed.us/r10/tongass/districts/discoverycenter/. Open daily 8am-5pm (May 9-Sept. 30); Tues-Sat, 10am-4:30pm (Oct. 30-May 8). Cost: $5/adult, free/under 7. Allow 45 minutes.

Swimming Pools
Along the Inside Passage

Few hotels in southeast Alaska come with swimming pools. But well-equipped public pools, listed in this chapter, offer daily open swims. Some are in public-school buildings, but don't let that stop you: These community resources welcome families. Schedules and fee structures are complex; call for details. Expect to pay about $3 an hour per adult (less for kids); some pools have family rates.

And should your visit coincide with a heat wave (it can happen), your young amphibians might even join their hardy counterparts in a cautious barefoot exploration at a rare sandy beach. ◙

Tongass Historical Museum   This small museum with a good collection of Native art and artifacts and historical displays will give you a taste of Ketchikan's lively past. Find U.S. President Truman's features on a totem pole, and admire a beautiful Chilkat blanket.
29 Dock St; 907/225-5600; www.city.ketchikan.ak.us/ds/tonghist/. Open daily, 8am-5pm (May 1-Sept. 30); Wed-Fri, 1-5pm, Sat 10am-4pm, Sun 1-4pm (Oct. 1-Apr. 30). Cost: $2. Allow 15-30 minutes.

Totem Heritage Center   This handsome museum is home to 33 historic totem poles collected from abandoned Tlingit and Haida villages in the Ketchikan vicinity. Displayed with them are other interesting Native artifacts and works of art. In summer, watch Native artists at work. There's a well-stocked gift shop.
601 Deermount St; 907/225-5600; www.city.ketchikan.ak.us/ds/tonghert/. Open daily, 8am-5pm (May 1-Sept. 30); Mon-Fri, 1-5pm (Oct. 1-Apr. 30). Tours, demos in summer. Cost: $4. Allow at least 30 minutes.

Animals, Animals

Deer Mountain Tribal Hatchery & Eagle Center   Across the creek from the Totem Heritage Center, this hatchery is set in a park that features a fish ladder and displays on the salmon life cycle. There are plenty of eagles on view, some being nursed back to health. However, tours of the center are expensive, and eagle-viewing opportunities abound in southeast Alaska. If you'll be visiting Juneau, the Macauley Salmon Hatchery is a better deal at $3 (see "Juneau" later in this chapter). You can reduce the cost here by buying a combined ticket for $9.95 that also gets you into the Totem Heritage Center.
1158 Salmon Rd. 907/225-6026, 800/252-5158. Open daily, 8:30am-4:30pm (summer); rest of year by appointment. Cost: $6.95. Allow 30 minutes.

Spectacles

The Great Alaskan Lumberjack Show Aimed at cruise-ship tourists, this show highlights the drama of man against log; it features ax throwing, log rolling, and pole climbing, and lets visitors get in on the act. Ironically, the skills showcased here are obsolete in today's timber trade. If time and money are limited, you can do better than this overpriced attraction.
One block from the cruise ship docks. 888/320-9049;
www.lumberjackshows.com. At least 3 shows daily. Cost: $30.60/adult,
$15.30/child 5-12, free/child under 5. Allow 1.5 hours.

Swimming

Ketchikan has two venues for swimming. **Mike Smithers Community Pool** (2610 4th Ave, 907/225-2010) has two pools along with a sauna and small fitness area. Kids under 4 swim free. **Valley Park Swimming Pool** (410/610 Schoenbar Rd, 907/225-8755) is located next to the Gateway Recreation Center (907/225-9579) with gym, sport courts, roller skating, and skateboarding.

The Great Outdoors

Hiking Excellent hiking opportunities abound in this area. Below are a few tried and true trails, offering a variety of challenges and benefits.

You'll need wheels to get to it, but **Ward Lake Nature Trail** is a good choice for families with young kids. It's an easy, level, 1.3-mile loop trail around a lake, set in temperate rainforest. Interpretive signs identify much of what you'll see. Look for deer, beaver, and migratory birds. In late summer, you'll see spawning salmon in Ward Creek. There are picnicking facilities and campgrounds in the area: phone 877/444-6777. *8 miles north on Tongass Hwy; right on Revilla Rd. Turn right at Ward Lake Rd. to the Ward Lake Day Use parking area. Allow 1 hour hiking time.*

Perseverance Lake Trail, located near Ward Lake, is a moderately difficult hike. You'll traverse 2.2 miles of rainforest and bog (most of the trail is on boardwalks), then ascend about 750 feet to Perseverance Lake. The trail passes through a variety of ecosystems, offering possible wildlife sightings, including black bears. In wet conditions, the boardwalk can get very slippery. *7 miles north on Tongass Hwy, off Ward Lake Rd. Allow 4 hours hiking time for the round trip.*

Deer Mountain Trail is a good bet for families with older children who are experienced hikers. Don't attempt it without good hiking boots, water, and raingear. The six-mile round trip takes you up about 3,000 feet and offers spectacular views of the entire region. If you lack the time or energy for the whole hike, go about a mile to the first overlook, where you'll catch a glimpse of nearby islands. Vegetation includes old-growth forest, wildflowers, and blueberries. You may find snow if you visit before late July. At the summit, the trail continues to Blue Lake and beyond. For information and trail conditions, pick up a hiking guide at the Ketchikan visitors bureau. *Trailhead is off Ketchikan Lakes Rd at the end of Fair St, past the City Park. Allow 4-6 hours.*

👉 **Parent Tip**

Instead of following the throng into the Village Store, walk down toward the waterfront to the Saxman Arts Co-op. The reasonably priced T-shirts, button blankets, jewelry, carvings, and more sold here are made locally. ◾

Sea Kayaking **Southeast Exposure** From May to September, these folks offer guided kayak trips, kayak instruction, and rentals. They supply everything needed to get out in the water. The 2.5-hour Tongass Narrows Waterfront tour is suitable for kids old enough to use a paddle. In double kayaks, you'll get a duck's eye view of Ketchikan's picturesque waterfront and more.

515 Water St; 907/225-8829; www.southeastexposure.com.
Cost: $50/adult, $30/child. Allow 2.5 hours.

Southeast Sea Kayaks This outfit rents kayaks and offers guided kayaking trips, including a 2.5-hour tour of the waterways around local islands in search of wildlife; several trips are offered daily ($68/adult, $49/child). Kids 6 and over are welcome; three-person kayaks can accommodate small paddlers. A four-hour trip to Orcas Cove (boat transportation included) in search of sea mammals, bald eagles, and interesting scenery is limited to six participants, and children must be over 12 ($129). Multiday trips include kayaking Misty Fjords and Tatoosh Rocks. Kayaking/hiking combo trips are also offered.

1430 Millar St; 907/225-1258, 800/287-1607; www.kayakketchikan.com.
Rentals available to experienced kayakers. Allow 2-4 hours and up.

Tidepooling ☺ At **Rotary Beach**, three miles south of downtown, there are a sheltered beach suitable for wading, plenty of tidepools, and a play-ground. The park includes picnic facilities and pit toilets. *3500 block of Tongass Hwy S.*

Excursions **Misty Fjords National Monument** This 2.3 million-acre park, accessible only by floatplane or boat, is one of the more spectacular sights along the Inside Passage. It features long fjords and natural canals, as well as rivers and streams from glaciers that continue to recede but once covered the entire region. The vegetation ranges from temperate rainforest (hemlock, spruce, and cedar) to muskeg and alpine. The Tlingit people, resident here for at least 10,000 years, left pictographs (pictures) and petroglyphs (rock etchings). Wildlife includes black and brown bears, Sitka black-tailed deer, wolves, all kinds of salmon and trout, and, of course, bald eagles, which can be seen posing majestically in treetops above Behm Canal and other waterways. Marine mammals include sea lions, whales, porpoises, and seals.

If you have less than a day to spend, you can still take a flightseeing trip, a wildlife cruise, or both. Options abound, but most are costly. In general, kids on a flight pay the same as adults unless they are seated on a parent's lap.

Staying in a Forest Service Cabin
by Christian Boatsman

The rustic Forest Service cabin we rented is located on Winstanley Island, east of Ketchikan in Misty Fjords National Monument—breathtaking scenery, incredible isolation, and perfect for the adventurous family. The 12-foot by 14-foot cabin, built and maintained by the U.S. Forest Service, is on a weather-protected salt-water beach about 30 air miles (50 boat miles) from Ketchikan. It is accessible only by floatplane or boat and there's no running water, gas or electricity. Its "amenities" include an outhouse 50 feet from the cabin, an ax for splitting firewood, four plywood bunk beds, and a wood-stove for heat. Fresh water must be carried from a small stream about a quarter-mile from the cabin.

It's not the Ritz, but for the adventurous family, this place is perfect! We had two families of four crammed into the cabin for five days and nights, and somehow we never got bored or on each other's nerves. It was perhaps the most beautiful and isolated place we've ever stayed. Except for a few

Check in advance about refunds if weather prohibits flying. Among the contenders for your business is **Taquan Air** (907/225-8800, 800/770-8800; www.taquanair.com), whose trips start at $89 for a 35-minute flight. Longer trips include hiking and wildlife spotting. There's a four-passenger minimum. **Promech Air** (800/860-3845; www.promech.com) offers a two-hour tour as well. Most flightseeing companies also offer charter aircraft to deliver you to Forest Service cabins. **Goldbelt Tours** (907/225-6044, 800/228-1905; www.goldbelttours.com), owned by Juneau's Native corporation, takes passengers on a 6.5-hour catamaran cruise to Misty Fjords ($150/adult, $125/child) with a naturalist on board. For multi-day kayak trips in Misty Fjords, see "Kayaking."

Saxman Native Village ☺   Tours of this village showcase Tlingit culture; if you have time for only one totem-pole park, make it this one. Owned by the Cape Fox Corporation (one of the Native village corporations established throughout Alaska by the Alaska Native Claims Settlement Act of 1973), the park features a Beaver Clan house, a large carving shed, and an extraordinary assortment of fine and unusual totem poles. Cape Fox Tours—a branch of the corporation—works with cruise-aligned tour companies to bring large groups of cruise passengers here. The tours efficiently move a nonstop flow of tourists through the village. Although the presentation is on the slick side, the tour is well worth taking and likely to interest most kids. Alaska Natives escort visitors to an orientation on Tlingit culture, teach them a few words of the challenging Tlingit language, then take them to the clan house where distant floatplanes heading up to Rudyard Bay, we saw no one else while we were there. We chartered a boat from Ketchikan to the cabin and brought four rented kayaks. The boat returned five days later to pick us up. We had to bring our food and as much water as we could, camp stoves, lanterns, sleeping bags and pads, flashlights, rain gear, and other necessities (the REI "solar shower" we brought was a hit!) A few of us circumnavigated the island (10 miles) in kayaks, and saw sea lions, bald eagles, and salmon. This was truly the trip of a lifetime, even for our 3-year-old!

On the downside, communication with the outside world was nonexistent. Had any of us required medical attention, this would have posed a problem. We had two contingency plans: 1) kayak to the middle of Behm Canal (less than a mile wide) to wait for a passing boat (but we saw none in five days), or 2) kayak five miles around the island to the U.S. Forest Service Rangers' floating Ranger Station and use their radio (we visited once via kayak, but didn't see anyone there). Luckily, we didn't have to test our contingency plans!

The Misty Fjords and Ketchikan areas have an annual rainfall of about 160-170 inches, which means it rains almost all the time, even during the summer months. July and August have the least rainfall and the most light. ▣

the Cape Fox Dancers perform dances (some feature very young Tlingit kids), and tell thrilling stories. You'll have a chance to see what those beautiful, intricate Chilkat blankets were designed for.

At the carving shed, eminent local carvers are available to answer questions. After a brief guided tour of the totem poles, visitors are turned loose in the big Village Store that sells souvenirs. Don't be rushed into the store; the totem poles are much more interesting. Be sure to check out the ridicule pole that caricatures William Seward, who negotiated the purchase of Alaska from Russia. Independent travelers can buy tickets at the Village Store. Call first (preferably the day before).

Saxman Village, 2.5 miles south of Ketchikan. Tours: Cape Fox Tours, 907/225-4846; www.capefoxtours.com/saxman. Call for details.
Cost: $35/adult, $17.50/child. Allow 2 hours.

Totem Bight State Historical Park   This attractive state park features 14 totem poles set along an easy walking trail and a reproduction Tlingit clan house set in evergreen forest overlooking the water. Parent reviewers report good tidepooling here. Brochures tell visitors about the poles and their meanings. City buses do not run here, so unless you've rented a car, you'll need to take a tour to reach it.

12 miles north of Ketchikan on Tongass Hwy. For information, contact the Ketchikan Ranger Station: 9883 N Tongass Hwy, 907/247-8574; www.dnr.state.ak.us/parks/units/totembgh/. Free.

Ketchikan Rain Derby

Just as Nenana has its ice classic, predicting when ice breakup will occur on the Nenana River, Ketchikan has a contest of its own: the rain derby. Contestants predict how much rainfall Ketchikan will receive for the year and for the month of December. The entrant whose guess comes closest to the actual totals receives $5,000; additional $100 prizes are awarded to the next five closest guesses. The $5 entry fee goes to Ketchikan's Chamber of Commerce. The highest rainfall recorded in Ketchikan was in 1999 (186.24 inches); the lowest in 1995 (88.44 inches). For more information, check out the Rain Derby Web page at www.ketchikanchamber.com/old_files/rainderby/. ◉

Calendar of Events

February
Festival of the North
907/225-2211; www.ketchikanarts.org
Month-long arts festival celebrating the arts, including dance, theater, literature, and music.

June
Annual Salmon Derby
907/225-2077
Runs three consecutive weekends, prizes.
Annual Salmon Run
907/225-5954

August
Blueberry Arts Festival
907/225-2211
Major arts & crafts festival with events such as slug races.

Resources

Greater Ketchikan Chamber of Commerce
P.O. Box 5957, Ketchikan, AK 99901, 907/225-3184; www.ketchikanchamber.com

Ketchikan Reservation Service
412 D-1 Loop Rd, 800/987-5337; www.Ketchikan-lodging.com.
Bed & breakfast reservations

Ketchikan Visitors Bureau ·
131 Front St, Ketchikan, AK 99901, 907/225-6166, 800/770-3300; www.visit-ketchikan.com

Alaska Marine Highway Terminal
On North Tongass Hwy; 907/225-6181

US Forest Service
Federal Building, Steadman & Mill Sts; 907/747-6671

SITKA

Sitka is blessed with a beautiful setting on Baranof Island. On clear days, Mount Edgecumbe, a 3,201-foot volcanic cone reminiscent of Japan's Mount Fuji, is visible across island-dotted Sitka Sound.

With 9,000 residents, Sitka is Alaska's fifth largest city. Because it is considerably west of other southeast Alaska communities, it's not included on all cruise ship itineraries. The larger lines include Sitka on about half their cruises. Cruises to Sitka are sometimes canceled due to rough weather. Alaska ferries serve Sitka year round.

Like much of the Inside Passage, Sitka is located inside the Tongass National Forest. It averages a mere 95 inches of rain annually (compared to Ketchikan's 162); summer high temperatures average in the low 60s, winter highs in the upper 30s. Sitka architecture includes lovely historic buildings and waterfront residences with attractive gardens. As befits its cultured past, Sitka is a sophisticated little community, full of fascinating historic sites, both Native and Russian; there's a lot to interest families, whether their pleasure is history, culture, or the great outdoors.

Sitka's rich marine environment has attracted some of the best outfitters in Alaska. The difficulty you may have is cramming a few interesting options into just hours. If so, prioritize carefully and plan to return someday to do the other 150 things you'd like to do!

History

Sitka has played a major role in Alaska history from the time of the early Tlingit people, whose magnificent art and culture is showcased around town. The Russians "discovered" Sitka at the end of the 18th century, when Alexander Baranof founded a settlement here with a charter from the Czar. The Tlingit did not take well to being colonized, however. After years of battles with the Native population, Russians established full control in 1804, and the city, called New Archangel, became the capital of Russian America. Sitka remained the capital, and a lively and cultured city, until Alaska was sold to the United States in 1867. The sale was concluded in Sitka, which served as the capital of American Alaska until 1900. But while Sitka had been a center of Russian culture for decades, the United States couldn't find a use for it; the town lost its centrality to territorial life and all but faded away. During World War II it came to life again, serving as an important air base.

Until recently, Sitka's economy depended on forest products and the fishing industry, but increasingly tourism is what sustains the town. Its gentle climate hasn't hurt either; Sitka has become an attractive place for Alaskans to retire. For such a small community, Sitka has a lot to offer culturally. It's home to Sheldon Jackson College, a small four-year liberal arts college. Every summer, the city hosts a major classical music festival and a fine-arts program for teenagers.

Getting to Sitka

Alaska Airlines (907/966-2266, 800/252-7522; www.alaskair.com) has daily jet flights to Sitka. The **AMHS** (907/465-3941, 800/642-0066;

www.dot.state.ak.us/amhs/) and major cruise lines visit Sitka (see "Getting There" and "Alaska Cruises"). The ferry ride from Ketchikan to Sitka takes 10 hours; from Sitka to Juneau is eight hours and 45 minutes.

Getting Around

Unlike Ketchikan and Juneau, Sitka's small harbor cannot accommodate huge cruise ships. Instead, cruise passengers are ferried in by tender. The AMHS ferry dock is several miles out of town; a **Sitka Tours** shuttle bus (907/747-8443, $5/one way, $7/round trip) meets all incoming ferries year round, as well as flights from May through September.

Tribal Tours operates a **Visitor Transit shuttle bus** (907/747-7290; $7/person/all-day pass) that circulates among Sitka's principal attractions including the **Crescent Harbor Shelter** (for cruise ship passengers disembarking from tenders), **Sheldon Jackson Museum**, **Sitka National Historical Park**, the **Alaska Raptor Center**, downtown, the **Tribal House**, and **O'Connell Bridge**. The bus operates May through September, Monday to Friday, 12:30-4:30pm

For land-based transportation, try **Arrowhead Taxi** (907/747-8888). Many locations, including some B&Bs, are best reached by water. **Sitka Water Taxi** (907/747-5970; home.gci.net/~snewell/) operates May to September in Sitka Sound; **EZC Transfer Company** (500 Lincoln St, Sheep Island, 907/747-5044) is a year-round water taxi.

Vehicles can be rented at the Sitka airport from **Allstar Rent-A-Car** (907/966-2552, 800/722-6927; www.allstarsitka.com) and **Avis** (907/966-2404, 800/478-2847; www.avis.com).

Places to Stay

Finn Alley Inn ☺ ($)
711 Lincoln St, 907/747-3655; www.ptialaska.net/~seakdist/finn/
FYI: Large room with bath & private entrance; breakfast; microwave/refrigerator; TV/VCR and videos.

This nonsmoking B&B is located in the basement of a historic waterfront residence. The premises come with a queen bed and sofabed. Rates are very reasonable.

❝ P A R E N T   C O M M E N T S ❞

"At Finn Alley Inn there was a series of videos in the room that featured local lore by local authors. These soon became my kids' favorite stories, and we were forced to seek out the books in the local bookstore and read them every night for the remainder of our trip!"

"It is great for a family—it felt like home. The caring host and hostess did everything they could to help us and make us comfortable during our two nights there. The breakfast and neighborhood were great."

The Sitka Hotel ($)
118 Lincoln St, 907/747-3288; www.sitkahotel.com
FYI: 57 rooms and suites, some shared baths, some kitchens; restaurant;
Laundromat; kids under 12 stay free

This attractive hotel dates from 1939 and has been beautifully restored.
The location is as central as they come.

Super 8 Motel ($)
404 Sawmill Creek Rd, 907/747-8804; www.super8.com/Super8/
FYI: 35 rooms; hot tub; Laundromat; pets OK (fee)

Westmark Shee Atiká ($$)
330 Seward St, 907/747-6241; www.westmarkhotels.com
FYI: 101 rooms and suites, restaurant

This is Sitka's largest and fanciest hotel; parent reviewers report the staff
is friendly and helpful. Rooms are not particularly large. VCRs are available
for rent.

66 PARENT COMMENTS 99

*"The hotel is located very close to the waterfront in
downtown Sitka. Most of the tourist attractions are
only a short walk away. We usually request
water-view rooms; not only do we prefer them,
but the other side of the hotel overlooks a busy
street and the noise can filter up to the rooms.
The Westmark has a good restaurant—standard
fare and a children's menu."*

Camping & Cabins

Two nearby campgrounds are managed by the Tongass National Forest (Sitka
Ranger District, 907/747-6671). By far the nicest is **Starrigavan Campground**
($8/site, 14-day limit), seven miles north of Sitka on Halibut Point Road, less
than a mile from the ferry terminal. It is very popular with RVers and tent
campers (there are six walk-in sites). Some sites front the water, others
Starrigavan Creek. (If you're here in late summer, you can witness the gory
spectacle of salmon spawning.) There's an artesian well with good drinking
water on the site; adjacent is **Old Sitka State Historic Site**, an old Russian set-
tlement, now a state park. There are interpretive signs and three excellent short
trails (two are accessible to wheelchairs), with trail-guiding brochures, suitable for
small fry to tackle. From May to October there's a campground host in residence.

Sawmill Creek Campground (seven miles east of town on Sawmill Creek
Rd., left on Blue Lake Rd.) has 11 sites and is free.

There are 24 **Forest Service cabins** around the vicinity of Sitka. Most
require boat or plane transport to access. For rentals, contact the Tongass
National Forest, Sitka Ranger District (201 Katlian St, 907/747-4220;

www.fs.fed.us/r10/tongass/recreation/cabin_info/sitkamap/sitka_map/).
Sitka water taxis can get you there and back, along with your kayaks, bikes,
and other gear. See "Getting There."

Places to Eat

Bayview Restaurant ☺
407 Lincoln St; 907/747-5440
Hours: Mon-Sat 5am-9pm; Sun 5am-8pm (spring-fall); Mon-Thurs 7am-8pm;
Fri-Sat 7am-9pm; Sun 8am-8pm (rest of year)

Located in a small mall overlooking Crescent Harbor, this is a gem of a
restaurant for families in a hurry. It's very popular with locals and visitors, so
chances are there'll be a line. Don't despair; they move customers through
quickly. The specialty is hearty Russian dishes; borscht is a good bet. There
is a full complement of American dishes along with a kids' menu. Lunch
specials are a good deal; prices are very reasonable for this part of the world.
Whoever finishes first can check out the Russian nesting dolls in the mall
shops.

Backdoor
104 Barracks St; 907/747-8856
Hours: Mon-Sat 7am-5pm; closed Sun

Sitka's literary coffeehouse has custom-roasted espresso, all kinds of baked
goods, soups, and juices. It's right behind Old Harbor Books, where local and
visiting bookworms all end up eventually. The food comes here from the
Mojo Café (203 Lincoln St, 907/747-0667. Hours: Mon-Sat, 6:30am-5pm,
Sun 9am-3pm.).

Kenny's Wok & Teriyaki
210 Katlian St. 907/747-5676
Hours: Mon-Fri 11am-9pm; Sat-Sun noon-9pm

In pricey Sitka, Kenny's is a popular choice with locals who need to feed a
hungry family on a budget. The menu offers a wide selection of Chinese and
Japanese favorites, with enough familiar options to tempt picky eaters.

What to See & Do

Stroll & Browse

Most tourists arrive by tender or shuttle bus at the Crescent Harbor. To get
your bearings, start from the **Visitor Center** (330 Harbor Dr, in Harrigan
Centennial Hall next to the Crescent Boat Harbor. 907/747-3225;
www.sitka.org. Open Mon-Wed 8am-10pm, Thurs-Fri. & most weekend
days, 8am-5pm [summer]; Mon-Fri, 8am-5pm [rest of year]). Pick up a walking
map here and orient yourself.

If time is limited, head up to Lincoln Street and turn right to get to the
Sheldon Jackson Museum and Sitka National Historical Park (see
"Museums"), Sitka's major sightseeing attractions. Stop in at **Saint Michael's**

Cathedral. This distinctive Russian Orthodox cathedral is a reconstruction of the 1848 original, which burned down in 1966. Many original icons and church artifacts were rescued and are on display. A flyer explains Orthodox Christian practices such as why they light candles before icons. There's a small store in the cathedral that sells gifts and religious items.

Lincoln & Seward. Open summer, Mon-Fri 9am-4pm. Check first on weekends; closed during services. Cost: free ($2 donation requested). Allow 20 minutes.

The large building that dominates Sitka's skyline west of the cathedral is the **Sitka Pioneer's Home**, built to house elderly Alaskans. Also in the vicinity are: a replica of a **Russian block house**, a reminder of Russia's war with the Tlingit, and, in the Lutheran Cemetery, the **grave of Princess Maktsoutoff**, wife of the last Russian governor of Alaska. These are more likely to interest adults than children, but kids might enjoy the restored Russian Bishop's House, which once served as a school (see "Museums").

Nestled among the historical sites are plenty of shopping opportunities. On Lincoln Street, drop into **Winter Song Soap Company** (419 Lincoln St, 907/747-8949, 888/819-8949) for locally made soaps and bath products. At the same address you'll find the **Sitka Rose Gallery** (907/747-3030, 888/236-1536), featuring work by some of Alaska's best-known Native artists. The **Russian American Company** (407 Lincoln St, 907/747-6228, 800/742-6448) has a broad selection of nesting dolls, including Alaska Native dolls, Russian antiques, and plenty of moderately priced Russian birch-bark crafts. You can find books by local authors at **Old Harbor Books** (201 Lincoln St, 907/747-8808), then take your purchases to the Backdoor for perusal while you sip a hot drink. **Fishermen's Eye Fine Art Gallery** (2 Lincoln St, Suite 2A, 907/747-6080) features work by local and Native artists and craftspeople.

Bus Tours

A variety of narrated historical tours are offered here, mostly aimed at cruise ship passengers. If you don't have the time (or energy) to take a walking tour on your own, one of these might be just the ticket. Many tours include a trip to the Raptor Center and parks. Some Tribal Tours include Native Alaska cultural events.

Tribal Tours (200 Katlian St, 907/747-7290, 888/270-8687; www.sitka.org/tribaltours/) has several options, starting with a one-hour tour. **Harbor Mountain Tours** (1210 Edgecumbe Dr, 907/747-8294. Cost: $15/adult, $10/child, group rates available) takes from 2 to 10 passengers in a van for a 1.5-hour tour, May through August. They'll customize to your taste and can arrange pick up, drop off, and flexible timing. **Sitka Tours** (907/747-8443) has a selection of longer tours, including a Ferry Stopover Tour ($12/adult, $6/child) timed to coincide with brief ferry layovers.

Parks

Baranof Castle Hill State Historic Site Despite the long name, it's a small park with views of Sitka and the waterfront. This is the site of the

Kids and Museums

According to the Travel Industry Association, 93 million Americans included at least one historic site, museum, or cultural event as part of their vacation in 2000. Alaska and the Yukon contain world-class museums, and there's a good chance your family will visit at least some. Children, however, do not always respond with enthusiasm to the prospect of a museum visit. Here are a few suggestions for generating interest:

• Call ahead and ask about family or kid programs and special exhibits that might interest your kids. Large museums often have dedicated children's rooms providing activities for a range of ages. The state Museum in Juneau has a Yukon Gold Rush computer game that can engage kids for hours. The Anchorage Museum of Art & History has a variety of children's programs and some for families.

Baranof Castle, where the Russians transferred control of Alaska to the United States. There's a walkway up the hill and interpretive panels along the way.

Sitka National Historical Park (see "Museums")

Whale Park This park is well worth a visit, especially during peak whale-viewing times (fall and winter). Two boardwalks with stairs lead down to the rocky shore. Interpretive signs and viewing scopes are provided. Along with whales, look for sea otters here. There's a small picnic shelter. *Four miles southeast of town on Sawmill Creek Rd.*

Museums

Isabel Miller Museum This small, interesting museum operated by the Sitka Historical Society is just the right size for kids. It covers a lot of ground: Tlingit basketry and carving, a 19th-century household parlor, and exhibits detailing Sitka's military history from the transfer of Alaska to the United States through World War II. A small gift shop includes books for kids on local culture and natural history.
In the Harrigan Centennial Bldg., 330 Harbor Dr. 907/747-6455; www.sitka.org/historicalmuseum. Open daily 9am-5pm (May-Sept.); Mon-Fri, 10am-noon, 1-4pm (Oct.-April). Cost: free ($3 donation requested). Allow 15-30 minutes.

Sheldon Jackson Museum ☺ This must-see museum houses more than 5,000 superb Alaskan Native artifacts, collected by Sheldon Jackson, a Presbyterian minister who acted as the state's education agent. Dr. Jackson founded the museum—Alaska's first—in 1895 to showcase and protect his finds; it was built of concrete to protect against fire. The museum is on the campus of Sheldon Jackson College, a small liberal arts college and Alaska's first institution of higher learning.

- Make sure kids are rested and fed. If kids have been cooped up in the car for awhile, give them a chance to run around before marching them into a museum.
- On arrival, ask at the reception desk for any materials, such as "treasure hunts," designed to help kids get the most from their visit. These materials aren't always advertised.
- Look for museums that feature hands-on exhibits. In Whitehorse, children can pan for gold at the MacBride Museum. at the Beringia Centre, there's a large kids' activity center, plus outside activities that relate to museum exhibits.

The Yukon Arts Centre has a children's art exhibit area where everything is hung at a young child's-eye level.
- Sometimes what fascinates a child in a museum isn't what the parent had in mind. Encourage kids to follow their interests rather than force them to see more than they can assimilate.
- A well-timed visit to the café or gift shop makes a welcome break. Always leave the museum before the kids are totally fed up; that way, they'll be more likely to enter the next museum in a happy frame of mind. ▣

This exceptional museum has lots of child appeal, too. At the center of the octagonal building are very old and weathered totem poles, around which are two concentric rings of exhibits. Fine woven baskets, masks, ivory and argillite carvings are among the highlights. Kids will enjoy peering into the glass-covered drawers containing Native Alaskan dolls and toys, including tiny dog sleds. Well-written descriptions accompany the exhibits.

In summer, Native artists demonstrate Alaskan crafts, and some encourage children to try their hands at basket weaving or embroidery. There's a small, excellent gift shop.

104 College Dr. 907/747-8981; www.museums.state.ak.us/Sheldon%20Jackson/. Open daily, 9am-5pm (mid-May—mid-Sept); Tues-Sat, 10am-4pm (rest of year). Closed holidays year round. Cost: $4, summer; $3, winter. Free/under 19. Allow 1 hour.

Sitka National Historical Park   At the end of Lincoln Street, on a little peninsula separating the town from the Indian River, is one of Alaska's oldest parks. This was the site of the Tlingit people's last stand against the Russians in 1804. Set in the 107-acre park's lush temperate rainforest, amid tall spruce, hemlock and cedar, are 11 totem poles. Kids will enjoy locating the next pole in the series along the one-mile loop—and in August, picking huckleberries from trailside bushes. The park fronts the water and walking through it is a magical experience. In 2002, the new **Visitor Center** opened. Among its attractions is 30-foot-high **Totem Hall**, which showcases some of the original totem poles (those outside are replicas). The center is also home to the **Southeast Alaska Indian Cultural Center**, where Tlingit artists work and demonstrate their crafts in summer; northwest Native-art classes are taught in winter. Also in the Visitor Center are exhibits of Native culture and art, a theater, and a bookstore operated by the Alaska Natural History Association.

Back toward town on Lincoln Street, you'll find the **Russian Bishop's House**, a National Historic Landmark administered by Sitka National Historical Park. It gives visitors a sense of what life might have been like for the Russian-Americans who spent the better part of a century here. Built in the early 1840s, the two-story building housed the Bishop and a succession of enterprises, including a school, a seminary, and an orphanage. The first floor contains exhibits chronicling the history of Russian America. The second floor, more likely to be of interest to kids, has been restored to its appearance when the Russian Bishop was in residence and includes some original furnishings.

In summer, the Visitor Center offers a variety of children's programs and ranger-guided walks.

Visitor Center: 106 Metlakatla St; 907/747-6281; www.nps.gov/sitk/.
Open daily, 8am-5pm (June-Sept); closed Sun (rest of year). Free. Allow 1 hour (including Cultural Center).
Southeast Alaska Indian Cultural Center: 106 Metlakatla St; 907/747-8061.
Open daily, 8am-5pm (summer); 8am-2pm, depending upon classes (rest of year).
Russian Bishop's House: 501 Lincoln St 907/747-6281. Open daily, 9am-5pm (May 15-Oct. 1); by appt. (rest of year). Cost: $3/adult, free/under 13. Allow 30 minutes.

Animals, Animals

Alaska Raptor Center ☺   Some cruise lines offer shore excursions just for kids to this popular family destination. The Center is a hospital for bald eagles and fulfills an educational mission. Each year, hundreds of bald eagles and other birds of prey are treated here; about 24 are permanent residents. Visitors move through stations with hands-on exhibits that teach about bald eagles, how they become injured, and how they are treated and rehabilitated. You can watch the staff at work. Kids ages 5-11 can participate in the Passport program (kids get a stamp at each station they visit). An outdoor trail teaches about raptor habitat; visitors can meet the feathered residents. At the end of the two-hour passport program, hot chocolate is served to the hard-working young participants. The center's excellent Web site is a good resource for kids.

1101 Sawmill Creek Rd. 907/747-8662, 800/643-9425;
www.alaskaraptor.org. Open Sun-Fri 8am-4pm. Cost: $10/adult, $5/under 13, $40/family membership. Allow 2 hours.

Wildlife Tours

Sea Life Discovery Tours ☺   This is the wildlife tour to take when the weather is lousy, waves are choppy out on Sitka Sound, and/or someone in your party is prone to seasickness. You'll spend the time cruising gently around the harbor in an oddly shaped, but comfortable, vessel. They refer to it as a "glass bottom" boat; in truth, passengers sit on a padded bench in the downstairs cabin and look through wide glass windows at crab, starfish, sea

Web Cams

Many Alaska communities and parks have installed Web cams that put video photos, refreshed every few minutes, on their Web sites. Sites in the southeast with Web cams include:

Eagle's Nest: http://12.18.170.100/

Lake Hood, Anchorage: www.alaskaairmen.com/web_cam/

Mendenhall Glacier Visitor Center:
www.fs.fed.us/r10/tongass/districts/mendenhall/webcam/

Tee Harbor, near Juneau: www.jeffuswilliams.com/teeharbor/index.php

Sheldon Jackson College, Sitka: www.sj-alaska.edu/OrcaCam/

View of Sitka Sound, Sitka: www.sitka.net/livewebcam/

Also see: Compendium of Alaska weather cams:
akweathercams.faa.gov/wxcams/map.php/ ▣

cucumbers, giant anemones, sculpin, rockfish, and gently waving grasses. The windows are positioned at exactly the right height for young kids.

On two-hour tours, a snack and drink are served, and a diver with a video camera leaves the boat to collect interesting sea life and show it to passengers via the camera. A naturalist describes what you're seeing and answers questions. There's a restroom, but the boat is not wheelchair-accessible. If claustrophobia strikes, climb up to the main level and breathe deeply on deck.
221 Harbor Dr; 907/966-2301, 877/966-2301;
www.sealifediscoverytours.com. Cost: call for details. Allow 2 hours.

Sitka Wildlife Quest   These tours are operated by Allen Marine Tours, a major supplier of marine wildlife tours to the cruise industry (non-cruise passengers may book day and evening cruises independently). This outfit does a first-class job of getting you to the sea otters and whales. Itineraries vary. A weekly cruise to St. Lazaria Island (see "Birdwatching") showcases local bird life. All cruises include naturalists. Binoculars are provided for every two or three passengers. Passengers board at the Visitors Dock across from the Centennial Building, 30 minutes before sailing. Reservations aren't required. Boats are comfortable, with restroom facilities, but motion sickness is a real possibility. Rates depend on the cruise chosen. Generally, children 3-12 pay about 60 percent of the adult rate; kids under 3 are free.
Allen Marine Tours. 907/747-8100, 888/747-8101; www.allenmarine.com
About 3 hours and up.

Swimming
Sitka's public swimming venues include the **Blatchley Pool** (601 Halibut Point Rd, 907/747-8670) and the **Sheldon Jackson College Pool** at the college's Hames P.E. Center (801 Lincoln St, 907/747-5231).

The Great Outdoors

Bicycling   Sitka is a great town for cycling. To outfit yourself, choose from **Southeast Diving & Sports** (105 Monastery St, 907/747-8279) or **Yellow Jersey Cycle Shop** (805 Halibut Point Rd, 907/747-6317; www.geocities.com/yellow_jersey_cycles/rentals/).

Birding   Birdwatchers have excellent options in and around Sitka. The **Starrigavan Platform**, at the start of the **Estuary Life Interpretive Trail** in the Old Sitka State Recreation Site (see "Camping"), is a popular choice. It's wheelchair accessible. Waterfowl, great blue herons, bald eagles, and songbirds are residents or visitors. The 65-acre **St. Lazaria National Wildlife Refuge** is harder to get to, but worth the effort. In addition to tufted puffins, demure murres and murrelets, cormorants, and auklets, marine mammals are often spotted. Trips are offered by Allen Marine (see "Wildlife Tours") and Sitka's Secrets (500 Lincoln St, #641, 907/747-5089; www.sitkasecret.com; 3-4 hour tours, $90/person).

Hiking   You'll find good hiking trails here, but there are bears around Sitka, all of them brown (i.e. grizzlies) so be sure to brush up on your good bear behavior.

The half-mile trail you'll find at **Halibut Point State Recreation Site** ☺ is a good bet for very young hikers; the park also has several picnic shelters and a beach suitable for combing. *4 miles north of Sitka on Halibut Point Rd. Allow 20 minutes.*

Beaver Lake Trail, which starts from the Sawmill Creek Campground (see "Camping"), is less than a mile. It's steep at first, but levels off; you'll go through forest, muskeg (with boardwalks), and continue to the lake, which is stocked with grayling for fishing. *Sawmill Creek Campground. Allow 1 hour.*

If you have the time, the 5.5 mile **Indian River Trail** makes a great family hike. You'll ascend gradually (a total of 700 feet), go through rainforest along the river, and finish up at a beautiful waterfall. You're likely to see plenty of wildlife along the way. *Off Sawmill Creek Rd. Turn left at Troopers Academy, walk around gate, follow road for .5 miles to pumphouse. Trailhead is just west of pumphouse. Park by roadside, outside gate. Allow at least 6 hours.*

Sea Kayaking   Guided kayak trips are provided by **Baidarka Boats** (320 Seward St, 907/747-8996; www.kayaksite.com), which also rents kayaks and gear. Tours and rentals start at half days and go up. No kayaking experience is required. Children 5 or older are welcome with an adult and are charged half price on guided trips.

Excursions

Flightseeing   With so many marine mammals to get up close and personal with, it doesn't make a lot of sense to rise up above it all; you're better off saving your flightseeing budget for Ketchikan, Juneau, or Denali. But if you've booked a Forest Service cabin or you've lucked out on one of those rare cloudless summer days, **Harris Aircraft Services** (400 Airport Rd, 907/966-3050; www.harrisaircraft.com) will get you there by air. You'll pay about $100/hour per passenger (a maximum of three or five passengers depending on the plane).

Calendar of Events

June

Sitka Summer Music Festival
907/747-6774; www.sitkamusicfestival.org
An annual classical music festival featuring family programming and brown-bag concerts.

Sitka Fine Arts Camp ☺
907/747-3085; www.fineartscamp.org
A program for teens (ages 12-18) offering theater, music, dance; visual, literary and Alaskan Native arts programming over a 15-day period. Examples of past classes include computer animation, Inupiak carving, jazz workshops, and Tlingit beading.

September

Mudball Classic Softball Tournament
907/747-3815
An annual Labor Day weekend tournament in which softball teams recruited nationwide play in Sitka.

October

Alaska Day Festival
October 14-18, 907/747-3512
A variety of events, including a parade that commemorates the day in 1867 when the United States purchased Alaska from Russia in Sitka.

November

Whalefest
907/747-7964; www.sitkawhalefest.org
Annual whale migration festival. Activities include educational cetacean seminars given by experts, whale-watching tours, and attendant merrymaking.

Resources

Sitka Ranger District
201 Katlian St, Ste 109, 907/747-6671
Hiking and Forest Service cabin rentals

Alaska Dept. of Fish & Game
304 Lake St, Rm 103, 907/747-5355 (fishing), 907/747-5449 (hunting)
Fishing & hunting license information

Chamber of Commerce
P.O. Box 638, Sitka, AK 99835, 907/747-8604; www.sitka.com

Sitka Convention and Visitors Bureau
303 Lincoln St, Sitka, AK 99835, 907/747-5940; www.sitka.org

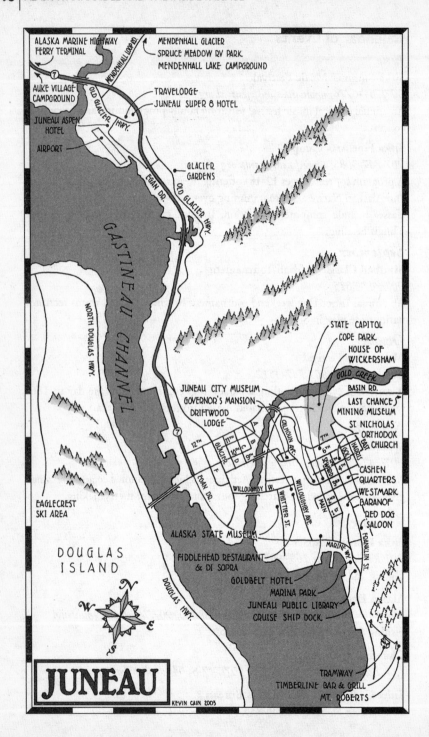

Books and Publications

Carlton, Rosemary. *Sheldon Jackson: The Collector*. Alaska State Museums, 1999. A study of the Presbyterian minister whose collection forms the basis for this great museum's exhibits.

Two short, but information-packed pamphlets from the Alaska Natural History Association are useful in exploring Sitka: *Carved History* is a guide to the National Historical Park's totems and their history. *For God and Tsar: A Brief History of Russian America, 1741-1867* is a succinct illustrated guide covering Russian history, trade, and the Russian Orthodox Church.

JUNEAU

Juneau, Alaska's state capital, is wedged tightly between water and mountains and separated from Douglas Island (today a bedroom suburb of Juneau) by Gastineau Channel. Home to the Auk tribe of the Tlingit people, as Douglas was home to the Taku, Juneau has a long and lively frontier history rooted in Alaska's first gold rush, nearly 20 years before the Klondike strike. Gold mining was the early engine of Juneau's economy; today, it's state government and tourism.

The city's population hovers around 30,000, very close to that of Fairbanks. Along with the state government, the University of Alaska Southeast is located here. One of the biggest draws is Mendenhall Glacier, although the city has enough interesting attractions of its own to keep visitors busy. Mount Roberts, which looms above the city and may be accessed by an aerial tramway from downtown, offers breathtaking views and nature trails. Glacier Bay and the spectacularly scenic Tracy Arm, a glacier-fed fjord, can be reached in day trips; many outfitters offer excursions to both.

Getting to Juneau

By Air   **Alaska Airlines** has frequent daily flights. The Yukon-based **Air North** (867/668-2228, 800/764-0407 [United States], 800/661-0407 [Canada]; www.flyairnorth.com) connects Juneau with Fairbanks; Vancouver, BC; Edmonton and Calgary, AB; and Yukon cities including Whitehorse, Inuvik, and Dawson City. They make the 50-minute flight between Whitehorse and Juneau three times a week.

By Sea   Every major cruise line stops at Juneau, as do the **Alaska ferries** (800/642-0066; www.dot.state.ak.us/amhs/)

Getting Around

The cruise ship dock is downtown, but ferry and airline passengers need transportation to get here. The airport is 9.5 miles north of Juneau, and the ferry dock is another five miles beyond the airport. Many local hotels offer free transportation to and from the airport. City buses run by **Capital Transit** (907/789-6901; www.juneau.lib.ak.us/pubworks/captrans/) stop at the airport, 8am to 5pm on weekdays ($1.25, exact fare only; kids under 6 ride free). Buses serve popular destinations, including Douglas Island, and can take you within a mile of Mendenhall Glacier.

You can rent a car or van from **Hertz** (1873 Shell Simmons Dr, 907/789-9494, 800/654-3131; www.hertz.com.) or **Rent-A-Wreck**, Juneau (2450-C Industrial Blvd, 907/789-4111; juneaualaska.com/rent-a-wreck/). Taxi service is provided by **Capital Cab** (907/586-2772) and **Juneau Taxi & Tours** (2 Marine Way, Ste 228, 907/790-4511; www.juneautaxi.com). The latter also offers tours of downtown Juneau and local sights, including Mendenhall Glacier, for which they charge $55 an hour per cab. Another option available May through September is to buy a day pass for the **Juneau Trolley Car** (245 Marine Way, 907/586-7433; www.juneautrolley.com; daily 8am-6pm. Cost: $12/adult, $8.50/child). This 30-minute narrated tour on a red trolley circulates through the city, stopping at 12 designated attractions to let you on or off. If weather is bad or your children are young, this could be a good bet. Otherwise, it's easy to walk the three-mile loop the trolley car serves. Most of these attractions are easily reached on foot from the cruise ship dock.

Bicycles can be rented and guided bike tours arranged through **Cycle Alaska** (907/780-2253; based in Douglas) and **Mountain Gears** (210 Franklin, 907/586-4327).

Places to Stay

Cashen Quarters (B&B) ☺ ($-$$)
303 Gold St, 907/586-9863; www.cashenquarters.com
FYI: 5 rooms & suites, kitchen, private entrance; yard, barbecue grill; laundry; pets OK on approval.
This historic house dates from 1914. For many years it was a small hotel; now it's a B&B with useful amenities for families. Furnished with sturdy antiques, each room has a kitchen; one suite accommodates up to six guests.

❝PARENT COMMENTS❞

> *"The owners were very helpful when we arrived, and had good suggestions for places to eat and destinations to visit. Although it was a bit of a walk from the heart of downtown, it was actually easier to begin longer journeys from here, since a taxi company was located one block away. One minus: our room was just outside the laundry room, which became a bit noisy in the late morning."*

Driftwood Lodge ($)
435 Willoughby Ave, 907/586-2280, 800/544-2239;
www.driftwoodalaska.comcom
FYI: 63 rooms & suites, some kitchens; free airport shuttle; bicycles for rent (including kids' bikes and trailers)

This hotel offers families affordable, roomy accommodations, including a couple of two-bedroom suites that accommodate six guests. Another important asset is its proximity to the **Fiddlehead Restaurant & Bakery** (see "Places to Eat"). Tours can be arranged here.

Goldbelt Hotel ($$-$$$)

51 Egan Dr, 907/586-6900, 888/478-6909;
www.goldbelttours.com/travel/lodging/hotel/
FYI: 105 rooms, restaurant; complimentary airport transportation
This high-end hotel is owned by the Juneau-based Alaska Native corporation.
Catering primarily to business and cruise travelers, it's not especially
child-friendly, but the location is convenient and scenic.

Juneau, Aspen Hotel ($-$$)

1800 Shell Simmons Dr, 907/790-6435, 888/559-9846;
www.aspenhotelsak.com
FYI: 114 rooms & suites, free breakfast; refrigerator/microwave; swimming pool,
spa; free airport, ferry, downtown shuttle

Juneau Super 8 ($)

2295 Trout St, 907/789-4858, 800/800-8000; www.super8.com
FYI: 75 rooms; Laundromat

Travelodge ($)

9200 Glacier Hwy, 907/789-9700, 888/660-2327; www.travelodge.com
FYI: 86 rooms; restaurant; indoor swimming pool; courtesy van

Westmark Baranof Juneau ($$-$$$)

127 N Franklin St, 907/586-2660, 800/544-0970; www.westmarkhotels.com
FYI: 196 rooms & suites, kitchen; restaurant and coffee shop

Camping & Cabins

Spruce Meadow RV Park (10200 Mendenhall Loop Rd, 907/789-1990; www.juneaurv.com) is a private RV park open year round, with full facilities, three miles from the ferry terminal and not far from Mendenhall Glacier. **Savikko RV Park** (907/586-5255) in Douglas has four RV slots without hookups (see "Parks" for amenities information and address).

The Tongass National Forest (907/586-8800; *www.fs.fed.us/r10/tongass/*) manages two area campgrounds, open summers only. Neither takes reservations. **Mendenhall Lake Campground** ($10-26/day depending on amenities; 68 camping sites, 7 walk-ins, 9 full RV hookup sites, 9 partial hookup sites; picnic tables, parking pads, water, restrooms, dump station) is 12 miles from Juneau, in view of the glacier. From the ferry, turn right and go 1.7 miles to Loop Road, left onto Loop Road, then 3.2 miles to Montana Creek Road, left again, and less than a mile to the campground. **Auke Village Campground** ($8/night; 12 sites, water, vault toilet; picnic tables, fireplaces) is close to the beach and hiking trails. It's on the Glacier Highway about 15 miles from Juneau and 1.5 miles from the ferry dock.

Five **Forest Service cabins** (907/586-8800; www.fs.fed.us/r10/tongass/recreation/rec_facilities/cabinlist/;$35/night) are also in the Juneau area.

Places to Eat

The Fiddlehead Restaurant & Bakery and DiSopra ☺
429 W Willoughby Ave, 907/586-1042; www.alaska.net/~fiddle/
Hours: daily, 7am-10pm (summer); 8am-9pm (rest of year)
This famous establishment is two restaurants in one, with a bakery on the side. Downstairs is the casual Fiddlehead, probably the best bet for families. Selections include pasta, Mexican, and eclectic dishes that appeal to kids (meatloaf, jerk chicken, burgers). Upstairs, the more formal DiSopra offers fine-dining choices. The bakery has breads, cookies, scones, muffins and more, along with espresso drinks. The quality is uniformly excellent.

Gold Creek Salmon Bake
1061 Salmon Creek Lane, 907/789-0052
Hours: Open mid-May-Sept for lunch daily, 11:30am-1:30pm; dinner:
Sun-Fri: 5:30pm-8pm; cost $29.40/adult; $19.95/child (including
transportation from downtown hotels)
This excellent, outdoor salmon bake is always teeming with cruise ship passengers, but it's big enough to accommodate a crowd comfortably. Along with salmon, there are ribs, baked beans, rice pilaf, salads, beverages, and—of course—blueberry cake. The lush, forested setting is enchanting; there are short trails to follow. Should you experience a sudden downpour, don't worry; tables are sheltered from the rain and well-placed stoves keep everything toasty.

The Red Dog Saloon ☺
278 S Franklin St, 907/463-9954; www.reddogsaloon/
Hours: weekdays 9am-11pm; weekends 9am-1am
Don't let the name stop you from coming here. Kids are welcome at this Juneau landmark that is also a full-service restaurant with a kids' menu. (Minors must be accompanied by parent or legal guardian.) The menu features child-pleasing favorites like the Deadhorse Gulch sandwich (barbecued beef brisket), Copper River Crab Cakes, and fish and chips. The owners operate a thriving souvenir business as well.

Timberline Bar & Grill
Top of Mount Roberts tramway;
Hours: 9am-9pm mid-May-Sept
With Juneau's finest view, this restaurant also gets high marks for its food and service. Choose from a range of seafood entrées and other selections, including vegetarian; there's a kids' menu. On weekends, there's often entertainment. A gift shop is in the same complex.

Patsy Ann: Juneau's Official Greeter

Patsy Ann, a pedigreed English bull terrier born in 1929, was one of Alaska's most famous residents. She was acquired by a Juneau dentist as a gift to his twin daughters. The relationship didn't work out, so Patsy Ann was passed on to another family, and that didn't work out either. Patsy Ann had bigger ideas: her loyalty was not to one family, but to all of Juneau. She would trot off to the docks to greet ships and their crews, mingling with longshoremen and sometimes leaping into the water to follow departing ships.

Patsy Ann, deaf from birth, knew when a ship was coming up Gastineau Channel and was there to greet it, begging for treats. Theories abound as to how she could tell a boat was coming in: did she feel the boat's vibrations?

Patsy Ann's image appeared on postcards, and tourists looked forward to meeting her when they arrived. She was not a handsome dog, but was full of character. Stories of her strong personality survive. In one, she interrupted a baseball game, taking the ball from the pitcher and playing with it for awhile before losing interest. Her lifestyle was hard on her; Patsy Ann got arthritis (jumping into the cold water chasing after ships didn't help) and finally died in her sleep on March 30, 1942. In her little coffin, Patsy Ann dove into Gastineau Channel for the last time.

Fifty years after Patsy Ann's death, the Gastineau Humane Society put up the large bronze statue in Marine Park that greets visitors today. The society collects funds from the sale of commemorative items to support the work of the animal shelter. Read more about Patsy Ann and other dogs who made a difference in Ruth Gordon's *It Takes a Dog to Raise a Village* (Willow Creek Press, 2000). ◙

What to See & Do

Stroll & Browse

The compact downtown is easy to negotiate on foot, but be aware that many streets suddenly turn into steep staircases. A stroller is a liability here; backpacks are a better choice. Many of Juneau's star attractions, restaurants, hotels, and shops are within walking distance of each other.

If you arrive via cruise ship, before you set off in search of adventure, stop by the **Marine Park Kiosk** (just north of the docks) and get a walking map from Visitor Center volunteers. On your way, notice the sculpture of the bull terrier Patsy Ann (see sidebar).

Close by is the **Juneau Public Library** (292 Marine Way; 907/586-5249; open Mon-Thurs 11am-9pm, Fri-Sun noon-5pm). An imposing building that sits above a parking garage over the channel, it's worth a visit just for the view.

Among downtown Juneau's historical sights is the **State Capitol** (4th &

Main) where daily tours are available (907/465-3800; Mon-Sat, 9am-4:30pm [mid-May—mid-Sept], free 30-minute tours every half-hour; Mon-Sat, 9am-4:30pm, [rest of year], self-guided tours). A few blocks up Calhoun, the **Governor's Mansion** (716 Calhoun Ave), dating from 1913, is an impressive sight. However, kids are likely to be more interested in the totem pole in front that tells the Tlingit story of how mosquitoes got into the world. (Pick up a copy of the *Totem Pole Walking Tour* brochure at the city museum for details.)

St. Nicholas Orthodox Church (326 5th St, 907/780-6320), dating from 1894, is one of Juneau's oldest buildings and is on the National Register of Historic Places. It's open mid-May to mid-September; Monday through Friday, 8:30am to 5pm. Tours are offered. (On weekends and to attend church services, check first.) It's open to visitors by appointment in winter.

Downtown Juneau offers many souvenir shops, where you can load up on smoked salmon and *ulu* knives, and some craft and fine arts galleries. **WmSpear Design** (174 South Franklin St, Ste 201, 907/586-2209; www.wmspear.com) sells Bill Spear's enamel pins, whose intricate subject matter ranges from anatomically correct fish to spaceships, reptiles, insects, Egyptian mummies, and more. At the **Juneau Artist's Gallery** (175 S Franklin St, 907/586-9891; www.juneauartistsgallery.com), a cooperative owned and operated by the local artists it showcases, you'll find high-quality art, jewelry, ceramics, and crafts.

Hearthside Books, with two locations (downtown, 254 Front St; 907/586-1726, and Nugget Mall, 8745 Glacier Hwy, 907/789-2750, 800/478-1000) has an excellent assortment of Alaskana and general-interest books with a good children's section strong on Native Alaskan books. **Rainy Day Books** (113 Seward St,907/463-2665; www.juneaubooks.com) has a large and eclectic selection of books new and used, and welcomes browsers.

Parks

Cope Park (Capital and Calhoun), next to Gold Creek, has climbing structures, swings for tiny tots and older kids, a tennis court, and ball field. There are picnic shelters, tables and grills, restrooms, and a drinking fountain. **Savikko Park** (end of Douglas Hwy on Third St) is a good choice but you'll need to drive or take the bus. At the park, you'll find popular Sandy Beach, which can be warm enough for wading and splashing in summer, as well as sport fields, tennis courts, swings and play structures, covered shelters, restrooms, and drinking fountains.

Glacier Gardens Rainforest Adventure Despite the name, this attraction is a tour of a 50-acre human-made garden. It's lush and beautiful, set on a mountainside with great views, but doesn't have a lot to offer children. A gift shop and café are on the premises.

7600 Glacier Hwy; 907/790-3377; glaciergardens.com. Open daily 9am-6pm (May 1-Sept. 30). Cost: $17.95/adult, $12.95/child 6-12, free/under 6. Admission includes guided tour on covered golf carts. (Wild Berry Café and Mocha Stand, 907/789-1980). Allow 1 hour.

☛ **Parent Tip**

Macauley Salmon Hatchery is also locally known as DIPAC (Douglas Island Pink and Chums). It's fun for kids to stand outside next to the salmon holding tanks and have water splashed up at them from hundreds of churning fish. It's a fisher's dream come true. For more fish fun, hire a taxi to drive you to Sheep Creek, southeast of town, where the salmon run. It's Juneau's best-kept secret, and July through October, you can practically cross the stream walking on the backs of fish! American bald eagles enjoy feeding here, so remember your telephoto lens. ◙

Museums

Alaska State Museum ☺ This is one of Alaska's best museums for both adults and kids. Downstairs, exhibits explain the history of Alaska's Natives and offer an in-depth look at the state's wildlife in a large natural history gallery. Upstairs, a large temporary area is devoted to traveling exhibits. In the children's room, kids can try on costumes, explore the Yukon Trail, play an interactive computer game about the Klondike Gold Rush, or, for the little ones, climb on a model of Captain Cook's ship Discovery. The excellent store has a wide selection of books and Native and Russian arts and crafts. Prices compare favorably with those at other Alaska museum stores.
395 Whittier St; 907/465-2901, 888/913-6873; www.museums.state.ak.us. Open Mon-Fri 9am-6pm; Sat-Sun 10am-6pm (mid-May-mid-Sept); Tues-Sat 10am-4pm (rest of year). Cost: $5/adult, $3/winter, free/18 and under. Allow at least 1 hour.

House of Wickersham This attractive Victorian house dates from 1898, and touring its restored interior will give you a feel for how well-to-do Alaskans of that era lived. Judge Wickersham was Alaska's first territorial representative to Congress and played an important role in the territory's development, introducing the first statehood resolution. He was also instrumental in creating the University of Alaska, the Alaska Railroad, and Denali National Park. The tour includes tea and an Alaskan snack, along with a great view.
213 7th St, 907/586-9001. Open daily 10am-noon and 1-5pm, except Wed (mid-May—Sept); by appt. other times. Cost: $1. Allow 30 minutes.

Juneau-Douglas City Museum Exhibits center on the history (especially gold mining) and life of Juneau and Douglas. Stop by early in your visit to the city and pick up a guide to Juneau's totem poles and other visitor information. Kids will enjoy the Children's Room, full of interactive and hands-on exhibits, including a dress-up closet with vintage clothing. There are traveling exhibits and a small gift shop.
4th & Main Sts, 907/586-3572; www.juneau.lib.ak.us/parksrec/museum/ index/php. Open weekdays 9am-5pm, weekends 10am-5pm (early May-late Sept). Fri & Sat noon-4pm and by appt. (rest of year); Cost: $3/adult, free/18 & under (summer); $2/adult; free/18 & under (winter). Allow at least 30 minutes.

Independent Sightseeing for Cruise Passengers

Experienced cruise travelers often book their own shore trips rather than going through the cruise line. The savings can be upwards of 20 percent. This is not always true, but if you are prepared to do a little research you can reap substantial savings. Here's what you need to know:

• Study the Shore Excursion booklet for your cruise. It may be mailed to you; often you can download it from the cruise line's Web site. Check the ship's itinerary, too. What hours will you be in port? Is the cruise dock downtown or will you need to take a tender to shore?

• Read up on the options offered by the cruise line and the kinds of activities available in each port—for example, helicopter glacier trips in Juneau, or wildlife cruises in Sitka. Scope out prices, options, and availability. Because you're booking independently, it's up to you to verify that you're working with a reputable outfitter. Ask how long they've been in business, whether they're members of the local Chamber of Commerce, and what training their guides have had.

• Before booking, ask about cancellation policies. Cruise ships rarely stay more than eight hours in any port, and often considerably less. If you're prevented from taking the tour because your cruise ship was delayed, can you get a full refund? Is more than one departure available, so that you can reschedule if necessary?

• Another option is to wait until you arrive in port to decide what to do. Of course, you run the risk of finding a tour you wanted is booked, but more often than not, space is available. When you arrive in port, you'll be greeted by a sea of outfitters on the dock. Many are fine and offer good value. If you've done a little homework you'll recognize some of the names. The advantage to this approach is flexibility; if the weather is rainy, taking a whale watching excursion on a comfy boat with a heated cabin may be more appealing than hiking on Mount Roberts. ◼

Last Chance Mining Museum   This museum, listed on the National Register of Historic Places, features the machinery once used in gold mining, along with the trains that transported miners and carted out the ore. *1001 Basin Rd, 907/586-5338; e-mail: glrrlg@alaska.net. Open 9:30 am-12:30 pm, 3:30-6:30pm daily, or by appt. Cost: $3/adult, free/under 11. Allow about 30 minutes.*

Animals Animals

Macauley Salmon Hatchery (formerly Gastineau Salmon Hatchery) ☺ This qualifies as a must-see. Guided tours introduce you to the salmon's life cycle, from egg through fry, and on to the return of the old geezers to spawn. (Here they milk the eggs from the salmon, which are then gutted and turned into fertilizer.) The hatchery's star attraction is a small but excellent saltwater aquarium, featuring unusual specimens of undersea life. Look for the Pacific spiny lumpsuckers, small greenish fish that look like tiny plastic wind-up toys released into the water to whirl around, their little tails a blur of motion. The large, eclectic gift shop has maritime toys, salmon snacks, and "fish eggs" (bubble gum).

2697 Channel Dr; 907/463-4810, 877/463-2486; www.dipac.net/visitor/. Open May 15-Sept 15, Mon-Fri, 10am-6pm, Sat-Sun, 10am-5pm. Cost: $3/adult, $1/child, $12/group pass good for 5 adults or 12 children. Allow 40 minutes.

Whale-Watching/Fishing Charters Whale watching tours are plentiful in Juneau between May and September. Some boats carry over 100 passengers and zip along at great speeds; others take fewer passengers and go more slowly. Many contract with large cruise lines, but also take independent travelers as space allows. Most outfitters offer a money-back guarantee that you will see wildlife of some kind (some report they spot humpback whales 95 percent of the time). You are likely to see some or all of bald eagles, humpback whales, orcas, sea otters, porpoises, and steller sea lions.

The following wildlife excursions are standouts. Each offers high-powered boats with heated cabins, outside viewing, and restrooms; and each provides transportation to and from the boat. **Dolphin Tours** (2 Marine Way, Ste. 115; 907/463-3421, 800/770-3422; www.dolphintours.com; 3-hour tours, April-Sept. Cost: $99.75/adult, $78.75/child 2-12, free/under 2) has five jet boats that carry from six to 30 passengers each. Tours include binoculars. **Orca Enterprises** (489 S Franklin St; 907/789-6801, 888/733-6722; www.alaskawhalewatching.com; three 3.5-hour trips daily in summer; by arrangement, rest of year. Cost: $103.95/adult, $82.95/child 5-12, free/under 5) takes up to 23 passengers out whale watching on its 42-foot jet boat. They offer fishing charters and longer excursions as well. **Juneau Sportfishing & Sightseeing** (907/586-1887; www.juneausportfishing.com) offers fishing charters (half-day $125/person, whole-day $215/person, tax extra) and assorted sightseeing tours.

Swimming

Families are welcome at the **Augustus Brown Pool** (1619 Glacier Ave, 907/586-5325). Here you'll find two public indoor pools, as well as a sauna and exercise room.

The Great Outdoors

Hiking From downtown Juneau, you can take several interesting hikes. With more time and your own transportation, many more possibilities open up. From downtown, the **Mount Roberts Trail** runs from the east end of 6th up to the visitor center (nearly 2,000 feet) and on to the summits of Gastineau Peak (3,666 feet) and Mount Roberts (3,819). For most families, hiking the first, steep 15 minutes that take you up to a breathtaking overlook is workout enough. One of the city's most interesting walks, about 1.5 miles, is up **Basin Road:** go north on Gold Street to 5th Street; turn right and go several blocks to East Street; turn left onto Basin Road. You'll leave the houses behind as you come into Gold Creek Basin. The giant mountain on your left is Mount Juneau. You'll cross a bridge over Gold Creek. A few hundred feet past the bridge, you'll arrive at the road to the Last Chance Mining Museum (see "Museums"). **Perseverance Trail**, accessible here, takes you 3.5 miles farther. If you plan to walk it, be sure to first pick up a map at the Visitor Center or Forest Service Center (see "Resources").

In summer, Juneau's **City Parks & Recreation** (155 S Seward St, Rm 218, 907/586-0428; www.juneau.org/parksrec/hike/saturday.php/) offers the **Juneau Hike Program,** with guided hikes around Juneau on Saturdays, geared to all ages and ability levels. Some, but not all, will be good choices for very young children. Call first to get the itinerary for the date you have in mind.

For a selection of hikes appropriate for all ages, *90 Short Walks Around Juneau,* by Mary Lou King (Taku Conservation Society, Trail Mix, etc., 1999) is a useful booklet that includes trail length, level of difficulty, access information, and full description.

Kayaking   For families with kids age 12 and over, **Alaska Discovery Wilderness Adventures** (5310 Glacier Hwy, 907/780-6226, 800/586-1911; www.akdiscovery.com/channel), in partnership with Goldbelt Tours, offers 6-to7-hour sea kayaking trips to the Channel Islands; no experience is required (mid-May-Sept. Cost $95). Trips include transportation to and from downtown Juneau, all equipment, a snack, a short hike through old-growth forest, and Native story telling. **Alaska Travel Adventures** (9085 Glacier Hwy, #301; 907/789-0052, 800/791-2673; www.alaskaadventures.com) has a 3.5-hour tour that goes to Smugglers Cove (May-Sept; Cost: $76/adults; $51/child 12 and under). Transportation, all equipment and a snack are included. **Alaska Boat and Kayak** (101 Dock St, 907/586-8220; www.juneaukayak.com) rents kayaks, starting at $40 per day for a single. They'll also deliver and retrieve kayaks where you need them.

Panning for Gold   However they're structured, local gold-panning tours observe the same protocols: prospectors large and small are guaranteed to find gold. Parents take note: most adventures include an opportunity for the successful prospector to purchase accessories with which to show off the find. The accompanying mine tours are interesting. Purveyors of local gold-panning outings are **Alaska Travel Adventures** (9085 Glacier Hwy, #301; 907/789-0052, 800/791-2673; www.alaskaadventures.com. May-Sept; 1.5 hrs. Cost: $37/adult, $25/child 12 and under. Cost includes pick-up and return) and **Goldbelt Tours** (76 Egan Dr, Ste 100; 907/586-8687, 800/820-2628, 800/478-3610; www.goldbelttours.com. Early May-Sept; 1.5 hours. Cost: $38.85/adult, $26.95/child).

River Rafting   Rafting on the gentle Mendenhall River, where rapids rarely go beyond Class 2, is a good bet for younger children. The scenery is lovely and you're likely to see wildlife, even if the weather is on the soggy side. (Who cares? You'll be covered head to toe in waterproof raingear anyway.) Several companies offer float trips, including **Auk Ta Shaa Discovery**, part of Goldbelt Tours (mid-May—mid-Sept; 4 hrs. Cost: $89/adult, $44.50/child under 17) and **Alaska Travel Adventures** (May-Sept; 3.5 hrs. Cost: $95/adult, $63/child under 13).

Skiing The **Eaglecrest Ski Area** (907/586-5284, 907/790-2000; www.juneau.org/eaglecrest) on Douglas Island is a rarity on the Inside Passage: a downhill ski and snowboarding area you can reach by car. It's open Thursday through Monday, 9am-4pm, and daily over Christmas and spring breaks. On Fridays, there's night skiing 4pm-9pm. They offer a variety of ski and snowboard schools and clinics, and the Little Tykes program for kids 3 and a half to 6, with many programs at various skill levels; a tubing area is open to kids 6 and older. Child rates and family ski passes and discounts apply. Equipment rentals are available for all ages. Just because it's Alaska, don't assume there'll be snow. Juneau gets mild winters and snow can be scarce early and late in the season. Trails aren't maintained in summer.

Take the Juneau Bridge to Douglas Island, and turn righ+t onto N Douglas; continue 7 miles to Eaglecrest Rd. Turn left and proceed 5 miles to Eaglecrest Resort.

Mount Roberts Tramway and Mount Roberts ☺ Yes, it's overpriced, but this ride that climbs up (straight up) Mount Roberts is worth the cost, especially if you're lucky enough to have clear skies. In six minutes, the cars climb from sea level to nearly 2,000 feet (the summit is at 3,819 feet). As you rise, you'll see Juneau spread out below you. The vista extends across Gastineau Channel to Douglas and Admiralty islands. At the top, there's a large building with gift shops, a restaurant, bar, and theater that shows a short, excellent film on Tlingit culture. A nature center and a host of trails, easy to challenging (including one you can take back down to Juneau), round out the attractions.

Take the opportunity to explore the excellent nature trails. Up to midsummer, you may encounter snow, and conditions can occasionally be muddy or slippery. All trails offer excellent views and interesting flora and fauna. The **Alpine Loop Trail** (.5 mile) is a good bet for young kids. **Gastineau Guiding Company** (907/586-2666; www.stepintoalaska.com) runs the attractive Nature Center, a short walk from the main visitor center, and offers a guided alpine walk (tramway included in the price) suitable for children able to walk comfortably over uneven terrain. If you decide to hike on your own, ask for tips at the Nature Center; the staff is knowledgeable and helpful. The center has books and assorted gifts (more interesting, affordable, and suitable for kids than what you'll find in the big Visitor Center). In a small video room, free wildlife videos are shown. Gastineau also offers other guided nature hikes in the Juneau vicinity.

490 S Franklin St; 907/463-3412, 888/461-TRAM; www.goldbelttours.com. Open daily, 9am-9pm (May-Sept); departs every 10 minutes. Cost: $21.95/adult, $12.60/child 7-12, free/under 7 (tickets good for unlimited trips throughout the day). Allow at least 2 hours.

Mendenhall Glacier ☺ This is just one finger of the enormous Juneau Icefield that blankets 1,500 square miles of the coast mountain range. The icefield—only 3,000 years old, extends north to Skagway and east to British

Glaciers

Glaciers are snow that has fallen and turned to ice. Over the past 750,000 years, the earth has experienced eight ice ages in which much of its surface has been covered by glaciers. In the last ice age, 32 percent of the land was covered with ice. We are at the end of an interglacial period (only 10 percent of the earth's surface is glacier-covered), due to enter a new ice age in the next few thousand years.

Most glaciers are in the polar regions, but major icefields still exist in North America, and visitors to Alaska and the Yukon have many opportunities to get acquainted with these enormous rivers of ice. Glaciers move when they attain a certain mass, a result of gravity on their sheer size. Today, some glaciers are advancing and others retreating. Some glaciers change direction, suddenly picking up speed or slowing down. Portage Glacier, near Anchorage, has been retreating rapidly in recent years; Hubbard Glacier has experienced sudden surges and retreats; in 1986, its speed increased to nearly 33 feet a day!

One of the most intriguing features of glaciers and icebergs is their intense aquamarine color. Just like water, the dense crystalline structure of glacier ice causes it to absorb the longer-wavelength red and yellow colors out of the visible light spectrum, reflecting only shorter-wavelength blues. As the ice warms and melts, it reflects all the light and appears white. A glacier seen close up will appear to have many different colors from white to aqua and deep blue. Glacier

Columbia. It advanced until the mid-1700s, then began a retreat that continues today. Throughout the 20th century, the glacier retreated an estimated 1.6 miles. Since 1998, the rate of retreat has increased to 150 feet a year. Although it is a huge glacier—1.5 miles wide in places—it can no longer be seen from the Mendenhall Glacier Visitor Center! Luckily, you need only take a short walk down to the lake and there it is.

Start at the **Mendenhall Glacier Visitor Center**, run by the Tongass National Forest and open year round. The Visitor Center has exhibits and shows a film about the glacier. Educational programs are offered year-round with guided hikes and programs for kids in summer. The well-stocked bookstore carries a wide selection of children's books on glaciers, geology and area wildlife.

If the weather is nice, you might want to take the bus from Juneau, get off at Mendenhall Loop Road and walk; it's about a mile. Dozens of tours will get you out here. A good, affordable choice is **Mendenhall Glacier Transport** (MGT). Their tour buses can be found at the cruise docks. A 2.5-hour tour includes 40 minutes at the Macauley Salmon Hatchery and 45 minutes at Mendenhall Glacier. The tour won't give you enough time to hike any trails except the .3-mile **Photo Point Trail**. A map of the trails is available at the ice crystals are larger than ordinary ice crystals, which means they melt more slowly. Children can try this experiment: put a bit of glacier ice and an ice cube about the same size in a drink and see which melts first.

Parent Ed
Alaska's Glaciers. Alaska Geographic, 1982. Everything you want to know about Alaska's glaciers.

Bohn, Dave. *Glacier Bay: The Land and the Silence.* Sierra Club-Ballantine, 1967. The story of Glacier Bay is told through archival and contemporary photos.

Foster, Scott. *Mendenhall Glacier: A River of Ice.* Alaska Natural History Association, 1999. This picture book, illustrated with photographs of the glacier, packs a lot of information about the geology and study of glaciers, and the plants and animals living in and alongside Mendenhall Glacier.

Glacier Videotapes
The Grand Glaciers of Alaska's Inside Passage. Alaska Natural History Association/KTOO. (37 minutes). This enticing video shows glaciers as experienced through kayaking, hiking, and flightseeing.

Voices from the Ice. Alaska Natural History Association. (17 minutes). You can also catch this video at the Begich Boggs Visitor Center at Portage Glacier (see "Anchorage and Environs").

Glacier Web Sites
All About Glaciers: nsidc.org/glaciers Scientific info on glaciers, including a comprehensive glossary of terms

Common Questions and Myths about Glaciers: ak.water.usgs.gov/ glaciology/FAQ.htm/www.glacier bay.org; Good info on glaciers. ▣

visitor center. If time allows, the **Trail of Time**, .5 mile, is an easy nature hike suitable for small kids that will take you about half an hour. Longer, more strenuous hikes give terrific views of the glacier and wildlife. The 1.5-hour **Moraine Ecology Trail** can be handled by small fry; if you visit in August or later, check out the spawning salmon. Bear are frequently sighted here, doing likewise. Berrying is good in late summer.

8465 Old Dairy Rd; take the Glacier Hwy north to Mendenhall Loop Rd; turn right and continue to the Visitor Center (the name changes on the way to Glacier Spur Rd). 907/789-6640; www.fs.fed.us/r10/tongass/districts/mendenhall/). Open daily 8-6:30pm (May-Sept); Thurs-Fri 10am-4pm, Sat-Sun 9am-4pm (Oct-April). Cost: $3/person. Summer children's programs, Sat 11am-noon. Mendenhall Glacier Transport, 907/789-5460; www.mightygreattrips.com. Early May-late Sept; 2.5-hour narrated tour to Mendenhall Glacier with stop at Macauley Salmon Hatchery; Cost: $25/adult, $15/child under 13.

Flightseeing The most interesting airborne tours of the Juneau Icefield are by helicopter that can land on the ice. This enormous mass of moving ice (North American's fifth largest icefield) stretches from British Columbia, in the east, to Juneau; one of its many arms is Mendenhall Glacier. Landing and walking on a glacier can be the experience of a lifetime.

TEMSCO Helicopters (1650 Maplesden Way; 907/789-9501, 877-789-9501; $160 and up), at the Juneau Airport, offers an expensive but unforgettable tour of Mendenhall Glacier. Start with a 30-minute orientation and safety video, then pull on glacier boots and (if necessary) raingear, climb aboard one of their many turbine helicopters, and get ready for spectacular views! The "Mendenhall Glacier Tour" ($169) includes 30 minutes of flight time and 25 minutes on the glacier. Other tours are the "Pilot's Choice Glacier Explorer Tour" ($239), which usually runs 1.5 hours, including 45 minutes on the glacier; a 2.5-hour glacier tour ($250), which includes a three-mile hike across the glacier (ages 12 and up); and a dog-sledding tour across glacier ice ($303). Passengers under the age of 12 must be accompanied by a parent or guardian. Passengers whose weight is 250 pounds or more are required to purchase a seat and a half at the time of booking. One minus: each helicopter seats four passengers (one in the front and three in the back), which means the person in the back center seat doesn't get a window. Passenger positioning is non-negotiable, since calculations made before take-off ensure proper weight distribution aboard the aircraft.

Coastal Helicopters (8995 Yandukin Dr, 907/789-5600; www.alaska one.com/coastal) offers a one-hour flight over the Juneau Icefield, landing on either Taku or Norris glacier ($173/seat). They provide the equipment you'll need. Children are not permitted to sit on parents' laps. A 90-minute tour takes in more glaciers ($290/seat; 3-seat minimum).

Era Aviation (907/586-2030, 800/843-1947; www.eraaviation.com) has two helicopter tours: a flightseeing tour with glacier landing (1 hour; $210/person) and one that includes dog-sledding on the glacier (1.75 hours; $349/person).

If landing on a glacier seems a bit too strenuous for your small fry, but you'd still like to see the landscape from the air, **Wings of Alaska** (8421 Livingston Way, 907/789-0790; www.flyingalaska.com) offers 40-minute floatplane tours from the Juneau waterfront over the glaciers ($135/adult, $104/child 2-12, free/lap child under 2) and a 3.5-hour trip that includes a two-hour stop at Taku Wilderness Lodge; the price of your trip ($199/adult, $156/child 2-12) includes a salmon bake at the lodge.

Excursions

Glacier Bay National Park and Preserve Northwest of Juneau, beyond Admiralty and Chichagof Islands and up Icy Strait, lies this extraordinary national park, designated as such in 1925 by President Calvin Coolidge. When Captain Cook sailed by in the *Discovery*, it was a bare indentation, the entrance blocked by sheets of ice. Less than a century later, John Muir found a deep bay and fjords into which tidewater glaciers (glaciers that terminate directly in the ocean) calved in thunderous explosions. Since then, the glaciers have continued to retreat at a rapid pace, uncovering land and reshaping the map.

Being surrounded by these moving, towering, deeply fissured walls of ice, hearing the crack of a calving glacier as enormous masses of ice cascade into the icy waters, and gazing at the deep blue icebergs bobbing everywhere is mesmerizing and unforgettable. Many visitors put it at the top of their

Alaska to-do list. Snow-covered peaks (up to 15,000 feet) dropping to glacier-sculpted fjords, tidewater glaciers, rich and diverse plant life, humpback whales, porpoises, seals, and seabirds make for a compelling experience.

Seeing Glacier Bay takes careful planning. Between June and August, the park strictly limits the number of large cruise ships and tour boats that can enter each day. Not surprisingly, tension exists between those who want to encourage tourism and who make a living by fishing or tourism, and those concerned about pollution from large vessels and loss of important animal species from stress and over-fishing. The National Park Service continues in its attempt to steer a course among the interest groups. Despite the restrictions, you can include Glacier Bay in your itinerary in several ways. Most cruise lines visit the bay on some cruises. You can fly to and stay at Gustavus, the nearest community, making short day trips to Glacier Bay (Alaska Airlines has scheduled service to Gustavus); or take a sight-seeing tour from Juneau, Skagway, or Haines. Some of these are multiple-day affairs that tend to be trying for kids. The bay can be reached only by sea or air.

Between Memorial Day and Labor Day, the **Glacier Bay Ferry** (877/774-8687; www.4seasonsmarine.com/glacier-bay-ferry/) makes a round trip four days a week between Juneau and Glacier Bay. Ferries leave Auke Bay for Gustavus at 10 a.m. and return from Bartlett Cove to Auke Bay at 5:30 p.m. (Mon, Wed, Fri, Sat; $69 one way, $195 round trip/adult; $34.50 one way, $49 round trip/child under 12). The trip takes three hours. You're likely to see bald eagles, humpback whales, sea lions, and seals along the way. Food service is minimal, so bring snacks along. Four Seasons Tours, which owns the ferry, also offers a whale-watching tour from Gustavus to Point Adolphus on days when the ferry runs. These tours leave Gustavus at 2 p.m. and return to Bartlett Cove at 5 p.m., in time for you to catch the ferry back to Juneau.

Note that although the ferry arrives in Gustavus, it departs from Bartlett Cove, several miles away. If you're staying in Bartlett Cove at Glacier Bay Lodge (the only accommodation in the national park), a free shuttle bus will pick you up from the Gustavus dock and take you to the lodge. If not, you'll need to arrange transportation from and to the ferry depending on where you are headed.

Glacier Bay Lodge (888/229-8687; www.visitglacierbay.com) is less expensive than most accommodation in Gustavus, and has hiking trails and the national-park ranger station on the premises. Rent kayaks, fishing gear, and bicycles here. Restaurant prices are steep, but the fare is excellent. The lodge can arrange tours: fishing charters, flightseeing, kayaking, and tours of Glacier Bay. For lodging and attractions in Gustavus, check the town's Web site: www.gustavus.com). The national park's Web site is a handy resource (www.nps.gov/glba/).

Tracy Arm A contrast to Glacier Bay and a terrific day trip from Juneau, is Tracy Arm, a deep fjord that lies south of Juneau and cuts 25 miles east of Stephens Passage, deep into the mainland. The fjord is narrow, about a mile wide. Enormous tidewater glaciers calving into pristine waters, waterfalls, and wildlife make this an unforgettable experience. (See Parent Tip next page.) Because negotiating Tracy Arm requires superior boating skills, be sure to sign on with a reputable, experienced tour.

☛ **Parent Tip: Tracy Arm Fjords**
by Christian Boatsman

Billed as one of the best-kept secrets in Juneau, a Tracy Arm Fjords glacier cruise is a great trip for the whole family. These are usually all-day excursions, departing at 9am and returning around dinner time. The glacier itself is massive and dwarfs even the largest cruise ships. Hundreds of mini blue-white icebergs fill the water at the base of the glacier, topped with sea lions seeking safety from killer whales. Several companies provide day tours of Tracy Arm Fjord, but many cater only to cruise ship passengers who must make reservations with their respective cruise lines; prices vary. However you plan your trip, ask about the availability of food onboard and if the boat is a high-speed catamaran (you'll spend more time at the glacier's edge and less time getting there and back). ◼

Auk Nu Tours (907/586-5137, 866/586-5162; www.goldbelttours.com) provides daily eight-hour excursions in a high-speed catamaran to Tracy Arm between mid-May and early September, departing Juneau at 9 am three days a week ($109/adults, $70/kids, including hot lunch). **Alaskatours.com** (413 G St, 907/277-3000) has tours three days a week departing at 9am from Juneau ($110/adults, $70.50 kids 3-12). **Adventure Bound** (215 Ferry Way;907/463-2509, 800/228-3875; www.adventureboundalaska.com) cruises depart at 8:30am from Juneau and return at 6pm (adults/$99,$59/ kids under 18). Food is available on board.

Admiralty Island National Monument   If seeing bears is high on your agenda, consider making a trip to Admiralty Island National Monument, a 30-minute flight or longer boat trip from Juneau. One bear- watching vantage point at **Pack Creek** is close to where you're dropped off; another is a one-mile walk along a scenic boardwalk to an overlook. Park rangers are available to answer questions and the area is well-marked for self-guided tours. You'll need a permit (between June and early September) from the Tongass National Forest (8461 Old Dairy Rd; 907/586-8790) which you can download at: www.fs.fed.us/r10/tongass/districts/admiralty/packweb/application.pdf. Fees are $50/adult during peak season (July 5-Aug 25) and $20 in June and late August to early September. Child (under 16) and senior permits are half the adult fee. **Alaskatours.com** has a day trip that includes flights to and from the island for $475 per person. They offer two-night camping excursions as well ($950). Some cruises to Glacier Bay include stops or "sail bys" at Admiralty Island.

Point Bridget State Park   Attractions at this popular state park range from meadowland and forest to rocky beaches with spectacular views. A boardwalk trail leads 3.5 miles from the parking pullout to the beach, where whales and sea lions are often seen and, at times, bears and spawning salmon (they often go together). There are two public use cabins in the park, and wilderness camping is permitted. You'll find several other interesting trails in this 2,800-acre park. *On the Glacier Hwy, 39 miles north of Juneau; www.dnr.state.ak.us/parks/units/ptbridg2/. Allow 6 hours for round trip.*

Calendar of Events

April
Alaska Folk Festival
907/463-3316; www.juneau.com/aff/
Week-long music, performance, dance festival of Alaska and Yukon musicians at Centennial Hall.

May
Juneau Jazz & Classics
907/463-3378; www.juneau.com/music/
A 10-day event celebrating spring and music, featuring jazz and classical music, and drawing musicians nationwide. Family concerts (low prices), free brown-bag concerts at local venues such as the Nugget Mall.

June
June-August, free evening concerts
907/586-2787
At Marine Park, Fridays, 7-8:30pm; entertainment by local musicians, dancers, dramatists.

Gold Rush Days
907/586-2497
Festival of logging, mining events at Gold Rush Fields.

Resources
Tongass National Forest
Forest Service Information Center, 8465 Old Dairy Rd, 907/586-8800

City of Juneau
www.juneau.com

Juneau Convention & Visitors Bureau
One Sealaska Plaza, Suite 305; 888/581-2201, 907/586-1737, www.traveljuneau.com

Books and Videos
Jettmar, Karen. *Alaska's Glacier Bay: A Traveler's Guide.* Alaska Northwest Books, 1997. This comprehensive handbook to the bay covers its history, geology, flora, and fauna, with photos and map.

Glacier Bay Handbook. National Park Service. One of a series of excellent NPS guidebooks.

Glacier Bay—The Grand Design. Alaska Video Postcards (35 minutes). The bay, up close and personal.

Raban, Jonathan. *Passage to Juneau: A Sea and Its Meanings.* Pantheon Books, 1999. This is a celebrated account of a journey up the Inside Passage in the context of the waterway's rich history of exploration.

HAINES

Lynn Canal extends from north of Juneau to Haines, which lies between the canal and the Chilkoot Inlet to the east, and the Chilkat Inlet and mouth of the Chilkat River to the west. Haines and Skagway, its closest neighbor, are 14 miles apart by sea, but separated by 360 miles plus two international borders by land. The greater Haines area, with 2,500 residents, has been largely bypassed by the cruise industry. Haines has a sheltered location, gently forested environment, and many homes with beautiful gardens. In Haines you'll find the little town that time forgot. Haines is most famous for the bald eagles that congregate here in droves when the salmon are running on the Chilkat River in November. By late in the fall, most of Alaska's spawning salmon have long gone to the big fertilizer factory in the sky, so hungry eagles vie for access to these last treats. During the summer, eagles can be spotted, but in far fewer numbers.

For families with younger kids who want to visit both Haines and Skagway, we recommend making Haines your base of operations with daytrips to Skagway via high-speed water taxi. Skagway is smaller, more expensive, has fewer services for families, and in summer is so overrun with cruise ship passengers that a kind of pedestrian gridlock develops.

Getting To Haines

By Air Regional airlines serving Haines are **Skagway Air Service** (907/766-3233; www.skagwayair.com; daily flights to Juneau and Skagway) and **Wings of Alaska** (907/766-2030; www.flyingalaska.com; Haines, Juneau, Skagway, and smaller communities). Both offer charter air services and/or flightseeing tours, as does **Air Excursions, LLC** (daily flights between Haines, Juneau, Skagway, and Gustavus; 907/766-2550, 800/354-2479; www.airexcursions.com). The **Haines Airport Terminal** is at Mile 4.5 Haines Highway (907/766-3609).

By Sea **Alaska Marine Highway System** (907/465-3941, 800/642-0066; www.dot.state.ak.us/amhs/) ferries serve Haines year round, with multiple weekly sailings in summer. **Silver Eagle Transport** (907/766-2418, 907/766-3324; kcd.com/akferry/. Cost: $25/adult one-way, $12/child; vehicle fees, calculated by vehicle length, start at $50), a 65-foot catamaran, carries up to 28 passengers and several vehicles between Juneau and Haines. Vessels depart from Ketknikoff Cove, four miles south of town, and arrive at Echo Cove on the Glacier Highway, 40 miles north of Juneau. Trips take 3.5 hours. Reservations are needed. There is a snack bar on board. **Chilkat Cruises & Tours** (142 Beach Rd, 907/766-2100; chilkatcruises.com. Cost: $40/adult, $20/child 2-12, free/under 2) runs a water taxi between Haines and Skagway with multiple daily sailings; the trip takes 35 minutes. Passengers are limited to a maximum of two pieces of luggage. Reservations are a good idea.

By Road Access to Haines is via the Haines Highway, a good paved road that runs 152 miles betweenHaines and the junction with the Alaska Highway in the small town of Haines Junction, Yukon Territory. The road crosses the international border. In summer, **RC Shuttle** (907/479-0079) runs buses from Haines to Fairbanks and points between. **Alaska Direct Bus Line** (800/770-6652) runs buses between Fairbanks, Tok, Skagway, and Haines.

Roadside Attractions

The 152-mile drive along the **Haines Highway** between Haines Junction, Yukon Territory and Haines is so scenic that it's worth renting a car just to drive it Allow about four hours for the drive and remember there is a one-hour time difference between the two ends of this highway. There are few services along the way, so fill your tank before you leave.

The Wrangell-St. Elias and Kluane National Parks (the world's largest contiguous national parkland), offer rugged peaks (Canada's tallest is here), sweeping forested vistas, and amazingly azure lakes. **Kathleen Lake Campground** (39 sites; kitchen area; picnic/day use area; restrooms; trails; camping; $10/site), the only established campground within mostly wild Kluane National Park, is about 17 miles from Haines Junction. This is a lovely place for a picnic; pick up the fixings at the supermarket in Haines Junction or, better yet, at the Village Bakery (see "the Alaska Highway and Yukon Territory"). Or, if you're headed north from Haines, pick up a scrumptious take-out meal at the Fireweed Restaurant (see "Places to Eat").

Dezadeash Lake, a few miles down the road, also has a Yukon public campground. At **Kluk̄shu**, 40 miles south of Haines Junction, Klukshu Craft Store and Museum sells local Native arts and crafts. From here to Chilkat Pass (3,493 feet) the views are extraordinary. There are plenty of places to park and look around. Forty miles from Haines is US Customs. This border station has a reputation for being suspicious of impecunious travelers; long waits are possible. After the border, you leave the frozen north behind and descend into lush rainforest and the Chilkat River valley. The road parallels the river and Chilkat Bald Eagle Preserve. Set the kids to work looking for those telltale spots of white at the tops of the evergreens.

Getting Around

Haines is actually two towns in one: Fort Seward, dating from 1903, was Alaska's first permanent army post. When it was decommissioned in 1945, it was purchased by veterans with a view toward making it the basis for a new community. Today it's a National Historic Landmark, and the remaining buildings, many of them officers' quarters, have been reborn as hotels, B&Bs, and shops. The cruise ship dock is here, along with art galleries, stores, and Native enterprises. Downtown Haines looks more like a traditional Alaskan small town; it's also where more mundane services are located.

Though Haines is small enough to get around on foot, families with very young kids might want to rent a vehicle. Try **Affordable Cars** (2nd Ave & Dalton St, at the Captain's Choice Motel; 907/766-3111, 800/247-7153 [U.S.], 800/478-2345 [Canada]; e-mail: capchoice@usa.net) or **Eagle's Nest Car Rental** (at the Eagle's Nest Motel, Mile 1 Haines Hwy; 907/766-2891,

---

☛ **Parent Tip: Cruise Ship Hours**

If there's a cruise ship in town, just about every establishment in town will be open for business, regardless of posted hours. But when the ships pull out, tired shopkeepers are likely to close their doors for a break. To find out when ships will be in, ask at the Visitor Center or check the cruise ship schedule on their Web site (haines.ak.us/hainesweb/events/). ◙

800/354-6009; www.eaglesnest.wytbear.com). **Avis** also rents cars here (at Chilkat Cruises, 121 Beach Rd; 800/331-1212; *www.avis.com*).

Taxi service is provided by **Yeshua Guided Tours** (907/766-2334; www.yeshuaguidedtours.com).

Sockeye Cycle rents bikes at 24 Portage Street, Fort Seward, up from the cruise ship dock (907/766-2869).

Places to Stay

Fort Seward Lodge ($)
39 Mud Bay Rd. 907/766-2009, 800/478-7772; www. ftsewardlodge.com
FYI: 10 rooms, 2 kitchenettes; some shared baths; restaurant; under 12 stay free; courtesy van; pets (fee)

This historic building, dating from the early 1900s, once housed Fort Seward's Post Exchange (PX). Today, it offers basic, comfortable accommodation at low rates. All rooms are nonsmoking. The location is close to the water, handy to Fort Seward and town services. The restaurant serves up hearty dishes, including an all-you-can-eat crab special, in season. Kids will enjoy the money-covered ceiling.

Hotel Halsingland ($-$$)
At Fort Seward. 907/766-2000, 800/542-6363; hotelhalsingland.com
FYI: 60 rooms, some family rooms, some shared baths; under 13 stay free; gift shop; courtesy shuttle; open mid-April-Sept

An excellent, affordable choice for families, this National Historic Landmark was the Commanding Officer's quarters with a view of the Fort Seward Parade Ground down to the water; an adjacent annex has additional rooms. In keeping with the slightly faded charm of this Victorian-era hotel, some rooms still have their original Belgian tile fireplaces and/or clawfoot tubs; some have views. There are several family rooms with three beds, tending toward the small side. A few rooms have shared baths and extra-low rates. All rooms are nonsmoking. The Commander's Room restaurant is a good dining choice (see "Places to Eat.")

❝ P A R E N T   C O M M E N T S ❞

"Hauling our suitcases up the steep stairs in the annex was
a bit of a trial, but our room had an amazing view. The
two doubles and one single bed were comfortable, but there
was practically no closet space. The staff was very nice and
made us feel welcome."

Mountain View Motel ($)
2nd Ave & Mud Bay Rd. 907/766-2900, 800/478-2902;
www.mtnviewmotel.com
FYI: 9 rooms, some family rooms, kitchenettes
   This small, no-frills motel close to Fort Seward and handy to downtown
has large family units and low prices.

Camping & Cabins

Several private and public campgrounds are close to Haines. But be aware that
large mosquitoes congregate here en masse in July and August.
   Chilkat State Park, seven miles south of town on Mud Bay Road (32 RV
sites, three tent sites; $5/site; picnic area, boat launch facilities, glacier views,
and trails [see "Hiking"]). There's a visitor center with telescopes through
which you can try to spot whales, eagles, and other local fauna. Five miles past
the ferry terminal on Lutak Road is **Chilkoot Lake State Recreation Site**,
with similar facilities to the state park ($10/site), but no visitor center. If you're
looking for tent-only campsites, try the waterfront **Portage Cove State
Recreation Site**, .75 mile south of town on Beach Road ($5/site).
   Hotel Halsingland operates the **Port Chilkoot Camper Park** behind the hotel
($20/site; wooded setting, picnic tables, full and partial hookups, laundry facilities,
and showers; tent campers welcome). A few miles past the ferry dock on Lutak
Road, **Salmon Run Campground & Cabins** (Mile 7 Lutak Rd; 907/766-3240;
salmonrunadventures.com; $13.50/site, showers, firewood, no hookups) has forest-
ed and streamside campsites and a few with views of Lutak Inlet. Primitive cabins
are available for $55 per night. The large **Haines Hitchup RV Park** (851 Main St;
907/ 766-2882; *www.hitchuprv.com*) has full services, starting at $24 per night.

Places to Eat

Commander's Room
In the Hotel Halsingland at Fort Seward. 907/766-2000, 800/542-6363;
hotelhalsingland.com
Hours: Open daily in summer, 7-9am, 5:30-9pm
This is the town's fine-dining establishment, but prices won't stress your wallet.
It's a good dinner choice for older kids, but the tranquil atmosphere might not
suit the fidgety set so well. The food is topnotch, especially fish; burgers are
also on the menu. Breakfast is especially good; try the peppered bacon.

Fireweed Restaurant
In Fort Seward, Building 37 on Blacksmith Rd, off Portage St. 907/766-3838
Hours: Open daily in summer from 11am; call for details
This place is a standout, accommodating fussy eaters and gourmet parents.
Selections range from scrumptious baked goods (available for takeout) to
pizza and delectable pasta dishes. Many dishes are prepared with organic
foods. Even if you don't have time for a meal, stop in for an espresso and
snack. Prices are higher-end for Haines, but still reasonable.

Just for the Halibut ☺
142 Beach Rd, Fort Seward. 907/766-2100
Hours: daily 11am-7pm (summer)
Stop in here for a quick lunch. Fish and chips, burgers, chili, a "dock dog," and other child-friendly items are on the menu. Root beer floats and espresso drinks can quench your thirst. Prices are low.

Port Chilkoot Salmon Bake
Parade ground, Fort Seward. 907/766-2000, 800/542-6363 (U.S.),
800/478-2525 (Canada); hotelhalsingland.com
Hours: Wed-Thurs evenings, April-Sept
This salmon bake, aimed at cruise ship tourists, is what you'd expect and fairly high-priced. On a warm summer evening, you may need reservations. The food, including locally caught sockeye salmon, is served in a replica Tlingit tribal house in the Parade Ground. If the weather is decent, this would be a good choice for messy little eaters. It's part of the Hotel Halsingland empire.

Mountain Market
151 3rd Ave S. 907/766-3340
Hours: daily 7am-7pm
At this large natural-foods market and bustling café, locals and visitors merge in a seamless line-up for lattes (coffee beans roasted here), sweet breads, soups, sandwiches, wraps, cookies, and more. Vegetarians and meat lovers are equally well served. If the weather is dreary, a fresh pumpkin spice cookie can put a smile on small faces. If the weather is sunny, dine outside.

What to See & Do

Stroll & Browse

Pick up a copy of the *Haines Visitor's Guide* and *A History Walking Tour* for Fort Seward at the Visitors Bureau on 2nd Avenue South. Haines is easy to navigate. To travel between Fort Seward and town, choose 2nd or 3rd Avenue or stroll along scenic Beach Road. Shops and galleries abound in both parts of town.

In Fort Seward, stroll around Officer's Row and the parade ground, where you can investigate the **Tlingit Tribal House** and the **Sea Wolf/Whale Rider Galleries** (907/766-2540; www.tresham.com), featuring Tlingit-inspired art, jewelry, and sculptures by Haines Native Tresham Gregg. At **Alaska Indian Arts** (13 Fort Seward Dr; 907/766-2160; www.alaskaindian arts.com) the work of Tlingit artists and carvers is for sale. Down toward the water on Portage Street, you can't miss **Wild Iris** (907/766-2300; e-mail: wildiris@wytbear.com); it's the building with the extraordinary flowers, fruit trees, and a rollicking veggie garden. Inside the shop, you'll find a superb collection of high-quality artwork, jewelry, and crafts by Native and local artists.

Downtown Haines also has its share of good galleries. Three options with affordable local arts and crafts are **Helen's Shop** (221 Main St; 907/766-2266), **Uniquely Alaskan Arts** (across from the Visitor Center; 907/766-3559) and **Windspirit** (109 2nd Ave S; 907/766-2858; e-mail: windspirit@mymail station.com). The **Bald Eagle Foundation** and **Sheldon Museum** (see "Animals Animals" and "Museums") have excellent gift stores, including books. You'll find a small selection of general interest books at the **Babbling Book** (223 Main St; 907/766-3356).

In summer, **Chilkat Dancers** (Tribal House, Fort Seward; 907/766 2160; cost: $10/adult, $5/child 4-14) perform in traditional costume, dancing and acting out myths and legends of the Tlingit people. This is a good bet for all ages. Among Alaska's excellent Native dance groups, this is one of the best. Hours dovetail with cruise ship schedules. Reservations are recommended.

If you're in search of a **playground,** there's one at the elementary school and another at the ballfield. Ask for directions at the visitor center.

Museums

Alaska Indian Arts This nonprofit cooperative showcases the work of Northwest Native tribes, especially Tlingit. Workshops and apprenticeship programs ensure Native arts are passed on. Here you can watch totem pole carvers, silversmiths, and more. This is the parent organization for the Chilkat Dancers. Much of the work is for sale. Prices are high, and so is quality. *13 Fort Seward Dr, 907/766-2160; e-mail: aiaio@seaknet.alaska.edu. Open Mon-Fri, 9am-5pm and by request; longer hours when cruise ships are in port (summer). Allow 30 minutes.*

Hammer Museum This quirky new museum has a collection of hammers on display—lots of hammers. Some are antiques and date back to colonial times. About 1,000 different kinds of hammer are exhibited, representing a wide range of trades and industries. Watch out for the owners' African Grey parrot, Casey, who does his best to entertain visitors (if he's in the mood). *108 Main St; 907/766-2374, 907/767-5674. Open May 1-Sept 15, 10am-5:30pm (and when cruise ships are in town). Cost: $2/person. Allow 20 minutes.*

Sheldon Museum and Cultural Center ☺ Don't miss the unusually fine Chilkat blankets and Native basketry upstairs in this excellent museum. If you've been at a loss to explain the complex Native moiety system (the division of a tribe into two metagroups, called moieties, prescribing rules for marriage) to your kids, you'll find a lucid explanation here. Downstairs is more recent history, including the story of building the Haines Highway. Videos, slide shows, and traveling and temporary exhibits are here; there's also a children's discovery tour (ask at the reception desk). The gift shop has a wide selection of items at various prices and the best selection in town of books on local Alaskana and natural history. *11 Main St, corner of Main & 1st, across from the small boat harbor. 907/766-2366; www.sheldonmuseum.org. Open Tues-Fri 10am-noon, 1-5pm, Wed-Thurs 7-9pm (mid-May-mid-Sept); Sun-Mon, Wed, 1-4pm, Tues, Thurs-Fri, 3-5pm (rest of year). Longer hours when cruise ships are in port. Cost: $3/adult, free/child under 12. Allow at least 1 hour.*

Animals Animals

American Bald Eagle Foundation ☺ This museum looks uninspiring from the reception desk, but is actually a good family attraction. Start by exploring hands-on exhibits (including animal skulls). The main exhibit is a diorama featuring Alaska wildlife, from insects and fish to bears and eagles. Kids can pick up a laminated card at the reception desk with a list of animals on display, and hunt for them in the diorama. Also check out the unusual colors of spawning salmon. A video of the eagles that gather in November will give you a taste of this event. If you're tempted to try locally made syrups (including high-bush cranberry, birch, rhubarb, and spruce tip), you'll find the best prices and selection in the gift shop. Special programs are sometimes scheduled. The founder, Dave Olerud, can often be spotted here, talking to visitors. His enthusiasm for bald eagles and the rich and astonishing natural history of the region is infectious.

Corner of 2nd Ave & Haines Hwy. 907/766-3094; baldeagles.org. Hours: Mon-Fri, 9am-6pm, Sat-Sun, 1-4pm (summer); Mon, Wed, Fri, 1-4pm (rest of year). Cost: $3/adult, $1/child 7-12, free/under 7.

Alaska Chilkat Bald Eagle Preserve In 1982, the state of Alaska set aside 48,000 acres near Haines to preserve bald eagle habitat. The Chilkat, Klehini, and Tsirku rivers run through the preserve and supply the birds with salmon. Along the Haines Highway (between miles 18 and 21) are pullouts where motorists can stop to ogle eagles. At the right time of year— between October and February—the numbers that congregate here are astonishing, as the photos on Haines brochures attest. An alluvial fan reservoir causes the water at the mouth of the Chilkat River to remain 10-20 degrees warmer than surrounding waters and hence it does not freeze over, making it possible for the eagles to continue their feasting into the winter.

If your visit coincides with the bald eagles' visit, be prepared for winter weather and only five to six hours of daylight. Dress in layers, including a waterproof top layer. Don't forget a hat, gloves, and good, waterproof footwear. During the festival, daily buses run visitors from town to the Preserve.

If you miss the festival and prime viewing season, by all means explore the highly scenic Preserve anyway. Take the boardwalk trail that runs through the forest to the river. It features interesting interpretive signs that describe the ecosystem, the habits of the bald eagle, and the lives of the original human inhabitants who used to come to the beach for eulachon, called "candlefish" because they are so rich in oil they were used as a light source. The nutritious oil was also an important food source and trade good for many tribes in the Pacific Northwest. NOTE: In July, the mosquitoes at the Preserve are ferocious. *Mile 18-21 Haines Hwy. Restroom available.*

Swimming The public is welcome to swim at the **Haines Pool** (Borough Public School Haines Hwy, between Main St and 3rd Ave, 907/766-2666). Check for a free-swim coupon in the *Haines Visitor's Guide.*

The Great Outdoors

Kayaking   **Alaska Kayak Supply & Deishu Expeditions** (425 Beach Rd, 907/766-2427, 800/552-9257; www.seakayaks.com) offers kayaking trips of varying lengths (4 hours: $85/person, full-day: $125/person). They take children age 7 or older. They also rent kayaks to those who have taken at least one trip with them or have kayaking experience (May-Sept, $35/single and $55/double 1-2 days).

Hiking   On the west side of the Chilkat Peninsula is **Chilkat State Park,** with several trails that kids can handle. The easiest, the **Battery Point Trail,** follows the shoreline two miles to a beach. The **Seduction Point Trail** is an easy 6.8-mile trek along beach and through forest. Chances of seeing wildlife are good. The round trip is too long for most kids, but the trail is worth following part of the way. The more challenging **Mount Riley Trail** ascends 2.8 miles to the mountain's summit. The terrific view ranges from Lynn Canal to Chilkat Inlet. For more ideas, pick up a copy of the brochure *Haines is for Hikers* at the Haines visitor center. For information on getting to the park, and camping options, see "Places to Stay."

River Float Trips   **Chilkat Guides** (907/766-2491; raftalaska.com. May-Sept, $79/adult, $52.50/child 7-14) takes passengers age 7 and older on Chilkat River float trips. The four-hour trip includes transportation to and from your accommodation in Haines and a snack. The trip is gorgeous; among the wildlife spotted are eagles, bears, and moose. **River Adventures** (907/766-2050, 800/478-9827) also offers Chilkat River float trips.

Tours   The Native-owned **Keet Gooshi Tours** (907/766-2168, 877/776-2168; www.keetgooshi.com. $71/adult, $44/child under 12) has a three-hour van tour that includes the Tlingit village of Klukwan, the Chilkat Bald Eagle Preserve, and the Bald Eagle Foundation. Adventurous kids can sample *sakwnaien*, Native fried bread.

Yeshua Guided Tours/Absolutely Alaskan Tours (907/766-2334; www.yeshuaguidedtours.com) takes visitors on a variety of excursions, including guided rainforest walks, fishing and river trips (kids must be 7 or older), and icefishing and snowshoeing in winter.

Sockeye Cycle leads bicycle tours of the area. See "Getting Around."

Flightseeing   The three air carriers that serve Haines offer flightseeing tours, including Glacier Bay flightseeing excursions, and all will arrange charters. See "Getting to Haines" for contact information.

Calendar of Events

July
Independence Day Celebration
907/766-2202
Parade, races, kids' fishing derby, Mount Ripinsky Run.

August
Southeast Alaska State Fair and Bald Eagle Music Festival
907/766-2476
This five-day fair has: farm animal and agricultural exhibits; food and cooking exhibits; Native and other fine arts; logging shows; children's stage; creative writing, musical composition, songwriting, and fiddle contests. The music festival is a highlight, with big names and plenty of good, homegrown talent ($5/person, free/under 6).

November
Alaska Bald Eagle Festival
907/766-2202; www.baldeaglefest.org
Events for the four-day festival include seminars on bald eagles, guided eagle viewing, photography workshops, release of rehabilitated birds into the wild, Tlingit dancing, and events at the Sheldon Museum. Many events are designed for families.

Resources
Borough of Haines
P.O. Box 1209, Haines, AK 99827; 907/-766-2231; cityofhaines.org

Haines Convention & Visitors Bureau
On 2nd Avenue South; 907/766-2234, 800/458-3579; P.O. Box 530, Haines AK 99827; www.haines.ak.us

Haines Chamber of Commerce
907/766-2202; haineschamber.org

Books
Anderson, Cary. *Alaska's Magnificent Eagles*. Alaska Geographic, vol. 24. 1997. Through color illustrations and photos, eagles are explored in depth.

SKAGWAY

Skagway sits at the top of Taiya Inlet, the narrow northern terminus of Lynn Canal. The town has fewer than 900 residents, but each summer thousands more come to shop and see the sights. Skagway owes its existence to an earlier horde of invaders: the prospectors who headed north in 1897 to strike it rich in the Klondike following news of the gold strike on Bonanza Creek. The quickest way to the Klondike was by boat from Seattle to Skagway, over White Pass to the Yukon via Lake Bennett (where prospectors had to stop and build boats to cross the lake), and on to Dawson City. The White Pass & Yukon Railway was built in 1899, running from Skagway to Lake Bennett and on to Whitehorse, easing the trip considerably.

The Gold Rush lasted only a few years, but the railway continued to move people and freight to and from Yukon mines and thus ensured the town's survival. During World War II, the trains hauled equipment and workers building of the Alaska Highway. The railroad died as a freight-moving operation in 1982, but six years later was reborn, in part as a tourism enterprise. Today, trains run only between Skagway and Lake Bennett. To reach Whitehorse from the lake, travelers must take to the road. However, the spectacular rail journey has become the most popular tourist attraction in southeast Alaska. Today, Skagway's success can be measured by the number of cruise ships arriving daily.

The town offers Klondike-flavored family activities to enjoy. Along with the popular train ride to Lake Bennett, you can hike some or all of the 33-mile *Chilkoot Trail* in the footsteps of long-ago prospectors. Klondike Gold Rush National Historic Park and the Gold Rush cemetery where colorful Klondike characters are buried are worth investigating. Although Skagway has plenty of accommodation, Haines, with lower prices and more services, may make a better base of operation.

Getting to Skagway

By Air Skagway is served by several local air carriers. **Skagway Air** (907/983-2218; www.skagwayair.com) has daily flights between Skagway, Juneau, Haines, and smaller communities. **Wings of Alaska** (907/983-2442; www.flying alaska.com) serves Juneau, Haines, and Skagway with scheduled flights, Monday through Saturday. Both also offer charters and flightseeing tours.

By Sea Skagway is the northern terminus for the southeast route of the **Alaska Marine Highway System** (907/465-3941, 800/642-0066; www.dot.state.ak.us/amhs/). The ferry dock is right downtown, next to the cruise ship docks. Ferries run between Skagway and Bellingham year round with many weekly sailings during summer months (see "Getting There" in Chapter 2). **Chilkat Cruises & Tours** (907/766.2100; www.chilkat cruises.com) runs a water taxi between Haines and Skagway. (See "Getting to Haines," this chapter). **Alaska Fjordlines** (907/766-3395, 800/320-0146; www.kcd.com/watertaxi/) connects Skagway, Haines, and Juneau. For all trips, reservations are recommended.

By Road Access to Skagway is via the **South Klondike Highway.** From the junction with the Alaska Highway, 12 miles south of Whitehorse, it's a scenic 99-mile drive over good paved road to Skagway. The international border is 6.8 miles south of the Alaska Highway junction. In summer, it's open 24 hours a day. Remember that identification is required for everyone, including children. Bus service between Skagway and Whitehorse is offered by **Alaska Direct Bus Lines** (907/277-6652, 800/780-6652; www.tokalaska.com/dirctbus/) four times weekly in summer, with connections to Anchorage, Fairbanks, and smaller destinations; the trip takes three hours.

Roadside Attractions

Plan on three hours to drive the 99 miles to Skagway, allowing time for stops. Remember that you'll be changing time zones: Alaska time is an hour behind Yukon time. About a mile before you reach Carcross, you'll come across an oddity: the **Carcross Desert** (Mile 67.3), billed as the world's smallest. There's a turnout with informational signs, where you can park and admire the arid windswept sand dunes. At the town of **Carcross**, 32 miles south of the Alcan junction, you can get a look at Lake Bennett, where thousands of prospectors stopped to build boats to transport themselves to the Yukon gold fields. At the **Visitor Reception Centre** (in the old train station; 867/821-4431; open daily 8am-8pm, mid-May-mid-Sept), pick up a walking guide and peer into a few of the town's old buildings. In summer, you can stop for ice cream at the 1909 **Watson General Store**.

As you wind your way up to **White Pass** (3,292 feet), the scenery grows increasingly spectacular. At the tree line is the aptly named **Tormented Valley**, with its odd rock formations and little lakes, both grim and beautiful. On your way down from the pass, a few miles after you pass Canadian Customs (for travelers going the other direction) you'll arrive at U.S. Customs. Lines, if any, usually move quickly.

Getting Around

Skagway Municipal and Regional Transit (SMART; 907/983-2743) operates between the cruise docks and points of interest in town, including the railroad terminal and Gold Rush cemetery. Tickets are $2.

Shuttle service between Skagway and the Chilkoot trailhead in Dyea, nine miles out of town, is provided by **Frontier Excursions** (907/983-2512, 877/983-2512; www.frontierexcursions.com; $10/person one-way).

Cars can be rented from **Sourdough Car & U-Haul Truck Rental & Bike Rentals** (6th & Broadway, 907/983-2523; e-mail: rental@aptalaska.net) or **Avis** (907/983-2247, 800/331-1212), which operates May through September from the Westmark Hotel.

May through September, **Sockeye Cycle** (5th Ave off Broadway; 907/983-2851) rents bicycles.

Places to Stay

Cindy's Place ☺ ($-$$)
Dyea Rd, 907/983-2674, 800/831-8095
FYI: Two cabins, free breakfast, refrigerator/microwave; hot tub; mountain bikes; courtesy transportation; negotiable rates for kids; open May-Sept
If you have wheels, this is one of the best family choices in Skagway. It's two miles out of town, but rides in or out are provided. Of the two cabins, the Columbine is the best for families, with a double bed and a twin bed in a sleeping loft. There's a discount if you use your own bedding and for stays of two or more nights. The log cabins are heated and cozy, and the baked goodies delicious.

Sgt. Preston's Lodge ($-$$)
6th & State St.; 907/983-2521; sgt-prestons@usa.net
FYI: 30 rooms, some family rooms, kitchens; kids under 13 stay free; gift shop; courtesy van; open year round
This comfortable motel has undergone renovation and expansion and offers an assortment of rooms and suites in several one-story buildings. Units vary in size; several have three beds. Rooms in the new buildings are very spacious. It's far

enough from downtown to avoid the noise and crowds, while close enough for the walk to be manageable for kids. This is a popular spot with international travelers and hikers.

❝ P A R E N T   C O M M E N T S ❞

"Our daughter enjoyed making trips to the candy jar in the lobby. The staff was friendly and knowledgeable; most of the other guests were Alaskans. Best of all, it was just two blocks from the Haven, where we discovered their fresh cranberry muffins and great milkshakes."

"Having free Internet access in the lobby was a huge help."

Westmark Skagway Inn ($-$$)

3rd & Spring, 907/983-6000, 800/544-0970; www.westmark.com
FYI: 195 rooms, box lunches; kids under 18 stay free; Laundromat; airport/ferry courtesy van

Accommodation in Skagway is at a premium in summer. In recent years, the town has lost its flagship hotel, The Golden North, and several others. Luckily the Westmark is still here, by far the biggest hotel in town. However, it's often fully booked by cruise tours, so don't assume there will be vacancies. It's best to book as far ahead as you can. Although small, rooms are comfortable. The location is conveniently downtown, but a block away from busy Broadway.

❝ P A R E N T   C O M M E N T S ❞

"We had two small kids, a stroller, and lots of baggage, and even though Skagway is small, it's a long walk to the ferry terminal. We were very grateful for the courtesy van. The Laundromat was a lifesaver! Turns out there are only two public Laundromats in Skagway and all the tour guides and summer staff do their laundry there."

Camping & Cabins

The loveliest campground, in Dyea where the *Chilkoot Trail* begins, is the **National Park Service Ranger Station & Dyea Campground** (9 miles from Skagway on Dyea Rd; 907/983-2921; 22 sites, pit toilets, picnic tables, and fire rings). You can stay for up to 14 days; booking is first come, first served. It's free, but you'll need a permit (ask at the Visitor Center or Skagway Police, 1st & State; 907/983-2232) and must bring your own water. NOTE: This is NOT recommended for RVs; the road between Skagway and Dyea is hair-raisingly twisty and narrow and, most of the way, dirt.

In town, RV campers can choose from **Pullen Creek RV Park** (take 2nd Ave to Congress Way; 907/983-2768, 800/936-3731; $24/RV site with full services), next to the ferry and cruise ship docks and the small boat harbor; they accept tenters but it will be noisy. A quieter option for tenters is **Hanousek Park** (14th & Broadway, 907/983-2768; water, pit toilets, picnic tables, fire rings,

Sleep in a Caboose

About five miles north of town, along the east fork of the Skagway River, the Tongass National Forest maintains a unique public use 'cabin'—actually, it's an old White Pass & Yukon Railroad caboose. Access to it during the summer months is via the railroad. The caboose sleeps up to six (one double bunk and four singles) and has a table, benches, oil stove and tank (for heat), and an outhouse. Water is available from a nearby stream but must be treated before use. As with all Forest Service cabins, visitors need to bring oil for the stove, sleeping bags and pads, cook stove and cooking paraphernalia, food, plates, and utensils. Be prepared to pack everything out.

You'll need to reserve and pay in advance. The caboose is next to the train line, so you won't have a long hike. There are good views of the river and Sawtooth Mountains, and black bears and mountain goats lurk in the vicinity. In the off season (when the train isn't running), you can hike along the tracks. A trail to Denver Glacier (about four miles) starts from the caboose.

Reservation info: 877/444-6777; www.fs.fed.us/r10/tongass/recreation/rec_facilities/jnucabins/denver_caboose/; $35/ night. Internet reservations: National Recreation Reservation System: www.reserveusa.com/cabins/. For train reservations: White Pass & Yukon Railroad, 800/343-7373; www.whitepassrailroad.com. ▣

and showers. Many seasonal workers, who nearly double Skagway's summer population, live here. **Skagway Mountain View RV Park** (12th & Broadway; 907/983-3333, 888/778-7700; www.alaskarv.com/pages/skagway/; $21/site) has full services and is a bit quieter.

Places to Eat

Skagway Fish Company
Small boat harbor, next to Stowaway Cafe. 907/983-3474
Hours: Daily in summer, 11am-10pm
If the Stowaway Café is a bit too sedate for your rowdy preschooler, head next door to the Skagway Fish Company, where even the noisiest toddler howls will blend in with the happy high volume of other diners. There are good steak and seafood selections, but the best bet for kids is the halibut and chips, a bargain in these pricey parts. Adults will find an Alaskan microbrew goes down well, too.

Corner Café
4th & State Sts, 907/983-2155
Hours: daily 11am-7pm (year round)
This is where the locals head for lunch and dinner. It's your basic local hangout with decent burgers and other kid-friendly fare. The weekend prime rib specials are good value.

Ristorante Portobello & Pizzeria
1st & Broadway, 907/983-3459
Hours: daily 11am-10pm daily (May-Sept)
This popular, touristy restaurant serves up decent burgers, fish and chips, and seafood entrées as well as pizza. The microbrew and wine selection is good, and the location (close to but not on the water) is pleasant. Reservations are recommended.

Stowaway Café
205 Congress Way, 907/982-3463
Hours: daily 4-10pm (May-Sept)
Although it's a bit of a hike from downtown, this waterfront café is well worth the effort it takes to get here. The bright aqua building is fronted by a cute, quirky garden. There's no kids' menu, but fish and chips or Pad Thai noodles should satisfy most youngsters. Grownups may want to try Dungeness crab, which can be hard to find in southeast Alaska (usually, it's previously frozen king crab). Desserts are superb: try peach bread pudding with bourbon sauce or, for the chocoholic in your party, chocolate truffle cake with raspberry sauce. Prices are moderate.

Sweet Tooth Café ☺
315 Broadway
Hours: 6am-3pm (year round)
This bustling little café on Skagway's main street serves up the best breakfast in town; French toast is one of the child-friendly choices. For lunch, try the hearty homemade soups and sandwiches on fresh-baked bread. There are often lines here, even before the cruise passengers arrive, so come early.

What to See & Do

As in other cruise ship towns, you'll find that restaurants, stores, and attractions open when the cruise passengers are in town, and close their doors when passengers leave. Non-cruise travelers might want to check the cruise ship schedule at the Visitor Center.

Stroll & Browse

Begin your stroll at the **Skagway Convention & Visitors Bureau** (2nd & Broadway, 907/983-2854; www.skagway.org. Open: 8am-6pm, May-Sept; 8am-5pm, rest of year). Pick up a free copy of the *Skagway Walking Tour* brochure. Broadway is the main street, and most town attractions line up on or close to it, including the major retail outlets. **Corrington's Museum of Alaskan History** (5th & Broadway, 907/983-2580; open daily 8:30am-7:30pm. Free.) combines a small museum with a large store carrying a wide selection of moderately priced arts and crafts. The museum offers a concise history of Native cultures and exploration of southeast Alaska. Notice the excellent baskets and unusual ivory-tusk scrimshaw artifacts. Allow at least 20 minutes here. Corrington's also runs the **Skagway Outlet Store** (7th & Broadway, 907/983-3331) up the street, with vast quantities of tourist icons like Eskimo *ulu* knives, T-shirts, sweatshirts, stuffed animal toys (moose, wolves, bear), and much more. Children will find plenty of kid-oriented souvenirs for sale. Prices are remarkably low and if you're on your way south via ferry or cruise ship you could have a hard time finding this selection at these prices anywhere else along your route.

If you've exhausted your child's tolerance for art galleries, jewelry stores, and craft emporiums, a visit to the **Kone Kompany** (5th & Broadway, 907/983-3439) which sells fresh fudge, ice cream, and candy along with fruit smoothies, should restore flagging spirits.

Echoes of Alaska (Broadway between 4th & alley, 907/983-2754) has high-quality Alaskan art. **The Rushin' Tailor** (Broadway between 6th & 7th; 907/983-2397) has a selection of Russian arts, along with some good, moderately priced local crafts. For the Mountie enthusiast, check out **Sgt Preston's Trading Post** (2nd & Spring, 907/983-2115) with plenty of RCMP-inspired regalia and toys. The only bookstore in town is **Skaguay News Depot & Books** (Broadway between 2nd & 3rd; 907/983-3354; www.skagwaybooks.com).

For families staying in Skagway, locating the necessities of life—from diapers to sipping cups to munchies—can be a challenge. Try the town's one grocery store, **Fairway Market** (State St & 4th, 907/983-2220). Also check out **You Say Tomato** (State & 9th, 907/983-2784), with a wide selection of natural foods and products and a good café, **Haven** (907/983-3553; open daily 6am-10 pm, Sun 6am-midnight) that serves espresso drinks, panini sandwiches, soups, and salads, along with breakfast sandwiches and cereals. Haven doubles as an Internet café.

Parks

Adjacent to the Skagway Museum & Archives is a large children's playground with swings, slides, and plenty of room for small fry to run around.
6th & Broadway

Klondike Gold Rush National Historical Park Think of the entire town as the park (with a branch in Seattle). There are 15 historic buildings in the park, along with the *Chilkoot Trail*, the old town site of Dyea at the Chilkoot trailhead, and a portion of the *White Pass Trail*. Start at the visitor center and pick up a park guide. Free ranger-led 45-minute walking tours of restored buildings in town are offered five times daily, starting at the visitor center, and are highly recommended. (There's a $2 fee per person for touring the Moore House at 5th & Spring.) A host of interesting evening programs is presented, including Robert Service poetry readings; schedules are posted in the visitor center, which also shows films on the Gold Rush in the auditorium.

Starting in June are daily guided tours of the Dyea town site, nine miles out of town. If you don't have wheels, see "Getting Around" or ask at the visitor center. Tours start at 2pm. The Park Web site has a lot of information and useful kid and educator links.
Klondike National Historic Park Visitor Center, 2nd & Broadway
907/983-2921, www.nps.gov/klgo/home/. Open daily 8am-8pm (June-Aug); daily 8am-6pm (May, Sept).

Museums

Corrington's Museum of Alaska History; see "Stroll and Browse."

Skagway Museum and Archives The museum is housed in the imposing and recently renovated and expanded McCabe College Building, dating from 1899, also home to Skagway's City Hall. You'll find a small, eclectic assortment of Native art and artifacts, a succinct history of Skagway and the Gold Rush, and traveling exhibits. The display on gambling in Skagway's early years is fascinating (check out the antique slot machines). There's a small gift shop. *7th Ave & Spring St, in the Historic District. 907/983-2420; e-mail: jmunns@skagwaymuseum.org. Open daily 9am-5pm (mid-May-Sept); hours vary rest of year. Cost: $2/adult, $1/student, free/child 12 and under. Allow at least 30 minutes.*

Culture

"The Days of '98 Show with Soapy Smith" ☺ In the tradition of Klondike revues throughout Alaska and the Yukon, this one offers a dollop of local Gold Rush history: the tale of Soapy Smith, an unsavory Skagway con man and saloon owner, who died in a shootout with town surveyor Frank Reid who, with other upright citizens, was attempting to clean up Skagway. (Both men are buried in the Gold Rush cemetery a few blocks away.) In song, dance, and lots of corny jokes (a few of which are very slightly risqué), the revue portrays events leading up to and including their confrontation. Parents be warned: if your children persuade you to sit in the front rows, you are likely to be tagged by the cast and forced onto the stage to participate in various scenes, one of which involves dancing the can-can. Fresh popcorn is sold before performances. *Eagles Hall, 6th & Broadway. 907/983-2545; shows 10:30am, 2pm, 8pm (mid-May-mid-Sept). Cost: $14/adult, $7/child 3-12, free/under 3. Allow about an hour.*

The Great Outdoors

Gold Mining **Klondike Gold Dredge Tours.** If you're curious about how gold gets out of the ground or stream bed, a visit to this restored gold dredge will answer some of your questions. Built in Seattle in 1936, the dredge made its way to Dawson City via Skagway. The restored dredge can be toured. The tour includes an interesting video. Panning for gold is included. There's a gift shop. *Mile 1.7 Klondike Hwy. 907/983-3175, 877/983-3175; www.klondikegolddredge.com.*

Hiking If you have time for only one hike, a trip to the **Gold Rush Cemetery** and **Lower Reid Falls** is a good choice. You can walk there easily: Go north from State Street to the railroad yards and cross the tracks to the cemetery. From the National Park Visitor Center, the trip is four miles round trip and level most of the way. The cemetery is charming, with grave 'stones' (many are painted wooden boards) set among the tall trees. Frank Reid has a large well-tended grave; Soapy Smith's is shunted to one side (for the story, see "Culture"). Allow two hours.

The hike to **Yakutania Point** takes you west along 1st Avenue and around the south end of the airport runway. (Some kids may be happy to stay awhile and watch small planes take off and land.) Crossing the footbridge, turn left and continue on the trail past the exercise stations to the viewpoint, where there are picnic sites and toilets. Allow about 90 minutes for the 1.5-mile round trip.

The most challenging trail in the park is the **Chilkoot Trail,** taken by thousands of hopeful miners headed to the Klondike. Canada required that each miner bring a year's worth of supplies: a ton each! Miners carried their loads in stages, moving them up slowly to the pass and beyond to the gold fields. At Lake Bennett, they stopped to build boats and wait for the ice to break up; in the spring they sailed across the lake and waterways to Whitehorse, then Dawson City on the Yukon River. On their arrival in 1898, the hopeful prospectors discovered that the gold fields had already been parceled out and nothing was left. To hike the entire 33 mile trail takes at least four days. Plenty of families do just that, but there's nothing to stop you from hiking a few miles from Dyea. Along the route you'll pass genuine relics of the Gold Rush; U.S. and Canadian ranger stations (you'll have to show your permit when you cross into Canada); nine maintained campgrounds, most with outhouses;cooking shelters;wildlife; and beautiful scenery. You can day hike on the trail from the U.S. side without the need to get a permit or pay a fee. However, to camp overnight on any portion of the trail requires a permit. It's best to obtain one in advance. Permits for those who arrive at the trail without reservations are limited to eight per day. All fees for use of the trail are levied in Canadian dollars. Permits for overnight use on the U.S. side of the border only cost $15. For the whole trail, hikers pay $35 per adult and $17.50 per child age 6 to 15. Canada limits the number of hikers on any given day to 50. On the Canadian side of the trail, day users are charged a $5 fee.

To get a handle on the options in summer, visit the **Chilkoot Trail Center** in the historic Martin Itjen house (Broadway between 1st & 2nd , 907/983-9234). *Trailhead 9 miles northwest of Skagway on Dyea Rd, in Dyea by the Taiya River bridge (For details, check with the National Park Service in Skagway.) 907/983-2921; www.nps.gov/klgo/chilkoot/. For Canadian hiking and permit information: 867/667-3910 , 800/661-0486; parkscan.harbour.com/ct/*

River Float Trips Skagway **Float Tours** (907/983-3688; www.skagway float.com) offers several trips suitable for families. The scenic float trip down the Taiya River is a good choice (3 hours, 45 minutes on the river; $65/adult, $45/child under 13). Because the river is gentle, young children are welcome, a rarity on float trips. Another option is the combined 1.8-mile hike and float trip (4 hours; $75/adult, $55/child).

Flightseeing A variety of glacier flightseeing tours is based in Skagway; see "Getting to Skagway" for contact information. Along with Glacier Bay tours, **Skagway Air** offers a 45-minute Gold Rush tour flight, well priced at $70 per adult and $50 per child, that includes Lake Bennett and the Juneau Icefield (see "Getting to Haines" for contact info).

Excursions

White Pass & Yukon Route Railway ☺   Hands down, this is Skagway's biggest attraction. Trains make the 3.5-4-hour round trip on a narrow gauge railway to the summit of White Pass two or three times daily, depending on the time of year. Saturdays, an eight-hour steam-train excursion is added, in which passengers continue 20 miles past the summit to Lake Bennett. During a two-hour layover, they have a box lunch and a guided tour by a park historian. There's also a tour, one-way or round-trip, to Whitehorse. However, at Lake Bennett, you'll be transferred to a bus for the rest of the trip as the train no longer goes all the way to Whitehorse. If you go to Whitehorse, you'll be buying two one-way tickets rather than a round-trip, because of the international crossing. Trains also carry Chilkoot Trail hikers from Bennett back to Skagway.

The trip is magnificent in any weather. The train climbs 2,865 feet in 27 miles. Just outside Skagway, it passes the Gold Rush cemetery. A little farther on is the Denver Caboose that the Forest Service rents out as a cabin (see "Camping"). Views are staggering: sheer cliffs drop to the rushing river below. The trip is narrated; you'll catch a glimpse of the old Chilkoot Trail, mossy and overgrown, but still visible. The best views are on the left as you go up (the right as you return from the summit). Although everyone switches sides at the summit, the most exciting part of the trip is the beginning, so it's worth finding a seat on the left if you can.

Kids will enjoy the two long tunnels and several high, scary trestles. Children are permitted to stand between cars if there's a parent with them; monitor small fry carefully, especially when in the tunnels; it's pitch dark for several minutes. There's no opportunity to disembark during the summit excursion. Free sodas and bottled water are included with your ticket price.

All trips involve crossing the international border into Canada and back again into the United States. However, if you're just traveling as far as the summit, you won't have to endure an official border crossing. But everyone, including children, is required to show proof of citizenship when tickets are purchased. On the Lake Bennett or Whitehorse excursions, you will need to clear customs and immigration.

The train depot is huge and includes an espresso bar and a store with railroad memorabilia, including a narrated video of the trip ($30). Small kids will enjoy watching the model train that circles the ceiling in one depot room. *907/983-2217, 800/343-7373; www.whitepassrailroad.com. Mid-May-mid Sept. Cost: White Pass Summit: $82/adult, $41/child 3-12; Lake Bennett Steam Train: $156/adult, $78/child 3-12; Whitehorse one way: $66.50/adult, $33.25/child 3-12; on all trips: free/child under 3.*

Wildlife and Fishing Tours   **Chilkoot Charters & Tours** (907/983-3400, 877/983-3400; www.chilkootcharters.com) has a bevy of tours, mostly but not only for cruise passengers. Wildlife cruises, king salmon and halibut fishing, tours of the city and to the summit of White Pass are all offered in various combinations, lengths, and prices. The three-hour City & White Pass Summit Tour with free gold-panning is a good value at $35 a head.

Calendar of Events

April
Mini Folk Festival
907/983-2276
This novel event consists of a day of folk music featuring southeast Alaska musicians in Skagway; on the second day, the festival packs up and moves to Whitehorse, Yukon.

June
International Softball Tournament
907/983-3021
Annual international softball tournament between teams from Alaska and Canada.

July
Independence Day celebrations (July 4)
907/983-1898
Parade, slow bike race, Ducky Derby (plastic ducky race), many family events.

Soapy Smith's Wake (July 8)
907/983-2234
A party orchestrated by the cast of the Days of '98 Show.

September
Klondike Road Relay
867/668-4236
A 110-mile Skagway-to-Whitehorse relay race over two days; international 10-person teams compete.

October
Abduct and Release—Skagway Paranormal Symposium (weekend before Halloween)
907/983-2854, 888/762-1898
A freewheeling conference that embraces UFOs, folk legends, urban legends, and ghosts.

Resources

Skagway Convention & Visitors Bureau
P.O. Box 1025, Skagway, AK 99840; 907/ 983-2854; www.skagway.org

Skagway Chamber of Commerce
P.O. Box 194, Skagway, AK 99840-0194; 907/983-1898; www.skagway chamber.org

Books
Clifford, Howard. Ed. *Soapy Smith, Uncrowned King of Skagway.* Sourdough Enterprises, 1997. Learn the story behind the legendary bad guy who inspired so much tourism.

Satterfield, Archie. *Chilkoot Pass: A Hiker's Historical Guide to the Klondike Gold Rush National Historical Park.* Alaska Northwest Books, 1973. This excellent history of the trail and its role in the Gold Rush is illustrated by archival photos.

5 Alaska Highway: Yukon Territory and British Columbia

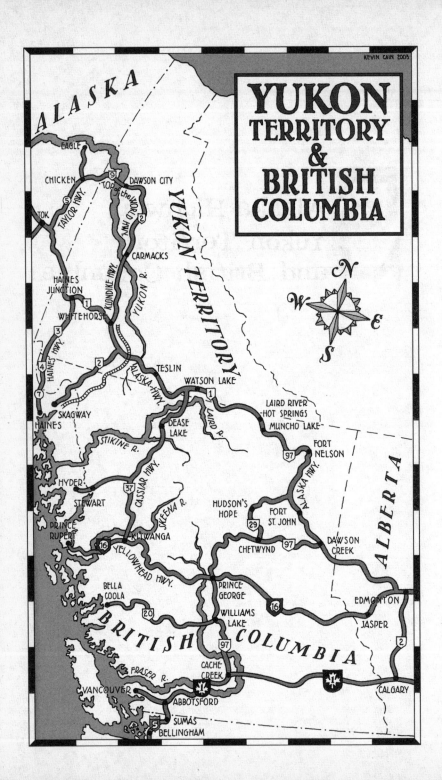

5 Alaska Highway: Yukon Territory and British Columbia

DRIVING THE ALASKA Highway is an adventure that will generate a lifetime of family memories. You'll pass through some of the loveliest, least-traveled lands on the continent while experiencing awesome scenery and encountering extraordinary wildlife: moose, caribou, bald and golden eagles, brown and black bears, cougars, and wolves. You'll discover a panorama of human history, from the days when First Nations hunted woolly mammoths in Beringia to the Gold Rush era when thousands of prospectors in search of gold turned tiny settlements into cities overnight. It's their trail you'll follow.

The Alaska Highway—also frequently referred to as the Alcan—is a paved road, usually two lanes, and in good condition except where under construction. Services are rarely more than 100 miles apart, usually less. Although every year more people drive the Alaska Highway, it often feels empty, without the stresses of freeway driving. For northern families, driving the Alaska Highway is no big deal: they've done it for three generations. But for the rest of us, a 2,000-mile road trip in the north with kids is not undertaken lightly. The Alaska Highway is nearly 1,400 miles long, requiring a minimum of four days to drive, preferably a week. Unless you have at least three weeks at your disposal, making the round trip by car will doom your family to spending most of their holiday inside a metal box.

If you're reluctant to risk the family car on a northern road trip, car-rental agencies can provide you with an Alcan-worthy vehicle. Fees tend to be higher than in the lower 48. Some companies allow one-way trips but charge a large drop-off fee. Check with Alaska-based car rental companies (see entries in "Anchorage") about drive-away opportunities; several seek drivers to make a one-way trip north or south and charge very low fees. Before renting, plan your itinerary and verify that your contract allows driving on the roads you have in mind. Some forbid driving on the Denali and Top of the World highways. In general, locally owned Alaskan agencies are less restrictive.

With planning, you can have your cake and eat it too. A popular approach is to drive one way and take the ferry home. Some Alaska-bound families team up: one family drives north, while the other family goes by ferry. Meeting in Skagway or Haines, the ferry travelers switch to the vehicle and drive home while the other family returns via ferry. If time and budget don't permit this, you can still craft a wonderful holiday driving part of the way.

Planning Your Trip
by Jan Faull

When traveling to Alaska by car, take advantage of the long periods of driving by planning fun and gratifying learning experiences. While you don't want to shove facts down your children's throats, do realize that kids, particularly ages 5-12, are usually interested and eager learners.

Prior to your vacation, go to the library and

stock up on fiction and nonfiction books about Alaska that will pique your children's interests.

Use car time to read aloud to your children. You'll ensure they learn about what they're seeing in an appealing way, and engage the entire family, including the driver, in a story of common interest.

Encourage each child to keep a combination

How this Chapter Is Organized

For the convenience of motorists, this chapter is organized by highway. Major sections give distances between destinations in miles (in Canada, distance is also given in kilometers). Side trips of special interest are also described at the end of this chapter starting on page 219. You'll read here about the west-access route from Vancouver, B.C., just north of the Canadian border, to the start of the highway in Dawson Creek, B.C. Then the text follows the entire Alaska Highway to its official end in Delta Junction, AK. (The extension between Delta Junction and Fairbanks, often considered part of the Alaska Highway, is described in chapter 10, "Fairbanks and the Interior.")

Also in this chapter is an alternate route that runs roughly parallel to the Alaska Highway between Whitehorse and Tok. Sometimes called the "Klondike Loop," this route runs north from Whitehorse to Dawson City, both in the Yukon, then west to the Alaska border, allowing a side trip to the historic town of Eagle. It eventually meets with the Alaska Highway a few miles east of Tok. The chapter also describes the Tok Cutoff, which connects the Alaska Highway with the Richardson and Glennallen highways, with road access to south central Alaska and Prince William Sound. The Richardson Highway is covered in chapter 10; the Glennallen is covered in chapter 6, "Anchorage and Environs."

Prices are given in the currency of the country described. Thus, in Whitehorse, prices are in Canadian dollars; in Tok, prices are in U.S. dollars.

journal-scrapbook. If your children are reluctant writers, you can take down their dictation, recording what they experienced each day. If you can afford it, buy each a Polaroid camera so your kids can snap a picture, record its significance, and paste it immediately in their memory book. Another option is to purchase disposable cameras. Help your children collect and read brochures and memorabilia and paste them in their memory books. Be sure to pack glue sticks, scissors and crayons for this project.

Help your kids learn to read a map, so they can follow the route you're traveling, check off distances, and note geographic and geological spots. Do realize that every historical or geological sight you'll visit has a gift shop. Kids will want to buy something—so set spending parameters before you go inside. One child may choose to collect a pencil from each gift shop along the way; another might purchase key chains.

Last, be aware of just how much input your children are receiving and how much information is too much. There will be times when a CD player or Game Boy is just what's needed to counteract tense car moments that inevitably arise—and when everyone, particularly the driver, needs a sanity break. ◼

What to Bring

When traveling in remote areas, where there may be long stretches between services, it's important to take along some essentials. Consider including these items when packing your car.

A good first-aid kit: Be sure you have one and that it's up to date. If you're not sure what to include, ask your healthcare provider for suggestions.

Alternative bedding: If your family has two or more kids, bring along a sleeping bag, and a good air mattress and pump. If a motel room is short on beds for every family member, having a bed in reserve helps ensure that everyone gets a decent night's sleep.

Entertainment for long travel days: Bring along car toys, travel games, and books. Hide some away to bring out on a dull stretch.

Towels: To take advantage of the many hot springs, lakes, and pools along the way, you will need to bring your own towels; pack at least one per person, plus sturdy, leakproof plastic bags for wet swimsuits and towels.

Waterproof footgear: Aquasox or sturdy rubber or plastic shoes that can be worn into a lake or hot springs or when tide-pooling at the ocean will be useful.

Cell phone: These are helpful in emergencies, but know that service may not exist in some locations. Check with your service provider about reception in Canada and Alaska.

Now, what to pack it all up in? Consider buying or borrowing convertible backpack/suitcases with zip-off daypacks. Inexpensive choices are widely available. These can fit into odd spaces when packing the car—and the daypack will come in handy on many occasions.

See "Introduction" for more ideas on what to bring.

Resources

The Milepost. Morris Communications. the bible of drivers in the north, this annual publication includes most major construction projects.

Road Conditions (British Columbia)
900/565-4997 (fee); 24-hour daily updates
250/774-7447 (reports on the Alaska Highway between Wonowon and Yukon border)

Road Conditions (Yukon Territory)
867/456-7623 (daily recorded updates)

Road Conditions (Alaska)
Alaska Road Conditions hotline: 800/478-7675
Highway Construction Office in Anchorage 800/478-7674 (recorded message); 907/269-0450; www.dot.state.ak.us/creg/const_nav/
Up-to-date highway construction information

Getting to the Alaska Highway

Your vacation begins when you pile the crew into your vehicle at home and set off into the unknown, but unless you live in northwestern Canada, you're facing two to three days of travel just to reach Dawson Creek, BC, where the Alaska Highway begins. There are many possible routes to choose from. The west-access route, described in this chapter, is the most popular and most direct. From Interstate 5, or from Vancouver and the lower mainland (for drivers starting in BC), motorists take the **TransCanada Highway** (Hwy 1) east from Vancouver (about three hours) and north to Cache Creek. The drive takes about 5.5 hours from Seattle. At the junction with Highway 97 in Cache Creek, the route continues north on 97 for 527 miles to Dawson Creek (about 12 hours). For information on attractions and accommodation in Seattle, Bellingham, and Vancouver, see "Getting There" and "Alaska Cruises."

It can be tempting to put pedal to the metal, ignoring all attractions until you reach the first mile of the Alaska Highway—but if you have time, take it slower. You'll enjoy some of the most spectacular roadside scenery and many attractions before reaching the Alaska Highway. Allow at least two days to reach Dawson Creek; three is better.

To the Alaska Highway from the East

If you're coming from east of British Columbia, you can access the Alaska Highway from its east-access route which takes you through Alberta's arid desert country where dinosaurs once roamed (and whose remains can be visited along the way). When the Alaska Highway first opened to nonmilitary traffic after World War II, this was the only route to reach it.

To reach the east-access route from the U.S., head north on Interstate 15 through Montana to the Canadian border, where I-15 becomes Highway 4, and on to Lethbridge, AB (101 km/63 miles north of the international border). From Lethbridge, the route runs west on Highway 3 to Fort McLeod

Family Road Trip:
A Teenager-Eye View

By Nick Webb

Teenagers: When going on a long car trip, especially to Alaska, you'll need every form of in-car entertainment you can find. If you take very little to entertain you, you will soon learn the hard way that all trees look very much the same after two hours. On the Alaska Highway, there are long stretches of road that offer nothing but forest on either side, a wall of trees that seems to run on forever—pretty dreary and mind-numbing.

Don't get me wrong: Alaska is a great place. There are tons of beautiful mountain vistas, waterfalls, glaciers, and sparse arctic tundra. There are great things to do, like visiting hot springs, hiking, and rafting, but getting there by car takes time. And let's face it: long hours in the car can be pretty boring if you have nothing to do.

So here is what you need to bring: If you enjoy reading, bring many books. If reading is not your style, then you'll have to bring something else to entertain your eyes. If you like to draw, bring art materials; if you have a portable game system, like a GameBoy, definitely bring that, and get some extra games.

Bring music, because that will make looking at trees more interesting. Include all your music; you never know when a craving for a certain song or performer will strike. Bring comic books, too. Everybody loves comic books (most people anyway).

If you like Mad Libs, these are a must—and they can entertain more than one person at a time. Mini board games are good to have as well. And finally, you'll need a cushion to sit on. A folded beach towel will do, but anything is better than the hard seat of a car. Trust me; I know from experience: Bring these items and your trip is sure to be much more interesting and worthwhile. ▣

(53 km/33 miles), then north on Highway 2 to Edmonton (463 km/288 miles). The final lap from Edmonton runs west on Highway 43 to Dawson Creek (590 km/367 miles). From Great Falls, MT, to Dawson Creek, the route is 1,394 km/867 miles.

A variant route with appeal for history buffs is available from Edmonton. Instead of going west on Highway 43, stay on Highway 2 and continue north through the historic town of Athabasca (171 km/106 miles), past Slave Lake to Donnelly (312 km/194 miles), then on Highway 49 to Dawson Creek (201 km/125 miles). This route runs 689 km/428 miles from Edmonton to Dawson Creek, adding about 96 km/60 miles to your trip.

Although less popular than the west-access route, this alternative has plenty of appeal for families, and you'll find several must-see attractions along way:

Head-Smashed-In Buffalo Jump Interpretive Centre Don't be put off by the gory name; this Unesco World Heritage Site is among the continent's most interesting aboriginal sites. For 6,000 years here, native hunters steered herds of bison toward and off a 30-foot cliff to their deaths. The meat was butchered and preserved in the camp below, feeding hundreds of people. The hunt was an important annual feature of First Nations culture until the near extinction of the bison in 1881 brought it to an end. At this extraordinary museum built into the cliff, visitors descend through five levels of displays including archeological finds, traditional stories of the hunt told by elders, and Blackfoot history. Guided tours are offered. In the café, sample buffalo meat along with more traditional deli fare. Outside are interpretive nature trails.

18 km north of Fort MacLeod on Hwy 785; 403/553-2731; www.head-smashed-in.com. Open year round.

Royal Tyrrell Museum in Drumheller This excursion will add a day to your trip, but what a day! In this large museum and paleontology research center, exhibits tell the story of life on our planet in fascinating detail. Wander through Dinosaur Hall, with 40 dinosaur skeletons, explore a Devonian Reef, learn about the Burgess Shale, and enjoy a living Cretaceous botanical garden. Educational programs for kids and families are offered, including digs and guided hikes. There's a large cafeteria. A 30 mile/50 km road network, the **Dinosaur Trail**, takes visitors through badlands; with access to nature trails that feature hoodoos.

North of Calgary on Hwy 2 to Hwy 72 (40.2 km). East on Hwy 72 to Hwy 9 (33 km); east on Hwy 9 to Drumheller (63 km); 403/823-7707, 888/440-4240. www.tyrrellmuseum.com. Open year round.

Calgary Zoo Along with the accoutrements of any world-class zoo, young visitors will enjoy the 6.5 hectare Prehistoric Park with amazingly lifelike and life-size dinosaurs set among living plants whose ancestors thrived alongside the dinosaurs. A large botanical garden showcases plants of Canadian habitats as well as rainforest and arid habitats, water gardens, and a butterfly garden. The zoo is open year round.

In Calgary. 1300 Zoo Rd NE; 403/232-9300, 800/588-9993; www.calgaryzoo.ab.ca/.

West Edmonton Mall It bills itself as the world's biggest mall, but it's not the shops that put it on our list; it's the underground submarine ride, water park (so big it has its own beach), aquarium, indoor amusement park, miniature golf, and ice-skating rink. Rest up in the mall's own hotel that caters to families with theme rooms including the Igloo, Canadian Rail, Polynesian, Truck, Hollywood, and World Waterpark.

In Edmonton. 87th Ave & 170th St; www.westedmall.com/events/events.asp. Open year round.

For one family's take on Jasper National Park in Alberta, as well as the train ride between Jasper and Prince Rupert, BC, see "Chapter 2: Getting There."

Resources

Alberta South Tourism Destination Region
2805 Scenic Dr, Lethbridge, AB Canada. T1K 5B7, 800/661-1222;
travelalbertasouth.com.
Comprehensive tourist information on southern Alberta, including road conditions

Discover Alberta
www.discoveralberta.com
Site with comprehensive tourism information on Alberta

Government of Alberta homepage
www.gov.ab.ca/home/about_alberta/

To the Alaska Highway from the West

The west-access route to the Alaska Highway runs from Seattle, WA, north on Interstate 5 and across the international border to the TransCanada Highway, then northeast to Highway 97 in Cache Creek, BC, and north on 97 to Dawson Creek. From Seattle to Dawson Creek is 817 miles.

TransCanada Highway:

Vancouver to Cache Creek (310 km/192 m)
With the occasional stop, this drive takes under four hours:
1) **Vancouver to Hope** (139 km/86 m)
2) **Hope to Cache Creek** (171 km/106 m)

1) Vancouver to Hope (139 km/86 m)

The first leg of the trip, from Vancouver to Hope on the TransCanada Highway, barely hints at the spectacular scenery to come. There are a variety of dubious kid attractions along the highway (such as Dinotown), but resist the siren call. Much more exciting options await after you reach Hope.

The last large town with all services until Williams Lake, Hope is the place to load up on supplies. You'll find shops and services along Water Avenue, Wallace Street, and the old Hope Princeton Highway. Tap water in the arid Cariboo is no treat for the taste buds, so if you haven't filled up the family water bottles, you might want to purchase bottled water here for this stretch.

2) Hope to Cache Creek (171 km/106 m)

Past Hope, as the highway turns north along the Fraser River canyon, you'll get tantalizing glimpses of the river swirling far below. Young tunnel connoisseurs should stay alert between Hope and Cache Creek to enjoy the road's many tunnels.

Siska Art Gallery & Museum If you need a stop to stretch your legs, check out this small gallery, run by the Siska Indian Band, that displays and sells traditional carvings in wood and soapstone, jewelry, beading, boxes, and various crafts. They also carry excellent jellies, teas, and soaps made from traditional plant food sources like chokecherry and elderberry.

10 km/6 miles south of Lytton on the TransCanada, 250/455-0072; free.

Hell's Gate Airtram If the weather is good, stopping to make this breath-taking trip across the Fraser River makes a fun diversion. You'll have a bird's eye view of the river, canyon, and fish-ways that help millions of salmon upriver to spawn each year. The ride takes just a few minutes each way, but with the interpretive displays, gift shop, fudge factory, and restaurant, you can easily spend an hour or more.

Boston Bar, on Hwy 1. Open daily mid-April-mid-Oct. $12/adult, $8/child 6-18, free/under 6; $32/family.

Cache Creek This rather disconsolate town of trailer parks and dusty streets, 171 km north of Hope, marks the start of the **Cariboo Highway,** the 446-km stretch of Highway 97 from Cache Creek to Prince George. This region is known as the Cariboo, site of a gold rush that preceded the Klondike Gold Rush by over 30 years, opening up the interior of the province to settlement.

Highway 97:

Cache Creek to Prince George (446 km/277 m)

1) **Cache Creek to 100 Mile House** (116 km/72 m)
2) **100 Mile House to Williams Lake** (90 km/56 m)
3) **Williams Lake to Quesnel** (121 km/75 m)
4) **Quesnel to Prince George** (119 km/74 m)

You can drive the full 446 kilometers in six hours. Two **side trips** offer gorgeous scenery and fascinating history. Driving the Chilcotin Highway, from Williams Lake to Bella Coola, takes two days (456 km/283 m) roundtrip. The side trip from Quesnel to Barkerville Historic Town requires at least five hours (82 km/51 m). See "Side Trips," page 219.

1) Cache Creek to 100 Mile House (116 km/72 m)

After you leave Cache Creek, the landscape turns to rolling hills and scenic lakes, set among stands of lodgepole and ponderosa pine. Although the gold rush is long over, there's something of a wild frontier feeling to the Cariboo, where cowboys are still found and rodeos, such as the Williams Lake Stampede, are major attractions.

100 MILE HOUSE

Many Cariboo towns were originally named to indicate their position on the Cariboo wagon road; of those that remain, only a few still bear those names; 100 Mile House is the largest, with 2,600 residents. Check with the **Visitor Info Centre** (422 Hwy 97; 250/395-5353, 877/511-5353; www.tourism.100mile.com) for suggestions on what to see and do in town.

☛ Parent Tip: Swimmer's Itch

Lakes in BC warm up enough for swimming, but before leaping in, check for warning signage about conditions such as swimmer's itch. Caused by a parasite carried by waterfowl and snails, the condition's symptoms are itchy skin and/or a burning sensation that can start within minutes of leaving the water. It's not dangerous, but it can be aggravating; too much scratching can raise blisters. It's not always possible to prevent swimmer's itch, but you can minimize its effects by showering or rinsing off after swimming and towel-drying thoroughly. Pack calamine lotion (which can be used for other bites and stings, too). ◨

Places to Stay

108 Resort ☺ (\$-\$\$)
4816 Telqua Dr, 108 Mile House
250/791-5211, 800/667-5233; www.108resort.com.
FYI: 62 rooms, some kitchens; restaurant; outdoor heated swimming pool, sauna, hot tub; Laundromat; playground; golf course, tennis courts, nature trails; tennis, canoeing, golf, horseback riding lessons; fishing pole, bike, and boat rentals; snowmachining & tobogganing; pets OK

The large rooms at this comfortable resort on 108 Lake, a few miles north of 100 Mile House, afford sweeping views of the grounds, golf course, and lakes; rooms come with private patios and good noise insulation. The atmosphere is relaxed and family-friendly. Board games can be checked out and VCRs rented. The large restaurant, in a separate building, has a kids' menu and serves half-portions of full entrées. There are 140 km of trails for use year round.

66 PARENT COMMENTS 99

"There's no lifeguard on duty at the pool and one end is six feet deep, so be sure to supervise kids. You can get lifejackets at the front desk."

2) 100 Mile House to Williams Lake (90 km/56 m)

This drive takes about an hour. On the way, you'll find attractive lake country and popular public and private campgrounds.

Lac La Hache Lined with rustic resorts and private and public campgrounds, this lake, 26 km/16 miles north of 100 Mile House, was reputedly named for the hatchet a hapless trapper lost in it while chopping a hole in the ice. **Lac La Hache Provincial Park** straddles the highway with a large, forested campground, a nature trail and, across the road, a day-use area on the beach with picnicking facilities and a playground. In summer, the water is warm enough for swimming. The lake is popular with fishers, boaters, and waterskiers, so reservations are recommended. As with all BC provincial parks, there are no electrical hookups for RVs.
281 First Ave N. 250/398-4414, 800/689-9025; www.discovercamping.com; 83 campsites, flush toilets, dump station, boat launch, fishing, beach, playground, interpretive trail; \$12/site, open mid-May-Sept.

WILLIAMS LAKE

This attractive town of 11,000, named for Shuswap Chief Willyum, overlooks a scenic lake. It's best known for the Williams Lake Stampede held in July.

Places to Stay

Drummond Lodge & Motel ($)
1405 Hwy 97 S; 250/392-5334; 800/667-4555; www.drummondlodge.com
FYI: 24 rooms, 6 are suites with kitchens, free continental breakfast;
Laundromat; small pets OK
It's basic, but comfortable and family-oriented. Decks and balconies afford good views of Williams Lake.

Super 8 Motel Williams Lake ($)
1712 Broadway Ave S, Highway 97; 250/398-8884; www.super8.com
FYI: 53 rooms

Places to Eat

Rendezvous Restaurant
240B Oliver St
Hours: 11am-8pm, Mon-Thurs; 11am-9pm, Fri-Sat; closed Sun
Like most Williams Lake eateries, this restaurant is family-friendly, running the steakhouse gamut from steaks, ribs, and burgers to pizza, pasta, and chicken. There is a kids' menu, too.

A&W Restaurant
1059 S Hwy 97; 250/392-2880
Hours: Open daily 6am-11pm
You'll find a good view and filling kid cuisine here.

What to See & Do

Williams Lake Stampede One of the country's biggest rodeos, this event is held around Canada Day (July 1); if you're thinking of attending, you'll need to plan ahead. Along with standard rodeo events (calf roping, steer wrestling) are barbecues and concerts.
Downtown at the stampede fairgrounds. 250/392-6585, 250/398-8388;
williamslakestampede.com.

Scout Island Nature Centre ☺ On a small peninsula jutting into Williams Lake, this marshy wetland hosts a plethora of feathered wildlife. There are several nature trails and a nature house full of critters dead and alive (don't miss the weird flat leeches), free pamphlets, and books on the local ecology for sale. From late June through early August, expect to find plenty of mosquitoes—it *is* a wetland, after all.
From Hwy 97, take Hwy 20 west; left on Mackenzie Ave S, right on Borland Rd; right again onto Scout Is. Rd. 250/398-8532; open daily, 8am-dusk;
visitor centre open Mon-Fri, 8am-4pm, Sun 1-4pm. Free.

Public Swimming Pools Along the Road

Swimming pools at lodgings along the roads north are few and far between. Fortunately, many communities fill the void with excellent public recreation centers and pools. Most offer daily open swims, some especially for families. Many centers have weight and fitness rooms, saunas, hot tubs, and sport courts. Even if you're just passing through, taking advantage of these facilities makes a welcome break from the road. Most pools and facilities are indoors (exceptions are noted). Fees usually range from $3-5 per adult or $7-12 per family. Some have summer drop-in programs for children that include a variety of fun activities. Pool information is included for Williams Lake, Prince George, Chetwynd, Hudson's Hope, Dawson Creek, Fort Nelson, Watson Lake, Whitehorse, Haines Junction, and Dawson City. Also check out Liard River Hot Springs and Takhini Hot Springs, which are suitable for kids. ▣

Swimming The **Sam Ketcham Memorial Pool** (in the Cariboo Memorial Recreation Complex, 525 Proctor St, 250/398-7665) has two swimming pools, hot tub, sauna, gym, and ice rink.

Resources

Williams Lake Visitor Info Centre
Hwy 97, south of junction with Hwy 20; 250/392-5025;
www.bcadventure.com/wlcc/
Information on lodging and local attractions; open year round

3) Williams Lake to Quesnel (121 km/75 m)

From Williams Lake, the highway follows the Fraser River 120 km/75 miles north to the attractive town of **Quesnel.** This town of 11,000 has all services, but there's not much for families to do here. Even so, you might want to stop and stretch your legs in the downtown **Riverfront Park and Trail** system with 5 km/3 miles of trails following the Fraser and Quesnel rivers.

4) Quesnel to Prince George (119 km/74 m)

A pleasant, if unexciting, 90-minute drive north of Quesnel on Highway 97 brings you to Prince George, with a population of 80,000, the largest city in BC's interior. There are few services on this stretch and no towns, so load up on supplies and snacks in Quesnel.

PRINCE GEORGE

Strategically situated at the intersection of two railroads and two major highways, Prince George is the last city Alaska- and Yukon-bound travelers will encounter for 1,843 km/1,145 miles (until Whitehorse). The second-largest town en route, Fort St. John, with 15,000 residents, is 300 miles north. Prince George makes an excellent overnight stop; you can relax in a comfortable hotel, shop for anything you need, and take in some interesting family attractions. From here north, communities along the highway dwindle in size and number.

Places to Stay

Esther's Inn ☺ ($)

1151 Commercial Dr; 250/562-4131, 800/663-6844; www.esthersinn.bc.ca.
FYI: 130 rooms: family rooms, suites, kitchens; restaurants; swimming pools, waterslide, hot tubs

The large, comfortable suites here and casual restaurant, the Papaya Grove, with kids' menu, couldn't be more family-friendly. Designed along Polynesian-fantasy lines, the hotel is two connected buildings; all rooms face an interior courtyard filled with ersatz greenery, real running water, three hot tubs (one large enough for swimming), and a small swimming pool. An attached building, open from March to October, houses the pièce de résistance: a three-story waterslide, two pools, and a hot tub. An added bonus: there are two lifeguards on duty; lifejackets are provided for younger sliders (not for use outside the waterslide building). Use of the slide is free to hotel guests; non-guests can use it for $3.25 a day.

❝ PARENT COMMENTS ❞

"This was our kids' favorite hotel on our vacation. They dashed from pool to pool for hours, while their parents trudged after them, carrying towels."

"The rooms in the annex are bigger, so better for families. Our unit was huge: two queen beds and a living room with a sofabed. The living rooms lack air conditioning, which could be a problem if it's really hot."

Mary Anna's Bed & Breakfast ($)

3931 Highland Dr; 250/962-8040; www.princegeorge.com/bnb/maryannas/
FYI: 2 rooms, suite, kitchenette; private bath; TV/VCR; pets OK

This appealing, family-friendly B&B is located in a private home in suburban Prince George.

❝ PARENT COMMENTS ❞

"We stayed in the family suite that comfortably slept four. The kitchenette had a small fridge, microwave, toaster, and hot plate. There were lots of games and books on hand. Breakfast was good and plentiful. The accommodations are very nice, but since the house is located in the middle of suburbia, families arriving by train might feel a bit trapped since it's a long walk to get to anything."

Ramada Hotel ($$; family specials)
444 George St; 250/563-0055, 800/272-6232; www.ramadaprincegeorge.com
FYI: 193 rooms; restaurant; pool, hot tub, sauna

Econolodge ($)
1915 3rd Ave; 250/563-7106, 888/566-6333
FYI: 30 rooms, some refrigerators; hot tub, exercise room

Camping

Close to town is a campground popular with families, **Blue Spruce RV Park** (3 miles west on Hwy 16; 250/964-7272; e-mail: bluesprucervpark@shaw.ca; 128 campsites, $16-22/site; hookups, picnic table, barbecue grate; showers, 2 dump stations, Laundromat; heated pool, mini-golf, store; open April-Oct).

Places to Eat

Northern Palace Restaurant
3788 W Austin Rd; 250/962-6838
Hours: daily, 11:30am-10pm
Head here for classic Chinese dishes at very reasonable prices. The restaurant has a suburban location.

The Pastry Chef
380 George St.; 250/564-7034
Hours: Mon-Fri 8:30am-5:30pm; closed Sun-Mon
Visit this popular bakery and order take-out sandwiches and pastries to enjoy on a picnic. The freshly baked European breads are superb.

You'll find big names in chain dining and fast food at the malls. See also Esther's Inn ("Places to Stay") and Books & Company ("What to See and Do").

What to See & Do

Shopping   Stock up on clothing, camping and outdoor gear, and in-car entertainment at one of PG's large malls: **Parkwood Place** (15th Ave & Victoria St), **Pine Centre** (on Hwy 97, just north of the Hwy 16 intersection), or **Spruceland Shopping Centre** (777 Rear Central). Pine Centre has a Roots outlet, with sportswear made popular by Canadian athletes. For books, choose between **Books & Company** (1685 3rd Ave; 250/563-6637; www.books-and-company.com), a large bookseller with an in-store café, and smaller, but well-stocked **Mosquito Books** (Parkwood Centre; 250/563-6495, 800/451-6495; e-mail: mosquito_books@mindlink.bc.ca). For a history of local First Nations, check out the **Prince George Native Art Gallery** in the Prince George Native Friendship Centre (1600 3rd Ave. 250/614-7726). Native arts and crafts are for sale along with a good selection of books for all ages.

Swimming   Prince George has two excellent aquatic centers. **Four Seasons Leisure Pool** (downtown in the Civic Plaza, 700 Dominion St, 250/561-7636; www.city.pg.ca/rec_culture/aquatics/fourseasons/) has three pools including a wave pool and tots pool, with diving, a water slide, spray fountain, and fitness center. The **Prince George Aquatic Complex** (next to Exhibition Park, 1770

Monroe St, 260/561-7633; www.city.pg.bc.ca/rec_culture/aquatics/aquatic centre.html) has a wave pool, diving tower, hot tub, and sauna. See also Esther's Inn in "Places to Stay."

Parks

Prince George has several fine parks. At **Fort George Park** (17th Ave & Taylor Dr), you'll find a playground and spray park, a small train, picnic shelters and restrooms, a tennis court, cemetery, and the excellent Exploration Place (see "Museums"). **Cottonwood Island Nature Park** (River Road, on the Nechako River) has a picnic shelter and pit toilets; it's part of an interconnected city trail system along with Fort George Park. **Connaught Hill Park** (Connaught Hill Dr & Queensway St) is open April through October. Along with flower gardens, the park offers terrific views of the city and surrounding area.

Museums

Fraser-Fort George Regional Museum   This popular attraction, along with the **Exploration Place,** located in Fort George Park, is a historical museum and science center combined. There are traveling exhibits, educational programs for adults and kids, and gift shop. An unusual feature is the online museum, with exhibits of interest to kids, including historic photographs illustrating how children lived in the city's early days.
250/562-1612; www.theexplorationplace.com. Open daily mid-May-mid-Oct, 10am-5pm; rest of year, Wed-Sun 10am-5pm. Cost: $10.95/adult, $8.95/child 3-12, free/under 3, $29.95/family.

Prince George Railway and Forestry Museum   Adjacent to Cottonwood Island Nature Park, here you'll find historic train cars to explore, two old train stations and historic buildings, and a gift shop.
850 River Rd. 250/563-7351; www.pgrfm.bc.ca. Open daily, May 15-Oct 31, 9am-5pm. Cost: $6/adult, $5/child 13-17, $3/child 6-12, free/under 6, $15/family.

Calendar of Events

May

Canadian Northern Children's Festival
250/562-4882; www.princegeorge.com/cncf/
Free, visual and performing arts festival with assorted concerts and performances

July

Celebrate Canada Festival, Fort George Park
July 1; 250/563-8525; www.multiculturalheritage.com/canada_day/
Canada's birthday (with giant cake) celebrated; multicultural festival, performances, children's activity center

Resources

Visitor Info Centre
1198 Victoria St; 250/562-3700, 800/668-7646; www.tourismpg.com

Alternate Route North
The Cassiar Highway: The Road Less Traveled
(718 km/446 m)

One of the loveliest routes to the Yukon and Alaska is via the Cassiar Highway (Hwy 37, also called the "Stewart-Cassiar Highway"), a 718-km/446-mile stretch of road connecting the Yellowhead and Alaska highways. What's more, by taking this route, you'll cut off 213km/132 miles from your trip. The highway is mostly paved, but there are long stretches of gravel; overall the road is rougher than the Alaska Highway, with services spaced farther apart. On the plus side, many travelers feel the spectacular scenery more than makes up for a few extra bumps.

The Cassiar Highway starts 241km/150 miles east of Prince Rupert (about a three hour drive) and 479km/298 miles west of Prince George (six hours). Whichever direction you travel, the scenery is terrific. Along the Yellowhead are several attractive towns, like **Smithers** (east of the Cassiar) and **Terrace** (west of the Cassiar), with full services. You'll also find plenty of campgrounds and some of the province's most scenic waterways as the road follows the Bulkley and Skeena rivers. Good opportunities for family hiking and boating can be found here. At Vanderhoof, 95km/59 miles west of Prince George, a side road leads to the historic town of **Fort St. James**, 59km/37 miles north.

Once you head north on the Cassiar, you'll find fewer parks and campgrounds—as well as fewer travelers competing for campsites. The landscape is wilder and you won't find many hiking trails suitable for small children. "Civilized" attractions are fewer and towns are small, though many have a quirky appeal. Families interested in First Nations history and culture will find several important historic sites along the way.

Roadside Attractions Along the Cassiar Route

The Hazeltons (Hazelton, South Hazelton, New Hazelton) Strictly speaking, these communities aren't on the Cassiar—they're 40 km/25 miles east of Highway 3—but are worth a visit. In Hazelton, at the confluence of the Skeena and Bulkley rivers, is **'Ksan Historical Village** (250/842-5544, 877/842-5518; www.ksan.org), an outstanding attraction showcasing the Gitxsan culture, with a museum, village with seven longhouses, arts and crafts for sale, and dance performances. Guided tours are offered ($10/adult, $8.50/child).

Kitwanga On the Cassiar Highway, 4.2km/3 miles north of the Yellowhead junction, is the site of **Kitwanga Fort National Historic Site.** Constructed by the Gitxsan people in the 18th century, the fort was the site of fierce battles among First Nations; interpretive signs explain the history. Kitwanga was on the "grease trail," the trade route for eulachon ("candlefish") oil that was a major Native trade corridor from British Columbia up through the Yukon and Alaska.

Gitanyow   Also known as Kitwancool, this small, historic First Nations community, 21 km/13 miles north of the Yellowhead and Cassiar junction, contains some of the province's oldest and best preserved totem poles; some have stood here for over a century. Plans are under way to open a museum.

Meziadin Lake Provincial Park   At this public park, 53 km/96 miles north of the junction, you'll find a lovely lakeside campground (46 sites, toilets, water, swimming, boat launch). This is bear country; bear-proof garbage containers are provided.

Stewart, BC, and Hyder, AK   On the Stewart-Hyder Access Road, 64.5 km/40 miles west of the 37, you can drive to these twin towns, separated by an international border station. The road is paved and richly scenic; along the way you'll pass impressive **Bear Glacier.** In Stewart, the larger of the towns, you'll find all services and **Toastworks,** a toaster museum (what are the odds?). The towns sit at the end of Portland Canal, one of the world's longest fjords, which begins north of Prince Rupert. Taking a short (28 km/17 mile) side trip to **Salmon Glacier** is highly recommended. The road is difficult, but sightseeing tours are offered from Stewart.

Telegraph Creek   This historic town of 300, dating from the Gold Rush era, has services and is accessed from the Cassiar at the town of Dease Lake. The 113 km/70 mile road is spectacular but not recommended for RVs or trailers. There are no services on the way; the town's setting overlooks the gorgeous Stikine River.

Boya Lake Provincial Park   Near the north end of the Cassiar Highway, 663 km/397 miles north of the junction, this park has an attractive campground (45 sites, picnic area, pit toilets, water, firewood, wheelchair access, swimming) with two nature trails suitable for all ages.

Resources

Fort St. James Visitor Info Centre
115 Douglas Ave, Fort St James, BC, V0J 1P0; 250/996-7023;
e-mail: fsjcham@qlynx.com; open year round

Hazelton Visitor Info Centre
Junction Hwy 16 & Hwy 62; Box 340 New Hazelton, BC V0J 2J0; 250/842-6071. Washrooms, gift shop, small museum. Open year round; call for details.

Hyder Community Association
Box 149, Hyder, AK 99923; 250/636-9148;
www.kermode.net/stewart/commerce-map/

Stewart Visitor Info Centre
222 5th Ave, Stewart, BC, V0T 1W0; 250/636-9224, 888/366-5999.
Open June-Aug

Stewart-Cassiar Tourism Council
Box 14, Stewart, BC, V0T 1W0; 866/417-3737

Highway 97:
Prince George to Dawson Creek (402 km/250 m)
1) **Prince George to Chetwynd** (302 km/188 m)
2) **Chetwynd to Dawson Creek** (100 km/62 m)

This five-hour drive can be dreary for kids. It's a good time to break out the car games and set the kids looking for wildlife. A side trip from Chetwynd to tiny Hudson's Hope (64 km/40 m) can help dispel the monotony (see page 222). Allow at least three hours.

1) Prince George to Chetwynd (302 km/188 m)

When you head north from Prince George, you leave the urban landscape behind for good. Rolling rangelands with horses and sheep gradually give way to the beautiful forested foothills of the northern Rocky Mountains. From here on, you may encounter bears or moose ambling across the road, and distances between towns and services increase. It's a good idea to check your gas tank routinely when you encounter a gas station. Between Prince George and the next sizable town, Chetwynd, there are few settlements.

Bijoux Falls Provincial Park At this small park 186 km/116 miles north of Prince George, take a driving break and admire the gorgeous waterfall just yards from the parking area. You'll find picnic tables, pit toilets, and hungry hordes of Stellers jays, the province's official bird. Just north of the park is **Pine Pass** (874m/2,867ft), from which the road descends to the majestic **Peace River Valley.** This is dam country: two huge dams on the Peace River supply 38 percent of the province's electricity, and more for export. Titanic towers, three abreast, carry hydroelectric lines stretching across the horizon.

CHETWYND

This small town, with 3,000 residents and all services, lines up along Highway 97 and a few parallel streets. Billing itself as the "Chainsaw Art Capital of the World," the town sports many large, well-executed sculptures of local fauna (bears, eagles, mountain goats, beavers, owls, prospectors). While it's not a top choice for an overnight, Chetwynd has acceptable accommodation and an excellent recreation center with a pool.

Places to Stay

Stagecoach Inn ($)
5413 S. Access Rd; 250/788-9666, 800/663-2744; e-mail: stagecoach@pris.bc.ca
FYI: 55 rooms, refrigerator/microwave, some kitchenettes; restaurant
"Basic" describes this hotel, just off Highway 97. However, the hotel's Chinese/Canadian restaurant (250/788-3388; open daily 6am-10pm) is attractive, with child-friendly offerings (chicken fingers, French fries, grilled cheese) and basic Chinese favorites; fortune cookies come with lottery numbers printed on the back.

Pinecone Motor Inn ($)
5220 53rd Ave on Hwy 97; 250/788-3311, 800/663-8082
FYI: 54 units, some suites, kitchenettes; restaurant
This hotel offers similar amenities to the Stagecoach Inn. Its restaurant is popular with locals and serves up a good breakfast.

Camping

Close to town, on Hwy 97, 3 km/2 miles north of the junction with Hwy 29, is **Westwind RV Park,** with campsites for tents and RVs (250/788-2199; 50 sites, $14-20/site; washrooms, free showers, hookups, dump station; Laundromat, playground).

If you're taking the Hudson's Hope option, scenic **Moberly Lake Provincial Park** (250/964-2243; wlapwww.gov.bc.ca/bcparks/explore/parkpgs/Moberly/; 109 sites, $14/site, water, pit toilets, no electrical hookups or showers, dump station, day-use picnic area [fee], playground, trails, swimming) on Highway 29, 25 km/15.5 miles north of Chetwynd, is the best of the local camping options.

What to See & Do

The modest **Little Pioneer Museum** (on Westgate Rd, off Hwy 97; 250/788-3358. Open July-Aug, Tues-Sat, 10am-5pm; admission by donation) showcases local history. The **Visitor Info Centre** (5400 N Access Rd; 250/788-1943; winter, 250/401-4100), housed in a real caboose, has information on nearby attractions and road conditions.

Swimming At the **Chetwynd & District Recreation Centre** (5400 N Access Rd, 250/788-2214; www.gochetwynd.com/recreation/), you'll find a pool, weight room, fitness and swimming classes, kid and family swims, and summer drop-in programs for children of all ages. In summer, you can swim at **Moberly Lake** (see "Camping").

2) Chetwynd to Dawson Creek (100 km/62 m)

The drive from Chetwynd to Dawson Creek winds among rolling, intensely green hills through which the placid Peace River flows. The Peace River Valley is large, extending east into the province of Alberta and north past Fort St. John.

DAWSON CREEK

This town of 12,000 makes the most of its lively history and location at Mile Zero of the Alaska Highway. It's definitely worth a look around although, for accommodation, families might prefer to drive to the larger city of Fort St. John and stay at a hotel with a pool. These will be in short supply until you reach Fairbanks. Although its hotels are pool-free, Dawson Creek has plenty of accommodation, too.

☛ **Parent Tip**

If you have the *Milepost* with you (and if your kids don't get carsick while reading), children can take turns alerting the family to upcoming sights. The *Milepost* is exhaustive in its detail; listing every interpretive sign, roadside turnout, garbage can, and anything else out of the ordinary. ◪

Places to Stay

Northwinds Lodge ($)
632 103rd Ave; 250/782-9181, 800/665-1759
FYI: 20 rooms, refrigerator, some kitchenettes
This basic motel is strictly no-frills, but adequate.

Peace Villa Motel ($)
1641 Alaska Ave; 250/782-8175; www.bc-biz.com/peacevillamotel/
FYI: 46 rooms, suites; refrigerator/microwave; Laundromat
Its location close to Boston Pizza and, in the other direction, the Pioneer Village, plus its Laundromat, give this basic motel a slight edge over others in town.

Ramada Limited ($)
1748 Alaska Ave; 250/782-8595, 888/298-2054; www.ramada.ca
FYI: 41rooms, refrigerator, free continental breakfast; microwave available on request

Super 8 ($)
1440 Alaska Ave; 250/782-8899, 800/800-8000; www.Super8.com.
FYI: 48 rooms; suites, free continental breakfast

Camping

At mile 1.5 of the Alaska Highway is **Mile "0" RV Park** (250/782-2590 (summer), 250/782-9595 (winter); 72 sites, tents OK, $12-17/site; hookups; free showers, Laundromat, dump station). It has pleasant, treed sites with picnic tables and a playground. Open May to September, it's located next to **Mile Zero Park** where kids can swim at **Rotary Lake** or visit **Walter Wright Pioneer Village**.

Places to Eat

Alaska Café
10209 10th St, 250/782-7040
Hours: Open daily 11am-10pm.
Dawson Creek's top dining choice is housed in the historic Alaska Hotel dating from 1928. Fare runs to hearty soups and sandwiches, burgers, and excellent pastries; there's a kids' menu, too.

If your kids pine for fast food, Dawson Creek (along with Fort St. John) is their last opportunity to indulge until you reach Whitehorse, several days away. Options include **A&W** (12000 8th St, 250/782-8775), **Dairy Queen** (821 102nd Ave, 250/782-3753), **Boston Pizza** (1525 Alaska Ave, 250/782-8585), and **Subway** (10500 8th St, 250/782-1740). There's an **Orange Julius** in the Dawson Mall.

What to See & Do

Shopping To beef up your store of reading materials, visit **Turn the Page** in the Dawson Mall (11000 8th St, 250/782-7243). For groceries, head for the **Dawson Co-op** (10200 8th St, 250/782-4858). If you're in town on a Saturday between 8:30am and 12:30pm, you can check out the **Farmer's Market**. From May to early October at the NAR Park the market sells fresh food, all kinds of goodies, and locally made crafts.

Northern Alberta Railroad (NAR) Park, Station Museum and Visitor Info Centre At this multipurpose facility you can get crucial road condition information; shop for maps, books, gifts, and souvenirs; and tour the excellent museum. A continuously playing video, The Alaska Highway, 1942-1992, offers a painless introduction to Alaska Highway history. You'll also find Alaska Highway exhibits and wildlife displays. Don't miss the reconstructed station rooms upstairs. Staff provides visitor information and answers questions. You can also pick up a walking-tour map here and explore town on foot.

Outside, there's a cairn commemorating Mile Zero of the Alaska Highway, where tourists line up to be photographed. The real Mile Zero, a block south, is also commemorated with a sign. Be careful, though; it's in the middle of a busy road.

900 Alaska Ave. 250/782-9595, 866/645-3022; www.pris.bc.ca/dcsm/.
Open daily 8am-7pm (summer); Tues-Sat, 10am-4pm (winter). Cost: $2 family donation requested.

Dawson Creek Art Gallery This gallery is in a distinctive local land-mark—a renovated grain elevator next to the museum. Youngsters will enjoy following the three-story walkway that winds up the inside of the elevator, lined with pictures and installations of traveling exhibits, work by local artists, and the interesting permanent collection (don't miss the photographic history of building the Alaska Highway). Gift shop offerings range from serious art objects to silly T-shirts and kid stuff.

816 Alaska Ave; 250/ 782-2601; www.pris.bc.ca/artgallery/. Open daily
9am-5pm (Victoria Day-Labour Day); Tues-Sat, 10am-5pm (rest of year). Free.

Walter Wright Pioneer Village The village, a popular attraction, is made up of relocated pioneer buildings along with some replicas: homes, two schools, store, churches, blacksmith shop, and other buildings. This living museum includes period furnishings and an attractive flower garden. **Mile One Café** (inside the Landry School building; 250/782-7144) is open for meals when the village is open; desserts are its specialty.

At Mile Zero Park, Hwy 97 & Alaska Hwy. 250/782-7144, 250/782-9595;
open daily 9am-6pm (mid-May-Aug). Cost: by donation.

Swimming **Centennial Swimming Pool** (105th Ave & 10th St, 250/784-3604; e-mail: recreation@mail.city.dawson-creek.bc.ca) also has a 150-foot water slide, hot tub, and saunas. Manmade **Rotary Lake**, in the park next to the pioneer village, is open for summer swimming, with restrooms, changing area, and picnic facilities. No lifeguards are on duty, so supervise small fry closely.

Resources

Visitor Info Centre
900 Alaska Ave, Dawson Creek, BC V1G 4T6; 250/782-9595,
866/645-3022; www.tourismdawsoncreek.com

City of Dawson Creek information
www.city.dawson-creek.bc.ca/

Alaska Highway:

Dawson Creek to Yukon Border (910 km/568 m)

This segment can easily be driven in a day and a half, but add time to enjoy the spectacular Northern Rockies and the crown jewel of the highway: the Liard River hot springs.

1) **Dawson Creek to Fort St. John** (76 km/47 m)
2) **Fort St. John to Fort Nelson** (378 km/236 m)
3) **Fort Nelson to Muncho Lake** (244 km/153 m)
4) **Muncho Lake to the Yukon border** (212 km/132 m)

1) Dawson Creek to Fort St. John (76 km/47 m)

The drive to Fort St. John begins in pastoral Peace River Valley farmlands, then descends with steep grades and switchbacks to the Peace River, crossed by a long bridge that was completed in 1960. At the south side of the river is popular **Peace Island Regional Park** (Mile 34; 250/789-9295, May-Sept.; 250/789-3392, rest of year; 32 campsites, $10/site, picnic area, firewood, toilets, water) which has a playground and nature trail. It's open for day-use 7am to 11pm. **Taylor Landing Provincial Park**, on the south side of the river, also has lovely views but no camping or picnicking facilities.

FORT ST. JOHN

This city of 15,000 is the oldest non-Native settlement on the BC mainland; it serves the oil and gas industry and a wide rural population. It's the second largest city on the Alaska Highway after Whitehorse, and your last opportunity to stock up on hard-to-find items for the trip north.

Places to Stay

Quality Inn Northern Grand ($$)
9830 100th Ave; 250/787-0521, 800/663-8312;
www.qualityinnnortherngrand.com
FYI: 123 rooms; restaurant, indoor pool, hot tub, sauna, exercise room
There are plenty of hotels in town, but only this one has a swimming pool. A White Spot Restaurant is located here, and the Northern Lights Restaurant is just a short walk away.

❝ P A R E N T   C O M M E N T S ❞

"The building is six stories tall, which qualifies as a high-rise here; from our room on the fifth floor we could see for blocks. The pool is quite large for a hotel, and the gym is pretty well equipped."

Ramada Limited ($)
10103 98th Ave; 250/787-0779, 888/298-2054; www.ramada.ca.
FYI: 73 rooms, suites; refrigerator/microwave; free continental breakfast, restaurant; Laundromat; free passes to North Peace Leisure Pool

Econolodge ($)
10419 Alaska Rd; 250/787-8475; www.choice.ca
FYI: 43 rooms, refrigerator/microwave, coffee shop, free breakfast

Camping

For RV camping with all the frills, try **Sourdough Pete's RV Park**, south of town (7704 Alaska Rd; 250/785-7664, 800/227-8388. (74 sites, $12-20/site; tenting sites, hookups, coin showers, Laundromat, dump station, store, open April-Oct).

Two nearby provincial parks (250/787-3407; www.discovercamping.ca. $12/site; pit toilets; playground; boat launch; open May-Oct) have campgrounds, but no hookups: **Beatton Provincial Park** (east off Alaska Highway Mile 49.5 on 244th Rd. 37 sites; lakeside sites, sandy beach, reservations) and **Charlie Lake Provincial Park** (east from junction with Hwy 29 at Alaska Highway Mile 53.7; 58 sites, dump station).

Places to Eat

Northern Lights Restaurant
9823 100th St, 250/787-9085
Hours: Mon-Sat 11am-9pm; closed Sun
This is Fort St. John's take on fine dining, but it works well for children, too. Italian and Greek dishes are on the menu; the small pizzas should satisfy the kids along with the mozzarella-stick appetizers. This place is popular with residents so expect a wait, especially on weekends and summer holidays.

White Spot
In the Northern Grand, 9830 100th Ave; 250/787-0521
Hours: Mon-Fri 6 am-10pm; Sat-Sun 8am-10pm
This Canadian chain will remind Americans of Denny's. There's a kids' menu and plenty of choices for picky eaters of all ages.

Calculating Mileage on the Alaska Highway

Calculating mileage for the Alaska Highway is a tricky business. The original ("historical") mileposts date from the early days of the highway. More than 60 years have elapsed since then, and the highway has experienced many changes beyond being paved. These add up to changes in actual mileage, creating a disconnect between the historical mileposts and actual mileage on your odometer.

Because Canada adopted the metric system in the 1980s, mileposts also indicate kilometers. Finally, many businesses along the Alaska Highway advertise their locations by giving their position using the historical mileposts. For the convenience of readers trying to identify where attractions can be found, we have used the historical milepost designations, unless otherwise indicated. ▣

What to See & Do

Shopping On the right as you drive into town is **Totem Mall** (9600 93rd Ave), the town's largest mall. For groceries, try the big **Overwaitea** at 10345 100th St (250/785-2985).

At the **Visitor Info Centre** (9923 96th Ave; 250/785-3033, 250/785-6037; open year round, 9am-5pm, until 8pm in summer) you can catch up on road conditions and weather. Next door is **Centennial Park.**

Fort St. John-North Peace Museum It's easy to spot this museum across Centennial Park; the oil derrick outside once stood along the Alaska Highway. Inside are artifacts from the region's long history of human habitation, going back 10,500 years. Reconstructed room interiors display pioneer life from the early 20th century and there are displays and videos on the Alaska Highway and local history. A small gift shop sells souvenirs, books, and videos. *9323 100th St; 250/787-0430; open daily 8:30am-5:30pm (summer), Mon-Sat, 9am-5pm (rest of year). Cost: $3/adult, $2/child, free/preschool and younger.*

Fish Creek Community Forest, adjacent to Northern Lights College (north on 100th 2 km/1.2 miles; turn right on Bypass Rd, then first left), has three self-guided nature trails suitable for kids.

Swimming **North Peace Leisure Pool** in Centennial Park (100th St, 250/785-7665) has a pool, wave pool, waterslide, spray, tots' pool, rapids channel, hot tub, steam room, and sauna open to the public.

2) Fort St. John to Fort Nelson (378 km/236 m)

During the 4.5-hour drive to Fort Nelson, the scenery changes from bucolic river valley to rugged terrain as you approach the Rockies. There aren't many roadside attractions. If you haven't done so already, break out activity books, travel games, stories on CD or cassette tape to pass the time.

Wonowon, at Mile 101, has gas, lodging, and food. **Mae's Kitchen** in **Pink**

Mountain (Mile 147, 250/772-3215; open daily except Sun, year round) serves up hearty meals all day; there's a small motel and gas station. In **Sikanni Chief** (Mile 162; keep your eyes peeled for moose) you can buy gas, and there's an RV park. The **Buckinghorse River Lodge** (Mile 175, 250/773-6468) has gas, free tenting, a small motel, and café; it makes a good ice cream or hot chocolate stop, depending on the weather. At Mile 233, **Prophet River** has all services. The rest of the way to Fort Nelson (Mile 300) has few services.

FORT NELSON

Fort Nelson, a long town with a population of 4,500, lining both sides of the highway, was once home to a major chopstick manufacturing plant; today oil, gas, and tourism are its economic engines. By the time you've arrived here, chances are good that everyone will be ready for a long break. Spend the night at a hotel with a swimming pool—or pass a fun hour or two at the museum, hiking, or taking a dip in the community pool.

Places to Stay

Fort Nelson Motor Hotel ($)
Mile 300 Alaska Hwy; 250/774-6971
FYI: 135 rooms, some kitchenettes, restaurant; indoor pool, sauna
Basic but comfortable, this hotel's big draw (need we say it?) is the pool.

Bluebell Inn ($)
4203 50th Ave S, Mile 300 Alaska Hwy; 250/774-6961, 800/663-5267;
www.pris.bc.ca/bluebell/
FYI: 58 rooms, kitchenettes, refrigerators; restaurant; store, Laundromat; kids
under 13 stay free
Probably the best family choice in town, the big draw for adults is the Laundromat.

Ramada Limited ($)
5035 51st Ave W; 250/774-3911; www.ramada.ca
FYI: 41 rooms, some refrigerators/microwaves, kitchenettes;
free continental breakfast

Travelodge ($)
4711 50th Ave S; 250/774-3911, 888/515-6375; www.travelodge.com
FYI: 70 rooms, restaurant; hot tub, sauna

Camping

The town's one and only campground, **Westend Campground & RV Park** (mile 300; 250/774-2340; 122 sites, $15-24/site, tent sites; showers, hookups; Laundromat; playground, miniature golf), is next to the museum and right on the highway.

☞ Parent Tip

Keep a close eye on small children at the Fort Nelson Heritage Museum. Outside is a haphazard collection of farm machinery and implements in various stages of disrepair, much of it rusty with sharp edges. Make sure kids are wearing protective footwear. ◙

Places to Eat

Dan's Neighbourhood Pub
4204 50th Ave N; 250/774-3929
Hours: daily 11am-midnight
Despite the name, this is Fort Nelson's best family option, serving decent pasta, burgers, and other child-friendly choices.

For lighter fare, there's a **Subway** in the Landmark Plaza (the strip mall in the center of town along the Alaska Highway) where you'll also find delicatessens and a confectionary shop. The Visitor Info Centre keeps an up-to-date list of where to go for ice cream. **Capp*A*Lu's** (4916 50th Ave N, 250/774-7222) has espresso, light meals, and snacks. For groceries, there's an **Overwaitea** a block off the highway on Airport Drive and an **IGA** on the south side of the highway.

What to See & Do

At the **Visitor Info Centre** (in the Recreation Centre, corner of Alaska Hwy & Simpson Trail; 250/774-2400, summer; 250/774-2956, rest of year) you can check on road conditions. Down the street is the Aquatic Centre (see "Swimming"). Next to the Recreation Centre is a skateboard park.

Fort Nelson Heritage Museum   Fans of quirky museums and old (very old) vehicles will love this one. There are some well-, and not so well-preserved fauna. (But where else will the kids see an albino moose, a deformed moose head, and a raging timberwolf?) The main building is jammed with pioneer relics. Check out the cache of beautiful silver trays and utensils hastily stashed in a nearby well, then forgotten for 130 years; watch videos on the Gold Rush and Alaska Highway in a postage-stamp-size theatre. Ask for the key to the trapper's cabin, with historically correct furnishings and an interesting, but historically incorrect, guitar made by museum volunteers from a tree burl. Vintage cars and trucks fill a large adjacent building and spill over outdoors. Ask the staff for a tour. There's a small gift shop in the main building.
North end of town, left side of Alaska Hwy; 250/774-3536; open daily in summer, 8:30am-7:30pm. Cost: $3/adult, $2/child 5-15, free/under 5, $6/family

Hiking   For an interesting family hike, head for the **Community Forest** (take Simpson Trail to Mountainview Dr). Among the three trails, the most interesting is the 4-km/2.5-mile **Native Trail**, which has interpretive signs about how area First Nations lived, hunted, and used local plants.

Swimming   As stopping places before and after this town are limited, you could do worse than schedule a long break at the **Fort Nelson Aquatic Centre**

Building the Alaska Highway

Plans to build a highway to Alaska had existed for years, but it took the bombing of Pearl Harbor on December 7, 1941 to turn them into reality. The road would allow troops in Alaska to be supplied and supported from the lower 48. The U.S. quickly authorized funds to build the highway through Canada (a month before the Canadian government gave the U.S. permission to build the road through its territory). And just three months later, construction started in Dawson Creek, BC, which had a population of about 600 people. Over the next eight and a half months, the entire Alaska Highway was constructed by seven U.S. Army Corps of Engineers regiments totaling around 11,000, with 16,000 additional U.S. and Canadian civilians.

Building the road was grueling. Conditions soon turned from cold and icy to hot, buggy, and muddy.

They cleared bush and built hundreds of bridges and over 8,000 culverts along the 1,400 miles. In November, 1942, the road officially opened.

The U.S. paid for the highway and Canada contributed the land. In 1946, the U.S. turned over the Canadian portion of the highway to Canada. The Alaska Highway opened to civilian traffic in 1947. Since then, it's been improved gradually to its generally excellent condition today. Many communities today exist solely because of their location along the highway. It remains a great feat of engineering and international cooperation, and is one of the world's most exciting roads to travel.

Resources

Many travel books track the Alaska Highway mile by mile, as well as the *Milepost*, a must-have for Alaska Highway drivers.

(Simpson Trail between 53rd & 54th, 250/774-2088) which has daily family swims in the pool, and a hot tub and sauna.

3) Fort Nelson to Muncho Lake (244 km/153 m)

From Fort Nelson the highway turns west, winding up to Summit Pass. Before tackling this stretch of highway, which has many hills and hairpin curves, you might want to take preventive steps against carsickness if your kids are susceptible. Some of the best scenery along the highway is here; keep a lookout for bears, too, often spotted along the roadside or right on the road! As the road climbs higher into the Rockies, look for Stone's sheep (shy, graceful thin-horn sheep, dark in color, with beautiful curving horns) and caribou. About 50 miles later, on the shoulders of **Steamboat Mountain,** which supposedly resembles an overturned steamboat, is the **Steamboat Mountain Café** (Mile 351; 250/774-3388), with meals, gas, a picnic and tenting area, RV sites, and a

Coates, K.S. and W.R. Morrison. *The Alaska Highway in World War II: The U.S. Army of Occupation in Canada's Northwest.* Toronto: University of Toronto Press 1992. This interesting historical look at the highway from a modern Canadian perspective takes a critical look at the mega-project and its effects.

Cohen, Stan. *The Trail of '42: A Pictorial History of the Alaska Highway.* Pictorial Histories, 1979. This popular history is also available in video cassette (60 minutes).

McAllister, Bruce and Peter Corley Smith. *Wings over the Alaska Highway.* Round Up Press, 2001. This book explores the role of aviation in building the Alaska Highway, including many archival photos.

Pratt, Verna E. *Wildflowers Along the Alaska Highway.* Alaskakrafts, 1992. A useful field guide for Alaska Highway drivers.

Alaska Highway Highway: 95th Engineer Regiment-Colored www. AlaskaHighwayhighway.com/. Three regiments of African American troops helped to build the Alaska Highway. This site tells the story, including historic photos, of the 3,695 black soldiers who contributed their labor to build the highway.

For Kids

Matheson, Shirlee Smith. *Flying Ghosts.* Stoddart Publishing, 1993. This young-adult novel about a teenager in Alaska during World War II has a setting that includes aviation and the building of the Alaska Highway.

McLaughlin, Les. *The Alaska Highway: An Audio History.* Sturgeon Sound. Compact Disc: 60 minutes. Listen to this CD starting at Mile Zero in Dawson Creek to hear the story behind what you see outside the car window. It's sold at gift shops and the art gallery in Dawson Creek. ◙

store. A few miles farther west is **Tetsa River Provincial Park** (25 campsites, pit toilets, water in summer, pets on leash, no reservations, arctic grayling fishing); and 11 miles past the park you can get gas, food, and accommodation at **Tetsa River Guest Ranch & Campground** (Mile 375, 250/774-1005).

About 15 miles farther is the eastern boundary of **Stone Mountain Provincial Park** and, about two miles on, **Summit Lake** and **Summit Pass** (4,250 ft./1,295 m). The higher elevations are above the tree line, so dramatic views are not obscured. The **Summit Lake Campground** (28 campsites, day use area, pit toilets, water in summer, pet restrictions, fishing at Summit Lake) offers panoramic views of the lake, the Rockies and rushing rivers. Several trails here are suitable for young kids. The **Erosion Pillars Trail**, a 1-km/.6-mile round trip, has views of hoodoos, those wacky rock formations that resemble demented sandstone mushrooms. The **Flower Springs Trail** includes alpine flowers, waterfalls, and lakes; it's 5.7 km/3.5 miles round-trip; allow two hours. The **Summit Peak Trail**, which gains 1,000m/3280ft in just 2.5 km/1.6 miles, is not recommended for young kids or anyone in less than very fit condition.

From Summit Pass, the road descends to the MacDonald River Valley, where you'll find trees again, as well as basic services and accommodation. At the **Rocky Mountain Lodge** (Mile 397, 250/232-7000) are food, lodging, and gas; camping is free when you fill up your tank. **Toad River Lodge** (Mile 422, 250/232-5401), has a motel, cabins with kitchenettes, restaurant, store, RV camping with hookups and dump station, Laundromat, and showers. (However, the campground is directly across the road from the airport.) Four miles on in a pleasant location is the **Poplars Campground & Café** (250/232-5465), with cabins, campground, hookups, shower, restaurant, store, and gas.

MUNCHO LAKE

Muncho Lake (it means "big lake" in the Kaskan language) is an extraordinarily beautiful body of water, whose remarkable milky aqua color is caused by its mineral content, high in copper. Even when the sky is a sullen gray, the water retains its lovely hue. The lake is long (over 12 km/7.5 miles) and deep (213 m/700 feet), with several islands. The setting, nestled in the peaks of the northern Rockies amid dense spruce forest, is idyllic. The small settlement at Milepost 463 on the east side of the lake has all services. Campgrounds and other accommodations fill up fast, so make reservations if visiting in summer. Area activities include hiking, fishing, flightseeing, and birding, and wildlife watching in summer; cross-country skiing, snowmachining, skating, snowshoeing, and aurora watching in winter.

Places to Stay
J&H Wilderness Resort
Mile 463 Alaska Hwy; 250/776-3453; $16-25/site; 72 sites; free showers; Laundromat; hookups, dump station; café; horseshoe pits; fuel; deli, gift shop FYI: 8-unit motel; RV campground on lake; air charters and flightseeing trips; fishing tackle and licenses

Northern Rockies Lodge ($-$$)
Mile 462 Alaska Hwy; 250/776-3481, 800/663-5269; www.northern-rockies-lodge.com FYI: 45 rooms; family rooms, some lakeside chalets, some kitchens; RV campground ($20-27/site), hookups; restaurant; playground; Laundromat; guided boating, fishing, flightseeing trips; gas station; store; pets OK; open year round

This attractive European-style lodge is warm and welcoming to families. Its owners, Swiss-born bush pilots, are the parents of two young boys. The lodge is an expansion of the Highland Glen Lodge next door. The new lodge, constructed of logs, is set well back from the lake, and several new lakeside chalets have been added. For a splurge, stay at the two-bedroom, two-bath chalet, with full kitchen, and deck ($300/night). Family rooms in the lodge have three beds. Only the lodge rooms have TVs, and no rooms have telephones. The RV campground is on the lakeshore with pull-through sites.

The lodge ambience is sumptuous, but fires crackling in the enormous fireplace make it feel homelike as well. The restaurant's deck overlooks the lake. The menu is distinctly European and remarkably good. Wienerschnitzel is a house specialty (the dinner menu runs to pork, but there are also chicken, seafood, and vegetarian options). There's no kids' menu, but burgers or grilled cheese and ham with French fries should go down well with most. Prices and quality are higher than usual in these parts. There's a standard breakfast menu along with a Swiss buffet that includes breads, muesli, cold cuts, and beverages.

The owner/pilots offer add-on tour packages to outpost cabins. Included are flights to the cabins, flightseeing, accommodation, and guided fishing trips, from one to seven days. Families are welcome. Packages can include flights from Vancouver or Edmonton. Guests receive a discount for meals and gas purchased at the lodge.

66 P A R E N T   C O M M E N T S 99

"At the Northern Rockies Lodge, our family room on the ground floor was small, with no closet, but it was spotless and the beds were fine. The adults were awakened early in the morning—our room was under the kitchen—but the kids slept through it all."

"The restaurant seemed a tad elegant for us after seven hours in the car, but our grubby kids were made to feel very welcome. We went for a walk after dinner and ran into some caribou strolling down the road. The morning we left, there was a Stone's sheep posing majestically on a rock outcropping above the highway."

Camping

Most area accommodation includes RV camping. You'll also find two campgrounds with 15 sites each—Strawberry Flats, Mile 457, and MacDonald, Mile 462—at **Muncho Lake Provincial Park** ($12/site, pit toilets, water, boat launch, fishing; open May-Oct). This mostly wild 88,420-hectare/341-square-mile provincial park extends from a little north of Toad River up the east side of Muncho Lake. No reservations are accepted at the popular campgrounds, so arrive early in the day to ensure a campsite.

4) Muncho Lake to the Yukon Border (212 km/132 m)

During the short (66 km/41 m) drive from Muncho Lake to Liard River (Mile 496), keep your eyes peeled for stone sheep, caribou, moose, and bears. Also be wary of hikers along the narrow, winding road.

☛ Parent Tip: Be Bear Aware

This is bear country. Even if the kids have heard the bear-safety lecture before, a little review or playacting an encounter won't hurt. They should be able to tell you, without stopping to think about it, what to do if they encounter wildlife. Running ahead along a trail, lagging behind, or just strolling along a paved roadside, can bring you suddenly face-to-face with a bear. Roadside turnouts have bear-proof garbage cans designed not just to keep the wilderness clean, but to keep bears away from humans and their litter. Bears, eternal optimists, sometimes wander by anyway in search of goodies. Keep kids close when stopping at a turnout. However empty the highway seems, do not stop your vehicle in the road to look at or photograph wildlife. Always pull over to the shoulder or into a turnout first. You can expect a long wait for a tow truck after a collision in these parts. ◨

LIARD RIVER

At Liard River you'll find one of the major tourist attractions along the Alaska Highway: the Liard River hot springs. Be sure to build in a couple of hours to enjoy the waters.

In addition to the campground at the springs (reservations recommended), lodging is available at the **Liard Hotsprings Lodge** (Mile 497, 250/776-7349; Rates: $-$$; 12 rooms, café, and tent and RV pull-through sites, dump station, showers, gas).

Liard River Hot Springs Provincial Park These wonderful pools in Liard River Hot Springs Provincial Park have been developed to retain their wild, natural beauty. The springs have generated a mini ecosystem that supports unusual plants and fish. About 150,000 people visit the springs annually.

The 1,082-hectare/4.2-square-mile park includes two developed hot springs, ranging between 42C/107F and 52C/126F degrees, that are reached via a boardwalk from the parking lot. There are changing rooms with lockers at the pool closest to the parking lot, known as the Alpha pool. A short distance from the pool you'll find the park's composting toilets, an environmentally proactive solution to the problem of waste disposal. Along the way to the Alpha pool are interpretive signs pointing out the fish and plants in the boreal forest: tiny chub, ostrich ferns, cow parsnips, carnivorous plants, and wild orchids. A short trek up a terraced hillside brings you to the "hanging gardens," a viewpoint for more local flora, most impressive in May and June. Moose enjoy feeding on the plants here and are often spotted around the park. Bears are also frequent visitors. A wild bison herd roams through the area, so be watchful on the highway, especially at dawn or dusk.

The Alpha pool is suitable for all ages. It's surrounded by plants and retains its natural appearance while subtle additions have made it safe and comfortable. At one end, the pool is quite shallow and cool—about kid bathtub temperature—with a small waterfall. A log, sculpted into a bench and artfully placed across the pool, separates the shallow end from the rest of the pool, which warms and deepens as you walk away from the shallow end. Benches placed under the water allow you to sit comfortably with the water up to shoulder or neck level. The bottom of the Alpha pool is soft, sandy gravel. Expect a good-natured crowd here, with travelers from all over. Only good swimmers who can tolerate fairly hot temperatures should attempt the Beta pool, a quarter-mile farther on. It is deep (about 9ft/3m) throughout.

In summer, check at the trailhead for interpretive and educational programs. And while you're soaking or watching the kids splash, check in with travelers who've driven in the other direction about road conditions they've encountered.

Mile 496; 52 sites, $15/site; water (summer only), pit toilets; day-use picnic area, playground, nature trails.

The BC/Yukon border is just 48km/30 miles north of Liard Hot Springs. There are few services along the way north until you reach Watson Lake about 225km/140 miles north, so be sure to fill your gas tank before heading out. The road descends out of the Rockies through lovely scenery and, in recent years, plenty of road construction; if you're forced to contend with much of it, the drive could take up to four hours.

Resources for Northern British Columbia

Northern BC Tourism Association
P.O. Box 2373, Prince George, BC V2N 2S6; 250/561-0432, 800/663-8843

Fort Nelson and Northern Rockies Regional District
Town Square, 5319 50th Avenue South, Bag Service 399, Fort Nelson, BC V0C 1R0; 250/774-2541; www.northernrockies.org

YUKON TERRITORY

The entire Yukon Territory has just over 31,000 residents in an area the size of Arizona, California, Delaware, and West Virginia put together. Two out of three Yukoners live in the capital city of Whitehorse. From the BC border, Yukon Territory runs north to the Beaufort Sea. Several good roads allow visitors to explore much of the Yukon.

The scenery is breathtaking just about everywhere and, except in the major tourist centers, you won't find huge crowds. Wildlife is plentiful (there are almost twice as many moose as people). The climate in summer tends to be much like the interior of Alaska, comfortable and sometimes even hot. Days are long: even at the southern border, you'll have around 19 hours of daylight. Night is a misnomer in Yukon summers; at best it's a sort of gentle twilight. Of course, in winter, the hours of daylight dip below six. Whenever you come, expect remarkably clear air, free of smog.

Yukon History

Human beings have inhabited Yukon Territory for at least 10,000 years, descendants of hunter-gatherers who pursued game across the Bering land bridge in the last ice age when a 2,400-km swath /1,243-mile swath of now-submerged grassland remained ice free and connected Asia and North America. Until European traders arrived in the mid-19th century, Yukon Natives lived sparsely throughout the territory, hunting in winter and fishing in the summer. Most first Yukoners were Athabascan; later, Tlingit arrived from the coast as traders; well into the days of European settlement they controlled access between the coast and the interior. The arrival of European trappers, traders, and eventually the Hudson's Bay Company, brought more settlement, and when Russia sold Alaska to the United States, American traders and whalers moved into the region. However, the lives of the Yukon's first inhabitants didn't change much until gold was discovered. In 1897, the Royal Canadian Mounted Police were authorized to maintain order in the territory, especially in light of the influx of thousands of miners. A year later, the Yukon achieved full territorial status with its own government. The impact of the Gold Rush on the First Nations was harsh. They were displaced from their communities and many succumbed to diseases carried into the north, such as typhoid fever.

While the population surge quickly subsided, it left in place a government and a transportation network: the railroad from Skagway to Whitehorse and the flotilla of sternwheelers on the rivers. Mining kept Dawson alive, while its pivotal position on the railway ensured that Whitehorse would thrive (it replaced Dawson as territorial capital in 1952). The building of the Alaska Highway, along with many airfields to support the war effort in World War II, brought new blood and new opportunities to the Yukon.

Today, Yukon Territory still depends heavily on mining: gold, silver, zinc, and lead. Tourism is an important and growing sector of the economy, but the territory's biggest employer is government. ▣

Klondike Gold Rush

From the time of the first California Gold Rush in 1849, successful strikes in southern and central BC saw a steady stream of prospectors headed north in search of riches. In August of 1896, George Carmack, his wife, Kate, a Yukon Native, and her two brothers, Tagish Charlie and Skookum Jim, struck gold on a tributary of the Klondike River called Bonanza Creek. Their success quickly drew other nearby miners and prospectors; among them, all the gold-bearing land was claimed within a few months and serious mining extracted astounding quantities of placer gold.

In July of 1897, nearly a year later, two steamships loaded with gold and newly wealthy miners arrived in San Francisco and Seattle. The U.S. was just pulling out of a four-year economic depression and the news of the strike on Bonanza Creek captured the front pages of newspapers in the U.S.

☛ **Parent Tip: Smoking in the Yukon**

Currently, smoking is not restricted in Yukon Territory restaurants. Restaurants may supply nonsmoking areas if they choose; many do not. Thick clouds of smoke can accompany a meal. One way to respond is to "vote with your feet" and leave, first politely telling whomever is in charge why you've chosen not to dine in this establishment. Of course, when there's just one place to eat, you're stuck. If so, take-out is probably your best option. ◼

---

and around the world, not to mention the imaginations of thousands.

Canada was especially attractive because, unlike the U.S., it did not prohibit non-citizens from staking claims. By the fall of 1897, thousands of hopeful prospectors were headed for the Klondike. Few were miners or had any experience with conditions in the far north; they were farmers, desk clerks, doctors, lawyers: city folk. Some prospectors brought wives and children. Estimates are that about 28,000 of these hopefuls arrived in Alaska in 1898 and hiked the grueling Chilkoot or White Pass trail up to Lake Bennett, most in winter. Alarmed at the influx of clueless southerners, Canada imposed a law requiring that each prospector prove sufficient resources to live in the Yukon for a year. A ton of supplies was held to be sufficient.

Once they had arrived at Skagway or Dyea, prospectors had to haul their supplies up to Lake Bennett, where they could take to the water to reach the Klondike. The Chilkoot Trail from Dyea was slightly easier than the White Pass trail from Skagway. Most carried their supplies on their own backs. They would hike five miles with one load, stash it, then return for the next consignment. They would make many successive trips over the 30-mile trail; estimates are that each prospector covered 1,800 miles just between Dyea and Bennett. In April 1898, an avalanche on the Chilkoot killed 53 prospectors. Those who had horses didn't fare much better: 5,000 horses died in that one year on the White Pass trail, causing it to be renamed Deadhorse Gulch.

Most prospectors arrived at Lake Bennett after the lake was frozen for the year. They camped here and built boats to be ready for the ice breakup that occurred in May. As few had experience in boating or boat building, not all of the vessels were a success. Thousands of boats sank and many prospectors drowned.

Those able to stay afloat made it to Miles Canyon, a scenic but dangerous passage just south of Whitehorse. (The name "Whitehorse" derives from the rapids whose frothy whitewater was reminiscent of white horses.) When the prospectors finally arrived in the Klondike, they discovered that all the gold was claimed. The Gold Rush was over.

Despite this terrible outcome, virtually no one regretted having made the trip. Some moved on to seek gold in Fairbanks and Nome; some stayed on and tried their luck anyway; some recognized opportunities other than gold mining. (Thousands of new residents in Dawson needed to be supplied with food, lodging, and entertainment.) Some simply turned around and returned home.

Among the earliest prospectors to arrive in the winter of 1897 was 21-year-old Jack London. After passing a miserable winter near Dawson, during which he got severe scurvy but no gold, he returned to California and mined the experience in his writings many times over. *White Fang* and *The Call of the Wild* owe their existence to London's northern adventure.

The other famous literary figure associated with the Klondike, Robert Service, did not arrive until 1909. A good listener, he was inspired by stories of the Gold Rush and his evocative poems brought the era to vivid life for readers around the world.

Getting to the Yukon Territory

By Air **Air Canada** (888/247-2262; www.aircanada.ca/) has multiple daily flights between Vancouver and Whitehorse, with connecting flights throughout North America and worldwide. **Air North** (800/661-0407 [Canada/Alaska], 800/764-0407 [Continental USA]; www.flyairnorth.com) connects Whitehorse with Vancouver, Calgary, Edmonton, Juneau, and Fairbanks, as well as Yukon cities including Dawson City, Old Crow, and Inuvik. **Era Aviation** (800/478-1947; www.era-aviation.com) flies between Anchorage and Whitehorse several times a week in summer, with connections in Anchorage to other Alaska cities and airlines.

By Road In addition to the Alaska Highway, the Cassiar Highway (Hwy 37) runs north from the Yellowhead Highway (Hwy 16) in BC to the Alaska Highway, just west of Watson Lake. The South Klondike Highway (Hwy 2) runs south from Whitehorse to Skagway, Alaska; the Haines Highway (Hwy 3) runs south from Haines Junction, YT, to Haines, AK. From Dawson City, YT, the Top of the World Highway (Hwy 9) connects with Alaska's Taylor Highway a few miles across the international border. Bus service between Yukon destinations and the rest of Canada and Alaska is available. **Greyhound Canada** (867/667-2223; www.greyhound.ca) serves destinations across Canada, as well as Dawson Creek and other northern BC towns. **The Dawson City Courier** (Whitehorse: 867/393-3334; Dawson City: 867/993-6688; www.dawsonbus.ca/ Cost: $90.75/one way; $163.35/round trip) has year-round service between Whitehorse and Dawson City, with multiple weekly departures along with service to Inuvik. For the most up-to-date information, check in with the **Visitor Centre in Whitehorse** (see "Resources"). If you're planning to get to the Yukon by bus from the Alaska Ferry or vice versa, be aware that in recent years, bus companies connecting destinations in the Yukon, Alaska, and BC have come and gone. Be sure to check (and verify close to travel time) that service providers still exist and travel to your destinations. The Holland America cruise line now owns **Gray Line Yukon** (867/668-3225; www.yukonweb.com/tourism/westours/), which in turn acquired Alaskon Express, and runs daily buses between Skagway and Whitehorse from mid-May to mid-September. It connects with Greyhound Canada buses.

By Sea Scheduled buses run between Whitehorse and Skagway, where the Alaska Marine Highway System serves various routes in Alaska and down to Washington State (see "Inside Passage") for details.

By Train The old **White Pass & Yukon Route Railway** connected

Rent an RV and See the Yukon

It doesn't come cheap, but one intriguing option is to rent an RV and head out on the Yukon's open roads. **Klondike Recreational Rentals** (107 Copper Rd, 867/668-2200, 800/665-4755; www.klondike-rv.com) rents trucks with campers and motor homes; the largest house up to five adults. Drivers are permitted to drive the Dempster Highway to Inuvik and other unpaved roads in northern BC, the Yukon, Alaska, and Northwest Territories. Read the small print carefully (notice the $1200 tow fee to Fairbanks if you break down on the road to Circle, for example). Bedding and kitchen gear can be included. Prices start at around $140 per day plus prep fees, mileage, and insurance. ◘

Whitehorse and Skagway by rail for over 80 years. Full service was discontinued in 1982; however, trains still run between Carcross, YT, and Skagway, and tours that combine train and bus travel between Skagway and Whitehorse are available. See "Skagway" in "Inside Passage."

Resources

Books for All Ages

Berton, Pierre. *The Klondike Fever: The Life and Death of the Last Great Gold Rush.* Carroll & Graf, 1958. This classic by the great Canadian author and son of a Klondike prospector brings the era to life.

London, Jack. *The Unabridged Jack London.* Running Press, 1981. This hefty paperback contains the Yukon novels and stories including "To Build a Fire," *The Call of the Wild,* and *White Fang.*

Morgan, Murray. *One Man's Gold Rush: Photographs of E.A. Hegg.* The story of the great photographer of the Klondike Gold Rush is accompanied by his powerful photos.

Murphy, Claire Rudolf and Jane G. Haigh. *Gold Rush Women.* Alaska Northwest Books, 1997. Fascinating stories of 23 women who played important roles in the Klondike and Fairbanks Gold Rush are illustrated with photos.

Service, Robert. *The Spell of the Yukon.* This volume appeared in 1916 and has remained a perennial favorite. It's also available on tape and CD.

Wilson, Graham. *The Klondike Gold Rush: Photographs from 1896-1899.* Wolf Creek Books, 1997. The story is told primarily through starkly evocative photographs.

Books Just for Kids

Murphy, Claire Rudolf and Jane G. Haigh. *Children of the Gold Rush.* Roberts Rinehart, 1999. Geared to kids 9 and older, this excellent volume examines the impact on children of the Gold Rush that consumed their parents, and their impact on Gold Rush communities.

Murphy, Claire Rudolf and Jane G. Haigh. *Gold Rush Dogs.* Alaska Northwest Books, 2001. Well-known dogs (Balto and Patsy Ann) and lesser-known canines are brought to vivid life.

Regional Resources

Parks Canada *(888/773-8888; www.parkscanada.gc.ca)* The federal agency responsible for national parks and national historic sites

Tourism Yukon *(Box 2703, Whitehorse, YT Y1A 2C6, 867/667-5340; www.touryukon.com)* Operates Yukon Visitor Reception Centers

Yukon Govt. Dept. of Renewal Resources, Fish and Wildlife Branch *(Box 2703, Whitehorse, YT Y1A 2C6, 867/667-5652; www.renres.gov.yk.ca)* Campground information, hunting and fishing licenses

Web sites

Yukon Web *(www.yukonweb.com)* A comprehensive site with information on all things Yukon

Yukon Info *(www.yukoninfo.com)* A well-organized site with useful information for travel planning

Yukon Information Links *(www.out-there.com/yt_info/)* Yukon travel and activities information

Yukon Wild *(www.yukonwild.com)* Government-sponsored site on Yukon adventure travel

Alaska Highway:
Yukon Border to Whitehorse (515 km/319 m)

You'll need at least seven to eight hours for this leg of the journey. Highway construction projects can slow traffic to a crawl; if a section requires a pilot car to lead vehicles, you can expect longer waits (as much as 30 minutes).

1) **Yukon border to Watson Lake** (70 km/44 m from Contact Creek)
2) **Watson Lake to Teslin** (263/163 m)
3) **Teslin to Whitehorse** (182 km/111 m)

1) Yukon Border to Watson Lake
(70 km/44 m from Contact Creek)

This stretch of highway crosses back and forth between British Columbia and the Yukon. The drive includes several pullouts with scenic views. If you need a break, at Historical Mile 570 you'll find picnic tables, firepits, outhouses, and a spectacular vista of the Liard River.

WATSON LAKE

This small town of 1,800 owes its existence to its strategic location on the Alaska Highway. Appearances to the contrary, there are a few unique attractions here for families. You'll find decent accommodation and food (but at a steep price), a community swimming pool, and an excellent visitor's center. The town is also the starting point of the **Robert Campbell Highway** (Hwy 4), which runs north to Ross River and Faro before meeting up with the Klondike Highway at Carmacks, 586 km/364 miles north of Watson Lake; the mostly gravel road runs through several historic Gold Rush-era towns.

Places to Stay

Belvedere Motor Hotel ($$)

Mile 635 Alaska Hwy. 867/536-7712; www.watsonlakehotels.com/Belvedere/
FYI: 48 rooms, some adjoining rooms, some refrigerators; coffee shop, restaurant; gift shop
This two-story hotel has standard-sized rooms. An adjacent motel unit provides additional housing. The coffee shop is your best bet for feeding kids. Soups, burgers, and daily specials are good and reasonably priced, but there is no nonsmoking section.

66 P A R E N T   C O M M E N T S 99

"Try to get a room on the first floor. There is no air conditioning, so the second floor rooms get very hot, and there's no elevator, just a very steep staircase. It was chilly outside, but like an oven in our room. All that daylight makes a difference! The breakfast in the café was first-rate and kid-friendly. Good hash browns."

Gateway Motor Inn ($$)

On the Alaska Hwy; 867/536-7712; www.watsonlakehotels.com/gateway/
FYI: 50 rooms, some kitchenettes, refrigerators; restaurant; pets OK
Another basic hotel, this one features Watson Lake's **Pizza Palace** (867/536-7744), a good dining choice for kids. It purports to have a non-smoking section, but parent reviewers found it saturated with cigarette smoke. Your best bet is to take the pizza back to your room.

Watson Lake Hotel ($-$$)

9th St N & Alaska Hwy. 867/536-7781
FYI: 48 rooms, family suite with kitchenette; restaurant, café; gift shop
The main plus for families is the family suite and location next to the Signpost Forest (see "What to See & Do").

Camping

There are two camping options in Watson Lake. Across the street from Wye Lake is the **Downtown RV Park** (Lakeview & 8th; 867/536-2646; 71 RV sites, $18+, no tents; hookups, showers, Laundromat; free RV wash with overnight stay). The **Watson Lake Recreation Park** (Mile 637; 55 sites, $12/site; pit toilets, water, fire pits; picnic shelters, playground, hiking trails, boat launch) is 1.5 km/.9 mile north of town on an access road off the Alaska Highway.

What to See & Do

Shopping By the time you've made it to Watson Lake, chances are good you're carrying a sizable shopping list. Prices and selection will be better at Whitehorse, but if you can't wait, you'll find **Hougen's Department Store** (Frank Trail & 8th St S; 867/536-7475) with clothing, souvenirs, and CDs along with fishing licenses and gear. **Watson Lake Foods** (867/536-2230) is a large grocery store with a bakery, deli, and ATM.

The Northern Lights Centre This attraction is heavily hyped on billboards and brochures from BC to Alaska. It consists of a tiny but interesting science center and a large planetarium showing locally made films on the region and the aurora borealis, as well as periodically changing films. Overall, it's an expensive disappointment. Still, if you have time to kill in Watson Lake and the weather drives you indoors, this is probably where you'll wind up. Steer the kids to the exhibits on Canada's role in space and the science behind the aurora. You can pick up children's science books and good-quality locally made items in the gift shop. *Frank Trail, 1 block off Alaska Hwy, 867/536-7827; www.watsonlakeinfo.com/ northernlightscentre/. Frequent daily shows, 12:30-8:30pm (mid-May-mid-Sept). Cost: $24/family.*

Signpost Forest This attraction is more interesting than it sounds, plus it's free. It dates from the building of the Alaska Highway in 1942, when a home-sick U.S. Army soldier from Illinois erected a homemade sign pointing to his hometown, with mileage. This started a trend that continues today. "Forest" is no exaggeration; long rows of walls, some as tall as old-growth evergreens, are covered with signs—road signs, freeway signs, warning signs, anything goes. In recent years, more homemade signs have been added to the mix, and enterprising entrepreneurs have set up kiosks where for a fee (about $7.50) visitors can paint a sign and post it in the forest. Unlikely as it sounds, you can easily spend hours here. Ingenious signs have been created by passers-through, with unusual materials including toilet seats and gold pans; one is painted on an old pair of leather gloves, another on an automobile whisk broom. The forest also includes construction equipment and machinery used to build the Alaska Highway. *At the junction of the Alaska Hwy & Robert Campbell Hwy; 867/536-2246. Free. Allow time for painting a sign; paint must dry before it can be mounted. Check with visitor centre for sign-painting information.*

Wye Lake This attractive lake is bordered by a park with a picnic area and trails, including a boardwalk trail with interpretive signs on the local flora and fauna. *8th St N & Hyland Ave.*

☛ Parent Tip:
Laundry—A Fact of Life

One of the gritty realities of life on the road is laundry—and a family of four is bound to generate plenty. You can cut down on the number of trips to the Laundromat with a little forethought:

Bring enough clothing to avoid having to do laundry more than once every five to seven days.

- Choose clothes that hide dirt or stains, can be hand-washed, and dry quickly.
- Pack detergent and fabric softener instead of paying a dollar or more for each wash load.
- Bring extra-large, sturdy plastic bags, preferably with handles, to get your clothes to and from the Laundromat.
- Hoard quarters for use at the Laundromat. Finding a source of quarters at 9pm in a small northern town can be harder than you think.
- Plan to stay at a hotel or campground with a Laundromat occasionally; these are noted in this book. ◙

Yukon Visitor Reception Centre/Alaska Highway Interpretive Centre This museum-cum-tourist information center behind the Signpost Forest has interesting exhibits on Alaska Highway construction and a small theatre that shows an excellent film on the highway's history and the political controversy it provoked between the U.S. and Canada.

Pick up information here on the road ahead, driving conditions, and what to see and do in the Yukon. One excellent resource is *Yukon's Wildlife Viewing Guide Along Major Highways* (Yukon Environment, 2002), a booklet that covers commonly spotted wildlife along each major territorial highway. In recent years, the Yukon government has sponsored the **Explorer's Passport** program in which visitors are given a passport to be stamped at select attractions. Those visiting all or a selection of designated destinations in the booklet are entered in a contest; in 2002 the grand prize was five troy ounces of Klondike placer gold. Some prizes are awarded automatically to those with a minimum number of stamps in their books. The booklets can be picked up at visitor reception centres and listed attractions.

Junction of Alaska & Robert Campbell Hwys, 867/536-7469. Open daily 8am-8pm (mid-May-mid-Sept).

Swimming   **Watson Lake Swimming Pool** (at the end of Swift Place, 2 blocks northeast of Alaska Hwy; 867/536-2246) adjacent to the recreation center and ballfield, this pool is open May to September. A few miles south of Watson Lake, pretty **Lucky Lake** with a sandy beach has what is reputed to be the only waterslide above 60 degrees north latitude. In summer, the lake actually gets warm enough for swimming. There are picnic tables and a trail that leads down to an observation platform overlooking the Liard River. The lake is stocked with rainbow trout.

Follow turnoff about 6 km south of Watson Lake.

2) Watson Lake to Teslin (263/163 m)

The Alaska Highway runs west from Watson Lake to Teslin; 21 km west of Watson Lake is the junction with the **Cassiar Highway (Hwy 37)**. For details, see "Highway 37: The Cassiar Highway, the Road Less Traveled."

Rancheria Falls Recreation Site   This lovely park makes an excellent place to stop and stretch your legs. There's no campground here, but there are picnic tables, outhouses, and an excellent trail through boreal forest to a beautiful waterfall, manageable by very small hikers. Notice the wildflowers, especially in early summer. The trail is about .5 km/.3 mile, partly on board-walk and is wheelchair accessible.

Mile 718 Alaska Hwy, about 121km/75 miles west of Watson Lake on the Alaska.

Continental Divide   Three km/1.9 miles past Rancheria Falls, the highway crosses the Continental Divide. A roadside interpretive sign marks the spot. From this point on, rivers flow north into the Yukon River basin and empty into the northern Beaufort or Bering seas.

Mile 721Alaska Hwy.

At **Walker's Continental Divide** (Mile 721; 867/851-6451) you'll find food, RV parking, hookups, gas, a motel, café, and gift shop. **Swift River Lodge** (Mile 733; 867/851-6401; open year round) has food, washrooms, gas, souvenirs, and a small motel.

TESLIN

At the confluence of Nisutlin Bay and Teslin Lake, the Hudson's Bay Company established a trading post in 1904. With a population of about 500, this historic Tlingit town, home of famous Yukon native George Johnston (see "George Johnston Museum") is definitely worth a visit. The area has a strong Tlingit history and presence today, showcased in its excellent museum and a new cultural center. The terrific local salmon bake is a good place to refuel and there are several accommodation choices.

Places to Stay

Dawson Peaks Resort & RV Park ($)

Mile 797Alaska Hwy; 867/390-2244; www.yukonweb.com/tourism/dawsonpeaks/
FYI: 3 lakefront cabins, 8 motel units, 28-site RV Park ($10-18/site, tents $8), with hookups, water, showers, dump station, fire pits & firewood, picnic tables, tents OK; restaurant, gift shop; boat and canoe rentals.

About 11 km/7 miles southeast of town on the Alaska Highway, this resort offers basic accommodation and a selection of chartered fishing trips, river-rafting trips, and land tours at reasonable rates. The triple-size cabins at $89 work for families.

Yukon Motel ($)

Mile 804 Alaska Hwy; 867/390-2575, 867/390-2443;
www.yukonmotel.com/
FYI: 7 rooms, restaurant, pets OK some units, souvenir shop; 70 RV sites, hookups, dump station, gas

Here's your best bet for accommodation in town with stuffed animals for sale (real animals).

See also "Mukluk Annie's."

Places to Eat

Mukluk Annie's Salmon Bake
Mile 812 Alaska Hwy; 867/390-2600
Hours: open daily 7am-10pm, salmon bake 11am-9pm

For any meal, this salmon bake—located nine miles west of town on the Alaska Highway—is your best option. The salmon bake is popular with tour groups; the ramshackle building is filled with row on row of long oilcloth covered tables. The food is excellent and if the kids whine "not salmon *again,*" barbecued beef and pork make excellent substitutes, and baked beans and cornbread usually go down well. Included in the price of your meal is a free houseboat cruise on Teslin Lake. Breakfasts here are also famous, especially the all-you-can-eat blueberry pancakes. There's also an RV Park (130 sites; hookups, tents OK, showers with fee, dump station, Laundromat, fire rings, free RV wash). All sites except those with hookups are free.

What to See & Do

George Johnston Museum   This small museum is an homage to Tlingit leader—trapper, entrepreneur, photographer/artist, and all-round fascinating character—George Johnston. His photos portray the history of his community in black and white, some of it tragic. Kids will relate to the photos of Tlingit children. Don't miss the displays that eloquently describe the impact that building the Alaska Highway had on the Tlingit. Also on display is Johnston's car, the first owned by a Tlingit and purchased before there were any roads to drive it on. Johnston used it on the ice for hunting; when game learned to vanish when they saw the gleaming black car against the white landscape, Johnston painted it white for camouflage). Other displays include antique basketry, embroidery, leatherwork, and tools. One exhibit depicts the life of the Tlingit through each season. The excellent store sells books, locally made moccasins, hide bowls, jewelry, and other crafts.
Mile 804 Alaska Hwy; 867/390-2550; www.gjkuseum.yk.net.
Open daily in summer, 9am-6pm. Cost: $2.50/adult, $2/senior, student, $1/child, $7/family.

Tlingit Heritage Centre   A not-to-be-missed attraction, just north of town, is this award-winning cultural center, opened in 2001. The building, sited on the sandy lakeshore, is fronted by five new totem poles representing each of the Tlingit clans: eagle, raven/crow, beaver, frog, and wolf. Exhibits detail the history of the Tlingit people and European settlement from the Tlingit perspective. Historically, the Tlingit were traders whose reach extended from the coast, up and down the Inside Passage, to the mountain passes and, eventually, over them into the Yukon Territory. They controlled access to and from the interior, trading on both sides of the passes and becoming agents for the Russians when they arrived in Alaska in the 18th century. The Yukon Tlingit are immigrants, descended from coastal Tlingit who migrated inland and intermarried with the local Athabascans.

Tlingit staff and volunteers circulate among visitors, pointing out interesting facets of exhibits and answering questions. The masks on display are of exceptional quality. Local carvers work with tribal elders to re-create earlier styles and also to put their own stamp on the art. Carvers work in the center and teach workshops here; they, too, are happy to talk to visitors and explain their work. A gift shop sells arts and crafts, books, and clothing. *Mile 779 Alaska Hwy; 867/390-2526. Open daily 9am-9pm (July-Aug); 10am-4pm (Sept 1-14). Cost: $5/adult, $4/student, $2/child 6-12, free/child under 6, $10/family.*

3) Teslin to Whitehorse (182 km/111 m)

From Teslin, the Alaska Highway turns north to Whitehorse. There are rushing rivers, dense evergreen and deciduous forests, and alpine meadows studded with flowers—wild roses, lupine, and bunchberry in pinks, blues, and whites. The lack of air pollution is a revelation; the sky is so clear that distances melt away. Leaving town, you'll pass over the **Teslin River Bridge**. At 584 meters/.36 mile, it's the third-longest water span on the Alaska Highway; its height allowed steamers to pass under it between Whitehorse and Teslin. Mile 866, **Jake's Corner**, is the junction with Highway 7, which leads to the small town of **Atlin,** BC, along a scenic 59-mile drive over mostly gravel road. Atlin, with all services, is located on beautiful Atlin Lake, much of which is surrounded by Atlin Provincial Park.

At Mile 861.3, about 40 km/25 miles west of the Highway 7 junction, the **Swan Haven Interpretive Centre** (Mile 891; 867/667-8291; www.environment yukon.gov.yk.ca) welcomes visitors in April and May, during the annual tundra and trumpeter swan migration north to their nesting grounds. In the third week of April, the Celebration of Swans is held, with programs for families and children. The Centre is closed the rest of the year, but you can park here and hike a short trail with interpretive panels and a view of M'Clintock Bay.

At Milepost 905 is the junction with the **South Klondike Highway (Hwy 2)** that runs south to Carcross and Skagway (see chapter 4, "Inside Passage"), where you can hook up with the Alaska ferries and cruise ships traveling the Inside Passage.

WHITEHORSE

With a population of over 23,000, Whitehorse is the largest city on the Alaska Highway, big enough to have a Walmart and other hallmarks of urbanization. Its pivotal location on the Yukon River and as the terminus of the White Pass & Yukon Railroad made it a key player in moving goods to the Klondike to support miners and mining, and moving the gold south. Today, Whitehorse is a modern city with several world-class attractions, including a unique museum dedicated to Beringia, the huge swath of present-day Yukon that remained ice-free during successive ice ages, supporting animals and humans when much of North America was uninhabitable. Most of the city lies on the banks of the Yukon River, while the airport, suburbs, and newer attractions are on the high bluffs overlooking the city.

Getting Around

The only city transit service in the Yukon, **Whitehorse Transit** operates buses throughout the city and suburbs (867/668-7433, cost: $1.50/adult). The **Whitehorse Waterfront Trolley** (daily in summer, 11am-7pm; $1/person), originally an electric streetcar from Portugal, now shuttles along the waterfront, stopping at popular tourist destinations including the Train Shed, Visitor Reception Centre, and Rotary Peace Park. Extended service is planned for the future.

Car rentals Whitehorse-based **Norcan Leasing** (213 Range Rd, 867/668-2137; www.norcan.yk.ca/) has outlets at the airport here and in Dawson City. Major names in car rentals can be found at the Whitehorse Airport.

Places to Stay

Best Western Gold Rush Inn ($$-$$$)

411 Main St; 867/668-4500, US/Canada: 800/780-7234; www.goldrushinn.com
FYI: 106 rooms, suites, restaurant, refrigerators; Laundromat; pets OK
This large hotel caters, as do most downtown Whitehorse hotels, to tour groups. Some rooms are designed for families and include bunk beds. The location, set back some blocks from the river, is close enough to walk to downtown attractions, but a bit quieter than some locations.

Edgewater Hotel ($$-$$$)

101 Main St; 867/667-2572, 877/484-3334; www.edgewaterhotel.yk.ca.com
FYI: 30 rooms, some kitchens, refrigerators; 2 restaurants
If you want a comfortable roost in the center of town, the Edgewater is just the ticket. A block from the water and close to museums and shopping, it makes a good base for exploring the city. Plus, it's the only hotel in Whitehorse with air conditioning, something you'll appreciate on a long, hot July evening. The Gallery Lounge serves informal meals daily. The more formal Cellar (open Tuesday through Friday, 11:30am to 1:30pm and Tuesday through Saturday, 5 to 10pm for dinner), the city's spiffiest fine-dining establishment, serves lunch and dinner.

66 PARENT COMMENTS 99

"We were very comfortable at the Edgewater Hotel. The only thing we missed was a Laundromat. Parents should know that once the Gallery starts serving alcohol (11am daily), it's off-limits to anyone under drinking age."

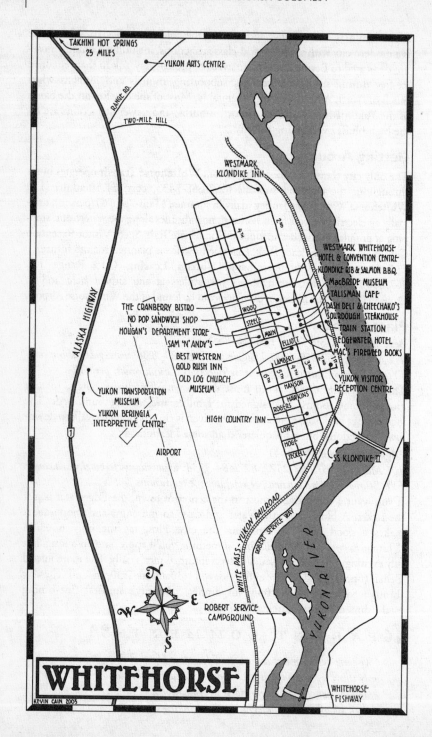

TAKHINI HOT SPRINGS 25 MILES

YUKON ARTS CENTRE

RANGE RD.

TWO-MILE HILL

WESTMARK KLONDIKE INN

ALASKA HIGHWAY

4TH

2ND

WESTMARK WHITEHORSE HOTEL & CONVENTION CENTRE
KLONDIKE RIB & SALMON B.B.Q.
MacBRIDE MUSEUM
TALISMAN CAFE
DASH DELI & CHEECHAKO'S
SOURDOUGH STEAKHOUSE
TRAIN STATION
EDGEWATER HOTEL
MAC'S FIREWEED BOOKS

THE CRANBERRY BISTRO
NO POP SANDWICH SHOP
HOUGAN'S DEPARTMENT STORE
SAM 'N' ANDY'S
BEST WESTERN GOLD RUSH INN
OLD LOG CHURCH MUSEUM

WOOD
STEELE
MAIN
ELLIOTT
LAMBERT
6TH 5TH 4TH 3RD 2ND 1ST
HANSON
HAWKINS
ROGERS
LOWE
HOGE
JECKELL

YUKON TRANSPORTATION MUSEUM
YUKON BERINGIA INTERPRETIVE CENTRE

AIRPORT

HIGH COUNTRY INN

YUKON VISITOR RECEPTION CENTRE

SS KLONDIKE II

1

WHITE PASS - YUKON RAILROAD

ROBERT SERVICE WAY

YUKON RIVER

N
W E
S

ROBERT SERVICE CAMPGROUND

WHITEHORSE FISHWAY

WHITEHORSE

KEVIN CAIN 2005

High Country Inn (**$$** off season; **$$-$$$** high season)
4051 4th Ave; 867/667-4471, 800/554-4471; www.highcountryinn.yk.ca
FYI: 100 rooms, restaurant; some with kitchenettes, hot tubs; family suite;
children under 12 stay free; weight room; pets OK (fee); free airport-hotel shuttle
Another of the large tour-group-oriented hotels, this one is situated too far from
downtown attractions to make it an easy walk for very young kids. On the other
hand, it's adjacent to the Aquatic Centre, the only public pool in town.

Westmark Klondike Inn (**$$-$$$**)
2288 Second Ave; 867/668-4747
*FYI: 99 rooms, coffee shop, gift shop; open May-Sept; not within walking
distance of downtown*

Westmark Whitehorse Hotel & Convention Center (**$$-$$$**)
2nd & Wood Sts; 867/393-9700
FYI: 181 rooms; restaurant, gift shop

NOTE: Name to the contrary, the **Stop-in Family Hotel** (314 Ray St,
867/668-5558; rates: $44 rooms, restaurant; Laundromat; hot tub, sauna)
is not especially recommended for families. The hotel's single family room is
situated in the basement, and the hotel's location in the concrete jungle two
blocks east of the Qwanlin Mall is less than appealing. On the plus side,
there is an enormous Laundromat.

Camping

Campers looking for an RV-free location can head south of town to the river-
front **Robert Service Campground** (on Robert Service Way, 2 km/1.2 miles
south of downtown; 867/668-6678 or 668-3721; www.yukonweb.com/
tourism/service/; 48 tenting sites, $14/site, showers, no hookups; firewood
[fee], store). The attractive location has plenty of trees, but fills up in summer.
In a nicer location south of town with wooded sites is **Pioneer RV Park**
(91091 Alaska Hwy, 867/668-5944; www.pioneer-rv-park.com; 150 sites,
$10-22/site, tents; hookups, showers, Laundromat, RV wash, breakfast at the
recreation center, store, daily bus service to Skagway).

Places to Eat

The Cranberry Bistro
302 Wood St; 867/456-4898
Hours: Mon-Fri 9am-7pm, Sat 9am-3pm
This attractive little spot specializes in healthy cuisine, offering soups and
salads for lunch. Try the fruit smoothies; the baked goods are first rate.

The Dash Deli/Cheechako's Sourdough Steakhouse
204B Main St; 867/393-2555; www.dashdeli.com
Hours: Mon-Fri 7am-9pm, Sat-Sun 9:30am-9pm

Two sides of the same coin, this establishment offers deli items in a casual restaurant that will suit most kids. There's a selection of panini and other sandwiches, soups, salads, fish and chips, and pb&j or grilled cheese for kids. Prices are among the lowest in the city. On the steakhouse side, you'll get more adult fare.

Klondike Rib and Salmon Barbecue
2116 2nd Ave; 867/667-7554
Hours: daily 11am-10pm, late May-mid-Sept
Head here for dinner when everyone is starving. Once you get over sticker shock, you'll enjoy an excellent meal. This ribs-and-fish emporium, housed in two historic buildings, gets very busy, but service is efficient. Lunches feature salads with burgers and sandwiches sporting names like "OK, Where's Bob? Sandwich" and "'Tree Hugger' Napoleon." Dinner entrées range from prime rib and barbecued chicken to fish and bison. Try the Yukon arctic char, a relative of the Dolly Varden; if you're feeling adventurous, go for wild game stroganoff. Microbrew beers are on tap.

No Pop Sandwich Shop
312 Steele St; 867/668-3227
Hours: Mon-Thurs 7am-8:30pm, Fri 7am-9pm, Sat 10am-8pm, Sun 10am-3pm
The soda pop-deprived child can choose from a variety of healthy sparkling drinks, juices, and floats (made with juice). This is the city's best bet for breakfast, offering eggs Benedict, omelets, pancakes, crepes, and croissants. For lunch, an array of sandwiches is on offer. The dinner menu is eclectic, ranging from quiche to cabbage rolls and burritos to Mongolian beef. Fresh-baked desserts round out the selections, along with espresso drinks and microbrews.

Sam 'n Andy's
506 Main St; 867/668-6994; samnandys@yt.sympatico.ca
Hours: Mon-Wed 11am-10pm, Thurs-Sat 11am-11pm, Sun 4:30pm-10pm
For Mexican cuisine, in short supply in northern BC and the Yukon, head to this charming restaurant housed in a cottage with a big yard. You're in for a superb meal that you can eat indoors or out. They have a light touch with traditional Mexican favorites; try the stuffed avocado salad for a light lunch, or the enormous guacamole salad for a larger one. The mud pie (a chocolate ice cream cake) makes a nice dessert. There's a kids' menu. They do takeout, too.

Talisman Café
2112 2nd Ave; 867/667-2736
Hours: Mon-Wed 9am-7pm, Thurs-Sat 9am-9pm, Sun 10am-3pm
Enter here and feel wafted back to the 1970s, if not farther. The food is fine—breakfast and lunch especially, and vegetarians, who often feel overlooked in the north, will find plenty to interest them.

What to See & Do

Stroll & Browse

Start your exploration of downtown Whitehorse at the large **Visitor Reception Centre**. This facility, like all Yukon government tourist information centers, is large, well staffed and funded. Skip the slick but insubstantial film shown in the theatre. The displays in the center offer much more specific, helpful information. The center offers a selection of CDs by Yukon artists. If you're thinking of tackling one of the Yukon's other highways, such as the Klondike to Dawson City or the Dempster Highway up to Inuvik, the knowledgeable staff can help you weigh the pros and cons.
100 Hanson St, 867/667-3084; open daily mid-May to mid-September, 8am-8pm.

If you have time, get your bearings by taking a guided tour with the **Yukon Historical & Museums Association**. Guides in historical dress lead tours (about an hour) of downtown Whitehorse. Alternatively, pick up self-guided tour maps at the Visitor Reception Centre.
At LePage Park, 3126 3rd Ave; tours Mon-Sat 9am, 11am, 1pm, 3pm, late-May-Aug; Cost: $2.

Stroll up Main Street, from the riverfront to the cliffs at **Teegatha 'Oh Zheh Park**. Stop in at **Mac's Fireweed Books** (203 Main St, 867/668-2434; www.yukonbooks.com) for books on the Yukon and a good general collection. **Midnight Sun Gallery & Gifts** (205C Main St, 867/668-4350; www.midnight sunyukon.com) has locally made arts and crafts and an impressive array of homemade fudge. **Paradise Alley** (206 Main St, 867/456-4228) sells good quality gifts from outside and within the Yukon. At **Coast Mountain Sports** (208A Main St, 867/667-4074), you can outfit the whole family, from hiking boots to fleece; they also sell tents, backpacks, and outdoor gear. Also on Main Street is the Hougen Centre; this small mall has a **Hougen's Department Store** (3rd & Main St, 867/668-6842) with an excellent assortment of Yukon souvenirs.

For good quality Yukon arts and crafts, try the **Yukon Gallery** (across from the Visitor Reception Centre; Lambert & 2nd Ave; 867/667-2391) or the **North End Gallery** (1116 1st Ave, Suite 118; 867/393-3590), where you can buy scrimshaw and jewelry made from fossilized woolly mammoth ivory and pictures made of tufted moose hair.

When you're shopped out, stop in at one of Whitehorse's many attractive coffee shops or bakeries for a latté or Italian soda, such as **Main Street Bäckerei/Kaffee Haus** (100 Main St, 867/633-6291) or the **Java Connection** (3125B 3rd Ave, 867/668-2196).

Museums

MacBride Museum The city's flagship museum is bigger than it looks and cleverly designed to interest children. Check out the new bear section, with intriguing videos on black and grizzly bears. Along with Yukon pioneer history is an excellent survey of Yukon geology. There's a detailed exhibit on gold mining and the lives of prospectors. Upstairs and outside, children can try their own luck panning for gold. Outside are also a Tlingit dugout canoe, an old house undergoing restoration, and a cabin once occupied by Sam McGee (yes, *that* Sam McGee). The large gift shop sells books, jewelry, and the like. *1124 First Ave (First Ave & Wood St); 867/667-2709; www.macbridemuseum.com. Open daily in summer, 10am-6pm; by appointment in winter. Cost: $5/adult, $3.50/child, $15/family. Allow at least 90 minutes.*

Old Log Church Museum This small, charming museum in a historic church tells the fascinating story of Anglican missionaries in the Yukon, describing the interaction of church and Native peoples especially well. Notice the vestments made of leather and intricately beaded. The missionaries came mainly from England and Scotland, bringing their hardworking wives, and most thrived. Kids will be enthralled by the story of Bishop Stringer, who had to eat his boots to survive an ill-fated trip west from Fort McPherson. The shreds of those boots are on display, and you can listen to a spellbinding narrative of the story. *3rd Ave & Elliott St; 867/668-2555. Open mid-May-Labour Day, Mon-Sat 10am-6pm, Sun 11am-4 pm. Cost: $2.50/adult, $1/child, free/under 6. Allow 30 minutes.*

SS Klondike II National Historic Site This historic sternwheeler is dry-docked in a park next to the river, just south of the Robert Campbell Bridge. To visit, you'll need to join a tour, which starts with a film (don't skip it; you'll get background information that will help you understand the tour) shown outside in a tent. There's a gift shop, and picnicking facilities.

Sternwheelers played a key role in Yukon and Alaskan history, from before the Gold Rush era well into the 20th century when aviation and highways edged out boat travel. The Yukon River was key in getting miners and their supplies to the gold and the gold back south. When the railroad from Skagway to Whitehorse became operational in 1900, the prime route to the gold fields was via sternwheeler from Whitehorse to Dawson. First the *SS Klondike I*, then this successor, made the difficult trip. *At the bottom of 2nd Ave; 867/667-4511, 800/661-0486; parkscan.harbour.com/ssk/. Open daily, 9am-7pm, mid-June-mid-Sept. Call for tour details. Cost: $5/adult, $2.75/student, $12/family. Allow at least 60 minutes for the tour (including video).*

Yukon Arts Centre More than an art gallery, the center houses programs including music and art camps for children. The Centre, on a hill west of downtown, offers a gorgeous view of Whitehorse, the Yukon River, and the hills and mountains beyond. This is also the site of Yukon College and of the Yukon Archives, open to the public.

The art gallery displays works by local and regional artists and mounts traveling exhibitions. The range of media and scope of the works is impressive. Notice the Eugene Alfred masks. Outside the building are sculptures and installations by Native artists depicting nature, spirits, and animals.

A **Kids' Grotto** includes a permanent kids' art gallery, with art made by children and hung at their eye level. Family art-related activities are held here on Sundays. Children's art classes, educational programs, including visiting artist lectures, are also held at the Centre.

80 Range Rd; 867/667-8577; www.yukonartscentre.org. Open Mon-Fri 11am-5pm, Thurs until 9pm, Sat-Sun noon-5pm (June-Aug); Tues-Fri 11am-5pm, Sat-Sun 1-4pm; until 9pm every third Thursday of each month (Sept-May). Admission by donation ($5/family suggested).

Yukon Beringia Interpretive Centre ☺ Beringia is the name given to the vast grasslands of Siberia, Alaska, and the Yukon that emerged during successive global glaciations. During the last ice age, a host of animal species thrived here, from the woolly mammoth to lesser-known species: the land sloth, short-faced bear, scimitar cat, giant beaver, and North American camel. Humans followed the game from Asia into the Americas during the last glaciation around 24,000 years ago, ancestors of today's First Nations.

Interactive exhibits tell the history of Beringia using geological and fossil evidence. The science behind glaciation is explored. A superb 20-minute film, made by Yukoners, describes the discovery of Beringia and features interviews with Native people, including a teenage boy, who made some of the significant finds shown in the museum. In galleries that include extraordinary art installations, you can listen to First Nations creation myths. Local Native lore, traced to this period, includes tales of great floods and precise instructions on how to hunt woolly mammoths. A traditional tale of a buried mammoth carcass proved so accurate that scientists were able to use it to locate and uncover a partially preserved mammoth.

A large alcove in the museum is set aside for kids to explore the science of Beringia with books, art supplies, puzzles, and research materials. Outside the building are statues of giant Beringian animals set among the trees. One interesting activity for kids centers around the revival of an ancient weapon: the *atlatl,* a tool used in hunting prior to the development of the bow and arrow. This device, once used worldwide, allows the user to throw a spear with a high degree of accuracy. The center has developed a set of atlatl games, such as atlatl "golf," that allow kids to safely explore these devices.

Camp Beringia, a program for 7- to 12-year-olds, is offered in summer. Kids come together from 9am to 4pm at a series of seven day camps and study archeology, geology, and paleontology. The cost is $20/per day per child. It's possible for visiting youngsters to enroll in some or all of these; contact the Centre for information. The Center's Web site has useful resources for teachers and for kids who want to learn more about Beringia.

Mile 915, Alaska Hwy, in Whitehorse, next to the Whitehorse International Airport; 867/667-8855; www.beringia.com; Open daily, mid-May-mid-Sept; May, Sept 9am-6pm, June-Aug 8:30am-7pm; winter and rest of year Sun 1-5pm and any day by appointment (with at least 7 days notice). Cost: $6/adult, $4/student, $8/combined ticket with Yukon Transportation Museum, $25/family pass (good for 1 year), free/under 6. Allow at least 90 minutes.

Yukon Transportation Museum Exhibits focus on the history of transportation in the Yukon. One contrasts the building of the Alaska Highway with the Canol Pipeline (an exercise in lousy planning). An exhibit on the role of aviation in the Yukon, which involved plenty of exciting crashes and mishaps, should get the attention of the museum-weary child. Several long videos are shown on the Gold Rush, as well as on mushing and the Yukon Quest dogsled race from Fairbanks to Whitehorse. Small kids will enjoy the enormous model train layout. There's a gift shop.
Airport, Alaska Hwy; Open daily, 10am-6pm. Cost: $5.25/adult, $3/child, $12/family. Allow 1 hour.

Kid Culture

Arts in the Park The Yukon Art Society provides lunch-hour visual and performing arts events each summer. Every Wednesday is family day, with activities and performances aimed at young children.
Le Page Park,3rd Ave & Wood St; 867/667-4080. Mid-June-mid-Aug; 11am-2pm, Mon-Fri. Free.

Frantic Follies Typical of the many song-and-dance shows you'll find in Yukon and Alaska Gold Rush country, the content of this one is a combination of vaudeville, mildly risqué jokes, a bit of history, and general silliness. It's about two hours long.
In the Westmark Hotel 2nd Ave & Wood St; 867/668-2042; vaudeville.yk .net/index2/. Open late May-early Sept. Cost: $19/adult, $9.50/under 12.

Yukon Summer Music Camp This annual week-long camp offers workshops for children preschool age and up in instrumental music (classical and jazz), fiddle music, chamber and orchestral music, voice, and movement. Adults are welcome at some classes; participants are of all levels of experience and ability. On the final day of camp, performances are open to the public.
At the Yukon Arts Centre; 867/667-8575; www.yukonmusiccamp.info

Swimming The **Whitehorse Lions Aquatic Center** (200 Hamilton Blvd; 867/668-7665) has two pools, waterslide, hot tub, water bikes, and a sauna. Also see "Takhini Hot Springs" in "Excursions."

Animals Animals

Muktuk Tours In summer, you can tour the working sled-dog kennels of Frank Turner, a 1995 Yukon Quest champion, and meet the furry residents. In winter, mushing tours are offered. There's a B&B here that welcomes families.
Mile 929 Alaska Hwy, 6 km past Klondike Hwy junction; 867/393-1799; www.muktuk.com

Whitehorse Fishway Near the Whitehorse Dam, this fishway, reputedly the longest wooden fish ladder in the world, was built in 1959. The Chinook (King) salmon who make their way here have already come from the Bering Sea 3,000 km/1,864 miles away, and they're not done yet.

Visitors can picnic here and read interpretive panels about the variety of fish who swim by (they include char, grayling and salmon). Inside, there are some small fish on display and a few other exhibits. Check out the underwater windows and walk up the ramp outside to a viewing platform. Watching the fish come up the fish ladder and the water pour out over the spillway is a mesmerizing sight. It can also be dangerous, as signs point out; keep a close eye on small kids. *Riverdale (Lewes Blvd to Nisutlin Dr); 867/633-5965. Open daily late May-early Sept, 8:30am-8:30pm.*

Yukon Game Farm & Wildlife Preserve Combine a trip to Takhini Hot Springs with a visit to the birds, bison, caribou, elk, and musk oxen at this park which breeds, rehabilitates, and reintroduces wildlife to the wild. *Km 8, Takhini Hot Springs Rd; 867/633-2922; www.yukongamefarm.com. Tours: 10am, 2pm, 5pm, 8pm. Cost: $12/adult, $6/child. Gray Line tours (867/668-3225) leave from Westmark in Whitehorse: $21/adult, $10.50/child.*

The Great Outdoors

Bicycle, canoe, kayak rentals **Fireweed Yukon Hikes and Bikes** (102 Wood St; 867/668-7313; www.yukonhikes.com) rents bikes and offers guided hikes and biking trips. **Kanoe People** (867/668-4899; www.kanoepeople.com) have rentals and also lead guided multiday trips. They can help you craft your own adventure. **Up North Adventures** (103 Stickland St; 867/667-7905, 867/667-7035; www.upnorthadventures.yk.ca) rents canoes and can help set up self-guided one-day trips.

Flightseeing Several Whitehorse-based companies offer panoramic flight-seeing tours, often in combination with hiking or sightseeing; some include overnight stays. **Alkan Air** (105 Lodestar Lane; 867/668-2107; www.alkanair.com) offers flightseeing tours, starting at $250/person. **Alpine Aviation** (867/668-7725; www.yuk-biz.com/alpineaviation/) offers flightseeing trips for the Chilkoot Pass, and Kluane National Park.

Hiking A popular local hike, *Miles Canyon*, starts from the Schwatka Lake day-use area (2.5 km; allow 45 minutes) and follows the old tramline route. Each summer, the **Yukon Conservation Society** (302 Hawkins St; 867/668-5678; www.yukonconservation.org) offers free hikes in the Whitehorse area; most are suitable for all ages. Their **Ed-Ventures for Kids** program offers two-hour hikes, twice a week, for children and parents.

Horseback riding Trail rides on the Trail of 1898 are offered at the **White Horse Riding Stable**, and horses can be rented by the hour or by the day. *Mile 912.5 Alaska Hwy; 867/633-3086, 867/667-2843; Open daily May-Sept, 9am-7pm*

River Trips On the **Yukon River Cruise**, the *MV Schwatka* takes you on a narrated 1.5-hour trip from just below the Whitehorse dam through Miles Canyon and many historical sights. *867/668-4716; www.yukonriverfollies.com/index2/. June-early Sept, several daily departures; call for details. Cost: $25/adult, $12.50/child 6-12, free/under 6. Reservations recommended. Shuttle service to and from dock from downtown Whitehorse; call Gray Line (867/668-3225) for details.*

Shadow Lake Expeditions (867/393-2232; www.shadowlake.ca/) offers half- and full-day road, river, lake, and hiking trips for all ages; prices start at about $90.

Excursions

Takhini Hot Springs   Visit this venerable small resort, 40 km/25 miles north of Whitehorse, on a cool day. On a warm day, even the most avid young water addict may have trouble staying in this hot water longer than a few moments. The resort is somewhat shabby, but kids and adults enjoy it anyway. The keyhole shaped pool has a moderately shallow end, separated from the hotter and deeper rounded end. When parent reviewers visited, the showers were barely working and the drinking fountain was nonfunctional. Bring drinking water to avoid dehydration. There are lockers in the change rooms. Bring your own padlock or rent a lock and key for $.25 (plus a $10 deposit). Towels and swimsuits are available for rent for $1.50.

There is a restaurant, store, picnic area, and large campground as well as hiking trails, horseback riding, and horse-drawn wagon rides. Tobogganing and skiing are offered in winter.

867/633-2706; www.takhinihotsprings.yk.ca. Pool cost: $6.50/adult, $6/youth, $5/child. Horseback riding: 10 minute pony ride ($6), half-hour ride ($18), one-hour ride ($25). RV Park with 88 sites ($10.25-16.50/RV site) and tenting area ($13.75/site); showers, Laundromat, dump station.

Calendar of Events

February
Yukon Quest Dog Sled Race
867/668-4711; www.yukonquest.org
1,600 km/1,000 mile sled-dog race from Whitehorse to Fairbanks; many family-friendly events and activities, including Junior Yukon Quest for mushers ages 14-17

May-June
Yukon International Storytelling Festival
867/633-755; www.yukonstory.com

June
Yukon River Quest Canoe Race
867/668-4711; www.polarcom.com/~riverquest
742 km canoe race between Whitehorse and Dawson City

July
Whitehorse Rodeo
867/668-2372

August
Yukon River Bathtub Race
Whitehorse-Dawson City, 867/667-2148

Klondyke Harvest Fair
867/668-6864

September
Klondike Trail of '98 International Road Relay
867/668-4236; www.sportsyukon.com
All-day, all-night relay race from Skagway to Whitehorse

Resources

Yukon Visitor Reception Centre/Whitehorse
100 Hansen St, Box 2703, Whitehorse, YT Y1A 2C6; 867/667-3084,
867/667-5340; www.touryukon.com

Whitehorse Chamber of Commerce
302 Steele St, Ste 101 (T.C. Richards Bldg), Whitehorse, YT Y1A 2C5;
867/667-7545; www.whitehorsechamber.com/

City of Whitehorse
Tourism, 2121 2nd Ave, Whitehorse, YT Y1A 1C2; 867/667-6401;
www.city.whitehorse.yk.ca/

Alaska Highway:
Whitehorse to the Alaska Border (483 km/300 m)
With no road construction, this drive should take no more than six hours. Interesting stops are well located along the road. While most hiking in this rugged region requires skill and experience, visitor centers and roadside pullouts allow even the smallest explorer to experience terrific scenery.

1) **Whitehorse to Haines Junction** (155 km/96 m)
2) **Haines Junction to Beaver Creek** (296km/184m; 32 km/20m farther to Alaska border)

1) Whitehorse to Haines Junction (155 km/96 m)

A pleasant drive brings you to **Haines Junction**, bordering the magnificent **Kluane National Park**. The junction with the **Klondike Highway** (Hwy 2), which runs north to Carmacks and Dawson City, is 11 km/7 m east of Whitehorse. See "North Klondike Highway" for details.

At Haines Junction, the Alaska Highway meets with the **Haines Highway** (Hwy 3) to Haines, Alaska. This historic route was used by the Chilkat people when trading eulachon oil for furs (the so called "grease trail"). Jack Dalton turned it into a Klondike supply trail in the 1880s. And in the 1940s, it was made into an alternative supply route to reach the interior of the Yukon from the Inside Passage. Today, the highway allows access to the Alaska ferries that serve Haines, and makes a beautiful day trip (or longer) from Haines Junction (see Chapter 4, "Inside Passage").

HAINES JUNCTION

With about 800 residents, this village sits at the edge of the largest contiguous public parklands in the world: Kluane and Wrangell-St. Elias National Parks, Tatsenshini-Alsek Provincial Park, and Glacier Bay National Park & Preserve. Collectively, this wilderness has been named a UNESCO World Heritage Site. Here you'll find the continent's second highest—Canada's highest—peak, Mount Logan (5,959m/19,550 ft). Surrounded by glaciated peaks, Haines Junction feels higher than its 1,956 feet/596 meters. With a wealth of wilderness to explore, the town has attracted outdoors people from across the world, some of who have settled permanently here, giving the village its cosmopolitan flavor. There is plenty of accommodation here, along with, fuel, food, and park headquarters, making it a good base from which to explore the neighboring parks.

Places to Stay

Alcan Motor Inn

Junction of Haines & Alaska Hwys; 867/634-2371, 888/265-1018; www.yukonweb.com/tourism/alcan/
FYI: 22 rooms, refrigerator/microwave, some kitchenettes; public Laundromat & showers; gift shop, pets OK; open year round
This comfortable motel (it was the Gateway in a former incarnation) has a strategic location and good views.

The Raven Hotel ($$)

181 Alaska Hwy; 867/634-2500; www.yukonweb.com/tourism/raven/
FYI: 12 rooms, restaurant; gift shop; children under 10 stay free; RV park (full hookups); open May-Sept.
Staying at this European-style inn qualifies as a splurge, but it's worth it. From well-appointed rooms to the lovely flower garden and first-rate restaurant, it's elegant yet comfortable and family-friendly. Owners Christine and Hans Nelles gave up professional careers in Germany to become Yukon innkeepers and the Raven is the fruit of their labors. For an extra $10 per person, breakfast is included. Open to the public as well as to hotel guests, the restaurant is strong on European entrées. There's no kids' menu; however, children's preferences are accommodated, and adult entrées can be made to serve two or more kids. European breakfasts feature fresh-baked breads, croissants and pastries, cold cuts and cheese. Call for hours; reservations are recommended.

66 PARENT COMMENTS 99

"The building is like an immaculate, oversize cottage. The kids loved it here; the rooms were large, the beds very comfortable, and having a zillion stations available via satellite TV didn't hurt, either. Finding this place in the middle of nowhere reminded us of a fairy tale."

Camping

In town, the **Kluane R.V. Kampground** (Mile 1016 Alaska Hwy; 867/634-2709, 866/634-6789; e-mail: kluanerv@yknet.yt.ca. 60 sites, full hookups, picnic tables, showers, Laundromat, dump station, firewood, fuel store, gift shop, hiking trails) has RV and tent sites amid a partly wooded and scenic location. The **Pine Lake Campground** (6.7 km east of Haines Junction, Mile 1012 Alaska Hwy; 42 sites [tent and RV], water, shelter, playground, boat launch, nature trail; open late May-early Sept), operated by the Yukon Government, has a lovely lake sandy beach.

Places to Eat

Village Bakery & Deli/The Fish Hook

Across from the Haines Junction Visitor Reception Centre; 867/634-2867
Hours: 7:30am-9pm

Among the fresh, eclectic offerings are sourdough pizza, deli sandwiches, fountain drinks (excellent shakes), vegetarian dishes such as spanakopita, espresso drinks, ice cream, smoked salmon, and creative pastries. Seating is outdoors on the deck (there is heated shelter as needed). Salmon barbecues are held from time to time.

See also "The Raven" in "Places to Stay."

What to See & Do

Shopping   **Madley's General Store** (103 Haines Rd; 867/634-2200; e-mail: medleys@yknet.ca) has a full range of groceries, a hardware department (with outdoor gear and supplies), a bank with ATM, and a post office.

Biking, Canoeing, Hiking, Kayaking, Rafting   Rent bikes and canoes from **Paddle Wheel Adventures** (867/634-2683; www.paddlewheeladventures.com) and take off on your own, or let them take you on a guided trip. Rent bikes by the hour or the day, canoes by the day. They also offer flightseeing, heli-hiking and fishing trips, and whitewater rafting trips of various lengths. **Kluane Ecotours** (219 Haines Rd, 27 km/17 miles south of Haines Junction; 867/634-2626; www.kluaneco.com) based at Kathleen Lake, offers day and multiday guided hikes, and canoe and kayak trips geared for various ages and abilities.

Horseback Riding   Take a day ride or arrange for a guided multi-day trip with **Yukon Trail Riding** (867/634-2386). Prices start at $20 an hour. Overnight trips start at $110 per day.

Swimming   At **Shakwak Valley Community Swimming Pool** (off Alaska Hwy, next to the skating rink and convention centre; 867/634-7105) there's an outdoor pool, open mid-May to September.

Excursions

Kluane National Park and Reserve   This park that takes up the southwest corner of Yukon Territory is huge, but only a tiny bit of it is accessible by road. What can be driven to is breathtaking. In addition to Mount Logan, the park has some of the largest icefields outside the polar regions.

☛ **Parent Tip—Feeding the Crew**

You'll find few restaurants or grocery stores between Haines Junction and Beaver Creek. And road construction can add an hour or more to the 4.5-hour trip. Although Burwash Landing has all services, parent reviewers have had dubious luck, at best, in feeding their kids there. To be safe, pack box lunches with you from Haines Junction. The Raven will prepare a box lunch on request. Takeout fare from Village Bakery is another excellent option; or go to Madley's General Store and purchase supplies for a car meal. Don't forget to carry water, too. ▣

Road access for the park is at Kathleen Lake on the Haines Highway and Sheep Mountain, northwest of Haines Junction along the Alaska Highway. (See "Inside Passage.")

The national park visitor center doubles as the Haines Junction Visitor Reception Centre. Staff dispenses information on hiking, traveling, activities, and conditions in the park, as well as on its natural history and inhabitants. Outfitters who guide visitors to the park can be found in Haines Junction and surrounding communities; ask at the visitor center.

An easy self-guided nature trail introduces visitors to the ecosystem of the park. An alcove with art supplies and information just for kids is a welcome addition at the well-equipped visitor centre. A theatre shows films on the park and region. *National Park main switchboard: 867/634 7250; parkscan.harbour.com/kluane/. Haines Junction Park Visitor Centre: 867/634-7207. Open daily mid-May-early Oct; most weekdays, rest of year. Yukon Visitor Reception Centre: 867/634-2345; open daily, 8am-8pm, mid-May-mid-Sept.*

Resources
The Village of Haines Junction
Box 5339, Haines Junction, YT Y0B 1L0; 867/634-7100; www.hainesjunctionyukon.com Tourist and City Information

2) Haines Junction to Beaver Creek
(328 km/204 m to Alaska border)

The 296-km/184-mile drive from Haines Junction to **Beaver Creek** rivals the northern Rockies for sheer scenic beauty. To the left are the high peaks of the Saint Elias Mountains, and to the right, after Milepost 1061, is beautiful, deep-blue Kluane Lake. Be sure to check on road conditions and construction work before leaving Haines Junction.

The **Spruce Beetle Interpretive Trail,** a 1.7-km loop (at Mile 1030) is 23 km/14 miles north of Haines Junction. It introduces the spruce bark beetle that has been devastating northern spruce forests in recent decades. Over 70 percent of the Kenai peninsula's forests have been killed by it. The beetle is a relative of the pine mountain beetle that has been eating its way through the forests of central and northern British Columbia and of the spruce budworm that has destroyed forests in eastern Canada and New England. Evidence is beginning to point to global warming as a cause of the beetles' transcendence; shorter winters and dormant seasons have given the beetles more time to proliferate.

A mile beyond the trail is **Bear Creek Summit**, the highest point on the Alaska Highway between Whitehorse and Fairbanks (1,004m/3,2094 ft). At km 1692/Mile 1052, you'll get your first look at **Kluane Lake**, the Yukon's largest. The small **Sheep Mountain Visitor Reception Centre** (open daily, mid-May-mid-Sept, 9am-5pm) at km 1706.6/Mile 1028.8is the second of the park's two visitor information centers. Stop for a restroom break (pit toilets) and to peek through the telescopes trained on the mountain where Dall sheep are often seen in spring and late summer (look for dots of white high up). Staff can answer questions; there are videos to watch and print information on the area. From 1 km north of here, you can take the short (.5 km) **Soldier Summit Trail** to a viewpoint overlooking Kluane Lake.

At Milepost 1072 is **Congdon Creek Campground** (81 sites, $8/site; dedicated tenting area, pit toilets, water, firewood, picnic tables, kitchen shelters; sandy beach, boat launch), the only public campground on Kluane Lake in a beautiful location. There's a short interpretive trail here.

Eighteen km/11 miles north is the tiny village of **Destruction Bay,** with all services. The town was built to support the construction of the Alaska Highway. It got its name from a storm that destroyed the encampment there in 1942.

Kluane Museum of Natural History At **Burwash Landing,** visit this excellent small museum that displays animals in natural settings. There are little nooks and crannies to explore with interesting tidbits of information on the Tutchone Indians and local flora and fauna. A tiny theatre shows films. The gift shop has locally made arts, crafts, and books. Families with small fry who are phobic about using pit toilets can take advantage of the flush toilets. Next to the museum is the self-billed "world's largest gold pan," 21 feet in diameter. *867/841-5561; e-mail: kluanemus@yknet.yk.ca; open daily, mid-May-mid-Sept, 9am-9pm. Cost: $3.75/adult, $2/child 6-16, free/under 6, $9.50/family.*

Between Burwash Landing and Beaver Creek you'll find all services and campgrounds, public and private.

BEAVER CREEK

Close to the Yukon/Alaska border, this small town of 112 offers no family attractions, but does have several comfortable hotels. For reasons not entirely clear, Beaver Creek boasts a large Westmark Hotel and a motel with one of the oddest family rooms you're likely to encounter in the Yukon.

Places to Stay

1202 Motor Inn ($-$$)
Mile 1202 Alaska Hwy; 867/ 862-7600; www.1202motorinn.com
FYI: 28 rooms, family suite, some kitchenettes; restaurant; kids under 12 stay free; RV park (hookups, water, dump station, showers); gas station, cash machine, showers; pets OK
Downstairs there's a café and a general store. There are basic motel rooms, sev-

eral with kitchenettes, but if you can, book the family suite upstairs. It's an over-the-top extravaganza: a huge room with two king-size beds, one double, and one single bed; a full kitchen featuring a log counter with seven stools; and a leather sofa, recliner, and armchair set around an enormous TV. Down a corridor is the two-room bathroom. Above it all, moose, deer, and elk trophies gaze down sternly.

❝ PARENT COMMENTS ❞

"Our daughter didn't want to sleep under the moose head, but she got over it. The kitchen was not fully furnished with dishes, although there were plenty of utensils. We were afraid the noise from the café below would keep us up, but the soundproofing was fine."

Westmark Inn Beaver Creek ($)
Mile1202 Alaska Hwy; 867/862-7501, 800/544-0970;
www.westmarkhotels.com
FYI: 174 rooms, restaurant; Laundromat; grocery store, gas station; RV park (hookups, tent sites, showers, dump station)

Places to Eat
Buckshot Betty's
Mile1202; 867/862-7111; e-mail: carmenhinson@sympatico.ca
Hours: 24/7, year round
This new restaurant is also the site of a campground (tents only) along with several cabins. The bakery receives good reviews.

Resources
The **Visitor Reception Centre**, at the south end of town (1,202 milepost) has a wildflower exhibit and information on the region.
On the Alaska Highway near the Westmark; 867/862-7321. Open daily, 8am-8pm mid-May-mid-Sept
The **Canada-US international border** is 32 km/20 miles north of Beaver Creek on the Alaska Highway. You'll gain an hour when you cross into Alaska.

Alaska Highway:
Alaska Border to Delta Junction (200 miles)
This stretch of highway has less exciting scenery than the previous stretch, but road conditions are fine and you should be able to cover the distance in under four hours. Even if you don't stay in Tok, its two fine family restaurants are worth investigating.
1) **Alaska Border to Tok** (92 miles)
2) **Tok to Delta Junction** (108 miles)
TIME SAVER: The Tok Cutoff: Tok to Glennallen (139 m)

1) **Alaska Border to Tok** (92 miles)

The drive to Tok takes you through the **Tetlin National Wildlife Refuge**, home to black and brown bears, wolves, coyotes, lynx, moose, caribou, and a host of birds. Stop in at the **Tetlin National Wildlife Refuge Visitor Center** (Mile 1229 Alaska Hwy; open daily June-Labor Day, 8am-4:30pm) for wildlife exhibits and videos, visitor information, nature talks, and a large observation deck with telescopes, looking out over the refuge. There's a restroom here as well. Several campgrounds are spaced along the Alaska Highway. At Milepost 1254, **Deadman Lake Campground** has 16 forested sites (pit toilets, firepits, picnic tables, boat ramp, no drinking water). A short self-guided nature trail leads to an observation deck overlooking the lake; bring binoculars to spot the many waterfowl. At **Lakeview Campground** (Milepost 1256.7; pit toilets, firepits, picnic tables, no drinking water) there are eight campsites next to Yarger Lake; this campground is not recommended for trailers or RVs longer than 30 feet.

The **Taylor Highway** (Hwy 5), which runs south from the town of **Eagle**, AK, joins the Alaska Highway at Milepost 1306. For information on driving this route, see "Top of the World and Taylor Highways," later in this chapter.

TOK

Tok sits at the crossroads of the Alaska and Taylor highways. Running southwest from Tok is the **Tok Cutoff**, a shortcut that connects Tok with the Richardson Highway (Hwy 4) to the southwest. Just to make things confusing, the Alaska Highway, which is Highway 1 in Canada, becomes Highway 2 when it crosses the border into Alaska. The Tok Cutoff (Hwy 1) joins the Richardson just south of Gakona and at Glennallen continues west to Anchorage as the Glenn Highway (also Hwy 1).

There's not much to do in Tok, but thanks to its pivotal location, it gets a lot of traffic. It has an abundance of good, affordable accommodation and two of Alaska's most family-friendly restaurants. Tok is a good place to load up on gifts at shops selling quality Alaska souvenirs.

Places to Stay

Golden Bear Motel ($)

907/883-2561; www.akpub.com/akbbrv/golde/
FYI: 60 rooms; pets OK on approval; restaurant; gift shop; RV Park (tents OK, picnic tables, showers, Laundromat, dump station); motel open year round
This comfortable motel is not fancy, but is convenient and reasonably priced. The gift shop here is worth investigating.

Westmark Inn ($$)

Junction of the Alaska & Glenn Hwys; 907/883-5174; www.westmark.com
FYI: 92 rooms, family rooms; restaurant; gift shop, open May-Sept.

☛ **Parent Tip**

If you have some shopping to do, take advantage of the gift shops in Tok, especially the enormous hotel gift shop at the **Westmark,** which has some of the best bargains in Alaskana in the state. They offer an extra-large selection of children's clothing, toys, and games and an excellent array of children's books on Alaska. If you're staying here, you're likely to be given coupons for the store to add to the savings. Big cruise-tour companies park busloads of tourists here, and it can be crowded. ◙

Young's Motel ($)
Mile 1313.3 Alaska Hwy; 907/883-4411
FYI: 43 rooms, restaurant
This simple motel offers little in terms of ambience, but the location next to Fast Eddy's (see "Places to Eat") is handy.

Camping

South of town is the **Tok River State Recreation Site** (south of town, at Milepost 1309; 43 campsites, $10/site; pit toilets, picnic tables, firepits, boat launch, nature trail; interpretive programs in summer.) Maximum vehicle length that can be accommodated here is 60 feet.

For in-town RV parks, see the **Golden Bear Motel** and **Gateway Salmon Bake.**

Places to Eat

Fast Eddy's
At Young's Motel, mile 1313.3 Alaska Hwy; 907/883-4411
Hours: 6am-midnight (summer); 7am-11pm (rest of year)
This large family restaurant is always busy, but efficient service makes for short waits. It's universally popular with travelers on the Alaska Highway. Offerings include hearty salads, pizza and pasta, burgers, seafood, and meat-and-potatoes entrées. The kids' menu includes dino (chicken) nuggets. Prices are moderately high and so is quality.

Gateway Salmon Bake
Mile 1312 Alaska Hwy; 907/883-5555 (summer), 520/685-2687 (rest of year); e-mail: salmonbake@tokalaska.com
Hours: Mon-Sat 11am-9pm, Sun 4-9pm
This first-class salmon bake is huge with a grill and picnic tables outdoors. A spacious indoor room has rows of picnic tables favored by salmon bakes. On the menu are halibut, salmon, and buffalo burgers, footlong reindeer hot dogs (real reindeer), baked beans, and a salad bar—all of which can be washed down with a bottomless lemonade or iced tea. Explore the quirky décor while your fish is on the grill. Antiques are everywhere; condiments are stowed in an antique, cast-iron wood stove with an enamel cover. Outside, a tiny, funky

shop sells locally made gifts, and a little antique shop has second-hand tchotchkes. If you don't have wheels, Gateway will pick you up from and drop you off at your hotel; call 907/883-5555 for the free shuttle. There's also an RV park here, but no hookups. Camping is thrown in free with your meal.

What to See & Do

At **Mukluk Land**, billed as "Alaska's Most Unique Family Visitor Park," you can view the "world's largest mukluk," the "Alaska Highway's largest mosquito," and some museum displays. There are dogsled rides and a kids' igloo (where very young kids can bounce their wiggles out), videos, more games, and of course, gold panning.

Mile 1317 Alaska Hwy; 907/883-2571; www.tokalaska.com/mukluk/. Open daily 1-9pm, June-Aug. Cost: $5/adult, $2/child (gold-panning $5 extra/person).

Calendar of Events

March
Race of Champions
907/883-6874
Sled Dog Race

Resources

Alaska Department of Fish & Game
Box 355, Tok, AK 99780; Milepost 1314.2 across Center St from the Mainstreet Visitors Center; 907/883-2971; www.state.ak.us/adfg/adfghome/

Mainstreet Visitors Center
Proclaimed as the largest natural log structure in the state, this large, well-staffed and well-equipped visitor center has everything needed for trip-planning statewide. *Milepost 1314. 907/883-5775; www. tokalaskainfo.com. Open daily 8am-5pm. May-Sept; until 7pm June-Aug.*

Tok Alaska Public Lands Information Center
P.O. Box 359, Tok, AK 99780
Milepost 1314. 907/883-5666, 5667. www.nps.gov/aplic/about_us/taplic/.
Open 8am-7pm (mid-May-Sept), Mon-Fri, 8am-4:30pm (rest of year)
Extensive information on public lands for tourists, knowledgeable staff

US Fish & Wildlife Service
Box 155, Tok, AK 99780
Across the Alaska Hwy from the Mainstreet Visitor Center at Milepost 1314.1.
Open 7:30am-5pm, Mon-Fri; 907/883-5312
Information on Tetlin National Wildlife Refuge, fishing licenses

2) Tok to Delta Junction (108 miles)

The final lap of the Alaska Highway features breathtaking views of the Alaska Range to the west, with three handsome, ice-covered peaks above 11,000 feet, rushing rivers, meandering streams, and deep blue lakes. At Mile 1332, **Moon Lake State Recreation Site** has a picnic area and sandy beach, 15 campsites ($10/site), with water and pit toilets. At Delta Junction, the Alaska Highway merges with the Richardson Highway. For practical purposes, the 96 miles from Delta Junction to Fairbanks is sometimes counted as part of the Alaska Highway, but its official end is in Delta Junction.

DELTA JUNCTION

This town of 3,000 has several tourist attractions and all services. Its biggest attraction, however, is closed indefinitely: the tour of TransAlaska Pipeline Pump St. #9, along with all the state's other pipeline tours, has been suspended owing to security concerns. Check with the **Delta Junction Visitor Center** for any changes to this policy. The center has historical displays, exhibits, restrooms and is well staffed. The monument marking the end of the Alaska Highway is also here, a photo op in the making.
Junction of Alaska & Richardson Hwys; 907/895-5068; open daily 8am-8pm. June-mid-Sept.

Places to Stay

Alaska 7 Motel ($$)
Mile 270.3 Richardson Hwy; 907/895-4848; www.alaska7motel.com
FYI: 16 rooms, refrigerators, some kitchenettes; kids under 11 stay free
This basic motel is clean and reasonably comfortable, with satellite TV.

Kelly's Alaska Country Inn ($)
1616 Richardson Hwy; 907/895-4667; www.kellysalaskacountryinn.com;
FYI: 21 rooms; refrigerators, some kitchens, kids under 12 stay free
Again, you'll find satellite TV here. Rooms are large and comfortable.

Camping

A good camping option just outside Delta Junction is the **Delta State Recreation Site** (Mile 267, Richardson Hwy; 25 sites, pit toilets, water, picnic area and covered shelter). Across the highway is the Delta River and beyond it, views of the Alaska Range. There's even an airstrip for "fly-in camping."

For other camping options, see "Big Delta State Historical Park."

Places to Eat

Alaskan Steak House & Motel
265 Richardson Hwy; 907/895-5175; www.wildak.net/~akstkhse
Hours: open daily 5am-10pm
This basic family restaurant serves up hearty meals.

Pizza Bella
265 Richardson Hwy; 907/895-4841, 907/895-4524
Hours: open daily, 10am-10pm
Bring the small fry here to get their fix of pizza at this popular restaurant which also serves pasta dishes, seafood, and steaks.

Buffalo Center Diner
Mile 265.5 Richardson Hwy; 907/895-4055
Hours: Sun-Thurs 6am-9pm, Fri-Sat 6am-10pm (summer); Sun-Thurs 6am-8pm, Fri-Sat 6am-9pm (rest of year)
Situated next to the Sullivan Roadhouse, this resembles any burger joint you'd find in the lower 48, except that it serves real buffalo. It's a friendly, no-frills place, popular with residents.

See also Rika's Roadhouse in "Big Delta Historical Park."

What to See & Do

Sullivan Roadhouse Historical Museum The town's outstanding tourist attraction, built in 1905 and beautifully restored, is the oldest remaining roadhouse in the interior of Alaska. There are old photos of the roadhouse in operation. Exhibits on how people were fed (including a vegetable garden) and the role played by roadhouses in Alaskan history give a feeling for life in the state's pioneer times.
Mile 267 Richardson Hwy; 907/895-5068 or 895-4415;
www.alaskan.com/sullivanroadhouse/. Open late May-mid-Sept, Mon-Sat 9am-5:30pm, closed Sun. Cost: free.

Big Delta State Historical Park This 10-acre park on the banks of the Tanana River is a National Historic Site. Pick up a walking-tour brochure and explore. The principal attraction is **Rika's Roadhouse**, a genuine 1909 roadhouse along the Valdez-to-Fairbanks Trail. The roadhouse was operated, then owned, by Swedish immigrant Rika Wallen from 1917 to 1947 (Rika lived on until 1969). Today, it houses a large restaurant and gift shop. Some of the roadhouse has been restored with period furnishings. Another interesting restored building is a Washington Alaska Military Cable and Telegraph System (WAMCATS) station designed to speed communications between Alaska and Washington, DC, which at the turn of the last century could take as long as a year. A sod-roofed cabin contains antique farming implements and tools.

There are flower gardens to admire and lots of grass to run across. But keep an eye on the whereabouts of young children: the wide, swiftly moving Tanana River has steep banks. This was the site of a construction camp for the Richardson Highway in the 1920s. There was no bridge then; crossing the Tanana required a ferry ride. Interpretive signs tell the interesting story of how truckers rebelled against paying the high ferry tolls levied by the government.

Rika's Roadhouse is a popular stop for tour groups; in mid-summer, you're likely to find several tour buses here whenever the roadhouse is open. Food is served cafeteria style; choices are limited but good; prices are fairly high. Reindeer dogs will appeal to kids with adventurous appetites, while grilled cheese sandwiches should satisfy the rest. Baked goods, made on the premises, are renowned, especially pies. The gift shop has a wide selection—and price range—of items, from the crudest of souvenirs to wolverine and ermine fur coats.

The well-equipped campground has 23 RV sites, $5/vehicle, picnic area, toilets, water, and dump station.

Mile 275 Richardson Hwy; Park open daily 8am-8pm. Rika's Roadhouse and Landing: 907/895-4201; www.rikas.com. Open: mid-May-mid-Sept 9am-5pm. Closed in winter. Cost: free.

Resources

Delta Junction Chamber of Commerce
PO Box 987LP, Delta Junction, AK 99737; 907/895-5068, 877/895-5068; www.wildak.net/chamber/

TIME SAVER: The Tok Cutoff: Tok to Glennallen (139 m)

The Tok Cutoff is a timesaver for motorists from Fairbanks or on the Alaska Highway headed to Anchorage and points south. Highway 1, the **Tok Cutoff** (strictly speaking, it's a northern spur of the Glenn Highway), runs southwest from Tok to the junction with the Richardson Highway (Hwy 4). The highways merge for 14 miles, then separate again. The Glenn Highway turns west to Anchorage, a scenic drive of 189 miles through a beautiful region of mountains and lakes where quite a few Anchorage residents have built summer homes.

The Richardson continues south 115 miles to Valdez, over spectacular Thompson Pass and close to Worthington Glacier. If you have the time, consider driving at least some of the Richardson Highway that runs between Delta Junction and Valdez. For details, see "Fairbanks and the Interior."

The road becomes increasingly scenic as you approach the Wrangell Mountains. Look for **Mount Sanford** to the south, a dormant volcano. The road follows the Tok and Little Tok rivers, goes through the small Athabascan community of **Mentasta Lake,** and climbs to **Mentasta Summit** (2,434 feet). The **Mentasta Lodge** (907/291-2324), 47 miles from Tok, offers accommodation, food, and fuel.

Porcupine Creek State Recreation Site, 61 miles south of Tok, has 12 campsites ($10/site), pit toilets, water, fire pits, picnic tables, and hiking trails. As you travel south, there are frequent turnouts where you can park and admire the view. Four miles later, at the junction with the Nabesna Road, turn off for the **Slana Ranger Station** (907/882-5238; open daily 8am-5pm, Memorial Day-Sept) with restrooms that feature flush toilets. Here at the border of **Wrangell-St. Elias National Park and Preserve** you can pick up information on the park and road conditions. From here, you can drive the 45-mile **Nabesna Road**—but only the first four miles are paved, and there are no public campgrounds. At **Gakona**, four miles before the junction with the Richardson Highway, the **Gakona Lodge** (907/822-3550), a historic road-house, is the site of a small restaurant, store, gift shop, cabins, and an RV park.

At **Gakona Junction**, the Glenn Highway Tok Cutoff joins the Richardson Highway and the highways merge for 14 miles before the Glenn Highway peels off, heading west to Anchorage.

👆 Parent Tip

There are few services along the Tok Cutoff, so make sure your gas tank and cooler are full before heading out of Tok. For groceries, try **Three Bear Foods** (Mile 1314 Alaska Hwy, 907/883-5195) or **Tok Saveway** (Mile 124.4 Tok Cutoff, 907/883-5389.) ▣

GLENNALLEN

Just east of the Glenn and Richardson Highway junction, Glennallen is a major population center in the Copper River Valley. All services are available, with motels, restaurants, and a large grocery store: **Park's Place** (Mile 188 Glenn Hwy, 907/822-3334; e-mail: parks@alaska.net). The **Copper River Valley Visitor Information Center** (junction of Richardson & Glenn Highways, 907/822-5555; open daily in summer, 8am-7pm) can fill you in on the many attractions in this area.

Places to Stay
New Caribou Hotel ($$)
Glenn Hwy; 907/822-3302; www.caribouhotel.com
FYI: 55 rooms & suites, restaurant, gift shop
This hotel is the largest and best equipped in town. The restaurant is a cavernous operation serving large tour groups efficiently.

Camping
Several excellent public campgrounds are in the vicinity. Try **Dry Creek State Recreation Site** (58 treed sites, $12/site, picnic and group sites, walk-in campsites). Note that mosquitoes can be a problem here.

For information on the Richardson Highway from Delta Junction to Fairbanks, and south from Gakona Junction and Glennallen to Valdez, see "Fairbanks and the Interior." For information on the rest of the Glenn Highway, see "Anchorage."

North Klondike Highway:

Whitehorse to Dawson City (536 km/333 m)

1) **Whitehorse to Carmacks** (180 km/112 m)
2) **Carmacks to Dawson City** (356 km/221 m)

The one-way trip takes seven hours from Whitehorse. Dawson's many attractions warrant at least two days. Driving the full loop to the Alaska Highway via the Top of the World and Taylor highways from Dawson adds at least another day. Side trips include the 15-hour drive north on the Dempster Highway from Dawson to Inuvik, on the Beaufort Sea (see page 224), and the shorter (105 km/65 m) side trip to historic Eagle, Alaska, on the Taylor Highway (see page 224).

1) **Whitehorse to Carmacks** (180 km/112 m)

The journey to Dawson City on the paved **North Klondike Highway** (Hwy 2) is lovely, and Dawson, as it's known here, is the most authentic and best-preserved Klondike community.

Buy gas before setting out from Whitehorse. Once you leave the Alaska Highway for Highway 2 (30 km/19 miles north of Whitehorse), you'll notice a decrease in traffic; there are no towns to speak of until you reach Carmacks. About 27 km/17 miles after the junction, you'll pass **Lake Laberge** on the east—yes, that Lake Laberge, where, according to Robert Service, "there are strange things done in the midnight sun by the men who moil for gold" (ask the kids to come up with a definition for 'moil'). There is a 16-site Yukon public campground here with water, picnic shelters, and pit toilets. Another Yukon public campground at **Fox Lake** (55.7 km/34.6 miles) has 33 sites, three of which are tent-only.

If you're in need of a snack and/or fuel break, **Braeburn Lodge** at km 88.8 has both, along with a few cabins and canoe rentals.

CARMACKS

The only town you'll encounter between Whitehorse and Dawson City, Carmacks has a population of 489, but seems smaller. Named for George Carmacks, the prospector who struck it rich on Bonanza Creek in 1896, the town was an important supply route on the way to the Klondike from Whitehorse. Sternwheelers stopped for supplies, as did prospectors. It has been home to the Tutchone and other First Nations for 10,000 years.

Places to Stay

Hotel Carmacks ($)
867/863-5221
FYI: 21 rooms; restaurant; 15 RV sites: Laundromat, showers, hook ups, dump station, grocery store and bakery, fuel
This hotel has been recently renovated and the location on the Yukon River can't be beat. However, the cigarette smoke can be thick, especially at the restaurant.

Camping

The town's best accommodation is at the beautiful **Tantalus Campground**, on the Yukon River just past the Visitor Center (tent and RV sites, water, picnic tables, and pit toilets). If you're hungry, pick up deli items at the hotel grocery store, head for the campground, and dine gazing over the river. There's a 2-km/1.2-mile boardwalk along the river with interpretive signs.

What to See & Do

Tage Cho Hudan Interpretive Center This museum showcases the life of the Northern Tutchones. Outside is a must-see for kids: a genuine woolly mammoth snare. Interpretive displays describe how human beings used to trap mammoths (a tricky task). Recent scientific discoveries in the Yukon have confirmed this fascinating bit of history.

Stop at the **Carmacks Visitor Reception Centre** (867/863-6330; open Mon.-Fri. 8:30am-5pm) for more visitor information.

2) Carmacks to Dawson City (356 km/221 m)

Between Whitehorse and Dawson City, Carmacks is your only reliable source of gas. Although a few small communities on the way have service stations, road traffic is infrequent, and there is no guarantee that there will be someone to sell you gas when you need it. Scenery is less spectacular than on other Yukon highways, but parent reviewers report more wildlife sightings.

Two kilometers out of Carmacks is the junction with the **Robert Campbell Highway** (Hwy 4) which runs east to Ross River, then south to Watson Lake.

At km 188/mile 116.8 from the Alaska Highway junction is the Yukon River's **Five Finger Rapids Trail**, with a picnic area and outhouses. The 1.5-km/.9-mile trail leads down to the rapids; it's a bit of a hike, and there are some stairs along the way, but it's manageable by small children. At km 237/mile 147.3, **Minto Resort** (867/633-5537; May-Sept) operates a campground, with tent and RV sites. **Pelly Crossing**, at km 270/mile 168, is an attractive Selkirk Indian community with all services.

At **Stewart Crossing**, km 340/mile 211.4, is the junction with the **Silver Trail** (Hwy 11), a popular side trip to the historic silver-mining communities of Mayo and Keno. It's paved the first 51 km/32 miles to Mayo, then gravel for 60 km/37 miles to Keno.

From Stewart Crossing to Dawson, the road winds into the mountains, getting steadily more beautiful. Watch for wildlife, including ptarmigan and rabbits wandering across the road. At km 364.9 is a Yukon government campground, **Moose Creek** (30 RV sites, 6 tent-only sites, $8/site, picnic tables, playground, hiking trails).

Perhaps the best photo op on the highway comes at **Tintina Trench Viewpoint** (km 460) where at a turnout you can stop to read about and see this titanic geologic feature: an 8-million-year-old trench along a fault line in the earth's crust that runs northwest-southeast for 725 km.

About 19 km/12 miles farther is the junction with the **Dempster Highway** (Hwy 5) that runs north to Inuvik in the Northwest Territories (see "Dempster Highway to Inuvik") As you approach Dawson, you'll start to see **goldmine tailings**. Soon, you'll be surrounded by these bare, high mounds (20-30 feet) of rock. This is what's discarded after the gold has been extracted during the dredge-mining process. These eerie mounds go on for miles, creating a strangely desolate, moon-crater effect. To understand how they were created, take a gold dredge tour in Dawson.

Roadhouses

Roadhouses have existed almost as long as roads. The need to "put up" for the night has not changed much over the centuries, though how we go about it certainly has. Today's chain hotels are just newer members of the same family that produced the roadhouses of Alaska and the Yukon.

Northern roadhouses were unique in that their existence was not merely a matter of comfort, but of life or death. In the northern interior's dark, icy winters, travelers needed to stop at frequent intervals, sometimes for days; horses and sled dogs needed a rest, too. A home could easily evolve into a roadhouse if it was conveniently placed along the road; strangers would drop by in search of a place to stay the night. Enterprising homeowners could make $2 a night per head—good money.

Some roadhouses evolved; others were planned. Some were awful, serving up horrific brews ("caribou stew") which contained awfully small bones! Beds were usually no more than a rough bunk without a mattress. And some were luxurious, with private bedrooms, comfortable furnishings, and delicious meals. A few, like Belinda Mulroney's establishments in Dawson City, evolved into genuine hotels.

During Gold Rush stampedes, roadhouses sprung up overnight, then disappeared when the prospectors did. Some developed reputations that survive to this day, like Rika's Roadhouse and the Sullivan Roadhouse along the Valdez-to-Eagle route. Several thousand road houses existed in the Yukon and Alaska prior to World War I. As transportation improved, with better roads and air travel, the need for roadhouses decreased.

Few roadhouses remain today. Many burned down; some simply decayed or were turned to other uses. A few are in private hands as homes. However, a number remain and can be viewed or toured.

The Sullivan Roadhouse Museum, in Delta Junction, and Rika's Roadhouse, nearby at Big Delta National Historic Site, make an excellent introduction to the northern roadhouse culture. Farther south, the Gakona Roadhouse has been reborn as the Gakona Lodge. The Copper Center Lodge, a roadhouse since 1898, still functions as a hotel in Copper Center.

In the Yukon, the famous Carmacks Roadhouse has been restored by the Yukon Government, and the Montague Roadhouse, moved from an earlier location, can be viewed at km 322.8 of the north Klondike Highway.

Historic Roadhouses Along the Yukon

www.nps.gov/yuch/Expanded/ roadhouses/roadhouses/

This site records the fate of roadhouses in the Yukon-Charley River National Preserve.

Explore North

www.explorenorth.com/library/ weekly/aa071000a/

This article examines the Sullivan Roadhouse and northern roadhouses in general. ◼

DAWSON CITY

Here we come to the Yukon's best tourist attraction: a living relic of the Klondike Gold Rush. The entire town, along the Yukon River, is authentically restored and maintained. Dawson still has dirt roads, some boardwalk sidewalks, and—among original buildings that survived several major fires in the early 20th century—accurately reconstructed sites, such as the Palace Grand Theatre.

Attractions include a tour of the town's historic buildings, including cabins once occupied by Jack London and Robert Service, where you can hear presentations on the authors and a gold dredge tour (much more interesting than it sounds). Be sure to take one of the Visitor Center's walking tours during your stay. With hiking, boating, and excursions, it's easy to fill several days here and still have items left on your to-do list.

Stay downtown to soak up the atmosphere. Hotels are mostly period pieces, with décor and ambience in keeping with the Klondike era. They're authentic to a fault; none has air conditioning yet, although a few hotels (noted) are starting to add an air-conditioned suite or two. Dawson's restaurants are varied, with good quality and moderate prices.

History

This small city of 2,000 has a fascinating history, which a visit brings to dramatic life. For thousands of years, the Han people, Athabascans, lived here at the confluence of the Yukon and Klondike rivers, where they had a summer fish camp. White trappers and traders arrived by the 1800s, and in 1896, the discovery of gold led to the massive Gold Rush (see "Klondike Days and Nights"). In two years, the town's population grew to 35,000. In 1898, Dawson became Yukon Territory's first capital (moved to Whitehorse in 1953). No more gold-rich land was left to claim, so by 1899 prospectors moved on to seek their fortunes first in Nome, then Fairbanks. While no unclaimed stakes were available to draw prospectors here, the gold mines remained immensely productive. To supply the miners and get the gold out of the Yukon, up to 250 sternwheelers at a time cruised the Yukon River from spring ice break-up until the river froze in the fall. Dawson gradually faded as a community, although mines continued to produce gold, and still do; the last of the huge dredges shut down in the 1960s. The desolate piles of tailings outside town are the legacy of six decades of mining by up to 35 dredges at a time.

The town hung on with a small but stable population, thanks to continued gold mining and the building of the Alaska Highway. However, Dawson was forgotten by the rest of the world until the Canadian National Film Board documentary *City of Gold*, nominated for an Academy Award in 1957, raised interest in Klondike Gold Rush history. The film was written and narrated by Pierre Berton, who was raised in Dawson, the son of a prospector who crossed the Chilkoot Pass in 1898. The popularity of the film (still shown at the Dawson City Museum) is credited with the drive to renovate the city's historic buildings and re-create Dawson as a tourist destination. Starting in the late

1950s, the federal government bought up properties and began the ongoing process of restoring them. Among the acquisitions was the gigantic Gold Dredge no. 4, which had rested, abandoned and full of frozen mud, for over 30 years. Today, 17 Dawson City buildings are owned and operated by Parks Canada and open to visitors.

Getting to Dawson City

If you can't drive to Dawson, there are other options.

By Bus The **Dawson City Courier** (Whitehorse: 867/393-3334; Dawson City: 867/993-6688; www.dawsonbus.ca/ Cost: $90.75/one way; $163.35/round trip) bus service connects Dawson City with Whitehorse and Inuvik, with daily service between the capital and Dawson in summer; four times weekly in winter.

By Air **Air North** (867/993-5110; www.flyairnorth.com) has scheduled service to Dawson City as well as flights to other BC, Alberta, and Yukon cities.

You can get just about anywhere in Dawson on foot, and tours run to nearby attractions. However, there is one vehicle-rental option: Budget (451 Craig St; 867/993-5644; www.Yukon.net/budget/).

Places to Stay

Dawson City Bunkhouse ($)

Front & Princess; 867/993-6164; www.bunkhouse.ca/
FYI: 31 rooms, family suite; open mid-May-mid-Sept
The attractive Bunkhouse is one of the best values in town. The family suite has two twins and a double bed. Save even more by getting a room with shared bath. Many European travelers stay here.

Downtown Hotel ($$)

Corner of 2nd & Queen; 867/993-5346, 800/661-0514;
www.downtownhotel.ca
FYI: 59 rooms, some connecting rooms; restaurant; Laundromat; hot tub; gift shop
Open year round, this attractive hotel is comfortable. There's no air conditioning, but rooms have fans. The corner room on the second floor of the main building is especially large. The annex is where you'll find the hot tub, centrally located.

❝PARENT COMMENTS ❞

"We loved our room, but the steep flight of stairs leading up to it was a challenge. The kids investigated the hot tub, but the thought of being submerged in hot, swirling water when it was 80 degrees outside at 10pm was not appealing, even to them."

"The staff is very friendly, especially in the dining room. The guest laundry is only available for a couple of hours each day, so plan accordingly."

☛ Parent Tip—Staying Cool

There is little shade in Dawson and temperatures in the 80s are not unusual in July. On a sunny day (think 20 hours of sunlight), it can get very hot indeed. Night never completely falls, so you can't count on the darkness to cool things off before the sun blazes out again. If you're here during a spate of hot weather, check out a hotel room before signing in. A ground-floor location, cross ventilation, and ceiling fan help keep the temperature manageable. Also, check that windows have good screens. Mosquitoes are plentiful here. ▣

Eldorado Hotel ($$)

Corner of 3rd & Princess St; 867/993-5451, 800/764-3536;
www.eldoradohotel.ca
FYI: 52 rooms, some air conditioned; some kitchenettes; free airport shuttle;
kids under 12 stay free; Laundromat; open May-Sept
This hotel has larger rooms than some; the air-conditioned suites and dining room can be worth the splurge to stay here.

Triple J Hotel ($-$$)

5th & Queen, next to Diamond Tooth Gertie's; 867/993-5323, 800/764-3555;
www.triplejhotel.com
FYI: 47 units (26 motel rooms, 1 suite, 20 cabins) most units have kitchens;
free airport shuttle; kids under 12 stay free; Laundromat; pets OK in some
rooms (fee); open mid-May-mid-Sept
It's the cabins with kitchenettes that put this place on our list. The location across from Diamond Gertie's casino may not thrill you, but it's downtown.

Westmark Inn Dawson ($$-$$$)

5th & Harper Sts; 867/993-5542; www.westmarkhotels.com
FYI: 131 rooms; restaurant; Laundromat, gift shop, open May-Sept

Camping

The only RV option downtown is the **Gold Rush Campground** (4th & York; 867/993-5247; www.goldrushcampground.com; 83 sites, $16-30, hookups, showers, Laundromat, and dump station, open mid-May-mid-Sept). A mile south of town is the **Bonanza Gold Motel & RV Park** (2.4 km south on Hwy 2; 867/993-6789, 888/993-6789; www.bonanza.gold.ca; 64 sites, $12-35/vehicle, hookups, showers, Laundromat, free RV wash and gold-panning); there are also 15 motel units here. South of town, but handy to out-of-town attractions like Gold Dredge No. 4 is **Guggieville Campground** (Klondike Hwy & Bonanza Creek Rd; 867/993-5008; www.yukoninfo.com/guggieville/; 100 sites, $11-24/vehicle, hookups, dump station, car and RV wash, showers, Laundromat, gift shop). They run a gold-panning operation with discounts to those who camp here; tenting is permitted. All three campgrounds are open May to September and fill up early in summer, so reservations are recommended.

The prettiest campground around Dawson is the public **Yukon River Campground** (Top of the World Highway; 98 sites, $8/site, pit toilets, picnic tables, wood, hiking trails, playground; open May-Sept). But to reach it, you need to take the free ferry across the river. The ferry is tiny, and waits in mid-summer can be long.

Places to Eat

Amica's Ristorante

401 Craig St (corner of 5th); 867/993-6800
Hours: daily 11am-11pm
This may be your best bet for straightforward fine dining and air conditioning. There's a range of pasta offerings and pizzas; try the "Dredge Vedge" (vegetarian pizza) or the "Mad Trapper" (chicken, broccoli, and dill).

Bonanza Dining Room

3rd & Princess (in the Eldorado Hotel); 867/993-5451
Hours: Daily 7am-9pm, Sat until 10pm
This is standard hotel dining (steaks, seafood); food is fine and so is the air conditioning.

The Grubstake

2nd & King; 867/993-6706
Hours: Sun-Thurs 11am-10pm, Fri-Sat 11am-11pm
Dine-in or take-out pizza, subs, or barbecued ribs. You can also get delivery ($5 in town, $8 out of town). Various specials are offered. Internet access is provided.

Jack London Grill

2nd & Queen (in the Downtown Hotel); 867/993-5346
Hours: Daily 6am-10pm, Fri-Sat until 11pm
You can eat in or outside on the deck. Lunch offerings are casual, with more fine-dining options at dinner. There's no kids' menu, but at dinner time children can dine off the lunch menu, which features burgers and grilled cheese and ham. Adults can wash their dinners down with a draft beer from the Yukon Brewing Co.

Klondike Kate's

3rd & King St; 867/993-6527; www.klondikekates.ca/
Hours: daily 6:30am-11pm
This is one of the best bets for families in Dawson. The hearty breakfasts include kid favorites like French toast or buttermilk pancakes, with adult offerings such as five different takes on eggs Benedict. For lunch, it's soups, salads, burgers, and sandwiches, while dinners feature a range of steak, chicken, and fish entrées with pasta specials. The kids' menu offers the mandatory items: chicken fingers, grilled cheese, corn dogs, and macaroni and cheese. While you're waiting for your food, pick up a copy of "Klondike Kate's Northern Menu" and read some of the entries: "Sweet & Sour Mosquitoes," "Caribou

Parmigiana" or the "Northern Salad: choice aspen leaves, fireweed & boiled porcupine needles…" The building dates from 1904, when it was a grocery.

Rio Grill
1066 Front St (Front & King); 867/993-5683
Hours are variable, open summer only
This little café, open in summer, has all-outdoor, covered seating. Burgers, Mexican dishes, and assorted specials are on offer; you'll find high quality and low prices. This is where to send your starving teens.

RiverWest
On Front St between Queen & Princess; 867/993-6339
Hours: Mon-Sat 7am-7pm, Sun 8am-6pm
If you come early, you'll likely find the Parks Canada staff here in fancy dress, fueling up on lattés and muffins before starting work, getting ready to do their takes on Robert Service or Klondike goodtime gals. The pastries are excellent here. For a quick breakfast before boarding the *Yukon Queen II* for a trip to Eagle, stop by for a heated breakfast bagel or wrap with eggs, tomatoes, and cheese. Wraps and sandwiches are excellent; a few choices are served hot. Along with the espresso drinks is a range of smoothies.

What to See & Do

Stroll & Browse
The best way to experience Dawson is on foot. As you explore the town, you'll notice the huge black bugs everywhere. These are the famous spruce bark beetles which have been decimating Canadian and Alaskan forests for some years now.

Shopping   Although the appeal of Dawson lies in its historic authenticity, there is a downside. The town is so much a living museum that it can take awhile to find a real grocery store. There is one, though: **Dawson City General Store** (Front & Queen, 867/993-5475) has just about everything you'll need; Dawson doesn't have a pharmacy. For duds, head to the **Raven's Nook** (2nd & Queen, 867/993-5530). A selection of gold nugget and mammoth ivory jewelry and other gifts can be found at **Klondike Nugget & Ivory Shop** (Front & Queen, 867/993-5432) and at **The Gold Claim** (3rd between Princess & Harper, 867/993-6387). You can find a selection of books at **Maximilian's Gold Rush Emporium** (Front & Queen, 867/993-5486), along with gifts and souvenirs. Cool down with a trip to **Klondyke Cream & Candy** (Front St, 867/993-6453); the ice cream is terrific, portions are large, and the cones are homemade.

Visit the **Dawson City Visitor Reception Centre** at Front & King before you undertake serious sightseeing. The large log structure is among the best staffed and organized in the Yukon. In addition to tourist information, they sell tickets for Parks Canada tours.

Walking Tour of Downtown Dawson City   To get inside some of the restored buildings, you'll need to join a conducted tour. Centre staff conducts tours several times a day in Klondike-era costume and character, and they're great fun. Tours take you inside the reconstructed **Palace Grand Theatre**, the **Red Feather Saloon**, the old bank, and the historic 1901 post office, where you can buy real stamps and post letters with a quaint rubber Klondike stamp. The 90-minute tour also includes **Paradise Alley** (where Dawson's sex workers plied their trade), a dressmaker, blacksmith, and newspaper printing office. With the **Parks & Partners pass**, tours are bundled together for a reduced fee, which includes tours of **Dredge No. 4**, the **Bear Creek Complex**, the downtown core, and the **Commissioner's Residence**. The **Author Avenue Program** includes the **Robert Service Cabin**, **Jack London Cabin**, and a waterfront tour including the **S.S. Keno** and **Dawson City Museum**. This is a lot of walking to cram into one day; only you can gauge whether your family is up to the legwork. *Starts from the Visitor Reception Centre, 867/993-5566; www.yukoninfo.com/dawson/kva/. Several tours per day. Cost: $5/adult, $2.50/child 6-16, free/under 6, $12.50/family. Parks & Partners Pass: $25/adult, $12.50/child 6-16, $62.50/family. Costs can vary with package selected; call for details.*

Commissioner's Residence   This home of the Queen's representative to the Yukon from 1901 to 1916 has been fully restored. Today, the house and gardens can be toured in summer. A two-hour afternoon tea includes a private tour of the residence. Although probably not a top choice for young kids, older children should enjoy it. *Front St near Church St; Tours daily, June-mid-Sept. Cost: $5/adult, $2.50/child 6-16, free/under 6, $12.50/family. Afternoon tea: $20/adult, $10/child 6-16, free/under 6, $50/family.*

Jack London's Cabin   It's a bit of a hike from downtown, so allow at least 20 minutes to walk from the visitor centre; it's worth the effort. This modest log cabin was occupied by Jack London, then moved here from its original location 120 km north of Dawson (only some of the cabin ended up in Dawson; the rest was moved to Jack London Square in Oakland, California). London journeyed north in search of gold in 1897, at the age of 21. The cabin features photos and artifacts showcasing London's life and Klondike history, but the main reason to come here is to hear the presentation given by Dick North, the Yukon writer who led the successful search for the cabin in 1965. North knew London's two daughters personally and brings the writer to vivid life. *8th Ave near Grant St. Open daily mid-May-mid-Sept, 10am-1pm, 2pm-6pm. Presentations at 11:30am & 2:30pm. Cost: $2. About an hour. For further details, check at Visitor Reception Centre.*

Robert Service Cabin   Robert Service lived in Dawson from 1909 to 1912 in this modest two-room cabin. Furnishings are not original but do date from the period. Presentations by Parks Canada staff include the history of Service's life and recitations of poetry. Service was a shy bank clerk from

Jack London and Robert Service

Pack with you, or purchase on your trip, stories by Jack London and poems by Robert Service. Older children will be enthralled by London's great story "To Build a Fire" (it may be a little scary for younger children), and kids of all ages will enjoy the Klondike poems of Robert Service. Read some of these works together before visiting the two cabins. Alternatively, purchase some of their works on tape or CD in Dawson and elsewhere and play them in the car on the drive to Dawson.

Several Web sites contain a rich assortment of resources on these prolific authors:

Jack London International (www.jack-london.org)

This is a comprehensive European Web site maintained by fans and family of Jack London (English and German).

Jack London Foundation (jacklondonfdn.org)

This organization sponsors an annual writing contest open to high school students, grades 9 through 12.

Robert W. Service (www.robertwservice.com)

Visitors to this Web site are greeted by the recorded voice of Service. The site contains some poems and facts about Service's life. ▣

Scotland who returned to that profession after a few years of travel around the US and Canada, whereupon he was sent to the Dawson bank. The Gold Rush was long over when he arrived, but he turned the stories he heard from Dawson residents into thrilling poems and a novel.

8th Ave (between Mission & Hanson). Open June–mid-Sept. Presentations: 10am, 3pm. Cost: $5/adult, $2.50/child 6-16, free/under 6, $12.50/family. About an hour. For further details, check at Visitor Reception Centre.

Robert Service Show Twice daily, Tom Byrne takes on the character of Robert Service, introducing audiences to his life and reciting his poetry.

Front St, next to Klondyke Cream & Candy, e-mail: robertserviceshow@yahoo.com. Shows at 3pm, 8pm, mid-May–mid-Sept. Cost: $8/adult, free/under 10. Reservations recommended. For further details, check at Visitor Reception Centre.

S.S. Keno This recently refurbished sternwheeler, built in 1922, can be toured. It was one of the many sternwheelers that once plied the Yukon River; her last trip was in 1960. The tour includes the same film shown on tours of the *SS Klondike II* (see "Whitehorse").

Front St, next to the Canadian Bank of Commerce. Open June–mid-Sept. Cost: $5/adult, $2.50/child 6-16, free/under 6, $12.50/family.

A popular local attraction, **Diamond Tooth Gertie's Gambling Hall** is indeed a casino, decked out as a Gold Rush gambling hall. The business is a locally owned nonprofit that reinvests in the community. However, entrance is restricted to adults 18 and over.

The real Klondike Kate

The identity of Klondike Kate is something of a mystery. The name is usually applied to Kathleen Rockwell, a teenage dance-hall girl from Kansas, who worked at the Palace Grand Theatre. Popularly known as the "Queen of the Klondike" and the "flower of the north," she made a fortune and used much of it to grubstake a man who eventually left her. Her turbulent life eventually led her to Oregon where she lived to the age of 80, dying in 1957. ◙

Museums

Dawson City Museum Housed in the handsome, neoclassical Old Territorial Administration Building dating from 1901, the museum features excellent compact exhibits on First Nations and Klondike history. There are daily showings of the film classic *City of Gold,* and educational presentations. Interesting First Nations basketry and bead work is on display, as are historic photographs A set of historic locomotives is outdoors.
5th Ave & Mission St, 867/993-5291; users.yknet.yk.ca/dcpages/Museum.html. Open daily10am-6pm, mid-May-mid-Sept. Cost: $7/adult, $5/student, $16/family.

Dänojà Zho Cultural Centre Located next to the river, the cultural center celebrates the Tr'ondëk Hwëch'in traditions. It features distinctive buildings, especially a round building encircled with metal stakes at uneven heights like upright spears. Inside, the center is air conditioned. Displays showcase traditional ways of life and include exhibits by Han artists. Don't miss the fascinating film on the successful effort to preserve the Han language, which at one point rested on only five Native speakers. Today, Native schoolchildren are taught the language in grades 1-8. Kids will enjoy this film, especially how high technology played a role in language instruction.
Front & York Sts, across from the Visitor Reception Centre, 867/993-6768; trondek.com/centre.html. Open daily late May-late Sept. Cost: $5.

Culture

Gaslight Follies Another Klondike-era vaudeville type show, this one is first-rate. It's held in the **Palace Grand Theatre**, a National Historic Site, rebuilt in 1962 to look just as it did in 1899. The revue includes song, dance, and silly jokes.
King & 3rd, 867/993-6217; www.dawsoncity.org/attr_pg.php. Open mid-May-mid-Sept; shows 8:30pm. Cost: $15/adult, $7.50/child (on main floor), $17/balcony. About 70 minutes.

Klondike Institute of Art and Culture The institute offers a variety of programs, workshops, and classes in all the arts, some designed for children. They offer wilderness art excursions (multi-day art camps) and host the Yukon Arts Festival during Discovery Days in August. There are also some artist residencies.
Odd Fellows Hall, 867/993-5005; www.kiac.org

☞ Parent Tip: Box Seats

The **Palace Grand Theatre** has loads of charm, but kids will enjoy themselves more if you purchase tickets for box seats. Since the main floor does not slope, seats are all at one height; children will have difficulty seeing over the heads of adults in front of them. The elegant boxes along the sides of the two balconies allow spectators an unobstructed view. Ticket proceeds go back into the upkeep of the theatre and Dawson's visitor attractions. Shows often sell out; reserve a day or two ahead if possible. ◙

The Great Outdoors

Flightseeing   With 20-minute helicopter flightseeing trips, **Trans North Helicopters** (867/668-2177; www.tntaheli.com; $90/person) flies over historic gold-mining locales around Dawson. **Sifton Air** (867/634-2916) offers one-hour Klondike tours at $125/person.

Gold Panning   If you have wheels, you can try your hands at gold panning for free on the **No. 6 Gold Claim** (from Klondike Hwy, turn onto Bonanza Creek Rd, follow past Gold Dredge No. 4 and look for signs), owned by the Klondike Visitors Association. You will have to bring your own panning equipment and only panning by hand is allowed. Check at the visitor center for places to purchase panning equipment, a small investment. Several local operators will set you up with pans and guarantee that you'll find gold (which has been seeded to ensure everyone takes some home). Usually, they'll also sell you jewelry or settings to show off your finds. **Bonanza Gold** and **Guggieville** RV parks offer gold panning (see "camping"). **Eureka Gold Panning Adventures** (867/633-6519; www.eurekagoldpanning.com) take visitors on multi-day gold-panning adventures. The best choice for kids is the half-day gold-panning tour; children under 12 are free; transportation to and from Dawson is provided at additional cost. **Goldbottom Mining Tours** (867/993-5023; www.goldbottom.com/goldbottom; 16 km/10 miles south of Dawson on the Klondike Hwy to Hunker Creek Rd. Follow it for 15 km/9 mi to the Roadhouse; look for signs) will let you try your luck for $2. For $5, they'll guarantee you find gold. Mine tours are $20; $35 including transportation to and from Dawson.

Guided Tours   **Gold City Tours** (867/993-5175; www.goldcitytours.info) offers options including a one-hour city tour, combined city and gold-mining tours, a Midnight Dome evening tour, and a 12-hour drive up the Dempster Highway to the Arctic Circle. Prices start at $12/adult, $6/child.

Hiking   The short **Crocus Bluff Nature trail** takes hikers to a panoramic viewpoint over the city. The 400-meter hike turns into a 1.5-km/.9-mile hike if you walk from the Visitor Center. To reach trailhead parking, follow King Street until it turns into the Old Dome Road, or take the New Dome Road from the Klondike Highway just south of town. Along the road past trailhead parking are **Dawson City's historic cemeteries**. You can pick up a cemetery

Klondike Days and Nights
Dawson 1897-99

Dawson City was founded at the confluence of the Klondike and Yukon rivers, the site of a seasonal Han fishing camp until the Gold Rush brought an influx of prospectors. In 1897, Dawson had 3,500 residents; a year later, the population was around 35,000, the largest of any town west of Winnipeg. Dawson's founder, Joe Ladue, was a prospector-turned-merchant who realized he could make a better living selling to the prospectors than being one. He staked 160 acres at the marshy riverside, and operated his sawmill and a saloon. As demand grew, he could supply both houses and land to build them on.

During the turbulent years from 1897 to 1899, Dawson was at times chaotic, but tall tales to the contrary, the RCMP generally had things under control. Handguns were illegal in Dawson (something that astonished American prospectors), which accounted for the vastly lower death and crime rate there than in Skagway.

The presence of gold and people quickly drew entrepreneurs selling just about anything, giving rise to the town's nickname as "the Paris of the North." Fashions from Paris, oysters and champagne, you could buy just about anything in Dawson at a price. Scarce household items could cost a fortune; brooms cost $17.

Gambling halls, saloons, and theatres were plentiful, but so were churches and banks. Dawson burned twice in these years, in fires reputedly started by the same dance-hall girl. The town was filled with journalists, who kept the Gold Rush and dreams of would-be prospectors alive with their vivid accounts of life in the Klondike.

The vast numbers who arrived in 1898 were just in time to experience crushing heat, mosquitoes, and muddy streets. Many were penniless and interested only in financing their trip back home. They hired themselves out as laborers, after auctioning off the gear they had carried thousands of miles on their backs. Many were ill or became ill in the crowded town. Two hospitals filled with typhoid patients. Those whose claims failed to produce were glad to sell out to the big corporations who eventually moved the dredges in.

The population trickled away, and the town diminished in size; by the time Pierre Berton wrote Klondike Fever in the 1950s, Dawson had fewer than 500 residents. Ironically, whereas the Alaska Highway gave life to some small northern communities and kept others alive, it did just the opposite for Dawson. The Yukon River was no longer the highway of choice for moving goods and people in the northern interior. The Alaska Highway made the sternwheelers irrelevant. ◨

walking tour brochure at the Dawson City Museum. Longer, more strenuous hikes can be taken up **Midnight Dome** (the 885-meter hill behind Dawson, which you can also drive). The **Ridge Road Heritage trail**, a new 32-km/20-mile hiking/biking trail, runs from town out to the goldfields. Pick up trail brochures at the Visitor Centre.

River Trips A two-hour Yukon River trip to a First Nations fish camp is offered by **Fishwheel Charter Service** (867/993-6447; daily 3pm. Cost: $32/adult, $10/child). Tours run year round; winter tours include travel by dog team or snowmachine. **Taiga River Tours** (867/993-5539; www.taigariver tours.com) offers customized one- or multi-day river trips for a minimum of four passengers, with prices starting at $140 per person per day.

Swimming The outdoor **Dawson City Swimming Pool** (Fifth & Turner, 867/993-7412) can be a welcome relief from relentless summer sun.

Excursions

Gold Dredge No. 4 Tour This may not sound like an appealing tour—but it is. You and your kids will be glad you went. This enormous machine is two-thirds the length of a football field and eight stories high; it looks like a strange combination of building and boat. It's the largest of its kind to have operated in North America. The tour takes you through every part of the dredge and paints a vivid picture of the life of a dredge operator; a film on how this dredge was hauled out of the frozen mud and cleaned (a process that took years) is shown here. *Turn off Klondike Hwy and follow Bonanza Creek Rd 12.3 km/7.8 miles.*

Midnight Dome For a panoramic view of Dawson City, the Yukon River, and the surrounding Klondike Valley, head up to the Midnight Dome, five miles out of town. In mid-summer, drive up around midnight and enjoy the brief sunset. *Take the Klondike Hwy south to New Midnight Dome Rd and follow to summit.*

River of Culture Tours For this First Nations-operated tour, visitors board a paddle wheeler that heads to Little Moosehide Island for a smoked salmon barbecue. Trips include storytelling, language instruction, and entertainment. *Little Birch Cabin on Front St, 867/993-5482; e-mail: rivercii@yknet.yk.ca; mid-June-mid-Sept: noon, 3pm. Cost: $47/adult, $35/child. Allow 2 hours.*

Yukon Queen II This 110-passenger catamaran, owned by Gray Line of Alaska, takes visitors on a river excursion from Dawson City to Eagle, Alaska, and back again. The all-day trip allows you to visit the historic town of Eagle and return to Dawson without the pain of driving 158 miles of washboard roads. The trip takes about 3.5 hours from Dawson (downstream) and over 4.5 hours back, with a couple of hours in Eagle. You'll need to buy tickets in advance. Since you'll be crossing an international border, you can't purchase round-trip tickets. But you can purchase return trip tickets in Eagle. You'll need valid ID, such as a passport or birth certificate, if you're Canadian or American. This information is faxed ahead to Eagle, so that the border crossing is a breeze. The trip includes lunch and dinner.

This boat moves along at quite a clip, and has comfortable indoor seating, with plenty of room for restless youngsters to stretch their legs. An upstairs area has comfortable sofas, books, and photos about the region and its inhabitants. Visitors are also welcome on the bridge, where four seats offer the boat's best views. Outside, a covered viewing area has more seating. Along the way you'll pass the sternwheeler graveyard, where old sternwheelers can be seen sadly disintegrating, and bits of Klondike history are brought to life by a narrator. See "Eagle" for information on what to see and do there.

Note that the boat's primary mission is to carry package-tour passengers to and from Eagle. Most are loaded onto buses when they get off the boat at either destination. The Eagle dock is about a mile out of town; however, there is almost always room on the bus waiting for cruise-tour passengers, which is free. *Gray Line ticket office on Front St, 867/993-5599. One trip in each direction daily, mid-May-mid-Sept. Cost: $130/one way.*

Calendar of Events

July
Dawson City Music Festival
867/993-5584; www.dcmf.com
Folk musicians from across Canada perform over three days.

August
Discovery Days Festival
867/993-5575, 877/465-3006; www.dawsoncity.org
A weekend of events celebrating discovery of gold in the Klondike; many family activities; Klassic Klondike Film Festival, bathtub race, Yukon Arts Festival.

September
Great Klondike International Outhouse Race, KVA
867/993-5575, 877/465-3006; www.dawsoncity.org
As it sounds—contestants race homemade, decorated outhouses in teams of five.

Resources

Klondike Visitors Association
P.O. Box 389W, Dawson City, YT, Y0B 1G0; 867/993-5575, 877/465-3006; www.dawsoncity.org

Dawson City Visitor Reception Centre
P.O. Box 389, Dawson City YT, Y0B 1G0; 867/993-5566; www.yukoninfo.com/dawson/kva/
Operated by Tourism Yukon and Parks Canada, open daily 8am-8pm, mid-May-mid-Sept. Provides information, conducts walking tours of Dawson, and sells tickets to Parks Canada attractions

Parks Canada
P.O. Box 390, Dawson City, YT, Y0B 1G0; 867/993-7200, 867/993-7237; e-mail: dawson.info@pc.gc.ca; www.parkscanada.gc.ca

Top of the World and Taylor Highways:
Dawson City to Tok (298 km/185 m)

This spectacular trip takes more time than you might think. The stretch from the Alaska border to Chicken is steep, unpaved, and very slow going. Expect to travel around 30 miles per hour for this stretch, about five hours between Dawson City and Chicken, plus four hours in transit to and from Eagle.

1) **Dawson City to Alaska Border** (109 km/68 m) **and Taylor Highway Junction** (add 18 km/11 m)
2) **Taylor Highway Junction to Tok** (106 miles)
See page 224 for side trip to Eagle, (65 miles).

1) Dawson City to Taylor Hwy Junction (127 km/79 m)

The thrilling, mostly paved **Top of the World Highway** rises from Dawson at 320m/1,050 feet to an elevation of 1,376m/4,515 feet in less than 80 miles. Eleven miles across the Alaska border, at the junction with the **Taylor Highway** (Hwy 5), you can head east to visit the tiny, historic town of Eagle, or continue west through the tiny community of Chicken to Tetlin Junction where the Taylor and Alaska Highways meet. This circle route is open only in summer, and the state of the road between the international border and Chicken can be very poor—mostly mud and gravel. If you're driving a rental car, this route may be prohibited; check the small print in your contract. There are several campgrounds along the way, and services are reasonably spaced, but make sure you head out with a full tank.

To get to this route, you need to take the tiny **George Black Ferry** (867/893-5441, 867/993-5344), a free Yukon Government service that operates 24 hours a day. Since it carries only a few vehicles at a time, pack some patience, especially when you see yet another enormous RV trailing an SUV take up the entire ferry. To avoid lines, don't take the ferry at peak times: 7-11 am and 4-7 pm in summer. Tour buses have priority between 6-9am and 5-9pm. Best time to head out is early afternoon. The ride itself takes only a few minutes.

The Top of the World Highway is aptly named, as the road follows a knife-edge ridge that separates the Dawson Range from the Ogilvie Mountains. Turnouts allow you to park and marvel at the scenery; several have outhouses, picnic tables, and trails. When you reach the summit, which is marked with a cairn at a rest area, take a look down at the tiny, lonely international border stations for Canada and the U.S. Like the highway, this border is open only in summer, mid-May to mid-Sept, and only 12 hours per day. *NOTE: Before you head out on the Top of the World or Taylor Highways to cross this border, verify the hours it will be open; these can change.* Remember to set your watches back an hour to Alaska time.

Gold Dredges

Dredges were brought into service in the Yukon when high volumes of gold could no longer be economically plucked from creeks by individual miners. The dredges were floated in water, and worked in a self-generated pond. A continuously moving line of wooden buckets, powered by electric motors, scooped up sandy soil from the bottom of the pond and dumped it in the dredge to be sifted; the heavy gold eventually fell to the bottom and was separated out. The rubble from which the gold had been extracted was deposited out the back. The dredge maneuvered in a circle, gradually scooping up deeper and deeper layers of silt. By the time a dredge had finished with a particular location, 96 percent of the gold had been removed. The miles of tailing piles you encounter along the Klondike Highway are left over from 50 years of dredging.

Before a dredge could start on a new area, workers had to clear the ground of every tree and shrub. The year's work started in icy spring temperatures; soon the heat soared, along with blackflies and mosquitoes. The dredge work continued until November or December. The dredges operated 24 hours a day; operating a dredge required eternal vigilance. A jam that kept the buckets from dumping the sifted gravel could sink the entire dredge in just six minutes.

Other old gold dredges can be viewed in Alaska (see "Fairbanks" and "Inside Passage").▣

In Alaska, the road quickly turns to gravel and mud, descending with sharp switchbacks and potholes. This route is not designed for huge RVs, although you'll find some of them here.

2) Taylor Highway Junction to Tok (106 miles)

The Taylor Highway from the junction with the Top of the World highway to the scrawny town of **Chicken** leaves a lot to be desired in terms of road condition, but the scenery is lovely. The road winds down in steep hairpin curves through tiny canyons. There are no services until you arrive at Chicken where you can get gas, food, park your RV, and do a bit of prospecting at the **Goldpanner** (Mile 66.8 Taylor Hwy; george@impulsedata.net). Although the town has a long history, there is no reason for families to linger.

The road from Chicken takes you through the **Fortymile National Wild and Scenic River**, maintained by the BLM (907/474-2350 [Fairbanks], 907/883-5121 [Tok Field Office].) Check at the Chicken Field Station (Mile 68.2) for recent river information. Sections of the river can be floated.

For the final 10 miles of the trip to Tok, you'll hook up with the Alaska Highway, which should feel almost crowded after your adventures on Klondike roads.

SIDE TRIPS

Each of the following five side trips offers significant attractions for families. If you can spare the time (you'll need a minimum of a half-day for the shortest trip up to several days for the longest trips), these detours can greatly enrich your family's experience.

Highway 97: (see page 144)
Side Trip on Highway 20, the Chilcotin Highway, from Bella Coola and the Discovery Coast (456 km/283 m)

Families with time to spare can drive the **Chilcotin Highway** (Hwy 20) 456 km/283 miles from Williams Lake to **Bella Coola**, a town of 800 residents on the beautiful Discovery Coast. Here, BC Ferries has service to and from Port Hardy on Vancouver Island (see Chapter 2, "Getting There") several days a week in summer.

Some of the highway is unpaved, and accommodation along it is sparse. Thanks to the final, hair-raising descent into Bella Coola, known as "the Hill," this route is not recommended for RVs. The scenic drive over Heckman Pass (1,542m/5,059 ft) traverses **Tweedsmuir South Provincial Park**, BC's largest provincial park, with two vehicle-accessible campgrounds ($12/site). Bella Coola is home to the Bella Coola Band of the Nuxalk First Nation; it is the only road-accessible coastal town along the 483-km/300-mile coastline between Powell River and Prince Rupert; all services are available. Before driving the Chilcotin, check on road conditions with the Williams Lake Visitor Info Centre.

Highway 97: (see page 144)
Side Trip on Highway 26 from Quesnel to Barkerville Historic Town (82 km/51 m)

East of Quesnel 82 km/51 miles on Highway 26 is one of the province's most interesting attractions: **Barkerville**, site of the Cariboo Gold Rush. Be on the lookout for moose as you wind your way into the mountains past rushing rivers and towering evergreens. You'll feel as if you're on the road to nowhere, with only an occasional passing motor coach to indicate you're headed to a popular destination. Near the end, you'll go through the grim but historic town of Wells.

BARKERVILLE HISTORIC TOWN ☺

Barkerville brings its history to life, re-creating an 1860s Cariboo Gold Rush town. When Billy Barker discovered gold in 1862 on Williams Creek, news of the strike quickly attracted thousands of prospectors, and the town mushroomed overnight. The boom lasted nearly a decade; in its glory days, Barkerville was the biggest city west of Chicago and north of San Francisco. Barkerville burned down in 1916, but was soon rebuilt. Today, it consists of 125 heritage buildings along several streets and boardwalks. Staff members in period dress conduct tours and answer visitors' questions. Spending the night will allow the kids to soak up even more history.

The town is at the end of a deep, narrow canyon. Against this backdrop, you'll see a large parking lot, filled with tour buses and cars. Make your way to the Visitor Centre, where you'll find tourist information, a well-stocked bookstore, mining exhibits, a theatre showing old-time movies, a room with an enormous camera where kids can pose for photos, washrooms (note that in Canada, restrooms are universally signed as "washrooms"), and an ATM.

There is a lot of ground to cover. If you have small kids, backpacks and strollers will make your visit more manageable. At the visitor centre, you can sign up for a **stagecoach tour** ($5/person) around town to get your bearings. Some buildings are museums; others are functioning shops, restaurants, and hotels. Visitors can enter or look into buildings including: a doctor's surgery, newspaper publisher's home, a post office, churches, stores, and many more. All have period furnishings. Kids will be intrigued by the school, where the 'schoolmaster' will answer their questions. The cemetery, too, is worth a visit.

Among the town's most interesting features is its replication of an authentic Chinatown, with an operational Chinese restaurant and a general store selling Chinese souvenirs. Displays describe immigrant life and tell the fascinating story of how Barkerville's Chinese residents belonged to a secret society bound to overthrow the Ching Dynasty.

Through hands-on exhibits, kids can learn how gold was mined, and pan for gold themselves. The Hotel Coffee Saloon serves snacks and light lunches. The fine bakery sells old-fashioned treats; try a flat Eccles cake, covered in currants and sugar sprinkles (go early in the day; they often sell out in summer). In the confectionary shop, along with assorted fudges, old-fashioned candies, such as sarsaparilla and horehound drops and rock candy, are sold.

Events and performances take place daily in summer, with celebrations on Canada Day (July 1). The "early justice" Court Sessions are not suitable for young kids.

On Hwy 26; 250/994-3302; www.barkerville.com. Open year round, 8am-dusk; attractions operate mid-May-mid-Sept. Visitor Centre open daily 8am-5pm, mid-May-mid-Sept. Cost: $8.50/adult, $5.25/youth 13-17, $2.50/child 6-12, free/under 6, $19.50/family. Some sites have additional fees. Package rates and group discounts available; call for details.

Places to Stay

Kelly, King Houses ($)
250/994-3328 (summer), 250/994-3312 (winter)
FYI: 3 rooms, shared baths (tubs); one private bath; full breakfast
Off the main drag but still in the historic town, these two B&Bs operate year round.

St. George Hotel ($$$)
250/994-0008, 888/246-7690; www.stgeorgehotel.bc.ca.
FYI: 7 rooms, some shared baths; connected rooms, family discounts; full breakfast; open May-Sept

This hotel is beautifully decorated in period furnishings and welcomes families. Staying here allows families to enter into the spirit of Barkerville in a big way. You can rent period clothing for everyone, so the kids can enjoy being part of the pageantry and become tourist attractions themselves.

Camping
Barkerville Provincial Park (800/689-9025, 604/689-9025; wlapwww.gov.bc. ca/bcparks/explore/parkpgs/barkervi/). This park maintains three camp-grounds nearby. All have drinking water and flush toilets; the two larger have free showers. **Lowhee** has 86 sites (*$15/site; dump station [fee]; accepts advance reservations);* **Forest Rose** (56 sites; $15/site) has a group cook site, but there are no picnic facilities in the park. **Government Hill** has 23 sites ($12/site).

Places to Eat
Lung Duck Tong
250/994-3458
Hours: daily 11am-7pm

This small restaurant in Barkerville's Chinatown serves traditional Chinese cuisine for lunch and dinner.

Wake-Up Jake
250/994-3259
Hours: Mon-Fri, 9am-6:30pm; Sat-Sun, 9am-8pm

Barkerville's full-service, sumptuously decorated restaurant features child-pleasing entrées, including pasta dishes.

Excursions
East of Barkerville, **Bowron Lake Provincial Park** is a world-famous canoe circuit of lakes warm enough for swimming, with groomed portage trails, pop-ular with outdoor-oriented families and groups. The full circuit (116 km/72 miles) takes 7 to 10 days, but shorter trips are possible. Reservations are a must. *27 km from Wells; $12/site; 25 primitive campsites. Canoe circuit reservations: 800/435-5622, (Canada & USA), 604/435-5622 (greater Vancouver area), 250/387-1642 (rest of North America & overseas).*

Calendar of Events
July
Dominion Day celebration
250/994-3302, ext. 29; www.barkerville.com/2002_events/
Games and activities for kids and families drawn from historical games from the 1870s.

December

Old-fashioned Christmas Celebration

50/994-3302, ext. 29; www.barkerville.com/2002_events/

Held on the three weekends preceding Christmas.

Highway 97: (see page 153)

Side Trip to Hudson's Hope (65 km/40 m)

From Chetwynd, if you can spare the time (you'll need at least three hours), the 64-km/40-mile drive up Highway 29 is recommended. Investigate the tiny historic town of Hudson's Hope and take a free fascinating tour of the nearby W.A.C. Bennett and Peace Canyon dams (completed by BC Hydro in 1967 and 1980 respectively). Plans to build more colossal hydroelectric projects were put on hold in the conservation-minded 1980s and are still in limbo. But the enormous power of the Peace River as it roars through the canyon here could someday be tapped again. BC Hydro owns much of the surrounding land and has set up recreational facilities on the enormous lakes created by the two dam reservoirs.

Peace Canyon Dam Dinosaur enthusiasts will enjoy a visit here. The smaller of the two Peace River dams, it's still a hefty 534m/1,752ft long and 50m/164ft high and generates power by reusing water released by the larger dam. Building the dam uncovered over 1,700 dinosaur footprints; many were removed for study before the valley was flooded to create 22.5 km/14-mile-long Dinosaur Lake.

Scheduled tours were canceled after Sept. 11, 2001, but Visitor Centre staff is on hand to answer questions or, with advance notice, set up a tour. The Centre has panoramic views of the dam and is a good place to spot golden eagles fishing. Interpretive displays describe the region's past from prehistoric days to the present. The towering full-scale statues of a mom and baby hadrosaur are likely to grab the kids' attention. Early horned dinosaurs, duckbills, and smaller carnivorous dinosaurs called the area home 100 million years ago.

A video shows how the enormous turbines, among the world's largest, were manufactured in Russia, shipped to Vancouver, then driven north along four-lane roads specially built for the purpose. Another film covers the discovery of dinosaur footprints, what they meant, and how they were investigated. There are restrooms, but no food or gift store.

From Hwy 29, 6 km south of Hudson's Hope, follow signs 1.5 km to Peace Canyon Dam and Generating Station. 250/783-5000; www.bchydro.com/recreation/northern/northern1197/. Open daily 8am-4pm, Victoria Day weekend-Labour Day; Mon-Fri, 8am-4pm, rest of year. Free. Allow 30 minutes.

Hudson's Hope This photogenic town with 1,122 residents, 64 km/40 miles north of Chetwynd, is where many of the dinosaur footprints unearthed when the dams were built ended up. Industrious, contemporary young hunter/gatherers occasionally find dinosaur fossils at the **Dinosaur Lake**

Campground (municipal campground off Highway 29, 250/783-9901; www.dist.hudsons-hope.bc.ca; 50 dry sites, $7/site; water pump, pit toilets, firewood, cooking boxes; swimming, hiking, fishing, boating; open May to September). **Hudson's Hope Museum** (10508 105th Ave; 250/783-5735; open daily Victoria Day-Labour Day weekends, 9:30am-5:30pm; admission by donation) is packed with exhibits on the area's history. Inside is a model of a small, perfect plesiosaur found during dam excavation, along with hadrosaur tracks and ichthyosaur fossils. Outside, a pioneer cabin can be viewed on request. Artifacts of pioneer life are on display along with First Nations relics. There is an excellent bookstore and a selection of local arts and crafts for sale.

Across the street is the **Visitor Info Centre** (250/783-9901; www.hhcn.prn.bc.ca/district/district/; open daily, Victoria Day-Labour Day, 8am-5:30pm) with information on community resources, such as nearby hiking trails and municipal campgrounds.

The **Hudson's Hope Pool** (in Centennial Park on Holland, 250/783-5519) is that northern rarity, an outdoor heated swimming pool, open from May to early September.

WAC Bennett Dam ☺ A scenic 24-km/15-mile drive west of Hudson's Hope brings you to this enormous dam. Much of the surrounding land is owned by BC Hydro and relatively undeveloped, so animal populations thrive. Keep your eyes peeled for moose, caribou, deer, wolves, and bears. The dam's scale is gargantuan; the enormous curving installation bridges the Peace River Canyon and is 2 km/1.2 miles across and 183 m/600ft high. It was constructed of rock from a glacial terminal moraine formed during the last ice age. Williston Lake, the vast reservoir created by building the dam, took five years to fill.

At the Visitor Centre, kids can explore hands-on exhibits on how electricity is generated with hydroelectric power, and peddle a bike to light up bulbs and make a radio work. They may be less thrilled with the film on constructing the dam (it will remind parents of "educational" films favored in school classrooms a few decades back). There are restroom facilities and a small café with moderately priced sandwiches, soup, drinks, and baked goods. Outside are interpretive displays and a picnic area.

A free, fascinating tour runs from the Visitor Centre down into the dam. Security is extremely tight. Visitors must leave everything behind, including purses, cameras, and backpacks. Boarding passes are required and issued at the reception desk. The bus ride down the steep road into the dam is thrilling; sit on the left side to spot wildlife. Inside the dam, hard hats are provided on request; kid sizes are available. The route leads through narrow tunnels where you can spot the tops of enormous spinning turbines. Noise can be deafening. *3 km south of Hudson's Hope, turn onto Canyon Dr and follow signs 21 km to the Visitor Centre. 250/783-5211; www.hhcn.prn.bc.ca/district/bc_hydro/bennett_dam/. Open daily, Victoria Day-Labour Day, 10am-6pm; tours leave every 30 minutes on the half-hour, 10:30am-4:30pm; rest of year by appt only (250/783-5000, 888/333-6667). Free. Café open 9am-6pm. Allow 1.5 hours.*

After you've explored the town and dams you can retrace your steps to Chetwynd or continue on Highway 29 for 75 km/47 miles to the junction with the Alaska Highway at Dawson Creek. Rugged vehicles and most cars will have no trouble driving the rest of Highway 29. However, the last few miles before reaching the Alaska Highway can be tricky driving, with steep switchbacks. Check with the Visitor Info Centre at Chetwynd or Hudson's Hope before choosing this route. Also, unless you backtrack on the Alaska Highway, you'll be passing up the opportunity to set out from the start of the Alaska Highway in Dawson Creek (a major photo op).

North Klondike Highway: (see page 201)
Side Trip on the Dempster Highway to Inuvik (774 km/481 m)

Just think—here you are, a mere 774 km/481 miles from Inuvik, Northwest Territories, an interesting multicultural town of 3,450 on the banks of the Mackenzie River, just 96.5 km/60 miles from the Beaufort Sea. Why not complete the drive across Canada from south to north? Driving to Inuvik on the Dempster Highway takes about 15 hours. The road, open year round, is mostly gravel, and conditions vary depending on weather and construction. Many families do drive the Dempster each year, but doing so involves planning. You'll need to carry several spare tires and be prepared for unexpected weather and road conditions. There is accommodation, food, fuel, and camping along the route.

Roadside attractions include **Tombstone Mountain** (2,193 m) and other peaks in the Ogilvie Range, **North Fork Pass Summit** (1,300 m), arctic circle turnout, arctic tundra, Fort McPherson, and the mighty **Mackenzie River**. The trip includes two ferry rides. Near Inuvik, you'll cross from the Yukon into the Northwest Territories. In Inuvik, cultural and adventure tours visit territorial parks and introduce visitors to the Dene First Nations. Visit a giant igloo-shaped church and tour the Aurora Research Institute, an arctic scientific facility. There are some galleries and shops to explore.

If the thought of doing more driving is less than appealing, the **Dawson City Courier** (867/993-6688; www.dawsonbus.ca) has frequent bus service between Dawson and Inuvik, and Air North (see "Getting to the Yukon Territory") has scheduled flights to Inuvik.

To find out more, visit the **Dempster/Delta Visitor Information Centre** (Front & King Sts, 867/777-3652 [Inuvik]; Open daily 9am-8pm, mid-May–mid-Sept) in Dawson City.

Top of the World and Taylor Highways:
(see page 217)
Side Trip on the Taylor Highway to Eagle (65 miles)

Eleven miles past the Alaska border is the junction with the **Taylor Highway** (Hwy 5), which connects the tiny town of Eagle, AK, 65 miles north of the junction, with the Alaska Highway, 10 miles east of Tok. The scenic, 65-mile drive north to this hamlet on the Yukon River can make good side trip. The historic town has services and attractions.

Road conditions are challenging, but bear in mind that huge tour buses full of geriatric passengers make this drive all summer long and so can you. Another option is to take a day trip from Dawson to Eagle and back on the *Yukon Queen II* (see "Excursions" in "Dawson City"). You'll have several hours to explore Eagle's attractions without the hassle of driving.

EAGLE

This is a tiny community, population 152, with loads of personality, interesting residents, and a few excellent attractions. Eagle was started by prospectors who arrived too late in the Klondike to strike it rich. In 1897, some of them wandered across the international border and started a town of their own, naming it after the large birds nesting on the bluffs above the Yukon River. Lots were sold to anyone who could muster a few hundred dollars, clear the land, and build a cabin within a year. Estimates are that 200 cabins went up that first year and the population soared to about 700. In 1899, Fort Egbert was built, as was a WAMCATS (Washington-Alaska Military Cable and Telegraph System) station; within four years the telegraph line went all the way to Valdez. (You can view a restored WAMCATS station at Big Delta National Historic Site, described earlier in this chapter.) Eagle City was the first town to incorporate and had the first federal court in interior Alaska. When a promised railroad line to Valdez failed to materialize and the telegraph was bypassed by wireless communication, Fort Egbert was closed. However, Eagle refused to die and continued to hang on until the Taylor Highway was built in 1953, giving the town road access to the rest of Alaska.

Places to Stay
Falcon Inn B&B ($)
220 Front St; 907/547-2254; aptalaska.com/~falconin/;
4 rooms and 1 suite, some shared baths
This attractive B&B has a prime riverfront location and great views—the most comfortable option in town.

Camping
The very basic **Eagle Campground** (16 sites for RVs and tents, outhouses, fire grills, picnic tables) is maintained by the BLM. There's no water, but you can access water from the Eagle public well house. At the **Eagle Trading Co.** (3 Front St, # 1; 907/547-2220), in addition to a basic café, you'll find a small motel, RV park with hookups, groceries, fuel, and Laundromat.

What to See & Do

Take some time to wander through town (it won't take long). If you're here in July, you'll find wild strawberries in profusion, ready to pick and eat. Also check out **Roald Amundsen Memorial Park**. Plaques tell the story of the famous explorer's two-month stay in Eagle after he mushed 1,000 miles from Herschel Island in the Beaufort Sea where his ship, the *Gjoa*, was stuck in the ice. (He went to Eagle to use the telegraph and wire for money.)

Eagle Historical Society and Museums First among the town's attractions is this complex, with exhibits strewn across several buildings, some dating from the 19th century. Museum tours are offered daily at 9 a.m. Videos and educational programs are also available. Most of the exhibits are contained in Judge Wickersham's first courthouse. The original courtroom has been maintained and exhibits describe what went on there. Downstairs, the history of Eagle is set out in several rooms. The school room features laminated copies of real papers and schoolwork done by children nearly a century ago. Eagle's children had a hand in designing several exhibits. A large gift shop in the courthouse sells locally made arts and crafts and a good selection of books. *907/547-2325; www.ealeak.org; open daily, May-Sept; tours 9am Cost: $5/adult, free/under 12.*

Yukon-Charley Rivers National Preserve Visitor Center The center has exhibits and books, and a video on the park. The staff can tell you about rafting and kayaking opportunities. The BLM maintains the five buildings that remain at the **Fort Egbert** site; there's an interpretive trail and exhibits. *907/547-2233; www.nps.gov/yuch/*

Boating Canoes and rafts can be rented from **Eagle Canoe Rentals** (907/547-2203; e-mail: paddleak@aptalaska.net).

6 Anchorage and Environs

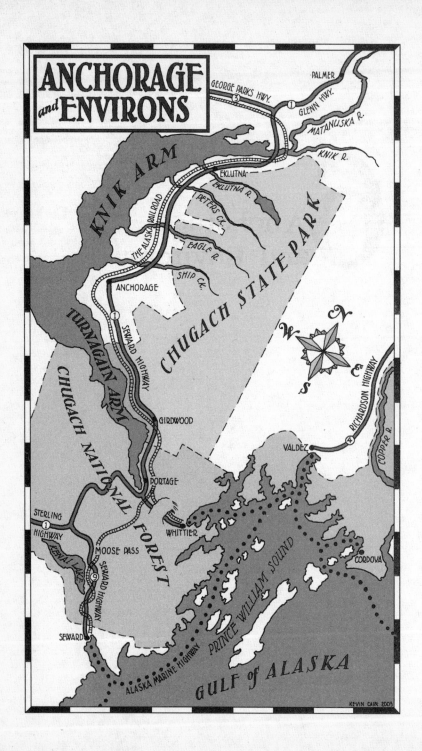

6 Anchorage and Environs

SOUTHCENTRAL ALASKA, CIRCLING the Gulf of Alaska, is bound to the north and west by the Alaska and Aleutian mountain ranges. Here, you'll find the state's largest city, Anchorage, and Alaska's "bread basket," the Matanuska valley, with a short but intense growing season. At the state fair in Palmer, produce of huge proportions is on display. Summer visitors will find the area pastoral and lush.

The region's weather is relatively balmy by northern standards: In January, Anchorage averages 15F degrees, in July 58F degrees; it gets less than 20 inches of rain a year, and less than 70 inches of snow.

Anchorage lacks the dramatic history of other Alaskan communities. Athabascan Dena'ina inhabited the region when Captain James Cook arrived in 1778. George Vancouver returned for a look in 1794, but settlement was sparse until construction of the Alaska Railroad began in 1915. Ship Creek housed a major camp to provide the railroad with workers and supplies, and the population quickly mushroomed into the thousands, but when the railroad was completed, dropped again. World War II brought the military into the area in large numbers, establishing Elmendorf Air Force Base and Fort Richardson. Through the Cold War, the military maintained a strong presence, and many Anchorage residents came here through this means. The discovery of oil brought an influx of business and wealth to the state's major urban center.

Getting to Anchorage

By Air Anchorage is the airline hub for the state. **Alaska Airlines** (800/252-7522; www.alaskaair.com) offers the most flights between Anchorage and cities in the lower 48, as well as the rest of Alaska and international destinations. For information on other airlines that fly to Alaska, see "Getting There."

By Rail The **Alaska Railroad** (800/544-0552, 907/265-2300; www.akrr.com) provides daily passenger service in summer between Anchorage and Fairbanks, with stops in Denali and other communities. Also in summer, trains run daily between Anchorage and Seward, with connection to Alaska ferries and cruise ships. Trains also make the short run daily between Anchorage and Whittier, on Prince William Sound. Winter service is less frequent and available only between Anchorage and Fairbanks. Seward-Anchorage and Anchorage-Whittier routes operate mid-May to mid-September. *Glacier Discovery*, a new service, provides service between Anchorage and

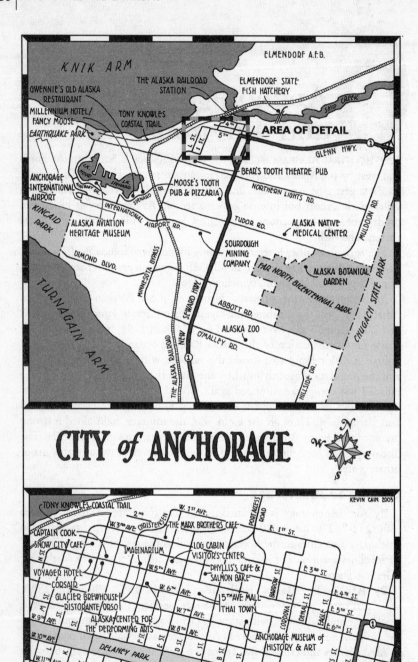

KNIK ARM

ELMENDORF A.F.B.

GWENNIE'S OLD ALASKA RESTAURANT

THE ALASKA RAILROAD STATION

ELMENDORF STATE FISH HATCHERY

MILLENNIUM HOTEL/ FANCY MOOSE

TONY KNOWLES COASTAL TRAIL

SHIP CREEK

EARTHQUAKE PARK

4TH

AREA OF DETAIL

5TH

L ST.

I ST.

GLENN HWY.

ANCHORAGE INTERNATIONAL AIRPORT

LK. HOOD

AIRCRAFT DR.

LK. SPENARD

BEAR'S TOOTH THEATRE PUB

SPENARD RD.

MOOSE'S TOOTH PUB & PIZZARIA

NORTHERN LIGHTS RD.

MULDOON RD.

KINCAID PARK

ALASKA AVIATION HERITAGE MUSEUM

INTERNATIONAL AIRPORT RD.

TUDOR RD.

ALASKA NATIVE MEDICAL CENTER

DIMOND BLVD.

SOURDOUGH MINING COMPANY

MINNESOTA BYPASS

FAR NORTH BICENTENNIAL PARK

ALASKA BOTANICAL GARDEN

CHUGACH STATE PARK

TURNAGAIN ARM

ABBOTT RD.

NEW SEWARD HWY.

ALASKA ZOO

O'MALLEY RD.

THE ALASKA RAILROAD

1

HILLSIDE DR.

CITY *of* ANCHORAGE

N W E S

KEVIN CAIN 2003

TONY KNOWLES COASTAL TRAIL

W. 1ST AVE.

2ND

CAPTAIN COOK

W. 3RD AVE. CHRISTENSEN

THE MARX BROTHERS CAFE

PORT ACCESS ROAD

E. 1ST ST.

SNOW CITY CAFE

IMAGINARIUM

LOG CABIN VISITOR'S CENTER

E. 3RD ST.

VOYAGER HOTEL

W. 5TH AVE.

PHYLLIS'S CAFE & SALMON BAKE

BARROW ST.

CORSAIR

W. 6TH AVE.

5TH AVE. MALL

CORDOVA ST.

DENALI ST.

EAGLE ST.

E. 4TH ST.

GLACIER BREWHOUSE/ RISTORANTE ORSO

W. 7TH AVE.

THAI TOWN

E. 5TH ST.

E. 6TH ST.

1

W. 9TH AVE.

ALASKA CENTER FOR THE PERFORMING ARTS

W. 8TH AVE.

ANCHORAGE MUSEUM of HISTORY & ART

W. 10TH AVE.

DELANEY PARK

FAIRBANKS ST.

GAMBELL ST.

HYDER ST.

INGRA ST.

W. 11TH AVE.

W. 12TH AVE.

G STREET HOUSE BED & BREAKFAST

Whittier, with connections to day cruises on Prince William Sound; check with Alaska Railroad for details.

By Road All major highways in the state, except the Alaska Highway, converge in Anchorage. The Glenn Highway (Hwy 1) connects Anchorage with Glennallen, 189 miles to the northeast, and to the Richardson Highway (Hwy 4) connecting Valdez and Fairbanks. Additionally, the Tok cutoff (about 11 miles north of Glennallen) runs northeast to Tok and the Alaska Highway. The drive from Anchorage to Tok is 328 miles using the cutoff; another 247 miles brings travelers to Fairbanks.

North of Anchorage, the Parks Highway (Hwy 3) goes to Talkeetna, Denali, Nenana, and on to Fairbanks, 362 miles in all. This is the major road connecting Anchorage and Fairbanks.

From Anchorage, drivers access the Kenai Peninsula from the Seward Highway (Hwy 6), which runs east along the north shore of Turnagain Arm to Portage, where drivers can make a detour to visit Portage Glacier and Whittier. South of Portage, the highway runs down to Seward. Just north of Moose Pass, the Sterling Highway peels off the Seward Highway and runs west and south to Soldotna, Kenai, and Homer.

Regional Resources

Alaska Public Lands Information Center
605 W 4th Ave, Ste 105, Anchorage, AK 99501; 907/271-2737;
www.nps.gov/aplic/

Department of Natural Resources Public Information Center
550 W 7th Ave; Anchorage, AK 99501-3557; 907/269-8400;
www.dnr.state.ak.us. Open Mon-Fri 10am-5pm.
Information on state parks and public-use cabins.

ANCHORAGE

Anchorage sits on the peninsula that separates Knik Arm and Turnagain Arm in Cook Inlet. With a population of over a quarter million, Anchorage is more than eight times bigger than any other Alaska city. It offers all the amenities of a modern urban center with few drawbacks. Although locals complain about rush hour traffic, visitors say "What traffic?" In minutes, you can get from downtown to the Glen Alps trailhead in Chugach State Park, with the great outdoors at your fingertips.

Anchorage has a diverse, well-integrated population that includes Native Alaskans, a thriving African American community, Latinos, Asians and Caucasians. A stroll through the Saturday Market makes a good introduction to local demographics.

For families, Anchorage offers a wealth of attractions in every category: great museums, an excellent zoo, a generous number of city parks, and shopping. You won't have to travel far to find outdoor recreation opportunities, from hiking and skiing to kayaking and flightseeing.

Getting Around

Many hotels offer free transportation to hotels from the airport and train station.

Anchorage has an efficient transit system: the **People Mover** (907/343-6543; www.peoplemover.org. $1.25/adult, $.75/child 5-18, free/under 5). Buses serve the greater Anchorage area, including Eagle River. If you plan more than one trip a day, get a day pass ($2.50). Note, however, that schedules are geared to serve weekday commuters. For routes and timetables, pick up the *Ride Guide* ($1) on buses, at bookstores, and visitor centers.

Taxis are plentiful, but expensive; try **Alaska Cab** (907/563-5353; www.alaskacabs.com) and **AAA Metro Cab** (907/677-7000). **Borealis Shuttle** (907-276-3600, 888/436-3600) serves airport passengers.

Unless your stay is very brief, you'll want to stay downtown, close to major attractions, or rent a car. Major hotels are clustered near the train station and 3rd and 6th Avenues. The big names in car rental can be found at Ted Stevens International Airport. You can also rent from **Affordable New Car Rental** (4707 Spenard Rd; 907/243-3370, 800/248-3765; www.ancr.com), an Alaska agency. They rent kids' car seats for $5 per day; reserve in advance.

Places to Stay

G Street House Bed & Breakfast ($$)
1032 G St; 907/276-3284; www.gstreethouse.com
FYI: 3 rooms; continental breakfast
This small B&B is located less than a mile from downtown Anchorage in a quiet, residential area. The top floor has been remodeled to accommodate guests and includes three very comfortable rooms—one with a queen bed, one with twin beds, and a suite with two rooms and two bathrooms. The shared sitting area upstairs is full of Alaskana—history books and photos. Guests are served a continental breakfast downstairs. Hosts Pam and Allen have their own kids, so there's no question about this B&B being family-friendly. Both are happy to provide suggestions for activities and directions, as needed.

66 PARENT COMMENTS 99

"Our family rented the suite—two bedrooms with a bath and a half-bath in the hallway between. My husband and I shared a double bed, and the girls had two single beds in their room."

"Proximity to downtown was a plus for us."

Voyager Hotel ($$)
501 K St; 907/277-9501, 800/247-9070; www.voyagerhotel.com
FYI: 38 room, kitchenettes (all rooms), free continental breakfast, all nonsmoking, complimentary parking (some restrictions)
This small hotel has a lot to offer families, with exceptionally large, comfortable rooms with kitchenettes. The Voyager is a mile from the train station and

Rent an RV in Alaska

To have your cake and eat it, too, fly up to Anchorage and slip into an RV for a week of adventure on the road. With children, RV camping makes sense. Packing and unpacking daily with small children as you move from one destination to the next can tire out the most energetic parent. If you don't have the weeks required to drive the Alaska Highway, you can still drive up to Denali National Park and Preserve, explore the scenic Glenn Highway east to the Richardson Highway, then drive down to Valdez, on Prince William Sound. Or explore the Kenai Peninsula and beyond (with advance planning) to Kodiak or Unalaska Island via Alaska Ferry. The possibilities are endless!

Most families with two children can do fine with a 20-foot vehicle. Rentals are less expensive in early June or September. During high season, expect to pay around $200 per day when you rent for a week or more. You'll still have to pay campground charges (usually about $15 per night), dump station fees, and for gas. But on the plus side, you'll can save money on meals and experience beautiful wilderness parks surrounded by the comforts of home. Modern RVs come with a refrigerator, microwave oven, stove, bathroom, and shower. Many have air conditioning along with heating. Bedding, towels, dishes, and cooking utensils are generally included with rentals. Few companies allow pets to travel in rented RVs.

Find out before booking which roads are prohibited. The Top of the World and Taylor highways are often off limits. However, many companies do allow travel on the Denali Highway.

Several companies in Anchorage rent campers and RVs.

ABC Motorhome Rentals (3875 W International Airport Rd; 907/279-2000, 800/421-7456) rents 20-30 foot RVs, campers, and cars. They'll allow you to drive one-way from the lower 48 to Alaska in spring or vice versa in fall.

Alaska Economy RVs (8825 Runamuck Pl, #4; 907/561-7723; 800/764-4625; www.goalaska.com) rents RVs and campers in several sizes.

Alaska Experience RV Rentals (3200 Mountain View Dr; 907/561-9800, 888/242-4359; www.akrvrentals.com). This outfit rents a deluxe camper and three sizes of RV.

Alaska Motorhome Rentals (800/254-9929; www.alaskarv.com) rents RVs in two sizes. Prices are on the low side. One-way trips between Seattle, WA and Alaska are allowed, but prices are steep.

Elmer, Howard. The RV Log Book and Journal. Whitecap Books, 2000. Keep a journal of your trip here with checklists for packing and room to record details of campgrounds and travel. ▣

walking distance from downtown attractions, though a long walk for very young kids. The staff is friendly and accommodating. Downstairs is Corsair, one of Anchorage's better fine-dining spots (see "Places to Eat"). The hotel gives discount coupons for guests to use here, but it's not recommended for small children; the wigglers in your party will be happier at the Glacier Brewhouse or Moose's Tooth.

66 P A R E N T   C O M M E N T S 99

"We were very comfortable here. What the kids liked best were the lamps that turn on when you touch them lightly (a feature of all the rooms) and the shampoo and bath gel dispensers in the shower. In addition to a large queen-size bed, there was a sofa which, when you pull the seat portion out, turns out to be a full double bed. It was much more comfortable and easier to set up than a sofabed. Our only quibble was parking. Although overnight parking is free, you have to pay for parking during the day."

Captain Cook ($$$)
939 W 5th Ave; 907/276-6000, 800/843-1950; www.captaincook.com
FYI: *547 rooms, 96 suites, 3 restaurants, coffee shop; athletic club: pool, hot tub, sauna, racquetball, massage; gift shops*
This independently owned, elegant downtown hotel epitomizes luxury in Alaska. Its three towers dwarf other buildings in the vicinity; views from most rooms range from good to phenomenal. The décor is appropriately reminiscent of Captain Cook and his voyages to Alaska and the South Pacific. Your children will likely find playmates in the large pool. Classes and workshops offered in the athletic club are available to guests.

Among the hotel's restaurants, Fletcher's, the upscale but child-friendly English pub/Italian eatery that serves pizza and pasta along with microbrews, is your best bet. You can also dine or snack at one of the two casual coffee shops.

66 P A R E N T   C O M M E N T S 99

"The staff was very pleasant and went out of their way to make us comfortable. The weather was horrible, so we spent a lot of time indoors. Between the shops and the pool, my daughter was in heaven. The pool (which is huge) is closed to kids some of the time, but with six hours available, it worked out OK. Our last day, the weather was nice and it got hot in our room; turns out the Captain Cook doesn't have air conditioning (I guess it's rarely needed). But we opened a window, and that did the trick."

Anchorage Chain Hotels

For more information about amenities at these hotels, see "Introduction."

Anchorage Marriott Downtown
820 W 7th Ave; 907/279-8000.
FYI: 392 rooms, suites, some kitchens; restaurant; health club, swimming pool, hot tub; Laundromat

Aspen Hotel
108 E 8th Ave; 907/274-2151, 888/559-9876.
FYI: 89 rooms, free breakfast; refrigerator/microwave; swimming pool, hut tub; Laundromat

Clarion Suites
325 W 8th Ave; 907/274-1000, 888/389-6575.
FYI: 111 suites, swimming pool, hot tub, exercise room; Laundromat; deli; free shuttle

Comfort Inn
111 W Ship Creek Ave; 907/277-6887, 800/228-5150.
FYI: 100 rooms, some suites; swimming pool, hot tub; Laundromat

Courtyard by Marriott
1025 E 35th Ave; 907/245-0322, 800,729-0197.
FYI: 154 rooms, some suites; restaurant; swimming pool, hot tub, sauna, exercise room; Laundromat

Econo Lodge
642 E 5th Ave; 907/274-1515.
FYI: 41 rooms, free continental breakfast; Laundromat, free airport and train shuttle.

Hampton Inn
301 Credit Union Dr; 907/550-7000, 800/426-7866.
FYI: 101 rooms, free breakfast bar; swimming pool, hot tub, exercise room; Laundromat

Hawthorn Suites
110 W 8th Ave; 907/222-5005, 888/469-6575.
FYI: 111 suites, free breakfast, swimming pool, hut tub, exercise room; Laundromat

Hilton Anchorage
500 W 3rd Ave; 907/272-7411, 800/445-8667.
FYI: 600 rooms, 2 restaurants ; pool, fitness room

Hilton Garden Inn
4540 A St; 907/729-7000, 800/445-8667.
FYI: 125 rooms, refrigerator/microwave; restaurant, swimming pool, fitness room; Laundromat; shuttle

Holiday Inn Downtown
239 W 4th Ave; 907/279-8671, 800/545-7665.
FYI: 251 rooms; restaurant; swimming pool, hot tub, fitness center; Laundromat; shuttle

Holiday Inn Express
4411 Spenard Rd; 907/248-8848.
FYI: 128 rooms; swimming pool, hot tub; Laundromat

Ramada Limited Hotel of Anchorage
207 Muldoon Rd; 907/929-7000.
FYI: 63 rooms, refrigerator/microwave (on request); free continental breakfast; shuttle

Residence Inn By Marriott
1025 E 35th Ave; 907/563-9844, 877/727-0197.
FYI: 148 suites, kitchens; free breakfast; swimming pool, hot tub, sauna, exercise room; Laundromat; shuttle

Sheraton Anchorage Hotel
401 E 6th Ave; 907/276-8700.
FYI: 375 rooms, suites; restaurants; fitness center, sauna, hot tub; gift shop

Springhill Suites
1025 E 35th Ave; 907/562-3247, 877/729-0197.
FYI: 122 suites, continental breakfast; swimming pool, hot tub; Laundromat

Super 8 Motel Of Anchorage
3501 Minnesota Dr; 907/276-8884, 800/800-8000.
FYI: 85 rooms, 1 with kitchen; Laundromat; shuttle

Westmark Anchorage Hotel
720 W 5th Ave; 800/544-0970.
FYI: 200 rooms; restaurant

Westmark Inn 3rd Avenue
115 E 3rd Ave; 907/272-7561, 800/544-0970.
FYI: 91 rooms; coffee shop; open May-Sept. ◼

Millennium Hotel Anchorage ($$$)

4800 Spenard Rd; 907/243-2300, 800/544-0553;
www.millennium-hotels.com/anchorage/
FYI: 248 rooms, refrigerators; 3 suites with hot tub, fireplace; Nintendo;
2 restaurants; health club: hot tub, steam room, sauna, exercise room;
Laundromat; gift shop; free shuttle to airport, downtown, Dimond Mall;
kids under 18 stay free

Aviation buffs will enjoy this hotel on Lake Spenard, connected to Lake Hood, location of the world's largest seaplane base. In summer, up to 800 flights a day take off and land here. Plus, it's a mile from Anchorage International Airport. The hotel has its own floatplane dock, and the lobby is a cross between a hunting lodge and a swanky airport lounge. Steer clear of the fine-dining option; kids will do better at the Fancy Moose (see "Places to Eat").

Places to Eat

Bear's Tooth Theatre Pub

1230 W 27th Ave; 907/276-4200; www.beartooththeatre.net
Hours: Call or check local listings for movie times

The Bear's Tooth offers instant entertainment for families: eat, drink and watch a movie! First, order pub food from a menu that includes Mexican fare, stone-baked pizza, wraps, soups, salads, desserts, Moose's Tooth beer, and wine (not to mention the more traditional popcorn and candy). Then find your seat equipped with a handy "bar table" (families tend to prefer the upstairs, where alcoholic beverages are not allowed) and before you know it, your meal will arrive. Then, enjoy the film! Movies are second run, admission price nominal.

Corsair

944 W 5th Ave; 907/278-4502
Hours: Mon-Thurs, 5-10pm; Fri-Sat 5-11pm; closed Sun, major holidays

This definitely qualifies as a splurge, but if you're longing for classic, elegant dishes (something flambéed, perhaps), you'll likely enjoy a meal at the Corsair. Seafood is always a good bet: very fresh and accompanied by an elegant European sauce. This is not a good choice for young children, but older kids should find something to enjoy. Dressing up is advised.

Fancy Moose ☺

In the Millennium Hotel, 4800 Spenard Rd; 907/243-2300
Hours: Open daily, 11-2am

As the Millennium Hotel's casual-dining option, this cheery, noisy hangout is just the ticket for squirrelly kids. Burgers, sandwiches, finger food, and a few heartier entrées are offered. In good weather, dine outside on the patio, and watch planes take off and land.

Glacier BrewHouse

737 W 5th Ave; 907/274-2739; www.glacierbrewhouse.com
Hours: Open daily in summer, 11am-11pm rest of year: Tues-Thurs 11am-10pm; Fri-Sat 11am-11pm, Sun, noon-9:30pm

Camping

Two municipal campgrounds, a short drive from downtown, operate in summer (generally May through October, depending on weather). **Centennial Campground** (8300 Glenn Hwy; 88 sites, 2 group sites, tent sites) and **Lion's Camper Park** (Boniface Pkwy between 6th Ave & DeBarr Rd; 50 RV sites, 10 tent sites). Both campgrounds charge $15/site, and have picnic facilities. Showers, firewood, and use of the dump station are provided for a fee. For details call 907/343-6986

(summer), or 907/343-4474 (winter); or check the Anchorage Parks and Recreation Web site at www.muni.org/parks/camp/.

For a good private campground in an attractive location, try **Anchorage RV Park** (1200 N Muldoon Rd; 907/338-7275, 800/400-7275; www.anchrvpark.com; 195/sites, no tents, $31-38; hookups, picnic tables, ice, groceries, gift shop, showers, Laundromat, pets OK) across from the Alaska Native Heritage Center. ◼

In summer, this is among the city's most popular restaurants; some days they stop taking reservations. The food should make up for any frustrations, though. "Eclectic" best describes the menu: Southwestern and Italian, with a bit of eastern Mediterranean and Thai thrown in. All dishes go well with the excellent microbrews. There's no kids' menu, but many items will suit small fry, and the staff are happy to prepare hot dogs, kid pasta, or grilled cheese sandwiches on request. For adults, halibut tacos and gourmet pizzas are delicious and easy on the wallet. Porcini-crusted salmon and blackened rockfish feature local seafood. The garlic mashed potatoes are famous. Don't forget to leave room for crème brulée.

Gwennie's Old Alaska Restaurant ☺
4333 Spenard Rd; 907/243-2090
Hours: Daily 6am-11pm
Gwennie's is an Anchorage institution and popular with families. The décor is suitably northern; a towering, stuffed grizzly glares down over the proceedings, reminding you you're in Alaska. Breakfasts are famous; the sourdough pancakes are a winner. There's a kids' menu, too.

The Marx Brothers Café
627 W 3rd Ave; 907/278-2133; Museum Café: 907/343-6193; www.marx cafe.com
Hours: Daily 5:30-10pm (summer); Tues-Thurs 6pm-9:30pm, Fri-Sat 5pm-10 pm, Sun 5:30pm-9pm; closed Mon (rest of year)
This is as good as it gets in Anchorage—and that's very good indeed. Located in a historic house overlooking Cook Inlet, the restaurant is small and popular, so reservations are a must. The emphasis is on fresh food beautifully prepared.

Noted for its large wine cellar, salads, seafood, and wild game dishes, the café is not the best choice for young kids. No fear; you can have your Chocolate Port Terrine Cake and eat it, too: Marx Brothers runs the Gallery Café at the Anchorage Museum. Stop in for lunch during a museum visit. The menu is smaller but just as good, featuring homemade soups, salads, and entrées; a kids' menu offers the usual.

Moose's Tooth Pub & Pizzeria ☺
3300 Old Seward Hwy; 907/258-2537; www.moosestooth.net
Hours: Sun-Thurs 11am-midnight; Fri-Sat 11am-1am (summer); Sun-Mon 11am-11pm; Tues-Thurs 11am-midnight; Fri-Sat 11am-1am (rest of year)
This is a perennial favorite with locals and visitors of all ages. There are soups, sandwiches, salads, and desserts, but nearly everyone comes for the pizza. Exotic combinations of toppings illustrate how pizza has morphed into world cuisine (Blackened Halibut and Spicy Thai Chicken). Luckily, lots of offerings will satisfy young diners, and custom-designed pizzas can be ordered. Wash it down with a microbrew or root beer float.

Phyllis's Cafe and Salmon Bake
436 D St; 907/274-6576
Hours: Daily 11am-midnight, May-Sept
This is your basic salmon bake in a city setting, with burgers, sandwiches, and other entrées. It's not cheap and the décor isn't a strong point but a cheery profusion of flowers makes up for a lot. To get the most for your dollars, spring for a full dinner—king crab legs are a good bet. For kids, try burgers, hot dogs, reindeer sausage or ribs. Hearty seafood chowder is served in sourdough bread bowls. Strawberry shortcake makes a nice conclusion. If there's a line, don't worry; service is fast and efficient, and if anyone gets antsy, send them next door to the Cook Inlet Bookstore for a browse.

Ristorante Orso
737 W 5th Ave, Ste 110; 907/222-3232
Hours: Open daily, Mon-Fri 11am-2:30pm, 4:30-11pm; Sat-Sun 4:30-11pm (summer); Sun-Mon 4:30-9:30pm; Tues-Thurs 4:30-10pm; Fri-Sat 4:30-11pm (rest of year)
Run by the folks who own the Glacier BrewHouse, Orso offers excellent Italian cuisine in a slightly more sedate setting. There's no kids' menu, but kids are welcome to dine off the bar menu, which features finger foods, sandwiches, and salads. Staff will gladly prepare kid favorites such as pasta with marinara sauce. Lunch includes a wide variety of pasta dishes. Molten chocolate cake is a dessert favorite.

Snow City Café ☺
1034 W 4th Ave (between K and L Sts); 907/272-2489
Hours: Mon-Fri 7am-4:30pm, Sat-Sun 8am-4pm
Best known for its tremendous breakfasts (served all day), this hip, casual spot in downtown Anchorage serves a wide selection of health-conscious foods.

☛ **Parent Tip:**

In Alaska, children are welcome to dine in the bar/lounge side of a restaurant. ◼

Choose a hearty egg dish (the huevos rancheros are particularly good), accompanied by a piece of warm, crusty bread or other baked treat. Gourmet teas and local favorite Kaladi Brothers Coffee are served, too. Daily lunch specials include seafood and vegetarian entrees, big bowls of steaming soup, and fresh salads. Their curried apple-squash soup is a pungent masterpiece! Service is fast and friendly, and picky eaters can make substitutions. There are magazines for browsing, and games for young ones to play while their parents nurse a second cup of espresso.

Sourdough Mining Company ☺
5200 Juneau St; 907/563-2272; www.alaskaone.com/aksourdough/
Hours: Open daily 11am-11pm; Sunday brunch 10am-2pm
Kids are likely to enjoy this touristy restaurant with a cheery chaotic rhythm, a chocolate waterfall, and a large gift shop. The premises replicate a historic mill house. The kids' menu carries items such as chicken nuggets cut in dinosaur shapes. Ribs are a specialty, but there's seafood, too. The signature dish is "korn fritters," which aren't bad. The ice cream bar with assorted toppings should please kids. Free round-trip shuttle service is offered from any Anchorage hotel.

Thai Town
#408, 5th Ave Mall, 320 W 5th Ave; 907/278-9889
Mall hours: Mon-Fri 10am-9pm; Sat 10am-8pm; Sun 11am-6pm
If your kids are shopping-mall age, you'll likely find yourself at this rather dowdy, downtown Anchorage mall. The large food court has many of the big names in fast food that kids will enjoy, but parents who like Thai food should head to this offshoot of a popular Thai restaurant in town. It's not much more than a kiosk, but the food is excellent, portions large, and prices low.

What to See & Do

Stroll & Browse

Orient yourself to the city by taking a self-guided walking tour of downtown after picking up a map at the **Anchorage Convention & Visitors Bureau log cabin** at 4th & F. In this cute, sod-roofed building you'll find tons of visitor info and knowledgeable staff.

Shopping You can find just about anything in Anchorage and much of it is located within the city's compact and easy-to-navigate downtown, mostly along 3rd, 4th, 5th, and 6th Avenues. Large, warehouse-style souvenir shops abound. Toward the end of the summer, prices drop. The **Fifth Avenue Mall** (320 W 5th Ave between C & D Sts) features standard names in retailing and fast food, a couple of toy stores, and several gift shops, including an **Alaska**

☛ **Parent Tip: Alaska Farmers' Markets**

Summer farmers' markets are a common sight in many Alaska towns. Some include craft fairs and live entertainment; others focus more on selling produce and food grown nearby. But all are likely to include Alaska-made preserves (fireweed jelly, highbush cranberry or spruce tip syrups), soaps and lotions, and a scattering of crafts. Most sell snacks, bakery goods, drinks, and sometimes complete meals. Visiting an Alaska farmers' market is a good way to rub elbows with local residents and get a taste of what it means to live here. Prices are almost always lower than in stores, and quality tends to be good. For up-to-date information on Alaska farmers markets check the U.S. Dept. of Agriculture Web site: www.ams.usda.gov/farmersmarkets/states/ak/ ◨

Wild Berry Products (907/562-8858) outlet and **Katherine the Great** (907/272-5283), which sells Russian dolls, crafts, and collectibles.

For high-quality, locally made arts and crafts, check out **Aurora Fine Arts Gallery** (737 W 5th Ave, Ste E; 907/274-0234) . The venerable **Artique** (314 G St between 3rd & 4th Aves; 907/277-1663) has beautiful artworks, from watercolors to sculpture, as well as jewelry and an assortment of crafts; works by prominent Alaska artists can be found here. The **Decker Morris Gallery** (621 W 6th Ave; 907/272-1489) is a major purveyor of Alaskan art. **Tundra Arts** (425 D St; 907/276-0190) is an Alaska artists' cooperative selling the work of its members.

For something completely different, head to the **Oomingmak Musk Ox Producers Co-op** (604 H St; 907/272-9225; www.qiviut.com) where you'll find items woven of *qiviut* (musk-ox hair), lightweight, soft, and very warm. The co-op consists of about 250 Native Alaskan women from remote northern coastal villages who weave the qiviut into scarves, stoles, hats, and more for all ages. Designs are complex and beautiful and prices are steep: a baby's hat will set you back more than $100.

Anchorage has two terrific independent booksellers: **Cook Inlet Book Company** (415 W 5th Ave; 907/258-4544; cookinlet.booksense.com) and **Cyrano's Bookstore** (413 D St; 907/274-2599).

Operating between mid-May and mid-September, the **Anchorage Saturday Market** (3rd Ave & E St; 907/277-5634; www.anchoragemarkets.com; 10am-6pm) is worth a visit. It's a combination farmers' market and craft fair with a bit of flea market thrown in. Be sure to sample some of the excellent food: corn dogs (made with real corn), reindeer sausage dogs, salmon quesadillas. Stroll among the giant cabbages ("three feet, wingtip to wingtip") and sample the birch syrups, berry vinegars, and jellies. Look for unique carved birch boxes sold by Siberian Natives. Listen to live music and pick up CDs by local artists. Wood carvings, basketry, jewelry, pottery, quilts, fiber arts, and toys are plentiful. All summer long, you can also sample locally grown produce, crafts, and munchies at the **Anchorage Farmers Market** (1001 Northway Dr; 907/746-1087; May-Oct Sat, 9am-2pm; e-mail: beans@Alaska.com).

☛ **Parent Tip:**

Before you shell out the hefty entrance fees for popular Anchorage attractions, check the Visitor Center, hotel lobbies, tourist brochures, and city guides for promotional offers and discount coupons that can save you a buck or more per ticket on many attractions. ◙

Alaska Experience Center   If you have limited time in Anchorage—or great weather—you can skip this attraction without feeling deprived. Otherwise, spend an entertaining hour or two watching a 40-minute film on scenic Alaska, shown on a giant screen, and taking in exhibits on the 1964 earthquake, including a 15-minute film that lives up to its promise to make the ground shake under your seat. The earthquake exhibits are better than the seedy ambience would lead you to believe. A large gift shop carries Alaska T-shirts and memorabilia. A word of caution: the Alaska film uses spectacular effects to create the sensation of flying in a small plane over Alaska; this could cause motion sickness in susceptible kids.

705 W 6th Ave; 907/3730; www.alaskavisitorscenter.com/images/alaskaexperience/. Open daily, 9am-9pm (summer); noon-6pm (rest of year). Cost: (Alaska Theatre) $6.99/adult, $3.99/child, 5-12, free/under 5; (Earthquake exhibit) $4.99/adult, $3.99/child; (combined ticket) $9.99/adult, $6.99/child. Allow 90 minutes.

Alaska Native Medical Center   This the finest medical establishment in Alaska (serving only Native Alaskans) and also the repository of some of the most amazing Native art produced in recent decades.

Before you enter the building, admire the bold exterior. The 380,000-square-foot center was built in 1996 with extensive input from the Alaska Native community. Each floor offers a large, beautifully displayed exhibit of Native-made masks, dolls, jewelry, clothing, sculpture, and much more. But don't take the elevator both ways; along the stairways are additional small display cases you won't want to miss!

Exhibits are housed in the lobby portions of each floor, but please be mindful of the fact that this is a working Medical Center. Only children who can be counted on to speak in low voices, avoid running, and yield right-of-way to patients and staff should be included on a visit here. Be sure to visit the Gift Shop; it has a small but lovely collection of Native art at fair prices.

4315 Diplomacy Dr, 907/257-1122 (gift shop).

Alaska Public Lands Information Center (APLIC)   One of four APLICs in Alaska (others are in Fairbanks, Ketchikan, and Tok), this one offers interpretive programs just for kids. APLIC is a consortium of federal and state agencies, including the National Park Service, Fish and Wildlife Service, Bureau of Land Management, Geological Survey, Forest Service, the Alaska Department of Fish and Game, Division of Tourism, and the Department of Natural Resources; together, they manage Alaska's public

lands. Staff at these visitor centers provide information on recreational opportunities in lands managed by the agencies. They also show films and videos, sell books and maps, and offer exhibits and educational programs.
605 W 4th Ave, in the Federal Bldg, corner of F St & 4th Ave; 907/271-2737. Open 10am-5:30pm, Mon-Fri (Sept-May); open daily 9am-5:30pm (rest of year).

Museums

Alaska Aviation Heritage Museum   In this interesting museum on the south shore of Lake Hood, view vintage, historic airplanes, restored by staff and volunteers, and exhibits on the thrilling history of Alaska aviation. One gallery tells the story of Alaska's bush pilots. In the World War II gallery, learn about the role of aviation—U.S. and Japanese—in the Aleutian campaign. A variety of films are shown, ranging from 30 minutes to an hour. Parents might want to think twice about letting kids see "I Wanna Be a Jet Pilot"; this could launch a career. The films, including vintage news coverage of the war in the Aleutians, are fascinating but may not be a good bet for very young kids. The short Disney film on bush pilots is a better choice. The museum store sells aviation memorabilia, including toys and models, along with aviation-related souvenirs.
4721 Aircraft Dr, Lake Hood; 907/248-5325; Hangar: 248-9838; home.gci.net/~aahm/. Open daily, May-Sept, 9am-6pm. Oct-April: Call for hours. Cost: $8/adult; $4/child 6-12, free/under 6.

Alaska Native Heritage Center   The state's premier Native-Alaskan attraction is expensive, and worth every penny. In a beautiful 26-acre natural setting, the center offers indoor and outdoor exhibits. On arrival, visitors are shown an excellent 15-minute film introducing Alaska's five Native groups: coastal, Aleut, Athabascan, Yupik, and Inupiaq. Indoor exhibits showcase each culture and include Native artists who demonstrate arts and crafts of their people. Hands-on activities are offered; kids can try their hands at beading in leather. The artists encourage questions. Storytelling an7d dancing performances are scheduled throughout the day. Outside, follow a trail that leads to reconstructed sites representing each of the five cultures, including dwellings and plants used in the culture. At each station, Native guides help you make sense of what you see and answer your questions. Educational programs for adults and kids are presented at the center, including art classes.

The large gift shop has a wide selection of books for all ages on Alaska Natives, along with arts and crafts. Canadians need to pay special attention to the signs that lay out rules for importing ivory to Canada. You can get a bite to eat in the café; there's an ATM in the lobby.
8800 Heritage Center Dr; 907/330-8000; www.alaskanative.net. Hours: 9am-6pm (summer); call for details (rest of year). Cost: $19.95/adult, $14.95/child 7-16, free/under 7.

Alaska State Trooper Museum   This museum is worthwhile for those interested in the peacekeeping business. It tells the story of Alaska's law enforcers through exhibits that include a restored 1952 Hudson Hornet patrol car, lots of badges, photos, and memorabilia. There's a small gift shop.

6th Ave between C & D Sts; 800/770-5050; www.alaska.net/~foast/.

Open Mon-Fri 10am-5pm; Sat noon-4pm. Free.

Anchorage Museum of History and Art ☺ One of the highlights of a trip to Anchorage is a visit to this elegant museum. On the ground floor are artworks about Alaskans and visitors, including Rockwell Kent. Standouts include the gallery of paintings by Alaska's best-known artist, Sydney Laurence. His luminous views of Mount McKinley and the Alaskan landscape convey their vast, expansive beauty more effectively than photography. The other must-see is the gallery of contemporary art by Alaska Natives. Observe how these artists combine traditional art forms with contemporary materials in breathtakingly original works. Steer kids toward the Children's Gallery, also on the ground floor, which features exhibits that are changed annually and are of special interest to children. Recently, the gallery featured artworks on the theme of "bugs." Temporary exhibits are also housed on the ground floor.

On the second floor is the Alaska Gallery, which leads visitors through Alaska's past, from prehistory to the present. A useful timeline helps visitors track the long history of Alaska Natives. Kids should enjoy the interesting dioramas.

Year round, the museum offers educational programs and art classes for kids and families. In summer, regular family nights are held in which local artists work at different stations around the museum with kids and parents to create arts and crafts. Jazz nights are also held. There is an excellent gift shop, along with the Gallery Café (see "Places to Eat"). In summer, when the museum is open late, the café serves appetizers.

121 W 7th Ave; 907/343-4326; www.anchoragemuseum.org. Open Sun-Fri 9am-9pm; Sat 9am-6pm (May 15-Sept 15); Tues-Sat 10am-6pm; Sun 1-5pm (rest of year). Cost: $5/adult $4.50/under 18.

The Imaginarium ☺ This charming science center is bigger than it looks from its mall entryway. Many hands-on exhibits are downstairs. There's a small planetarium, marine-life touch tank, and some appealing reptiles, including a small alligator, a couple of demure boa constrictors, and Monte, a large python. One popular exhibit is on the science of bubbles. Exhibits on plasma state and the science of the aurora help explain the physical principles behind nature's greatest light show. Scheduled programming is offered for kids of various ages. Exhibits change periodically. The tiny, but excellent store is jam-packed with science books, games, and toys.

737 W 5th Ave, Ste G; 907/276-3179; www.imaginarium.org. Open Mon-Sat 10am-6pm; Sun noon-5 pm. Cost: $5/adult, $4.50/child 2-12, free/under 2.

The Oscar Anderson House Museum If your family enjoys historical homes, you'll love the Oscar Anderson House. Built in 1915, this was one of the first privately owned wood-frame homes in Anchorage. The house stands much as it has for all those years; although a loving restoration has provided a facelift. It's fun to let the mind wander and imagine what it might have been like to be among the first non-Native people to settle in Alaska (Anderson claimed he was the 18th person to arrive in what would later become Anchorage). Oscar and Elizabeth Anderson raised three children. Kids will enjoy hearing how they lived, seeing what they wore, and what toys they owned. Guides offer an interactive tour, asking visitors to guess about some of the house's mystery items.

420 M St, near Elderberry Park; 907/274-3600. Open daily mid-May–mid-Sept, daily noon-4pm. Cost: $2/adult, $1/child 5-12.

Parks

Alaska Botanical Garden   This 110-acre park lies within **Far North Bicentennial Park** (whose 4,000 acres abut Chugach State Park) and features northern perennials, a rock garden, and herb garden. The **wildflower trail** introduces visitors to common local wildflowers. The 1.2-mile **Lowenfels Family Nature Trail** makes a good hike for young kids, with plenty of wildlife on view; check Campbell Creek for spawning salmon in summer. New trails and a children's garden are planned. The garden Web site includes a kids' page with gardening resources for children. Nearby is the Bureau of Land Management's **Campbell Creek Science Center** (6881 Abbott Loop Rd; 907/267-1247), whose mission is to promote understanding of nature. The center offers scheduled educational programs for kids, generally presented through schools. Call for details.

East on Tudor Rd, right on Campbell Airstrip Rd; take first left; park at Benny Benson School; 907/770-3692; www.alaskabg.org. Open 9am-9pm. Free admission.

Delaney Park   This long rectangular park was once the city's airfield. Today, it's a great place for kids to race around. Among the amenities are picnic facilities, a playground, wading pool, and flower gardens.

Between 9th and 10th Aves, and A to P Sts.

Earthquake Park   This park, which intersects with the Tony Knowles Coastal Trail, has signage describing the effects on Anchorage of the Good Friday earthquake in 1964.

Access from W Northern Lights Blvd or via Tony Knowles Coastal Trail.

Tony Knowles Coastal Trail   On a sunny summer day, you'll share this lovely 11-mile, paved trail along the Knik Arm waterfront with a cross-section of Anchorage families on foot, in-line skates, and bikes. In winter, it's used for cross-country skiing. The park begins at the west end of downtown. **Elderberry Park** (5th Ave & M St) abuts the trail and has playground equipment. Also within view is **Oscar Anderson House** (see "Museums"). From downtown, the trail runs southwest, past Earthquake Park, to Kincaid Park, at Point Campbell, the southern tip of the blunt peninsula that separates Knik Arm from Turnagain Arm.

Along the route you'll pass nesting waterfowl; **Westchester Lagoon** (about a mile south of the north end of the trail) is a good place to look. The

---

☛ **Parent Tip**

The coastal trail is worth exploring if the weather cooperates. Pack a picnic lunch and don't forget binoculars to check out birdlife along the way. Check with the Audubon Hot Line (907/338-2473), where a recorded message lists recent bird sightings in the refuge and Anchorage area. **Warning:** The wide, flat expanses of muddy beach stretching west from the trail to the water can be enticing for children. But under no circumstances should you allow them to venture onto the mudflats. Walking on the mudflats, anywhere between Knik Arm and Turnagain Arm, can be deadly! Not only do they contain quicksand, but deadly bore tides can race in far faster than any child can run. You'll see warning signs at intervals along the trail; take them very seriously. ▣

Anchorage Coastal Wildlife Refuge starts at Point Woronzof, about halfway along the trail, and runs south along Turnagain Arm to Potter. Although the most popular site for wildlife viewing is farther south (see "Potter Marsh"), birds are abundant all along the trail.
Access at west end of 2nd, 5th, 9th Aves; Earthquake Park, Kincaid Park.

Kincaid Park   This large (1,400 acres), popular wilderness park has 43 miles of dirt trails for biking, hiking, running, and, in winter, skiing. Moose, bears, and other wildlife are often sighted here, so be vigilant. Hills in the park offer views of downtown, Knik Arm, Cook Inlet, Mount McKinley and other peaks.
Access from west end of Raspberry Rd (off Minnesota Dr) or south end of Tony Knowles Coastal Trail; 907/343-4474.

Animals Animals

Alaska Zoo ☺   This excellent zoo specializes in northern fauna. You'll find a few exotic species including Siberian tigers, Bactrian camels, and llamas, but all come from cold climates. An exception is the lone African elephant. If you've been unlucky with bear sightings, you'll see them here, including black and brown bears, and a Kodiak bear. Other animals include musk oxen, Dall sheep, moose, and wolverines. Programs for children and families are offered throughout the year. A well-equipped gift shop sells stuffed animals, assorted books and toys. There's a snack bar and summer picnic area.
4731 O'Malley Rd; 907/346-1088; www.alaskazoo.org. Open daily, 9am-6pm; Sat-Sun, 9am-6pm (summer); daily, 10am-5pm (rest of year). Cost: $8/adult, $5/child 12-17, $4/child 3-11, free/under 3.

Elmendorf State Fish Hatchery   Throughout the summer, various species of salmon can be spied through the salmon-viewing area here. You'll find King salmon from late May through July; Coho visit August through mid September.
North bank of Ship Creek, near Reeve Blvd & Post Rd 907/274-0065; www.sf.adfg.state.ak.us/statewide/hatchery/. Open daily, late May-Sept., 8am-10pm. Free.

Raising Children in Alaska

By Bridjette March

Although in most ways raising children in Alaska is not very different from raising children anywhere, some differences merit consideration. Bridjette March, born and raised in Anchorage, has raised two children in Alaska and offers thoughts on what "northern" parenting entails.

When They're Small

For infants and early toddlers, life is not too complex in a cold climate. Parents must make sure that coats, boots, mittens, and hats are appropriate to protect the child at very cold temperatures. When transporting them, you make sure you have the necessary equipment to survive a vehicle breakdown. I always packed a duffle with plenty of down accessories: extra coats, Sorrel boots with liners (dry), mittens instead of gloves, scarves (never left hanging out of a jacket where they could be caught in a snow machine or sled), turtlenecks, and even face masks. Today, all these come in polypropylene fabrics.

As They Grow

One of the most important tasks in northern childrearing is making sure your child gets physical exercise. Once they hit school age, this can take the form of sports or gym class. Younger children can be taken to programs such as "Kinder Gym" or to playgroups.

As the kids grow, having lots of space for indoor play is helpful. One family I know with triplet boys and two other sons built a very large, basic home with a gymnasium at the basement level.

Respect the Wildlife

Anchorage has an "urban moose population" of around 120. It's important to alert children in areas where moose can frequent front yards about moose habits. Recently, at my home in Anchorage, I awoke to loud banging on my front door; and on investigation I discovered a cow moose had kicked it. I tried to shoo her away from our lovely mountain ash tree, but to no avail.

Wolf Song of Alaska This small museum-cum-advocacy group-cum-store is dedicated to wolves. Exhibits introduce visitors to wolf physiology and social life, and explain how wolves interact with their environment. You can also participate in an Adopt a Wolf program. The Howling Puppy gift shop sells cute wolf toys, books (some for kids), artwork, and assorted memorabilia.

6th & C St. Mall; 907/274-9653, 907/688-9653; www.wolfsongalaska.org. Open daily in summer; hours vary, rest of year. Call for details. Cost: $4/adult, $2/child 6-18, free/under 6.

Lighten Up

The coldest days in Alaska are also the darkest. At Point Barrow, the sun does not rise for several months. In Fairbanks and Anchorage, it gets dark just after lunch and remains that way until 10 or 11am the next morning. So kids get up in the dark, go to school or work, and come home in the dark. Seasonal Affective Disorder (SAD) can cause depression in people living in such climates; children, too, can be affected. One treatment is extended exposure to special fluorescent lights. Getting out and involved in social activities can also help; it's important for children develop the habit of staying active in the winter.

Beginning December 21, the light comes back, at a rate of six minutes a day, until we wind up with 20 hours of sunlight each day in June! Children in Alaska are used to this and tend to extend bedtimes with the light. On the summer solstice, a baseball game begins in local parks at midnight and goes until . . . whenever.

Hike Off Your Blues

One of the wonderful things about living in Alaska is the accessibility to the outdoors and activities such as skiing, fishing, boating, and hiking, literally in your own back yard. Anchorage also has a wonderful system of bicycle and running trails. In winter, these become cross-country ski trails. In winter, I made a cross-country ski track in the backyard for my young son to ski around; the same backyard became a baseball or football field in summer. Many folks put ice-skating rinks in their yards.

Go Fish

Ship Creek, which runs through downtown Anchorage, has a salmon derby in summer. Anyone can go down and fish, and lots of high-school kids spend late-night hours there.

Alaskan Athletes

Sports in which Alaskan kids excel include cross-country skiing, downhill skiing, and snowboarding. Olympians include Tommy Moe, who won the gold medal in downhill skiing, and snowboarder Rosy Fletcher. We've also produced some NHL hockey players, most notably Scott Gonzales. These athletes grew up hiking nature trails, skiing in our wonderful mountain ranges, and playing at local public hockey rinks. ◼

Active Fun

Ice Skating In winter, you can skate on one of five outdoor, city-maintained rinks. Westchester Lagoon is maintained as a city outdoor rink from around mid-December for as long as its safe to skate on. Other city-maintained outdoor rinks are at Goose Lake, Jewel Lake, Cheney Lake, and Lake Spenard. You can rent skates from **Champions Choice** (3901 Old Spenard Hwy, Ste 12; 907/563-3503) or buy used skates at **Play It Again Sports** (2636 Spenard Rd; 907/278-7529; www.playitagainsports.com).

For ice skating in summer, there are several choices. **Ben Boeke Ice Arena**

(334 E 16th Ave, 907/274-5715; www.benboeke.com) has two rinks, along with a coffee shop. Ice-skating classes and skate rentals (preschool age and up) are offered. Farther afield, the **Harry J. Mc Donald Memorial Center** (mile 2.2 Old Glenn Hwy; 907/696-0051, Eagle River; 907/696-0052; www.custom cpu.com/themac) offers an Olympic-size rink with other facilities, including a jogging track lining the perimeter of the ice rink. Skating lessons for all ages and ability levels are offered, along with ice-hockey instruction. You can rent skates here for all ages. Family discounts are offered for admission, skate rentals, and lessons.

Swimming Anchorage is blessed with many opportunities for watery fun. A top choice is the **H2 Oasis Waterpark** (1520 O'Malley Rd; 907/344-8610, 888/426-2747; www.h2oasiswaterpark.com. Open daily 10am-10pm; $19.95/adult, $14.95/child 2-12, free/under 2). A "lazy river" ride circles the park; other features include a wave pool, and "watercoaster," a lagoon with a pirate ship and water cannons, an enclosed slide, and more. There's also a game room, snack bar, and gift shop. Kids under 13 must be accompanied by an adult.

For a less overwhelming experience, visit one of the city's six municipal pools (located in Anchorage high schools). **West Pool** (1700 Hillcrest Dr; 907/274-5161) is lucky enough to have its own waterslide along with the pool. For locations and schedules, contact **Anchorage Parks and Recreation** (907/343-4476; www.muni.org/parks/pools/; fee: $5.25/adult, $3.50/3-18, free/under 3).

Kid Culture

Alaska Center for the Performing Arts The city's fine-arts center includes several live performance facilities. Nature films are shown on the IMAX screen at the Discovery Theatre. Educational programs and workshops, some for kids are offered. Backstage tours for school-age kids can be arranged (907/263-2920). *621 W 6th Ave; 907/263-2900; www.alaskapac.org*

Anchorage Concert Association This nonprofit brings classical music to town and includes education for all ages in its mission. Contact them for information on upcoming programs of interest to children and families. *430 W 7th Ave, Ste 200; 907/272-1471; www.anchorageconcerts.org*

Summer Music Conservatory The Anchorage Music Festival offers programs for kids of various ages over a week in mid June. Kids 6-11 can attend Orff Camp; music instruction in a variety of instruments is offered for kids ages 11-18. *Anchorage Music Festival, PO Box 103251, Anchorage, AK 99510-3251; 907/276-2465; www.festivalmusic.org*

Anchorage Symphony Orchestra In addition to its regular concert schedule, the ASO has outreach programs to schools. An annual family concert is held on Halloween. *400 D St, Ste 230; 907/274-8668; www.anchoragesymphony.org*

Music in the Park From June through August, free concerts are offered twice a week in downtown Anchorage. *4th Ave & E St; 907/279-5650; www.ancdp.com/pages/Events/musicpark/. Wed, Fri noon-1pm.*

The Great Outdoors

Bicycling   Anchorage roads are not particularly bike friendly. But the extensive trail system in and around the city, used for biking in summer, makes for great family bike outings. See "Parks" for ideas. To rent bikes, head to **Downtown Bicycle Rental** (333 W 4th Ave; 907/279-5293; alaska-bike-rentals.com), where bikes for all ages are available. Bikes come with helmets, lock, and map. The **Bike Exchange** (211 E 4th Ave; 907/276-2453) also has bikes for rent.

Flightseeing   A host of choices confronts visitors interested in seeing the view from above. **Era Aviation** (907/248-4422, 800/478-1947; www.era-aviation.com) offers a 1940s twist on the standard flightseeing tour: in a DC3, restored in 1940s décor with corroborating touches like vintage magazines and big band recordings. You can choose Denali, Harding Icefield, Prince William Sound, and Lake Chakachamna (over the Alaska Range) tours. A 90-minute trip runs $225 per person.

Rust's Flying Service (907/243-1595, 800/544-2299; www.flyrusts.com) offers trips taking off from Lake Hood to points near (Chugach Mountains) and far (Denali National Park); longer bear-watching flights are offered. Prices start at $89 per person for a 30-minute flight.

Hiking   Many city parks are big enough to feature extensive trail systems ideal for family hiking. See "Parks." **Chugach State Park** offers terrific hiking for families, from easy scenic hikes a few miles from downtown, to challenging trails suitable for experienced hikers only. Public-use cabins can be rented in the park. Bear in mind that you're in high mountains here, and that even the easiest hikes can be dangerous if you don't pay attention to where you're going. Alaska's most popular hike, to the summit of **Flattop Mountain**, has seen plenty of injuries and even deaths. Your kids may see their Anchorage counterparts dashing along the trail, but resident youngsters likely have made the trip many times. Bears and other wildlife hang out here. Keep young kids close and establish ground rules for older kids. Hiking in groups of two or more is recommended.

If you have time for only one hike, head up to the **Glen Alps Trailhead**, where you'll find plenty of parking. For very small children, the mostly paved **Anchorage Overlook Trail** (a .25-mile loop, wheel accessible) brings you to breathtaking views of the city, Cook Inlet, and the Alaska Range. If conditions are good, you can see Mount McKinley. If you have at least two hours and your kids can handle the steep, three-mile round trip, the **Flattop Mountain Trail** is highly recommended. You'll gain 1300 feet in 1.5 miles. Allow plenty of time and supervise kids carefully. The mountain and water views are terrific. This area is prone to avalanches in winter.

Access to Glen Alps Trailhead: take Old Seward Hwy south; turn east onto O'Malley Rd; at Hillside Dr turn right, then left onto Upper Huffman Rd; follow to Toilsome Hill Dr; turn right and follow to parking lot. 907/269-8400; www.dnr.state.ak.us/parks/units/chugach/.

For information on the many other hikes in the park, check in town at APLIC or at the Eagle River Nature Center (see "Northeast of Anchorage").

Skiing   For downhill skiing, the top local choice is **Alyeska Resort**, in Girdwood (see "Southeast of Anchorage"). Closer to town is the **Hilltop Ski Area** (off Abbott Rd, near Hillside Dr; 907/346-1407; www.hilltopskiarea.org) with lessons for children and families (907/346-2169), ski school, and equipment rentals. Adults can expect to pay between $25 and $30 for a day's rental of skis or snowboard and boots; kid rentals are a little less. For most families, the best deal is the family rental rate of $72 for four people. Hills range from easy to difficult; there are several ski jumps. Hilltop is a nonprofit, owned and operated by Youth Exploring Adventure. They also offer after-school programs for kids.

City park trails are turned into cross-country ski trails in winter, groomed and some lighted for night skiing.

Calendar of Events

January
Weekend Races in Winter
Alaskan Sled Dog & Racing Association
Tozier Memorial Track, 907/562-2235.

Anchorage Folk Festival
University of Alaska Anchorage; 907/566-2334; www.anchoragefolkfestival.org
Since 1990, this annual event has featured Alaska artists. In summer, they offer a fiddle camp.

March
Iditarod Sled Dog Race ☺
907/376-5155; www.iditarod.com
The state's most famous sled dog race starts from downtown Anchorage (but unseasonably warm weather caused the 2003 Iditarod to be moved to Fairbanks) and runs 1,049 miles to Nome. The Junior Iditarod for young mushers occurs a week earlier. Many family and kid-oriented events center around the Iditarod.

April
Native Youth Olympics ☺
907/265-5981
Alaska Native young people compete at traditional games.

June
The Anchorage Festival of Music Summer Solstice Series
907/276-2465; www.festivalmusic.org
A week of concerts leads up to the solstice.

Three Barons Renaissance Fair
907/868-8012; www.3barons.org
Here's an opportunity to let out your inner medieval peasant.

Resources

Audubon Society
Audubon hotline, 907/338-2473

Anchorage Chamber of Commerce
441 W 5th Ave, Ste 300, Anchorage, AK 99501
907/272-2401; www.anchoragechamber.org

Anchorage Convention & Visitors Bureau
524 W 4th Ave, Anchorage AK 99501; 907/276-4118; www.anchorage.net

Department of Natural Resources Public Information Center (state parks)
550 W 7th Ave, Ste 1260, Anchorage, AK 99501-3557
907/269-8400; www.dnr.state.ak.us

Log Cabin Visitor Information Center
4th Ave & F St; 907/274-3531

Books

Alaska Geographic. *Anchorage.*
Audubon Society. *A Field Guide to Birding in Anchorage.*
Nienhueser, Helen D. and John Wolfe, Jr. *55 Ways to the Wilderness in Southcentral Alaska.* The Mountaineers, 1994. This book catalogues hikes in the vicinity of Anchorage and the Kenai Peninsula.
Zimmerman, Jenny. *A Naturalist's Guide to Chugach State Park.*

SOUTHEAST OF ANCHORAGE

The Seward Highway hugs Turnagain Arm southeast past Girdwood to Portage, where it turns south onto the Kenai Peninsula. At Portage, drivers can head east to Prince William Sound via the **Whittier-Portage Glacier Access Road** or continue south to Seward and Homer. While the drive to Girdwood is only 37 miles (48 to Portage), there are several attractions along the way worth a stop, especially if the weather is nice. The view is magnificent.

Potter Marsh About 10 miles outside Anchorage, just after the Rabbit Creek Road exit, is a pullout and boardwalk featuring interpretive signs that leads through several miles of the **Anchorage Coastal Wildlife Refuge.** The marsh is home to varied migrating birds, waterfowl, and other animals. Moose are abundant, and in the higher elevations you can sometimes spot Dall sheep. About two miles farther along the highway, in a restored train car, is the **Kenai Peninsula Visitor Center** (907/336-3300; www.kpvc.org; open daily in summer, 8am-5pm). There's also a small snack bar and a few items for sale. Here, too, is the **Potter Section House**, headquarters for **Chugach State Park** (907/345-5014; open Mon-Fri 8am-4:30pm; www.dnr.state.ak.us/parks/units/chugach/turnagan/). The historic 1929 house was built to house and service Alaska Railroad crews. Today, you'll find information on the park and some exhibits. Take a look at the awesome rotary snow plow for trains. There are restrooms, and a flower garden in summer. Across the street, is the trailhead for the **Turnagain Arm Trail,** with parking. This fairly easy trail runs parallel to the Seward

---

☛ Parent Tip

If you can, try to arrive at Beluga Point just after low tide to experience the bore tides. The sight of the tidal waters rushing in is breathtaking. You'll need a tide table and a little luck. Most coastal visitor centers in Alaska have tide tables or you can check a tide table Web site (www.freetides.com). The closer you are to a full or new moon, the lower the low (spring) tides will be. To calculate low tide at Beluga Point if you're coming from Anchorage, add 2 hours and 15 minutes to the Anchorage low tide. Do not venture onto the mudflats where the sand acts like quicksand! ▣

Highway for about nine miles with good wildlife viewing and lots of wildflowers in spring.

McHugh Creek Picnic Area   About three miles east of Potter Marsh, this picnic area has great views, tables, paved paths, restrooms, and a viewing platform with interpretive displays. Several trails start here.

Beluga Point   As the name suggests, visitors here stand a good chance of spotting these attractive animals. Have binoculars handy.

Indian Valley Mine National Historic Site   The tiny settlement of Indian sits directly across Turnagain Arm from Hope; both were sites of a Gold Rush (see "Kenai Peninsula"); today, you can stop to check out the remaining historic buildings and have a shot at panning for gold yourself. The small museum has a gift shop along with gold-pan kits that contain "paydirt."
Mile 104 on Seward Hwy; 907/653-1120; www.indianvalleymine.com. Open daily mid-May-mid-Sept 9am-9pm. Cost: $1/person (gold-panning $3-20).

GIRDWOOD

This small town 40 miles southeast of Anchorage, with a population of about 2,000, was founded as the site of gold-mining operations; today, it's a tourist destination with easy access to hiking, boating, and wildlife sightseeing in summer and the state's best skiing in winter.

Places to Stay

Alyeska Prince Hotel, Alyeska Resort ($$$)
907/754-1111, 800/880-3880; www.alyeskaresort.com
FYI: 307 rooms, refrigerators; 4 restaurants, 2 coffee shops; tram, fitness center, swimming pool, hot tub, spa; nature trails, skiing, snowboarding, fishing and sightseeing tours
The Alyeska Prince bills itself as the state's premier destination resort, and it's hard to disagree. Nestled under Mount Alyeska, the resort makes the most of its gorgeous location year round. The resort is owned by a Japanese corporation and caters to Asian visitors. Among its restaurants, only the Pond Café is recommended for young kids (see "Places to Eat"). The coffee shops also serve kid cuisine. Seven Glaciers Restaurant offers fine dining; to get here, you'll

Baby Beluga

Many children know Raffi's song "Baby Beluga." In Alaska, kids have an opportunity to see these small intriguing white whales in the wild. They are a common sight year round on Turnagain Arm east of Anchorage and also off the bluffs in the town of Kenai. Belugas have no dorsal fins; to spot them, look for white ovals just under the surface of the water an hour before or after high tide.

Belugas live on a diet of fish and shellfish and travel in small groups. Babies are a dark gray, which fades to white by the time they reach age 5. Their life expectancy ranges from 30 to 50 years in the wild. Belugas are boisterously social and very noisy. Their sounds have been likened to an orchestra tuning up or a herd of cows mooing.

Although their only natural enemies are ice (they can become trapped in it), orcas (killer whales), and the occasional polar bear, Alaska Belugas have been endangered by whaling and pollution. The population in this area is estimated at around 250.

Resources

Raffi, *Baby Beluga*. Crown, 1997. The lyrics to Raffi's song are featured in this picture book.

Schuch, Steve. *A Symphony of Whales*. Harcourt Brace, 1999. This picture book tells the story of a young Russian girl who is instrumental in saving thousands of Beluga whales.

Enchanted Learning (www.enchanted learning.com/subjects/whales/species/ Beluga/). This Web site has information and kid activities related to Beluga whales.

National Oceanographic and Atmospheric Administration (NOAA); nmml.afsc.noaa.gov/education/cetace ans/beluga2/. You'll find detailed information on Belugas with links to information on the Alaska Beluga population.

Ocean Conservancy (www.ocean conservancy.org/dynamic/issues/fish /belugaWhales/belugaWhales/). This Web site is devoted to conserving marine animals, including the Beluga whale. ◼

need to take the tram (the fare is included for diners). For a quick meal with a view, try the Glacier Express (see "Alyeska Tram"). The Teppanyaki Katsura Restaurant is a Japanese steakhouse, not a great choice for kids.

For families, staying here makes most sense if you're here to enjoy skiing or other outdoor amenities the resort has in abundance. The nature trails, maintained as part of the Chugach National Forest, can be fun to explore in summer. The resort can save you the trouble of setting up wildlife cruises, kayaking, rafting, and other trips. The tram to the top of the mountain is a fun ride for all ages.

High season is winter (November to May depending on weather conditions); the large mountain ski area has downhill skiing for all levels of ability. The Mountain Learning Center (907/754-2280), a ski and snowboarding school, offers classes, courses, and packages for kids ages 3 and up, families, and adults at all levels. Group and private instruction is available. Ski and snowboarding equipment can be rented at the resort, which also has a repair shop. Night skiing, snowshoeing, heliskiing, cross-country skiing, and dogsledding are offered as well.

66 P A R E N T   C O M M E N T S 99

> *"We sprang for one of the cheaper rooms, barely within our budget, but it was large and even had a partial view of the mountains. The towel racks are heated; make sure small kids know this or they could get burned. Our kids found their way to the pool by instinct, but adults were not so lucky. The pool is at one end of the resort, a really long way from a lot of the rooms. If there are younger kids in your family, ask for a room close to the pool. There are stringent rules for showering before entering the pool."*

Bud & Carol's B&B ($$)

Arlberg Dr & Brighton Dr, 907/783-3182; www.budandcarolsbandb.com
FYI: 2 B&B suites, hot tubs, TV/VCR, continental breakfast; rental discounts on snowboard/ski equipment

This B&B, operated by the couple who also own the town ice cream shop (see "Places to Eat") is close to the Alyeska Resort and offers comfortable accommodation for families. Rates cover room and breakfast for two; you'll pay $15 more for each child.

Places to Eat

Alpine Diner & Bakery

Girdwood Station Mall; Alyeska Hwy & Seward Hwy; 907/783-2550
Hours: Open daily 6am-11pm

Drop in for a quick, high-calorie breakfast before you hit the road for the Kenai Peninsula, or the trail or ski slopes. They serve full meals, too, but quality is uneven, and you're better off sticking with the baked goods they're known for. The pecan bars are highly recommended.

The Bake Shop

Alyeska Boardwalk (3 miles up Alyeska Hwy; left at Arlberg, right at Olympic Circle and follow signs); 907/783-2831; www.thebakeshop.com
Hours: Open daily 7am-7pm; open Sat till 8pm

This small shop is redolent with the scent of baked goods, spicy soups, and gourmet espresso. Everything here is homemade from natural ingredients. Breakfast is served until 1pm daily: omelets, huge sweet rolls, sourdough pancake stacks. For lunch there's always a hearty soup brewing and if you have room, try the bakery's famous Alyeska cookie or a slice of vanilla butter cake. Their jams and jellies are available for sale and make nice gifts. A nice gift shop is just downhill from here, offering Native art, jewelry, and small sculptures at reasonable prices.

☛ Parent Tip

Skiing on Mount Alyeska is considered difficult at best; some have rated the ski area among the top five most challenging in the U.S. There are several good beginner runs, but these get quite crowded. Families that include strong skiers—or at least strong adult skiers—will do fine here, as will young beginners. But options are very limited for older learners and intermediate skiers. You'll have more choices and pay less at Hilltop in Anchorage. ▣

The Ice Cream Shop
In the Tesoro Mall; 907/783-1008, 907/783-3182; www.theicecreamshop.com
This excellent purveyor of ice cream treats offers flavors from the traditional to only-in-Alaska varieties. Two choices popular with adventurous eaters are Fireweed and Honey or Ginger, Cinnamon, and Berry. Among the beverages offered are espresso drinks.

The Pond Café
In the Alyeska Prince Resort, 1000 Arlberg Ave; 907/754-1111; restaurant: 907/754-2248
Hours: Open daily 7am-10pm
It's not exciting, and prices are high, but you'll get classic, well-prepared hotel food and a kids' menu.

What to See & Do

Alyeska Tram Even if you don't stay at the resort, take a trip up in the tram. In winter, the tram takes 3.5 minutes to reach the 2,334-foot summit; 7 minutes in summer. Each car holds up to 60 passengers, and waits are short. The views of Turnagain Arm and mountains are spectacular. At the top, follow a short trail to Alyeska Glacier. If you're dining at the Seven Glaciers, your tram ticket is free. In summer, a better choice for families is to buy a tram/lunch combo ticket (offerings include burgers and hot dogs and other child-friendly fare).
At the Alyeska Resort. Ticket office: 907/754-2275. Cost: $16/adult, $13/adult hotel guest, $12/Alaska native, $10/student 8-17, $7/under 8. Tram/lunch combo: $19/adult, $15/student 8-17, $12/ under 8.

Alaska Wildlife Conservation Center If you've been frustrated in your search for Alaska's large wildlife, make a trip to this drive-through wild animal park with bison, moose, Sitka black-tailed deer, elk, caribou, musk oxen, and bears. The mission is not just to show off wildlife; orphaned animals are rescued, nursed to health, and released in the wild. The large, well-stocked gift shop carries Alaskana, and the snack bar has treats.
Mile 79 Seward Hwy; 907/783-2025; www.alaskawildlife.org. Open daily in summer: 8am-8pm; winter: open daily 10am-5pm to dusk. Cost: $5/adult, $3/child 4-15, free/under 4.

Crow Creek Mine If you missed out on Klondike tourist attractions, you can pan for gold here; for almost a half century, this mine produced respectable quantities of gold. Staff will outfit you with panning gear and give a demonstration of how it's done. The mine closed in 1940, and visitors are told that more gold remains in the ground than was ever removed. Tour historic buildings dating from the original 1898 mining camp, including a blacksmith's shop, mess hall, bunkhouse, and barn. There's a gift shop and camping is allowed (no hookups or water).

2 miles on Alyeska Hwy to Crow Creek Rd, turn left and follow 3.5 miles to mine. 907/278-8060; www.crowcreekgoldmine.com. Open daily, May 15- Sept 15: 9am-6pm. Cost: $8/adult, $4/under 13 (includes mining); camping: $5.

Girdwood Center for Visual Arts Works by local artists are exhibited here and a variety of arts and crafts are for sale. The center offers classes and workshops in different media.

Off Alyeska Hwy on Hightower Rd. 907/783-3209; www.girdwood.org. Open daily, May-July.

Chugach National Forest This is the nation's second largest national forest, with 5,400,000 acres. This huge chunk of land extends around Prince William Sound from Cape Saint Elias in the east, encompassing Cordova, Valdez, and Whittier, and on to the northeast Kenai Peninsula up to Seward. The forest has 16 road-accessible campgrounds, many public-use cabins, and more than 200 miles of trails. **Winner Creek Gorge Trail**, one of the forest's most kid-friendly, starts from the Alyeska Resort grounds close to the tramway (follow signs) and runs 2.5 miles through beautiful forested terrain; look for berries in summer. The trail continues on as the **Upper Winner Creek Trail**, for eight more miles; this portion is suitable for families with experienced hikers or older kids.

907/743-9500; www.fs.fed.us/r10/chugach/

Portage Glacier Eleven miles east of the Alyeska Highway turnoff on the Seward Highway is the ghost town of Portage. Only the dead trees and occasional sagging building provide a clue to the devastation caused by the 1964 earthquake. From its junction with the Seward Highway, the Whittier/Portage Glacier Access road runs east to Whittier (see sidebar). The glacier, five miles long and a mile wide, runs into Portage Lake, which in turn gives rise to the Portage River that runs into Turnagain Arm. Even if you're not going all the way to Whittier, drive five miles east of the Seward Highway to the Chugach National Forest **Begich, Boggs Visitor Center.** The center was named for two politicians, Nicholas Begich, U.S. Representative from Alaska, and U.S. Senate Majority Leader Wade Boggs, whose plane disappeared in the vicinity in 1972. (This site is among the state's most visited; expect a crowd.)

The attractive center, built on the glacier's terminal moraine, has all the amenities one could ask for—except a view of the glacier it was designed to showcase! Portage Glacier has receded so fast that it is no longer visible from the center. To see it, you'll need to take one of the many cruises offered. However, if you're going to visit the Kenai Peninsula, you might opt to skip a cruise and visit Exit Glacier in Kenai Fjords National Park instead (see "Kenai Peninsula"), where kids on foot can get close to the glacier.

Whichever course you take, don't skip the visitor center. Among its features of interest to kids are the large chunks of genuine iceberg, and a display of ice worms, tiny black, threadlike beings that writhe and curl in the water. Also at the center are displays on the glacier and an excellent film, "Voices from the Ice." A variety of educational programs are offered in summer. Take an "ice worm safari" with a park ranger (a half-mile walk). Although you can't see the glacier from the lake any more, there are still likely to be icebergs on view, and there are several interpretive trails to follow. The **Byron Glacier Trail** takes you .75 miles along a runoff stream. A variety of cruises are offered to the glacier itself. Among them is the one-hour **Portage Glacier Cruise** on the *M/V Ptarmigan*, offered by Gray Line (Holland America Tours; 800/544-2206; mid-May-mid-Sept. Cost: $25/adult, $12.50/child 2/11, free/under 2), leaving from Portage Lake.

Nearby the visitor center is the **Williwaw Campground** (60 sites, $12/site, toilets, water, tables, firepits, dumpsters, nature trail). Head here in late August and September to get ringside seats at the spawning salmon spectacle. *Visitor Center: Open daily 9am-6 pm, Memorial Day to Labor day; 10-4 Sat-Sun, Labor Day to Memorial Day. 907/783-3242 (GRD) or 783-2326 (BBVC) for current hours. Campground: 877/44-6777.*

Calendar of Events

April
Alyeska Resort Spring Carnival
907/754-2209
This carnival is a popular spring event and features silly ski activities (the Slush Cup is awarded), amid a festive atmosphere.

July
Girdwood Forest Faire
907/783-2931
A family-oriented festival with arts and crafts, music, food, games, and sports events.

September
Alyeska Blueberry & Mountain Arts Festival
907/754-1111
This annual festival at the Alyeska Prince Resort celebrates berries, accompanied by food, music, arts and crafts events.

Resources
Girdwood Chamber of Commerce
PO Box 222, Girdwood, AK 99587-0330

Girdwood Resort Association Web site
www.girdwoodalaska.com

Chugach National Forest (office in Anchorage)
3301 C St, Ste 300, Anchorage AK 99503; 907/743-9500; www.fs.fed.us/r10/chugach/

Whittier

At the west end of Passage Canal, a narrow fjord leading west from Prince William Sound, is the tiny town of Whittier, separated by only a few miles from Cook Inlet. For years, Whittier has been accessible by train from Anchorage and Seward; recently, the train tunnel was expanded to allow vehicular traffic. Whether you get here by train or car, make it a day trip; services and attractions in Whittier are limited. Most children (and some adults) will find the tunnel the biggest draw, a case of getting there being nearly all the fun. Once in Whittier, there's little to do except take a scenic and wildlife-rich but fairly pricey cruise on the Sound, or turn around and go back.

The town was constructed during World War II as part of the war effort. Engineers literally blasted through mountains to create rail access to an alternative ice-free port in case Seward was attacked by the Japanese. Cold War concerns kept the military here until 1960.

The town is an oddity: dreary concrete buildings surrounded by extraordinary natural beauty. Half of Whittier's 300 residents live in a monolithic 14-story high rise, the Begich Tower. Once a military building, it's been reborn as condominium housing. The even bigger Buckner Building has not been renovated. A few hotels and B&Bs (one of which is in the Begich Tower), a smattering of restaurants, and a gift shop or two round out the amenities. Several wildlife cruises leave from here and combined tunnel/cruise trips have become popular with cruise passengers and tour groups.

Inside the tunnel the road, which shares the tunnel with the train, is one lane. Travel direction is one way, changing at specified intervals (generally every half hour). All road traffic is prohibited when trains are in the tunnel. The road is open daily year round, 6am-11pm in summer; shorter hours in winter. Expect line ups waiting to drive through the tunnel in summer. Be sure to check schedules before heading out. The round-trip drive through the tunnel costs $12 for cars, and between $25

Books

Johannsen, Neil and Elizabeth. *Exploring Alaska's Prince William Sound: Its Fiords, Islands, Glaciers & Wildlife.* Alaska Travel Publications, 1975. This is a useful guide to outdoor attractions in the region.

Lethcoe, Nancy. *An Observer's Guide to the Glaciers of Prince William Sound.* This book details the many varied glaciers in this area.

East of Anchorage:
Glenn Highway to Glennallen

From Anchorage, the **Glenn Highway** (Hwy 1) runs northeast, parallel to Knik Arm past Eagle River and Eklutna to Palmer, home of the Alaska State Fair in the heart of the Matanuska Valley, Alaska's "breadbasket." The highway and $35 for RVs or trucks pulling trailers, depending on size.

To reach the tunnel, take the Whittier/Portage Glacier Access Road from the Seward Highway, 48 miles southeast of Anchorage.

Resources
Alaska Marine Highway System 907/272-7116 (Anchorage), 800/642-0066; www.dot.state.ak.us/amhs/. Alaska ferries run between Valdez, Whittier, and Cordova.

Alaska Railroad 800/544-0552, 907/265-2300; www.akrr.com. Glacier Discovery runs between Anchorage and Whittier; mid-May to mid-September. One way takes 2 hours, 20 minutes; fares are $55/person, plus Prince William Sound cruise add-ons.

Phillip's Cruises and Tours 907/276-8023, 800/544-0529; www.26glaciers.com/whittier/. Their 4.5-hour, 26 glacier day cruise is coordinated with Alaska Railroad Glacier Discovery service; the boat is a large catamaran with all services. A less expensive option by motor coach can be substituted

for the train. Expect to pay about $190 round trip per an adult, including rail or bus fare. Kids under 12 will pay about $100. Children under 2 ride free on bus or train, but must pay for the cruise.

Prince William Sound Cruises & Tours 800/992-1297; ww.ciritourism.com Four- and six-hour sightseeing cruises from Whittier are offered. Tour prices are comparable to Phillip's.

Whittier Tunnel 907/611-2584, 877/611-2586; www.dot.state.ak.us/creg/whittier tunnel/. Access the tunnel schedule by phone or Web site; tunnel information is broadcast on 1610 AM (Portage) and 530 AM (Whittier).

Whittier Chamber Of Commerce PO Box 607, Whittier, AK 99693, 907/472-2493

Taylor, Alan and Christine Taylor. *The Strangest Town in Alaska: The History of Whittier, Alaska, and the Portage Valley.* Kokogiak Media, 2000. Whittier just might be that strange; this entertaining book makes a strong case for it. ▣

continues to Glennallen and the junction with the Richardson Highway running from Fairbanks to Valdez. Also from Glennallen, the Tok Cutoff runs northeast to Tok and the Alaska Highway. The Glenn Highway is a lovely drive; the road is paved and open year round. You'll pass glaciers and major recreation areas, such as Lake Louise.

Anchorage to Palmer (42 m)
Palmer to Glennallen (147 m)
Sidetrip to Lake Louise (34.4 miles round trip)

Anchorage to Palmer (42 m)
Thirteen miles northeast of Anchorage, the scenic, paved Eagle River Road leads 12 miles east into Chugach State Park, ending at the park's **Eagle River Nature Center.** Along with natural history exhibits, the center has year-round

...ner, staff lead daily nature hikes. Books, maps, and ...shop. For a family hike, try the **Rodak Trail**, an easy ...ver pond and valley views. The three-mile **Albert** ...views and is groomed for cross-country skiing in ...art from the center. Public-use cabins and yurts are ...e reserved with the nature center in advance. *...07/694-2108; www.ernc.org; Sun-Thurs ...-Sat 10am-7pm, June-Aug; Tues-Sun 10am-5pm, May, Sept; Fri-Sun 10am-5pm, rest of year. Free entrance; $5/parking fee.*

For another short family hike, at Mile 25.2 of the Glenn Highway, take the Thunderbird Exit and drive east to the **Thunderbird Falls Trailhead**. This pleasant two-mile round trip is an easy hike through birch forest to a 200-foot waterfall. Watch kids carefully; the cliffs over the falls are too steep to climb on.

Eklutna   At Mile 26.3, the Eklutna Road leads to the tiny hamlet of Eklutna and nearby points of interest. **Eklutna Historical Park** is an unusual attraction that offers a unique look at Native history in southcentral Alaska. The site dates back to 1650, making it the oldest continually inhabited Athabascan (Dena'ina) site in the region. The Dena'ina first encountered white explorers here in the late 1700s, and were later influenced by the arrival of Russian missionaries.

The park includes several buildings of historical interest. The Eklutna Village Heritage House has exhibits portraying the lifestyle and art of area Natives; a small gift shop sells Native and Russian crafts. The Russian Orthodox Church, originally built in the 1830s and reconstructed in the 1970s, is listed on the National Register of Historic Places. The interior is remarkable; pause over the beautiful collection of Russian icons, many of them centuries old. Next door is a newer church, where services are still held. Walk through the understated but intriguing Eklutna Cemetery, where colorful "Spirit Houses" are placed over many graves (a custom said to be a melding of Athabascan and Russian Orthodox traditions). Color combinations identify a specific family or clan. *Mile 26 Glenn Hwy. 907/696-2828; www.eklutna.com. Open daily, 8am-6pm (mid-May-mid-Sept). Cost: $6/person, free/under 7.*

Continue east on the Eklutna Road for 10 miles to reach **Eklutna Lake Recreation Area** in Chugach State Park. The seven-mile-long lake is the park's largest and provides water to Anchorage. From here, the 13-mile **Eklutna Lakeside Trail** climbs to Eklutna Glacier. It's an easy hike, following the lakeshore for the first seven miles. It's groomed for skiing in winter. There's a large campground with 50 sites, $10/site, 23 picnic sites, water pumps, picnic tables, firepits, pit toilets, and a campground host in summer. *907/26908400; www.alaskastateparks.org*

At Mile 29.6, you can turn off onto the **Old Glenn Highway** for a pleasant drive or stay on the Glenn Highway; either way brings you to the town of **Palmer,** with over 4,000 residents, the heart of Alaska's agriculture region and home of the Alaska State Fair. Taking the Old Glenn Highway allows you to drop in on the **Reindeer Farm**, where youngsters can visit with reindeer, moose, and elk. Kids are encouraged to feed the inmates. Also here, you can go horseback riding ($35/hour, ages 10 and up). Corral rides are a good deal for small cowpokes at $5 for five minutes.

Mile 11.5 (7 miles south of Palmer) At flashing yellow light, turn onto Bodenburg Rd; go 3/4 mile; 907/745-4000; www.reindeerfarm.com; open daily 10am-6pm, May-mid Sept. Cost: $5/adult, $3/child 3-11, free/under 3.

Palmer   Palmer has a unique history. In 1935 colonists were brought from the American Midwest to establish farms, a New Deal social experiment that, despite some failures, proved to be a long-term success. Social workers selected the families to transport here (those of hardy Scandinavian heritage were thought most likely to have what it took to survive in the frozen north); some of their descendants live here still.

Pick up visitor info at the **Log Cabin Visitor Center** (723 S Valley Way; 907/745-2880; www.palmerchamber.org; open daily, 8am-6pm, May 1-Sept 15; Mon-Fri 9am-4pm, winter). The small **Colony Museum** downstairs is worth a quick look. A short walk from the visitor center at 316 Elmwood Ave is **Colony House** (907/745-1935; open in summer, Mon-Sat noon-4 pm. Cost: $2/adult, $1/child), a restored home dating from the original Matanuska colony.

Another family attraction is the **Musk Ox Farm**. This nonprofit organization raises musk ox domestically, the world's only such farm. Crossing the Beringia land bridge from Asia during the last ice age, these impressive shaggy ungulates survived where giant beavers and woolly mammoths were not so lucky. Some still survive in the wild, though the species was nearly hunted to extinction by the 1860s. The soft *qiviut* apparel sold at the Oomingmak Co-op in Anchorage is made from their wool. Entry fees include a tour of the farm. There's a gift shop.

Mile 50.1 Glenn Hwy; 907/745-4151; www.muskoxfarm.org. Open daily, 10am-6pm, Mother's Day-late Sept; by appt, rest of year. Cost: $8.50/adult, $7/child 13-18, $5.50/child 6-12, free/under 6.

For a bite to eat, head for **Vagabond Blues** (642 S Alaska St; 907/745-2233; open Mon-Thurs, 7am-9pm, Fri 7am-10pm, Sat 8am-10pm, Sun 9am-5pm), a trendy spot with lunch fare that includes healthy and hearty wraps, sandwiches, and salads. Homemade soups are served in colorful pottery bowls and accompanied by hunks of fresh-baked bread. The setting is quiet and relaxed.

Hatcher Pass/Independence Mine State Historical Park   For active families, it's worth the drive to Hatcher Pass (3,886 ft) to enjoy hiking, kayaking on the "Little Su" river, or skiing. If your goal is simply sightseeing, the drive from Palmer is pretty, and there is history to be viewed at the 760-acre park. This former site of the Alaska Pacific Consolidated Mine Company includes two historic gold mines. What remains—prospector bunkhouses, mining tunnel, assay office, and the collapsed mill—can be visited.

There are many hiking trails in the area; several are recommended for families. For specific trail information, call Mat-Su/VCR Area Headquarters in Wasilla, 907/745-3975. If you hike late summer, take a container for blueberries.

The **Hatcher Pass Road** continues on from the pass west 49 miles to Willow south of Talkeetna. While it's among the area's loveliest roads and has been upgraded, some of it is unpaved and in poor condition. However, driving the improved sections is highly recommended.

Mile 17 Hatcher Pass Rd off Fishhook Rd, approximately 12 miles from Palmer. Drivers on the way to or from Denali can access Hatcher Pass from Wasilla, via the Wasilla-Fishhook Road.

Palmer to Glennallen (147 m)

From Palmer, the road becomes gradually wilder, with the Talkeetna Mountains to the north and the Chugach Mountains to the south. Along the road are a number of pleasant campgrounds, and several recreation areas offer attractions for families.

About 60 miles east of Palmer is **Matanuska Glacier**, a finger of the enormous **Chugach Icefield**, source of the mighty Matanuska River. It's 27 miles long and four miles wide at the terminus. All access to this glacier lies through private property; to set foot on or close to it, you'll have to pay an entrance fee. At **Glacier Park Resort** (Mile 102 Glenn Hwy; 907/745-2534, 888/253-4480) payment of about $7 will get you close to the glacier, a short hike away. The resort has a basic campground along with snacks, gift shop, and guided and flightseeing tours; camping is covered by the entrance fee.

If you're not inclined to pay for the privilege of ogling ice, a number of attractive viewpoints along the highway offer more distant, but still terrific, views. You can drop by or camp at **Matanuska Glacier State Recreation Site** (Mile 101; 12 sites, $10/site, toilets, water pump, dumpster), with nature trails offering beautiful glacier vistas. Another 12 miles brings you to **Sheep Mountain Lodge** (Mile 113.5; 907/745-5121; www.sheepmountain.net; 10 cabins, restaurant, hot tub, sauna. Rates: $$; open year round) which has hiking trails.

At Mile 129.5, **Eureka Summit**, at 3,322 feet the highest point on the highway, is marked by a turnout with great mountain views.

Side Trip to Lake Louise (34.4 miles round trip)

Thirty miles beyond Eureka Summit is the **Lake Louise Road.** The first few miles are paved, but most of the 20-mile road is well-maintained gravel, leading

The Iditarod Trail Dog Sled Race: An Alaskan Tradition

By Rose Williamson

Whether you know it personally or through folklore, you probably think of Alaska as a rough, wild land, full of environmental challenges and inhabited by a tough and independent people. No Alaskan tradition embodies this image—and the attendant reality—better than the Iditarod Trail race. Run annually by a slew of hardy, mostly-Alaskan mushers and their hardier sleddogs, this grueling race typifies the environmental and psychological challenges and rewards of life up north.

A Little History

The origin of an Iditarod Trail can be traced to the Alaskan Gold Rush of the 1880s, when this rough roadway was used to transport equipment and miners to the interior of Alaska, and to bring the gold back out. But the trail as it exists today owes its origins to the diphtheria-serum run of 1925, when 20 sled teams combined their efforts to transport life-saving antitoxin from the train station at Nenana to Nome (itself one of those far, distant places), stricken by a deadly diphtheria epidemic.

The 672 miles between Nenana and Nome were covered relay-style. The last leg was run by Gunnar Kaason, guided by the able lead-dog Balto (since honored in countless ways, including an animated feature film and a statue in New York's Central Park).

Forty years later, musher Joe Redington, Sr. and Alaska historian Dorothy Page joined forces to commemorate the tradition of dog sledding. A 27-mile race was held in 1967 to bring attention to mushing; in 1973, the race route was extended to follow a part of the old Iditarod Trail.

The Trail and the Race

Today, upward of 60 sleds depart Anchorage each March 1 for the Iditarod Trail race, nicknamed "The Last Great Race on Earth." The route covers more than 1,000 miles of frozen terrain, on which mushers can expect to encounter everything from ice storms and ill-tempered wildlife to sleepless nights and hallucinations. From Anchorage, the Iditarod route winds into the Matanuska and Susitna valleys and through the Alaska Range, then passes by or through a number of tiny villages in the interior of Alaska to Nome, on the southern coast of the Seward Peninsula. Along the way are checkpoints where mushers can stop to eat, provide dog care, shift their load, or catch a bit of shut-eye. Between checkpoints at Ophir (population: 0) and Kaltag (population: 234) the trail splits; teams follow the northern route in even-numbered years, the southern route in odd.

About the Dogs

Sled dogs are Alaskan huskies, which are not actually a "breed" as defined by the American Kennel

continued on page 264

Iditarod Trail Dog Sled Race

continued from page 263

Club. Rather, these Alaskan huskies hail from a long line of canines raised in Native Alaskan villages and bred to pull sleds. Commonly called "Alaskan village dogs," these animals acclimate well to extreme cold and are considered to be the fastest, most reliable sled dogs in the world. For centuries, northerners have depended upon these dogs for transportation and for survival.

All Alaskan huskies share certain physical traits, including a physiology adapted to high calorie-intake, a willingness to pull, and the ability to change gaits comfortably. Most are black-and-white or gray in coloring, with thick coats that protect them in below-freezing temperatures.

Young animal lovers enthralled with the idea of the Iditarod may nevertheless worry about the treatment of these canine athletes on the trail. Rest assured; race regulations—not to mention the great bond between the mushers and their teams—dictate that the dogs will be treated with great care throughout their training and during the race. Prior to entering the race, each sled dog must pass a physical exam conducted by an authorized veterinarian. Along the route, mushers are required to provide the team with a certain amount of food per dog, and to carry eight pairs of booties for each. Race rules disallow inhumane treatment: "any action or inaction that causes preventable pain or suffering" to a dog. As with any athletes, some dogs do suffer injury: those requiring special care can be left at any of a number of designated "dog drops" along the route, where they will be transported to receive the treatment they need.

Resources

Iditarod Trail Sled Dog Race Headquarters
The headquarters provide visitors with a good understanding of the history of the Iditarod, and particulars of training and running sled dogs. The log museum houses race memorabilia and Native artifacts. *Mile 2.2 Knik-Goose Bay Rd, Wasilla; 907/376-5155, 800/545-6874; www.iditarod.com. Open daily 8am-7pm (summer), Mon-Fri, 9am-5pm (rest of year). Free (wheeled "dog sled" rides, $5).*

Knik Museum and Dog Mushers Hall of Fame
This historic building includes exhibits about the Knik gold rush (beginning 1897) and the Iditarod Trail race.
Mile 14 Knik-Goose Bay Rd, southwest of Wasilla; 907/376-7755; www.iditarod.com. Open Wed-Sun, noon-6 pm (June-Aug). Cost: $2.

Publications

Freedman, Lew. *Iditarod Classics: Tales of the Trail from the Men & Women Who Race Across Alaska*, Epicenter Press, 1992. Freedman has collected the timeless Iditarod Trail stories of some 20 experienced mushers (teens and older).

Paulsen, Gary. *Puppies, Dogs and Blue Northers: Reflections on Being Raised by a Pack of Sled Dogs*, Harcourt Brace & Company, 1996. This well-known children's writer (*Hatchet, Dogsong*) and his illustrator wife have made an avocation of training sled dogs (ages 10 and up).

Paulsen, Gary. *Winterdance: The Fine Madness of Running the Iditarod.* Harvest Books, 1995. The author has twice run the Iditarod Trail race and recounts some of his adventures here (ages 10 and up).

Riddles, Libby and Tim Jones. *Race Across Alaska: First Woman to Win the Iditarod Tells Her Story.* Stackpole Books, 1988. Each chapter covers a leg of the historic Iditarod Trail race won by Riddles in 1985 (teens and older).

Riddles, Libby. *Storm Run: The Story of the First Woman to Win the Iditarod Sled Dog Race,* Sasquatch Books, 2002. The picture-book look will appeal to little ones, but there is actually a lot of sophisticated information here (ages 6-10).

Web Sites
Official Web site of the Iditarod Trail Sled Dog Race Headquarters www.iditarod.com

www.dogsled.com. From this Web site, follow the Iditarod Race and get in-depth information on the competitors. (Their motto is "All the adventure, none of the frostbite").

Films
Balto. Universal Studios, 1995. This animated feature for kids, rated G, is short on historical accuracy in places, but there's enough substance to interest young kids in finding out what really happened. ▣

to one of the loveliest lakes in Alaska, surrounded by mountains and dotted with islands, an enchanting spot to spend a few days. Stop along the road for great views of **Tazlina Glacier** and **Tazlina Lake**. The road terminates at the Lake Louise, where you'll find several lodges and the attractive **Lake Louise State Recreation Area** with campground (52 sites, $10/site, toilets, water pumps, firepits, covered picnic tables, picnic shelter, trail, boat launch).

Among the resorts, **The Point Lodge at Lake Louise** is the top choice, perched on a promontory overlooking the lake. Open year round, the lodge is a spacious inn with a homey feel; children are made very welcome. The common rooms are encircled by a wide deck. There are also several small rustic cabins. The lodge provides power via its own generator. Guests dine at long tables, family style. The entire lodge can be booked for large groups. Sunsets in late summer last all night; in winter, auroras are the big draw.

Mile 17.2, Lake Louise Rd. 907/822-5566; 800/808-2018 www.thepoint lodge.com. Rates: $-$$. 13 rooms, suite; 4 cabins (some shared baths); meals, boats, floatplane dock, helicopter parking

Glennallen is another 28 miles east of the Lake Louise Road junction. See "The Road North" for what to see and do in the vicinity.

Calendar of Events

August-September
Alaska State Fair
Palmer Fairgrounds 2075 Glenn Hwy; 907/745-4827; www.akstatefair.org

The state's largest fair has the traditional farm animal and 4H Club exhibits (featuring reindeer and muskoxen) along with craft booths, live entertainment, preserves and produce, including 90 pound cabbages and other giant vegetables.

Resources

Matanuska-Susitna Convention and Visitors Bureau
HC01 Box 6166 J21, Palmer, AK 99645; 907/746-5000;
www.alaskavisit.com

Mat-Su Borough Parks & Outdoor Recreation
350 E Dahlia Ave, Palmer, AK 99645; 907/745-9631; www.co.mat-su.ak.us

Greater Palmer Chamber of Commerce
PO Box 45 Palmer, AK 99645; 907/745-2880: www.palmerchamber.org

Books

Gwin, Sally. *Mosquito Girl.* Royal Fireworks Press, 1997. This young adult novel tells the story of a teenage girl in the 1930s whose family has immigrated from Minnesota to the Matanuska colony.

7 Kenai Peninsula

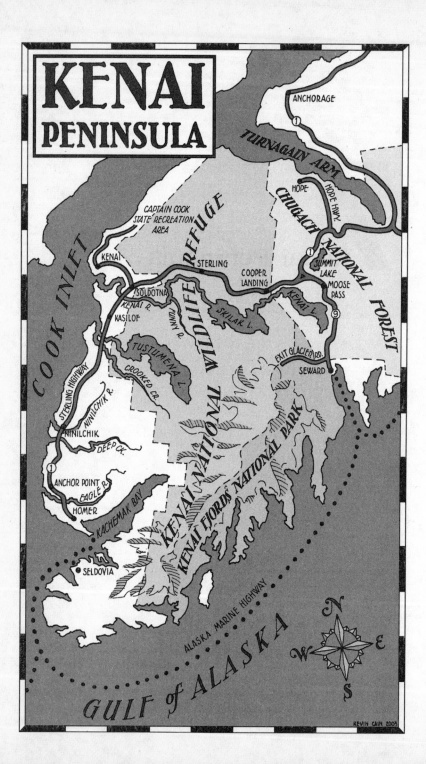

7 Kenai Peninsula

JUST 50 MILES from Anchorage, the Kenai Peninsula offers rich recreational possibilities. This is where Anchorage residents head on weekends to fish or hike; some moor pleasure boats at Seward. Kenai Peninsula destinations don't involve long road trips; the two principal towns, Seward and Homer, are 127 and 224 miles from Anchorage, respectively.

The peninsula is southwest of Anchorage across Turnagain Arm, a deep inlet running east from Cook Inlet. To the east is Prince William Sound; Kennedy Entrance separates the peninsula from Kodiak and islands to the south.

Most of the peninsula is federally protected land including Chugach National Forest, Kenai Fjords National Park, and Kenai National Wildlife Refuge. Attractions are many: Visit the Harding Ice Field in the national park, fish for salmon and go river rafting at Cooper Landing and Soldotna; enjoy attractions at Alaska's premier aquarium, the Alaska SeaLife Center, in historic Seward. Picturesque Homer offers one of the state's best and most family-friendly museums and other amenities of a much larger community. From Homer, hop an Alaska ferry to Kodiak and the Aleutian Islands or take a short trip across Kachemak Bay to tiny Seldovia.

To best enjoy the Kenai Peninsula, you'll need several days. If time is very short, however, you can visit Seward as a long daytrip from Anchorage. Peninsula weather is variable, with a moderate (for Alaska) climate. Average winter temperatures range between 0 and 24 degrees Fahrenheit. In summer, lows run in the upper 40s, while a warm day usually tops out at 68 degrees. One pleasant feature of the climate is the absence of heavy precipitation.

While some winter sports are available, such as cross-country skiing, most visitors come in summer when the region offers wonderful boating, hiking and camping, and some of the world's best sportfishing. To take advantage of these opportunities, you'll likely want to sign on with professional outfitters. A principal attraction for kids is the abundant wildlife. Moose are king; in fact, they are a hazard on the road, or perhaps we should say humans are a moose hazard (road signs record the yearly moose kill). Bears are around, but they are shy. You'll have more luck seeing Dall sheep and eagles. The most abundant wildlife is maritime. You'll spot Beluga whales from the Kenai bluffs, flotillas of sea otters in Kachemak Bay, and humpback whales and orcas on the trip to Seldovia from Homer.

History

For thousands of years, the Kenai Peninsula was home to the Kenaitze, Dena'ina Athabascan natives. Captain James Cook, the first European to venture here, landed at Anchor Point on the southwest coast in 1778. Shortly after, Russian fur traders colonized the area and stayed until 1867 when Alaska was purchased by the U.S. The oldest town on the peninsula is Kenai with many historic Russian buildings. More evidence of Russian settlement can be seen in Ninilchik and Seldovia.

In the 1880s and '90s, prospectors discovered gold on Resurrection Creek. One find triggered an intense but short-lived gold rush in 1896, bringing 3,000 prospectors to Hope and Sunrise. Most left following news of the far-bigger Klondike strikes. Hope continued to exist, barely; today, the historic district in this hamlet of about 200 residents can be toured.

Fishing has been an economic mainstay throughout peninsula history, but the discovery of oil in Cook Inlet in 1957 soon overshadowed other industry. Today, the oil and gas industry employs about a third of peninsula residents, most of who reside in the Kenai-Soldotna area. However, tourism is a growth industry as well. Most of the large cruise ships that tour the Inside Passage start from or arrive at Seward on their one-way cruises. Passengers arriving in Seward generally go straight to Anchorage (or a cruise ship) without spending much time here.

Getting To the Kenai Peninsula

By Air   Era Aviation (907/248-4422, 800/866-8394; www.eraaviation.com) serves Kenai and Homer with multiple daily flights to and from Anchorage.

By Sea   Most major cruise lines offer one-way cruises between Seward and either Vancouver, BC, or Seattle. Some cruise lines also serve California ports. See "Alaska Cruises" for details.

The **Alaska Marine Highway System** (AMHS: 907/235-8449, 800/382-9229; www.akmhs.com) runs ferries between Seldovia, Homer, Kodiak, and points west. Crossings between Seldovia and Homer are just under 2 hours. Between Homer and Kodiak, crossings are 9 hours, 30 minutes. Cross-gulf service is offered between Seward and Valdez, connecting with Juneau as well as to Homer and Kodiak. The Seward-Valdez run takes 9 hours, 30 minutes. Service varies according to time of year.

By Train   The **Alaska Railroad** ☺ (907/265-2494, 800/544-0552; akrr.com. Cost: Anchorage to Seward oneway, $55; roundtrip, $90) runs trains daily each way between Anchorage and Seward, with stops at **Girdwood**, mid-May through mid-September. The trip takes about 4 hours, 25 minutes and is strongly recommended for families. From Anchorage, as the train follows the **Turnagain Arm** coastline southeast to **Portage**, sit on the right and scan the water for Beluga whales, white ovals just beneath the surface of the water. Look for dainty little spouts from these mammals.

Watch for powerful bore tides—swift-moving walls of water that come surging into Turnagain Arm, the second most powerful in the world after those in maritime Canada's Bay of Fundy.

The train passes the ghost town of Portage, destroyed in the Good Friday earthquake of 1964. You'll pass **Spencer** and **Bartlett glaciers**, **Moose Pass**, and **Trail Lake**. A few miles before reaching the station in Seward, the train crosses the **Resurrection River**. Keep binoculars and camera handy; chances of spotting wildlife are excellent. In the mountains look for **Dall Sheep** (tiny dots of white to the unaided eye); look for moose and eagles everywhere. Railroad staff point out spots of interest and any passing wildlife. Trains have a dining car and gift shop.

By Road The **Seward Highway** (Hwy 1) is a gorgeous 127-mile drive on a good, paved road with many scenic distractions and opportunities for interesting side trips. The highway is a designated a National Forest Scenic Byway and "All-American Road," one of only 15 U.S. highways to be so named. (For information on the trip between Anchorage and Portage, such as about Potter, Girdwood, and Portage Glacier, see "Anchorage and Environs.") From Portage, the road rises to **Turnagain Pass** at 998 feet. There's a scenic view turnout with parking area and restrooms here.

Forty-three miles south of Portage, the Seward Highway splits in two. The Seward Highway continues over Moose Pass as Highway 9. **The Sterling Highway**, now designated Highway 1, turns west. It runs through Cooper Landing, 11 miles west of the Sterling Highway turnoff, and continues 48 miles west to the busy town of Soldotna. Here, the **Kenai Spur Road** runs 11 miles northwest to Kenai and north to the popular Captain Cook State Recreation Area. From Soldotna, the Sterling Highway runs south through the historic towns of Ninilchik and Anchor Point before reaching its end in Homer, a trip of 85 miles. From here, you can hop a ferry or water taxi to Seldovia, across Kachemak Bay.

By Bus Frequent bus service is provided between Seward and Anchorage by the **Alaska Parks Connection** (800/208-0200; www.alaskatravel.com. Twice daily service, Mid-May-mid-Sept. Cost: $49/adult, $24.50/child 4-12, free/under 4). Note that you must provide a car seat for all children under age 4. The **Homer Stage Line** (907/235-2252; 907/399-1847 [van phone]; homerstageline.com) connects Homer, Kenai, Soldotna, Seward, and Anchorage year round (service less frequent Sept-May). Fares run $28 to $48 one way in summer, depending on your destination. For five dollars more, they'll drop you off at the Anchorage Airport. **Kachemak Bay Transit** (907/235-9101, 877/235-9101) has daily service between Anchorage and Homer. And **Seward Bus Line** (Anchorage: 907/563-0800; Seward: 907/224-3608; www.sewardbuslines.com) offers daily, year-round service between Anchorage and Seward at $40 one way, $75 round trip with a $5 drop-off fee for the Anchorage Airport.

Regional Resources

Alaska State Parks
Kenai Area Office, PO Box 1247, Soldotna, AK 99669; 907/262-5581;
www.dnr.state.ak.us/parks/units/

Chugach National Forest
3301 C Street Anchorage, AK 99503; 907/743-9500;
www.fs.fed.us/r10/chugach/

Kenai Fjords National Park
National Park Service, PO Box 1727, Seward, AK 99664; 907/224-2132;
www.nps.gov/kefj/

Kenai National Wildlife Refuge
P.O. Box 2139, Soldotna, AK 99669-2139; 907/262-7021;
e-mail: fw7_kenai_comment@fws.gov

Kenai Peninsula Tourism Marketing Council
14896 Kenai Spur Hwy, Ste 106A; Kenai, AK 99611; 907/283-3850;
www.kenaipeninsula.org

The Seward Highway:
From Portage to Seward (80 m)

While it's possible to drive this portion of the road in about 90 minutes, there is every reason to take your time and stop for a picnic, hike, or to investigate an interesting byroad.

Hope Consider a detour along the pretty, paved 18-mile Hope Highway. It intersects with the Seward Highway, 23 miles south of Portage, and leads northwest to this mini-Gold Rush town. When gold was discovered in nearby Sixmile Creek around 1888, several thousand people came to this area over the course of a decade. Mining prospered well into the 1900s, then dwindled. What little remains of Hope today is supported by recreation, especially fishing. The Klondike this isn't, but Hope's a cute little town. If you're camping, there's an attractive U.S. Forest Service campground at the end of Hope Highway: **Porcupine** (24 sites, $10/site, tables, pit toilets firepits, dumpster, water, campground host). The **Hope Point Trail** starts close to the camp-ground entrance, but a better choice for family hiking is the five-mile **Gull Rock Trail.** The trail can be muddy at times. For a snack or meal, check out **Tito's Discovery Café** (Mile 16.5, 907/782-3274) or the **Seaview Café** (end of Main St, 907/782-3300; home.gci.net/~hopeak/) where you can also pan for gold. The Seaview has a few cabins and an RV Park as well.

The small **Hope-Sunrise Historical and Mining Museum** (907/782-3740; www.advenalaska.com/hope. Open Memorial Day-Labor Day, Fri-Mon, noon-4pm. Free) in an old log building bears witness to the Turnagain Arm Gold Rush of 1896 in photos, exhibits, and old gold-mining equipment. For more infor-mation contact the **Hope Chamber of Commerce** (PO Box 89 Hope, AK 99605; www.advenalaska.com/Hope/).

A few miles south of the Hope Highway junction is scenic **Summit Lake**, at mile 45.8 of the Seward Highway. In addition to the lodge, there's a USFS campground, **Tenderfoot Creek** (27 sites, $10/site, toilets, tables, firepits, dumpsters, boat launch) at Mile 46.

Summit Lake Lodge ($)
Mile 45.8 Seward Hwy; 907/244-2031; www.summitlakelodge.com
FYI: 6 rooms; restaurant; gift shop; fishing, cross-country skiing, hiking, and tours
Located near Summit Lake, the lodge was completed in 1954, using logs from nearby Chugach National Forest and tongue-and-groove pine from Washington state. It was rebuilt after the 1964 earthquake, which left only the fireplace standing. Inside is an old-fashioned bar (complete with enough cigarette smoke to gag a grizzly) and a light-filled restaurant that's very pleasant for breakfast, available until 2 pm. Lunch fare includes burgers, soup, salad and a few Mexican dishes. The motel portion of this establishment has six very small rooms, each with a tiny bath. Also on the premises is a gift shop that serves espresso and ice cream.

66 PARENT COMMENTS 99

"Our room was so small, there were only the two single beds, plus they put an extra mattress on the ground for me. Unfortunately, the three women in the next room were old college classmates reuniting for the weekend, and the thin walls did nothing to buffer their partying."

"The rooms were very small, but there was something rustically charming about the experience. Breakfast at the restaurant was delightful, and my daughter topped it with an ice cream cone at the gift shop."

Moose Pass This tiny community of about 200, at Mile 29 perched on the edge of Trail Lake, is renowned locally for its summer solstice festival each June. The area is beautiful and offers good accommodation and food at the **Trail Lake Lodge** (907/288-3101, 888-395-3624; www.traillakelodge.com. Rates: $-$$; 35 rooms, some shared baths, restaurant, open year round, kids under 11 stay free). It offers lodge and motel rooms. If it's open, dine out on the beautiful log pavilion overlooking the lake. Snacks, groceries, souvenirs, visitor info, and fishing licenses can be had at **Estes Brothers Groceries & Waterwheel** (Mile 29.5 Seward Hwy; 907/288-3151; www.moosepass.net/estesbros/; open daily in summer, 8am-7pm Mon-Sat, 8am-6pm Sun; closed Tues in winter). For area information, contact the **Moose Pass Chamber of Commerce & Visitor Bureau** (PO Box 558, Moose Pass, AK 99631) or visit the Moose Pass community Web site: www.moosepass.net.

SEWARD

At the end of beautiful **Resurrection Bay** is this town of 3,000 residents. This is a working city, with plenty of business activity but a relatively lackluster town core. The town was 90-percent destroyed in the Good Friday earthquake of

Moose

They can be a comical sight, these enormous mammals with huge, camel-like heads, rounded ears, and spindly legs supporting barrel-shaped, humpbacked bodies. Moose are nature's plain janes: they lack the elegance of deer or the impressive majesty of caribou and elk. But they grow on you. It is virtually certain that in your northern travels you'll encounter a moose or two.

The largest members of the deer family, moose are found across the northern hemisphere. Moose live about 25 years. Only the males grow antlers, which are broad and curved. Alaska moose are larger than their east coast relatives; the average Alaska bull moose weighs half a ton. And moose are nothing to trifle with. Cows are very protective of their young, who remain with their mothers for about a year. Look for moose in wooded areas. Their favorite food is willow, birch, and aspen. In summer, moose gravitate toward ponds with water plants. It's not uncommon to see a moose standing in a lake or stream, head down and yanking at something, probably a pond lily. The theory is that these plants are high in needed sodium.

Moose are not endangered; Alaska has about 175,000. But they are vulnerable to humans as well as wolves and bears, who prey on them. Every year, hundreds are killed by Alaska motorists. And the collisions don't do motor vehicles any good either! When you spot a moose from a car, it's best to pull over to the side of the road and observe from a discreet distance.

Moose are rarely aggressive to humans, but it does happen, usually in the fall during mating season or when a mother is defending her calves. Never approach a calf that appears to be by itself; the mother is

1964, when oil-storage tanks and oil-tank rail cars burst into flame, and much of the waterfront collapsed into the bay. Tsunamis 30 feet high rolled in half an hour after the quake, causing further ruin. In the end, only 13 people in Seward died; but 86 homes were destroyed and many more badly damaged.

Resurrection Bay was named by Alexander Baranof in 1792 when he arrived seeking shelter on Resurrection Sunday; he later established a ship-building enterprise here. The town is named for William Seward, Abraham Lincoln's Secretary of State, who negotiated Alaska's purchase from Russia. The town's history has been fairly industrial; as one of the state's few ports ice-free year round with land access to the interior, it's harbored shipping concerns, fisheries, a coal terminal, ferry and cruise docks, and tourism.

Although Seward lacks the charm and rich cultural life of Homer, it has several unique and stellar attractions: the Alaska SeaLife Center, access to Kenai Fjords National Park, and some of the state's most important sled-dog kennels.

Gigantic cruise ships visit Seward in summer. Visitors also arrive by train, ferry, and road (see "Getting to the Kenai Peninsula"), but it's the cruise ships you'll notice; the major lines that offer one-way Alaska sailings either depart somewhere nearby and will interpret this as a threat to her offspring. If a moose approaches you, back off. Although it's a bad idea to run away from a bear, it's a very good idea to run away from a moose! They rarely follow (although a moose can run up to 35 miles an hour). If the worst happens, and a moose attacks, roll up into a ball and cover your head.

Moose and dogs don't get on; if you have a dog with you, don't let it run after the moose. Most important of all, never feed a moose. It's illegal and at best will cause the moose to expect to be fed the next time it encounters a human, then behave aggressively when no food is forthcoming.

And finally, there is the question of "moose nuggets." Yes, those hard little pellets, about the size of large hazelnuts, sold in gift shops (sometimes coated with gold paint) are really hardened moose poop. Moose digest and use nearly everything they consume in fall and winter (it takes a lot of fuel to keep a moose warm in Alaska), so these hard little pellets represent a small part of what moose consume. Still, estimates are that a moose produces 380 nuggets a day for nine months. If there are 175,000 moose in Alaska—well, have the kids do the math!

Resources

Numeroff, Laura. *If You Give a Moose a Cookie* (HarperCollins, 1985); *If You Give a Moose a Muffin.* (Scott Foresman, 1991). These two popular picture books illustrate cause and effect.

Go Moose! (www.gomoose.com) This fun kid-oriented Web site is devoted to everything moose; contains facts (including recorded moose calls), activities, and trivia.

Moose World (www.mooseworld.com). This comprehensive site has science, fun facts, and an excellent kids' page.

U.K. Moose Site (www.smouse.force9.co.uk).This site blends science and trivia including TV shows and films that feature moose or moose references. ▣

from or arrive at Seward. Cruise lines offer add-on packages for sightseeing in Seward and the vicinity, as well as connections to the Anchorage airport and land tours (see "Alaska Cruises").

Getting Around

Public transport of sorts, **Seward's Trolley,** runs between downtown Seward and the small boat harbor along Resurrection Bay.
Daily service May-Sept, 10am-7pm. Cost: $2/adult, one way; $4/all day.

Cars can be rented from **Hertz Rent-A-Car** (604 Port Ave; 907/224-4378). Water taxi service to Caine State Recreation Area and Thumb's Cove is provided by **Miller's Landing** (Beach Dr 907/224-5739; www.millerslandingak.com) and **Weather Permitting** (328 3rd Ave; 907/224-6595; www.watertaxiak.com).

Places to Stay

Seward Windsong Lodge ($$$)
Mile 0.5 Exit Glacier Rd; 907/224-7116, 888/959-9590;
www.sewardwindsong.com
FYI: 108 rooms, 3 suites, microwave, refrigerator (suites), VCRs; hot tub

(suites); restaurant; shuttle service; all nonsmoking, kids under 12 stay free with parents; open mid-April-mid-Oct

Owned by a Native corporation based in Anchorage, the Windsong's rooms are on two levels, set in a forested area, not far from Exit Glacier. If you don't have a car, the lodge's shuttle system will take you the two miles into Seward proper. (Once in town, you can use "Seward's Trolley" to ease your travel-weary feet while seeing the sights.) Rooms are nice and quite spacious. Suites accommodate up to six guests. The lodge is small but beautiful, and houses a gift shop and an espresso bar. A few steps through the woods bring you to the affiliated Resurrection Roadhouse (see "Places to Eat") and a satisfying meal at breakfast, lunch, or dinner.

66 PARENT COMMENTS 99

"We didn't have a car, and were afraid that the distance to town would be a bother. It turned out that the free shuttle service was very convenient—it dropped us right at the attractions we wanted (Kenai Fjords Tour, Alaska SeaLife Center). One day we hiked into town, just for the fun of it."

"The lodge has a nice collection of videotapes. One evening we went out for dinner and left our older kids to order pizza and watch a movie."

Van Gilder Hotel ($$-$$$)

308 Adams St; 907/224-3079, 800/204-6835; www.VanGilderHotel.com
FYI: 24 rooms; open year-round

Located in the heart of Seward, the well maintained Van Gilder Hotel was built in 1916 and is on the National Register of Historical Places. Rooms are graced with period antiques, as well as modern amenities such as phones and cable TVs.

There are a few two-room suites, perfect for families (these are view rooms, so they can be spendy during the high season). Each has a queen bed in the main room and a queen bed and a Murphy bed in the adjoining room. Other options are view rooms with a queen bed and a twin bed, or non-view rooms with either a queen bed and a twin Murphy bed, or two double beds.

66 PARENT COMMENTS 99

"I thought this place was quite charming and accommodating. Our room had brass beds and quilts. My husband, the historian, got lost in their collection of old books and photos about Alaska."

"As you might imagine, this older building does not have a lot of soundproofing. I don't think I'd choose it if I had an infant who wakes at night, or an active toddler. My older children loved the ambience, and loved being allowed to walk 'to town' by themselves!"

Harborview Inn ($-$$)
804 3rd Ave; 907/224-3217
FYI: 12 rooms

The Harborview is a popular spot for families, perhaps because of its location (less than a mile from downtown) and price. Although it is essentially a two-story motel, the hewn-log and stone fireplace exterior and views of Seward and the harbor from some rooms add an Alaskan flavor. Any of the rooms would be adequate for a family. The only other room is a deluxe suite with Jacuzzi—perhaps better suited to honeymooners than a family.

66 P A R E N T   C O M M E N T S 99

"I guess the best part of this place, for families, is the relaxed attitude of the proprietors. They are accommodating to kids, and helpful in terms of suggesting appropriate activities."

Camping

The **Seward municipal campground** is right on the beach (south of Van Buren on Ballaine Blvd; Seward Parks & Recreation: 907/224-4055). You'll find hundreds of tents and RV sites ($15/site, restrooms, water, showers, hookups, some sites; mid-April-Sept). The view and convenient location can't be beat; noise is another story. Tenters might be more comfortable heading back up the Highway to the **Kenai Fjords National Park Campground** at Exit Glacier, where there are walk-in tenting sites with water. See "Excursions." For RV camping with all the bells and whistles, **Miller's Landing** (3 miles south of town on Lowell Pt Rd; 907/224-5739; www.millerslandingak.com; $25/night) has hookups, free hot showers for campers, a store, fishing licenses, boating rentals, and a lot more; there are tenting sites along with several rustic cabins as well.

Places to Eat

Resurrection Roadhouse
On Exit Glacier Rd, adjacent to Seward Windsong Lodge; 907/224-7116 (courtesy shuttle)
Hours: Open daily, late April-mid-Sept, Sun brunch

This recent addition is not your typical Alaska "roadhouse." The ambience is somewhat austere when there are not many diners. The view of the Resurrection River Valley is always great, though, and the food is satisfying. Alaskan fare includes a number of seafood specialties (the halibut is nice, or try the Dungeness crab cakes), as well as original pasta dishes. Alaskan brews are on tap.

Our youngest reviewer was well pleased by the individual-size pizza she ordered from the kids' menu, but bigger eaters might also order an appetizer, soup, or salad.

Railway Cantina
Small boat harbor 1401 4th Ave; 907/224-8226
Hours: open daily till 8pm
Here you'll find kid-friendly Mexican food in a casual setting. Eat in or take out.

Ray's Waterfront
Small boat harbor; 907-224-5606
Hours: open daily 11am-11pm; April-Sept
This is downtown Seward's fine-dining option, open for lunch and dinner. The place is wildly popular, so reservations are essential. It may not thrill very young kids, although it is boisterous enough to lend cover to the occasional shrill kid vocalization. But if your crew likes pasta and/or seafood, you'll all do fine here. Go for salmon, halibut, king crab, or whatever else is fresh. The macadamia-encrusted halibut is famous. There's also prime rib. The décor features former denizens of the deep, suitably mounted, and a harbor view. Prices will put a dent in your wallet.

What to See & Do

Stroll & Browse

If you're driving, on your way into town at Mile 2, stop at the **Chamber of Commerce Visitor Center** (2001 Seward Hwy; 907/224-8051; www.sewardak.org) and pick up travel information.

Seward's downtown is compact and perfect for strolling, but if little legs grow weary, catch the trolley (see "Getting Around"). The harbor is a good place to begin your stroll. If you're considering a fjords cruise, stop into the **Kenai Fjords National Park Visitor Center** for information or reservations. Across the street is the **Harbor Creamery** (307 S Harbor St; 907/224-8818).

The main drag, **3rd Avenue**, features a number of T-shirt and gift shops. Stop at the **Seward Visitor Information Center** (3rd St at Jefferson; 907/224-3094; open daily 9am-5pm, June-Aug) for maps and information, and to make reservations for special activities. The center is housed in a historic rail car, appropriately named *Seward*.

Northland Books & Charts (234 4th Ave; 907/224-3102) has a huge collection of Alaskan books, maps, and marine charts. Stop in at **Ranting Raven** (228 4th Ave, 907/224-2228) for a good, quick meal. Here you will find pick-me-ups in the form of gourmet espresso and tea, baked goods, soups, and sandwiches; their lemon shortbread cookies are to die for. They also have a nice collection of Alaskan crafts. Across the street, the **Starbird Studio** (221 4th Ave; 907/224-8770, 888/868-8770) has interesting gifts.

Bardarson Studio (1317 4th Ave; 907/224-5448, 800/354-0141; bardarson @seward.net) has a particularly nice collection of unique items by Alaskan artists, including Rie Muñoz, Gail Niebrugge, and Dot Bardarson (the proprietress). And a bonus for parents: there's a video room and a playroom for children! The **Resurrect Art Coffeehouse Gallery** (320 Third Ave; 907/224-7161) is a combination art gallery and café, housed in a former Lutheran church.

Museums

Resurrection Bay Historical Society / Seward Museum   This small museum contains a patchwork of Seward history, from beautiful Aleut basketry and Native ivory carvings to old photos and pioneer artifacts. Exhibits on the devastation caused by the Good Friday earthquake are especially impressive. Kids are likely to be interested in reading accounts written by Seward second-graders of how it felt to live through the 9.2 earthquake. The tiny diorama of Rockwell Kent's log-cabin studio, with tiny easels and paintings, and miniature sacks of provisions, should appeal to kids. Evening programs on the history of the Iditarod and of Seward are offered in summer. The small gift shop includes books on the area.

336 3rd Ave; 907/224-3902. Open daily, May-Sept, 10am-5 pm. Rest of year, call for hours. Cost: $2/adult, $.50/child, free/preschool. Allow 30 minutes.

Animals Animals

Alaska SeaLife Center ☺   Built in large part with funds from the Exxon Valdez oil-spill-litigation settlement, this is Alaska's premier aquarium. It's situated on Resurrection Bay, and its mission is to introduce visitors to the extraordinary life of Alaskan waters, rehabilitate wounded marine animals, and educate the public on the need to protect the fragile marine environment. Hands-on exhibits introduce children, step-by-step, to the process of rescuing and rehabilitating a seal pup. In a touch tank, kids can handle seastars, chitons, hermit crabs, and sea cucumbers. Some of the ocean's more unusual denizens are on display: notice the other-worldly basketstar, tiny shrimp, and giant king crabs. Viewing areas allow visitors to see sea lions below and above the water. Look through high powered telescopes trained on the bay to observe marine wildlife many miles away and participate in research on animal behavior. Educational programs for all ages are offered. The small snack bar has the usual food items along with an impressive selection of homemade fudge.

301 Railway Ave; 907/224-6300, 800/224-2525; www.alaskasealife.org. Open daily, May 1-mid-Sept, 9am-9:30pm; winter, 10 am-5pm. Cost: $12.50/adult, $10/child 4-16, free/ under 4. Allow 90 minutes.

The Great Outdoors

Biking   Seward lends itself to bicycling, especially the **Iditarod National Historic Trail** (see also "Hiking"). Stop in at the visitor center for trail maps. You can rent bikes at the **Seward Bike Shop** (411 Port Ave; 907/224-2448).

Dog Sled Riding   A visit to kennels offers a chance to see sled dogs up close and learn about how they are raised, trained, and worked. It's an interesting visit—summer or winter. Many sled dogs train in summer by pulling big carts (essentially sleds on wheels). It's fun to see them racing along from a distance, and truly exhilarating to ride in the cart behind them! Kids especially will enjoy meeting the dogs and experiencing a trail ride; at the end, they can visit and hold the new pups awaiting their first harnesses. Once you've done a dog sled ride, you'll no longer question the conventional wisdom that these dogs love to pull, perhaps even LIVE to pull.

Sea Otters

One of the highlights of a wildlife cruise in coastal Alaska is the chance to observe sea otters up close. A flotilla of furry mammals cruising by on their backs, casually nibbling on a bit of shellfish or cradling a pup, is an unforgettable sight. Sea otters are playful, not just with other otters but with seals. But whether future generations will be able to enjoy the sight is still in question; sea otter populations are endangered.

Perhaps more than any other factor, sea otters were responsible for bringing the Russians to North America. In search of sea otter pelts, Russian trappers hunted these mammals nearly to extinction in the eighteenth and nineteenth century. Hunting continued after the purchase of Alaska by the United States in 1867. By 1911, populations had dropped so low that it was no longer economical to hunt sea otters; the few remaining were covered in the Fur Seal Treaty, signed that year by the U.S., Russia, Japan, and Great Britain. It is estimated that only 2,000 Alaska sea otters were in existence at that time; by the 1970s numbers had grown to over 100,000. However, the Exxon Valdez oil spill in 1989 killed thousands. Sea otters depend on the ability of their fur coats to keep them warm in the icy waters they live in. When those coats become soiled or matted by pollution, such as that caused by oil spills, they can no longer provide insulation. Today, the Alaskan sea otter population is estimated at 75,000.

That figure represents 90 percent of the world's sea otter population. Besides pollution, killer whales have been feeding on sea otters in large numbers. One theory is that stellar sea lion populations, which once formed a large part of the orca's diet, have been declining, so they've substituted sea otters.

Where to Learn More

Alaska SeaLife Center, Seward

Pratt Museum, Homer

Kingston, George J. *The Exciting Adventures of Hydra & Muste Otter: Life in the Big Sea.* G Sharp Productions, 2001. Through the lives of two sea otters, the world they inhabit is brought to life.

Meeker, Claire Hodgson. *Lootas, Little Wave Eater: An Orphaned Sea Otter's Story.* Sasquatch, 1999.

Smith, Roland. *Sea Otter Rescue: The Aftermath of an Oil Spill.* Puffin, 1999. Kids will enjoy this first-person account of the effort to rescue thousands of sea otters following the Exxon Valdez oil spill.

Defenders of Wildlife—Sea Otter Page (www.kidsplanet.org/factsheets/otter/). This site contains sea otter facts for kids and animations.

Monterey Bay Aquarium (www.mbayaq.org/lc/activities/book_pups_supper/). The aquarium is famous for its sea otter program, including volunteers who play with orphaned sea otters. This animated online story includes interactive games and information for kids and teachers. ◾

Best-known in the Seward area is **Seavey's IdidaRide Sled Dog Tours**, run by Mitch Seavey, who placed fourth in the Iditarod in 1998, 11th in 2002, and 12th in 2003. It runs in the family; Mitch's father, Dan, helped start the Iditarod in the early 1970s, and was the third-place finisher in the first race in 1973.

Seavey offers three types of summer tours. The most popular is the 1.25-hour Wilderness Sled Dog Ride & Tour, offered five times daily, which allows participants to ride a custom-wheeled sled along a two-mile woodland trail. The musher discusses the dogs and their training and answers questions. The daily four-hour Real Alaska Tour includes a dog sled ride, lunch at nearby Resurrection Roadhouse, a trip to Exit Glacier, and a quick spin through downtown Seward. If you're short on time, take the Ididaride Kennel Tour (15 to 30 minutes), guided by a junior musher.

Located outside Seward, off Old Exit Glacier Rd (Turn onto Old Exit Glacier Rd at Mile 3.7 Seward Hwy, then follow the road for 1.1 mile.) 907/224-8607 (summer), 907/260-3139 (winter), 800/478-3139; www.ididaride.com Cost: Wilderness, $39/adult, $19/child under 12, free/under 2; Real Alaska, $116/adult, $71.50/2-11

Hiking   The **Iditarod National Historic Trail** starts at Trailhead Park (4th Ave & Railway St) and goes all 2,300 miles to Nome. You can enjoy hiking the first few miles that take you along the beach and up parallel to the Seward Highway toward Snow River.

See also "Excursions."

Horseback Riding   One way to get out and into the wilderness is on horseback. **Bardy's Trail Rides** takes kids 7 and older (younger kids may be able to ride if they've had prior riding experience).
907/224-7863; www.sewardhorses.com. May-Aug; 2 rides daily, noon and 3pm; $65/2-hour ride.

Sea Kayaking   If your family is adventurous, consider viewing Resurrection Bay from sea kayaks. **Kenai Fjords Tours** offers a full-day guided excursion along the shoreline of Caines Head State Recreation Area, where encounters with sea life are common. Instruction is provided by experienced guides, so no prior experience is necessary. **Miller's Landing** (866/541-5739; www.millerslandingak.com/kayaking/) has classes, tours, and rentals ($40/day single, $50/double).

Excursions

Caines Head State Recreation Area   There was a fort here during World War II. Today, the remains of **Fort McGilvray**, above and below ground, are open to exploration. Beautiful beaches and fantastic views make this a popular destination. However, it's best for families with older kids. To get here, you'll need to park at Lowell Point and hike 4.5 miles; some of the trail is along the beach and accessible only at low tide, so having a tide table, and sticking to a plan for getting in and out, are essentials. Most visitors will have to camp out before returning (depending on what time of day the low tides occur). There are rustic campsites available along with a couple of public-use cabins that

---

☛ **Parent Tip:**

Kenai Fjords Tours also offers the **Marine Science Explorer Program** for kids, grades 3-12. In a five-hour trip into the park aboard the *M/V Fjordland*, students participate in experiments, including seawater and plankton analysis, and study seabird and marine mammal adaptations as well as the fjord ecosystem. A Prince William Sound variant is offered by **Prince William Sound Cruises & Tours**, based in Whittier. For information on both, contact the Marine Science Explorer Desk at Kenai Fjord Tours. For Seward trips: 800/478-8068; for Prince William Sound: 800/270-1238. E-mail both at kftscience@ciri.com. ◙

---

must be booked well in advance. Another way to visit is by boat. Kenai Fjords has a guided kayak trip here (see "Sea Kayaking").

Park at Lowell Point State Recreation Site (3 miles south of Seward). Seward Ranger Office: 907/224-3434; www.dnr.state.ak.us/parks/units/caineshd/. DNR Soldotna: 907/262-5581; cabin reservations: 518/885-3639, 877/444-6777.

Kenai Fjords National Park   These 600,000 acres of picturesque fjords and glaciers (including Harding Icefield) afford as much "Alaska" as one could hope for at any one destination. Wildlife includes sea lions, porpoises, sea otters, whales, and a wide variety of sea birds. One small portion of the park is accessible by land (see "Exit Glacier"). Otherwise, you'll need to visit by sea. **Kenai Fjords Tours** (800/478-8068) offers a variety of day cruises.

The most popular trip, and arguably the best option for families, is the six-hour **National Park Tour** ($109/adult, $54/child under 12), which has several daily departures and covers approximately 110 spectacularly scenic miles, including a stop at Holgate Glacier. Here, passengers can hear, and sometimes see, the dramatic calving of huge chunks of ice from the face of the glacier. The tour includes a deli-style lunch or dinner, served on board. The 8-hour version of this cruise (departs daily, 10am; $125/adult, $62/child) includes a stop at Fox Island for a salmon bake lunch.

The **Northwestern Fjords Tour** (about nine hours; departs daily, 9am; $149/adult, $74/child) travels roughly 150 miles into the park and visits the fjord for which it is named; breakfast and lunch are served. If time is short, there's plenty to be seen on the shorter Resurrection Bay Tour. Three, four, and five hour options are offered, starting at $56/adult, $28/child.

Exit Glacier ☺   This glacier is the only portion of Kenai Fjords National Park that can be accessed by car. A finger of the huge Harding Icefield, it's well worth a visit and makes an ideal family outing for all ages. There are plenty of scenic stops along the road with views of the Resurrection River. From the parking lot at the campground, an easy half-mile trail with interpretive signage leads to the glacier. In summer, rangers are available to answer questions. Many animals hang out here, including moose, bears, wolverines, marmots, bald eagles, and songbirds. Much of the trail is paved and wheel accessible.

The Kenai Fjords National Park Tour: A Kid's Eye View

By Sara Heermans

We went on the six-hour Kenai Fjords. It goes between some islands and coves, which were good places to spot wildlife (be sure to bring binoculars!). The trip is long, perhaps too long for young children, because there is a lot of cruising between the wildlife sightings. However, seeing a variety of wild animals really makes up for the length of the trip. For younger kids, I would suggest taking entertainment, including books, CDs, GameBoy, or a deck of cards.

On our cruise, we saw tons of birds—cormorants, eagles, oyster-catchers, kittiwakes, puffins, a lot of murres—and the cutest was a family of parakeet auklets on a cliffside. We saw a black bear on the hill (far away!), sea otters, harbor seals, and whales.

I would suggest getting in line early so your family can get a good location in the warm cabin. There are tables for playing games and eating (my sister took a nap on the bench). The lunch they serve is nothing close to gourmet, so I would recommend bringing some lunch or snacks, especially if you are bringing children or you are a vegetarian (most of the meals have meat in them).

The most fun was when we stopped at a HUGE glacier and ate lunch right next to it. The glacier was very cold (bring extra-warm coats, even in the summer), but it was still very fun and different from anything I have ever done or seen before. The captain tells everyone to be really quiet and we all stood there and listened for the ice breaking off the glacier (called calving). It sounds like a muffled crack and then you hear or even see the ice splash into the water. The captain also explains about the glacier and why it looks blue.

Also, the cabin is very warm and there is a snack bar with some candy and chips. So I would recommend this trip for anyone interested in wildlife, but kids should have things to do in between stops.◼

The **Upper Loop Glacier Trail** is manageable by young kids, with supervision, and offers up-close views of the glacier. Don't allow kids to get too close to the glacier, which is retreating quickly and unstable.

Experienced hikers may want to hike the **Harding Icefield Trail** (3.5 miles one way), which follows the flank of Exit Glacier to an overlook of the icefield (which covers some 300 square miles of the park with snow and ice accumulations thousands of feet thick).

From Mile 3.7 Seward Highway, just north of Seward, take Exit Glacier Rd 9 miles. NPS Headquarters: 907/224-3175; Visitor information: 907-224-2132; www.nps.gov/kefj/.

Calendar of Events

August
Silver Salmon Derby
907/224-8051; www.sewardak.org/silver_salmon_derby/

Resources

Alaska State Parks
Kenai/PWS Area Office, PO Box 1247, Soldotna, AK 99669
907/262-5581; www.dnr.state.ak.us/parks/units/caineshd/

Bureau of Land Management
Anchorage Field Office, 6881 Abbott Loop Rd, Anchorage, AK 99507-2599;
907/267-1246, 800/478-1263; www.anchorage.ak.blm.gov/inhthome/

National Park Service
P.O. Box 1727, Seward, AK 99664; 907/224-3175 (headquarters);
907/224-2132; www.nps.gov/kefj/ (visitor information)

Seward Convention & Visitor Bureau/Chamber of Commerce
P.O. Box 749, Seward, AK 99664; 907/224-8051; www.sewardak.org

Books

Kent, Rockwell. *Wilderness: A Journey of Quiet Adventure in Alaska.* Alaska Natural History Association. This tells the story of the great artist's sojourn on Fox Island near Seward.

Rea, CJ. *A Whale's Tale from the Supper Sea.* Bas Relief Publishing Group, 1999. This picture book weaves the stories of local marine animals and natural history together for younger kids.

Sterling Highway:
From Seward Highway Junction to Soldotna (57m)

The Sterling Highway leaves the Seward Highway at Tern Lake Junction, 90 miles south of Anchorage. The scenic drive offers access to rustic resorts and small communities that depend on tourism—primarily fishing, hunting, hiking, and boating, most of which is concentrated between Cooper Landing and Sterling.

COOPER LANDING

A small community along the Kenai River, Cooper Landing was originally home to Kenaitze people. Gold was discovered here by Russian and later American prospectors in the 19th century. The town has grown slowly to its current population of around 300. Beautiful, 24-mile-long Kenai Lake, the Kenai River that originates from it, and the Russian River, set among the Kenai mountains, all add up to a world-renowned sport salmon-fishing center. Several small resorts cater to families. Family activities include river rafting, fishing, and hiking.

Places to Stay
Kenai Princess Wilderness Lodge ($$-$$$)
Bean Creek Rd (turnoff at Mile 47.8 Sterling Hwy; 907/595-1425,
800/426-0500; www.princesslodges.com
FYI: 86 rooms, decks, wood stoves; restaurant; exercise room, hut tubs; gift shop;
nature trails, tours; RV park (29 units, showers, Laundromat, grocery store);
open May-Sept.
This attractive facility consists of a large lodge and smaller buildings each
containing several units. The log buildings are arranged on a hillside and
feature terrific views. Larger units have separate living areas with porches. The
restaurant is in the main lodge. Espresso drinks and snacks can be purchased
at the gift shop. The Kenai Princess is one of an assortment of wilderness
lodges that cater primarily to Princess cruise-tour passengers. Reservations are
strongly recommended.

66 PARENT COMMENTS 99

"We loved it here. Our unit was fabulous, set above the
main lodge with an incredible view of the mountains.
The wood stove came with wood and good operating
instructions. Guests should know that the Laundromat
is way down in the RV Park. You'll need to drive your
laundry to it."

"There are two nature loop trails: one is a half mile and
one is a full mile. Both are suitable for small kids. Pick up
a map and guide at the front desk. There are stairs here
and there, so don't bring a stroller."

Gwin's Lodge ($-$$)
14865 Sterling Hwy at Milepost 52; 907/595-1266; www.gwinslodge.com
FYI: 11 rooms, cabins, some full kitchens, separate bedrooms; restaurant, general
store, fishing charters
Built in the 1950s and gradually enlarged, this attractive lodge is a local
institution. The newer chalets are especially good, affordable bets for families
with full kitchen, bedroom, and sleeping loft. The excellent restaurant, open
around the clock in summer, is a fine family choice, especially the hearty
breakfasts. The Little Angler's menu features the usual choices. At the store,
you can outfit the family for fishing and river floats; guests receive a 10-percent
discount.

Camping
There are two U.S. Forest Service campgrounds in the vicinity. At Mile 52.8 is
the **Russian River Campground** ($13/single site, 84 sites, 3-day limit; flush
toilets, water, picnic tables, fire pits, dumpster, hiking trails, fish cleaning
station) with terrific mountain views. Across the highway is the **Kenaitze**

Indian Tribe Interpretive Site (however, parent reviewers reported that it was closed during their entire visit). For information call 907/283-4321. The smaller **Cooper Creek Campground** (at Mile 50.7 Sterling Hwy; $10/single site; 26 sites; 3 tent sites, pit toilets, picnic tables, water, fire pits, dumpster) is set among cottonwood and spruce trees. Both campgrounds are open mid-May through mid-September. For reservations call 877/444-6777; www.reserveusa.com.

Places to Eat

Sunrise Inn Café
At Milepost 45 Sterling Hwy. 907/595-1222; www.alaskasunriseinn.com
Hours: daily 8am-9pm
The food here is hearty and child-pleasing. Breakfasts feature the usual, including several takes on waffles and pancakes stuffed with eggs, bacon, and veggies. The "Pig Vomit Omelet" is a cardiologist's nightmare, but more moderate, if less colorful, choices are available. For lunch, buffalo chili, assorted burgers, and blackened fish sandwiches are offered. A few fine-dining options are trotted out for dinner; pasta entrées should appeal to the picky eater in your party.

What to See & Do

There is no downtown to explore in Cooper Landing; the only street to speak of is the Sterling Highway. Watch kids carefully; traffic can be heavy in summer. For a cheap thrill, take the tiny **Russian River Ferry** (Mile 54.8; 6am-11pm; round trip cost: $5/adult, $4/child 3-11) across the Kenai River to the mouth of the Russian River. Parking, toilets, boat launch, dumpster, fish cleaning, and tenting facilities are here.

Shopping **Shrew's Nest** (mile 48.4 Sterling Hwy; 907/595-1257; e-mail: shrewsnest@arctic.net) has a selection of Alaska gifts, videos for rent, fishing and outdoor gear for sale, fishing licenses, hardware, and a tanning salon. For groceries, head to **Cooper Landing General Store** (Mile 48.2; 907/595-1677) or **Hamilton's Place** (Mile 48.5; 907/595-1260) which also has fuel.

Fishing, River Rafting, and Watery Adventure Several outfits offer Kenai River float trips suitable for kids. You're likely to see some wildlife, but because the river is bound to be full of fishers, chances of catching a glimpse of shyer animals is unlikely. Along with five varieties of salmon, you can fish for trout and Dolly Varden. From mid-May through September, **Alaska Wildland Adventures** (Milepost 50.1; 907/595-1279, 800/478-4100; www.alaskarivertrips.com) offers a two-hour Kenai River scenic float trip (multiple daily departures; $45/adult, $29/child 5-11); children must be at least 5 years. For their seven-hour Kenai River canyon float trip ($110/adult, $89/child 7-11), kids must be at least 7. In all cases, children must weigh at least 50 pounds (required for flotation devices to work). All equipment is provided. The longer trips feature Class II rapids.

> ☛ **Parent Tip:**
>
> This area is known as a "combat fishing zone." Outfitters tell chilling stories of local medical clinics that specialize in extracting fish hooks from various parts of the human anatomy. Make sure kids understand not to get too close to other fishers. ◙

They also offer a variety of half- and full-day fishing packages suitable for families, which include all fishing gear. Prices start at $125.

Alaska River Adventures (907/595-2000, 888/836-9027; www.alaska riveradventures.com) offer similar trips to those of Alaska Wildland, at similar rates. Children are welcome. Fishing charters can also be booked through Gwin's.

Hiking   Hiking part of the 21-mile **Russian Lakes Trail,** starting at the U.S. Forest Service Russian River Campground, is doable by small kids. You'll see first-hand evidence of the devastation caused by the spruce bark beetle here along with river and mountain views.

Horseback Riding   You can get into the beautiful country surrounding Cooper Landing on horseback. **Alaska Horsemen Trail Adventures** (1/10 Mile Quartz Creek Rd., mile 45 Sterling Hwy.; 907/595-1806; www.alaska horsemen.com) offers two-hour and half-day horseback rides twice daily each. Shorter rides are a good bet for young kids.

Resources

Cooper Landing Chamber of Commerce and Visitors Bureau
PO Box 809, Cooper Landing, AK 99572; 907/595-8888; www.cooperlanding chamber.com

Kenai River Sportfishing Association
PO Box 1228, Soldotna, AK 99669; 907/262-8588; www.kenairiversport fishing.com

SOLDOTNA

The drive to Soldotna from Cooper Landing takes you through the **Kenai National Wildlife Refuge** and the heart of the spruce bark beetle's munching grounds.

Soldotna is at one end of an extended urban zone; Kenai at the other. This area is home to oil and gas industry workers. Kenai, 11 miles west on Cook Inlet, is much the prettier destination, but Soldotna is conveniently positioned right on the Sterling Highway 48 miles west of Cooper Landing. The town straddles the Kenai River and hosts an assortment of fishing derbies.

There's something unnerving to adults about suddenly finding clusters of giant car dealerships and megamalls in what has felt like wilderness, but many children will cheer at the sight of familiar stores and fast food places. Even so, Soldotna doesn't have much to recommend it to families. Distances between amenities are short, but involve crossing busy roads. The attractive B&Bs on the Kenai River are primarily oriented to adults on fishing junkets. Several establishments do provide acceptable family accommodation, however, and the town features two family-friendly restaurants. The Aspen Hotel provides a rare perk for peninsula accommodation: a swimming pool.

Soldotna has a short history. Opened for homesteading in 1947, it grew slowly until oil and gas began to be extracted from Cook Inlet in the 1950s. Today, about 4,000 people reside here. Added to 7,000 in Kenai, this adds up to the biggest community on the peninsula.

Kachemak Bay Transit and Homer Stage Line both provide bus service to Soldotna from Anchorage and the peninsula (see "Getting There"). For scheduled air service and local car rentals, see "Kenai."

Places to Stay
Kenai River Lodge ($$)
393 Riverside Dr; 907/262-4292; www.kenairiverlodge.com
FYI: 25 rooms, 2-bedroom suite with full kitchen, refrigerators; outdoor barbecue facilities, boat moorage
With a location right on the river, you can all but fish out your window. All rooms offer river views. There's no restaurant, but you can walk (with caution, this is a heavy-traffic area) to several restaurants including Mykel's (see "Places to Eat").

Soldotna, Aspen Hotel ($$-$$$)
326 Binkley Circle; 907/260-7736; www.aspenhotelsak.com
FYI: 63 rooms, refrigerator/microwave, free continental breakfast; swimming pool, hot tub
See "Hotel Chains" in the Introduction for more information.

Camping
Soldotna has two good city campgrounds on the river. The large campground at **Centennial Park** on Kalifornsky Beach Rd (turn right after crossing the Kenai River bridge; $11/night, 200 sites, picnic tables, firepits and wood, restrooms, water and dump station [extra fee], boat launches, fishing) next to the Visitor Center complex, is the more centrally located. This pleasant, wooded park includes substantial disabled camping, parking, and fishing access. Several sites are on the river. The smaller **Swiftwater Campground** off E Redoubt Ave, .5 mile east of Sterling Hwy ($11/night, 40 sites, picnic tables, firepits, toilets, water and dump station [extra fee], boat launch, fishing) also has fishing access. Day use fees at both are $5; boat launch is $7, including day fee. There are no hookups for RVs at either campground. For camping information, call the Soldotna Sports Center office at 907/262-3151.

Places to Eat

Mykel's Restaurant

In the Soldotna Inn; 35041 Kenai Spur Hwy; 907/262-4305;
www.mykels.com
Hours: Open daily Sun-Thurs, 11am-3pm, 5pm-10pm; Fri-Sat, open till 11pm
(summer); Tues-Sun open 11am-3pm, 5pm- 9pm, Fri-Sat, open till 10pm,
closed Mon (rest of year)

Appearances to the contrary, this restaurant with its dim lighting and fancy cocktail-lounge atmosphere has good food and welcomes kids with a menu of their own, featuring tried-and-true favorites. For adults, it's fish, of course, or prime rib. For dessert, the lemon-lime pie is a winner. Prices are on the high side, but within the normal range for Alaska.

Sal's Klondike Diner ☺

44619 Sterling Hwy; 907/262-2220
Hours: Open daily 24 hours

It's a fair distance from the Klondike, but this cheery and venerable Soldotna institution serves up just what weary prospectors probably visualized when they were panting up the Chilkoot Trail: miner-sized portions of good, hearty food, well prepared. The kids' menu offers the usual, with a few surprises, such as the happy-face pancakes. Prices are remarkably reasonable, and the service is efficient and friendly.

See also River City Books & Espresso Café in "What to See & Do."

What to See & Do

Shopping It's hard to picture urban sprawl in a city of 4,000, but that's just what Soldotna offers. The news isn't all bad; the price of gas in Soldotna will probably come as a pleasant surprise. So, seize the day, pretend you're back home for a few hours, and head for the malls to pick up any of life's necessities: the latest CDs or cool, new action figures. Don't assume you can wait to buy this stuff in Homer. Homer residents drive here to stock up. When you tire of the familiar names, head to **River City Books & Espresso Café** (43977 Sterling Hwy; 907/260-7722), the only bookstore in the area. They have an excellent assortment of Alaskana and children's books. The café serves excellent bistro cuisine.

For local information, stop at the well-equipped **Soldotna Visitor Information Center** (off the Sterling Hwy next to Centennial Park; 907/262-1337; open daily May-Sept 9am-7pm; open Mon-Fri 9am-5pm, Sat noon-5pm rest of year). You can also check out the small **Soldotna Historical Society and Museum** (Centennial Park Rd, just south of the river off the Sterling Hwy; 907/262-3756; www.geocities.com/soldotnamuseum/; open May 15-Sept 15 or by appt Tues-Sat 10am-4pm, Sun noon-4pm. Free) behind the Visitor Center. The "homesteaders' village" features several small log buildings with settler-era furnishings. Behind the Visitor center is the **Classic Fishwalk**, a walkway with interpretive signs that descends down to the river.

Fishing There are many outfitters, guides, and package deals available for fishing. Most of these are probably not a great choice for young kids. However, the city has placed **fishwalks** in parks along the river to provide free public access to the river and the meals swimming by in it. For fishing gear and license, try just about any store. **Hooked on Fishing Gifts** (34870 Keystone Dr; 907/260-3151; www.hookedonfishinggifts.com; call first) has an assortment of halibut and cod *otolith* jewelry (ask the small aquarium aficionado in your family to tell you what otoliths are) and some very nice cloth baby books. Besides Centennial and Swiftwater parks, there are fishwalks at **Rotary Park** (cross Kenai River bridge; left 2.5 miles on Funny River) and **Soldotna Creek Park** (left on States Ave from Sterling Hwy). Between 10am and 2pm, June to September, the **Central Kenai Peninsula Farmers Market** (Park St between the Senior Center & Post Office (907/262-5463) sells locally grown produce, snacks, artworks, and gifts.

Parks with Playgrounds Soldotna created a number of parks where small people can safely run. You'll find playgrounds and picnic tables at **Aspen Park** (Kenai Spur Hwy & Marydale Ave), **Riverview Park** (Kobuk St across the river from Centennial Campground), and **Farnsworth Park** (Sterling Hwy & Kenai Spur Hwy).

The **Kenai National Wildlife Refuge Visitor Center (KNWR)** is located in Soldotna, and highly recommended. Here you can view displays on refuge wildlife and watch a variety of free wildlife films. Hike the one-mile nature trail and pick up information on hiking and recreational opportunities in the Refuge. An Alaska Natural History Association Bookstore has a good selection of nature books and videos for adults and kids.

The nearly two-million-acre refuge extends from the Kenai Mountains in the east all the way to Cook Inlet. First set aside in 1941 as the Kenai National Moose Range, it was given its present name and more land in 1980. The refuge is home to brown and black bears, wolverines, moose, caribou, Dall sheep, beluga whales, eagles, loons, songbirds, and much more. The KNWR is operated by the U.S. Fish & Wildlife Service, dedicated to preserving the habitat that supports the animals here and educating the public on the wildlife that depends on our goodwill.

There are 13 campgrounds in the Refuge between Soldotna and Cooper Landing, accessed from Shilak Lake Loop Road and Swanson River Road, which run from the Sterling Highway east of Soldotna. On Friday and Saturday evenings, June through August, KNWR campgrounds offer nature programs, including campfires, hikes and nature walks, and wildlife films. There is also a Junior Ranger program for kids, with self-guided activities available at the visitor center. The KNWR has a variety of educational and youth programs such as the Youth Conservation Corps. Write or call for details.

Top of Ski Hill Rd (turn off Sterling Hwy at Milepost 97.9). Open Mon-Fri 8am-4:30pm; Sat-Sun 10am-6pm (summer), till 5pm (rest of year).

Resources

Kenai National Wildlife Refuge
PO Box 2139 Soldotna, AK 99669; 907/262-7021;
(kenai.fws.gov/employment/ycc/).

Soldotna Chamber of Commerce
44790 Sterling Hwy, Soldotna, AK 99669; 907/262-9814;
www.soldotnachamber.com

Alaska Department of Fish and Game (Soldotna)
907/262-9368; Information on fishing licenses, clam digging

Alaska State Parks
514 Funny River Rd, Soldotna, AK 99669; 907/260-4882

City of Soldotna
177 North Birch St, Soldotna, AK 99669; 907/262-9107;
www.ci.soldotna.ak.us; Parks and recreation info

KENAI

An 11-mile drive from Soldotna along the Kenai Spur Highway, the city of Kenai has a population of 7,000. More live in the surrounding suburbs. The urban area extends west from the Sterling Highway and Soldotna along the Kenai Spur Highway to the north; the Kalifornsky Beach Road to the south runs between Cook Inlet and the Sterling Highway. Between those two roads is a fair bit of urban and suburban development.

The town is much more a working community than a tourist-oriented one. Accommodation is limited; a number of B&Bs are located in the vicinity, some with terrific locations on the water and marine views. The Kenai Visitors and Convention Center has up-to-date info on these.

Kenai is served by Era Aviation and Kachemak Bay Transit and Homer Stage Line. See "Getting to the Kenai Peninsula" for details.

History

The city of Kenai is the oldest community on the peninsula, the longtime site of a Dena'ina community. Russian fur traders made this a base in 1791, Fort St. Nicholas; it was the second permanent Russian settlement in Alaska. However, the Dena'ina successfully attacked the Russian fort in 1797. The same year, Sitka was chosen over Kenai to be the capital of Russian America. But the Kenai Russian settlement continued and the Russian Orthodox religion was successfully established here. Visitors will notice the term "Kalifornsky"; this does indeed derive from California. The son of a Dena'ina chief took the name "Kalifornsky" (the Californian) after a visit to a Russian fort in California. Kenai's native population was devastated twice by epidemics. Smallpox killed about half the local Dena'ina in 1838. The world influenza epidemic of 1918 also decimated local populations, but their descendants survive and make up a vital part of the local population.

Getting Around

You can rent a car from **Great Alaska Car Company** (10288 Kenai Spur Hwy; 907/283-3469), **Hertz Rent a Car** (325 Airport Way; 800/478-7980) and **Payless Car Rental** (907/283-6428). Taxi service is provided by **Inlet Taxi** (907/283-4711).

Places to Stay
Kenai Merit Inn ($)
260 South Willow St; 907/283-6131, 800/227-6131; www.kenaimeritinn.com
FYI: 60 rooms, free continental breakfast, pets OK (some rooms), free airport pickup, kids under 6 free
This hotel delivers the basics. The breakfast is minimal. Across the street is the Kenai Recreation Center, open to the public, with exercise facilities, sauna, and teen club.

Camping

The best camping in the area is at the public campgrounds in Soldotna and at Captain Cook State Recreation Area (see "Excursions"). However, for RVers who want to be in town with hookups and other amenities, seek out **Beluga Lookout RV Park** in Kenai Old Town, with a view overlooking Cook Inlet. *929 Mission Ave; 907/283-5999, 800/745-5999; e-mail: belugarv@ptialaska.net; 75 full hookups, pull -throughs, picnic tables, restrooms, showers, Laundromat, grills, fishing charters; open May-Sept.*

Places to Eat
Charlotte's
115 S Willow St; 907/283-2777
Hours: Mon-Fri, 7am-5pm, Sat 9am-3pm
This excellent café in a strip mall gets crowded at lunchtime with local office workers. Soups and salads are excellent. Kids should enjoy the array of sandwiches on offer. Leave room for the excellent desserts.

Paradiso's
PO Box 2917; 907/283-2222
Hours: Mon-Fri 11am-11pm, Sat-Sun, 11am-midnight
You'll find a medley of Greek, Italian, and Mexican specialties here. The best bet for kids is pizza or pasta. Quality is variable, but portions are large and so is the kid-friendliness. Prices are high.

Veronica's Coffee House
604 Peterson Way; 907/283-2725
Hours: Daily 9am-6pm (May-Oct)
This little café house makes a great stop for lunch when you're strolling through historic Kenai. Espresso and other drinks, pastries, and light lunches are served. If the kids aren't too fussy, you should be able to feed them well. It's located in a historic house whose small rooms offer beautiful views over Cook Inlet. If the weather is good, dine outside.

What to See & Do

Shopping   Like Soldotna, Kenai has no downtown shopping district to speak of. For souvenirs, your best bet is the visitor center gift shop.

Challenger Learning Center   Like all members of the network of U.S. space-science education centers, this one features programs almost exclusively for school groups. Families are welcome to look at the exhibits in the lobby and shop in the gift shop. Science camps for kids are offered in summer. If your children will be here long enough to take advantage of a two-week camp, contact the Center for details.

9711 Kenai Spur Hwy; 907/283-2000; www.akchallenger.org.

Kenai Visitors & Cultural Center   This visitor center is part museum, part store, and part dispenser of information. Built in 1992 to commemorate the city's 200th birthday, it features exhibits from Dena'ina, Aleut, and Russian cultures. Displays showcase recent Kenai history and the local economy. There are wildlife displays and information on nearby national and state parks, along with occasional traveling art exhibits. In summer, the center puts on interpretive programs.

11471 Kenai Spur Hwy; 907/283-1991; www.visitkenai.com. Open Mon-Fri, 9am-8pm; Sat, 10am-7 pm; Sun, 11am-7pm (summer); Mon-Fri, 9am-5pm; Sat, 10am-4pm, closed Sun (rest of year). Cost: $/3adult (museum only).

Old Town Kenai Self-Guided Walking Tours   Explore the historic buildings in town with the help of the *Old Town Kenai Walking Tour* brochure, available at the visitor center. Starting from the visitor center, the tour takes in Moosemeat John's cabin, the original headquarters for the first incarnation of the KNWR, the Moose Range. You'll pass several homesteader cabins (dating from before 1920) and Kenai's early public buildings; but the most interesting are three Russian buildings: the Parish House Rectory (1881), the Holy Assumption Russian Orthodox Church (1894), and the chapel of Saint Nicholas (1906). The last is named after a priest, Father Nikolai, who is remembered for bringing smallpox vaccine to the peninsula.

If the kids get whiny on this admittedly low-priority attraction for kids, schedule a stop at Veronica's Coffee House (see "Places to Eat") for an Italian soda. If the weather is good, stroll over to **Erik Hansen Scout Park** and gaze out at the volcanoes straight ahead and the sandy beach below and search for whales. *Start from visitor center. Free guided tours in summer.*

Saturday Open Air Market   In summer, check out the local Saturday farmer's market.

Central Peninsula Sports Center; 907/283-3633. June-Aug 10am-5pm.

The Great Outdoors

Beachcombing   You can't swim here, but the attractive beach with expansive volcano views is just fine for beachcombing and playing "catch me if you can" with the waves. There are outhouses.

At the end of Spruce Dr, accessed from the Kenai Spur Hwy, north of the visitor center.

Front Row Seats on the Ring of Fire

Alaska makes up a large arc in the "ring of fire," the roughly circular band of volcanoes that ring the Pacific ocean from the Andes Mountains in the southern hemisphere, up through the Cascade Ranges of North America (including Mount Saint Helens), north to the Aleutian Islands, curving across the north Pacific to Russia's Kamchatka Peninsula and down through Japan, the Philippines, and South Pacific Islands to New Zealand. Throughout the ring, active, dormant, and extinct volcanoes are interspersed. From the Kenai Peninsula, viewers have ringside seats to observe three magnificent volcanoes: **Mount Redoubt** (10,197 feet) directly west of Kenai, **Mount Iliamna** (10,016 feet), a little farther south, and **Augustine**, farther south, a perfect cone on its own island. To remember which is which, residents use the acronym "AIR," which means, reading left to right, Augustine, Iliamna, Redoubt.

The youngest of the three, Augustine, erupted in 1986 over a five month period, generating mud- and pyroclastic flows, its plumes of airborne ash disrupting air traffic. Iliamna, over twice as tall, hasn't had a major eruption in 250 years, but monitoring shows plenty of seismic activity inside with the real possibility of future eruptions. Mount Redoubt experienced huge, successive eruptions from 1989 through 1990. Ash coated the Kenai Peninsula and debris flooded the waterways, threatening to breach the huge oil storage tanks at the oil terminal; costly measures were required to prevent catastrophic oil spills. Estimated cost of these eruptions was $160 million, making this the second costliest eruption in U.S. history.

Resources

Alaska Volcano Observatory (www.avo.alaska.edu)
Look up individual volcanoes, check their level of activity; and learn about recent active volcanoes.

Global Vulcanism, Smithsonian National Museum of Natural History (www.volcano. si.edu/gvp/)
This site takes a planetwide look at volcanoes with links to international volcano sites.

Volcanic and Geologic Terms (volcano.und.nodak.edu/vwdocs/glossary/)
Visitors can look up terms like "pyroclastic," "aa," "pahoehoe," and "stratovolcano" here.

Volcanoes: FEMA for Kids (www.fema.gov/kids/volcano/) Here, the young worrier in your family can learn about volcanoes and other disasters, and how to meet them prepared.

Volcano World (volcano.und.nodak.edu/vwdocs/kids/kids/)
This site has abundant activities, information, and links for children and teachers.

Books

Alaska's Volcanoes: Northern Link in the Ring of Fire. Alaska Geographic Society, Alaska Northwest Books, 1977.
This is an illustrated guide to Alaska's role in the Ring of Fire.

Healey, Larry. *Angry Mountain.* Dodd Mead,1983
In this novel for middle school age and older kids, a teenager sent to Alaska must figure out how to survive an erupting volcano. ◼

Cross-Country Skiing   The **Kenai Nordic Trails**, maintained by the city, are groomed cross-country ski trails of varying lengths, all suitable for beginners. No motorized vehicles are allowed.

Lawton St, by Kenai Middle School. Contact Kenai Parks & Recreation Dept for details: 907/283-3855, 907/283-7926.

Excursions

Nikiski Pool and Recreation Center   This recreational jewel is 12 miles north of town on the Kenai Spur Highway. The drive takes you past the oil and gas refineries that fuel the local economy. A mile past the Tesoro Refinery, at Mile 23.4, turn left onto Pool Side Avenue. Under a huge dome is a complex with a large pool and a 136-foot water slide, hot tub, and rain umbrella. There's a dedicated kid swim area, too. Beneath the dome, the walls are glass, bringing in natural light and views of wildlife.

Outdoors are a lakeside picnic area, nature trails, ball fields, and a seasonal ice-skating rink. In winter, the trails are used for cross-country skiing; in summer, they're used for walking and running. A series of fitness stations is placed along one trail. RVs are welcome to camp in the parking lot here (however, there are no restrooms or hookups).

Pool Side Ave & N Kenai Rd; 907/776-8800. Pool: daily swims year round. Cost: $3/pool, $6/water slide.

Captain Cook State Recreation Area   Another 12 miles beyond the Nikiski Center on the Kenai Spur Highway is this 3,460-acre state park on Upper Cook Inlet, offering recreational opportunities and two campgrounds (Mile 35.5 Kenai Spur Hwy; 907/262-5581; www.dnr.state.ak.us/parks/units/captcook/.)

Not far from the entrance is **Bishop Creek Campground** ($10/site 15 tent sites, toilets, water, picnic area, and a trail to the beach). A little farther on is beautiful, clear **Stormy Lake**, which gets warm enough for swimming in summer. A staircase leads down to the water from the parking lot. Change room and outhouses are provided. A picnic area is farther on (not by the lake) and a boat launch is nearby. Drive to the end of the park where the **Swanson River** flows into Cook Inlet against a backdrop of snowcapped mountains. Here at **Discovery Campground**, ($10/site, 53 sites, toilets, water, and picnic tables) there's a day-use picnic area and a nature trail to the beach, along with a campground.

You can pick berries, hike, and beachcomb here—but be very careful on the mudflats; the tide can come in several times faster than a child can run. Some have found agates on the beach. You can go boating and fishing on the Swanson River and Stormy Lake. And of course, there's the wildlife. Among the many animals that call the park home are bald eagles, moose, bears, beavers, muskrats, wolves, and coyotes. In the water, watch for beluga whales and harbor seals. And above, you may spot bald eagles, sandhill cranes, trumpeter swans, loons, and songbirds. On Saturdays, June through August, there are natural history programs at Discovery Campground. Call for details.

Calendar of Events
June
Kenai River Festival
907/260-5449; www.kenaiwatershed.org
Free, annual family festival with music, arts and crafts, and environmental learning programs, put on by Kenai Watershed Forum

Resources
City of Kenai, Parks & Recreation Department
227 Caviar Street, Kenai, AK 99611; 907/283-3855; www.ci.kenai.ak.us

Kenai Chamber of Commerce
402 Overland Street, Kenai, AK 99611; 907/283-7989; www.kenaichamber.org

Kenai Visitor and Cultural Center
11471 Kenai Spur Highway, Kenai, AK 99611; 907/283-1991; www.visitkenai.com

Sterling Highway:
Soldotna to Homer (78 m)
The Sterling Highway turns south at Soldotna. At first impression, the prospect is dismal: miles of dead spruce trees, killed off in the last few decades by the spruce bark beetle. Over 70 percent of the peninsula's spruce forest is dead. Logging the dead trees is a growth industry and a necessity in order to reduce the risk of forest fire.

From **Clam Gulch** (22 miles south of Soldotna), the road mostly follows the spectacular coastline. The road is for the most part on high bluffs above the sea, with beach access at several points along the way. You'll seldom be more than a few miles from a public campground and/or picnic area between Soldotna and Homer, 78 miles south.

At Mile 117.4, the **Clam Gulch State Recreation Area** has a picnic area, 116 campsites with tables, picnic shelter, toilets, and water ($5/day use, $10/campsite). The park is .5 miles off the highway. It gets windy here and the high bluffs can be dangerous. There's a short, but steep beach access road. To drive to the beach you'll need 4-wheel drive; you can also hike down.

Ninilchik   A stop at this historic town (Mile 135.6) with 700 residents can make a welcome break from cramped car quarters. The town offers abundant salmon, trout, and halibut fishing, especially on the Ninilchik River and Deep Creek, which flow into Cook Inlet. Ninilchik has a few attractions. Check out the **Russian Orthodox Church**, built in 1900 (turn off the Sterling Hwy onto Coal Street). Drive down Mission Avenue to old **Ninilchik Village** on the beach. The town's a bit dispiriting—decaying buildings standing forlorn in the wind (mostly destroyed in the 1964 earthquake)—but in clear weather, your attention will be on the extraordinary view of Mounts Redoubt and Iliamna and, of course, the ocean.

Clam Digging

The beaches south of Kasilof down to Anchor Point are famous for razor clams. Their rectangular shells contain delicious clams many times the size of the better-known steamer clam. To try your hand at digging razor clams (early summer is best), all you need is a fishing license, clam shovel, bucket, rubber boots, and old clothes—and a very low (minus) tide. Once you've got your clams, you have to figure out how to clean and cook them. RVers may have the wherewithal with them. For everyone else, booking with one of the out-

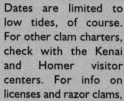

fitters that charter clam digs is smart. **Ninilchik Charters** (based in Ninilchik; 888/290-3507; www.ninilchik.com/clams/) has sites in Ninilchik and Homer. Dates are limited to low tides, of course. For other clam charters, check with the Kenai and Homer visitor centers. For info on licenses and razor clams, contact the Soldotna branch of the Alaska Department of Fish and Game (907/262-9368). Tide info: NOAA Tide Information (co-ops.nos.noaa.gov/cpred2 .html#AK). ◙

If you're in camping, hiking, or picnic mode, the **Ninilchik State Recreation Area** has four campgrounds in the vicinity. The **Ninilchik River Scenic Overlook**, along with camping and picnicking, has a nature trail above the river, with interpretive signs. At the **Ninilchik View Campground** is a staircase down to the beach (Camping fees: $10/site except Ninilchik Campground, $5/site; day use fees: $5). A scattering of B&Bs and outfitters offering fishing charters are located here. In August, the town hosts the **Kenai Peninsula State Fair**, 907/567-3670. For more information, contact the **Ninilchik Chamber of Commerce** (PO Box 39164, Ninilchik, AK 99639; 907/567-3571; www.ninilchikchamber.com).

Anchor Point Another 22 miles bring you to this town of about 1,000. For the best view of the three volcanoes (Iliamna, Redoubt, and Augustine) on the highway, stop at the paved turnout at mile 142.5. Like Ninilchik, Anchor Point is famous for its sportfishing. This is where Captain Cook arrived in 1778, seeking the Northwest Passage; he lost an anchor here, giving rise to the name. The public **Anchor River State Recreation Area** and **Stariski Recreation Site** have campgrounds ($10/site; $5/day use). For info on attractions in Anchor Point, contact the **Anchor Point Chamber of Commerce** (PO Box 610, Anchor Point, AK 99556; 907/235-2600; www.anchorpointalaska.info).

HOMER

The gem of the Kenai Peninsula, for scenic beauty and culture, is this attractive town of 4,000 at the end of the Sterling Highway. To the west are the high volcanic peaks of the Alaska Range, while to the south and east are the Kenai

Mountains. At the southern end of Cook Inlet, Kachemak Bay reaches up into the peninsula, sheltering a rich variety of marine wildlife. The Alaska Maritime National Wildlife Refuge and Kachemak Bay State Park offer many recreational opportunities. Across Kachemak Bay, the historic town of Seldovia is a popular destination, accessible by sea and by air.

The sprawling town of Homer has much charm; its focal point is the Homer Spit, a 4.5-mile-long narrow finger of land extending into Kachemak Bay. It's the focus of Homer's maritime activities, with pleasure- and working-boat harbors, cruise and ferry docks. At the tip is a resort and close by are art galleries, bistros, and restaurants, all with enviable views. The rest of Homer offers some sandy beaches and high bluffs with spectacular views.

Homer has attracted a disproportionately high number of intellectuals and artists (some say that Homer features the highest number of PhDs per capita of any US city). Good hotels and B&Bs, along with excellent restaurants, happily accommodate family travelers. One of the state's best museums, the Pratt, is here, too. With many hiking, wildlife-spotting, boating, and cultural opportunities, Homer is a top destination for families.

Allow six hours for the 224-mile drive from Anchorage (without major stops or detours). Era Aviation, the only scheduled airline serving Homer, offers multiple daily flights between Homer and Anchorage. Alaska Marine Highway System ferries connect Homer with Seldovia, Kodiak, and Seward. (See "Getting to the Kenai Peninsula.") The new cruise ship dock on the spit was designed to lure more cruise ships to Homer. Several mid-size cruise lines are putting Homer on their itineraries: **Alaska Sightseeing Cruise West** (800/580-0072; www.cruisewest.com) and a floating condominium, **ResidenSea's The World** (800/970-6601; www.residensea.com). European cruise lines also stop in.

History

For thousands of years, the Kachemak Bay area was home to Alutiiq people, whose territory extended from Prince William Sound to Kodiak and surrounding islands. More recently, Dena'ina Athabascan people inhabited the area. Oddly enough, what brought European settlers here was neither fur trade nor fishing, but coal mining, an industry that continued from the mid 1800s until the turn of the last century. The town got its name from Homer Pennock, a combination confidence man and entrepreneur who arrived in search of gold in 1896 but abandoned the search to head for the Klondike when news of the strikes there arrived. Homer shrank over the 20th century, at one point slipping to about 300 residents. But the growth of fishing and canning kept the area alive. Homer and Seldovia have experienced devastating fires, and the Good Friday earthquake of 1964 did great damage, especially to Seldovia, whose canneries were destroyed. The Homer spit dropped between four and six feet. Throughout Homer's history, hopeful homesteaders have tried farming here. The land is rich enough but short and cool growing seasons have limited crop output. However, locally grown produce enhances restaurant menus and the Homer Farmers Market.

Getting Around

To see Homer properly, you'll need a vehicle.

On Land For car rentals, try **Adventure Alaska Car Rentals** (1368 Ocean Dr; 907/235-4022, 800/882-2808; www.adventurealaskacars.com), **Polar Car Rental** (3720 FAA Rd, #125; 907/235-5998, 800/876-6417; e-mail: polarcar@ptialaska.net); or **Hertz/Pioneer** (3720 FAA Rd, #123; 907/235-0734; www.hertzofhomer.com). Taxi service, 24/7, is provided by **KacheCab** (907/235-1950; e-mail: kachecab@xyz.net) and **Chux Cab** (907/235-2489).

On Water For destinations that aren't accessible by road, such as **Seldovia and Kachemak Bay State Park**, transportation is provided by water taxis that often offer sightseeing and wildlife tours as well. **Bay Excursions Water Taxi & Tours** (907/235-7525; www.xyz.net/~bay/), **Jakalof Ferry Service** (907/235-6384, 907/235-2376; www.jakolofferryservice.com), **Mako's Water Taxi** (907/235-9055; makoswatertaxi.com), **Rainbow Tours** (907/235-7272; www.rainbowtours.net), **Smoke Wagon Water Taxi** (907/399-3455; homer watertaxi.com), and **Tutka Bay Taxi** (907/235-7166; www.tutkabaytaxi.com).

Places to Stay

Beeson's B&B ($-$$)

1393 Bay Ave; 907/235-3757, 800/371-2095; www.beesons.com
FYI: 4 rooms, large family room, apartment, breakfast; exercise room, hot tub
This B&B warmly welcomes families. The family room has bunk beds and easily sleeps five; the apartment sleeps seven. The location is close to the Spit and has terrific views of the bay and mountains. Each room has a TV and the living room has a 52-inch TV.

66 PARENT COMMENTS 99
> *"The kids liked having bunk beds to sleep in for a change, instead of sharing a bed. We had to walk through chilly outdoors to get to the gazebo and the hot tub. But once we were there, it was heaven."*

Driftwood Inn ($-$$)

135 Bunnell St; 907/235-8019; www.thedriftwoodinn.com
FYI: 21 rooms, family suite with kitchen, some shared baths; Laundromat; picnic area with barbecue; RV Park (22 sites, $26-29/site, hookups, showers, firepits and wood, picnic area)
It's a bit funky, but the Bishop's Beach location is a winner. Families will be comfortable in the suite, which is a good deal in these pricey parts.

66 PARENT COMMENTS 99
> *"The best part for us was the location. We were a block from Two Sisters Bakery and our kids could hang out at the park with local kids. The suite was huge, with a dining table and six chairs along with a fridge, microwave, and sink. Staff is friendly."*

Heritage Hotel ($$)

147 E Pioneer Ave; 800/380-7787; www.alaskaheritagehotel.com
FYI: 33 rooms, two Jacuzzi suites; kitchen (shared); restaurant, bakery next door

Entering the lobby of this vintage log-cabin establishment, you'll feel as though you've stepped into the wild west, even though you're in downtown Homer. Built in 1948, the Heritage is a sprawling wooden hotel that offers accommodations both economical and deluxe.

Other than the two suites, most of the rooms are small and the amenities basic. There is a common kitchen area where you can keep baby bottles or snacks cold, or prepare a meal.

66 PARENT COMMENTS 99

"It was nice to set out on foot from the hotel and find several attractions (and an espresso stop) within easy walking distance."

"We liked the Western feel to this place. We had to squeeze four people into a smallish room, but it didn't matter. No one sits in the hotel room in Homer, anyway."

Land's End Resort ($$-$$$)

4786 Homer Spit Rd; 907/235-0400, 800/478-0400; www.lands-end-resort.com
FYI: 80 rooms, restaurant, spa (indoor pool, outdoor hot tub, sauna, exercise room, massage); gift shop, tours

A stay here definitely qualifies as a splurge. Perched at the tip of the Homer Spit, this is truly Land's End. Views from the bayside rooms extend across the bay to the mountains. Sit on your deck and watch sea otters and harbor seals cavort just feet away. One of the pluses here is the warm welcome for families with nautical-theme rooms that come with porthole windows, Murphy beds and trundle beds, and kids' menu at the restaurant. However, kids have limited hot-tub access.

66 PARENT COMMENTS 99

"We all loved the hot tub; it was sheer bliss to sit in the twilight and watch the birds while we soaked. The exercise pool could be dangerous for small kids when the wave action is turned on."

"The proximity of the beach is a lifesaver for families, especially if your room begins to feel smallish. One day, my 11-year-old spent more than an hour skipping flat stones on the bay."

Camping

Between April and October, the City of Homer operates two **city campgrounds** (907/235-1583; RVs $10/site, tents $6/site, water, restrooms, garbage, 14-day limit). There are no hookups, but the city operates two RV dump stations (fee $2). The fee office is across from the Fishing Hole on the Spit. For privately operated camping, try the **Homer Spit Campground** (4611 Homer Spit Rd; 907/235-8206; $26+ per site, hookups, pull-throughs, showers, Laundromat, dump station, bookings for fishing and recreation), with an unbeatable view at the end of the Spit. Tenters should note the campground is right on the beach and gets very windy. See also the Driftwood Inn.

Places to Eat

Boardwalk Fish & Chips ☺
4287 Homer Spit Rd; 907/235-7749
Hours: Daily 11am-10pm, summer only
The claim to fame of this cheery, no-frills restaurant is its "fish on a stick." Fresh halibut indeed comes wrapped on a stick. The novelty should appeal to kids, and the taste will appeal to everyone. Wash it down with a glass of decent chardonnay in a plastic cup, while the kids figure out how to eat their fish, and gaze out the window on a view that far more expensive restaurants would envy.

Café Cups
162 W Pioneer Ave; 907/235-8330
Hours: Daily 7:30am-9pm
You can't miss this place, graced as it is with four large, colorful sculptures of teacups. However, neither the menu nor the ambience here (including a small dining area with tables set close together) has much to recommend itself to kids (at least little ones).

Grownups are likely to love the food. The breakfast is mythic, especially the eggs Benedict and the bagels and lox. Lunch and dinner dishes emphasize fresh seafood and lean toward the Asian in taste and presentation. The restaurant is in a converted house, and the décor is colorful and fun.

Captain Pattie's Fish House
On the Homer Spit; 907/235-5135
Hours: Daily 11am-10pm
This popular seafood restaurant with a great Spit location specializes in halibut, salmon, and a range of shellfish dishes, simply prepared. All are excellent, though not cheap. A few steak and chicken dishes are available. However, this is not the best choice for vegetarians. The kids' menu offers fish and chips, grilled cheese, and chicken fingers at affordable prices.

Chart Room Restaurant
Land's End Resort; 4786 Homer Spit Rd; 907-235-0406;
www.lands-end-resort.com
Hours: Mon-Fri, 11am-9pm, Sat-Sun 8am-9pm
The Chart Room is one of Homer's fine dining establishments, but it's perfectly child-friendly, too. As you might expect, seafood specialties top the list of choices. The kid menu features the usual; fish and chips (especially the chips) got top marks from child reviewers.

Fresh Sourdough Express Bakery and Café
1316 Ocean Dr; 907/235-7571; www.freshsourdoughexpress.com
Hours: Daily 7am-9pm
This spot is often busy, but somehow manages to feel relaxed and inviting. The food is carefully prepared, using fresh ingredients. Breakfasts here are Alaskan in size and include a number of scrambles and other specials. At midday, choose from grilled items, filled croissants, soups, salads, and sandwiches. For dinner, there's an eclectic menu that includes veggie lasagna, New Zealand lamb and much more.

There's a kids' menu with favorites; alternatively, the young ones might enjoy the soup du jour—a hearty concoction such as halibut chowder. The service is friendly and patient. There's a play area out front; ask for a window booth so you can watch them play while you linger over coffee.

The Homestead
Mile 8.2, East End Rd; 907/235-8723
Hours: Open daily in summer, 5-10pm, April-May, Wed-Sat 5-9pm
This is where residents go to celebrate a special occasion. It's a lovely drive out, and the attractive log building high above the town adds to the sense of occasion. The food is justly renowned, featuring elegant seafood and steak dishes. Prices are high. This is recommended for families with older kids. Reservations are a must.

Two Sisters Bakery & Espresso
106 Bunnel St; 907/235-2280
Hours: Mon-Fri, 7am-4pm, Sat 7am-2pm
This tiny bakery/restaurant, next to the Bunnell Gallery near Bishop's Beach, is the perfect place for breakfast. Try the whole wheat sticky buns with pecans. They have casual choices for lunch and dinner, too, including sandwiches, foccacia, and pizza. Everything is delicious and homemade and smells heavenly. If it's nice outside, take your tasty treats to the picnic tables at the beach.

What to See & Do

Stroll & Browse
You can see Homer on foot, but you'll need a vehicle to get from one neighborhood to another. Most shops and restaurants on the Spit are clustered near the tip. If you're staying at Land's End, these are within strolling distance. Downtown, it's a fair walk from the Pratt Museum to shops on Pioneer Avenue, down Main, Heath, or Lake Street to the Homer Bypass, and through the slough to Bunnell Street—and you'll cross some busy roads.

Start with a trip to the **Homer Visitor Information Center** (201 Sterling Hwy; 907/235-7740; www.homeralaska.org; open daily in summer). This new facility has a colorful stained glass depiction of Kachemak Bay, set in the floor.

If you're looking to stretch your legs and see the sights, begin on the **Homer Spit**. This four-mile-long finger of land is chockablock with tiny tourist shops and eateries, as well as headquarters for many businesses. You'll also find the small boat harbor, a bit of public camping, the Alaska Marine Highway terminal, and the infamous **Salty Dawg Saloon** (near the end of the spit; opens at 11am, March-November).

Shopping   Homer is the best place to shop for high-quality Alaska arts and crafts on the Kenai Peninsula. It also has a stellar bookstore. You'll find most shops along Pioneer Avenue or out on the Spit. There are a few shops and galleries on Bunnell Street, too, near Bishop's Beach. Among the standouts is **Ptarmigan Arts Studios & Gallery** (471 E Pioneer Ave; 907/235-5345; www.ptarmiganarts.com) with a superb selection of high-quality work by local artists in just about every medium. Nearby, the **Fireweed Gallery** (475 E Pioneer Ave, Ste C; 907/235-3411; www.xyznet/~homerart/) has similar offerings, with an emphasis on Eskimo art, including dolls, and an assortment of Alaska goodies (jellies, teas, honey). It's definitely a touristy experience, but **Alaska Wildberry Products** (528 E Pioneer Ave; 907/235-8858) is bound to appeal to kids. The large store is a scheduled stop for cruise tours and often crowded. It's got a huge selection of Alaska souvenirs, T-shirts, and food items. One plus is the taster's stand where you can sample those odd-sounding goodies you've encountered elsewhere. This successful locally grown business also has outlets in Anchorage and Juneau. Also on Pioneer Avenue is the new location of **The Bookstore** (332 E Pioneer Ave, #1; 907/235-7496, 888/635-BOOK), where you will find a superb collection of Alaskana, a large children's section with dedicated kids' area, and a small café.

Down at the **Bunnell Street Gallery** (106 W Bunnell St; 907/235-2662), serious art collectors can find works by some of Alaska's top artists.

Of special interest to outdoor enthusiasts is the **Nomar Store** (104 E Pioneer Ave; 907/235-8363, 800/478-8364; www.normaralaska.com) which sells quality homemade outerwear and luggage. You can also order their sturdy products online.

When you want a break, stop at **Espresso Express** (280 W Pioneer Ave; 907/235-3688). In summer, stop into their "satellite" shop on the Spit. Or walk or ride down to **Homer Brewing Company** (1411 Lakeshore Dr; 907/235-3626; Mon-Sat, noon-8pm, Sun noon-6 pm). It's fun to sample the brew before you buy. Because of the way they're bottled, these home brews will go flat—ask the folks how long you have to down your purchase. There's a fun selection of logo shirts, hats, and paraphernalia on sale.

If you're here on a Saturday June through August, check out the excellent **farmers market** (Ocean Dr across from the Sourdough Express Bakery; 907/235-4029; 10am-2pm) with high-quality gifts—pottery, jewelry, textiles, clothing, art—along with fresh food and delicious snacks. Prices are lower than in the shops and you'll find unusual items such as moose- or caribou-antler jewelry.

The Big Spill

On Friday March 24, 1989, four minutes after midnight, the *Exxon Valdez*, a huge oil tanker that had taken on 53 million gallons of oil earlier that night at the Alyeska Pipeline Terminal in Valdez, hit Bligh Reef, went aground, and began to leak oil. The damage caused 42,488 barrels an hour to gush into the water, eventually fouling much of pristine Prince William Sound with crude oil. Over 13 million gallons leaked out over the next few days and would prove the biggest oil spill in U.S. history.

Immediately, efforts were made to contain the spill and minimize the disaster. However, the damage could not be contained. The existing procedures and policies to follow in case of a problem proved very weak; in the critical time immediately following the spill, little effective action was taken to address it.

A few days later, 300 square miles of oil slick began to hit the beaches. Fisheries were destroyed, salmon and herring hatcheries ruined, thousands of sea otters and even more seabirds killed. Many Alaska Natives who depended on hunting and fishing lost their livelihood. First the local community, then Alaskans from farther away, and eventually volunteers from around the globe arrived to try to help. Fishermen skimmed the water for oil, rescued wildlife and took them to hastily assembled wildlife shelters. Heart-wrenching photos of sea otters, covered in thick black sludge, appeared in newspapers worldwide. Within weeks of the spill, the town of

Bishop's Beach Park   At this attractive park at the foot of Main Street, your kids will find plenty of playmates. Time your visit for the lowest tides and you'll be rewarded with the sight of tide pools teeming with creatures. Remember that tides can come in fast; be aware of when the tide turns. It gets windy on the beach; kids need warm clothes and appropriate footwear.

Swimming   Kachemak Bay is not warm enough for swimming. The **Homer High School Pool** (600 E Fairview Ave; 907/235-7416) is open to the public; call for details. Also check out the **Bay Club** (2395 Kachemak Dr; 907/235-2582www.homerbayclub.com).

Museums

Alaska Maritime National Wildlife Refuge (AMNWR)   The small visitor center will be replaced by a new center in 2004, a joint project of the Kachemak Bay National Estuarine Research Reserve (KBNERR) and AMNWR, with many displays and exhibits, a theater, and expanded programs. In the meantime, stop in for information on the refuge, a look at the displays, and to view the wildlife videos. Check for special programs (some just for kids), including guided walks, birding, and beachcombing.
Visitor Center: 451 Sterling Hwy; 907/235-6961; alaskamaritime.fws.gov; open daily, Memorial Day-Labor Day, 9am-6pm. Free.

Valdez had more than tripled in size to 11,000. Thousands of volunteers 'washed' rocks free of oil. Many strategies were tried and many failed; some helped, but the impact of these efforts was small. Eventually, the spill reached as far as the Alaska Peninsula; over 1,500 miles of coastline were coated in oil from Prince William Sound to the Gulf of Alaska and lower Cook Inlet.

Given the wild and remote area, estimates of wildlife loss are not exact. A U.S. Dept. of Fish and Wildlife study estimated that 350,000-390,000 seabirds died as a result of the spill. Estimates of sea otters lost range from 3,000-5,000, and even 14 years later, their populations have not fully recovered.

Federal legislation, which will take effect in 2015, requires that all oil tankers have double hulls as a protection against leaks. Other changes include closer monitoring of ships passing through Valdez Narrows and better contingency plans for responding to an emergency. But opinion remains divided as to how much progress there has been in preventing future spills.

Where to Learn More

Seward SeaLife Center, Seward

Pratt Museum, Homer

Exxon Valdez Oil Spill Trustee Council (www.oilspill.state.ak.us/facts/details/)

NOAA Web page for kids on oil spills and their impact (response.restoration.noaa.gov/kids/spills/)

Markle, Saandra. *After the Spill: The Exxon Valdez Disaster Then and Now.* Walker and Company, 1999.

Roderick, Jack. *Crude Dreams: History of Oil in Alaska.* Epicenter Press, 1997. ▣

Pratt Museum / Homer Society of Natural History   Along with traditional Alaska museum features (native history, European settlers) this museum has a large natural history section, the highlight of which is remote cameras that kids can operate to observe wildlife on Gull Island and McNeil River State Game Sanctuary. Kids will enjoy a visit to the tide pool tank when the inmates are fed (4 p.m. on Tuesdays and Fridays). Downstairs, "Darkened Waters" is a superb exhibit on the Exxon Valdez oil spill and its grim aftermath. A version of this exhibit traveled across the United States in recent years. Notice the beautiful quilts; the museum serves as an art gallery with provocative works by Alaskan artists. The museum store is one of the best shops in town for native Alaskan arts and crafts.

Outside is a large botanical garden with plants representing different local habitats. Pick up an interpretive guide. Among the plants is a locomotive engine, discovered in Jackolof Bay in 1980, whose origins are shrouded in mystery. A homestead cabin can also be explored.

The best and most child-friendly museum feature is the **Forest Ecology Trail**. Each year, artists are selected to create installations that are set among the forest trees in summer. Kids enjoy following the trail and trying to spot the next artwork. Around a bend in the trail, children might discover shimmering strands of glass beads, suspended from delicately interwoven branches of a birch tree, or a poem hung on a line between two trees, like laundry. Entries from previous years sometimes are left, deliberately, to be assimilated by the forest. The hunt for the next installation reveals how subtle the line between art and nature can be. There are trail guides to the art and to the forest. *3779 Bartlett St; 907/235-8635; www.prattmuseum.org. Open daily 10am-6pm, May-Sept; Tues-Sun noon-5pm, Oct-April. Closed Jan. Cost: $6/adult $3/youth (6-18), free/under 6, $20/family.*

The Great Outdoors

Bicycling Young cyclists will enjoy the ride from downtown on Ocean Drive out to the end of the Spit and back. You can rent bikes at **Chain Reaction Sports** in the Lakeside Mall downtown (3858 Lake St #2; 907/235-0750) and **Homer Saw & Cycle** (1532 Ocean Dr; 907/235-8406; www.homersaw.com).

Fishing Anglers of all ages fish here for halibut, for which Homer is world famous. Charters also take fishers to the bays and streams around Kachemak Bay, where salmon runs occur from late spring through late summer. To help you identify which of the 50-plus fishing outfitters best suit your family's needs, visit **The Bookie** on the Spit (4460-A Homer Spit Rd; 907/235-1581, 888/335-1581; alaskabookie.com).

Flightseeing Several companies offer flights over Kachemak Bay, the ice fields and lakes of Kenai Fjords National Park, and bear-viewing excursions to Katmai National Park. Prices for a full-day bear-viewing trip will run close to $500 a person. **Kachemak Bay Flying Service** (907/235-8924; www.alaskaseaplanes.com) offers a range of flights from 30 minutes to an hour on a restored luxury biplane as well as modern float planes. Rates start at less than $100 per person for a short flight. Also try **Homer Air** (2190 Kachemak Dr, 907/235-8591, 800/478-8591; www.homerair.com).

Hiking Many hikes around Homer are suitable for families. If time is limited, the best option is to make for the beach. Start from Bishop's Beach and head west toward Anchor Point or east to the Spit. Pick a time when the tide is low for safety and tidepooling opportunities.

The **Calvin & Coyle Nature Trail**, a loop of just under a mile, makes a good hike for young kids. It's close to town; you'll find trail guides at the trailhead. The trail can be muddy; boots are recommended. It was developed by the **Kachemak Heritage Land Trust** (395 E Pioneer Ave; 907/235-5263), which leads guided hikes on this and other local trails in summer. Call for details.
Take East End Rd 1 mile out of town; turn right on Mariner Dr; Parking at trailhead.

Somewhat more difficult, but still a good family hike, is the 6.7 mile **Homestead Trail**. The trail brings you up through forest and meadows up to Diamond Ridge Road. As you ascend, you'll get panoramic views of Cook Inlet and good chances of encountering wildlife. With kids, the full one-way trip can take up to four hours. Be sure to pick up map and trail guide at the trailhead. There are several road access points along the way. If it's an option for you, leaving a second vehicle at another access point can shorten the trip considerably. Check at the visitor center for details.

Take Sterling Hwy west out of town and turn right on Rogers Loop Rd. Park at Trailhead. For a shorter hike, drive up Diamond Ridge Rd to Rucksack Dr.

Horseback Riding   At **Trail's End Horse Adventures** (11.2 Mile East End Rd; 907/235-6393), half-day and longer rides are offered in the Homer area.

Kayaking   Kachemak Bay offers many opportunities for family kayaking. Check out **Seaside Adventures Eco Tours** (66685 Cranberry Ct; 907/235-6672, 800/335-1581; in winter: 907/235-0603; www.ptialaska.net/~seaside/; $125/adult, $115/under 12) which leads guided kayak trips that include beach and intertidal exploration for all ages and levels of experience. **True North Kayak Adventures** (907/235-0708; www.truenorthkayak.com) offers guided trips, half days or longer.

You can rent kayaks from **Bay Excursions Water Taxi and Tours** (907/235-7525; www.xyz.net/~bay/; $45/single per day, $65/double; reduced fees for rentals of 3 days or longer). They also lead guided tours.

Winter Activities   Winter temperatures in Homer are relatively balmy for Alaska, not too much under freezing. Cross-country skiing and snowshoeing are popular, and there's a network of groomed trails in the Baycrest-Diamond Ridge area. There's even a bit of downhill skiing suitable for beginners and young kids at Ohlson Mountain, run by the **Kachemak Nordic Ski Club** (www.xyz.net/~watson/knsc/). For ice skaters, there's a rink behind Homer Middle School, as well as skating on Beluga Lake.

Excursions

Carl E. Wynn Nature Center   This 130-acre nature center is located along the bluffs above Homer. The lovely woods and meadows, donated to the Center for Alaskan Coastal Studies in 1990, represent several plant communities found at the edge of the boreal forest. The Center is best known for its birding opportunities and mountain wildflowers.

Only a small portion of Center lands have been developed; the rest provide wildlife refuge. Stop first at the Interpretive Cabin, a short distance from the parking lot, to get self-guiding maps of the area. Then enjoy the nature trails (including 800 feet of boardwalk) and the sights from two viewing platforms. Or take a regularly scheduled tour. Be sure to apply mosquito repellent; the bugs here are fierce.

On Skyline Dr, 1.5 miles from the top of East Hill Rd. Open daily 10am-6pm. Tours depart: 10am, noon, 2 & 4pm (mid-June-Labor Day). Cost: $5/adult, $4/senior, $3/child.

The Center for Alaskan Coastal Studies ☺ Between late May and the beginning of September, this nonprofit environmental education organization offers natural history tours across Kachemak Bay, overnight trips to their Peterson Bay Field Station, guided hikes, oceanographic exploration, and more. These trips are highly recommended for families. School programs and some just for kids are also offered.

Especially recommended is the four-day Junior Naturalist program. This camp takes kids ages 9 to 12 to the Wynn Nature Center for two days and to the Peterson Bay Field Station for two more; the last two days include an overnight stay in a yurt. Kids need transportation to and from the center and the boat, as well as sack lunches for the first three days. Sleeping bag and pad and appropriate gear is also required. Cost is $150. Two sessions are offered, one in July and one in August.

4014 Lake St; 907/235-6667; www.akcoastalstudies.org

Kachemak Bay State Park This park has 200 miles of pristine coastline teeming with wildlife, including sea otters, whales, seals and porpoises, seabirds, and an assortment of Alaskan land mammals (moose, bears, mountain goats, wolves). The intertidal zone contains a rich variety of creatures.

The park is accessible only by floatplane or boat. (See "Getting Around" for water taxi and air taxi service.) Prices for round trip water-taxi service to the park start at $50/adult and $30/child 2-12. Depending on your destination in the park, prices may be higher.

The tides here are among the world's strongest, and currents can be very tricky. Boaters need to be knowledgeable and well prepared. Once on land, there are over 80 miles of trails. Camping is permitted in most of the park and some campsites have pit toilets, fireplaces, picnic tables, and tent platforms; nine public-use cabins have been added in recent years. Water is plentiful but it needs to be purified.

For most families, the best way to access the park is through the Center for Alaskan Coastal Studies or by kayak or sightseeing tour. However, adventurous, experienced families can and do camp in the park. Water and air taxis can deliver you to trailheads and cabins as you arrange. There's a public dock at Halibut Cove Lagoon, with nearby ranger station, public restrooms, public-use cabins and trails. The **Southern District Ranger Station** (907/235-7024), four miles west of Homer on the Sterling Highway, can give you information, maps, brochures, and advice on visiting the park.

800/770-2257, 907/262-5581, or 907/235-7024: reservations, information.

Whale watching/Wildlife viewing As with fishing charters, there are dozens of whale-watching and wildlife outfitters to choose from. Check with the visitor center or the Bookie (see "Resources").

Calendar of Events

May

Kachemak Bay Shorebird Festival
907/235-7740; www.homeralaska.org/shorebird/
This celebration of local shorebirds, includes guided birdwalks, lectures, cruises and tours, arts and craft fair, activities and concerts for kids, and a wooden boat festival.

July

KBBI Concert on the Lawn

907/235-7721

This all-day event has live music, food, and fun, put on by Kachemak Bay Broadcasting, Homer's public radio station (KBBI 890 AM).

August

Kenai Peninsula Orchestra Summer Strings Festival

907/235-8678; www.xyz.net/~smokybay/festival/

This annual weeklong classical music festival in Homer offers concerts, master classes, and workshops.

Resources

Alaska Bookie

PO Box 195 Homer, AK 99603; 907/235-1581, 888/335-1581; alaskabookie.com

Books trips and various activities, accommodation; on Homer Spit

Homer Referral Agency

PO Box 1264, Homer, AK 99603; 907/235-8996, 907/235-8998

Makes referrals to B&Bs, hotels, tours and activities

Homer Visitor Information Center

201 Sterling Hwy, PO Box 541, Homer, AK 99603; 907/235-5300, 907/235-7740; www.homeralaska.org

Kachemak Bay State Park

PO Box 3248, Homer, AK 99603; 907/235-7024; www.dnr.state.ak.us/parks/units/kbay/kbay/

Books

Homer Alaska Visitor's Guide (Online); Homer Tribune; 907/235-3714; akms.com/htguide/

Kenai Peninsula Vacation Guide, 14896 Kenai Spur Hwy, Ste 106A, Kenai, 99611; 907/283-3850; www.kenaipeninsula.org

Bodett, Tom. *Williwaw!* Alfred A. Knopf, 1999. This thrilling young adult novel describes the adventures of two children who live with their father on an island near Homer, left on their own, whose misadventures lead them into danger: a sudden, violent storm.

SELDOVIA

The town of Seldovia is a bit of an enigma. Located across Kachemak Bay from Homer, it's at once a small, hard-working, no-nonsense Alaskan fishing village and a quaint and magical place to visit. With a population of 309 and a handful of "attractions," Seldovia is a good destination for families who want a chance to kick back. That's not to say there aren't plenty of active pursuits here as well—Seldovia is a premier choice for fabulous hiking, biking, and kayaking experiences.

Russians settled Seldovia (the name comes from the Russian word for "herring") in the 1800s and established a thriving fur trade here; this makes it one of the oldest settlements in the Cook Inlet area. In 1867, with the purchase of Alaska by the United States, many Russians returned to their mother country, but their heritage remains evident.

The 1964 earthquake changed Seldovia forever. The land subsided four feet, allowing high tides to wash over the boardwalk and into its buildings. The waterfront boardwalk was replaced and renewed with fill from surrounding hills so the town could be rebuilt on higher ground, above high tides. The most important reclamation project, though, was that of the townspeople, who struggled to reestablish their lives and livelihoods. From the destruction came a village with two reliable sources of revenue: fishing and tourism.

Although Seldovia is inaccessible by car, there are motor vehicles in Seldovia, brought here by ferry. Most accommodations provide shuttle services around town, if needed. Several boats provide service from Homer. Most runs take 75 minutes, and some longer runs include tours. The Alaska Marine Highway System operates the **Ferry M/V Tusteumena** (907/234-7868), which sails between Homer and Seldovia on Tuesdays. The ferry leaves Homer at 10:30am, and leaves Seldovia to return at 4pm. The layover in Seldovia is four hours. (In summer, the ferry also runs on Sundays, but in the wee hours of the morning.) The route is also served by several water taxis. **M/V Rainbow Connection** (907/235-7272) and **Mako's Water Taxi** (see "Getting Around" under "Homer"); both sail daily in summer, leaving Homer at 9am and Seldovia at 4:45pm. Winter runs vary. (Cost: $50/adult, $45/senior and child for either service).

To add a wildlife or bird tour onto your transportation, check out **M/V Denaina Seldovia Tours** (907/235-7847, 800/478-7847; www.central charter.com). Operating May 15 through Sept 15, this company runs daily tours that leave Homer at 11:30am and Seldovia at 5pm, allowing three hours in the village. Tour costs vary. On weekends, they sail the same route sans tour, leaving Homer at 8:30am and Seldovia at 5pm. (Cost: $45/adult, $40/senior, $35/child under 12.) **Air taxi** service is quick (15 minutes) and inexpensive ($50-60). Try **Homer Air Taxi** (907/235-8591, 800/478-8591; www.homerair.com daily flights on the half-hour in summer, less often in winter) and **Smokey Bay Air** (907/235-1511; call for flight times).

Getting Around

The key word here is "walk." Most of what you'll need or desire is within a few blocks of where you are at any given time. If you wish transportation to Jakalof (for ferry dock or trailhead, for example), inquire at your place of accommodation; most offer a shuttle service.

Places to Stay
Alaska Dancing Eagles Cabin and Bed & Breakfast $$ (house), $$$ (cabin)
*End of Old Seldovia boardwalk (P.O. Box 264, Seldovia 99663); 907/278-0288
(winter), 907/234-7627 (summer); www.dancingeagles.com*
*FYI: 4 rooms (house), cabin; full breakfast, kitchen (cabin); hot tub (sometimes);
shuttle service*
This B&B is situated on a bluff where the Seldovia Slough meets the bay,
providing sterling views in several different directions. The amenities are basic,
but the scenery and gourmet breakfast compensate for any lack of luxury.

The four bedrooms on the second floor of the main house are small but
cozy, each with a scenic view; they share the main-floor bath. Other shared
areas include a large living room, a dining space, and a TV area. One of the
four bedrooms has a double bed and two built-in singles. Otherwise, families
should book two rooms.

The separate cabin is located across a dock-like patio from the main house.
It, too, has a lovely view of the harbor and is quite charming. There's a bedroom
on the main floor, and sleeping accommodations for four in the loft.

66 PARENT COMMENTS 99
*"The kitchen made the cabin a worthwhile investment for
our family. Cooking there saved us money, plus there aren't
very many restaurants in town!"*

*"Standing on the B&B deck, we were visited by a bald
eagle, which swooped low over our heads and then landed
nearby. It was a thrill!"*

Seldovia Seaport Cottages ($-$$)
313 Shoreline Dr.; 907/234-7483; www.xyz.net/~chap
FYI: 4 cottages, kitchenettes
Affordable and comfy, these cottages are a great choice for families. Located
along the Seldovia Slough, each cottage has a kitchen and bath, and sleeping
capacity can be extended with rollaway beds. If you've got a big group, request
the larger cottage, which sleeps six-plus.

66 PARENT COMMENTS 99
*"These cottages are rustic in a way that really fits their
surroundings. Our family enjoyed borrowing mountain
bikes and biking around town."*

Places to Eat
The Mad Fish
221 Main St; 907/234-7676
Hours: Open daily, noon-2:30pm, 5pm-8pm
In this, the town's nicest restaurant, the atmosphere is relaxed and comfortable.
Located on Main Street across from the small boat harbor, The Mad Fish is

Getting There Can Be Half the Fun

By Rose Williamson

"I hear they had about 40 whales by Seldovia when the boat went in yesterday," said the hotel clerk as I checked out of my Homer hotel. "No fair," said another clerk behind her. "I went out two days ago and we only saw eight!"

We chose Rainbow Tours (see "Getting There") for the trip across Kachemak Bay from Homer to Seldovia. Their boat, the 65-foot *Rainbow Connection*, departs Homer's Cannery Row Spit and makes the trip to Seldovia in about 1.25 hours. After dropping passengers (like us) in Seldovia, it proceeds to open waters on a whale-watching tour ($75/adult, $60/child 11 and under).

The ride is very smooth and comfortable. There's a roomy and warm indoor cabin, a hold for storing luggage, and a snack bar. My 11-year-old was pleased, upon invitation, to join the captain in the wheelhouse where she got a quick lesson in navigating the waters. Some commentary is also provided on the ship's public address system.

And although we didn't see any whales before disembarking in Seldovia, we had a lovely ride. The *Rainbow Connection* went on to spot two pods that day! ▣

easy to spot—the wooden building sports bright pink and blue trim. Inside it's light and airy, and offers a view of the harbor.

The menu is almost as much fun as the décor. Recommended for lunch is the Fresh Catch Salad, topped with the grilled fish of the day (try it with the house blueberry vinaigrette). There are also a number of meat and fish entrées, a selection of burgers, and a kids' menu with burgers and chicken. At dinner there are a number of signature dishes.

The Buzz Coffee House & Espresso Café
231 Main St; 907/234-7479
Hours: Open 6:30am-5:30pm, closed Wed (March-Sept)

If you hail from any of the urban centers in the lower 48, you'll be heartened to find a coffeehouse in this unlikely place! The Buzz makes an espresso worthy of Seattle or Chicago, and you can sip it while you watch the action down at the harbor. You can also order a specialty tea, smoothie, or Italian soda.

Breakfast foods include baked items, including The Buzz breakfast burrito (say that five times quickly). Italian dishes, soup and chili, and quiche headline the lunch menu. There's a patio outside and tables, games, and newspapers inside. The help here won't be hurried; don't expect "fast" food (or drinks) as you run to catch your boat.

What To See & Do

Stroll & Browse

You can see most of Seldovia on a short stroll down **Main Street**. Start at the historic boardwalk just south of the harbor, where you'll find a quaint collection of cottages and a few small shops. Then, as you walk north along the main drag check out **Sweet 'n' Clean** (226 Main St), a combination Laundromat, café, and ice cream parlor!

Tarry along the harbor and scrutinize the fishing and pleasure boats. A fun place to shop is the **Alaska Tribal Cache** (907/234-7898, 800/270-7810; www.alaskatribalcache.com), located along the water just past the boat launch. Here you'll find native-made foods (try some of the preserves made from local berries) and crafts. You'll find reading material at the **Tidepool Café & Bookstore** (267 Main St; 907/234-7502; www.ptialaska.net/~tide/where.html). It's open year round, 6am to 3pm. They also serve dinners, Wednesday through Saturday, from 5 to 8 pm. The view is excellent and meals are eclectic and affordable.

With eating and shopping behind you, head up the small hill to your right, to **Saint Nicholas Church**, built by Russian Orthodox in 1891.

The Great Outdoors

Hiking Highly recommended for families, the **Otterbahn Trail** is a short, moderately easy hike that begins behind the Susan B. English School. A group of high school students was instrumental in blazing the trail, which winds for 1.5 miles through old-growth forest to Outside Beach. The calm shoreline is a frequent resting place for kayakers.

In 2001, construction began on **Rocky Ridge Trail**, designed to provide an additional hike within walking distance from town. This moderately difficult trail, approximately 2.5 miles in length, is recommended for experienced hikers. Beginning at the Slough Bridge, take Rocky Street to the section-line road and cross the small wooden bridge. Above the bridge is the trailhead, from which the trail is well marked. You will climb quite steeply, then follow the ridgeline to Reservoir Road. Take the road down and circle back to the Slough Bridge. Bears have been spotted along this trail.

Water Activities The beautiful waters around Seldovia offer rugged coastline and beaches to explore, as well as wildlife and sea life. Kayaking is a great way for families to explore these waters, given proper equipment and instruction. To schedule a sea kayak tour or outfitted trip, contact **Kayak'atak Alaskan Paddling Adventures** (PO Box 109-KP, Seldovia, 99663; 907/234-7425; www.alaska.net/~kayaks/). With kayaking experience, you can rent single or double kayaks by the hour; call for prices.

Across the Bay Tent & Breakfast (907/345-2571 [winter], 907/235-3633 [summer]; www.tentandbreakfastalaska.com) provides a customized outdoor package that includes tent and breakfast ($58/person/day), tent and all meals

Putting Alaska in Perspective with Kids

By Jan Faull

Before taking children to Alaska museums, prepare yourself and them for what you'll witness about the earthquake that occurred in 1964. Anchorage and Valdez have museums dedicated to the earthquake, and many others include vivid exhibits on the subject. The Seward museum displays letters by 2nd graders describing what they experienced on that Good Friday in 1964. While these exhibits make for fascinating reading and wonderful lifelike experiences, they might scare and worry some children.

Most preschoolers will experience an earthquake exhibit as an imaginative experience similar to a Star Wars or Wizard of Oz movie. It's out of their realm of understanding and experience to begin to grasp what actually happened. If they dwell on the topic, ask lots of questions, and continually bring it up, rather than sweeping their interest under the rug with distractions, embrace the topic by reading them simple books, offerings bits of information, and providing opportunities with water, dirt and blocks so children can play about the event, and thus come to terms with what they don't understand.

Children in elementary school are the ones who might provide

($85/person/day), guided sea kayak tour ($95/person/day), and mountain bike rental ($25/person/day).

If fishing is your thing, you'll find big halibut and king salmon—along with a number of other fish—in the Seldovia area. They offer several charter packages, day trips or multiday with accommodation provided. Transporation can also be provided from Homer. To plan a trip, contact **Seldovia Fishing Adventures** (PO Box 121, Seldovia, 99663; 907/234-7417).

Calendar of Events

July

4th of July Celebration
www.kash.net/alaska/july4/
Probably the biggest day of the year in Seldovia, this "old fashioned Fourth" includes a parade, canoe jousting and other friendly competitions, and food booths.

Resources

Tide Tables for Seldovia
(NOTE: Seldovia has 30-foot tides; be aware of these.)
www.seldovia.com/nav_tides/

the biggest challenge to parents. They're old enough to know the earthquake and tsunami really happened but they're not old enough to understand that the likelihood of it happening again is minimal. They want the facts but don't have enough mental wherewithal to put it into perspective.

For the child who is concerned, it's important to give them something specific to do if an earthquake takes place again, like getting under a table, or standing in a doorway. By teaching them how to respond, children fill competent and in control rather than fearful.

Let children know what protective measures are in place for school-aged children in Alaska. It's also important to explain to school-aged kids that although there's a lot children can do in such situations, parents, teachers and emergency response units are in place to take care of them in an emergency.

Talk about their fears and clarify any misunderstandings. Don't overwhelm them with information but rather listen carefully to their questions and comments, see what a child is really trying to understand. A little disruption in their mind and emotions is normal as they attempt to absorb the new information that's coming their way.

Young teens are the ones who will thoroughly absorb all the information about the earthquake and tsunami. This is true particularly for ones who are interested in science, geology and natural disasters. There's a lot for them to learn if they're so inclined. ▣

Seldovia Chamber of Commerce
PO Drawer F, Seldovia, AK 99663. 907/234-7612; www.xyz.net/~seldovia

City of Seldovia Web site
www.seldovia.com

Seldovia Summer Gazette
PO Box 97, Seldovia, AK 99663
Free paper published May through September and distributed throughout the village.

8 The Southwest: Kodiak Island and Dutch Harbor/Unalaska

8 The Southwest: Kodiak Island and Dutch Harbor/Unalaska

ALASKA'S SOUTHWEST ISN'T all that far from the state's largest population center—Kodiak is just 252 miles from Anchorage. But it's a 5.5-hour drive, plus a 10.5-hour boat ride, making it remote in a way that mileage doesn't capture. At 800 miles from Anchorage, Unalaska Island is even more remote. But thanks to daily airline service and affordable public transportation via the Alaska Marine Highway System, with planning this region is accessible. And parents who take the time to plan a visit here are enthusiastic about what they find: extraordinary scenery, a fascinating history, and a warm and welcoming local population. With some of the world's best kayaking and wildlife viewing, this region is truly a great bet for families.

If there is one place in Alaska in which travel plans can easily go awry, however, this is it. It is not uncommon for airports to be socked in or seas to be too rough to allow passage for several days. Try to build in time at either end of your trip to allow for delays, and bring extra clothing, books, toys, and a generous helping of patience. Travel insurance is strongly recommended for flights, cruises, and tours to the area (see "Booking an Extended Trip into the Outback").

The climate on Kodiak and the Aleutian Islands is mild. Average winter low temperatures don't fall below about 25 degrees Fahrenheit, whereas average summer highs are around 62 degrees. Precipitation ranges from 7.4 inches in January to 3.7 inches in July, the driest month. However, any month can be plenty wet. High-quality raingear for everyone is a must. As elsewhere in Alaska, dressing for the weather will enhance your family's enjoyment.

Regional Resources

Alaska Department of Fish & Game
907/465-4100; www.state.ak.us/adfg/adfghome/

National Weather Service for Southcentral Alaska
800/472-0391; pafc.arh.noaa.gov/pubfcst.php

Parent Ed.

Dyson, George. *Baidarka*. Alaska Northwest Books, 1986. A history of the Aleut kayak that includes author's experience, reflections, and gorgeous photos.

Fields, Leslie Leyland. *The Entangling Net: Alaska's Commercial Fishing Women Tell Their Lives*. University of Illinois Press, 1997.

Lord, Nancy. *Green Alaska: Dreams from the Far Coast.* Counterpoint, 2000. An account of the 1899 Harriman Alaska Expedition that included Kodiak, Unalaska, the Aleutian, and Pribilof Islands.

Walker, Spike. *Nights of Ice: True Stories of Disaster and Survival on Alaska's High Seas.* St. Martin's Press, 1999.

Walker, Spike. *Working on the Edge: Surviving in the World's Most Dangerous Profession: King Crab Fishing on Alaska's High Seas.* St. Martin's Press, 1993.

Web Sites

These online teaching resources cover native Alaskan history, education, languages, and cultures. www.alaskool.org

The Alaska Native Knowledge Network (www.ankn.uaf.edu)

Alaska's Native Heritage Center; www.alaskanative.net

Comprehensive Web page on native Alaskans; sled.alaska.edu/native/

Kid Stuff

Bartok, Mira and Romanl, Christine. *Alaskan Eskimo and Aleut Stencils.* With these stencils, kids can make a hunting hat, finger mask, scrimshaw ornament, and more.

Ferrell, Nancy. *Alaska: Land in Motion.* This is actually a geography text for kids, grades 3-6, that looks at all of Alaska's regions and covers the powerful natural forces, including earthquakes and volcanoes, that have shaped it.

KODIAK ISLAND

Probably the biggest draw for visitors to Kodiak is the hope of seeing the world's largest land-based carnivore, the Kodiak brown bear, in its native— and only—habitat. In fact, the Kodiak National Wildlife Refuge, devoted to preserving the bear and its fellow fauna, covers two-thirds of Kodiak Island. If you plan ahead and take a flightseeing trip, your chances of seeing a bear are excellent.

Bears aside, there are plenty of other good reasons to pay Kodiak a visit. Home to the Alutiiq people for about 9,000 years, Kodiak was 'discovered' by the Russians (whose interest was sea otter pelts) in the 18th century. Kodiak became the first capital of Russian Alaska. Today, the island supports about 14,000 people, nearly half residing in the town of Kodiak, the largest fishing port in the United States.

Getting To Kodiak

By Sea Taking the ferry can be the most interesting, affordable, and exciting way to visit this region, but it takes time and planning. **Alaska Marine Highway System ferries** (907/486-3800; www.akferry) make the trip between Homer and Kodiak three times a week.

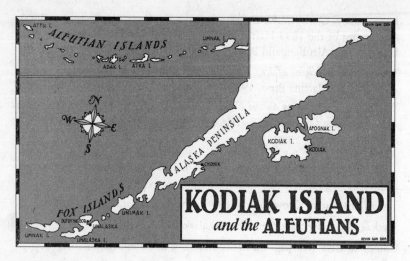

CruiseWest (800/580-0072; www.cruisewest.com), a small cruise line, sails both to Kodiak and Dutch Harbor.

By Air This is by far the easiest way to get to Kodiak. **Alaska Airlines** (800/252-7522; www.alaskaair.com) offers multiple daily flights between Anchorage and Kodiak. **Era Aviation** (800/866-8394; www.eraaviation.com) flies daily between Anchorage and Kodiak.

Getting Around

Kodiak tends to sprawl. Renting a car to deal with the distances, some steep hills, and weather conditions is the most convenient option for getting around. It will also allow you to enjoy the island's 100 miles of scenic road. But if you're here for only a day or two, you can probably make do with a taxi or two (although these are notoriously expensive) and the local bus system. Some hotels offer free shuttles to and from the airport, and many tours will pick you up and drop you off at your hotel.

KATS (Kodiak Area Transportation System) While Kodiak does not have a full-time transit system, the Kodiak Area Transportation System (KATS) runs buses at rush hour. Buses stop at the airport, Best Western, Shelikof Lodge, and Harbormaster's Office, among other sites. (907/486-8308. Mon-Fri 6:30-8:30am and 4:30-6:30pm. Cost: $2/person, one way; exact change required. Call for details.)

Car rentals **Budget Rent a Car** (budget@eagle.ptialaska.net) has two locations: at the Kodiak State Airport (1200 Airport Rd; 907/487-2220) and downtown, close to the ferry terminal at (508 Marine Way 907/486-8550). **Rent-a-Heap** (carrent@ptialaska.net) also operates at the same two locations: the Kodiak State Airport (907/487-4001) and 508 Marine Way (907/486-2220).

Places to Stay

Best Western Kodiak Inn ($-$$)

236 Rezanof Dr; 907/486-5712, 888/KODIAK-4; www.kodiakinn.com
FYI: 80 rooms, restaurant; refrigerators/microwaves; hot tub; pets OK (deposit); free airport shuttle

Conventions and tour groups stay here. Apart from a breathtaking stuffed Kodiak brown bear in the lobby, it's short on atmosphere but long on comfort. Rooms are spacious and quiet.

66 PARENT COMMENTS 99

"Staff were very friendly and informative. Our ferry didn't leave until late evening, and the staff kept our luggage safe for us after we checked out."

Buskin River Inn ($$-$$$)

1395 Airport Way; 907/487-2700, 800/544-2202;
www.kodiakadventure.com/buskin/
FYI: 50 rooms, four suites; refrigerators; guest laundry; restaurant; pets OK (in smoking rooms only); free airport shuttle; sightseeing packages

This comfortable hotel is a good choice if you're renting a car. It's close to the airport but far from downtown, so you need transportation to get around.

Russian Heritage Inn ($-$$)

119 Yukon St; 907/486-5657; e-mail: rhkodiak@ptialaska.net;
www.ak-biz.com/russianheritage
FYI: 25 rooms, suites, one unit with full kitchen; refrigerators/microwaves; kids stay free; bike and stroller rentals, guest laundry; pets OK; convenience store, picnic area

This rather basic inn is a good choice for families looking for kitchen facilities and is handy to downtown. Discounts are offered for long-term stays.

Teal House B&B

3300 Wilton White Way; 907/486-3369; www.tealhouse.com
FYI: four rooms; breakfast, access to full kitchen, freezer; no smoking or alcohol; shared baths; portacrib, cots, highchair available; TV, VCR can be borrowed; guest laundry; sunroom with fitness equipment; outdoor hot tub; accessible; small pets OK on approval

About a 10-minute drive from downtown, this spacious, comfortable B&B welcomes families and can provide books and activities for kids and accommodate small-fry eating preferences. When a single party rents the entire B&B, there's a 10-percent discount. You can negotiate discounts for longer stays.

66 PARENT COMMENTS 99

"The bookcase has a variety of books ranging from Alaskana and books of local interest to the history of the Gold Rush... There are many games and puzzles to entertain the active child and appropriate toys for toddlers."

The Big One:
1964 Earthquake and Tsunami in Kodiak

by Betty E. Marriott

Good Friday 1964 certainly stands out in my mind, but not because of the lovely dinner we had planned with friends. At 5:36 p.m. my husband, Dick, had just returned home from work, and I was tending to my daughter, Wendy, almost a year old, when suddenly things began to shake! Six months pregnant and feeling unsteady, I grabbed Wendy and plopped myself down on the couch. Dick stood with his legs spread-eagled and grasped a chair and table to avoid falling. The chandelier was swinging ominously above his head and I worried that it would fall.

Dick staggered to the battery-operated radio to catch the local news. A frantic announcer reported that Alaska had experienced an earthquake of immense magnitude. He urged everyone to seek high ground, as a tidal wave was threatening. He braved the airwaves as long as he felt he could, then frantically signed off with, "Ladies and Gentlemen, this is your last warning: get to higher ground immediate-

ly." (We were later saddened to hear that the announcer had failed to leave the station, which was located near the water, in time. Attempting to drive away, he was caught in the impending waves and drowned.)

Our home was located high up in the city of Kodiak, and I noticed that cars were whizzing by to get up to Pillar Mountain. We stayed put, figuring that one couldn't go much higher, anyway. We had canned chicken soup over a camp stove that night—no company for dinner and no sukiyaki.

The next few days were cold and fearful, the aftershocks unnerving. It was the end of March, still winter in Alaska. Temperatures were freezing, and we were without power or heat. At night we used flashlights and candles, dressed in ski clothes, and used all the blankets we could muster together to stay warm. We huddled around the radio to listen to the increasingly discouraging news.

We learned that the earthquake had registered a punishing 8.6 on the

Camping

See "State Parks."

Places to Eat

The Chart Room/Best Western Kodiak Inn

236 Rezanof Dr; 907/486-8807
Hours: Daily 7am-2pm; 4-10pm

Here is where Kodiak residents head for a spot of fine dining. The food is good, portions are large, but it's all fairly expensive.

King's Diner

1941 Mill bay Rd. 907/486-4100
Hours: Mon-Sat 5:30am-3pm; Sun 6:30am-3pm

Richter scale (in recent years, this figure has been revised upward to 9.2, one of the very highest magnitudes ever recorded on the planet). Damage in downtown Kodiak was significant: a huge fishing boat was tied to a telephone pole next to the elementary school, the Fish and Game office and local businesses were gone, liquor bottles were floating in Potato Patch Lake. Dick, who was doing research for the state Department of Fish and Game, was concerned about biologists working at the Kitoi Bay Fish Hatchery. When the men were finally brought back, it was learned they had spent a night in an open boat tied to a tree. The hatchery was gone, and they were shaken but okay.

Reports came in of devastating damage statewide, caused by the quake itself and the tidal wave that followed. In Anchorage, about 75 houses in Turnagain Heights slid from the bluff onto the tide flats. Downtown, 4th Avenue opened into large fissures, and area theaters, businesses, and cars fell into them. In Valdez, oil tanks exploded and, according to a previous resident, "the town was like Armageddon."

(Valdez was eventually relocated as the ground was too unstable to allow rebuilding.) Tsunamis, together with land subsidence and uplift, destroyed or damaged fisheries and canneries.

Our families in Seattle were frantic. All telephone communication was lost; there was no way to communicate with them and assure them of our safety. "Kodiak Island has sunk!" was broadcast over the radio and television. (True, parts of the island had sunk significantly, but the island did not disappear from the map!) My mother-in-law heard a television announcer say that a pregnant woman was seen running up a mountain, and she thought, "Oh, no, that can't be Betty!" But soon, ham-radio operators generously volunteered their services, and we were able to communicate with our anxious families.

Our little family was happy to be alive and together. We were cold, but we still had our home. Our refrigerator was not too full, but we had staples and canned foods to eat. We assessed our damages. The tiles had cracked all the way down the length of the kitchen floor, but damages were few. We were lucky. ◼

Good truck-stop cuisine makes this a perennially popular spot with locals for breakfast and lunch. Prices are low and menu items include child-friendly favorites like burgers and spaghetti. The location by the municipal airport is another plus for families: watch the small planes take off and land while you wait. Homemade pies go down well for dessert.

El Chicano
103 Center St; 907/486-6116
Hours: Mon-Sat 11am-10pm; closed Sun
This popular Mexican restaurant serves up the expected fare in hearty portions.

Harborside Coffee & Goods
216 Shelikof St; 907/486-5862
Hours: Mon-Thurs 6:30am-9pm; Sat 6:30am-10pm; Sun 7am-8pm
Duck in here for a steamy latté, hot chocolate, or bowl of soup during a

Kodiak downpour, and you'll find plenty of locals doing likewise. Choose from the excellent selection of child-friendly baked treats while recharging your sightseeing batteries.

Henry's Great Alaskan Restaurant
512 Marine Way; 907/486-8844
Hours: Mon-Thurs 11:30am-9:30pm; Fri-Sat 11:30am-10pm; Sun noon-9pm
At first glance, the ambiance does not say "family restaurant," but the menu will soon allay fears. Ignore the smoky, barroom feel of the place, and plunge on in. (But if air quality is a concern, you'll probably want to dine elsewhere.) There's a kids' menu, and reliable, child-approved standbys include burgers, pasta, and chicken-fried steak. You can be well fed here for a reasonable price.

What to See & Do

As the weather is at best variable, explore downtown or hike over to Near Island when it's dry, and save the museums and shops for the downpour you'll likely encounter eventually.

Stroll & Browse

Downtown Kodiak is crammed with interesting things to see and do, all within a few blocks. Start out by getting your bearings and a map at the **Visitor Center** (see "Resources"). As you leave the Center, notice the *Star of Kodiak*, to your left. This old World War II Liberty ship, the last ever built to carry troops in that war, is now a fish cannery, not an uncommon fate for old ships in Alaska.

From the Visitor Center, follow Marine Way as it curves up to meet Shelikof Street. There, you'll find the **St. Paul Boat Harbor & Shelikof Waterfront**. From this street you can get a good view of Kodiak's busy fishing industry. A series of interpretive signs help you make sense of what you see.

Before you turn back to the shops, stop in for a snack at **Harborside Coffee & Goods** (see "Places to Eat"). Back on Marine Way at the Mall, you'll find several gift stores. **Norman's** (414 Marine Way, 907/486-3315) carries an assortment of gifts and books of local interest. You'll find the widest assortment of local artworks and crafts at **The Treasury** (104 Center Ave; 907/486-0373), which serves as Internet café and Kodiak's principal bookstore.

The Russian Orthodox community in Kodiak is alive and well. To get a feel for its rich history, visit the Diocesan Museum in St. Herman's Seminary (see "Museums"). You can take the guided tour of the **Holy Resurrection Russian Orthodox Church,** offered daily in summer (410 Mission Rd, 907/486-3854, $1); services, open to the public, are held several times a week. Next to the church, explore the enchanting store in a small, round kiosk-like building on the grounds. You'll find nesting dolls, intricate Christmas ornaments, scarves, carved boxes, jewelry, and much more. Prices are low for authentic Russian arts and crafts. Call the church for hours.

For a complete change of pace, cross the street to the **Alaska Department of**

Fish and Game where you'll find a variety of sea life on display (211 Mission Rd; Mon-Fri 8am-5pm. Free.). Exhibits include a touch tank that kids will enjoy.

At 713 Rezanof Street, in a *barabara* sod house—a reconstructed, authentic Alutiiq dwelling—the **Alutiiq Dancers** perform June through August (907/486-4449; $15). The dancers are one of Kodiak's most popular attractions, so reservations are a good idea. Allow about 30 minutes.

Parks and Viewpoints

Walk across the Near Island Bridge to **North End Park**, stopping in the middle to view the busy harbor below. The park, just on the other side of the bridge, features easy trails down to the water, suitable for small children to explore. There are lovely picnic sites, and if you're lucky, you'll have a great view of town and other islands. In July and August, locals come here to pick salmonberries.

You'll get a fabulous view of the city and surrounding areas from the summit of 1400-foot **Pillar Mountain**. You can drive up via the gravel-surfaced Pillar Mountain Road (take Hillside Drive to Pillar Mountain Road), or hike up from downtown if your kids are older; pick up a map and directions at the Visitor Information Center.

Baranof Park (between Baranof & Chichenof Sts, east of Powell) has a playground with climbing structure and swings.

Museums

Alutiiq Museum and Archaeological Repository This fascinating museum showcases the vibrant culture of the Alutiiq people from prehistoric times to the present. Along with historic artifacts, artworks, archival photographs, and more, the museum offers educational programs—often in tandem with schools and community organizations—that are of interest to families, such as archaeological digs and cultural workshops. A well-stocked gift store features work of native Alaskan artists. For a taste of the culture, visit the museum Web site, which describes the Alutiiq world in detail and includes archaeological resources for children.

215 Mission Rd; 907/486-7004; www.alutiiqmuseum.com. Open Mon-Fri 9am to 5pm; Sat 10am-5pm; Sun by appt. (June-Aug); Tues-Fri 9am-5pm; Sat 10:30am-4:30pm (Sept-May). Cost: $2/adult; free/under 13.

Baranov Museum/Kodiak Historical Society This charming museum is small, but jam-packed with fascinating relics of Kodiak's colorful, multicultural past. It's housed in an old Russian fur warehouse. This National Historic Landmark, dating in part from the mid-19th century, is one of Alaska's oldest.

Exhibits cover the natural and human history of Kodiak Island and the Aleutian archipelago, including prehistoric and later artifacts of the Alutiiq-Aleut culture; several stuffed animals; Russian carvings, samovars, and clothing; a host of paintings and historic photographs, a re-created Kodiak sitting room, and a couple of pioneer kitchens. Don't miss the beautiful basketry in the Basket Room.

A Kodiak-bear video is shown in the gift shop, where you'll find an excellent assortment of Russian arts, crafts, and jewelry, although prices are usually lower at the gift shop outside the Russian Orthodox Church.
101 Marine Way (Erskine House); 907/486-5920; www.baranov.us. Open: Mon-Sat 10am-4pm; Sun noon-4pm (summer and Crab Festival); Mon-Sat 10am-3pm; closed Thurs, Sun and all Feb (rest of year). Cost: $2/adult, under 13/free. Allow at least one hour.

Kodiak Military History Museum Housed in an ammunition bunker at Miller Point in Fort Abercrombie State Historical Park, this museum is a National Historic Landmark. When the kids tire of racing along the trails or peering into tidepools at Fort Abercrombie, suggest a visit to this interesting facility. Like the Aleutians, Kodiak Island played an important role in plans U.S. defense plansfor the defense of the United States during World War II. Bunkers were built and guns emplaced at Fort Abercrombie to support the effort, though Kodiak was never bombed. Wartime memorabilia, photos, and documents tell the story of the role played by Kodiak and the Aleutians in the war. There is a small gift store.
In Fort Abercrombie State Historical Park, 1623 Mill Bay Rd; 907/486-7015; www.kodiak.org. Open Mon, Wed, Sat 1-3pm; Sun.2-3pm; winter, other times by appointment; call for details. Cost: $2/adult; free/children under 12. Allow at least 30 minutes.

Diocesan Museum of the History of the Russian Orthodox Church This small museum tells the story of the first Christian church in Alaska (1784) and of Saint Herman, a missionary born near Moscow and sent to Alaska. He lived out his long life in Kodiak and nearby Spruce Island. Displays of historic religious art and artifacts of the church's long history are shown here.
In St. Herman's Theological Seminary, 414 Mission Rd; 907/486-3524; e-mail: stherman@ptialaska.net. Open Mon-Fri 10am-4pm or by appointment. Free.

Animals Animals

The wildlife is abundant here, even by Alaska standards. Along with eagles and bears, you'll find buffalo herds. Many whales summer here, while orcas reside year-round. Allow an extra day or two to get to the wildlife, and you are not likely to be disappointed.

Birdwatching Along with one of the state's largest year-round populations of bald eagles, puffins, and other seabirds, plenty of ducks and songbirds call Kodiak home. One of the best ways to see these is on a hike with the **Kodiak Audubon Society** (907/486-6498; e-mail: tidepool@ptialaska.net). From mid-May through mid-September, Society members lead hikes, usually on Saturdays, starting from the Visitor Information Center. If you'd rather head out on your own, be sure to pick up the Society's trail guide, *Hiking on Kodiak*, available at the Visitor Information Center, which offers maps and detailed descriptions of popular hikes for wildlife viewing.

The Kodiak Brown Bear

Technically they are members of the brown bear family that includes grizzlies, but the Kodiak brown bear has been separated from other family members for at least 12,000 years. They are unique in their size: They can be nearly 11 feet high and weigh up to 1,500 pounds. Kodiak bears rarely harm humans; only one person has been killed in the past 70 years by a Kodiak bear.

These magnificent animals are found only on Kodiak and nearby islands and have been protected since 1941. Most of Kodiak Island provides them with abundant healthy food and water. Plenty of local outfitters can help you get close enough to the bears to observe and photograph them. Each year several hundred permits are issued for hunting the bears, too.

The Kodiak bear population is estimated at nearly 3,000, by and large a healthy group that lives on salmon, berries, herbs and plants, and anything else they can find (bears are omnivores). The bears stay with their mothers for about three years before setting off on their own, and can live up to 30 years. While most hibernate for seven months or more, new mothers hibernate a month or two longer, and occasional males don't hibernate at all. One of the mysteries of bear hibernation is how they manage to conserve so much muscle and bone mass after months with no food or exercise. Scientists have been studying this phenomenon for clues that may eventually help astronauts in space.

Resources

Parent Ed

Great Bear Foundation. *Field Guide to the Grizzly Bear*. Sasquatch Books, 1992.

Kodiak Bears & the Exxon Valdez. Kodiak Brown Bear Trust. Richardson, Tim and Cline, Dave, eds. 2000.

Treadwell, Timothy. *Among Grizzlies: Living with Wild Bears in Alaska*. HarperCollins, 1997.

Kid Stuff

Cartwright, Shannon and Gill, Shelley. *Alaska's Three Bears*. A Paws IV Book, Sasquatch.

Hoshino, Michio and Colligan-Taylor, Karen. *The Grizzly Bear Family Book*. North South Books.

Videos

Alaska's Grizzlies. This hour-long video should whet kid appetites for visiting bears in their native habitats.

The Bear (1989, video-92 minutes). This marvelous film, by Jean-Jaques Annaud, released in movie theaters, tells the story of a Kodiak bear cub who, after his mother is killed, bonds to an adult male.

The Biggest Bears. Sky River Films (Video, 22 minutes) ▣

Flightseeing/Bear Watching

The good news is that you are very likely to see a Kodiak bear when you sign on to a bear-watching trip. But it will take time and a hefty chunk of change. Expect to pay at least $350 per person for a flight and/or boat trip into the island's interior, nearby islands, or Katmai National Park on the Alaska

Peninsula. To maximize your chances of seeing bears, schedule your visit when the salmon are running in July and August. The exact timing changes from year to year; check with the Kodiak National Wildlife Refuge Visitor Center for up-to-date bear sightings.

Kodiak National Wildlife Refuge (KNWR) Visitor Center At the Visitor Center, located close to the airport, several miles out of town, you'll find wildlife displays, films, books, and information on recent bear sightings. You can also book public-use cabins. Kids will enjoy exploring the **Audubon Buskin View Trail**, an easy nature trail behind the Visitor Center. Family programs are offered every Saturday during summer months. The KNWR itself is another 25 miles southwest of the Visitor Center. Its nearly two million acres encompass most of Kodiak Island and extend to a few others, including 50,000 acres of Afognak Island. While giant brown bears are the big draw, the KNWR shelters plenty of other mammals and sea birds, too.
1390 Buskin River Rd; 907/487-2600; www.r7.fws.gov/nwr/kodiak/kodnwr/.
Open Mon-Fri 8am-4:30pm; Sat-Sun noon-4pm (mid-June-mid-Sept);
Mon-Fri 8am-4:30pm (rest of year).

Andrew Airways This company offers a variety of package tours. There's a three-hour flightseeing/bear-viewing package at $355/per person (two-person minimum) and a four-hour trip at $450/per person. Hip boots, snacks, and beverages are provided. A combination glacier/bear-viewing charter is also available, along with several shorter trips and ground-based trips. Van service to and from the charters is provided.
At Kodiak State Airport; 907/ 487-2566; www.andrewairways.com.

Highline Air A bear-watching tour of four-and-a-half hours (two-person minimum) costs $395/per person. Lunch is included and time is built in on the ground for photos. Children above toddler age are welcome. If you book four seats, you'll receive a 10-percent discount.
1829 Mill Bay Rd; 907/486-5155.

Sea Hawk Air A bear-watching trip of four to five hours costs $420/adult, two-person minimum, June 1-September 15. Some discounts and specials apply; check for details. Customized fishing packages are also available. Children 12 and under are $300. Prices go down, the larger the party. Children of all ages are permitted to fly.
907/486-8282, 800/770-4295; www.seahawkair.com.

Swimming The only place to swim in town is at the **Kodiak High School Swimming Pool**, owned and operated by the Kodiak Island Borough and open to the public.
At Kodiak High School. 722 Mill Bay Rd; 907/486-9263. Call for hours.

The Great Outdoors

Berry Picking In Kodiak, July through August is the season for salmonberries and blueberries. North End Park, on Near Island, is a good bet, as are the state parks. Check with the Visitor Center for more tips on where to look. And remember that bears love berries, too.

Booking an Extended Trip into the Outback

A wide variety of outfitters take visitors on all sorts of adventures on Kodiak and neighboring islands and over to Katmai National Park on the Alaska Peninsula. Many provide lodging and equipment rental along with guide service. All of these can be costly, so it pays to do some homework first.

Begin by shopping around and doing some research. Is there a particular animal you want to see? Find out when sightings are most likely, and check tide tables and weather patterns (see "Resources") that might impact sightings. If you can, combine two or more activities to maximize your chances of success in at least one—for example, berry picking and bear watching. When you've got a handle on the options, contact the Kodiak Convention Center and Visitor Bureau (see "Resources") and ask for a list of outfitters for the kind of trip you are interested in. Contact them and ask lots of questions: how long they've been in business, which business associations they belong to (such as the Chamber of Commerce), and what experience they have with children. Being willing to accept children on a trip is not the same thing as providing an excursion designed with kids in mind. Do they provide snacks and/or meals? If so, will kids like them? Do they carry kid sizes of gear, such as hip boots for fishing? Last but not least, ask about the outfitters' weather-related cancellation and refund policies. Does the outfitter offer an alternative trip if flights are grounded? Kodiak can be windy and foggy at any time of year. It may be worthwhile to obtain travel insurance. ▣

Fishing Just about every outfitter on Kodiak Island includes guided fishing trips in their menu of options. **David's Family Guide Service** specializes in taking families, including very small fishers, on a variety of adventures, also including wildlife viewing and wildflower hunting.
Mile 35 Chiniak Hwy; PO Box 266 Kodiak, AK 99615; 907/486-3715.

Fossil Hunting Fossil Beach is a perennial favorite with local families and schools. In recent years, intriguing finds, such as the discovery of an ancient sea mammal, something like an elephant and around 15 million years old, have been made here. (See "Pasagshak River State Recreation Site" under "State Parks.")

Horseback Riding Several ranches and outfitters on the island offer horseback riding. Kodiak has plenty of wide-open spaces with expansive vistas, and riding can be a terrific way for families to get out into the island's spectacular scenery and enjoy its abundant wildlife. **Northland Ranch Resort** (907/486-5578), a working ranch, provides basic accommodation, meals and assorted activities that include berry picking, fossil hunting, beachcombing and hiking, as well as riding ($45 for a two-hour ride). Fishing is available, but bring your own tackle. The **Kodiak Cattle Company** (907/486-3705; chiniak.net/buffalo/) ranch farms buffalo and offers hunting and fishing excursions for visitors who can also stay or camp here. Horseback riding fees are per person and assume a minimum of two people: $60/three hours; $75/four hours; $150/all day. The location, about 50 miles south of the town of Kodiak, includes wilderness beaches. The Company can provide transportation to and from the ranch. At **Red Cloud Ranch** (Mile 8, Anton Larsen Rd; 907/487-4566) you can book trail rides by appointment. Fees start at $35/person, per hour. Pony rides for kids in the corral are $5/ride. Helmets are provided.

Sea Kayaking   Kodiak's combination of mild weather, numerous inlets, bays and tiny islands to explore, gorgeous scenery, and abundant critters to observe adds up to some of the best kayaking anywhere on the planet. Outfitters suggest that you don't book too far in advance, owing to the uncertain weather conditions that prevail in this part of the world.

While most outfitters gladly accept very young kayakers, make sure your child is up to sitting still in a kayak for several hours before booking what can be an expensive outing. Also, it is essential that kids be dressed warmly, with gloves and hats. **Kodiak Kayak Tours** (907/486-2722; e-mail: fish2live@aol.com) offers two guided four-hour sessions daily, at 9am and again at 2pm ($50/person). No experience is required and all ages are welcome. Gear and life vests are provided, but bring a waterproof jacket and outdoor clothing. In addition to other trips, **Mythos Expeditions Kodiak** (907/486-5536; www.ptialaska.net/~mythosdk/mythos/kayak) offers guided kayaking trips suitable for small fry. Kayaks are also available for rent. Their two-hour tours around Kodiak harbor islands and nearby bays are a good bet for youngsters and offer glimpses of whales, sea birds, ducks, seals, sea lions, sea otters, and—with a little luck—whales. Be sure to bring raingear, gloves, sturdy footwear, and, of course, binoculars. Tours include instruction. Cost: $50/person, two-hour guided tour and instruction; $100/person, four-hour guided tour and instruction. Mythos also takes family groups on extended trips aboard the Mythos, a refitted commercial salmon-fishing boat that can take up to six passengers. Trips can be customized and include whale and bear watching, birding, and fishing.

Outdoor Equipment Rentals   You can rent bicycles from **58 Degrees North** (1231 Mill Bay Rd, Kodiak, AK 99615-6409. 907/486-6249; thowland@ptialaska.net). For kayaks and other outdoor gear, try **Kodiak Kamps** (PO Box 4111, Kodiak, AK 99615-4111; 907/486-5333; e-mail: aair2@gci.net). At **Mythos Expeditions Kodiak** (PO Box 2084, Kodiak, AK 99615; 907/486 5536; www.ptialaska.net/~mythosdk/mythos/kayak) kayaks, singles and doubles, can be rented in Kodiak or on-site at Shuyak Island State Park (see "Excursions"). Prices for singles range from $139.95 each for three days up to $404.95 for 10 days; doubles run from $169.95 for three days up to $504.95 for 10 days. For Shuyak there is a three-day minimum rental. Advance reservations are recommended.

Excursions

Kodiak's roads are well worth exploring; car rentals may be more affordable for families than a sightseeing road tour. Combine a trip to Fort Abercrombie with a drive to the end of the Monashka Bay Road and explore the sandy beach (about 24 miles roundtrip from downtown). You can also head north from town on scenic Anton Larsen Bay Road (about 24 miles round trip). For a longer excursion, head south to Pasagshak Bay and Narrow Cape or take the Chiniak Highway east to Cape Chiniak. Note that while all routes are scenic, only 20 miles of the island's roads are paved. The *Guide to Kodiak*, available at the Visitor Center, includes detailed information on driving Kodiak roads.

Alaska Spaceport And now for something unexpected: a genuine rocket-launching spaceport! At Alaska's new commercial spaceport, satellites are launched for military and commercial clients. This state-of-the-art facility is open for tours every Friday at 10am by arrangement (call for appointment first). Tours take about an hour and are free.

From downtown Kodiak, go 30 miles west on Rezanof Dr W; turn right onto Pasagshak Rd; continue on to the launch facility; 907/487-2812; www.akaerospace.com.

State Parks

For contact information on state parks, see "Resources."

Buskin River State Recreation Site Just a few miles southwest of Kodiak, a little north of the state airport and adjacent to the Kodiak National Wildlife Refuge Visitor Center, this 168-acre state park has trails and beaches, as well as picnic shelters and campsites. The biggest draw is the excellent sport fishing. There's a wheelchair-accessible fishing platform. Late in the summer, you can watch hordes of spawning salmon return up the river, leaping, expiring, and decomposing before your eyes.

From downtown Kodiak, south on Rezanof Dr for 4.1 miles. Watch for the park sign.

15 campsites (14-day limit, $10/day per vehicle), picnic area, two shelters, trails, beach.

Fort Abercrombie State Historical Park ☺ If you have time to visit only one state park, make it this one. Besides the military museum (see "Museums"), the 186-acre park features good trails and beaches, a swimming lake, fishing, and some of the best tidepooling anywhere. The views make this a great place to spot puffins, whales, sea lions, and sea otters. From late June through August, weekly naturalist programs are offered at 7pm at the Visitor Center.

North on Rezanof Dr 3.7 miles; turn right onto Abercrombie Dr. and follow to the park. 907/486-6339; FYI: 13 campsites (seven-day limit, $10/night per site), water, toilets, picnic areas, one covered picnic shelter, beach for swimming, trails, canoeing/kayaking

Pasagshak River State Recreation Site At 20 acres, this is the smallest of Kodiak Island's three state parks. It offers salmon fishing and a good beach. (Combine a visit here with a trip to the fossil fields and Kodiak Launch Facility, and Fossil Beach. Parking and hiking down to Fossil Beach is recommended, as the road is rough.)

30 miles west on Rezanof Dr W.; right on Pasagshak Road just past the

Archaeological Digs

If the thought of a working vacation appeals to your crew, you might want to consider joining an archaeological dig helping to excavate archaeological sites brimming with fascinating finds from early Afognak Alutiiq and Aleut cultures. Two major digs, one on Afognak Island near Kodiak and one in Unalaska, welcome amateur archaeologists and provide any training needed, along with an unforgettable experience. This can be a great way for families to learn about Alaska's rich cultural history while having fun at the same time.

While it's a great bet for preteen and older kids, this is not a good choice for the smaller fry. However, younger kids can watch archaeologists at work in the Museum of the Aleutians in Dutch Harbor/Unalaska and get a sense of what happens after a find is uncovered.

Dig Afognak Kids over 12 can participate with you in this fascinating project, excavating Afognak Alutiiq sites on Afognak Island. For a week, participants work in the field with archaeologists and Alutiiq natives. Opportunities for island exploration exist, but this is primarily a working vacation. Transportation, housing in heated tents, food, training, and education—scientific and cultural—are included in the cost. Visitors provide their own sleeping bags. The program is sponsored by the Afnognak Native Corporation and has been underway since 1994. Visitors can arrange in advance for a shorter or longer stay.

Afognak Native Corporation, 215 Mission Rd, Ste 212, Kodiak, Alaska 99615. 800/770-6014; www.afognak.com/dig/regframeset.htm. Cost: $1,650/person.

Margaret Bay Archaeological Project The Museum of the Aleutians sponsors archaeological digs all summer long. Unlike Dig Afognak, these digs don't require travel to another island. Here's what one parent reviewer reports:

"Digs go on all summer and anyone may participate. My daughters and I took part, and it was exciting for me when I found a labret! During the summer of 2001, a significant find was made at the dig. An effigy was discovered, contributing to the cultural understanding of the peoples who lived here long ago. There are opportunities not only to participate in the project site, but to listen to enriching evening lectures presented by the museum staff and visiting faculty. I highly recommend this activity for families. Not only is it educational, but it impresses upon children the need for careful gathering of data and documentation in a fun but scientific way. And who doesn't like to play in the dirt!"

Museum of the Aleutians, 907/581-5150; www.aleutians.org ▣

Kalsin River, continue nine miles. Continue on Pasagshak Road to reach the Launch Facility, and to the end of the road to get to the fossil cliffs.

FYI: 12 campsites, (14-day limit, no fee), a picnic area, potable water, and toilets.

Shuyak Island State Park For families with kids pre-teen and older, who are prepared for a few days in the wilderness and enjoy kayaking, this state park is highly recommended. Encompassing most of the 47,000-acre island, it is popular with kayakers, and many local outfitters offer transportation and guided trips to the island. Mythos has kayaks here for on-site rentals. Features include Sitka spruce forest, wild coastline and beaches, and wildlife. While there are a few hiking trails, conditions are rough and your best bet is to take to the water. Sheltered inlets, channels, and bays are numerous. There are four public-use cabins and primitive camping is possible. While park rangers keep an eye on visitors, the island is definitely a wilderness experience and visitors must be as self-sufficient as possible, bringing in all supplies. (Although there is some potable water at the cabins, it must be treated first.) Deer hunting is permitted on the island (check with the Alaska Dept. of Fish & Game). In late summer, the island features good salmon fishing. The weather is changeable and so are sea conditions. For information on renting cabins, check the State Park Web site (www.ptialaska.net/~kodsp/application.html) or call (see "Resources").

Calendar of Events

January
Russian Christmas and Starring
907/486-3854
Because of its retention of the Julian calendar, the Russian Orthodox Church celebrates Christmas later than western Christian churches do. These festivities include the tradition of "Starring," in which a choir, accompanying a large Christmas star, visits homes of the community faithful and sings. You'll find Starring observed throughout Kodiak Island villages.

Russian New Year and Masquerade Ball
907/486-3854
Another Russian Orthodox tradition is a New Year's feast featuring Russian food, and followed by a masked costume ball. Costumes are judged and, at midnight, celebrants unmask. Participation is open to all and is free.

April
Whalefest
907/486-3737, 907/481-1719; www.koc.alaska.edu/whalefest/ ☺
This annual Kodiak tradition celebrates the return of migrating whales to Alaskan waters. Activities take place over almost two weeks and include whale observation, Native Alaskan traditions, stories, and games, and art and literary happenings. Marine scientists give educational workshops, and much of the fun is hands-on.

May
Koniag's Kodiak Crab Festival
Kodiak Chamber of Commerce, 907/486-5557 ☺
This five-day rite of spring includes a fishing derby, carnival, games, golf tournament, bike races, live music, art festival (in which crabs play a significant role), and plenty of silly fun.

July

Independence Day Celebrations
907/486-8636
Includes fireworks and a multicultural parade

MainStreet Kodiak's Rainfest
Downtown ☺
A one-day, kid-oriented party with face painting, pony rides, games and races, and more.

Kodiak Bear Country Music Festival
Kodiak Lions Club, 907-486-6117
This annual music festival embraces many kinds of music, including bluegrass and homegrown Alaskan performers.

September

Kodiak State Fair and Rodeo
State Fair Grounds, 907/487-4440
A Labor Day weekend traditional event.

Resources

Kodiak Island Convention and Visitors Bureau
100 Marine Way; 907/486-4782; www.kodiak.org
The Visitor Information Center, located next to the Alaska Ferry dock, is open Monday to Friday 8am-5pm, year-round and in summer, Saturdays 10am-4pm, and Sundays 1-9pm (and usually later on weeknights, at least until the ferry gets in). Depending on staffing, they may close for lunch. The **Kodiak Chamber of Commerce** (907/486-5557) is located downstairs in the same building.

Alaska State Parks, Kodiak District
1400 Abercrombie Dr, Kodiak, AK 99615; 907/486-6339;
www.ptialaska.net/~kodsp/
Displays, naturalist programs, tidepool walks, camping, public-use cabins.

Parent Ed.

Griggs, Robert F. *The Valley of Ten Thousand Smokes.* National Geographic Society, 1922.

Harvey, Lola. *Derevnia's Daughters: Saga of an Alaskan Village.* Sunflower Press, 1991.

Katmai Country. *Alaska Geographic Society,* 1989.

Keith, Sam. *One Man's Wilderness: An Alaskan Odyssey.* Graphic Arts Center Publishing, 1999.

Kodiak. Alaska Geographic Society, 1982.

☛ Parent Tip:

Unalaska's Tsunami Warning System prepares the island to meet the challenge of a tsunami (tidal wave) should one occur, as they have been known to. Once a month, to test the system, a siren goes off briefly, usually at noon on the 15th. If they happened to see some alarming exhibits elsewhere in Alaska on the damage done by the 1964 tsunami, kids may be reassured to know this advance-warning system is in place. However, if you hear a loud siren that keeps on wailing—especially if it's neither noon nor the middle of the month—it's time to postpone the explanation and move to higher ground! ▣

UNALASKA ISLAND

This island with the intriguing name is one of the pearls in the 1,300-mile-long Aleutian island chain that trails off the tip of the Alaska Peninsula as it curves southwest. The Aleutians separate the warm Japanese current of the north Pacific from the colder northern waters of the Bering Sea, a major cause of the region's ferociously high seas, powerful winds, and famous mists. Yet when the fog clears, the scenery is breathtaking and unobscured by trees, which are almost nonexistent here. The highest point on the island is Mount Makushin, an active volcano of 6,680 feet. In fact, the Aleutians themselves are the tops of volcanoes—some quite active—in the Pacific Ring (or Rim) of Fire; the islands mark the place where two tectonic plates converge.

While the island's permanent population barely exceeds 4,000, at the height of the fishing season it can increase to as many as 10,000. The climate is harsh, yet hospitable enough to have nourished the rich Aleut/Unangan culture for 9,000 years.

The Aleutians are closer to Japan than is anywhere else in Alaska, and visitors will find many reminders of World War II here. During the war, Japan bombed Dutch Harbor twice, and invaded and occupied several western islands. Most of the island belongs to the Ounalashka Corporation, one of Alaska's 200 village Native corporations, and to do just about anything in Unalaska requires a permit from them. (See "What to See and Do.")

Oh yes: The word "Alaska" derives from an Aleut word, "Alaxxsa," describing the Alaska Peninsula. As it passed through Russian and other non-indigenous hands, the word became Alaska. The derivation of Unalaska is "Ounalashka," another place name, not a negation of Alaska.

Getting To Unalaska

Unalaska/Dutch Harbor is still the richest fishing port in the U.S., but signs are growing that the resources won't last forever. Gradually, tourism is gaining importance in the local economy. Recently, several smaller cruise lines have begun to make annual stops here.

By Air For most visitors, flying is the best way to get here. Try to get seats on the right side of the plane, where you'll have a fine view of Mounts Iliamna and Redoubt on your way from Anchorage, if weather allows.

Alaska Airlines offers daily flights between Anchorage and Dutch Harbor that take a little over two hours. Expect to pay premium prices in summer. To keep fares reasonable, research promotional fares and Internet wholesalers. If you plan to take advantage of a package sightseeing tour, you'll find they often include airfares to the island from Anchorage. Visitors who plan to take the ferry one way might want to take **PenAir** (907/ 581-1383; 800/448-4226; www.penair.com/) back to Anchorage. This airline flies ONLY out of, not into Dutch Harbor.

By Sea For scenic beauty and affordability, the Alaska ferry (907/486-3800; www.akferry), the same *M/V Tustumena* that serves Kodiak, is unbeatable. Once a month, between April and October, the *Tusty* travels down the Alaska Peninsula and Aleutian chain to Dutch Harbor. Ferries stop at Chignik, Sand Point, King Cove, Cold Bay, and False Pass before arriving at Unalaska. The trip takes a little under 62 hours and can be quite rough.

At least three smaller cruise lines include Unalaska/Dutch Harbor in itineraries. These are **CruiseWest** (800/580-0072; www.cruisewest.com. See "Getting There" in "Kodiak" for details), **Clipper Cruise Line** (314/655-6700, 800/325-0010; www.clippercruise.com/), and **Society Expeditions** (800/548-8669; www.societyexpeditions.com/). In the volatile world of cruising, things change quickly. Be sure to research and choose carefully.

CITY OF UNALASKA/DUTCH HARBOR

Yes, the city is called Unalaska, too, like the island. The Port of Dutch Harbor, however, retains its own name and identity, which can be plenty confusing. Unalaska, the town, sits on the northwest tip of Unalaska Island. Dutch Harbor sits on the southern tip of Amaknak Island, separated from Unalaska by the "Bridge to the Other Side." Each has its own post office, but for all practical purposes, the two make up one extended town. Airline flights are ticketed to Dutch Harbor, not Unalaska, just to add a bit more complexity. Given the intricacies of nomenclature here, it is a good idea to confirm which one is meant (think Minneapolis-St. Paul). Residents can be a bit touchy about names. Call the whole town Dutch and you'll be corrected.

Getting Around

If you rent a car, remember there are only 38 miles of road, six of which are paved. Consider springing for four-wheel-drive. **BC Vehicle Rental**, 907/581-6777; e-mail: checker@arctic.net, and **North Port Rentals**, 907/581-3880, both at the airport, rent all kinds of vehicles.

There are far more taxi companies than car-rental outfits—and taxis are usually a better bargain. You can choose from **Alaskan Taxi**, 907/581-2129; **Aleutian Taxi**, 907/581-1866; **Blue Checker Cab Co.**, 907/581-2186; **Dutch Harbor Express**, 907/581-6666; **Harbor Express**, 907/581-1381; and **Mr. Cab**, 907/581-2624.

Places to Stay

The Grand Aleutian Hotel ($$-$$$—weekly rates lower)
498 Salmon Way; 866/581-3844, 800/891-1194; www.grandaleutian.com
FYI: 112 rooms; 2 suites for up to six guests, with wet bars and refrigerators; children under 12 stay free; restaurants; box lunches prepared on request; some whirlpool tubs; VCRs at front desk; gift shop, tours and charters; free airport transportation; pets OK (deposit required)

If you hope to stay here in summer, reserve a room as early as possible. Promotional packages are available during the Halibut Derby and for archaeological dig participants. Visitors with relatives in Unalaska may be able to receive local (lower) rates. In any event, remember that rates are often negotiable.

66 PARENT COMMENTS 99
"The rooms provide a gorgeous view of mountains or of Margaret Bay and display work of local artists. You can rent videos next door."

Carl's Bayview Inn ($$—weekly rates lower)
606 Bayview; 907/581-1230, 800/581-1230; e-mail bayview@arctic.net
FYI: 47rooms, 8 kitchenette units, 6 suites; pool tables, darts; guest laundry; grocery store

This is the only hotel actually in the town of Dutch Harbor. Rates are reasonable. Families with small children take note: Carl's boasts the largest bar in Dutch Harbor.

Places to Eat

Airport Restaurant
Unalaska Airport; 907/581-6007; call for hours
Here's where to go for your pizza fix. Delivery is available for $5.

The Chart Room/Grand Aleutian Hotel
Airport Beach Rd; Unalaska; 907/581-3844
Hours: Mon-Sat 6pm-11pm; Sun brunch 10am-2pm; dinner 6pm-10pm
This is the island's fine-dining choice, specializing in fresh seafood and Pacific Rim cuisine. Prices are high, but so is the quality. While it's probably not a great choice for kids, the view, service, and food may be worth it. On Wednesday nights, there's a popular seafood buffet.

Margaret Bay Café /Grand Aleutian Hotel
907/581-3844
Hours: Daily 7am-3pm
In addition to breakfast, a lunch buffet is served from 11:30 am to 1:30 pm. This is a good bet for families—casual dining with a view, plus there's a kids' menu.

What Are They Catching?

Everywhere you go, you'll see signs of the enormous fishing industry that keeps the town humming. Just what are they catching? Along with all kinds of crab, fishers are  pulling in halibut and lots of pollock, the versatile fish that is made into surimi (faux crab, sometimes marketed as krab), and the fish sticks the kids often enjoy. ◼

Amelia's Restaurant
Airport Beach Road & East Point Rd; 907/581-2800; call for hours
Hearty breakfasts, plus burgers and shakes for lunch, are on the menu; Mexican offerings round out the selections.

Tino's Steakhouse
11 N 2nd St, Dutch Harbor; 907/581-4288
Hours: Daily 8am-11pm
Highly rated Mexican food, including halibut tacos, is offered here along with the usual hearty fare.

What to See & Do

Whether you're staying at the Grand Aleutian on Amaknak Island or at Carl's Bayview on Unalaska, you're within walking distance of quite a few local attractions. The bad news is that to see everything, you'll need transportation. A taxi should suffice.

Stroll & Browse

Not far from the Russian Orthodox cathedral and the Visitor Center, you'll find **Nicky's Place** (Front Beach Rd & 2nd St, downtown Unalaska; 907/581-1570). Enjoy a good selection of books and gifts to peruse or some espresso. Next door to Carl's Bayview Inn is **Carl's General Store** (907-581-1234; open 9am-midnight), with just what you'd expect. Should the weather cooperate, you'll find a small **Town Park** on Broadway with playground equipment and a gazebo for picnicking. The Community Center and Unalaska City School are close by. The latter has Aleutian art on display (you're welcome to drop by and view it; check in first at the school office) and a replica of a *barabara* on school grounds. This is where you'll find the community swimming pool.

On Amaknak island, shop for gifts at the **Grand Aleutian Gift Shop** (in the hotel; 907/581-5093) and the **Museum of the Aleutians gift shop** (907/581-5150). Check out the **Alaska Commercial Company** (on Salmon Way, across from the Grand Aleutian, 907/581-1245), a general store that sells clothes, fishing licenses and gear, and gifts. It also has a small display of prehistoric and Russian artifacts. The store also features a **Burger King**,

The Boy Who Designed the Alaska State Flag

Near the church is the site of the Jesse Lee Home, a Methodist orphanage built in 1890 and later moved to Seward. Here its most famous resident, Bennie Benson, a 13-year-old Aleut boy from Chignik, won a contest to design a flag for Alaska in 1926 for which he received $1,000 and a watch. When a design was needed for the new state flag in 1959, Bennie's simple, elegant design featuring the eight stars of the Milky Way and Polaris, the North Star, symbolizing Alaska, was chosen.◙

Unalaska's only fast-food-chain outlet. Next door, the **Ounalashka Corporation** has art and artifacts on display that you can check out when picking up your land-use permit.

Holy Ascension Russian Orthodox Cathedral If you've seen a picture of Unalaska, chances are it included this beautiful church's onion-shaped dome, probably surmounted by a bald eagle. A National Historic Monument that dates from 1894, the church includes earlier elements from the mid-19th century. It received an expensive renovation in 1996. Not only the building is of interest; inside is a remarkably rich assortment of historic Russian icons and other items, one of the largest in Alaska. Next to the church is the **Bishop's House**, dating from 1882, shipped from San Francisco and reassembled here.

No photos are allowed inside the church. If you attend a service, tradition requires that hats be removed. Benches are for the use of elders and people with disabilities. Males sit on the right, females on the left. As always, it helps to talk to kids first about manners during religious observance.

On Broadway, near Carl's. 907/581-1747. Local tour companies include the Cathedral in tours. To visit on your own, ask for help at the Visitor Bureau or visit before services (summer only; church opens to public Sat at 6pm, Sun 9am). Cost: $5 donation requested.

Sitka Spruce Tree Park There are no trees native to the Aleutians, but in 1805, the Russians transplanted some Sitka spruce to Unalaska. Today, three trees from those original transplants survive. These National Historic Landmarks, and some of their smaller offspring can be viewed in this park. *Follow Biorka Dr off Airport Beach Rd.*

Museums

Museum of the Aleutians This fairly new museum has become an important resource for the study and preservation of Aleutian history and culture, from Aleut/Unangan prehistoric times to the present. The museum's distinctive curved roof represents a *barabara*, a semisubterranean Aleut dwelling. Permanent exhibits focus on native culture, the Russian-American era, and the role played by the islands in World War II. The delicate basketry

World War II and the Aleutians

The westernmost Aleutian islands lie just 1,000 miles from Japan. In June 1942, the Japanese bombed Dutch Harbor, where there was a new U.S. military outpost. The bombing was a diversion intended to draw U.S. forces away from Midway Island in the South Pacific, and although it failed in that respect, it marked the beginning of a terrible ordeal for the Aleut people. The Japanese followed up the bombing by taking and occupying the islands of Kiska and Attu, whose residents were captured and taken as prisoners to Hokkaido. The U.S. began a successful but bloody campaign to regain the islands, a process that took nearly a year and during which the U.S. military occupied several nearby islands, evacuating Aleut residents from their homes to internment camps in southeast Alaska. The Aleuts were subjected to terrible living conditions, housed in old canneries with inadequate food and heat. Mortality rates were high both in Japan and in the U.S. internment camps. After the war, when the Aleuts were permitted to return, they found their homes and communities razed. This sad and unsavory story is little known outside Alaska. An excellent film about the episode, with documentary footage, is shown at the University of Alaska Museum (see "Resources").

Parent Ed

Garfield, Brian. *The Thousand Mile War: World War II in Alaska and the Aleutians.* University of Alaska Press, (reprint from original Bantam Books ed., 1969).

Kohlhoff, Dean. *When the Wind Was a River.* University of Washington Press, 1995. This book depicts the wartime deportation from their homes and its impact on the Aleut people.

Aleut Evacuation. (60-minute video.) This video about the evacuation of Aleut islanders by the U.S. military during World War II is available for sale from the University of Alaska Museum (www.uaf.edu/museum/) and libraries. Appropriate for adults and kids 10 and above. ◪

is extraordinary. Visitors can peer through laboratory windows to see archeologists at work. The museum sponsors digs open to public participation (see "Archaeological Digs"). Recent finds include ornamented whalebone digging sticks used to dig up edible roots and a tiny mask made of pumice. The gift shop is your best bet in Unalaska for high-quality local arts and books about the region and its people.

907/581-5150; www.aleutians.org. Open Mon-Sat 10am-5pm; Sun noon-5pm. (June 1- Sept 30); Wed-Sat 11am-4pm; Sun noon-4pm. Closed Mon and Tues (Oct 1-May 31). Cost: $4/person.

The Aleutian World War II National Historic Area This 134-acre park, jointly managed by the US Park Service and the Ounalashka Corporation, once housed Fort Schwatka. Throughout the park, visitors will see the scars left by trenches, the remains of gun emplacements, ammunition magazines,

> ### ☞ Parent Tip: Raising a Young Birder
>
> Get your young future birders up to speed with a field guide for the trip. The following offer a good introduction to the birds you'll encounter in Unalaska.
>
> *Arctic Nesting Shorebirds.* This kit helps kids learn how to recognize shorebirds and includes online resources.
>
> *Bizarre Birds.* Peterson Field Guides for Young Naturalists. Houghton Mifflin, 1999.
>
> *Shorebirds.* Peterson Field Guides for Young Naturalists. Houghton Mifflin, 1999.
>
> The National Audubon Society Web site introduces visitors to the whiskered auklet, an important resident of the Aleutian Islands and popular among birders visiting Unalaska. www.audubon.org/bird/watch/wau/wau/
>
> Kids can also explore the Kids Watchlist (www.audubon.org/ bird/watch/kids/), a list of birds whose continued existence the Society seeks to ensure.
>
> Birders of all ages—but kids especially—will enjoy the bird trivia, jokes, songs, and quizzes on this site: www.birder.com ▣

and interpretive displays. The Visitor Center, new in 2001 and housed in the Aerology Building at the airport, explains the history of the war here and the enormous impact it had on the Aleut/Unangan people who were either made prisoner by the Japanese, who occupied the westernmost islands, or evacuated and interned in southeast Alaska by the U.S. military. Exhibits also describe the lives of the thousands of men and women stationed here. Documentaries and movies, along with photos and archival materials, flesh out a picture both heroic and grim. A visit here can be combined with a hike up Mount Ballyhoo, most of which is located within the park.
2716 Airport Beach Rd, at the Unalaska Airport. 907/581-1276; www.ounalashka.com/Aleutian; www.nps.gov/aleu/. Call for hours.

Animals Animals

No, they're not dinosaurs, but fossil remains of the **demostylian** on display at the Ounalashka Corporation may intrigue kids anyway. Once upon a time about 30 million years ago, these bizarre, extinct ungulates (something like a small, bucktoothed marine hippopotamus) hung out in the Aleutians and Kodiak.

Few land mammals and no bears reside on Unalaska, but small herds of **wild cows** and **horses**, **naturalized citizens**, can be glimpsed on the northeast end of the island. **Sea lions** and **sea otters** are plentiful.

Birding Unalaska's varied and unique bird life is a major draw for visitors. Leading the list of rare feathered denizens is the whiskered auklet, a small, demure, diving seabird, gray with white whiskers. You can book a tour to visit it in its native haunts. To help your young ornithologists get up to speed, a good place to start is searching for tufted and horned puffins. With their bright orange beaks, they're hard to miss and fun to watch flying. Ducks, seabirds, songbirds, and raptors also call Unalaska home. To see bald eagles, head out to the landfill on Summer Bay Road, where you're likely to find a few inspecting the pickings. The Visitor Center map includes tips on where to see which birds.

Classes and Workshops   The week-long **Unangan Culture Camp** is held each August at Humpy Cove, offering classes in elements of Aleut culture such as basket weaving, bentwood hat-making, seal-skinning, and use of local plants. (Call the Qawalangin Tribe, 907/581-2920 for details.) At the **Aleutian/Pribilof Center** (907/581-1666; www.iac.uaf.edu/ AleutianPribilof/), classes for adults and kids range from mask making to kayak building.

Swimming and Fitness Facilities   For swimming, head to the **Unalaska Pool** (on Broadway in the Unalaska City School. 907/581-1649; $3; call for details). At the **Community Center** (Near 5th & Broadway; 907/581-3416), exercise facilities, sport courts, and an indoor track are open to the public.

The Great Outdoors

Most of Unalaska Island, as well as neighboring islands, is owned by the Ounalashka Corporation, so you'll need to buy a land-use permit if you wish to hike, camp, bike, picnic, pick berries, or just visit the area. This Native corporation sells permits on a daily or monthly basis. Permits for hiking and access cost $6/person per day. Camping costs $11 per person per day. Nonprofit groups with fewer than 11 people can camp, hike, or picnic for $10 per day. For more than 10 people, add $2 per person per day. The best bet for most families will be to invest in a monthly pass. Monthly permits for an individual or family cost $20, valid for a month from time of purchase. Contact the Ounalashka Corporation for details (907/581-1276).

Bicycling   If the weather cooperates, biking can be a great way to see the island. You can rent bikes from **Aleutian Adventure Sports** (PO Box 921181, Dutch Harbor, AK 99692; 888/581-4489; www.aleutianadventure.com).

Hiking   The most popular hike accessible for all ages is up **Mount Ballyhoo** (1,634 feet). It's off Ballyhoo Road, northeast of the airport on Amaknak Island. Walk, don't try to drive up unless you have four-wheel drive. Views are spectacular, but cliffs are abrupt and very steep. Keep the kids close. Also, the extremely slim but not impossible chance that you might come upon unexploded ordnance exists, so it's best not to touch any bits of metal junk that might be lying around. Allow three hours for the four-mile round trip. **Bunker Hill** (421 feet), also on Amaknak Island, is an easier climb, but has less sweeping views. For directions, pick up a driving-tour brochure at the Visitor Center.

On Unalaska Island, the **Agamgik Trail** has been in use for 8,000 years. To reach it, drive or bike northeast of downtown on Summer Bay Road to Summer Bay (past the landfill and eagles).

The 1912 Novarupta Eruption

In June of 1912, less than two months after the *Titanic* sank, the world's biggest volcanic eruption since the end of the 19th century occurred not far from Kodiak Island. The rain of ash on the Alaska Peninsula from several new vents—collectively referred to as the Novarupta eruption—transformed life in Kodiak and surrounding islands. At the same time, Mount Katmai, a 7,000-foot peak nearby, imploded, raising intriguing and still perplexing questions about why and how this sequence of events took place. Today, what's left is the area known as the Valley of Ten Thousand Smokes, in Katmai National Park. Although the smoking vents have died down since 1912, the area is still very much an active part of the Ring of Fire.

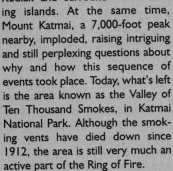

Estimated to be more than 10 times as powerful as the 1980 eruption of Mount Saint Helens, the 1912 eruption was preceded by several large earthquakes. Residents of nearby villages had been warned to flee, and conse-quently no one died in the eruption. Novarupta showered ash so thick (more than seven cubic miles, expelled in 60 hours) that for two days Kodiak Island was in utter darkness. The ash made it as far south as Vancouver, BC, where acid rain from the eruption reportedly ate holes in clothes hanging on clotheslines! Some reports say that the eruption burned the fur off the backs of Kodiak bears. Buildings collapsed from the weight of ash on their roofs.

Today, many flightseeing tours can take you to Katmai National Park and the Valley of Ten Thousand Smokes (see "Flightseeing" in the Kodiak section).

Exciting Volcano Resources

Decker, Robert, and Decker, Barbara, *Volcanoes*: San Francisco, Freeman, 1989 US Geological Web site: vulcan.wr.usgs.gov/Volcanoes/Alaska/description_1912_eruption_novarupta/

Katmai National Park Web sites: www.nps.gov/katm/ and www2.nature.nps.gov/grd/parks/katm/ ◙

Berrypicking   Even out here in the north Pacific, berries are abundant. According to the Alaska Chamber of Commerce, local berries grow huge, resembling "raspberries on steroids." Reports a parent reviewer: "During the summer months, the area is extremely beautiful with a profusion of wildflowers in bloom and plump salmonberries and blueberries on the bushes. Berry picking is an incredible experience! Salmonberries are about an inch in diameter, sweet and juicy. I was familiar with small, pale, dry salmonberries, and they were not my favorite—until I found the ones in Dutch!" Unlike the rest of Alaska, there are no bears on Unalaska to compete with you for the goodies. All that's required is a daily picking permit from the Ounalashka Corporation. Popular berrying spots include **Strawberry Hill** and **Pyramid Peak**, south of town.

West from Homer: A Ferry Odyssey

Taking the Alaska ferry from Homer to Kodiak and beyond to Dutch Harbor/Unalaska is an adventure. The Gulf of Alaska is often choppy, and big swells are the norm, not the exception—but if you can stomach the ride, you'll be rewarded with magnificent scenery and abundant wildlife.

Alaska families regularly make the crossing aboard the M/V Tustumena. Although one of the Alaska Marine Highway System's smaller ships, it's sturdy and comfortable. It makes the return trip from Homer and Seldovia to Kodiak three times weekly, and once a month goes all the way to Dutch Harbor /Unalaska. The trip from Homer to Kodiak, the most traveled section, takes about 10 hours. Ferries run year round to Kodiak and make the once-a-month trip along the Aleutian chain from April to October.

Even for the short trip between Homer and Kodiak, consider booking a stateroom. The Tusty can carry 36 vehicles and has 8 four-berth cabins and 18 two-berth cabins. The latter do not have bathroom facilities, but being able to lie down comfortably in choppy seas can be well worth the price. (If you tend toward queasiness, get motion-sickness patches from your physician or take medication for this purpose.) Sailings from Kodiak to Homer are at night. Passengers can usually board an hour or so

before sailing, so there's ample time to get youngsters tucked into bed and, with luck, to sleep before you leave Kodiak.

If your destination is Unalaska/Dutch Harbor, reserve a stateroom for a ferry ride that can take three days and three nights sfrom Kodiak, five days from Seldovia, and four from Homer. Reservations are recommended about eight months in advance. The young and adventurous can snooze in sleeping bags on the deck or the lounge. The food is good and the gift shop stocked with toiletries and other necessary items. On the ferry, the Forest Service and the U.S. Fish and Wildlife Service present educational lectures and slide shows pertaining to the many small towns and scenic attractions along the route. Short stops are made at charming villages along the way, and everyone charges off at Chignik to buy pastries at the Chignik Bakery! During the ferry's October voyage, the crew gives pumpkins out to the children in the villages along the way.

Wheelchair-accessible cabins on the MV Tustumena should be arranged through central AMHS reservations at 800/642-0066. If a grandparent wishes to accompany your family, check on special rates for seniors and passes for persons with disabilities or for disabled veterans." ◼

Excursions

Flightseeing **PenAir Charters** (907/581-1383; www.penair.com) can arrange a flightseeing trip to nearby islands and volcanoes, such as **Okmok Caldera** on **Umnak Island**, about 75 miles southwest of Unalaska, a spectacular and occasionally active volcano. The island has black-sand beaches. A variety of intriguing flight options exist.

Island Services Historical/Cultural Bus Tour These bus tours can accommodate groups from 20 to 200. Tours feature Aleut culture, World War II sites, the Russian Orthodox cathedral, and shopping.
PO Box 214, Unalaska, AK 99685; 907/581-3880.

The Extra Mile Tours These tours cover historical and World War II sites as well as birding and flower-identification. Tours can be customized. Cost: $40/person, two-hour tour; $75/person, four-hour tour.
PO Box 322, Unalaska, AK 99685; 907/581-6171; e-mail: xmitours@arctic.net, www.unalaskadutchharbortour.com.

A.L.E.U.T. Tours With a native guide, tour the town and major local sites, with an emphasis on the history, culture, and community of the Aleut/Unangan people. Tours take from two to three hours. Cost: $40/person. Free pickup and dropoff.
PO Box 156, Unalaska, AK 99685 907/581-6001; e-mail: akaleut@arctic.net.

Aleutian Adventure Sports Sailing charters, guided trips, sea kayaking, mountain biking, and bike rentals are offered by these outfitters.
888/581-4489; www.aleutianadventure.com.

Calendar of Events

January
Russian Orthodox Christmas Eve and Starring
907/581-6001
Russian Orthodox New Years Eve
907/581-6001

May-August
World Record Halibut Derby
907/581-2612
The Derby holds weekly $100 drawings that go to the biggest halibut caught that week. A $100,000 prize goes to anyone who breaks the world record. There's a category open to kids under 16, with prizes.

Resources

Alaska Maritime National Wildlife Refuge—Aleutian Islands Unit
907/592-2406; e-mail: aleutianisland@fws.gov;
www.r7.fws.gov/nwr/akmnwr/akmnwr/

Ounalashka Corporation
400 Asalmon Way, P.O. Box 149, Unalaska, AK, 99685; 907/581-1276;
www.ounalashka.com

Unalaska/Port of Dutch Harbor Convention and Visitors Bureau
Burma Road Chapel on the corner of 5th & Broadway; PO Box 545, Unalaska,
AK 99685; 907/581-2612, 877/581-2612; www.arctic.net/~updhcvb

Parks Culture and Recreation, Unalaska
907/581-1297; ci.unalaska.ak.us/parks.

Books

Campbell, L.J. *The Aleutian Islands.* Alaska Geographic Books, 1995.

Dutch Harbor, Alaska. Unalaska Pride

Hudson, Ray, *Moments Rightly Placed: An Aleutian Memoir.* Epicenter Press, 1998.

Veniaminov, Ivan. *Notes on the Islands of the Unalashka District* (trans. by Lydia T. Black and R.H. Geoghegan). University of Alaska and Limestone Press, 1991.

9 Talkeetna, Denali National Park, and Environs

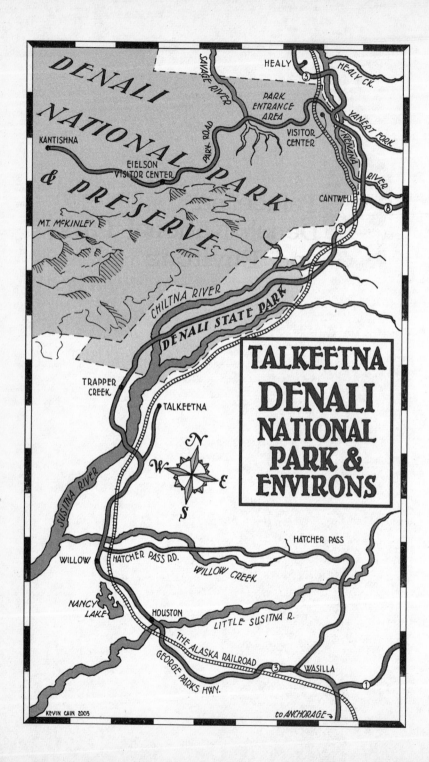

9 Talkeetna, Denali National Park, and Environs

ON A BEAUTIFUL day in Anchorage, you can see the massive form of Mount McKinley looming alone on the northern horizon. The mountain—the tallest in North America at 20,232 feet—is called Denali, "the high one," in the Athabascan language. While both names are correct, most Alaskans prefer "Denali." Either way, the mountain is an extraordinary sight, and the closer you get, the more awesome it becomes. For a sense of how Denali has inspired artists, visit Sydney M. Laurence's mystically luminous paintings at the Anchorage Museum of History and Art (see "Anchorage and Environs").

While the mountain is the region's biggest draw, many visitors come away with no more than a few tantalizing glimpses of its flanks. Often shrouded in clouds for weeks at a time, Denali is visible only one day in three. Luckily, there is plenty to see and do in the vicinity, even when the mountain is in hiding. There's a long list of wildlife here: grizzlies, moose, Dall sheep, wolves, and caribou are among the 37 mammal and more than 150 bird species to be found in the area. The landscape, too, is awe-inspiring. In summer, visitors can float the Nenana River, watch a free sled-dog demonstration at park headquarters, take an all-day bus trip deep into the park, or hike a host of trails of varying difficulty.

Early in its history, the park's caretakers took dramatic steps to restrict visitor access in order to preserve the park and its wildlife for future generations. At the same time, innovative and effective efforts were made to bring visitors into the park. Park-operated buses transport sightseers, hikers, and campers, regulating their numbers.

Between Anchorage and the national park lies the charming town of Talkeetna (rumored to be the model for Cicely, Alaska, in the 1990s TV show *Northern Exposure*). The ambience is as close to "typically Alaskan" as you'll find. In recent years, Talkeetna has become a staging area for mountain-climbers. On the way to Denali, Talkeetna makes a good place to break your journey.

As with so much of Alaska, weather conditions in this region are subject to extreme and sudden variation. If you visit in July, you might encounter 80F-degree temperatures; then again, it could snow. As always, dress in layers, bring waterproof gear and extra clothing.

Getting To Denali

By Alaska standards, this region is quite accessible. Talkeetna is less than 100 miles from Anchorage. Mount McKinley, surrounded by Denali National Park and Preserve, is farther from Anchorage than it looks—237 miles north—but a five-hour drive will get you there. About halfway to the national park is Denali State Park, less traveled and chock-full of remarkable scenery, mountain views, and wildlife. Visitors coming from Anchorage or Fairbanks should allow a minimum of three days to scratch the surface of what this area has to offer.

By Train The most comfortable way to reach Talkeetna and Denali National Park is via the **Alaska Railroad** (907/265-2494, 800/544-0552; www.akrr.com), which makes two 12-hour trips daily between Anchorage and Fairbanks, with stops at Talkeetna and Denali, mid-May to mid-September. Trains leave in each direction at 8:15 am daily. From Anchorage, you'll arrive in Talkeetna at 11:25am and Denali at 3:45pm. Traveling from Fairbanks, you'll reach Denali at noon and Talkeetna at 4:40pm. The rest of the year, service is once a week in each direction (Saturday, trains head north from Anchorage; Sunday, south from Fairbanks), many more stops are added, and passengers can flag the train between stops.

Round-trip adult fare between Anchorage and Talkeetna during peak season (June-Aug) is $150; between Anchorage and Denali, $250. From Fairbanks, round-trip peak adult fare is $100; to Talkeetna, $200. Children between ages 2 and 11 ride half price; kids under 2 are free. Fares are about 20 percent lower during the Value Season (May and September). Off season, service is weekly in each direction, more stops are added, and passengers are allowed to flag the train between stops. Online booking is offered.

In summer, most cars are dedicated to cruise tours, with separate dining and sightseeing facilities. However, each train accommodates non-tour passengers with dining, lounge, gift shop, and observation cars. Summer staff includes Alaskan students whose job it is to point out wildlife and spots of interest . For the best views, sit on the right going north from Anchorage and on the left from Fairbanks. Some of the most spectacular scenery is north of Denali, so—if you can—consider riding the rails all the way to Fairbanks.

By Road The George Parks Highway (Hwy 3) is the shortest of two well-traveled corridors connecting Fairbanks and Anchorage. The Parks Highway is the only paved, direct route to Talkeetna, which is located on a 14-mile spur road that meets the Parks at Mile 98.7. Road conditions are good and the views are extraordinary.

Cruise/tour companies run buses and several local companies provide bus service along the Parks Highway. Vans serving Seward, Anchorage, Talkeetna, and Denali National Park several times a day from mid-May to mid-September are run by the **Alaska Park Connection** (800/266-8625; www.alaskacoach.com. Seward-Talkeetna: $82/adult; Seward-Talkeetna: $100/adult; Anchorage-Talkeetna: $41/adult; Anchorage-Denali: $59/adult.

To Camp or Not to Camp

If you're planning on tent camping in Alaska, do your research ahead of time. You'll need to plan for the possibility of bear encounters, and you might be surprised at some of the lengths campers go to in order to keep the furry visitors at bay. In addition to the usual camping gear, you'll need a system for storing and disposing of food. Bears are attracted by all kinds of scents, including bug juice, sunscreen, soap, and detergent. Denali Park Visitor Center staff ask campers to 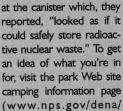 watch a video on bears and offer free bear-resistant food canisters to use while camping. One family decided against camping after they took a look at the canister which, they reported, "looked as if it could safely store radioactive nuclear waste." To get an idea of what you're in for, visit the park Web site camping information page (www.nps.gov/dena/home/visitorinfo/camping/home/). Also see "Bear Basics" in Chapter 1 before committing your family to camping out in bear country. ◪

Children under 13 pay half fare). Kids under 4 must travel in a car seat. The trip is 10.5 hours from Seward to Denali; 6 hours from Anchorage to Denali. Another option is to catch the van (**Denali Overland Transportation**; 800-651-5221, 907/733-2384) that runs between Anchorage and Denali.

The Parks Highway:
Anchorage to Talkeetna (113 m)

The Parks Highway starts 35 miles north of Anchorage at the junction with the Glenn Highway. (For attractions on the Glenn Highway, see "Anchorage and Environs.") If you have time, stop in at the **Matanuska-Susitna Convention & Visitors Bureau** (Mile 35.5 Parks Hwy; 907/746-5000; www.alaskavisit.com) where there's an abundance of travel information; you can book accommodation here. The center is open daily, May 15-Sept 15, 8am-6pm.

Wasilla A few miles farther on the Parks bring you to this historic town, with several attractions of note, such as the **Dorothy G. Page Museum** (323 Main St; 907/373-9071. Open Mon-Sat, 9am-6pm. Cost: $3/adult, free/under 12) and the **Old Wasilla Town Site Historical Park.** The museum offers local and natural history exhibits. Kids will especially enjoy visiting the early-day dentist's office, complete with mystery instruments. Out back is the Old Wasilla Town Site with seven original structures, including a prospector's cabin, railroad worker's cabin, old Wasilla schoolhouse (1917), barn, blacksmith shop, and public bath (Wasilla residents held meetings in the sauna). On Wednesday afternoons in summer, the **Wasilla Farmers Market** (300 Boundary Ave, town site park behind Wasilla Museum; 907/376-5679; e-mail: lemarhea@hotmail.com. Open June-Sept, Wed 3pm-6pm) is held here.

Bonding Along the Iditarod Trail

By Jay and Ryan Holtan

Jay: Planes fly fast, but they're nothing to watching your children grow up! One moment you're gassin' 'em up with good food and advice, then before you know it, they sprout wings and fly away. Along the way, though, are those moments that are better than anything you can buy with a VISA card. One such moment for me came in 1996, when my 10-year-old son, Ryan and I went on a 10-day, 1,000-mile "dog chase," following the Iditarod Trail from Anchorage to Nome, AK.

Our adventure was by private airplane—an airplane with less horsepower than most cars built today. Winter tent camping for days along the way was trying, but the glow of tent and northern lights, not to mention the excitement of watching the dogs come through the checkpoints, more than made up for the sub-zero temperatures. We both learned more than most people would believe possible—and not just practical things like navigation, flying, and staying warm. I learned was how dearly I loved my son as he

was then and as the young man I could see he would become. Here's how it appeared from his viewpoint, looking back from the perspective of a high-school senior.

Ryan: When most children look back fondly on their childhoods, they might remember visiting grandma, or selling lemonade on the corner. I remember soaring at 2,000 feet through the frosty air of the Alaska interior.

When I was 10, my father and I flew the historic Iditarod Trail, following the mushers along their harrowing 1100-mile race. The methodical packing of my Dad's 1954 bush plane went without a hitch and concluded with the customary phone-book riser to help the 4'10" kid see out.

The first leg of our journey began with a trip through Rainy Pass, a temperamental valley that cuts through the Alaska Range just southwest of Mount McKinley. Flying through icy mountain passages, with just 300 to 400 feet clearance on either side, is more

For a real meal, try **Evangelo's Restaurant** (Mile 40 Parks Hwy; 907/376-1212; open daily 11am-10pm, Sat-Sun until 11pm), a mainstay in this area for nearly two decades, recently moved to a new, larger building. Don't be put off by the odd location and bland exterior. The interior is comfortable and the food is simply great. It's an excellent choice for families, and the wait staff is happy to split orders or substitute. Entrées are large and include thick pizza, pungent pasta, and a variety of chicken and seafood dishes.

Wasilla is also headquarters of the **Iditarod Trail** (Mile 2.2 Knik Rd; 907/376-5155; www.iditarod.com), with a small museum and gift shop (open like driving a Volkswagen with wings than flying in a 747, and it is truly an exhilarating experience.

Our first night found us tent-bound at 25 degrees below zero on Fairwell Lakes. Within the confines of our cozy tent, my Dad and I whiled away the hours playing poker with a battered deck of cards I discovered in the survival kit. Early the next morning, we made our way north toward Cripple, the halfway point to Nome. A major checkpoint along the trail, the village was a beehive of activity with bush planes landing every 10 minutes and mushers spooning out food for their dogs. While in Cripple, I found myself around the fire with new-found friends, whittling diamond willow. Among these was a long-time volunteer veterinarian from Montana, who gave me one of his carvings.

From Cripple, we continued north toward the Yukon River and Nome. Looking out over the frozen Yukon River, covered in the morning ice fog, I could see the mushers heading out onto this winter highway. We arrived in Nome a full day ahead of the expected arrival of the first musher, and spent the next two days wandering around the historic downtown and meeting the mushers as they arrived. From its classic main street bordered by weathered wood-plank buildings, to its streets filled with fur parkas adorned with Native embroidery, there are few places that retain the traditional Native way of life as completely as Nome.

Leaving Nome was bittersweet, but as we winged our way home, I reflected on all I had experienced in those amazing 12 days. Now, as I look through the photo album of our trip, I remember the great moments and the remarkable way the trip has shaped my life. More and more I find myself hiking or skiing through the backcountry, in search of new horizons. It seems that an Alaskan adolescence, like an Alaskan childhood, also has a way of changing you. The invisible boundary between work and play begins and ends for me at the trailheads of Alaska's wilderness. My dad's guidance and knowledge has served me well in Alaska, whether I'm avoiding treacherous slopes or prying a few more nickels and dimes from my tent-mate with a well-bluffed pair of nines. ▣

daily 8am-7pm [summer]; Mon-Fri 8am-5pm [rest of year]. Free). A video on the great race is worth seeing.

Transportation buffs might enjoy a visit to the **Museum of Alaska Transportation and Industry** (Mile 47, Parks Hwy; 907/376-1211; www.museumofalaska.org. Open May-Sept, 9am-6pm; open Sat only [rest of year]. Cost: $8/adult, $5/student, $14/family). With 20 acres, the museum's collection includes examples of just about every kind of transportation, including aircraft and rolling stock. Steam train rides are offered on Saturdays during the summer; call for details.

Wasilla to Talkeetna (71 m)

As you continue on the Parks Highway, you'll notice that this is "cottage country," Alaska style. The landscape is dotted with lakes and vacation homes within handy distance from Anchorage and its suburbs. About 10 miles west of Wasilla at Mile 52 and three miles west of the highway, you'll find **Big Lake**, an old-time resort destination with swimming, boating, and fishing in summer and cross-country skiing and snow machining in winter. You'll also see signs of the devastating 1996 Miller's Reach fire that destroyed more than 400 homes. **The Klondike Inn** (907/892-6261), rebuilt after the fire, includes a motel, restaurant, lounge, and boot moorage on the lake's northern shore. **Rocky Lake State Recreation Site** has 10 campsites, with outhouses, fire pits, and water. **Big Lake North Recreation Site** (60 campsites) and **Big Lake South Recreation Site** (20 campsites) have similar facilities ($10/camping fee; $5/day use). Before traveling, check to be sure these are open; in 2002, several sites were closed or services cut back due to state budgeting issues. Check with the Department of Natural Resources for updates (907/269-8400; www.dnr.state.ak.us/parks/).

Mile 67 is the turnoff for **Nancy Lake State Recreation Area** (www.dnr.state.ak.us/parks/units/nancylk/), an attractive spot for a picnic or campout. The **Nancy Lake State Recreation Site** has 30 campsites ($10/night), toilets, boat launch facilities, and plenty of picnic sites. Six miles farther along Nancy Lake Road, you'll find the **South Rolly Lake Campground**, with about 100 campsites ($10/night), toilets, water, fire pits, canoes for rent, and boat launch facilities. Nancy Lake has public-use cabins for rent; these are especially popular thanks to their proximity to Anchorage, so you'll need to book far in advance ($35/night; pay only in person or by mail: DNR Public Information Center, 550 W. 7th Ave, Suite 1260, Anchorage, AK 99501-3557; 907/269-8400; e-mail: pic@dnr.state.ak.us/). There are several easy nature trails and berries—cranberries, blueberries and raspberries—to pick in July and August (make sure your kids know how to recognize poisonous baneberries). Sadly, mature spruce in this area are being destroyed by the spruce bark beetle that has ravaged forests elsewhere in Alaska and British Columbia. The area is popular with canoeists. Wild residents include moose, black bears, and the occasional grizzly.

TALKEETNA

Reminiscent of our movie-inspired notions of the wild west, this funky, forested little town consists of a Main Street and a large square of grass where townsfolk and tourists gather. Talkeetna is situated at the confluence of three rivers (the Susitna, the Chulitna, and the Talkeetna) and flanked by the majestic Alaska Range. Its historic buildings have earned it status on the National Register of Historic Places. On a spur road 14 miles off the Parks Highway at Mile 98.7, Talkeetna makes a convenient stop for Denali-bound visitors. Not surprisingly, tourism is the bread and butter of Talkeetna, the primary staging area for mountain-climbing assaults on Denali. Many flightseeing trips over the mountain and park originate here, and river rafting is popular.

Talkeetna makes an interesting stop on the long trip between Anchorage and the national park or Fairbanks. Here and there, on clear days, you'll find brilliant views of Mount McKinley. But don't let clouds stop you—Talkeetna is a fun spot for families, regardless of the weather.

Places to Stay

Talkeetna Alaskan Lodge ($$-$$$)
Mile 12.5 Talkeetna Spur Rd; 907/733-9500, 888/959-9590, 907/733-9545; www.talkeetnalodge.com
FYI: 201 rooms (4 adjoining rooms) on 2 levels, some suites; restaurant, espresso bar; hot tub; gift shop; free shuttle between lodge and railroad station. Children under 12 stay free; maximum 4 guests per room; nature trails
This big, comfortable hotel serves mostly large tour groups, so it's not the best choice for experiencing Talkeetna's quirky charms. The lodge has a lot to offer in comfort and scenery. The impressive lobby (kids will enjoy picking out the animal shapes in the smooth-stone fireplace) with floor-to-ceiling windows offers panoramic views of the Alaska Range and Mount McKinley. Lodge rooms are nicely appointed and roomy; annex accommodations are more modest.

The lodge offers casual lunch dining at the Susitna Café and a formal evening meal at the Foraker restaurant. Breakfast is served in both restaurants. There's a large deck and hot tub in back, overlooking the mountains.

❝ P A R E N T   C O M M E N T S ❞
> *"One of my fondest memories of Alaska is sitting on the lodge's back deck early one morning, sipping a latté and gazing contentedly at the incredible and incomparable Mt. McKinley."*

Swiss-Alaska Inn ($-$$)
In east Talkeetna, by the boat launch; 907/733-2424; www.swissalaska.com
FYI: 20 rooms, restaurant, kids under 12 stay free
This inn offers basic comforts in a pleasant setting.

Talkeetna Roadhouse ($)
Main St; 907/733-1351; www.talkeetnaroadhouse.com
FYI: 7 rooms, shared baths, kids under 13 stay free; café, bakery (lunch & dinner only); all non-smoking
Funky and "rustic ambience" are words that describe this accommodation. If you're looking for the real Alaskan experience, this is the place for you. Built in 1917 by freighter Frank Lee, the building was purchased in 1944 and turned into a roadhouse. There are seven dormitory-style rooms—each is tiny, with various configurations of beds, bunks, and desks, and bathrooms down

the hall. There's a charmingly rustic salon and dining room, with a piano (locals stop in occasionally to tickle the ivories) and dusty bookshelves holding everything from well-worn classics to modern tour guides, and ancient kids' games to videotapes. The bakery is an Alaskan institution.

66 PARENT COMMENTS 99

"If you don't mind the absolute lack of amenities, this is a place where kids can be kids and adults can relax. Our family visited during the Moose Dropping Festival, and it was fun to be at the center of things—amid noise, dust, and bustle."

Places to Eat

Café Michele
Mile 13.75 Talkeetna Spur Rd; 907/773-5300
Hours: daily 11am-4pm, 5:30-9pm, Sun brunch 9:30am-4pm (summer);
Thurs 5-9pm, Fri-Sat 5-10pm, Sun brunch 11am-4pm (winter);
closed Jan-March
Located in a log cabin, this café has an inviting look, inside and out. Enjoy indoor dining in a light, airy space, or eat outside when the weather is agreeable. The cuisine leans toward the Mediterranean, and ranges from hearty soups and salads to carefully prepared pastas, local fish, and meat. If smaller appetites dictate sharing, don't hesitate to ask: your server will accommodate whenever possible. Among appetizers offered, the Mediterranean Sampler is especially appealing.

Talkeetna Roadhouse
Main St; 907/733-1351; www.talkeetnaroadhouse.com/meals/
Hours: 6:30am-1pm (breakfast), 11:30am-3pm (lunch)
This is definitely the place to go for hearty, frontier breakfasts. The dining is family style, so be prepared to share your table; the area can get pretty packed. The normal plates are huge and overflowing, so consider sharing a plate, or order à la carte (a world-famous cinnamon roll and a strong cup of coffee is an excellent choice). For lunch, try a sandwich on fresh-baked bread and a hearty bowl of soup. Along with the restaurant, you'll find Talkeetna's principal bakery has all kinds of tempting goodies for sale.

What to See & Do

Stroll & Browse
Although there's not much to the Talkeetna town center in terms of acreage, during the drier months there always seems to be something going on. Begin your visit at **Village Park**. This grassy square, at the intersection of Talkeetna Spur Road and Main Street, is a central gathering point, especially during the Talkeetna Winterfest in December and the Moose Dropping Festival in July. Stop into the **Talkeetna Visitor Center/Mountain Gifts**, in the Three

German Bachelors' Cabin adjacent to Village Park (look for the "Welcome to Beautiful Downtown Talkeetna" sign), and pick up a Walking Tour brochure and suggestions from the helpful folks here on where to go and what to do.

Stroll up and down Main Street and the spur road, and check out the restaurants and shops—and some of the accommodations—available in Talkeetna. Worthy of note (especially if you're short on diapers) is **Nagley's Store**, first opened in the 1920s and still the only spot in town for groceries.

When you've done all the perusing you're up for, stroll to the end of Main Street and cross the gravel parking area to the **confluence of the rivers**. This is a lovely, serene spot—good for skipping stones and contemplating the universe. Likely you will see river rafts and jetboats on the river—check them out to determine whether this is an adventure you think your young ones could enjoy (for more information, see "River Trips").

Museums

Museum of Northern Adventure   Part museum, part tourist shop, this museum is housed in a small building on Main Street across from the post office. There's not a lot here, but kids will enjoy the dioramas and life-size wax figures, as well as oddities such as the original cook stove from the Talkeetna Roadhouse. *Mile 14.5 Talkeetna Spur Hwy (across from the post office); 907/733-3999. Open daily, 10am-6pm (summer). Cost: $2/adult, $1/over 65 & under 13; $5/family.*

Talkeetna Historical Society Museum   If you visit only one museum, make it this one (look for the "little red schoolhouse" south Main Street). The schoolhouse opened its doors in 1935, and today it houses a fascinating collection of local memorabilia, including photos, tools, toys, and commemorative items. Don't miss the mountaineering displays, which feature a comparison of the art of climbing, past and present, and the scale model of Mount McKinley fashioned by a Seattle mapmaker. Take a peek into the Ole Dahl Cabin, the oldest existing structure in town, to see how one trapper lived during the first part of the 20th century. *In 4 bldgs, corner of 1st Alley and Valley Airstrip; 907/733-2487. Open daily, 10:30am-5pm, (May-Sept); weekends, 10:30am-5pm, rest of year. Cost: $2.50/adult, free/under 12.*

River Trips

Talkeetna means "Where the Rivers Meet," and many visitors like to experience those waters personally. You can get a sense of the rich variety of scenery and wildlife here on a raft trip. Unlike some Alaska rivers, these tend to be quiet enough for very small children.

Denali View Raft Adventures   These folks offer a selection of floats, such as a two-hour trip on the Talkeetna River featuring a beaver dam up close and personal, a three-hour trip on the Susitna offering great views of Denali (if the mountain cooperates), and a five- to six-hour tour that includes both rivers. Children 4 and older are welcome. Trips include transportation, raingear, snacks, and drinks. Stops along the way allow small legs to stretch.

☛ Parent Tip: Choosing a River Trip

Before choosing a river trip, ask your outfitter a few questions: Will raingear and boots be provided? Hats and gloves? If so, do they carry a variety of children's sizes? Will there be snacks? Hot drinks? (It can get mighty chilly out on the river!) Do they offer boat-safety training before you board? Will the trip allow for bathroom stops? While trips longer than three hours generally build in restroom stops of some kind, shorter trips may not. Consider in advance how you'll handle bathroom emergencies, and discuss with the outfitter before booking. ▣

877/533-2778, 907/733-2778; www.alaskaone.com/denviewraft: $55/adult, $30/child under 13; 3-hour: $75/adult, $50/child under 13; 5-6 hour: $125/adult, $95/child under 13.

Mahay's Riverboat Service   Services include "safaris" aboard the Talkeetna Queen jetboat, along with more adventurous trips. There is an onboard restroom. The McKinley Safari features a short nature walk with a visit to a trapper's cabin from the early 1900s and an introduction to local flora and fauna (which can include black and grizzly bears). Although the nature walk is leisurely, the trail can be rough in parts; wear sturdy walking shoes and carry babies in backpacks. The trip includes a cruise along 10 miles of the Susitna River. Choose from multiple daily departures. Longer trips offer stunning scenery, but are probably too much for families with young children. The Deluxe Wilderness Safari takes passengers on a 50-mile, 3.5-hour cruise of the Susitna, twice daily. Fishing packages are available; call for details.
800/736-2210; www.mahaysriverboat.com. Cost: McKinley Safari: $50/adult, $25/child under 6; Deluxe Wilderness Safari, $95/adult, $47.50/child under 6.

Talkeetna River Guides   This outfit offers trips of various lengths and destinations, including the "Grand Slam": a flight to Denali National Park, a lunch, and a float. Children must be accompanied by an adult. The shortest option is a two-hour narrated float trip on the Talkeetna River in search of wildlife and views of Denali, with multiple daily departures; custom trips can be arranged. Raingear, boots, and binoculars are provided. A four-hour trip on the Chulitna River (transportation from Talkeetna included), into Denali State Park offers rich wildlife-viewing opportunities in a less-traveled area. The Grand Slam, which comes with an optional flightseeing trip, would be best for older kids. Prices vary depending on the size of your party. Charges drop a bit if you omit the flightseeing. All trips include lunch. Overnight trips can be arranged.
800/353-2677; 907/733-2677; www.talkeetnariverguides.com. Cost: 2-hour trip, $54/adult, $22/child under age 12; 4-hour trip, $84/adult, $42/child under 10; Grand Slam with flightseeing trip, $379/adult (party of 2), $349/adult (more than 2).

☛ Parent Tip: Avoiding Hypothermia

Hypothermia, a serious condition, comes about when your body loses heat faster than it's created. If severe enough, it can cause death. Even when the temperature is well above freezing, you can get hypothermia if conditions are right—for instance, an unexpected soaking on a chilly raft trip. Your first line of defense is to dress appropriately: in layers with clothing that breathes. Sweat-soaked clothing will make you cold. Always bring a change of clothing for long hikes or day trips and keep it dry (waterproof plastic bags should do the trick). Waterproof outerwear is a must, including hats and gloves. Finally, make sure everyone has plenty of water and high-calorie snacks when you head out. Trail mix, granola bars, dried fruit and nuts, even chocolate are good choices. If the activity is strenuous, take frequent breaks and pass around the water and snacks. For clothing guidelines, see "Dressing Your Child for Alaska." The Forest Service Web site lists hypothermia guidelines at www.fs.fed.us/r10/naturewatch/miscpages/hypothermia/ ▣

Fishing   Several local guides offer river trips (half-day, full-day, or overnight) to fish for trout, grayling, and five salmon species. Call **Talkeetna Fishing Guides** (800/318-2534, 907/733-3355) or **Mountain River Adventures** (907/733-4453, www.mtnriver.com). Either take your catch home (guides help with packing) or release the fish back into the river.

Flightseeing   Talkeetna has some of the best and most affordable mountain flightseeing in Alaska, and you'll pay less than at Denali. You can take short, scenic flights to view wildlife, explore glaciers (and sometimes land on them), and learn about history and geology. Remember that chances are good that a flight will be delayed or canceled due to poor weather conditions. Ask about refund policies for canceled flights before you pay. If time is very tight and rebooking at a later time is not an option, you might want to refrain from advance booking. You risk not being able to go at all if flights are full, but at least you won't have paid for that privilege!

K2 Aviation (800/764-2291, 907/733-2291;www.flyk2.com) is the largest of the area operators. Flights start at $120 per person and they have many options. **McKinley Air Service** (800/564-1765, 907/733-1765; www.mckinley airservice.com), billed as "two babes and a bird," offers flights "manned" by two female pilots, one of whom has run the Iditarod and operates a kennel. Check in advance to see whether you can combine your flightseeing trip with a visit to some junior sled dogs. Fares for flights start at $120/person. Another well-known service is **Doug Geeting Aviation** (800/770-2366, 907/733-2366; www.alaskaairtours.com), run by a long-time bush pilot with more than 25 years of experience running sightseers around the mountain. Tours start at $105/person.

Calendar of Events

July

Moose Dropping Festival
907/733-1234; www.north-to-alaska.com
Parents brace yourselves: Throughout Alaska, moose droppings—AKA moose nuggets—turn up in gift stores in forms both virtual and real (dried) to the delight of children of all ages. This popular '70s-style festival features music, food, crafts, and a number of events spread throughout the woods. Don't miss the Mountain Mama competition (a race where women attempt to complete a course that includes chopping wood and shooting an arrow, all while carrying a 10-pound "baby") or the famous moose nugget toss.

December

Talkeetna Winterfest
907/733-1234; www.north-to-alaska.com
This month-long solstice festival includes the Parade of Lights, tree trimming contest, and a gingerbread-house building contest (with adult and child categories). Especially popular is the Bachelor Society Ball/Wilderness Woman Contest, at which women can bid on the bachelors.

Resources

Talkeetna Chamber of Commerce
Box 334, Talkeetna, AK 99676; 907/733-2330; www.talkeetna-chamber.com

TalkeetnaDenali Visitor Center
Parks Highway at Talkeetna Spur Rd; 907/733-2688; 800/660-2688; www.alaskan.com/talkeetnadenali/. Open daily 8am-8pm, mid-May-mid-Sept

Talleetna Ranger Station
B St, off Main S; 907/733-2231
Open daily, mid-April—Labor Day, 8am-6pm; remainder of year, Mon-Fri 8am-4pm
Information on mountaineering and interpretive programs

Talkeetna to Denali National Park (153 m)

As you head north out of Talkeetna, fill your gas tank if necessary—there are few gas stations for 100 miles until you reach Cantwell. The trip north on the Parks Highway (Hwy 3) from its junction with Talkeetna Spur Road is an easy, tree-lined drive with now-and-again views of the Alaska Range. It's a pretty straight shot to Cantwell (Mile 210), a tiny town located at the junction with the Denali Highway (Hwy 8). If you don't stay the night in Talkeetna on the way to Denali, consider the **Mount McKinley Princess Wilderness Lodge** at Mile 133.1 (800/426-0442; www.princesslodges.com/mcKinley/). As with other Princess lodges, you'll need to book this one well ahead; it's often full of tour groups. Open from mid-May to mid-September, it has 238 rooms, a restaurant and coffee shop, fitness center, and hot tubs. There is a main lodge with guest rooms grouped in smaller buildings, nature trails, and great views. Rates are moderate to high.

Denali State Park   From Mile 132 to 169, the highway bisects Denali State Park, not to be confused with Denali National Park and Preserve. While much smaller than the national park, the state park's 325,000 acres of wilderness afford some of the best views of Denali and the Alaska Range, along with plenty of bears. The assortment of wildlife is as rich and varied as you'll find anywhere in the state. Arctic terns breed here, along with songbirds and water birds. There's a staffed Visitor Contact Station at the Alaska Veterans Memorial (Mile 147.1), which also offers the best view of Denali.

Wilder and less overrun with tourists than the national park, the state park has three campgrounds. At the south end of the park you'll find **Lower Troublesome Creek Campground** ($5/vehicle, 20 sites, water, toilets, picnic sites and shelter). The **Chulitna Confluence Trail** here is an easy 1.2-mile hike for small folk.

A bit farther north is **Byers Lake Campground** (68 sites, $10/site, toilets, water, picnic sites, firewood). Here you can rent canoes and kayaks by the hour ($10 and up) or by the day through **Susitna Expeditions** (907/892-6916, 800/891-6916 [in Alaska]). Susitna also leads guided nature hikes from the campground ($35/person). There's a five-mile loop nature trail suitable for kids to explore.

At the northern end of the park is **Denali View North Campground** (23 sites, $10/vehicle, toilets, water, picnicking). Also in the park are two popular, public-use cabins for rent ($35/night); one can be accessed by car. To rent, contact **Mat-Su Area Headquarters** in Wasilla at 907/745-3975 or the **Public Information Center** in Anchorage at 907/269-8400.

Cantwell, at Mile 209.9, marks the junction of the Parks and Denali highways. You'll find gas and supplies here. The Denali Highway, mostly unpaved, but remarkably scenic, is the 136-mile route that connects the Parks with the Richardson Highway. The latter roughly parallels the Parks Highway to the east of the Alaska Range, and runs from Valdez on Prince William Sound north to Fairbanks. If you're up for a spot of adventure and don't mind the bumps, driving some or all of the Denali Highway makes a great trip (see "Driving the Denali Highway" in "The Road North").

Mount McKinley is rarely visible throughout an entire day, so if you happen to spot it along the way, take the opportunity to stop, stare, point, and shoot; this could be your one and only opportunity, not to be missed. The 27-mile stretch from Cantwell to the Park entrance is wild and lovely, though mountain views become scarcer as you approach the national park itself. Settle back and enjoy the woods. If stomachs are rumbling, watch for the **Perch Restaurant and Resort** at Mile 224 (see "Places to Eat").

Diary of the Train Ride to Denali

We made our trip to Denali from Anchorage in early September. At first the kids were a bit downcast that we were not boarding one of the gleaming Princess or Holland America cars proudly emblazoned with company logos. We explained that they were for tour passengers and pointed out that we'd be in the same car as 'real' Alaskans. For our non-group, there were two ordinary passenger cars, one combined passenger-observation car, and a dining car. We were the second party to board and were able to snag one of only four sets of facing seats with tables between, good for games on the 12-hour trip.

Owing to our early start in Anchorage (we had to be at the station to pick up our tickets at 7 am), we had breakfast onboard and were glad we had. Emily and I chose the fruit, yogurt and cinnamon roll, while Mike and Nick enjoyed eggs and reindeer sausage. Prices were comparable to a mid-range Anchorage restaurant, and it was all delicious.

Over the next few hours, the kids explored the four cars at our disposal. Friendly staff lent us books on Alaska, some for kids, and made their way through our cars, talking to everyone. Most proved to be high school seniors. Spots of interest were pointed out over the P.A. system (that's how we got to see a black bear fishing in a shallow river). We learned later that Alaska Railroad always designates one of the passenger cars as a quiet car; here, passengers can sleep undisturbed by announcements. Around lunchtime, the scenery became more interesting. There was a polite stampede to the observation car; passengers would stay for half an hour or so, soaking up the view, then leave, allowing others to observe. We passed shallow rivers, milky blue laced with white water, and watched as a bald eagle roosting in a tall evergreen stretched its wings and flew parallel to the train for 10 thrilling seconds. Most exciting, we occasionally spotted Denali peeking from behind veils of cloud.

Lunch was equal to breakfast in quality. The kids split a burger, and the adults shared an appetizer plate of smoked salmon, smoked halibut, beef and salmon jerky, cheeses, fruit salad, rolls and crackers.

On arriving in Denali, we were met by about 50 ancient school buses painted white, along with several elegant tour buses. There was some confusion as not all buses posted their destinations. By asking, we finally located our hotel bus and confirmed with the driver where it was headed. The cheery driver helped with our baggage and we were off to our hotel and Denali adventure.◘

DENALI NATIONAL PARK AND PRESERVE

The park is the size of Vermont and it takes planning to get more than a taste of what it has to offer. With 360,000 visitors per year, mostly in summer, Denali ties with Glacier Bay as Alaska's most visited park. Human and vehicular access to the park is strictly controlled (see "Accessing the Park Sidebar"), to maintain a pristine habitat for park wildlife. Although the park is open year round, most facilities in it are open only mid-May to mid-September. There are two visitor centers, seven campgrounds, a few roads, and trails close to the park entrance suitable for small fry to tackle. Family park-entrance fee is $10.

Not to be missed are the sled-dog kennels and free sled-dog demonstration at park headquarters. In the backcountry are several rustic lodges where you can get enjoy the tranquility and the wildlife. The stunningly beautiful Nenana River runs along the eastern edge of the park. The best river views are from the train or on a float trip, offered by several local outfitters (see "River Rafting").

Your first step in planning a trip here is to decide whether to act as your own travel agent or book a package tour. The latter will certainly be less work. But it's not hard to create your own customized Denali visit with a little research and planning. If you decide to book a tour, you'll find a bewildering choice of options. Just about every cruise company has tours to Denali; you don't have to sail on a cruise ship to book one of these (see "Getting There" for company listings). The Alaska Railroad offers tours, and most Denali-area hotels will gladly set you up.

Getting Around

If you're arriving by train, a confusing array of hotel shuttle buses will greet you at the station, along with the park-run Riley Creek Shuttle bus. The park buses are free, too; however, they don't stop at the hotels. When you make your hotel reservation, ask how to get from the station to your hotel and how to distinguish your shuttle bus from others.

Accessing the Park

To ensure that its wild habitat remains free from human encroachment, a variety of ingenious schemes limit the number of visitors who can drive, hike, camp, and bike here. Motorists, with a few exceptions, are allowed to drive only the first 15 miles into the park. From early May until the shuttle buses run, the Park Road is open to all motorists. However, weather is often poor and most facilities are closed. For four days every mid-September, 400 lucky motorists are permitted to drive the entire Park Road each day (see "Road Lottery"). Also, if you have secured a reservation at Teklanika Campground (a three-day minimum stay is required) at Mile 30 in the park, you can drive in, even during the summer months. With your reservation, you'll get a permit good for one trip in and one trip out. ◼

Taking the Grandkids to Alaska
By Liz Kinneberg

I suppose it all began when I first read Robert Service in a thin, leather-bound book, at around age 10. I have always been fascinated by "The North" and when I married Dave, I discovered his father had been to Alaska during the Gold Rush of 1898. Andrew Kinneberg worked on the railroad through White's Pass out of Skagway, and later got to Nome when they were mining the beaches for gold. I felt I had to see that faraway place for myself. After a trip on a small cruise ship through the Inside Passage, we were hooked. Subsequent trips took us to Prince Rupert, on the Alaska ferry, with stops in Wrangell and Skagway. From Haines we drove to Chitna, where we traveled on a small plane to visit the old Kennicott mine near McCarthy. Everything there seemed to be frozen in time—back when the mill was closed in 1938. My husband, a retired miner from the Lower 48, loved every minute at Kennicott.

In an effort to keep the next generation hooked, we introduced our two granddaughters to Alaska. The girls flew into Anchorage from Los Angeles. Kate, 10, and her sister Emma, 11, arrived, loaded with toys and games they'd brought to fill the six-hour flight. We got into the Suburban and made the two-hour drive to Talkeetna where we stayed at the Talkeetna Alaskan Lodge, with Mt. McKinley (Denali) in glorious view. The girls loved the funky town of Talkeetna, the moose and caribou we saw along the way, as well as a 5-

If you have your own wheels, getting into the park from the Parks Highway is a piece of cake; turn left at Mile 237.4, where the highway meets the Park Road, which winds 90 miles into Denali National Park. The park entrance is located just west of the junction. A little farther along the Park Road is the main Visitor Center. (The other Visitor Center, Eileson, is at Mile 66 of the Park Road.)

A few miles farther down the Park Road is the Park Headquarters. Here you'll find the kennels where daily demonstrations of sled dogs in action are held. There are campgrounds along the Park Road, some of which can be accessed by private vehicle and some that can be reached only by the park's shuttle buses.

Area accommodation, dining, and services stretch out along the highway from about seven miles south of the park entrance to 11 miles north in the small town of Healy. If you don't have your own vehicle, staying in "Glitter Gulch," the strip of lodgings, restaurants, gas stations, and stores within a mile of the park entrance at Mile 238, is recommended. From here, you can catch a free shuttle bus or van to the Park Visitor Center, or—if you have the time—walk the path to the Center. If you're seeking budget accommodation, or a B&B, Healy has several options. Check with the Greater Denali/Healy Chamber of Commerce (see "Resources").

star outhouse. (No McDonald's here.) What a first day—nothing like it in Southern California!

The next morning, we drove to Denali National Park and boarded a bus for the all-day trip to Kantishna Roadhouse, where we planned a four-day visit. (In retrospect, I wish we had flown out; 90 miles [twice] is a long time to spend on the bus.) Kantishna Roadhouse was everything promised and more (for example, they made no claim to have mosquitoes, but did they ever)! We had a cabin near the lodge, and enjoyed a hay ride, panning for gold, and horseback riding. The management graciously provided us with fishing poles and sack lunches, and we went fishing on Wonder Lake. The canoe trip was beautiful and our guide, who had homesteaded in Manley Hot Springs many years ear-lier, was a source of wonderful tales about Alaska and dog teams. The girls, true to their mining heritage, relished the gold panning and even collected enough to put into little necklaces—nice mementos.

For our next adventure, we took the girls along the Denali Highway and spent a night at Tangle Lakes where we caught some Arctic grayling. We spent the following day in the Mat/Su Valley northeast of Anchorage, and the girls delighted in a visit to the Musk Ox Farm. In the morning, we were off to the airport to send the girls back home to a mother who hadn't had a good night's sleep since they left. One thing is certain: those girls will get back to Alaska before too much time has passed. Kantisha Roadhouse did a laudable job of keeping the Alaska spirit alive for the next generation. ◨

Entrance Area Park Shuttle Buses From mid-May to early-September, the park operates two free shuttle buses from the entrance area. The **Riley Creek Loop Bus** shuttles between the Visitor Center, **Riley Creek Campground**, **Horseshoe Trailhead**, and the train station. One complete loop takes 30 minutes.

The **Dog Sled Demo Bus** runs between the Riley Creek Campground, Visitor Center, and Park Headquarters, where the Dog Sled demo takes place. Buses leave the campground 40 minutes and the Visitor Center 30 minutes before each demo (see "Dog Sled Demos" for details). Even if you have a vehicle, you'll need to take the bus to the demo, as no parking is provided there. The ride is 10 minutes.

For $2 each way (kids under 15 ride free), the **Savage River Shuttle Bus** carries passengers 15 miles into the park, to the Savage River Campground. Buses travel on the off-hour, and the one-way trip takes about an hour. Unlike the shuttles that go deeper into the park, none of these requires reservations. (For other park shuttles, see "What to See & Do.")

Other Forms of Transportation You can rent a car from **Teresa's Alaskan Car Rentals** in Healy (907/683-1377; http://www.denalicarrental.com).

Given the far-flung nature of services along the Parks Highway, the **Denali Taxi Service** (907/683-2504) can come in handy if you need a quick trip back to the hotel before the shuttle bus is scheduled to depart.

Places to Stay

Denali Princess Wilderness Lodge ($$-$$$)
Mile 238.5 Parks Hwy; 800/426-0442; www.princesslodges.com
350 rooms; restaurants; fitness center, 3 outdoor hot tubs; Laundromat; gift shop;
free shuttle to the park visitor center and train station; open mid-May-mid Sept
One of Princess's four Alaska Wilderness Lodges, this one shows its age a little, but is still comfortable. It's perched on a bluff with a spectacular view of the Nenana River, directly below. The large gift shop sells clothing, souvenirs, and books. Staff will book tours and excursions for guests. Although the main restaurant has a kids' menu, it caters to older, quieter diners. So if the weather is good, pick up a pizza from Lynx Creek (see "Places to Eat") and dine at one of the outdoor tables overlooking the river.

66 PARENT COMMENTS 99
"Our need to do serious laundry was approaching critical, so we really appreciated the good-sized Laundromat."

"Through trial and error we learned it was easiest to eat dinner in our room. The casual-dining option closed early, the fine-dining restaurant was intimidatingly quiet, and the bar was crowded and noisy. Helpful staff suggested we could order burgers from the bar and bring them back to our room, and that worked fine."

Denali River Cabins ($$)
Mile 231.1 Parks Hwy; 800/2300-7275; www.denalirivercabins.com
FYI: 54 cabins; restaurant; sauna; Laundromat; tour desk; open late
May-mid June
The best thing about this property is the river that runs through it; the glacier-fed Nenana River offers a refreshing break from time spent on the road or sightseeing in the park. Each small cedar cabin comes with private bath and either two double beds or a double and a single. Some have decks overlooking the river. There's a lodge/gift shop, restaurant, and two-story motel structure (the motel rooms are clean and reasonably spacious, but lack character).

66 PARENT COMMENTS 99
"The first night we were there they had a musher scheduled to give a talk and demonstrate how the sled dogs work, which was really interesting."

"We were disappointed at how small and close together the cabins were, but then the kids made friends with others staying close by, and that was a big plus."

☞ Parent Tip: Deciding Where to Stay

If you're not camping, you have three main location choices for where to stay near Denali. All have pros and cons. You can stay south of the park; 11 miles north in Healy (Mile 248.7); or at "Glitter Gulch," close to the park entrance.

Staying south of the park can be an attractive option; it's quieter and the scenery is especially gorgeous. Hotels are equal in quality to those elsewhere, but because they are about seven miles from the Visitor Center and the family-friendly activities there (such as the free sled dog demonstration at Park headquarters and easy hikes) and lack casual dining and shopping options, you'll be dependent on the shuttle bus schedule.

The small town of Healy (Mile 248.7) offers accommodation at a more modest rate than you'll find closer to the park (see "Resources").

"Glitter Gulch," close to the Park Entrance and the hub of park activity, is also most convenient, especially if you don't have a car. Most hotels here offer free shuttle service to the railroad station and into the park, or you can walk in on your own (about a mile).

Hotel brochures and Web sites don't necessarily identify their locations as miles from the park entrance. So before booking, check the mile number of the hotel you're considering. If it's around 231, you'll need transportation to reach park activities. If it's around 238, you'll be close to where the action is.

A word of caution to parents of young kids: Most of the area's big hotels still cater primarily to older visitors without children. While families are heading here in ever-larger numbers and kid-friendly amenities, once almost nonexistent, are gradually appearing, plenty of hotels still seem not to welcome kids with open arms. Before booking, ask a few questions: What is there for kids to do in the immediate vicinity of the hotel (i.e. without requiring a vehicle)? Do hotel grounds have nature trails or space for small children to run off excess energy? What are the dining options? If you decide against booking, let them know why. If parents want improved family amenities, they need to make their needs clear. ◙

Grande Denali ($$-$$$)

Mile 238 Parks Hwy; 907/683-8500, 866/683-8500; www.grandedenali.com
FYI:154 rooms, 6 cabins with refrigerator/microwave; kids under 13 stay free with parents; restaurant; Laundromat (open 24 hours); gift shop; free shuttle to train station and around park entrance area

The cabins are the draw here for families. Each has a deck and comes with a queen bed, and one double and one twin sofa/sleeper. With the refrigerator and microwave, you can rustle up something to feed the small fry when the fine-dining atmosphere of local restaurants gets to them. The Grande has quite a view, too, perched on the mountainside above the highway and Nenana River.

Camping

Camping in Denali National Park can be a thrilling experience, but the commercial RV parks don't have a lot to recommend them. They tend to be dreary roadside parking lots, tree-free and in earshot of vehicles whizzing by. Most are miles from the park entrance and local amenities. In contrast, the park campsites are beautiful wooded spots, well worth a little forethought.

Park Campgrounds

You'll need to reserve well in advance to secure a campsite in one of the seven park campgrounds. All are open for tent camping, and three accept RVs and campers with vehicles. There are no dump stations for RVs anywhere in the park. A nonrefundable fee ($4) is charged for all park campground reservations. Pets are allowed in the campgrounds only and must be on leash at all times. Generators may be used from 8-10am and 4-8pm.

Riley Creek Campground, a quarter-mile off the Parks Highway and open year round is within walking distance of Glitter Gulch and the Park Visitor Center. Entrance Area shuttles stop here. The down side is that proximity to traffic and the Visitor Center make it fairly busy, though quiet hours are in effect from 10pm to 6am.
100 sites, tents and RVs, $16/site; flush toilets, water (summer only), firewood for sale

Savage River Campground, at Mile 13 of the Park Road, is smaller and chances of encountering wildlife are better. It's open May to September.
33 RV and tent sites, $6/site; chemical toilets, drinking water; no fires allowed, stoves only.

Teklanika Campground, at Mile 30 of the Park Road, is open May to September. Your reservation allows you to drive to and from the campground only; during your stay, your vehicle must remain parked at the campground.
53 sites for RVs and tents, $12/night, 3-night minimum, flush toilets, water.

Campers must use park shuttle buses to get to the other four campgrounds. These are not the best choice for families with small children even if you all can hoist packs, sleeping bags, food, and equipment. Most of the park is trail-free wilderness, not suitable for younger children. But if you're experienced campers with older kids, you might want to tackle a backcountry trip. If so, you'll need a permit, which must be issued in person at the Visitor Center no more than a day before you plan to go.
Reservations: 907/272-7275, 800/622-7275 (national); fax: 907/264-4684 (download a fax form at www.nps.gov/dena). Reservations are accepted starting in late February.

Commercial Campgrounds

The closest campground to the park is **Denali Rainbow Village & RV Park** (Mile 238.6 Parks Hwy; 907/683-7777; www.denalirvrvpark.com). All services are available and tents are permitted. Prices start at $18. Next closest is **Denali Riverside RV Park** (Mile 240 Parks Hwy; 888/778-7700; www.alaskarv.com), also offering all services.

Books

Alaska's Bears: Grizzlies, Black Bears, and Polar Bears. Alaska Pocket Guides. Alaska Northwest, 1998.

Markle, Sandra. *Bears.* Atheneum, 2000. A picture book with fine photos describes North American bears for small children.

Shelton, Gary. *Bear Encounter Survival Guide.* Pallister, 1997. A useful handbook on bear-safety.

Bear Facts Web Sites

Comprehensive bear site: www.bears.org

A comprehensive, kid-friendly site on bears in general: www.bearden.org

Bear Safety Web Sites:

US Scouting Bear Safety Tips: www.usscouts.org/safety/safe_bea/

Forest Service Bear Sense Web site: www.fs.fed.us/r10/naturewatch/misc pages/bearsafety/

Yukon Bear Tips: www.environmentyukon.gov.yk.ca/fishwild/bearsafety/

North American Bear Center, Kid's Page: http://wlapwww.gov.bc.ca/ bcparks/explore/misc/bears/bearsaf/

Mountain Nature.com Bear Facts: www.mountainnature.com/ Wildlife/Bears/

Places to Eat

Denali Salmon Bake ☺
Mile 23 Parks Hwy; 907/683-2733; e-mail: Kevin@denalipark.com
Hours: open daily 5am-11pm
Across the Parks Highway from the Glitter Gulch hotels, this cheery, rustic salmon bake is the place to head when the crew is starving. There's a kids' menu and lots of room at picnic tables indoors and outdoors (heated). All-you-can-eat breakfasts include sourdough and blueberry pancakes and reindeer sausage. For lunch and dinner you'll get burgers, steaks, ribs, fish, salads, and more. The food is hearty, good, and plentiful. Unlike some salmon bakes, this one serves more than just blueberry cake for dessert.

Lynx Creek Pizza ☺
Mile 238.6 Parks Hwy; 907/683-2547
Hours: open daily 11am-11:30pm, mid-May-mid-Sept
This fabled institution is close to the park entrance and most hotels, and perennially popular with just about everyone. Count on it to be crowded and loud. The pizza is just fine and prices, for the area, reasonable. Caesar and chop-chop salads and Panini sandwiches round out the offerings. Parents can wash it all down with a pitcher of beer. If you have room, order ice cream cones for the road.

Perch Restaurant and Resort
Mile 224 Parks Hwy; 888/322-2523, 907/683-2523;
Hours: open daily, 6am-10pm (summer); Fri-Sat, 5pm-9pm, Sun 10am-3pm
(rest of year)
Literally "perched" on a hill overlooking the surrounding forest, the Perch is a light-filled spot with a lovely back deck. Meals begin with a platter of delicious bread, and entrées include pasta, fish, and meat. The children's menu offers spaghetti and fish and chips, or kids can choose from a few lighter selections of soup and salad.

What to See & Do

Everyone's first stop is the **Denali National Park Visitor Center**, half a mile from the park entrance on Park Road. It is a hub of activity and information from May to September. There are numerous notices and handouts on the park and its wildlife residents, an excellent bookstore, and knowledgeable staff. Take the time to read the message boards with information on bear sightings and park happenings. Attend the park orientation sessions which offer important tips on handling wildlife encounters. Find out when staff-led campground talks and nature walks are scheduled. It gets crowded at times, and there's nowhere to get a bite to eat, but this will be corrected when the new visitor center opens in 2005 on the site of the old park hotel (torn down in 2001). The new location will include a food court, bookstore, exhibit area, and theater.
Mile 1, Park Rd; 907/683-2294; www.nps.gov/dena/. Open daily June-mid-Sept, 7am-8pm; open daily May and late Sept, 10am-4pm; closed Oct-April.

Sled-dog demonstration ☺ Using sled dogs is an old tradition at Denali. During the summer, 40-minute demonstrations on the history of sled dogs and the work they do, are offered three times per day, at the kennels at Park Headquarters. As a grand finale, the ranger hitches up the dogs and takes them for a spin around a training track. You'll have a chance to ask questions, visit the sled shed, and shake some paws.
Park Headquarters; 10am, 2pm, 4pm. Shuttle bus leaves Riley Creek Campground 40 minutes before each session, stopping at Visitor Center. Free.

Park Bus Tours Tan school buses are a common sight on Denali roads. Together with the privately run Wilderness Trails bus tours, park-operated half-day and full-day tours are the only ones offered, so make reservations as early as possible. While several departure times are offered, your best bet for spotting wildlife and seeing the mountain is in the morning, the earlier the better.

Of the tours, the half-day **Natural History Tour** is the best bet for kids. Buses go to Primrose Ridge at Mile 17. Count on plenty of unscheduled stops along the way. Whenever someone spots wildlife, the bus pulls over to the side of the road, and a sedate stampede of octogenarians festooned with camera gear ensues. Scheduled stops include Primrose Ridge, a look at a

---

☞ **Parent Tip**

At the park visitor center, you can check out a **Discovery Pack**, a new feature for kids, introduced in 2002. These kits contain fun and educational tools and hands-on family activities to take out into the park. You'll need to leave a deposit and return the pack when you're done.

Like other national parks, Denali has a **Junior Ranger Program**. Pick up an activity guide at the visitor center (there is a version for 4-8 year olds, and another for the 9-14 set). Kids fill out the guide as directed, then turn in the completed guide to park staff at the visitor center. Kids who've answered questions correctly are awarded a junior ranger badge. ▣

---

park ranger cache cabin, and a Native American interpretive display. Snacks and hot beverages, usually cider or cocoa, are served on the way. The buses are not very comfortable and don't have restrooms, but as most driving is on paved road and stops are frequent, that shouldn't be a problem. (Even kids in potty training won't need to stop as often as the bus does.) You will see wildlife, but that may mean microscopic dots of white (Dall sheep on the mountainside) or dark brown (a moose strolling through the taiga, a half-mile away). If the weather cooperates, you'll have spectacular views of Denali. If the weather is cloudy, you might do better to substitute a shuttle trip to Savage River and take the loop hike there.

The six- to eight-hour **Tundra Wildlife Tour** is not a great bet for children under 12. Buses travel to Toklat River (Mile 53), all but the first 15 miles on gravel road. Wildlife sightings are more frequent than on the shorter tour, but parents will have to decide whether that prospect compensates for a full day of bumping over potholes. This tour includes box lunches and hot drinks. A shorter version (three to four hours) is offered in early to mid-May and in mid-September.

Reservations: 800/208-0200; Natural History Tour: 3 departures early, mid-morning, afternoon daily. Cost: $40.50/adult, $24.50/child under 12. Tundra Wildlife Tour: 2 departures early morning, afternoon daily; $74/adult, $52/child under 12 (summer); $51/adult, $29.50/child under 12 (mid-May, mid-Sept).

Kantishna Wilderness Trails This privately operated bus tour takes you all the way to the **Kantishna Roadhouse** at the end of the park road (Mile 91). The all-day round trip tour includes lunch at the Roadhouse, panning for gold, and a sled dog demonstration. The buses are painted differently, but are basically the same as other park buses—not terribly comfortable. Children under 5 are not permitted; all children pay full fare.

800/942-7420; www.denaliwildlifetour.com/. Tours start from Denali Bluffs Hotel at 6:30am, McKinley Chalet 6:40am; return to hotels about 8pm. Cost: $115/person, snacks, lunch, park entrance fee included.

The Great Outdoors

Bicycling Cyclists are free to use roads in Denali and to reserve space on the shuttle buses (be sure to mention the bike when you reserve). Some rules apply; pick up a copy of these up at the Visitor Center. You must keep to the roads; riding on trails or in the backcountry is not allowed. **Denali Outdoor Center** (888/303-1925, 907/683-1925; www.denalioutdoorcenter.com; Mile 238.5 Parks Hwy) rents mountain bikes for half-day ($25), full-day ($40), or multiple-day ($37/day) trips. They offer a variety of biking tours as well. Helmets and water bottles are included. Tours include van shuttle.

Hiking Within yards of the Visitor Center are several excellent hikes for families with young kids. You'll find maps for these at the Visitor Center.

The **Horseshoe Lake Loop Trail** (3 miles, allow 1 hour) winds down through taiga forest for 200 feet to a lovely oxbow lake. The forest is spectacular in autumn (mid-August through September), with yellow-leaved aspen and birch, green moss and spruce trees, and crimson-leaved shrubs. The trailhead is across the railroad tracks, a short walk from the Visitor Center. Alaska Railroad trains cross here several times a day. Keep an eye on your small train aficionados who may be more thrilled than you are at the prospect of seeing a train go by just a few feet away. Pick up a trail brochure at the trailhead and make your way down to the lake where you can inspect a beaver lodge and dam.

The **Taiga Trail** (2 miles round trip, allow about an hour) is a pretty walk. In late summer, look for crowberries and blueberries. The trail provides access to the **Rock Creek Trail**, somewhat more strenuous (4 miles round trip, allow about 4 hours) and the **Mount Healy Trail**, which climbs about 1700 feet to a scenic overlook (4.5 miles round trip, 4 hours). If you aren't up for the whole trip, you can hike as far as the benches (2 miles round trip, 1.5 hours).

Guided Hikes The park's Education Program staff lead free hikes in summer designed especially for families with kids age 5 and older. Offered Monday through Friday, these can be a great introduction to park flora and fauna. Check at the Visitor Center for details.

Deeper into the Park Highly recommended for all ages is the **Savage River Loop Trail** (3 miles, 1.5 hours, plus bus or car travel) at Mile 15 of the Park Road. The Savage River shuttle (catch it at the Visitor Center; $2/adults—exact fare only, free/under 15) makes frequent trips out, or you can drive and park at the small lot at the trailhead. The trail winds along the banks of the Savage River, deep into an ever narrowing canyon. It gets very windy here, so be sure to bring hats or scarves.

Park Shuttles The park's green shuttle buses carry visitors on multiple daily trips to Kantishna, with many stops along the way. They'll also drop you off wherever you like and pick you up on the way back when you flag them down, if there's room. No permits are needed if you're just doing a day hike, but it is always a good idea to check in with the Visitor Center first.

Kids 15-17 ride at reduced rates; 15 and under ride free. However, like adults, kids need reservations. Some buses are wheelchair accessible. Expect to pay anywhere from $17-33 for an adult, depending on how far you go. Special deals are available. You'll pay a $6 fee for any cancellations.

Flightseeing The principal flightseeing attraction is, of course, the mountain—but it's often shrouded in clouds. If you are lucky enough to catch the mountain on an "out" day, you might want to splurge on a flight. Several one-hour options are available at Denali. (If you miss out on a flight here, don't despair; a lot of Denali flights also originate in Anchorage.) Try **Denali Air** (907/683-2261; www.denaliair.com), which offers one-hour flights daily at hourly intervals in the summer when the weather cooperates. **Era Aviation** (800/843-1947;www.eraaviation.com), a local airline, has frequent 50-minute flights from Denali, as well as from Talkeetna and Chulitna. For other carriers, see "Talkeetna."

River Rafting It would be a shame to spend time at Denali without getting out on the Nenana River, where you'll see wildlife not visible on park roads. The river makes a great family float trip, especially if you visit in late summer, when the colors are glowing around you. Eagles are often visible from the water. A variety of options exist, many of which involve Class IV and V rapids and are not suitable for young kids. Shorter Nenana float trips are tamer, but still exciting for kids. Outfitters provide all the gear you'll need. Some provide transportation as well. Most outfitters accept children 12 and older; some restrictions apply to younger kids.

Alaska Raft Adventures (800/789-7238, 907/683-7238; www.raft denali.com) has a three-to-four-hour trip that accepts kids 5 and older ($65/adult, $55/child 5-10). They'll help you figure out how to get to their departure point. **Denali Raft Adventures** (888/683-2234, 907/683-2234; www.denaliraft.com) has two-hour and four-hour options suitable for the 5- to 10-year-old set (several daily departures; two hours: $62/adult, $52/child 5-11; four hours: $112/adult, $102/child 5-11). They provide free transportation to and from Denali hotels and the train station. **Denali Outdoor Center** (see "Bicycling") also offers raft outings including a two-hour trip ($60/adult, $30/child 5-10). For families with older kids, they rent inflatable kayaks and offer guided kayaking trips.

Resources

Alaska Natural History Association (ANHA)
750 W 2nd Ave, Ste 100, Anchorage, AK 99501-2167; 907/274-8440; www.alaskanha.org

Denali National Park
PO Box 9, Denali Park, AK 99755; Headquarters: 907/683-2294; www.nps.gov/dena/
Be sure to check out their sled-dog page for kids: www.nps.gov/dena/backup2/ kennels/dogbios/dogpages/doghouse/

Denali State Park
Contact the Denali Ranger at 907/745-3975;
www.dnr.state.ak.us/parks/units/denali1/

Greater Healy/Denali Chamber of Commerce
PO Box 437, Healy, AK 99743; 907/683-4636;
www.denalichamber.com/index/

Sled Dog Central
www.sleddogcentral.com
This kid-friendly site is devoted to sled dogs and mushing and includes many useful links.

Parent Ed

Collier, Michael. *The Geology of Denali National Park.* Alaska Natural History Association, 1989. This short guide explains Denali's landforms and the forces that shaped them.

Forbes, Sheri. *The Nature of Denali: Entrance Area Trail Guide.* Alaska Natural History Association, 1992. If you plan to hike the trails around the park entrance and visitor center, this compact guide will come in handy.

Heacox, Kim. *Denali Road Guide.* Alaska Natural History Association, 1996. This guide, organized by milepost along park roads, helps you make sense of the scenery and wildlife you'll encounter when you travel on a park shuttle bus.

Murie, Adolph. *A Naturalist in Alaska.* University of Arizona Press, 1990. First published in the 1960s, this award-winning book is still the best introduction to the park and its wildlife by a naturalist who devoted most of his career to the park and whose influence is still felt in the way the park is managed today.

Pratt, Verna. *Wildflowers of Denali.* Alaskakrafts, 1993. This short, useful guide is organized by color.

Washburn, Barbara. *Accidental Adventurer.* Epicenter Press, 2001. This fascinating memoir by an otherwise down-to-earth mother of three tells how she came to be the first woman to climb Mount McKinley in 1947.

Waterman, Jonathan. *In the Shadow of Denali: Life and Death in the Shadow of Alaska's Mount McKinley.* Lyons Press, 1998. Essays explore the lure of the mountain and the people who respond to it.

Just for Kids

Corral, Hannah, and Kimberly Corral, Ray Corral. *My Denali: Exploring Alaska's Favorite National Park with Hannah Corral.* Alaska Northwest Books, 1995. This picture book written by a 12-year-old naturalist doesn't whitewash the sometimes brutal world animals live in. Best for kids 10 and up.

Miller, Debbie S. *Disappearing Lake: Nature's Magic in Denali National Park.* Walker, 1999. In this picture book, Miller explores seasonal changes in the

The Road Lottery

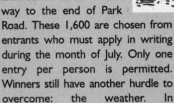

Every September for each of four days, usually the 13th through 16th, 400 lucky winners of the Denali Road lottery are allowed to drive all the way to the end of Park Road. These 1,600 are chosen from entrants who must apply in writing during the month of July. Only one entry per person is permitted. Winners still have another hurdle to overcome: the weather. In September, weather can be spectacular and warm enough for shirt sleeves. Or it might be snowing, in which case the road will be closed. (If so, you're out of luck). You can drive only on the day to which you've been assigned. On average, over 10,000 entrants apply each year, so it's a long shot. Still, if you know you'll be in the area, why not give it a try? Send your entry to Road Lottery, Denali National Park, P.O. Box 9, Denali Park, AK 99755. Good luck! ◼

park through the story of a seasonal lake. A good way to introduce kids to the park's rich ecosystem.

Yanuchi, Lori. *Running with the Big Dogs: A Sled Dog Puppy Grows Up in Denali National Park, Alaska*. Ridge Rock Press, 1998. This great read-aloud picture book introduces kids to Denali sled dogs. A portion of sales supports the Denali National Park sled dog kennel.

Activity Books and Homeschool Curriculum

Denali Adventures: Activities for Young People, Alaska Natural History Association. This includes games and puzzles for the 4-10 year old set.

Palmer, Mary. *Denali Curriculum: Climbing America's Highest Peak*. Paws IV, 1996. This multi-disciplinary curriculum for grades 3-6 centers around the mountain and comes with lessons and worksheets.

Videos

Denali: Alaska's Last Great Wilderness. PBS Home Video, 1997. One of the *Living Edens* series, this one-hour video showcases the park and wildlife in it. Parents of younger kids take note: although most of the video makes good viewing for little ones, it does show a moose calf stalked and killed by wolves.

Winter Patrol: Denali by Dog Sled. Alaska Natural History Association, 1997. This 25-minute video has interesting facts about the raising and training of Denali sled dogs.

10

Fairbanks
and the Interior

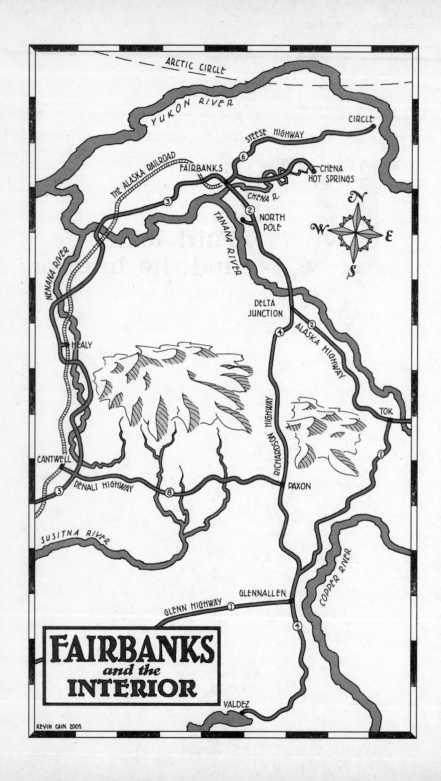

FAIRBANKS
and the
INTERIOR

KEVIN CAIN 2003

10 Fairbanks and the Interior

NOWHERE IN ALASKA will the visitor experience the sheer immensity of the state more spectacularly than in the interior, especially the Tanana Valley. Here, vistas extend from the sweeping heights of the Alaska Range in the south to the White Mountains in the northeast; and in every direction, more peaks loom far off, distant and alluring. Between mountain ranges stretch vast expanses of taiga, flat lands, and boreal forest through which flow Alaska's most important rivers. The mighty Yukon and Tanana rivers, and the sternwheelers that once served the communities along their banks, played a vital role in the history of the interior and they still offer plenty to attract family visitors today.

From Fairbanks, the regional center and home of the University of Alaska, the intrepid motorist can reach an assortment of hot springs resorts, and beyond the Arctic Circle as far as Deadhorse, almost to the Arctic Ocean. Tour operators drive or fly visitors to the Arctic Circle, the Brooks Range, and Prudhoe Bay.

The climate here is more extreme than in southern Alaska. Winter temperatures in Fairbanks can drop to 70F degrees below zero, while on a long summer day they may reach the 80s. Luckily, a dry climate lessens the impact of these extremes. Much of this region is classified as a sub-Arctic desert, averaging fewer than 14 inches of precipitation per year. It's rare for a family outing to be interrupted by an unexpected downpour. A summer visit is likely to yield sunny skies by day and starry heavens by night—what there is of it. Not surprisingly, the region provides some of Alaska's best aurora-viewing. In early spring and mid-to-late September, you can enjoy the celestial light show, but not until well after midnight; Fairbanks averages 20 hours of sunlight a day during June and July. While it's true that only north of the Arctic Circle will you find genuine "midnight sun," in much of the Alaska and Yukon interior, the sun barely dips below the horizon all summer. On the plus side, a gorgeous sunset can last all night. However, if you intend to camp out, give some thought to how children might be affected by the absence of night-time darkness.

For families, a visit to the region might require a little more planning than for other Alaska destinations, but the effort is repaid with some of the state's best recreation and weather. Whether it's hiking, bicycling, berrying, horseback riding, river rafting, and canoeing in summer; or cross-country skiing, mushing, and snowshoeing in winter, Alaska's interior offers something for just about every family.

What to Bring

When packing for the interior of Alaska, remember that winter lows are likely to be colder than any you've experienced, while summer highs can rival those in the U.S. Midwest.

Winter If you're here for a spot of aurora watching in February, expect average low temperatures of -15F degrees, and highs that aren't likely to top 10F degrees. Mitts, hats that cover most of the face, thick socks, and long underwear are all musts. Remember that auroras are visible at night when temperatures are lowest. If you aren't used to a cold climate, pack warmer clothing than you think you'll need, and bring extra mitts, socks, and hats with you in a daypack on outings. Kids always lose these, and here, such losses can be not only a nuisance but an emergency.

Summer If there's one place you're likely to need hot-summer clothing in Alaska, it's Fairbanks. With long hours of daylight, the potential for blistering sunburns arises, so be sure to break out sunscreen and hats or sun visors, and make sure that your kids are well covered outdoors.

Remember that summer nights here are warm and bright. Lightweight sleepwear is recommended. And if your kids (or you) are bothered by light at night, consider packing sleep masks. Although most hotels have blackout curtains, often some light will get through.◙

Getting To Fairbanks and the Interior

The interior is accessible to visitors by air, road, and train.

By Air **Alaska Airlines** (800/252-7522; www.alaskaair.com) flies between Fairbanks and most Alaskan cities, connecting to destinations in Canada and the lower forty-eight. **Air North** (867/668-2228, for Canada: 800/661-0407, for USA: 800/764-0407; www.airnorth.yk.net) connects Fairbanks and Juneau to destinations in the Yukon and Northwest Territories.

By Train Unquestionably, the train is the most relaxing and fun way to approach Fairbanks. The **Alaska Railroad** (800/544-0552, 907/265-2494; www.alaskarailroad.com) offers daily service between Anchorage and Fairbanks, with stops in Wasilla, Talkeetna, and Denali National Park from mid-May through mid-September; trains depart at 8 am. In winter, trains run less frequently. The trip takes 12 hours each way. In summer, most trains consist of cars dedicated to tour companies and cruise lines. However, each train also includes ordinary passenger cars, observation and dining cars, and a gift shop. For a description of the trip from Anchorage to Denali see "Denali." The trip from Denali to Fairbanks takes you through spectacular gorges, with glimpses of the frothy Nenana River (for the best view heading north, sit on the right side of the train). Gradually, as you leave the park behind, the terrain becomes pleasantly forested.

☛ Parent Tip

If you leave Fairbanks by train, stop in at the **Tanana Valley Model Railway Club** (280 N. Cushman St.; www.tvrr.org) next door to the train station. Here, volunteer model-railroading enthusiasts guide visitors around elaborate model layouts from 7-8 am daily. The wait for your full-size train will fly by as your children try to locate the bear eating a salmon, the moose walking through town, and many more vignettes of Alaskan life hidden among the tiny villages along the model-train tracks. ◼

By Road Two major paved highways lead to Fairbanks. The George Parks Highway (Hwy 3), skirting the eastern edge of Denali National Park, connects the city to Anchorage. The drive is 358 miles and takes about eight hours. From Denali, the drive is about three and a half hours. The Richardson Highway (Hwy 4) extends from Valdez through Copper Center up to Delta Junction, where it joins with the Alaska Highway for the last 100 miles into Fairbanks; the trip from Valdez is 364 miles and eight hours. For driving conditions, check with the **Alaska Department of Transportation** Web site (www.dot.state.ak.us/stwdplng/planresc/road_cond/). For the latest weather forecast for the Fairbanks area, call the **Alaska Weather Line**, 907/458-3745. For road conditions and weather by phone, call 800/478-7675 for a recorded message.

Roadside Attractions

Along the George Parks Highway A little more than halfway between Denali and Fairbanks is the historic town of **Nenana**, where the Tanana and Yukon rivers meet. Its location made Nenana an important site, first for native Athabascan hunting and fishing camps and later for Alaska travelers and settlers. By the early 20th century, it was a railroad-construction boom town (U.S. President Warren G. Harding drove in a golden spike here in 1923, marking the completion of the railroad between Seward and Fairbanks). Today, **Nenana** makes a good place to break the journey between Denali and Fairbanks. Stop in first at the log cabin **Nenana Visitor Center** (at the turnoff from the Parks Highway onto A street; 907/832-9953; open Memorial Day-Labor Day), then visit the **Alaska Railroad Museum** (in the historic depot at the end of Main St; open daily, 9am-6pm in summer). Check out the **Alfred Starr Nenana Cultural Center** (415 Riverfront; 907/832-5520; open daily 9am-7pm in summer), stroll through a gift shop or two, and finish with a burger at the **Monderosa Bar & Grill** (Mile 309, Parks Hwy; 907/832-5243). If you want just a snack, the **A Frame Service Station** at Mile 304.5 Parks Hwy sells fast food and groceries, along with gas.

Ten miles before you reach Fairbanks, you'll see the turnoff for **Ester**. If you have time, check out the attractions in this bedroom suburb of Fairbanks. See "Ester Gold Camp" under "Excursions" for details on what's here. While there

The Nenana Ice Classic:

How a Game of Chance Became a Test Case on Global Warming

In 1917, railroad engineers in Nenana were waiting for the ice to break up on the Tanana River so that they could continue work on a railroad bridge. To pass the time, they bet on when the breakup would occur. A total of $800 was collected from participants who guessed the date and time of the ice breakup. The contestant who picked the time closest to actual breakup won the pool. That was the birth of the Nenana Ice Classic, a uniquely Alaskan event that signals the arrival of spring, when the rivers of the interior become navigable. For each of the past 85 years, breakup has occurred between April 20 and May 20, usually between 9am and 9pm; the event now attracts worldwide interest.

Half the annual proceeds go to the town of Nenana and to cover contest expenses; the rest goes into a pool paid to the lucky winners. Today, the pool is more than $300,000 annually. The size of the overall payoff depends on how many entrants participate; how much an individual wins depends on how many correct entries are received. In 2001, winners came from as far away as Wisconsin and Japan.

Not surprisingly, with so much at stake, great care is taken to make sure the time of breakup is recorded accurately. Each February, during a community festival (Tripod Days), a black and white structure, the "tripod," is raised on the frozen Tanana River. The tripod is attached by cable to a clock mechanism in town. When the ice breaks up, the tripod falls, and the motion trips the cable, which stops the clock.

Raphael Sagarin, a Stanford University scientist, realized that the records kept on the Ice Classic might yield interesting results on climate change and global warming. If trends showed the ice breaking up earlier each year, this would suggest that winters were getting shorter. After studying the record, Sagarin reported in the journal Science in 1992, that ice breakup was occurring 5.5 days earlier today than in 1917.

Family Activity Use the information provided on the Ice Classic Web site to predict the next breakup. (Dates and times of breakup for each year are listed on the site, along with median dates and times and other useful information.) Discuss how to make the most accurate prediction. What other factors might influence ice breakup besides global warming? To test your hypothesis, you might want to enter the contest. Each entry costs $2 and must be mailed to: Nenana Ice Classic, Box 272, Nenana, AK 99760.

To learn more about the Nenana Ice Classic, visit the official Web site at www.ptialaska.net. ◾

is a hotel at Ester Gold Camp, it's not a great choice for families. There are campsites and an RV park here.

Along the Richardson Highway You'll notice the ranks of impressive military aircraft visible from the highway as you approach **Eileson Air Force Base**, 20 miles south of Fairbanks. The base offers free, weekly bus tours of the base and some of its aircraft (907/377-3148; www.eilelson.af.mil; 10:30am-noon Fri., Memorial Day-Labor Day). Visitors should arrive at the main gate, on the Richardson Highway, at 10:15 am. Parking is available. Groups of 15 or more can call and arrange customized tours; these need to be set up at least two weeks in advance. Since the events of September 11, 2001, security at the Air Force Base has tightened. Adults should bring photo identification, and call ahead to confirm tours.

About 12 miles before you reach Fairbanks is the town of **North Pole**. The town was built around Santa, as its street names (Santa Claus Lane, St. Nicholas Drive) attest. Now a bedroom suburb of Fairbanks, North Pole is home to **Santa Claus House**, which sells Santa memorabilia, Christmas ornaments, and the like; several of Santa's reindeer hang out here when not on their Christmas rounds. Also, visitors can obtain a customized letter from Santa ($7.50) or purchase a square inch of North Pole real estate (also $7.50). Santa can be spotted year-round, listening to Christmas-present agendas. You'll find many major fast-food chains and other conveniences here. For a local treat, get an ice cream cone at North Pole's branch of **Hot Licks** (see "Places to Eat"), across the parking lot from Santa Claus House. On Fridays in summer, check out the North Pole Farmers Market at the North Pole Plaza parking lot under the red and white canopy (between June 1-Sept. 15, from 3-7 pm; 907/488-2242). The **Santaland RV Park & Campground** (125 Saint Nicholas Dr; 907/488-9123, 888/488-9123; www.santalandrv.com) has the usual amenities and offers shuttle service to Fairbanks tours. The **Visitor Center Log Cabin** (2550 Mistletoe Dr; 907/488-2242; open May-Sept.) can fill you in on Santa-related happenings. Also here is the Chena Lakes Recreation Area (see "Excursions" later in this section) with campsites and a host of recreational options.

FAIRBANKS

Fairbanks is one of many interior communities that owes its existence to the Gold Rush. Beginning as an accidental trading post, it quickly grew into a town when gold was discovered nearby a year later. However, as the gold proved hard to get at (the weather and the permafrost didn't help), the boom didn't last long. But Fairbanks got a new lease on life when first the Alaska Railroad and later the Alaska Highway were built and kept the town humming. Fairbanks and the surrounding suburbs continue to grow steadily, with a population now of nearly 100,000. As the largest city on the continent north of Anchorage, Fairbanks has just about every amenity you're likely to need. The University of Alaska is known for its cutting-edge research in science and technology, and visitors will find this sprawling city full of interesting things to explore. Visiting Pioneer Park, Alaska's only theme park, cruising the scenic Chena River aboard a sternwheeler, or admiring the sandhill cranes in Creamer's Field, families can easily pass several fun-filled days in Fairbanks.

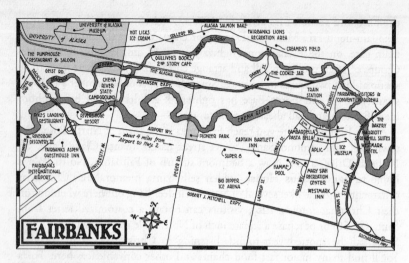

Getting Around

Fairbanks feels a lot bigger than it is—thanks to urban sprawl. Motorists beware: A bewildering network of freeways, more in keeping with a city 10 times the size, surrounds and traverses Fairbanks. Be sure to bring a good map.

Fairbanks does not lend itself to exploration on foot. Many hotels offer free shuttle service to and from the airport and train station. **The Metropolitan Area Commuter System (MACS)** offers limited bus service in Fairbanks and the surrounding area. Bus schedules are available at malls, the Visitor Center, and on the buses. You can also get information over the phone and online (907/459-1011; www.co.fairbanks.ak.us/Transportation. Cost: $1.50/adult, $.75/child K-12, free/under 5 with full-paying companion; $3/day pass). In recent years MACS has been free November through March.

Car Rentals The big names in car rental are well represented in Fairbanks. However, expect rental agreements that forbid driving on many of the more interesting local highways, which tend to be gravel. If you want to explore farther afield, rent from a local player, **Arctic Rent A Car** (907/479-8044, 800/478-8696; www.arcticrentacar.com), which offers good rates and allows driving on roads usually prohibited by other rental agencies. Some conditions apply, and vehicle options and mileage are limited. **Affordable Car Rental** (907/452-7341, 800/471-3101) offers unlimited mileage on all kinds of vehicles, including SUVs, vans, and trucks.

Places to Stay

Forget-Me-Not Lodge and Aurora-Express ☺ ($-$$)
1540 Chena Ridge Rd; 800/221-0073;
www.aurora-express.com
FYI: 10 rooms; some shared baths, kitchen (one unit), two 2-bedroom units; free full breakfast; plug-ins for parking in winter; smoke-free premises; TV or telephone in dining car only

This one-of-a-kind B&B is well worth a stay for just about any family. Perched on a ledge on a hillside above Fairbanks sits the Aurora Express, a complete train on a short length of track. There's an engine, available for exploring (with close parental supervision), a tank car, a Pullman sleeping car (called the National Emblem), two train cars (the National Domain and the Arlene), a caboose, and a dining car. The caboose, the sleeping car, the National Domain car (divided into four suites), and the Arlene (a two-bedroom suite with kitchen) have wildly original décor and many little touches that add charm and comfort. Next door is Forget-Me-Not Lodge, the home of owners Mike and Sue Wilson, with three more rooms. But who wants to stay in a house when there's a train at hand?

Mike and Sue have three kids and welcome families warmly. For families with kids under 12, they recommend the National Emblem or the Arlene. The former sleeps up to seven, with two bathrooms; kids will enjoy sleeping in their own roomettes. Part of the car is a roomy living area. The Arlene, which sleeps up to four, is the best choice for families with very young kids. It's decked out in the cheery blue and yellow of the Alaska Railroad, and there's a toddler-sized bed in a room decorated with Thomas the Tank Engine toys, an engine quilt, and train posters.

A superb, ample and child-friendly breakfast is served in the dining car, where you'll also find the telephone. A wide selection of videos is available for kids and adults. Don't miss the home video that shows how they got the train cars to the B&B.

66 PARENT COMMENTS 99

"We stayed in the Pullman. It was very hot outside, but the car stayed cool with the help of a fan. The kids loved having their own rooms. We noticed these could be locked from inside, which could be an issue for toddlers."

"The breakfast was out of this world. The banana French toast was a big hit with our kids. And they were offered hot chocolate with whipped cream without having to ask."

Captain Bartlett Inn ($-$$)
1411 Airport Way; 907/452-1888, 800/544-7528; 800/478-7900 (in Alaska); www.captainbartlettinn.com
FYI: 197 rooms, connecting rooms, a/c, children under 18 stay free; restaurant; pets OK (fee)
From the minute they step through the swinging doors, kids will be mesmerized by the towering, stuffed brown bear in a glass case that dominates the lobby. The log-cabin ambience, along with the hotel's faded carpet and flowered wallpaper, contribute to the old-Alaska feel of this funky and fun establishment. The rooms are fine, and the Musher's Roadhouse restaurant features good, hearty food in huge portions and a kids' menu with the usual child-pleasing offerings.

❝ PARENT COMMENTS ❞

*"We were put off by the location on Airport Way, which is
pretty dreary, but once inside, we were pleasantly surprised.
Service was friendly and the restaurant served us breakfast
in record time so we could make our train."*

River's Edge Resort ($-$$)
*4200 Boat St; 907/474-0286, 800/770-3343; www.riversedge.net
FYI: 94 cottages; restaurant, room service; free airport/train station shuttle
service; seasonal RV Park (mid-May to mid-Sept); Laundromat, free showers,
tent camping*

This resort has a gorgeous setting on the banks of the Chena River. There are
bike and walking paths to explore and plenty of grounds for small legs to get a
workout.

Chain Hotels

Comfort Inn ☺ ($-$$)
*1908 Chena Landings Loop; 907/479-8080, 800/424-6423;
www.3.choicehotels.com.
FYI: 74 rooms; free continental breakfast; pool, hot tub; Laundromat*

Fairbanks, Aspen /Guesthouse Inns ($$-$$$)
*4580 Old Airport Rd; 888/595-2151; www.aspenhotelsak.com
FYI: 97 rooms, family suites, TV/VCR, refrigerator/microwave; free continental
breakfast; pool, hot tub, exercise room; Laundromat*

Marriott Springhill Suites ($$)
*575 1st Ave; 907/451-6552, 888/287-9400; www.springhillsuites.com
FYI: 140 rooms; free continental breakfast; refrigerator/microwave; pool,
hot tub, sauna, exercise room; Laundromat; free airport shuttle; free parking*

Super 8 ($-$$)
*1909 Airport Rd; 907/451-8888, 800/800-8000; www.super8.com
FYI: 77 rooms; laundry; free airport shuttle, pets OK*

Westmark Fairbanks Hotel and Conference Center ($$-$$$)
*813 Noble St; 907/456-7722, 800/544-0970; www.westmarkhotels.com
FYI: 244 rooms, restaurant, Laundromat, a/c*

Westmark Inn Fairbanks ($$)
*1521 South Cushman; 907/456-6602, 800/544-0970;
www.westmarkhotels.com
FYI: 170 rooms, closed Sept-May; restaurant, Laundromat, a/c, free parking*

Camping

See Santaland RV Park and Chena Lakes Recreation Area earlier in this section, and Chena River State Recreation Site later in this section.

Places to Eat

Alaska Salmon Bake (Pioneer Park) ☺

3175 College Rd; 907/452-7274, 800/354-7274; www.akvisit.com
Hours: daily 5-9pm, mid-May-mid-Sept

This outdoor restaurant consistently appears on lists of Alaska's best salmon bakes. It offers a kids' menu with hot dogs as well as smaller portions from the adult menu (which offers salmon, ribs, halibut, steak dinners with all-you-can-eat salad bar, dessert, and non-alcoholic beverages; alcohol is extra). Dessert is, of course, the ubiquitous blueberry cake. There's a fixed price for all meals. Combine dinner here with a trip to Pioneer Park and the Palace Theatre and Saloon. Bus service is provided between here and many local hotels and campgrounds between 4:30 and 9:15 p.m. Somewhat perplexingly, the salmon-bake area is surrounded with old mining artifacts—chalk it all up to the eclectic theme-park experience.

The Bakery Restaurant

69 College Rd; 907/456-8600
Hours: Mon-Sat 6am-9pm; Sun 7am-4pm

You could easily miss this excellent old-style family restaurant tucked away among the giant superstores in mallsville. It's worth making an effort to track down. Here, you'll find a wide assortment of breakfast options, as well as salads, soups, deli sandwiches, and burgers. Prices are among the lowest in Fairbanks, and portions are large. The kids' menu features the usual. Some heartier fare is offered, including steak and seafood. There are even a few Chinese options. All menu items are served all day. Take out is available at a charge of 25 cents per order.

The Cookie Jar ☺

1006 Cadillac Court; 907/479-8319
Hours: Mon-Sat 6:30am-9:30pm; Sun 8am-7pm

Don't let the name mislead you: This is a great bet for full meals. Located close to Creamer's Field, this busy, nonsmoking restaurant makes a good lunch stop. The kids' menu features items such as corn-dog nuggets and pepperoni pizza on French bread. Baked goods are superb, as are salads, soups and pastas. Prices are reasonable, and service is excellent. Take out is available.

Gambardella's Pasta Bella

706 2nd Ave; 907/456-3417
Hours: Mon-Thurs 11am-9pm; Fri-Sat 11am-10pm; Sun 4-9pm; open to 10pm nightly in summer

Here is where locals head for fine dining. The bistro occupies several attractive rooms in an older downtown building. In summer, you can also dine outside on the fenced patio facing the Chena River. The menu features traditional Italian dishes and nontraditional desserts (try the Snickers pie). Pizza is offered, and there is a kids' menu.

Hot Licks Homemade Ice Cream
3453 College Rd; 907/479-7813; www.hotlicks.net
Hours: daily noon-9pm, April-Sept (may be open later in summer; call for details); closed rest of year
Hot Licks is located adjacent to Gulliver's Books, not far from the University on College Road. Stop in at this popular kiosk for an ice cream or shave ice, and sample homegrown flavors like Alaska blueberry, Aurora Borealis (Alaska cranberries and blueberries swirled in vanilla ice cream), or Prudhoe (industrial-strength chocolate), served in a variety of cone options. Benches are provided for seating. Soda fountain drinks are on offer, and with 24-hours notice, you can order an ice cream cake. Kid-size cones are a deal.

Pike's Landing Restaurant & Lounge
4438 Airport Way; 907/479-7113
Hours: Daily, 11am-10pm
The dining room has a kids' menu, but rambunctious youngsters and their parents will feel more comfortable on the Patio, where burgers and lots of other kid-friendly fare is available. This has a great waterside location. Sunday brunch is served.

The Pump House Restaurant and Saloon ☺
1.3 Mile Chena Pump Rd; 907/479-8452; pumphse@ptialaska.net; www.pumphouse.com
Hours: Mon-Sat 11am-2pm, 5pm-10 pm; Sun 10am-2pm (summer); Mon-Fri 4pm-1am; Sat noon-1am; Sun 10am-2pm (rest of year)
This riverside restaurant was once a pump house for gold and is now a National Historic monument with its own dock. Diners can arrange to be dropped off by the *Discovery III.* The Chena River Shuttle also stops here.

Set in sweeping, landscaped grounds, there's a large dining room furnished with sturdy Klondike-era antiques. Kids may be happier dining in the glass atrium, open at the river end, from which they can watch the river traffic pass by. This is a good place for parents to sample offerings from Alaska's fine microbreweries. It can be noisy and chaotic, and it's not cheap. But food is good and plentiful, there's a kids' menu, and if the kids get squirmy, just take them for a stroll outside.

Second Story Café
In Gulliver's Books; 3525 College Rd; 907/474-9574
Hours: Mon-Fri 9am-9pm; Sat 9am-8pm; Sun 11am-6pm
It's easy to find yourself spending longer than you'd planned in Gulliver's (see "What to See & Do"). This charming café makes a good stop for a quick meal or a snack. A variety of bagels, wraps, and sandwiches are offered, along with soups, salads, and a welcome assortment of espresso drinks and smoothies. Prices are low.

What to See & Do

Stroll & Browse

Fairbanks lacks much of a downtown core suitable for strolling or browsing through. But there are a few places where you can get a feel for the character of the town. The Chena River Walk follows the river as it winds through downtown. In summer, you can stop at Gambardella's for a meal in their outdoor patio.

Close to the University of Alaska, you'll find a small cluster of interesting shops along College Road that include **Gulliver's Books** (3525 College Rd; 907/474-9574, 800/390-8999;www.gullivers-books.com), Fairbanks' premier bookstore. If you're hungry, check out the Second Story Café on the second floor, or pick up ice cream or an espresso drink at Hot Licks a little farther down College Road (see "Places to Eat"). You can also step into **The Magic Carpet** (3535 College Rd; 907/2323; www.themagiccarpet.net) for gifts and clothing from far-away places.

Pioneer Park ☺ This funky theme park/open air museum feels like a cultural attic. Formerly known as Alaskaland, its name was changed to Pioneer Park in 2002. All kinds of interesting odds and ends of Alaskan history have been deposited here. Built in 1967 to mark the 100th anniversary of Alaska's purchase from Russia, the park occupies 44 acres of central Fairbanks. Over the years, new features have been added and the park is now an important cultural resource for the city.

On first wandering in, you may feel bemused at a seemingly random assortment of attractions and architectural styles. Persevere and you'll be rewarded with a unique, enjoyable, and family-oriented experience. There's a tiny **Native Village,** suitable for exploration by very small anthropologists, and **Gold Rush Town**, a somewhat hokey reconstructed frontier town in which souvenir shops and candy are interspersed with nuggets of pioneer history in historic buildings. You'll find several museums here, too, along with miniature golf, an antique carousel, a dance hall, and a civic center. A narrow-gauge train, the **Crooked Creek and Whiskey Island Railroad,** chugs around the perimeter during the summer (daily, 11am-9pm, closed for dinner from 4-5pm. Cost: $2/adult, $1/child 12 and under, free/under 4).

Kids will enjoy peering into the restored **Harding Car**, on the National Historic Register, from which President Warren G. Harding saw the wonders of the Alaskan landscape on his 1923 visit. Harding was in Alaska to drive in the golden spike in Nenana, marking the completion of the Alaska Railroad.

The pièce de résistance is the *SS Nenana*, a historically significant stern-wheeler that once served communities along the Yukon and Tanana rivers. The lovely boat, designated a National Historic Landmark, is open to visitors ($5 suggested donation). Inside, you'll find extensive fascinating dioramas depicting the riverside towns and gold mines that once depended on the *Nenana* for survival. Visit the pilothouse and check out the tiny cabins. Restoration is ongoing.

When hunger calls, head to the Alaska Salmon Bake for supper (see "Places to Eat"). Or, if you can think this far ahead, bring a box lunch from the Cookie

Aurora Watching
by Brooke Whipple

There's no denying the magic of seeing the aurora dance overhead for the first time. Even for seasoned Alaskans, the magic endures. From low white curtains of light draping the sky to pulsating ribbons of arching color, the aurora is a spectacular sight. Visitors and locals alike are treated to auroral displays as early as late August, just as soon as the nights become dark enough to see it. This is an ideal time of year for those wanting to see the aurora while experiencing the milder temperatures of autumn. Good aurora viewing continues through the winter until late March.

For families wanting to experience this jewel of Alaska, some planning is required. Care must be taken to ensure that everyone is properly outfitted for such an adventure. Winter nights in Alaska can be bitterly cold.

Warm hats, mittens, coats, winter pants, boots, and face masks are a necessity. Another nice amenity is disposable hand warmers that are activated with a few quick shakes. These can be tucked into mittens and boots for extra warmth. Aside from proper outerwear, dressing in layers and limiting prolonged exposure to the cold are the best bets for enjoyable aurora viewing. Although daily forecasts for aurora displays are made by the Geophysical Institute at the University of Alaska Fairbanks (www.pfrr.alaska.edu), it is still a natural phenomenon and subject to the whims of Mother Nature. The best auroras are commonly viewed between midnight and 3am, but can occur at any time before or after this. The combination of cold, clear nights, patience, and luck all play a

Jar (see "Places to Eat") and dine al fresco. There are plenty of picnic tables, restrooms, a sturdy playground, and grassy spaces for running. The salmon bake and some picnic tables have covered seating.

Pioneer Park is open year round, but most attractions close between Labor Day and mid-May.

2300 Airport Way (at Peger Rd); 907/459-1087;
www.co.fairbanks.ak.us/Parks&Rec/Alaskaland/. Open daily, 11am-9pm. Free.

Palace Theatre and Saloon (Pioneer Park)   The "Golden Heart Revue" tells the history of Fairbanks with song and dance. Such shows are a feature of Alaska and Yukon communities that aim to conjure up the 'olden days.' This one is short and lively enough to fit a child's attention span.

907/452-7274, 800/354-7274; www.akvisit.com. Open mid-May to mid-Sept; shows daily, 8:15pm (sometimes a 6:30pm show is added in summer).
Cost: $14/adult, $7/child.

Tanana Valley Farmers Market   Visitors unaware of Alaska's extraordinarily intense growing season will be astonished at the variety and, especially, the size of the produce available here. You'll also find baked treats and a selection of crafts. Most of the offerings come from local artists. If you're looking for gifts, this is a great bet. Prices compare favorably to those charged in area craft shops.

factor in successful aurora viewing.

Chena Hot Springs Resort caters to winter travelers in search of a northern lights-viewing vacation. Family winter activities at the resort include dog sledding, cross-country skiing, snowmobiling, and sleigh rides. For aurora viewing, the resort offers a heated, glass-front cabin on a hill above the lodge for use at no charge; or for a modest fee, take a snow coach to the top of a nearby mountain for 360 degree vistas of the afternoon sunset and midnight aurora. At the top, enjoy hot cocoa or tea in a heated Yurt while waiting for the skies to dance. The resort rents arctic gear in adult sizes S, M, L, and XL. This includes parkas, pants and Alaska's famous bunny boots. Good luck and happy aurora hunting!

Resources

Akasofu, S.I. *Aurora Borealis: The Amazing Northern Lights.* Alaska Geographic reprint, 1994. A straightforward guide to the aurora with gorgeous photos.

Davis, Neil. *The Aurora Watcher's Handbook.* University of Alaska Press, 1992. A basic guide to the aurora with pictures and glossary.

Falck-Ytter, H. *The Aurora: The Northern Lights in Mythology, History, and Science.* Anthroposophic Press, 1985.

Savage, Candace. *Aurora: The Mysterious Northern Lights.* Sierra Club Books, 1994

Walsh Shepherd, Donna. *Auroras: Light shows in the Night Sky.* Franklin Watts, 1995

Videos

Aurora: Rivers of Light in the Sky. Sky River Films (30 minutes; available from the Alaska Natural History Association; 605 West Fourth Ave., Suite 105, Anchorage, AK 99501; 907/271-3290; www.alaskanha.org)

For Kids

Dwyer, Mindy. *Aurora: A Tale of the Northern Lights.* Alaska Northwest Books, 1997.▣

College Rd & Aurora; 907/456-3276; www.tvfmarket.com. Open Wed-Sat, mid-May-Sept. Call for hours.

University of Alaska Guided Walking Tour   Perched atop a ridge, the University of Alaska offers the best views in Fairbanks. The breathtaking panorama extends across rolling taiga and boreal forest to distant mountains, and Mount McKinley is sometimes visible. The campus includes several lakes and extensive ski trails. In the summer, two-hour, student-led guided walking tours of the campus are offered. If you have time, consider packing a picnic lunch and spending the day here. Tours start at the University of Alaska Museum. You can also pick up a map at the museum and head off on your own. *907/474-7581; Mon-Fri 10am, June 1-Aug 31.*

Arctic Region Supercomputing Center (ARSC)   Computer enthusiasts young and old will enjoy a tour of this facility located on the University of Alaska campus. Visitors are shown a video production lab, experience a virtual-reality demo, and get an up-close-and-personal look at how ARSC uses the latest in supercomputing technology to study the Arctic environment. *Butrovich Bldg on Yukon Dr; 907/474-6935; www.arsc.edu. Weekly tours June-Aug. Call for details.*

Geophysical Institute   Here, scientists research earthquakes, tsunamis, volcanoes, the aurora borealis, climate, space physics, and many other subjects. The Geophysical Institute Web site offers links to the Alaska Volcano Observatory, aurora forecasts, and pages that record recent volcanic and earthquake activity. Children may enjoy checking out this site before visiting in person.

Tours are offered in summer, and details are posted on the Web site shortly before the season's tours begin. Check the Web site or call for details. *C.T. Elvey Bldg, 903 Koyukuk Dr; 907/474-7558; www.gi.alaska.edu. Weekly tours.*

Georgeson Botanical Garden Tour (U of A)   Here, in the Western Hemisphere's northernmost botanical garden, even verdure-loathing youngsters will be wide eyed at the sight of truly enormous cabbages and squash. Native plants, herbs, wildflowers, and much more are on display in the garden's five acres; a nature trail introduces visitors to plants common to the boreal forest.

Signs that Fairbanks kids have had a hand in the garden are everywhere, from creative mosaic paving stones to special planting beds. There's an excellent gift shop, well stocked with garden-themed gifts, soaps, lotions, botanicals, seeds, jewelry, and books. During the summer, two-hour classes for kids are offered on subjects ranging from kitchen chemistry to earthworms. Call for details. *Agricultural and Forestry Experiment Station; 907/474-5651. Open for self-guided viewing 7 am-8pm, May-Sept.; guided tours by reservation only, June 1-Sept. 1, Fridays at 2 pm (except holidays). Cost: free/self-guided, $1 donation requested. Guided tours: $2, (All tours $25 minimum).*

International Arctic Research Center Tour (U of A)   The International Arctic Research Center (IARC) studies global climate change and other scientific issues in the context of the arctic environment, in cooperation with other countries. Tours are offered during summer months and information is posted on the Web site shortly before the season tours begin. Young visitors will have fun exploring the interactive CD-ROM *Aurora Alive* (907/474-2722; www.aurora alive.com) developed by the center and the Geophysical Institute; with it, they can learn about auroras and even develop their own aurora creation myth. *930 Koyukuk Dr 907/474-7413; e-mail: info@iarc.uaf.edu; www.iarc.uaf.edu/welcome_syun/. Summer tours. Check Web site, call, or e-mail for details.*

Museums

Dog Mushing Museum   This museum bills itself as "the most comprehensive dog-mushing exhibit in the world." Sleds, mushing gear and garb, and memorabilia are featured. Visitors can view mushing videos in the theater. There's also a gift shop. *250 Cushman St, Courthouse Square; 907/456-6874. Open Wed-Sun, 10am-4pm (May); daily, 9am-6pm (June-Labor Day); call for hours. Cost: $2.*

Ice Museum   Here you can check out videos of past winners of the World Ice Art Championships (see "Calendar"). Along with photos of past entries, there is a display of current ice sculptures.

Lacey Street Theater, 500 2nd Ave (at Lacey St); 907-451-8222. Open daily, 10am-9pm, May 28-Sept 15. Cost: $9/adult, $8/senior, $5/child 6-12, free/under 6.

Pioneer Air Museum   Owned and operated by the Interior and Arctic Alaska Aeronautical Foundation (IAAAF) which works to preserve Alaska's unique aviation history, Pioneer Air Museum contains 16 vintage aircraft, memorabilia, and displays on Alaskan aviation and aviators—all housed in a golden dome.

In Pioneer Park/Alaskaland; 907/452-2969, 907/451-0037. Open daily, Memorial Day-Labor Day, 11am-9pm. Cost: $2/adult, $5/family.

Pioneer Hall   This museum showcases memorabilia of early Fairbanks, including paintings, and offers a taped narrative of Alaska history, "The Big Stampede Show," five times a day during the summer.

In Pioneer Park/Alaskaland. 907/456-8579. Open daily, Memorial Day-Labor Day, 11am-9pm.

University of Alaska Museum ☺   This extraordinary museum is densely packed with fascinating exhibits, yet manages to feel spacious. A vastly expanded museum will open in 2005, complete with café and learning center. There is a lot more here than first meets the eye; small though it is, allow at least two hours for a visit.

Highlights include Blue Babe, an amazingly well preserved, mummified bison about 36,000 years old, many examples of Alaskan wildlife, and enormous gold nuggets. Exhibits include interesting videos. Curators give frequent talks on Alaska's natural history and cultures. There's a large collection of Native Alaskan children's toys, many in drawers at a small child's height, that can be pulled out . Leave time to explore the ample gift shop and bookstore. Prices can be fairly high, so shop carefully.

907 Yukon Dr; 907/474-7505. Open 9am-5pm, Mon-Fri; noon-5pm, weekends (Sept 16-May 14); daily 9am-7pm, daily (May 15-Sept 15); closed Thanksgiving, Christmas, and New Year's Day. Cost: $5/adult; $4.50/senior, 60 and over; $3/youth, 7-17; free/6 and under; $8/group, eight or more; $2/youth group, eight or more. $50/family annual pass. Free parking across the street from the museum.

Kid Culture

The Fairbanks Light Opera Theater *(PO Box 72787, Fairbanks, AK 99707; 907/456-3568; www.flot.org) offers "FLOT, Jr.," a weeklong theater workshop for kids ages 7-12 in June.* The **Fairbanks Drama Association & Children's Theatre** *(PO Box 73610, Fairbanks, AK 99707; 907/451-4378)* provides children's theater classes for a variety of age groups, some in conjunction with FLOT. Subjects include improvisation, storytelling, and musical theater. Students range from 4 to 18 and classes are offered in two two-week sessions. Call for details. Check with the **Fairbanks Arts Association** (907/456-6485) for current kid-oriented culture events.

Alaska Native Dolls

For children, a highlight of a visit to the University of Alaska Museum in Fairbanks and the Sheldon Jackson Museum in Sitka is the chance to view their extensive collections of dolls and human figurines.

Dolls have played an important part in Eskimo cultures since at least 100 BC, and the tradition continues. The dolls you'll see in these museums are extraordinary delicate and exact human replicas. Hunters sport tiny bows and arrows; mothers carry infants on their backs. Whalers sit in tiny kayaks, in perfectly made parkas trimmed with real fur.

Eskimo dolls were highly functional. Role-playing with dolls taught children important life skills: how to care for a baby, how to make a spear, how to hunt. In making clothing for a doll, a child learned how to sew. Children, isolated from the larger community beyond the family during cold dark winters, could interact with their dolls, maintaining social skills. Adults applied dolls to different purposes. Shamans used them in healing and religious ceremonies. These were often carved from ivory, wood, or whale baleen.

With European contact, doll-making craft and the use of dolls changed. They were made for and sold to collectors. In recent years, interest in the authentic art of Alaska Native dolls has prompted a reevaluation of the role dolls have played in Native Alaskan cultures and a respect for the rich traditions they represent.

For More Information
Jones, Suzi, ed. *Eskimo Dolls.* University of Washington Press, 1995.

Lee, Molly, C. ed. *Not Just a Pretty Face: Dolls and Human Figurines in Alaska Native Cultures.* University of Alaska Museum, 1999. ▣

Parks

Chena River State Recreation Site   Don't confuse this 29-acre city park with the Chena River State Recreation Area, a huge state park 30 miles northeast of Fairbanks. This city park has trails, riverside picnic facilities, restrooms, and boat launch facilities, along with 60 vehicle campsites and five walk-in sites. Campers can stay here for a maximum of five consecutive nights June 10-Aug 10 and for 15 consecutive nights the rest of the season.
South bank of the Chena River. University Ave, north of Airport Way. Check with the Public Lands Information Center in Fairbanks for fee information at 250 Cushman St; 907/456-0527, www.dnr.state.ak.us/parks/units/chena/.

Fairbanks Lions Recreation Area (Noyes Slough)   Across College Road from Creamer's Field (see "Animals, Animals"), this site has a playground, sheltered picnic area, restrooms, and boat launch.
College Rd & Danby St.

See also "Chena Lakes Recreation Area" and "Chena River State Recreation Area" later in this section.

The **Fairbanks North Star Borough Department of Parks & Recreation** lists and briefly describes its parks on its Web site: www.co.fairbanks. ak.us/Parks&Rec/guide/. For information, call 907/459-1070.

Animals, Animals

Creamer's Field Migratory Waterfowl Refuge / Alaska Bird Observatory ☺ This bird sanctuary is located at the site of Creamer's Dairy, opened at the turn of the century and interior Alaska's largest and most successful dairy farm until it closed in 1966. (The farm buildings and machinery are intact and well preserved; plans are underway to open them to the public.) During the farm's years in operation, birds dropped by on their migratory routes in increasing numbers, while others settled in for the summer or remained year round. Today, visitors can expect to see geese, ducks, songbirds, owls, and other wildlife. Especially impressive are the sandhill cranes, which often hang around all summer. You'll find high-powered binoculars set up on tripods here and there to facilitate viewing. The cranes often pose in elegant groups around the ponds. The setting includes rolling fields interspersed with birch and aspen boreal forest. The Alaska Bird Observatory has a viewing area near the visitor parking lot.

Stop at the Visitor Center first to check out the wildlife displays and be introduced to the animals who make Creamer's Field their permanent or seasonal home; staff are available to answer questions and give directions. There's also a small gift shop and restrooms.

Three popular nature trails here are easily navigated by small visitors. The two-mile Boreal Trail leads through forest and wetlands, and includes a small observation tower; pick up a trail guide in the Visitor Center. The shorter Wetland Trail, wheelchair-accessible during snow-free months, leads visitors along the margin of a seasonal pond. The Farm Road Trail takes visitors along the open fields. Be aware that in July and August, the mosquitoes party non-stop on the Boreal Trail.

Friends of Creamer's Field offer various family programs year round, from guided nature hikes to educational programs. In summer, a day camp is offered for kids 4-14.

1300 College Rd. Visitor Center open Tue-Fri, 10am-5pm; Sat, 10am-3pm (summer); Sat, 10am-4pm (winter), 907/459-7307. Free. For Alaska Bird Observatory programs call 907/451-7059; www.alaskabird.org. For naturalist-led walks and other programs, call Friends of Creamer's Field: 907/452-5162; www.creamersfield.org.

Large Animal Research Station (LARS) This popular attraction at the University of Alaska offers public tours introducing visitors to resident reindeer, caribou, and musk oxen. Concerns about possible transmission of foot-and-mouth disease have led to some restrictions. Visitors who have been out of North America recently are asked to wait at least five days after their return before visiting; concerns about possible outbreaks could lead to tours being cancelled, so call before you come. Displays offer information about what you're seeing.

Picking Berries

From rain-soaked southeast Alaska to the windswept Aleutian Islands, from the Kenai Peninsula to the vast interior, a northern summer means berries. Perhaps it's because the growing season is so short and local fresh fruit is never taken for granted that Alaskans adore berries.

Visiting families can join in the fun, too. Berry picking is permitted and encouraged just about everywhere. Visitor center and tourist information offices often have handouts on where and when to pick berries, with illustrated guides to help identify them. Some varieties will be familiar: Blackberries and red huckleberries are abundant in the panhandle; raspberries and many strains of blueberries grow over much of Alaska and the Yukon. Tiny, delicious wild strawberries are found in the southeast, the Aleutians, and interior (west Yukon and east Alaska). But don't limit yourself just to familiar varieties. Look for cloudberries in midsummer, crowberries in late August, and low-bush cranberries in September.

Be sure to take a good field guide. A few kinds of berries are highly toxic; eating just a few baneberries could kill a small child. Make sure the kids know to check with you before eating. Another point to keep in mind: Bears love berries at least as much as humans do. Be alert and keep small kids and pets close by.

Books

Bowen, Asta. *The Huckleberry Book*. American Geographic Publishing, 1988. The history of huckleberries and their use with folklore and recipes.

Pratt, Verna E. *Alaska's Wild Berries*. Alaskakrafts, 1995. Excellent, compact field guide with photos; including poisonous berries. ▣

Binoculars are a must. Tours last about an hour. The gift shop sells interesting items including musk-ox wool clothing items and caribou and musk ox jewelry. *Take Farmers Loop to Ballaine Rd; turn left on Yankovich Rd; farm is one mile up on the right; 907/474-7581; www.uaf.edu/UAF/visitors.html. Tours June-Aug, Tues, Thurs, Sat, 11am and 1:30pm; Sept, Sat 1:30pm. Cost: $5/adult, $4/senior, $2/student, free/under 7. Platform viewing year round.*

Active Fun

Bicycling, Hiking, and Cross-Country Skiing   Like many Alaska communities, Fairbanks is a great place for biking; pick up a bicycle map at the Visitor Center. The **Chena River Walk** is a popular destination for strolling and bicycling.

Birch Hill Recreation Area   Here you'll find several miles of trails for hiking in summer and cross-country skiing in winter (trails in winter are lighted at night). There is a display map at the entrance, along with restroom and picnicking facilities. This is a good spot for berrying in late summer. *2.8 miles north of Fairbanks, off Steese Expwy. Follow signs from turnoff for 2.3 miles.*

Skarland Trails (U of A) This network of interconnected trails on the west ridge of the University of Alaska campus can be hiked and biked in summer and skied in winter. There are camping and picnic facilities available. *University of Alaska campus.*

You can rent a variety of outdoor gear including bicycles, canoes, and camping equipment by the day or week from **Para Tours** (907/479-PARA (7272), 866/236-7272; www.paratours.net). They also offer a host of tours throughout the state.

Canoeing For family group outings, try **CanoeAlaska** (907/883-BOAT; www.canoealaska.net), which leads guided canoe trips and accepts children (for family groups, there must be at least one adult per young child). A variety of trips are offered and trips can be customized. They also offer canoeing workshops and clinics (must be 10 or older; call for details).

Mushing Mushing enthusiasts can check out **Alaskan Tails Of The Trail with Mary Shields** (907/455-6469; www.maryshields.com). The first woman to finish the Iditarod, Mary Shields also competed in the Yukon Quest. Tails Of The Trail offers tours in summer for adults and children over 8 ($25/adults, $20/children under 12).

Sun Dog Express (907/479-6983; www.mosquitonet.com/~sleddog/) offers a selection of mushing tours from 5 to 90 minutes in length. Teams of sled dogs take you over typical sledding terrain—over tundra and permafrost, through forests, and among the wildlife. It's essential to dress appropriately. That means insulated boots with at least two pairs of socks, warm mittens and hats; dressing in layers is a must. Facial protection may be necessary. Check the Web site or call for suggestions. Kids 3 and over are welcome (if under 12, they must be accompanied by an adult). Prices vary from $10/person for short group tours to $100/adult, $50/child for 90-minute tours. There is also a half-day mushing school ($250/person). Their motto is "If there's enough snow, we go." No snow? In summer, demos and dog-cart rides are offered to give you a taste of mushing ($25/person).

Several Web sites offer abundant mushing information and educational links. Try www.dogsled.com and www.sleddogcentral.com.

Ice-Skating The large Big Dipper Ice Arena features one indoor and three outdoor ice rinks. *1920 Lathrop St; 907/459-1076.*

Racket Sports You'll find court sports included among the attractions at **Pioneer Park** (2300 Airport Way (at Peger Rd); 907/459-1087; www.co.fairbanks.ak.us/Parks&Rec/Alaskaland/. Open daily, 11am-9pm. Free). The **Mary Siah Recreation Center** has tennis courts and volleyball courts. See also "Swimming." (1025-14th Ave; 907/459-1081; call for hours.)

Spectator Sports The Alaska **Goldpanners** are the pride of Fairbanks. Games, including the famous Midnight Sun game (see "Calendar"), are held at Growden Memorial Park. *Near the intersection of Wilbur & Airport Rd.; 907/451-0095; goldpanners.com.*

Swimming   Fairbanks has several community centers with public pools. Those operated by Parks & Recreation all charge the same fees. However, schedules vary for each. Call for open swim times.

Open daily; closed major holidays. Hours vary; call for details. Cost: $3.50/adult (18-59), $1/senior, $2.50/ages 12-17, $2/4-11, free under 3; $8/family. Showers are $2.

At the **Mary Siah Recreation Center** (1025-14th Ave; 907/459-1081) you'll find a large indoor pool, sauna and Jacuzzi, and a weight room for users age 14 and over; various classes are offered. The **Robert Hamme Pool** (901 Airport Way; 907/459-1086) and **Wescott Pool** (8th St, North Pole; 907/488-9402) are also open to the public.

Excursions

Riverboat Discovery III ☺   If there is a "must-do" tourist activity in Fairbanks, this is it. *Discovery III* is the third in a highly successful line of sternwheeler sightseeing boats operated by the Binkley family, longtime Fairbanks residents. The first, *Discovery I,* was launched by Jim and Mary Binkley in 1950. Today, their grandchildren carry on this tradition on the well-appointed *Discovery III.* The 3.5-hour round-trip sailings offer a variety of sights and photo ops, and introduce you to a wide range of things typically Alaskan. The boat is huge. For the best kid-friendly view, sit on the left side on the trip out. Ample inside and outside seating is provided. Interesting sights abound on both sides of the boat; monitors mounted on both sides of the boat display passing sights. (However, if it's very sunny, it can be hard to make out what's on the screen unless you sit inside.)

Children will appreciate the free drinks and terrific homemade donuts. The boat is well equipped with restrooms, and there is a gift shop, plus two snack bars that offer hot dogs, reindeer sausage, and a selection of child-friendly snacks.

While the commentary and activities are scripted and slick, the tour is fascinating. You'll learn a lot about Fairbanks, its residents past and present, famous visitors, and the cultural and natural landscape. From the unusual sight of the meeting of the waters (where the Chena and Tanana rivers come together) to the visit to a fully re-created Athabascan village, you'll definitely get your money's worth. Other interesting stops include a fish wheel and a salmon-skinning demonstration.

For most kids, the highlight is a trip past the Trail Breaker Kennel, owned by Susan Butcher, four-time winner of the Iditarod, and her husband, David Monson, a past winner of the Yukon Quest. While the boat hovers offshore, passengers are treated to the sight of sled dogs in training. Note the dog merry-go-round and other fun features of sled-dog life. One of the kennel staff (often Susan Butcher herself) introduces various dogs, discusses their care and feeding, and shares mushing anecdotes. Passengers are encouraged to ask questions.

Although the boat is large, it's worth booking early in summer. Large tour companies and cruise lines book many of their passengers on the riverboat, so space can quickly fill up. Before and after the trip, you'll be encouraged to visit the enormous dockside gift shop, also part of the enterprise.

1975 Discovery Dr; 907/479-6673, 866/479-6673; reservations@ riverboatdiscovery.com. Sailings daily, 8:45am, 2pm, mid-May–mid-Sept. Cost: $39.95/adult, $29.95/child (3-12), free/under 3. Reservations required.

Chena Lakes Recreation Area   This park, 15 miles southeast of Fairbanks, exists thanks to the U.S. Army Corps of Engineers who built it in the late 1960s following a disastrous Chena River flood that submerged much of Fairbanks. Engineers built a dam and levee, and created several lakes to control river flooding. Today, the area and lakes, complete with sandy beaches, are popular spots for swimming, boating, picnicking, and hiking on 12 miles of groomed trails in summer and cross-country skiing and mushing in winter. There are two boat ramps, and boats and canoes can be rented. A volleyball court, RV parking, and 82 campsites for vehicles and tents round out the amenities.

The lakes are worth a look even if you don't have time to do more than marvel at the extraordinary engineering feat building them entailed. Pay the modest day-use fee, drive to the end of the road, park and climb the gravel embankment that overlooks the miles of levees into which water from the river can be diverted to avoid flooding.

In North Pole. From the Richardson Hwy, turn east on Laurence Rd. Drive 3.5 miles, then turn left at the Lake Park sign. Open year round. Day use fee: $3; campsite fee: $10.

Ester Gold Camp   About a century ago this was a thriving city full of placer miners and goldpanners. When the pickings became slimmer, gold dredges replaced them, and gold mining continued until the 1950s. When gold became scarce, the camp became a tourist attraction. Listed on the National Register of Historic Places, Ester Gold Camp is a perennially popular attraction. Wander around the historic buildings, including a blacksmith shop that now houses the gift store. The dining hall buffet dinner includes hearty, child-friendly fare (open daily, 5-9pm). Afterwards, take in a show at the **Malamute Saloon** (shows daily at 9pm, May–Sept., additional shows 7pm, July only. Cost: $14/adult; $7/child, 3-12; free/under 3) where you'll get your fill of Robert Service-related song and dance.

Also at Ester Gold Camp is the **Northern Lights PhotoSymphony** (open Memorial Day–Labor Day, $8/adult, $4/kid 3-12, free/under 3), a big-screen slide show housed in the Firehouse Theater and showcasing auroral displays. Probably not the best choice for small children, its 45-minute shows give you a taste of auroral splendor. The 45-minute show runs nightly at 6:45 and 7:45pm. In July, a 6pm show is added Wednesday through Saturday.

In Ester. Turn left at MP 351 on the Parks Hwy; follow the Old Nenana Hwy for .5 mile; 907/452-7274, 800/354-7274; www.akvisit.com/ester. Open May–Sept.

The small community of **Fox**, with a population of about 300, lies a few miles northeast of Fairbanks. Here or nearby, you'll find several popular attractions.

Gold Dredge No. 8   For those who, when they hear the phrase "gold mining," picture a prospector leading a donkey laden with pans, this huge dredge will come as something of a surprise. At 250 feet long and five stories high, this is one big machine. The only dredge open to the public in Alaska, this one was responsible for millions of ounces of gold mined from Goldstream and Engineer Creeks between 1928 and 1959. Holland America bought this National Historic Site and renovated it in the late 1990s, adding other genuine artifacts of mining and mining-camp life. Prehistoric finds, including a giant tusk more than nine feet long, are on display. The full four-hour tour includes a "miner's buffet lunch" and the opportunity to pan for gold, of course. Visitors can omit the lunch. Snacks are available for sale, and there is a gift shop.

Take Steese Expwy to Goldstream Rd; turn left, then left again on Old Steese Hwy. Dredge is about .3 mile on right; 907/457-6058. Open daily, 9:30am-6pm, Memorial Day-mid-Sept. Tours are scheduled hourly. Cost: $29.95 (with lunch), $21 (without lunch).

El Dorado Gold Mine   This attraction, like the Riverboat Discovery, is owned and operated by the Binkley family. As with the riverboat, this two-hour tour is wellorganized and fun. From the old Fox train station, the Tanana Valley Railroad train transports visitors through a permafrost tunnel to a historic goldmine camp to learn about gold mining past and present. You'll finish with a chance to pan for gold (success guaranteed). Free coffee and cookies are provided. A free shuttle transports visitors to and from five locations in Fairbanks.

Mile 1.3 Elliott Hwy, Fox; nine miles northeast of Fairbanks. 907/479-6673, 866/479-6673; www.eldoradogoldmine.com. Open: Cost: $27.95/adult, $19.95/child, 3-12, free/under 3.

Poker Flat Research Range   This is the only university-owned, scientific rocket launch facility in the world. Administered by the Geophysical Institute of the University of Alaska, its instruments track satellites and carry out research on a variety of scientific projects, including auroras, climate, the upper atmosphere, and more. Tours are offered every other week during summer months. For details, check the Geophysical Institute Web site.

A 30-minute drive north of Fairbanks on the Steese Hwy, north of Fox.
For information, contact the Geophysical Institute Public Information Office at 907/474-7942; www.pfrr.alaska.edu.

NOAA/NESDIS Command & Data Acquisition Station (Satellite Tracking Station Tour)   This station with the long name is the continent's farthest north civilian-operated satellite tracking station. Its mission is to track, relay, and receive information to and from satellites in orbit. The information is used by the National Weather Service, among others, to help with weather forecasting. Researchers also use data collected to track ice breakup on Alaska rivers, investigate maritime oil spills, and study environmental conditions. Tours are offered on request in summer (call first).

1 Eisele Rd; 13.6 miles north of Fairbanks on Steese Hwy; take turnoff on right, northbound for NOAA/NESDIS; 907/451-1200; www.fcdas.noaa.gov/html /station_info/. Free tours June-Aug between 8am-5pm, Mon-Sat; call Shift Manager to arrange a tour for rest of year, 907/451-1222.

High Arctic Trips A number of outfitters run day trips by motor vehicle on the Dalton Highway to the Arctic Circle and back. Some go farther, transporting visitors by land and air to the Arctic Ocean. **Trans Arctic Circle Treks** offers trips from Fairbanks. Their one-day round trip to the Arctic Circle includes stops at historic viewpoints, lunch by the Yukon River, a look at the Alaska Pipeline and, on arrival at the Arctic Circle, presentation of a certificate you can use to prove you've been there (4825 Glasgow Dr; 907/479-5451; www.arctictreks.com. Cost: $119/person). Considerably more expensive are two- and three-day trips to Prudhoe Bay and beyond. See "A Trip to Prudhoe Bay" for an account of what you're in for.

Calendar of Events

February

Yukon Quest Dog Sled Race
U.S.: 907/452-7954; Canada: 867/668-4711; www.yukonquest.org
This race between Fairbanks and Whitehorse covers rugged terrain. There is easy access for visitors to watch some of the race from various checkpoints along the course. For younger mushers, there is a Junior Yukon Quest.

March

Tripod Days, Nenana Ice Classic
Nenana (See "The Nenana Ice Classic."), World Ice Art Championships and Kids Park, Fairbanks ☺, Ice Park, Phillips Field Rd; 907/451-8250, 800/327-5774; www.icealaska.com/hist/
Watch sculptors from around the world create amazing works of art in ice, some of them huge. There's a Kids Park, a playground made entirely of ice. Sculptures remain on display until they melt, usually by month's end. Park entry fee: $8/adult/$8, $3/child 6-12, free/under 6. A season pass ($15 adult, $5/child) and other discounts are offered; call for details.

June

Yukon 800 Boat Race, Fairbanks to Galena, on the Chena, Tanana, and Yukon rivers
907/488-4627

Midnight Sun Festival (street fair)
Fairbanks, 907/452-8671

July

Fairbanks Summer Arts Festival
University of Alaska, PO Box 80845, Fairbanks, 907/474-8869; www.fsaf.org
Concerts, plays, master classes, workshops, performances take place over two weeks.

Many of these are suitable for children. Ice skating for all ages and experience levels and dance workshops for ages 12 and up are offered.

World Eskimo-Indian Olympics
Fairbanks, www.weio.org

August

Tanana Valley State Fair
800 College Rd; 907/452-3750; www.tananavalleyfair.org
All the usual events are offered, along with an indoor craft market and midway. There's a free shuttle to the fairgrounds; call or check with Web site for details (Cost: Adults/$8, kids 6-18/$5, under 6/free).

November

Athabascan Fiddling Festival
Fairbanks; Athabascan Fiddlers Association, 907/452-1825

December

Winter Solstice Celebration
Fairbanks, 907/452-8671

Resources

Fairbanks Chamber of Commerce
*250 Cushman St, Ste 2D Fairbanks, AK 99701; 907/452-1105;
www.fairbankschamber.org*

Fairbanks Convention & Visitors Bureau
*550 First Ave, Fairbanks, AK 99701-4790; 907/456-5774;
www.explorefairbanks.com*

Alaska Public Lands Information Center (APLIC)
*250 Cushman St, Ste 1A, Fairbanks, AK 99701; 907/456-0527;
www.nps.gov/aplic/center/*
The APLIC provides information to the public about national parks and forests, fish, game, wildlife, and more. This is a great resource for obtaining maps, planning trips and hikes, and learning about Alaska's natural history, flora, and fauna.

Books

Balzar, John. *Yukon Alone: The World's Toughest Adventure Race.* Henry Holt, 2000.

Cole, Dermot. *Fairbanks: A Gold Rush Town that Beat the Odds.* Epicenter Press, 1999.

Fairbanks. Alaska Geographic, 1995. A reprint of an in-depth look at Fairbanks from the *Alaska Geographic* magazine.

Firth, John. *Yukon Quest: 1000-Mile Dog Sled Race.* Lost Moose Publishing, 1998.

Scully, Julia. *Outside Passage: A Memoir of an Alaskan Childhood.* Random House, 1999.

For Kids

Morey, Walt. *Scrub Dog of Alaska.* Buchanan Resources, 1989

Rand, Gloria. *Baby in a Basket.* Cobblehill Books/Dutton, 1997. (The exciting, true story of a mom and two daughters who had a sleigh accident on the way from Fairbanks to Seattle in the winter of 1917).

Rand, Gloria. *River of Life.* Clarion, 2000. This read-aloud book follows a year in the life of an Alaska river and the life it supports).

CHENA HOT SPRINGS

The Chena River State Recreation Area and Chena Hot Springs Resort are popular destinations for tourists and locals alike. The former congregate here in summer; the latter in winter. Whatever the season, the attractions include gorgeous scenery, spectacular auroras, abundant wildlife, and a rich assortment of recreational options. July and August is the peak season for mosquitos, so visitors may want to time a visit for early or late summer. From mid-September on, the aurora is visible. In addition to the resort, several campgrounds and public-use cabins are available. The road is paved and well-maintained all the way.

The paved road from Fairbanks to Chena Hot Springs takes a little over an hour to drive, but allow extra time to check out the river and assorted wildlife you are very likely to encounter along the way.

Getting There

The Chena River State Recreation Area is accessed via Chena Hot Springs Road (take the Steese Expressway north toward Fox to the Chena Hot Springs Road at Mile 4.9). Chena Hot Springs Resort is roughly 60 miles northeast of Fairbanks at the end of Chena Hot Springs Road (56.5 miles, 91 km).

Once you leave the Steese Expressway, you're in the country. If you're in need of a rest stop, gas, snacks, fishing gear, or licenses, stop at **Tack's General Store,** in Two Rivers, the only town on the road (Mile 23.5; 907/488-3242; open 8 am-8 pm year round).

Roadside Attractions

Chena River State Recreation Area (www.dnr.state.ak.us/parks/units/chena/index/) encompasses 254,000 acres of recreational possibilities. While most of the hiking trails are extensive and at least moderately difficult, the **Angel Rocks Trail** can be handled by young hikers. The 3.5-mile round trip begins at mile 48.9 of Chena Hot Springs Road; allow 3-4 hours. A longer option allows hikers to continue all the way to the Resort and offers spectacular views. The Resort offers guided trips along several of these trails, a good option for beginners.

Places to Stay

Chena Hot Springs Resort ☺ ($-$$$)
Mile 56.5 Chena Hot Springs Rd; 907/452-7867, 800/478-4681;
www.chenahotsprings.com

Family Hikes in the Chena River State Recreation Area

By Brooke Whipple

After traveling long distances by car, plane, train, or bus around Alaska, a stretch of the legs and a little fresh air may be just what the adventurous family needs to rejuvenate. A fine place to start is *Angel Rocks*, a 3.5-mile hike northeast of Fairbanks at Mile 49, Chena Hot Springs Road. It was voted Alaska's "best day hike" by the readers of *Alaska Magazine* in 2001, and rewards hikers with outstanding views of the Angel Creek valley and the surrounding hills. (From the air, the rock formations are said to look like an angel.) The hike begins at the parking lot, follows the North Fork of the Chena River for a bit, and then climbs through the woods, winding its way around giant granite spires and outcroppings that provide excellent platforms for picture taking. Along the trail, hikers will pass through areas that were burned by the West Fork Chena fire in May 2002. The scars are quite noticeable in one section, but starkly beautiful nonetheless and should not deter hikers from experiencing this trail. Having reached the top, hikers can return the way they came or continue along the ridge and loop down the other side and back to the parking area. NOTE: The trail can be hard to follow on the far side of the loop, especially since the fire. Always take a trail map (you can pick these up at the trailhead), and tell someone where you are going and when you expect to return.

Wildlife sightings may include ducks, moose, squirrels, and the always-friendly gray jays that swoop and glide closely overhead. Not far from the trailhead, hikers can walk out onto a beaver dam and witness this wonder first hand. In the fall, an abundance of wild berries and beautiful colors stretches as far as the eye can see.

This hike is suitable for families and children who are in moderate to good shape. The trail gains approximately 1000 feet in elevation. There are great views within a mile of the trailhead though, so families looking for a shorter hike, or those with younger children, can still enjoy a portion of this hike. Although there may be some wet sections along the trail in spring and early summer, sneakers and hiking boots are suitable footwear. Watch out for granite pebbles on the trail in the steeper sections; they act as marbles. And don't forget to bring bug repellent!

For families seeking a short and easy hike, *Chena Hot Springs Resort's Nature Trail*, just over a mile in length, is a great choice. The trail is quite wide and suitable for strollers or bicycles. Along the way, the trail parallels a stream and circles a beaver pond, and hikers may see beavers, moose, fox, or squirrels. (For a glimpse of the beavers themselves, try this hike in early morning or the evening. I've counted six at one time!) A bridge leads over scenic Monument Creek, which hosts arctic grayling and supports myriad songbirds and waterfowl. Frequent interpretive signs allow hikers to learn about local flora and fauna. ◼

FYI: *Restaurant; family suites, kids under 13 stay free; indoor heated pool, hut tubs, outdoor hot-springs pool, outdoor hot tub, massage; horseback riding, guided river rafting, fishing, canoeing, guided hikes, orienteering, mountain bike rentals, gold-panning, van tours, ATV tours, flightseeing tours; (winter) cross-country skiing, snowshoeing, ice skating, dog sled rides, mushing school, snowmachine rentals, ATV rentals, snow cat rides, horse sleigh rides, winter clothing rentals; gift shop, laundry, transportation to and from Fairbanks; RV and tent camping sites; pets OK*

The sprawling grounds of this relaxed resort contain an eclectic assortment of buildings and cabins. The new wing, M, is a good choice for families, close to the main building and pools, and with spacious, comfortable rooms. There is no air conditioning, but large ceiling fans keep things cool. Cabins without electricity or plumbing are available for a truly rustic experience. In the main building is a rambling restaurant and bar, gift shop, and reception area. There's a large recreation building and the pièces de résistance: the pools including a large hot-spring fed indoor pool and three hot tubs. Outside, the sandy-bottom hot-spring "lake," which is off limits to those under age 18. In winter, resort guests float dreamily in the steamy waters, watching the aurora pulse and stream overhead.

The restaurant serves a varied assortment of dishes (try the fish and game specialties). There's a kid's menu (with the usual items), with prices lower than you'd expect for the location, and portions are huge. A generously sized duck salad or pasta with Portobello mushrooms are good adult choices. For break-fast, try the blueberry pancakes.

The resort provides an impressive list of guided activities and tours, year round. Costs can quickly add up. Children ages 6-12 are usually half-price; 5 and younger are free. Many activities are oriented specifically to kids, such as Mini-Z-Rides (snow machines) in winter and special horseback rides in summer. If you're not familiar with the area, taking a guided hike here can be a good introduction to the beauties of the Chena River Recreation Area. For most activities, kids 6 and older can participate, provided they're accompanied by an adult.

Visitors may be surprised to learn that winter, not summer, is the high season here. The spectacular winter auroras are one reason, along with the wide variety of winter sports. Book early, especially if you plan to come in September. The resort has become very popular with international travelers in recent years and some weeks are booked up a year or more in advance.

66 PARENT COMMENTS 99

"The kids spent most of their time running between bodies of water. Be aware of the picturesque, rusty farm equipment scattered around the grounds; you'll need to watch younger kids carefully. The staff is very friendly and tolerant of the kids."

Public Use Cabins

There are six public-use cabins (see "Public-Use Cabins" in the "Introduction" for a general description of amenities and rental information) in the Chena River State Recreation Area. Two of these—the North Fork Cabin (mile 47.7 Chena Hot Springs Rd, sleeps six) and the Chena River Cabin (mile 32.2, Chena Hot Springs Rd, sleeps nine)—can be accessed by road, a rarity.

Camping

There are three developed campgrounds in the Chena River State Recreation Area. **Rosehip Campground**, at mile 27 of the Chena Hot Springs Road the closest to Fairbanks, has 37 campsites, toilets, water, dumpsters, picnic tables, river access, and fishing. There are no shelters. Twelve miles east at Mile 39.5, you'll find **Tors Trail Campground**, with 24 campsites, toilets, water, dumpsters, picnic tables, river access, and fishing. A little farther (Mile 42.8) is **Red Squirrel Campground**, with 12 campsites, toilets, water, dumpsters, picnic shelters and tables, fishing and swimming. Be prepared for bear encounters; this is home to black and brown bears. Check with the Division of Parks and Outdoor Recreation of the Alaska Department of Natural Resources (907/451-2695; www.dnr.state.ak.us/parks/units/chena/) for up-to-date information on recent bear sightings.

Richardson Highway:
Fairbanks to Valdez (364 m)
1) **Fairbanks to Paxson** (284 km/177 m)
2) **Paxton to Valdez** (306 km/190 m)

Two main highways connect Fairbanks to Anchorage and southcentral Alaska: the George Parks Highway (described in Chapter 9) and the **Richardson Highway** (Hwy 4) which connects Fairbanks to the town of **Valdez** on pristine **Prince William Sound** with its numerous fjords, surrounded by the Chugach Mountains. The Alyeska Pipeline follows roughly the same path as the highway, carrying oil from the North Slope in the Arctic down to the pipeline terminal at Valdez, from where it is shipped to the lower 48. Because the major tourist attraction in Valdez, the Alyeska Pipeline Terminal tour, is closed indefinitely, few attractions there now draw visitors by road. But the drive is outstanding, offering access to the Denali Highway, two mountain passes above the tree line, and the chance to get close to a very large glacier (Worthington). And Valdez itself has a lot to offer families who are outdoors enthusiasts.

The Richardson and Alaska Highways converge at Delta Junction. At Glenallen, the Glenn Highway (described in Chapter 6) runs west to the Matanuska-Susitna Valley, Anchorage, and the Kenai Peninsula. Travelers to and from the lower 48 and the Yukon can shorten their trip by taking the Tok Cutoff, which runs between Tok, on the Alaska Highway, and meets the Richardson at Gakona Junction (see Chapter 5).

Although the Richardson is paved and in excellent condition, it's less traveled than other Alaska highways, and towns and services are fewer. You'll need to keep an eye on your gas tank and calculate how far it is to the next service center before you pass on filling up. You can drive the full highway in under nine hours, but with scenic stops and byways to investigate, it's best to allow two days.

1) Fairbanks to Paxson (177 m)

Along the 80 miles from Delta Junction to Paxson, the road cuts between two glaciated arms of the Alaska Range. Views become steadily more spectacular as the road twists and turns. The biggest consistent presence in the landscape, apart from the mountains, is the straight white seam of the Alyeska Pipeline as it cuts through the landscape, never far from the road.

The **Fielding Lake State Campground** (two miles west on a gravel road and about 65 miles south of Delta Junction) makes a good rest stop. It's above the tree line, with seven free campsites, picnic tables, and pit toilets. A few miles south toward Paxson, the road crests **Isabel Pass** (3,280 feet), named for one of the Klondike's more intriguing heroines, **Isabel Barnette** (see "The real Klondike Kate"). Nearby is beautiful **Summit Lake,** with views of Gulkana Glacier back to the northeast. Along the lake are some vacation homes and a few B&Bs.

Paxson has little to recommend it to families, but you'll find gas and services here; it's also the junction with one of Alaska's loveliest roads: the 134-mile **Denali Highway.**

Side Trip: Denali Highway (134 m one way)

This gem of a highway runs west from Paxson, meeting up with the **George Parks Highway** (Hwy 3) at **Cantwell,** 27 miles south of the entrance to Denali National Park. The Denali Highway is paved for the first 21 miles west of Paxson, then turns to gravel until three miles short of Cantwell. Due to its unpaved status and distance from amenities such as tow truck and cell phone service, most rental car contracts forbid driving on this highway, which is closed in winter. This is not a drive to be undertaken without forethought. But many consider it the most beautiful highway in Alaska. You are literally surrounded with breathtaking mountains as the road rises up to **McLaren Summit** (4,086 feet). The drive features some of the longest vistas on any Alaska highway.

If you can't drive the entire way, going as far as **Tangle Lakes** (the end of the paved section) will give you more than a taste of what the highway offers. The Bureau of Land Management (BLM) administers the **Tangle Lakes Archeological District** here, where evidence of over 10,000 years of human occupation has been found. There are plenty of turnouts where you can stretch your legs and bring out the camera. Note that it's illegal to remove artifacts found in the Archeological District. The **Tangle Lakes BLM Campground** on Round Tangle Lake has 25 campsites, water, pit toilets, and tables. Several small resorts in the Tangle Lakes area provide gas, food, and lodging. The road has curves; although these probably won't bother most children, you might want to take precautions against kid carsickness if yours are especially susceptible.

2) Paxson to Valdez (190 m)

South of Paxson, in the 71-mile drive to Glennallen, the scenery continues to be breathtaking as the road crosses many rivers and creeks offering good fishing for lake trout, grayling, and various salmon species. Stop and check for spawning salmon. The sight of thousands of brilliant-red, wild, pre-spawning salmon is worth seeking out (and a much less gruesome sight than post-spawning salmon).

Copper Center   Close to this small town, about 10 miles south of Glennallen, consider splurging on a stay at the new **Copper River Princess Wilderness Lodge** (Brenwick Craig Rd, Mile 102 Richardson Hwy, Copper Center; 907/822-4000, 800/426-0500; www.princesslodges.com/copper/; ($$-$$$); 85 rooms & suites, restaurant; open May-Sept). This resort offers stunning views and is four miles from the new Wrangell-St. Elias National Park Visitor Center. A host of activities and tours is offered, from flightseeing to river rafting. The hamlet of Copper Center itself is much more charming than the name implies and worth a short detour off the Richardson, onto the well-marked Copper Center Loop. This well-preserved community dates from 1896.

About 12 miles south of Copper Center on the last 100-mile lap to Valdez, you can stop and marvel at the pipeline (which is much bigger than it looks) at the **Pipeline Interpretive Viewpoint**, a well-marked turnout with parking and interpretive signs. This is as close as you can get to the pipeline in these security-conscious times.

The last 40 miles as you approach Valdez are particularly stunning. The road winds deep into the Chugach Mountains. Near the summit of **Thompson Pass** (2,678 feet), **Worthington Glacier State Recreation Site** is a must-see. From a large parking area, paved trails lead to various viewpoints from which you can ogle the ice. It's something to ogle, too. In summer, park rangers operate a small visitor center with information on the glacier and surrounding area, as well as gifts and books for sale. Visitors are warned to keep a good distance from the glacier; chunks occasionally break off and fall (a tourist was killed this way at Exit Glacier, on the Kenai Peninsula, in 2000). Two miles past the summit is one of the state's most beautiful campgrounds, **Blueberry Lake State Recreation Site** (10 sites, $12/night, some covered picnic tables, pit toilets, water, fire pits). Perched high above the Keystone Canyon, the park offers stupendous views. From Thompson Pass, you descend into Keystone Canyon and are joined by the Lowe River; notice **Bridal Veil Falls**, 13.8 miles out of town.

VALDEZ

With 4,300 residents, Valdez sits at the end of Prince William Sound, location of the disastrous 1989 oil spill when the Exxon Valdez oil tanker ran aground at Bligh Reef, spilling nearly 11 million gallons of crude oil and coating over 1,200 miles of rocky beach. Wildlife was destroyed in vast numbers; the impact of the spill on local wildlife populations is still to be finally determined.

While the town itself is lackluster, it's encircled by high mountains whose deep-mossy-green flanks rise up to jagged, snow-capped peaks, like a glossy calendar of the Alps. These extremes are reflected in the town's history. The magnitude 9.2 Good Friday earthquake of 1964, its epicenter just 45 miles west of Valdez, completely destroyed the town, killing 33 people. Valdez was rebuilt four miles away at a more stable site, its present location. In the 1970s, the oil pipeline terminal gave the city a new lease on life and brought tourism; but after 2001, most cruise lines pulled out of Valdez when the pipeline tours were canceled in the wake of security concerns. For families, the main reason to come here is to enjoy the extraordinary environment: Sea kayaking, river rafting, and hiking are among the pastimes available.

Valdez is also served by the **Alaska Marine Highway System** (800/642-0066; www.dot.state.ak.us/amhs/) which runs between Valdez and Whittier (6.75 hours) and between Valdez and Cordova (5.5 hours) year round. Scheduled airline service to and from Anchorage is provided by **Alaska Airlines** (800/252-7522; www.alaskaair.com).

Places to Stay

Best Western Valdez Harbor Inn ($-$$)
100 Fidalgo Dr; 907/835-3434, 888/222-3440; www.valdezharborinn.com/
FYI: 90 rooms, refrigerator/microwave; restaurant, coffee shop, gift shop;
Laundromat; airport/ferry shuttle; children under 13 stay free
This is the nicest choice in Valdez, located on the harbor and close to shops and restaurants.

Totem Inn ($$)
144 East Egan Dr; 907/835-4443; www.toteminn.com
FYI: 44 rooms, refrigerator/microwave, restaurant with kids' menu, gift shop,
no cribs or rollaways; Laundromat; kids stay free

Aspen Hotel ($$$)
100 Meals Ave; 907/835-4445; www.aspenhotelsak.com/Valdez/
FYI: 78 rooms, refrigerator/microwave; free breakfast; exercise room,
Laundromat

Camping

The downtown RV parks resemble RV dealerships more than campgrounds: rows of vehicles crowded close together with no landscaping. For anything resembling attractive ambience, you'll need to head out of town. The best choice for tenters and those who crave a bit of greenery is **Glacier Campground** (241 N Harbor Dr; 907/835-2282; 101 sites: $10/site; picnic tables, grills, pit toilets), which accommodates tents and RVs on attractive wooded sites next to a creek and waterfall; a day-use picnic area is available. For downtown convenience and full RV services, try **Bear Paw Camper Park** (101 N Harbor Dr; 907/835-2530; www.akpub.com/akbbrv/bearp/; 150 sites: $22 and up; restrooms and showers free, full hookups, Laundromat, dump station). It also has some tent sites.

Places to Eat

Alaska Halibut House
Fairbanks St & Meals Ave; 907/835-2788
Hours: open daily 6am-10pm
This is a good choice for a meal. It's no-frills, but the fish is fresh and prices are low for Valdez. Kids will likely enjoy the fish and chips; for the seafood phobic, burgers or barbecued beef sandwiches go down well, and yes, they have chicken nuggets.

Lunch Box Sandwich Shop
103 Harbor Ct; 907/835-9500
Hours: call for hours
This place has just what you'd expect; they'll make up box lunches to take with you on outdoor adventures.

Mike's Palace
201 N Harbor Dr; 907/835-4686
Hours: open daily 11am-11pm)
The pizza lovers in your party will like Mike's. It has many other offerings including seafood, popular Italian entrées, Mexican menu, and a kids' menu.

What to See & Do

Shopping A few shops downtown carry the usual in Alaska tchotchkes. **Anne's Place** (200 Egan Dr; 907/835-4336) has gifts, souvenirs, and clothing; nearby **Northwind Floral & Gifts** (129 Egan Dr; 907/835-4483) has Alaskana gifts and souvenirs. **Alaskan Fine Gifts** (201 N Harbor Dr 907/835-3155) sells a better than average assortment of locally made goodies and crafts, along with a selection of books on the region. To get out and see the area, you can rent a bike from **Beaver Sports** (316 Galena St; 907/835-4727; $6/hour includes helmet and lock). They also rent skis, snowshoes, and tubes in winter. If you get thirsty while shopping, **Latte Dah** (100 Meals Ave, in Harbor Court; 907/835-3720) can fix you up with espressos or smoothies, depending on your age and the weather. **Howling Wolf Coffee** (inside 3 Bears Market on Egan Dr; 907/835-8700) has excellent espresso.

Valdez Museum and Historical Archive This museum offers a thumbnail sketch of Valdez since European exploration. Among the more interesting exhibits is the story of the Exxon Valdez oil spill and its impact on Valdez. Ask staff for a copy of the history hunt or other family activities designed to help kids orient themselves to the museum; they'll receive a prize on completion. In spring, the museum showcases the artwork of local students. In summer, an annual quilt exhibit showcases unusual quilts and fiber arts. The **Museum Annex Warehouse** offers an old but riveting documentary on the Good Friday earthquake and its aftermath; there's also a model of pre-earthquake Valdez *217 Egan Dr; 907/ 835-2764 or 835-5800; www.alaskanet/~vldzmuse/index/; Open Mon-Sat 9am-6pm, Sun 8am-5pm (Memorial Day-Labor Day); Mon-Fri*

1-5pm, Sat 12-4pm (rest of year). Cost: $3/adult; $2/student 14-18, free/under 14, $1.50/annex admission. Museum Annex Warehouse: 436 S Hazelet; open daily, summer only, 9am-4pm. Allow 30 minutes at each site.

Alaska Cultural Center It may be a bit of a hike if you don't have a vehicle, but it's worth the exercise. This small museum in the airport showcases the extraordinary collection of Maxine Whitney, who amassed a fascinating, high-quality collection of Native Alaskan artifacts and art. Many of the pieces here will interest children, such as the tiny ivory animals, tusk carvings, amulets, and spirit carvings. Notice the intricate Russian prayer rug made from furs by Eskimos.

300 Airport Rd, Valdez Airport Terminal, 907/ 834-1690; e-mail: vnpa@uaa.Alaska.edu. Open daily 9am-6pm (May 15-Aug); closed Sept-May 15. Cost: $4/adult, free/under 18. Allow 30 minutes.

Cruises Prince William Sound is one of the loveliest waterscapes in Alaska. For a tour of its attractions, **Prince William Sound Tours & Cruises** (small boat harbor tour dock, 907/835-4731, 877/777-2805; www.princewilliamsound.com) has two sightseeing trips; prices start at $76/adult, $38/child 2-11 (6 hours).

Flightseeing You can take a one-hour Prince William Sound tour with **Era Helicopters** (907/835-2595, 800/843-1947; www.eraaviation.com; $215/person).

Hiking There are many interesting trails around Valdez. However, a look around will show you that sooner or later they will have to go up, up, up. Also, bears love it here; berries and rushing rivers filled with fish are powerful draws for the furred set; rehearse your bear strategies. The visitor center has trail maps and recent information on bear sightings. The **Dock Point Trail** (by the Small Boat Harbor, off Kobuk Dr) is an easy .75-mile loop with observation platforms and a view of Valdez Bay. The **Mineral Creek Trail** (take Mineral Creek Dr about 5.5 miles) is an easy 1.75-mile round trip along a scenic creek with waterfalls. Pick up trail maps at the visitor center.

Kayaking and River Rafting Several outfitters offer guided sea kayaking trips suitable for the youngest paddlers. **Anadyr Adventures** (225 Harbor Dr; 907/835-2814, 800/865-2925; www.anadyradventures.com) has no age limits for their 3-4hour Duck Flats kayak excursion (along the town's waterfront; $55/adult, $49/child). Longer day and multi-day trips are also offered, some limited to older children and adults and/or advanced paddlers. They also rent boats to experienced kayakers. **Pangaea Adventures** (101 N Harbor Dr; 907/835-8442, 800/660-9637; www.alaskasummer.com) offers similar trips in the same price range. For your rafting needs, **Keystone Raft & Kayak Adventures** (Mile 16.5 Richardson Hwy 907/835-2606, 800/328-8460; www.alaskawhitewater.com) offers a variety of excursions; the Keystone Canyon float trip down the Lowe River is suitable for children 5 years and older (higher age limits apply for passengers who book through cruise lines).

Swimming **Valdez Pool** (at Valdez High School, 319 Robe River Dr; 907/835-5429) has two swimming pools.

Calendar

April
World Extreme Skiing Competition (WESC)
650/888-9311
Free skiing competition

August
Gold Rush Days
907/835-2984
Lots of kids' and family activities during this celebration of the Gold Rush and the town's role in it

Resources

"One Call Does It All"
P.O. Box 2197-MP, Valdez, AK 99686; 907/835-4988
Free reservation service for accommodation, outfitters, tours, and transportation

Valdez CVB Visitor Information Center
200 Chenega St, P.O. Box 1603, Valdez, AK 99686; 907/835-4636, 800/770-5954; www.valdezalaska.org.

Index

INDEX

100 Mile House, 144-45; lodging, 145
108 Resort (100 Mile House), 145
1202 Motor Inn (Beaver Creek), 193-94

A

A&W Restaurant (Williams Lake), 146
Abduct and Release—Skagway Paranormal Symposium, 134
Admiralty Island National Monument, 114
Afognak Island, 332
Airport Restaurant (Unalaska/Dutch Harbor), 337
air travel, 26-28; to Anchorage, 229; to Bellingham, 36; with children, 27; to Dawson City, 206; to Fairbanks, 380; to Haines, 116; to Inside Passage, 72; to Juneau, 99; to Kenai Peninsula, 270; to Ketchikan, 75; to Kodiak Island, 320; to Prince Rupert, 38-39; to Seattle, 62; to Sitka, 87; to Skagway, 125; to Unalaska/Dutch Harbor, 335-36; to Vancouver, 66; to Yukon Territory, 170
Alaska: appropriate clothing, 14-15; buses to, 28-29; campgrounds, 11; cruises, 44-68; derivation of word, 335; mystery books set in, 58-59; raising children in, 246-47; restaurants, 11-12; road and weather resources, 31-32; state flag, 339; taking grandchildren to, 364-65; traveling to, 26-41; visitor information/resources, 19-21; Web cams, 95. See also Inside Passage; Interior Alaska; Kenai Peninsula; Kodiak Island; Southwest Alaska
Alaska Aviation Heritage Museum (Anchorage), 242
Alaska Bald Eagle Festival, 124
Alaska Bird Observatory (Fairbanks), 395
Alaska Botanical Garden (Anchorage), 244
Alaska Café (Dawson Creek), 155

Alaska Center for the Performing Arts (Anchorage), 248
Alaska Chilkat Bald Eagle Preserve (Haines), 122
Alaska Cultural Center (Valdez), 411
Alaska Dancing Eagles Cabin and Bed & Breakfast (Seldovia), 311
Alaska Day Festival (Sitka), 97
Alaska Experience Center (Anchorage), 241
Alaska Folk Festival (Juneau), 115
Alaska Goldpanners , 397
Alaska Halibut House (Valdez), 410
Alaska Highway, 136-226; advice for teenagers on a road trip, 141; Alaska border to Delta Junction, 194-200; calculating mileage, 159; construction of, 162-63; Dawson Creek to Yukon Territory border, 157-67; equipment/supplies for, 139; getting to from the east, 140-43; getting to from the west, 143-54; map, 136; resources, 140; side trips, 219-26; trip planning, 138-39; Whitehorse to the Alaska border, 189-94; Yukon Territory border to Whitehorse, 172-89; Yukon Visitor Reception Centre/Alaska Highway Interpretive Centre (Watson Lake), 175
Alaska Indian Arts (Haines), 121
Alaska interior. See Interior Alaska, 378
Alaska Marine Ferry System. See Alaska Marine Highway System
Alaska Marine Highway System, 33-40, 72, 75, 125, 259, 270, 310
Alaska Maritime National Wildlife Refuge, 304
Alaska Native Heritage Center (Anchorage), 242
Alaska Native Medical Center (Anchorage), 241
Alaskan Steak House & Motel (Delta Junction), 198
Alaskan Tails Of The Trail with Mary Shields (Fairbanks), 397
Alaska Panhandle. See Inside Passage

Alaska Pass, 34

Alaska Public Lands Information Center (Anchorage), 241-42

Alaska Railroad, 229-31, 259, 270; to Denali National Park, 350; to Fairbanks, 380

Alaska Railroad Museum (Nenana), 381

Alaska Raptor Center (Sitka), 94

Alaska Salmon Bake (Fairbanks), 387

Alaska SeaLife Center (Seward), 279

Alaska 7 Motel (Delta Junction), 198

Alaska Spaceport (Kodiak Island), 331

Alaska State Fair. *See* state fairs

Alaska State Museum (Juneau), 105

Alaska State Trooper Museum (Anchorage), 242-43

Alaska Wildberry Products, 303

Alaska Wildlife Conservation Center, 257

Alaska Zoo (Anchorage), 245

Alberta, 140-43; resources, 143

Alcan Highway. *See* Alaska Highway

Alcan Motor Inn (Haines Junction), 190

Aleutian Islands: during World War II, 340; map, 320

Aleutian World War II National Historic Site, 340-41

Alpine Diner & Bakery (Girdwood), 254

Alutiiq Museum and Archaeological Repository (Kodiak Island), 325

Alyeska Blueberry & Mountain Arts Festival (Girdwood), 257

Alyeska Prince Hotel/Alyeska Resort (Girdwood), 253-54

Alyeska Resort Spring Carnival (Girdwood), 257

Alyeska Tram (Girdwood), 255

Amelia's Restaurant (Unalaska/Dutch Harbor), 338

American Bald Eagle Foundation (Haines), 122

Amica's Ristorante (Dawson City), 208

Anchorage, 228-51; activities/attractions, 239-50; air travel to, 229; area east of, 258-66; area southeast of, 251-58; biking, 249; calendar of events, 250; camping, 237; chain hotels, 235; culture for kids, 248; driving to, 231; farmers' market, 240; flightseeing,

249; hiking, 249-50; ice skating, 247-48; lodging, 232-36; map, 228, 230; museums, 242-44; music, 248; parks, 244-45; resources, 231, 251; restaurants, 236-39; RV rental, 233; shopping, 239-40; skiing, 250; swimming, 248; trains to, 229-31; transportation in, 232; wildlife, 245-46

Anchorage Coastal Wildlife Refuge, 245, 251

Anchorage Concert Association, 248

Anchorage Festival of Music Summer Solstice Series, 250

Anchorage Museum of History and Art, 243; Web site, 20

Anchorage Symphony Orchestra, 248

Anchor Point, 297

Anchor River State Recreation Area, 297

Annabelle's Famous Keg and Chowder House (Ketchikan), 77

archaeological digs, 332; Tangle Lakes Archeological District, 407

Arctic Circle, trips, 401

Arctic Region Supercomputing Center (Fairbanks), 391

art: Anchorage, 240; Anchorage Museum of History and Art, 243; Fairbanks Summer Arts Festival, 401; Girdwood Center for Visual Arts, 256; Homer, 303; Juneau, 104; Klondike Institute of Art and Culture (Dawson City), 212; Siska Art Gallery & Museum, 143-44; Sitka Fine Arts Camp, 97; Yukon Arts Centre (Whitehorse), 185. *See also individual entries for festivals, events, and museums*

Arts in the Park (Whitehorse), 186

Aspen Hotels/Guesthouse Inns, 9; Fairbanks, 386; Juneau, 101; Soldotna, 288; Valdez, 409

Athabascan Fiddling Festival (Fairbanks), 402

Atlin, 178

Audubon Society Web site, 21

Auk Nu Tours, 114

aurora borealis (northern lights), 390-91; Northern Lights Centre (Watson Lake), 174

B

Backdoor (Sitka), 90

Bakery Restaurant, The (Fairbanks), 387

Bake Shop, The (Girdwood), 254

Baranov Museum/Kodiak Historical Society (Kodiak Island), 325-26

Barkerville: calendar of events, 221; camping, 221; excursions, 221; lodging, 220-21; restaurants, 221

Barkerville Historic Town, 219-22

Barkerville Provincial Park, 221

baseball: Alaska Goldpanners, 397

Bayview Restaurant (Sitka), 90

bears: Kodiak brown, 327; resources, 20, 369; safety tips/precautions, 17-18, 166, 351; watching on Kodiak Island, 327-28; Web site, 20

Bear's Tooth Theatre Pub (Anchorage), 236

Beaver Creek, 193-94; lodging, 193-94; resources, 194; restaurants, 194

Beeson's B&B (Homer), 299

Bella Coola, 219

Bellingham: activities/attractions, 38; ferries, 36; lodging, 38; transportation to, 36-37

Beluga Point, 252

beluga whales, 253, 270-71

Belvedere Motor Hotel (Watson Lake), 173

Bennett (W.A.C.) Dam, 223

berry picking, 396; Unalaska/Dutch Harbor, 343

Best Western: Gold Rush Inn (Whitehorse), 179; Kodiak Inn (Kodiak Island), 321, 322; Valdez Harbor Inn, 409

bicycle rental: Denali National Park, 372; Haines Junction, 191; Haines, 118; Homer, 306; Kodiak Island, 330; Seward, 279; Unalaska/Dutch Harbor, 342; Whitehorse, 187

bicycling: Anchorage, 249; Denali National Park, 372; Fairbanks, 396-97; Homer, 306; Seward, 279; Sitka, 96; Unalaska/Dutch Harbor, 342

Big Delta State Historical Park, 199-200

Big Lake, 354

Bijoux Falls Provincial Park, 153

bird-watching: Audubon Society Web site, 21; Fairbanks, 395; for children, 341; Kachemak Bay Shorebird Festival, 308; Kodiak Island, 326; Sitka, 96; Swan Haven Interpretive Centre, 178; Unalaska/Dutch Harbor, 341-42. See also eagles; *individual entries for state, provincial, and national parks, forests, and refuges*

Bluebell Inn (Fort Nelson), 160

Blueberry Arts Festival (Ketchikan), 86

Blueberry Lake State Recreation Site, 408

Boardwalk Fish & Chips (Homer), 301

Bonanza Dining Room (Dawson City), 208

books: about Alaska, 21-23; mysteries set in, 58-59

border crossings, 16-17

Bowron Lake Provincial Park, 221

Boya Lake Provincial Park, 152

British Columbia, 143-67, 219-24; map, 136; northern, resources, 167; road and weather resources, 32

Buckinghorse River Lodge, 160

Buckshot Betty's (Beaver Creek), 194

Bud & Carol's B&B (Girdwood), 254

Buffalo Center Diner (Delta Junction), 199

Burwash Landing, 193

buses: to Alaska/Yukon Territory, 28-29; in Anchorage, 232; to Dawson City, 206; to Denali National Park, 350-51; in Denali National Park, 365; in Fairbanks, 384; Juneau, 99-100; Kenai Peninsula, 271; Ketchikan, 76, 77; Kodiak Island, 320; in Skagway, 126; to Skagway, 125; in Whitehorse, 179; to Yukon Territory, 170

Buskin River Inn (Kodiak Island), 321

Buskin River State Recreation Site, 331

bus tours, Sitka, 91

Buzz Coffee House & Espresso Café, The (Seldovia), 312

C

cabins: Chena River State Recreation Area, 406; Denali River Cabins (Denali National Park), 366; Forest Service, 10-11, 84-85; Haines, 119; Juneau, 102; Sitka, 89-90; sleeping in a caboose (Skagway), 128; Tongass National Forest, 77

caboose, sleeping in (Skagway), 128

Cache Creek, 144

Café Cups (Homer), 301

Café Michele (Talkeetna), 356

Caines Head State Recreation Area, 281-82

Calgary Zoo, 142

Camp Beringia (Whitehorse), 185

campgrounds in Alaska and Canada, 11

camping, 11; Anchorage, 237; Barkerville, 221; bear safety, 351; Carmacks, 202; Chena River State Recreation Area, 406; Chetwynd, 154; Cooper Landing, 285-86; Dawson City, 207-8; Dawson Creek, 155; Delta Junction, 198; Denali National Park, 368; Denali State Park, 361; Eagle, 225; Fort Nelson, 160; Fort St. John, 158; Glennallen, 201; Haines, 119; Haines Junction, 191; Homer, 300-1; Juneau, 101-2; Kenai, 292, 295; Ketchikan, 77; Kodiak Island, 331-33; Muncho Lake, 165; North Pole, 383; Prince George, 149; Seward, 277; Sitka, 89; Skagway, 127-28; Soldotna, 288; Tok, 198; Valdez, 409; Watson Lake, 174; Whitehorse, 181. *See also individual entries for state, provincial, and national parks, forests, and recreation areas*

Canada: campgrounds, 11; road and weather resources, 32. *See also* Alberta; British Columbia; Yukon Territory

Canadian Northern Children's Festival (Prince George), 150

canoeing: Eagle, 226; Fairbanks, 397. *See also* canoe rental; kayaking

canoe rental: Haines Junction, 191; Whitehorse, 187

Cantwell, 361, 407

Captain Bartlett Inn (Fairbanks), 385-86

Captain Cook (Anchorage), 234

Captain Cook State Recreation Area, 295

Captain Pattie's Fish House (Homer), 301

car rental, 29; for Alaska Highway, 137; Anchorage, 232; for Denali National Park, 365; Fairbanks, 384; Haines, 118; Homer, 299; Juneau, 100; Kenai, 292; Ketchikan, 76; Kodiak Island, 320; Seward, 275; Sitka, 88; Skagway, 126; Unalaska/Dutch Harbor, 336; Whitehorse, 179

Carcross Desert, 125-26

Cariboo Highway (Highway 97): Cache Creek to Prince George, 144-50; side trips, 219-24

Carl E. Wynn Nature Center (Homer), 307

Carl's Bayview Inn (Unalaska/Dutch Harbor), 337

Carmacks, 202-3; activities/attractions, 202-3; camping, 202; lodging, 202

Carnival Cruise Lines, 52-53

Cashen Quarters (Juneau), 100

Cassiar Highway (Highway 37), 151-52, 176; resources, 152

Celebrate Canada Festival (Prince George), 150

Celebrity Cruises, 53-54

Center for Alaskan Coastal Studies (Homer), 307-8

Challenger Learning Center (Kenai), 293

Charlotte's (Kenai), 292

Chart Room: Homer, 301; Kodiak Island, 322; Unalaska/Dutch Harbor, 337

Chena Hot Springs, 403; hiking, 403; lodging, 403-5; traveling to, 403; traveling to, 403-6

Chena Hot Springs Resort, 403-5

Chena Lakes Recreation Area, 399

Chena River State Recreation Area, cabins, 406; camping, 406; hiking, 403, 404

Chena River State Recreation Site, 394

Chetwynd, 153-54; activities/attractions, 154; camping, 154; lodging, 153-54; swimming, 154

Chicken, 218

Chilcotin Highway (Highway 20), Williams Lake to Bella Coola, 219

children: air travel with, 27; anticipating earthquake fears of, 314-15; raising in Alaska, 246-47; Web sites for, 20-21

Chilkat State Park, 119

Chilkoot Trail, 132

Christmas Celebration (Barkerville), 222

Chugach National Forest, 256

Chugach State Park, 251-52, 259-60

Cindy's Place (Skagway), 126

clam digging, 297

Clam Gulch State Recreation Area, 296

Clarion Inns/Suites, 8

clothing, summer and winter, 13-15, 380

Comfort Inns/Suites, 8; Fairbanks, 386

Commander's Room (Haines), 119

Commissioner's Residence (Dawson City), 210

Continental Divide, 176

Cookie Jar, The (Fairbanks), 387

Cooper Landing, 284-87; activities/attractions, 286-87; camping, 285-86; fishing/float trips, 286-87; hiking, 287; horseback riding, 287; lodging, 285; resources, 287; restaurants, 286

Copper Center, 408

Copper River Princess Wilderness Lodge (Copper Center), 408

Corner Café (Skagway), 128

Corrington's Museum of Alaskan History (Skagway), 129

Corsair (Anchorage), 236

Courtyard, 9

Cranberry Bistro, The (Whitehorse), 181

Creamer's Field Migratory Waterfowl Refuge (Fairbanks), 395

cross-country skiing: Fairbanks, 396-97; Girdwood, 253-54; Homer, 37; Kenai, 295

Crow Creek Mine (Girdwood), 255-56

cruises/cruising, 44-68; affordable, 60; basics, 44-52; cruise lines, 52-59; glacier, 114; Homer, 298; independent shore trips, 106; Inside Passage, 72; to Juneau, 99; Kenai Peninsula, 270; Kodiak Island, 319-20; Marine Science Explorer Program, 282; Parent Tip, 47, 51; preboarding strategies, 65; Prince William Sound Cruises & Tours, 282; resources, 59-61; Seattle-based, 61-62; staying healthy during, 52; Tracy Arm Fjords, 114; Unalaska/Dutch Harbor, 336; Valdez, 411; Vancouver-based, 65-66. *See also* ferries; river trips

D

Dänojà Zho Cultural Centre, 212

Dan's Neighbourhood Pub (Fort Nelson), 161

Dash Deli/Cheechako's Sourdough Steakhouse (Whitehorse), 181-82

Dawson City, 205-16; activities/attractions, 209-11; air travel to, 206; buses to, 206; calendar of events, 216; camping, 207-8; culture, 212; excursions, 215-16; flightseeing, 213; gold panning, 213; hiking, 213-15; history, 205-6, 214; lodging, 206-7; museums, 212; resources, 216; restaurants, 208-9; river cruises, 215-16; swimming, 215; tours, 213; walking tour, 210

Dawson City Bunkhouse, 206

Dawson City Museum, 212

Dawson City Music Festival, 216

Dawson Creek, 154-57; activities/attractions, 156; camping, 155; lodging, 155; resources, 157; restaurants, 155; swimming, 156

Dawson Creek Art Gallery, 156

Dawson Peaks Resort & RV Park (Teslin), 176

"Days of '98 Show with Soapy Smith," 131

Deer Mountain Tribal Hatchery & Eagle Center (Ketchikan), 81

Delaney Park (Anchorage), 244

Delta Junction, 198-200;

activities/attractions, 199-200; camping, 198; lodging, 198; museums, 199; resources, 200; restaurants, 198-99

Delta State Recreation Site, 198

Dempster Highway (Highway 5), 203; to Inuvik, 224

Denali (Mount McKinley), 349, 361

Denali Highway (Highway 8), 360, 361, 407

Denali National Park and Preserve, 363-75; access to, 363; activities/attractions, 370-73; biking, 372; buses to, 350-51; bus tours, 370-71; camping, 368; children's activities, 371; driving to, 350; flightseeing, 373; hiking, 372; lodging decisions, 367; lodging, 366-67; map, 348; resources, 373-75; restaurants, 369-70; river rafting, 373; road lottery, 375; shuttle buses, 365, 372-73; trains to, 350, 362; transportation in, 363-64, 365; traveling to, 350-51; visitor center, 370

Denali Princess Wilderness Lodge (Denali National Park), 366

Denali River Cabins (Denali National Park), 366

Denali Salmon Bake (Denali National Park), 369

Denali State Park, 361; camping, 361

Denali View Raft Adventures (Talkeetna), 357-58

Destruction Bay, 193

Diamond Tooth Gertie's Gambling Hall (Dawson City), 211

Diocesan Museum of the History of the Russian Orthodox Church (Kodiak Island), 326

Discovery Days Festival (Dawson City), 216

Discovery III (Fairbanks), 398-99

DiSopra (Juneau), 102

Dog Mushing Museum (Fairbanks), 392

dogs: Patsy Ann, 103

dog sledding: Alaskan Tails of the Trail with Mary Shields (Fairbanks), 397; demonstration (Denali National Park), 365, 370; Dog Mushing

Museum (Fairbanks), 392; Fairbanks, 397; Iditarod Trail Dog Sled Race, 263-65; Muktuk Tours (Whitehorse), 186; Race of Champions (Tok), 197; resources, 374; Seavey's IdidaRide Sled Dog Tours (Seward), 281; Seward, 279-81; Sun Dog Express (Fairbanks), 397; Web site, 21; Yukon Quest Dog Sled Race (Fairbanks), 401; Yukon Quest Dog Sled Race (Whitehorse), 188

dolls, Alaska Native, 394

Dominion Day (Barkerville), 221

Downtown Hotel (Dawson City), 206

Driftwood Inn (Homer), 299

Driftwood Lodge (Juneau), 100-1

driving: Alaska Highway, 136-226; to Alaska/Yukon Territory, 28; to Anchorage, 231; to Bellingham, 36; to Chena Hot Springs, 403; to Denali National Park, 350, 364; to Fairbanks, 381; to Haines, 116-17; to Kenai Peninsula, 271; to Prince Rupert, 39; resources, 29-20; road and weather conditions, 31; to Seattle, 62; to Skagway, 125; to Vancouver, 65; to Yukon Territory, 170. *See also* car rental

Drumheller: Royal Tyrrell Museum, 142

Drummond Lodge & Motel (Williams Lake), 146

Dry Creek Recreation Site, 201

Dutch Harbor. *See* Unalaska/Dutch Harbor

E

Eagle, 225-26; activities/attractions, 226; boating, 226; camping, 225; lodging, 225; museums, 226

Eaglecrest Ski Area (Juneau), 109

Eagle Historical Society and Museum, 226

Eagle River Nature Center, 259-60

eagles: Alaska Bald Eagle Festival (Haines), 124; Deer Mountain Tribal Hatchery & Eagle Center (Ketchikan), 81; Haines, 122

Earthquake Park (Anchorage), 244

earthquakes: anticipating children's fear of, 314-15; Good Friday 1964 earthquake, 322-23; Web site, 20

Econolodge, 9; Fort St. John, 158; Prince George, 149

Edgewater Hotel (Whitehorse), 179

Eileson Air Force Base, 382-83

Eklutna, 260

Eklutna Historical Park, 260

El Chicano (Kodiak Island), 323

El Dorado Gold Mine (Fox), 400

Eldorado Hotel (Dawson City), 207

Elmendorf State Fish Hatchery (Anchorage), 245

Eskimo dolls, 394

Eskimos. *See* Native culture

Ester, 381-82

Ester Gold Camp, 399

Esther's Inn (Prince George), 148

events. See festivals/events

Exit Glacier, 282-83

Exxon Valdez oil spill, 304-5

F

Fairbanks, 383-403; activities/attractions, 389-401; air travel to, 380; biking/hiking/cross-country skiing, 396-97; buses, 384; calendar of events, 401-2; canoeing, 397; chain hotels, 386; dog sledding, 397; driving to, 381; excursions, 398-401; ice-skating, 397; lodging, 384-86; map, 378, 384; museums, 392-93; open-air museums, 389-90; parks, 394-95; resources, 402-3; restaurants, 387-88; swimming, 398; tennis, 397; theater for children, 393; trains to, 380; transportation in, 384; traveling to, 380-81; wildlife, 395-96

Fairbanks Summer Arts Festival, 401

Falcon Inn B&B (Eagle), 225

Fancy Moose (Anchorage), 236

Far North Bicentennial Park (Anchorage), 244

farmers' markets, 240; Kenai, 293; Homer, 303; Tanana Valley, 390-91; Wasilla, 351

Fast Eddy's (Tok), 196

ferries, 32-41; Alaska Highway shuttles, 137; Alaska Marine Highway System, 33-40, 72, 75, 125, 270, 310; amenities, 35-36; Auk Nu Tours, 113, 114; George Black Ferry, 217; Haines, 116; Homer to Kodiak and Unalaska/Dutch Harbor, 344; to Inside Passage, 72; to Juneau, 99; Kenai Peninsula, 270; to Ketchikan, 75; to Kodiak Island, 319; Parent Tip, 36; to Prince Rupert, 39; to Seldovia, 310, 312; to Sitka, 87-88; to Skagway, 125; to Unalaska/Dutch Harbor, 336. *See also* cruises

Festival of the North, 86

festivals/events: Anchorage, 250; Barkerville, 221; Dawson City, 216; Fairbanks, 401-2; Girdwood, 257; Haines, 123-24; Homer, 308-9; Juneau, 115; Kenai, 296; Ketchikan, 86; Kodiak Island, 333-34; Palmer, 266-67; Prince George, 150; Seward, 284; Sitka, 97; Skagway, 134; Talkeetna, 360; Tok, 199; Valdez, 412; Whitehorse, 188-89

Fiddlehead Restaurant & Bakery (Juneau), 102

Finn Alley Inn (Sitka), 88

Fireweed Restaurant (Haines), 119

fishing: Cooper Landing, 286-87; Homer, 306; Kodiak Island, 329; Seldovia, 314; Skagway, 133; Soldotna, 290; Talkeetna, 359; World Record Halibut Derby (Unalaska/Dutch Harbor), 345

flag, Alaska state, 339

flight times, 28

flightseeing: Anchorage, 249; Dawson City, 213; Denali National Park, 373; Haines, 123; Homer, 306; Juneau, 111-12; Ketchikan/Misty Fjords National Monument, 83-84; Kodiak Island, 327-28; Sitka, 96; Skagway, 132; Talkeetna, 359; Unalaska/Dutch Harbor, 345; Valdez, 411; Whitehorse, 187

float trips. *See* rafting/float trips

Forest Service cabins, 10-11, 84-85. *See also* cabins

Forget-Me-Not Lodge and Aurora-Express (Fairbanks), 384-85
Fort Abercrombie State Historical Park, 331
Fort Nelson, 160-62; activities/attractions, 161-62; camping, 160; hiking, 161; lodging, 160; restaurants, 161; swimming, 161-62
Fort Nelson Heritage Museum, 161
Fort Nelson Motor Hotel (Fort Nelson), 160
Fort St. James, 151, 152
Fort St. John, 157-59; activities/attractions, 159; camping, 158; lodging, 157-58; museums, 159; restaurants, 158; swimming, 159
Fort St. John-North Peace Museum, 159
Fort Seward Lodge (Haines), 118
Fortymile National Wild and Scenic River, 218
fossil hunting, Kodiak Island, 329
Fox, 400
Frantic Follies (Whitehorse), 186
Fraser-Fort George Regional Museum, 150
Fresh Sourdough Express Bakery and Café (Homer), 302

G

Gakona Junction, 200
Gambardella's Pasta Bella (Fairbanks), 387-88
Gaslight Follies (Dawson City), 212
Gateway Motor Inn (Watson Lake), 173
Gateway Salmon Bake (Tok), 196-97
Geophysical Institute (Fairbanks), 392; Poker Flat Research Range, 400; Web site, 20
George Black Ferry, 217
George Johnston Museum (Teslin), 177
George Parks Highway (Highway 3), 350, 360, 381; Anchorage to Talkeetna, 351-54; roadside attractions, 381-82; Talkeetna to Denali National Park, 360-61
Georgeson Botanical Garden Tour (Fairbanks), 392

Girdwood, 252-58; activities/attractions, 255-57; calendar of events, 257; lodging, 252-54; resources, 257-58; restaurants, 254-55; skiing, 253-54; trains to, 270
Girdwood Center for Visual Arts, 256
Girdwood Forest Faire, 257
Gitanyow, 152
Glacier Bay Ferry, 113
Glacier Bay Lodge, 113
Glacier Bay National Park and Preserve, 112-13
Glacier BrewHouse (Anchorage), 236-37
glaciers, 110-11; Exit Glacier, 282-83; Glacier Bay National Park and Preserve, 112-13; Matanuska Glacier, 262; Mendenhall Glacier, 109-11; Portage Glacier, 256-57; Salmon Glacier, 152; Tracy Arm, 113, 114; Worthington Glacier State Recreation Site, 408
Glennallen, 201; camping, 201; lodging, 201
Glenn Highway (Highway 1), Anchorage to Glennallen, 258-62
Goldbelt Hotel (Juneau), 101
Gold Creek Salmon Bake (Juneau), 102
Gold Dredge No. 4 Tour (Dawson City), 215
Gold Dredge No. 8 (Fox), 400
gold dredges, 218
Golden Bear Motel (Tok), 195
gold mining: El Dorado Gold Mine (Fox), 399; Ester Gold Camp, 399; Gold Dredge No. 8 (Fox), 399; Hope-Sunrise Historical and Mining Museum, 272; Independence Mine State Historical Park, 261-62; Skagway, 131; tailings, 203
gold panning: Crow Creek Mine (Girdwood), 255-56; Dawson City, 213; Goldpanner, 218; Indian Valley Mine National Historic Site, 252; Juneau, 108
Gold Rush, Klondike, 168-70
Gold Rush Cemetery (Skagway), 131
Gold Rush Days: Juneau, 115; Valdez, 412

Grand Aleutian Hotel (Unalaska/Dutch Harbor), 337

grandchildren, Alaska trip with, 364-65

Grande Denali (Denali National Park), 367

Great Alaskan Lumberjack Show, The (Ketchikan), 82

Great Klondike International Outhouse Race (Dawson City), 216

Grubstake, The (Dawson City), 208

G Street House Bed & Breakfast (Anchorage), 232

Guesthouse Inns/Aspen. *See* Aspen Hotels/Guesthouse Inns

guides/outfitters: High Arctic trips, 401; Kodiak Island, 329; Talkeetna River Guides, 358

Gwennie's Old Alaska Restaurant (Anchorage), 237

Gwin's Lodge (Cooper Landing), 285

H

Haines, 116-24; activities/attractions, 120-23; calendar of events, 123-24; camping/cabins, 119; driving to, 116-17; flightseeing, 123; hiking, 122; kayaking, 123; lodging, 118-19; museums, 121; rafting/float trips, 123; resources, 124; restaurants, 119-20; swimming, 122; tours, 123; transportation in, 117-18; wildlife, 122

Haines Highway (Highway 3), 117, 189

Haines Junction, 189, 190-93; activities/attractions, 191-92; biking/canoeing/hiking/kayaking/rafting, 191; camping, 191; excursions, 191-92; horseback riding, 191; lodging, 190; resources, 192; restaurants, 191; swimming, 191; takeout food, 192

Hammer Museum (Haines), 121

Hampton Inns/Suites, 9

Harborside Coffee & Goods (Kodiak Island), 323-24

Harborview Inn (Seward), 277

hatcheries: Anchorage, 245; Juneau, 105, 106-7; Ketchikan, 81

Hatcher Pass, 261-62

Hazelton, 151, 152

Head-Smashed-In Buffalo Jump Interpretive Centre, 142

Healy: car rental, 365; lodging, 367

Heen Kahidi Dining Room & Lodge (Ketchikan), 77

Hell's Gate Airtram, 144

Henry's Great Alaskan Restaurant (Kodiak Island), 324

Heritage Hotel (Homer), 300

High Arctic trips, 401

High Country Inn Whitehorse, 181

Highway 1 (Glenn Highway): Anchorage to Glennallen, 258-62

Highway 1/Highway 9 (Seward Highway), 271, 272-73; Portage to Seward, 272-73

Highway 1 (Sterling Highway), 271; Seward Highway Junction to Soldotna, 284-87; Soldotna to Homer, 296-97

Highway 1 (Tok Cutoff): Tok to Glennallen, 200-1

Highway 2 (Klondike Highway), 189; North, Whitehorse to Dawson City, 201-3; North, side trips, 224; South, 125-25, 178

Highway 3 (George Parks Highway), 350, 360, 381; Anchorage to Talkeetna, 351-54; roadside attractions, 381-82; Talkeetna to Denali National Park, 360-61

Highway 3 (Haines Highway), 189

Highway 4 (Richardson Highway), 361, 381; Fairbanks to Valdez, 406-8; roadside attractions, 382-83; side trip, 407

Highway 4 (Robert Campbell Highway), 173

Highway 5 (Dempster Highway), 203

Highway 5 (Taylor Highway), 195; side trip to Eagle, 224-26

Highway 8 (Denali Highway), 360, 361, 407

Highway 9/Highway 1 (Seward Highway), 271, 272-73; Portage to Seward, 272-73

Highway 20 (Chilcotin Highway),

Williams Lake to Bella Coola, 219
Highway 26: Quesnel to Barkerville Historic Town, 219-22
Highway 29: Chetwynd to Hudson's Hope, 222-24
Highway 37 (Cassiar Highway), 151-52, 176
Highway 97: Prince George to Dawson Creek, 153-57; Cariboo Highway, Cache Creek to Prince George, 144-50; side trips, 219-24
hiking: Anchorage, 249-50; Chena River State Recreation Area, hiking, 403, 404; Cooper Landing, 287; Dawson City, 213-15; Denali National Park, 372; Fairbanks, 396-97; Fort Nelson, 161; Haines, 122; Homer, 306-7; Juneau, 107-8; Ketchikan, 82; Seldovia, 313; Seward, 281, 283; Sitka, 96; Skagway, 131-32; Unalaska/Dutch Harbor, 342; Valdez, 411; Whitehorse, 187. *See also individual entries for state, provincial, and national parks, forests, recreation areas, and refuges*
Hilton Hotels, 9
Holiday Inn/Express, 9
Holland America, 54-55
Holy Ascension Russian Orthodox Cathedral (Unalaska/Dutch Harbor), 339
Homer, 297-309; activities/attractions, 302-8; art galleries, 303; biking, 306; calendar of events, 308-9; camping, 300-1; cross-country skiing, 307; excursions, 307-8; ferry to Kodiak and Unalaska/Dutch Harbor, 344; fishing, 306; flightseeing, 306; hiking, 306-7; history, 298; horseback riding, 307; kayaking, 307; lodging, 299-300; museums, 304-6; resources, 309; restaurants, 301-2; transportation in, 299; whale/wildlife watching, 308
Homer Brewing Company, 303
Homestead, The (Homer), 302
Hope, 272
Hope-Sunrise Historical and Mining Museum, 272

horseback riding: Cooper Landing, 287; Haines Junction, 191; Homer, 307; Kodiak Island, 329-30; Seward, 281; Whitehorse, 187
Hotel Carmacks, 202
hotel chains, 8-10; Anchorage, 235; Fairbanks, 386; Seattle, 64; Vancouver, 64. *See also individual entries*
Hotel Halsingland (Haines), 118
Hot Licks Homemade Ice Cream (Fairbanks), 388
hot springs: Chena Hot Springs, 403-6; Liard River Hot Springs Provincial Park, 166-67; Takhini Hot Springs, 188
House of Wickersham (Juneau), 105
Hudson's Hope, 222-23
Hyder, 152
hypothermia, 359

I

Ice Cream Shop, The (Girdwood), 255
Ice Museum (Fairbanks), 392-93
ice skating: Anchorage, 247-48; Fairbanks, 397
Iditarod National Historic Trail, 281
Iditarod Trail Dog Sled Race, 263-65; flying along route of, 352-53; Web site, 21
Imaginarium, The (Anchorage), 243
Independence Mine State Historical Park, 261-62
Indian Valley Mine National Historic Site, 252
information, 19-21
insects, 18-19
Inside Passage, 37, 70-134; air travel to, 72; cruising, 72; ferries to, 72; history, 71-72; map, 70; resources, 72-74. *See also individual entries*
Interior Alaska, 378-412; map, 378; packing for, 380. *See also* Fairbanks
Inter-Island Ferry Authority, 75
International Arctic Research Center Tour (Fairbanks), 392
International Softball Tournament (Skagway), 134
Isabel Miller Museum (Sitka), 92

J

J&H Wilderness Resort (Muncho Lake), 164
Jack London Grill (Dawson City), 208
Jack London's Cabin (Dawson City), 210
Juneau, 99-115; activities/attractions, 103-4; air travel to, 99; calendar of events, 115; camping/cabins, 101-2; excursions, 112-14; ferries to, 99; flightseeing, 111-12; gold panning, 108; hiking, 107-8; kayaking, 108; lodging, 100-1; map, 98; museums, 105-6; official greeter, 103; parks, 104; rafting/float trips, 108-9; resources, 115; restaurants, 102; skiing, 109-11; swimming, 107; transportation in, 99-100
Juneau-Douglas City Museum (Juneau), 105
Juneau Jazz & Classics, 115
Just for the Halibut (Haines), 120

K

Kachemak Bay Shorebird Festival, 308
Kachemak Bay State Park, 308
Kantishna Roadhouse (Denali National Park), 371
Katmai National Park, 343
kayak rental: Kodiak Island, 330; Whitehorse, 187
kayaking: Haines, 123; Homer, 307; Juneau, 108; Seldovia, 313-14; Valdez, 411. See also sea kayaking
KBBI Concert on the Lawn (Homer), 309
Kelly and King Houses (Barkerville), 220
Kelly's Alaska Country Inn (Delta Junction), 198
Kenai, 291-96; activities/attractions, 293-95; beachcombing, 293; camping, 292; cross-country skiing, 295; excursions, 295; festivals/events, 296; history, 291; lodging, 292; resources, 296; restaurants, 292; swimming, 295; transportation in, 292; walking tours, 293

Kenai Fjords National Park, 277; tours, 282, 283
Kenai Fjords Tours, 282
Kenai Merit Inn (Kenai), 292
Kenai National Wildlife Refuge, 287; visitor center (Soldotna), 290
Kenai Peninsula, 268-315; air travel to, 270; buses, 271; driving to, 271; ferries to, 270; history, 270; map, 268; resources, 272; trains to, 270-71; traveling to, 270-71
Kenai Peninsula Orchestra Summer Strings Festival, 309
Kenai Peninsula State Fair, 297
Kenai Princess Wilderness Lodge (Cooper Landing), 285
Kenai River Festival, 296
Kenai River Lodge (Soldotna), 288
Kenai Spur Road, 271
Kenny's Wok & Teriyaki, 90
Keno (S.S.), 211
Ketchikan, 75-86; air travel to, 75; calendar of events, 86; camping/cabins, 77; excursions, 83-85; ferries to, 75; flightseeing, 83-84; funicular, 80; galleries, 78, 80; hiking, 82; lodging, 76-77; museums, 80-81; parks, 80; Rain Derby, 86; resources, 86; restaurants, 77-78; sea kayaking, 83; swimming, 81, 82; tidepooling, 83; totem poles, 79; transportation in, 76
Ketchikan Creek, 78-80
Ketchikan Rain Derby, 86
Kids' Grotto (Whitehorse), 184-85
Kincaid Park (Anchorage), 245
King and Kelly Houses (Barkerville), 220
King's Diner, 322-23
Kitwanga Fort National Historic Site, 151
Klondike Gold Rush, 168-70
Klondike Gold Rush National Historical Park, 130
Klondike Highway (Highway 2), 189; North, Whitehorse to Dawson City, 201-3; North, side trips, 224; South, 125-26, 178. See also Klondike Loop
Klondike Institute of Art and Culture (Dawson City), 212

Klondike Kate, 212
Klondike Kate's (Dawson City), 208-9
Klondike Loop, 138. See also Klondike
    Highway
Klondike Recreational Rentals, 171
Klondike Rib and Salmon Barbecue
    (Whitehorse), 182
Klondike Road Relay (Skagway), 134
Klondike Trail of '98 Road Relay
    (Whitehorse), 189
Klondike II (S.S.) National Historic Site
    (Whitehorse), 184
Klondyke Harvest Fair (Whitehorse), 188
Kluane Ecotours (Haines Junction), 191
Kluane Museum of Natural History
    (Burwash Landing), 193
Kluane National Park and Reserve, 117,
    191-92
Klukshu, 117
Kodiak Bear Country Music Festival, 334
Kodiak brown bears, 327
Kodiak Island, 319-34;
    activities/attractions, 324-33; air travel
    to, 320; berry picking, 328; bird-
    watching, 326; buses, 320; calendar of
    events, 333-34; camping, 331-33;
    cruises to, 319-20; excursions, 330-
    31; ferries to, 319; ferry from Homer
    to, 344; fishing, 329; flightseeing/bear
    watching, 327-28; fossil hunting, 329;
    Good Friday 1964 earthquake and
    tsunami, 322-23; horseback riding,
    329-30; lodging, 321; map, 320;
    museums, 325-26; outdoor equipment
    rental, 330; outfitters/guides, 329;
    parks, 325; resources, 334;
    restaurants, 322-24; sea kayaking,
    330; state parks, 331-33; swimming,
    328; transportation on, 320; traveling
    to, 319-20; wildlife, 326-28
Kodiak Military History Museum
    (Kodiak Island), 326
Kodiak National Wildlife Refuge, visitor
    center (Kodiak Island), 328
Kodiak State Fair and Rodeo, 334
Koniag's Kodiak Crab Festival (Kodiak
    Island), 333
'Ksan Historical Village, 151

L

Lac La Hache, 145
Lake Laberge, 202
Lake Louise, 262-65
Land's End Resort (Homer), 300
Landing, The, Best Western (Ketchikan),
    76
Large Animal Research Station
    (Fairbanks), 395-96
Last Chance Mining Museum (Juneau),
    106
laundry, 175
Liard Hotsprings Lodge, 166
Liard River, 166-67
Liard River Hot Springs Provincial Park,
    166-67
Little Pioneer Museum (Chetwynd), 154
London, Jack, 210, 211; Jack London's
    Cabin (Dawson City), 210
lottery, Denali Road, 375
Lunch Box Sandwich Shop (Valdez), 410
Lung Duck Tong (Barkerville), 221
Lynx Creek Pizza (Denali National
    Park), 369

M

Macauley Salmon Hatchery, 105, 106-7
MacBride Museum Whitehorse, 183-84
Mad Fish, The (Seldovia), 311-12
Mae's Kitchen (Pink Mountain), 159-60
Mahay's Riverboat Service (Talkeetna), 358
MainStreet Kodiak's Rainfest, 334
maps: Alaska/British Columbia/Yukon
    Territory, 6; Anchorage, 228, 230;
    British Columbia/Yukon Territory,
    136; Fairbanks, 384; Inside Passage,
    70; Interior Alaska/Fairbanks, 378;
    Juneau, 98; Kenai Peninsula, 268;
    Kodiak Island/Aleutian Islands, 320;
    Talkeetna and Denali National Park,
    348; Whitehorse, 180
Margaret Bay Archeological Project, 332
Margaret Bay Café/Grand Aleutian
    Hotel (Unalaska/Dutch Harbor), 337
Marine Science Explorer Program, 282
Marriott/Springhill Suites, 9; Fairbanks,
    386

Marx Brothers Café, The (Anchorage), 237-38

Mary Anna's Bed & Breakfast (Prince George), 148

Matanuska Glacier, 262

Matanuska Glacier State Recreation Site, 262

Mendenhall Glacier (Juneau), 109-11

Meziadin Lake Provincial Park, 152

Midnight Dome (Dawson City), 215

Midnight Sun Festival (Fairbanks), 401

Mike's Palace (Valdez), 410

Milepost, 155

Millennium Hotel Anchorage (Anchorage), 236

Mini Folk Festival (Skagway), 134

Misty Fjords National Monument, 83-84

Moberly Lake Provincial Park, 154

Moon Lake State Recreation Site, 197-98

moose, 274-75

Moose Dropping Festival (Talkeetna), 360

Moose Pass, 273

Moose's Tooth Pub & Pizzeria (Anchorage), 238

mosquitoes, 18-19

Mountain Market, 120

Mountain View Motel (Haines), 119

Mount Alyeska, skiing, 255

Mount McKinley (Denali), 349, 361

Mount McKinley Princess Wilderness Lodge, 360-61

Mount Roberts/Mount Roberts Tramway (Juneau), 109

Mudball Classic Softball Tournament, 97

Mukluk Annie's Salmon Bake (Teslin), 177

Mukluk Land (Tok), 197

Muktuk Tours Whitehorse, 186

Muncho Lake, 164-65; camping, 165; lodging, 164-65

Muncho Lake Provincial Park, 165

Museum of Alaska Transportation and Industry (Wasilla), 353

Museum of Northern Adventure (Talkeetna), 357

Museum of the Aleutians (Unalaska/Dutch Harbor), 339-40

museums. *See individual entries for museums, subjects, and towns*

mushing. *See* dog sledding

music festivals/events: Anchorage, 248, 250; Dawson City, 216; Fairbanks, 402; Homer, 309; Juneau, 115; Kodiak Island, 334; Sitka, 97; Skagway/Whitehorse, 134; Whitehorse, 134, 186

musk ox: Musk Ox Farm, 261; Oomingmak Musk Ox Producers Co-op, 240; *qiviut*, 240, 261

Mykel's Restaurant (Soldotna), 289

mysteries set in Alaska, 58-59

N

Nancy Lake State Recreation Site, 354

National Audubon Society, Web site, 21

Native culture: Alaska Cultural Center (Valdez), 411; Alaska Native Heritage Center (Anchorage), 242; Alaska Native Medical Center (Anchorage), 241; Alutiiq Dancers (Kodiak Island), 325; Alutiiq Museum and Archaeological Repository (Kodiak Island), 325; archaeological digs, 332; dolls, 394; Eklutna Historical Park, 260; Isabel Miller Museum (Sitka), 92; Kenai Visitors & Cultural Center, 293; Kitwanga Fort National Historic Site, 151; 'Ksan Historical Village (Hazelton), 151; Museum of the Aleutians (Unalaska/Dutch Harbor), 339-40; Native Youth Olympics (Anchorage), 250; River of Culture Tours (Dawson City), 215; Saxman Native Village (Ketchikan), 84-85; Sheldon Jackson Museum (Sitka), 92-93; Sitka National Historical Park (Sitka), 93-94; Tage Cho Hudan Interpretive Center (Carmacks), 202-3; Tlingit Heritage Centre (Teslin), 177-78; Totem Bight State Historical Park (Ketchikan), 85; Tr'ondëk Hwëch'in Cultural Centre (Dawson City), 212; Unangan Culture Camp,

342; World Eskimo-Indian Olympics (Fairbanks), 402

Native Youth Olympics (Anchorage), 250

Nenana, 381

Nenana Ice Classic, 382, 401

New Caribou Hotel (Glennallen), 201

Ninilchik, 296

Ninilchick State Recreation Area, 297

Nikiski Pool and Recreation Center (Kenai), 295

NOAA/NESDIS Command & Data Acquisition Station, 400-1

No Pop Sandwich Shop (Whitehorse), 182

Northern Alberta Railroad Park, Station Museum and Visitor Info Centre (Dawson Creek), 156

Northern Lights Restaurant (Fort St. John), 158

northern lights (aurora borealis), 390-91; Northern Lights Centre (Watson Lake), 174

Northern Palace Restaurant (Prince George), 149

Northern Rockies Lodge (Muncho Lake), 164-65

North Klondike Highway. *See* Klondike Highway, North

North Pole, 383; camping, 383

Northwinds Lodge (Dawson Creek), 155

Norwegian Cruise Lines, 55-56

Novarupta eruption, 343

O

oil spill, *Exxon Valdez*, 304-5

Old Log Church Museum (Whitehorse), 184

Old Sitka State Historic Site, 89

Oomingmak Musk Ox Producers Co-op, 240

Oscar Anderson House Museum (Anchorage), 243-44

outfitters/guides: High Arctic trips, 401; Kodiak Island, 329

P

Paddle Wheel Adventures (Haines Junction), 191

Palace Grand Theatre (Dawson City), 212, 213

Palmer, 261; resources, 267

Panhandle. *See* Inside Passage

Paradiso's (Kenai), 292

Parks Highway. *See* George Parks Highway (Highway 3)

Pasagshak River State Recreation Site, 331-32

Pastry Chef, The (Prince George), 149

Patsy Ann, 103

Paxson, 407

Peace Canyon Dam, 222

Peace Villa Motel (Dawson Creek), 155

Perch Restaurant and Resort (Denali National Park), 370

Phyllis's Cafe and Salmon Bake (Anchorage), 238

Pike's Landing Restaurant & Lounge (Fairbanks), 388

Pinecone Motor Inn (Chetwynd), 154

Pink Mountain, 159-60

Pioneer Air Museum (Fairbanks), 393

Pioneer Hall (Fairbanks), 393

Pioneer Park (Fairbanks), 389-90

Pipeline Interpretive Viewpoint, 408

Pizza Bella (Delta Junction), 198

Point Bridget State Park, 114

Point Lodge at Lake Louise, The, 265

Poker Flat Research Range, 400

Pond Café, The (Girdwood), 255

Porcupine Creek State Recreation Site, 200

Port Chilkoot Salmon Bake (Haines), 120

Portage Glacier, 256-57

Pratt Museum/Homer Society of Natural History (Homer), 305-6

prices, 13

Prince George, 147, 148-50; calendar of events, 150; camping, 149; lodging, 148; museums, 150; parks, 150; resources, 150; restaurants, 149; swimming, 149-50

Prince George Railway and Forestry Museum, 150

Prince Rupert: activities/attractions, 39-40; ferries, 38; lodging, 39; train service to, 30-31; transportation to, 38-39

Prince William Sound: cruises, 259, 282, 411; *Exxon Valdez* oil spill, 304-5

Prince William Sound Cruises & Tours, 282, 411

Princess, 56-57

Prophet River, 160

Pump House Restaurant and Saloon, The (Fairbanks), 388

Q

qiviut, 240, 261. *See also* musk ox

Quality Inns/Hotels/Suites, 9; Northern Grand (Fort St. John), 157

Quesnel, 147

R

Race of Champions (Tok), 197

rafting/float trips: Cooper Landing, 286-87; Denali National Park, 373; Haines, 123; Haines Junction, 191; Juneau, 108-9; Skagway, 132; Talkeetna, 357-58; Valdez, 411. *See also* river trips

railroads. *See* trains

Railway Cantina (Seward), 278

rain, 15

Ramada, 10; Dawson Creek, 155; Fort Nelson, 160; Fort St. John, 158; Prince George, 149

Rancheria Falls Recreation Site, 176

Raven Hotel, The (Haines Junction), 190

Ray's Waterfront (Seward), 278

recreational vehicles. *See* RV rental

Red Dog Saloon(Juneau), 102

Rendezvous Restaurant (Williams Lake), 146

rentals. *See* bicycle rental; canoe rental; car rental; kayak rental; RV rental

Residence Inns, 9

resources. *See individual entries for subjects and towns*

restaurants, 11-12; Yukon Territory, smoking in, 169. *See also individual entries for towns*

Resurrection Bay Historical Society/Seward Museum (Seward), 279

Resurrection Roadhouse (Seward), 277

Richardson Highway (Highway 4), 361, 381; Fairbanks to Valdez, 406-8; roadside attractions, 382-83; side trip, 407

Rika's Roadhouse (Delta Junction), 199

Rio Grill (Dawson City), 209

Ristorante Orso (Anchorage), 238

Ristorante Portobello & Pizzeria (Skagway), 129

River of Culture Tours (Dawson City), 215

Riverboat *Discovery III* (Fairbanks), 398-99

river rafting. *See* rafting

River's Edge Resort (Fairbanks), 386

river trips/riverboats, 398-99; choosing, 358; Dawson City, 215-16; Fairbanks, 398-99; Talkeetna, 357-58; Whitehorse, 187

RiverWest (Dawson City), 209

roadhouses, 204; Kantishna Roadhouse (Denali National Park), 371; Resurrection Roadhouse (Seward), 277; Rika's Roadhouse (Delta Junction), 199; Sullivan Roadhouse Historical Museum (Delta Junction), 199; Talkeetna Roadhouse, 355, 356

road lottery, Denali, 375

Roald Amundsen Memorial Park, 226

Robert Campbell Highway (Highway 4), 173

Robert Service Cabin (Dawson City), 210

Robert Service Show (Dawson City), 211

Rocky Mountain Lodge, 164

rodeos: Kodiak State Fair and Rodeo, 334; Whitehorse Rodeo, 188; Williams Lake Stampede, 146

Royal Caribbean International, 57-59

Royal Tyrrell Museum (Drumheller), 142

running: Annual Salmon Run (Ketchikan), 86; Klondike Road Relay (Skagway), 134; Klondike Trail of '98 Road Relay (Whitehorse), 189

Russian Bishop's House (Sitka), 94

Russian Christmas and Starring (Kodiak Island), 333

Russian Heritage Inn (Kodiak Island), 321

Russian New Year and Masquerade Ball (Kodiak Island), 333

Russian Orthodox Christmas Eve and Starring (Unalaska/Dutch Harbor), 345

Russian Orthodox New Year's Eve (Unalaska/Dutch Harbor), 345

RV parks. *See* camping

RV rental: Anchorage, 233; Yukon Territory, 171

S

safety, 15-16; bears, 17-18, 166, 351; hypothermia, 359

St. George Hotel (Barkerville), 221

St. Lazaria National Wildlife Refuge, 96

salmon, 105; Deer Mountain Tribal Hatchery & Eagle Center (Ketchikan), 81; Elmendorf State Fish Hatchery (Anchorage), 245; Ketchikan Creek, 78-80; Macauley Salmon Hatchery, 105, 106-7; Salmon Derby/Run (Ketchikan), 86; Silver Salmon Derby (Seward), 284; Whitehorse Fishway 186-87

Salmon Glacier, 152

Sal's Klondike Diner (Soldotna), 289

Sam N' Andy's (Whitehorse), 182

Santa Claus House (North Pole), 383

Satellite Tracking Station Tour, 400-1

Saxman Native Village (Ketchikan), 84-85

Scout Island Nature Center (Williams Lake), 146

sea kayaking: Ketchikan, 83; Kodiak Island, 330; Seward, 281; Sitka, 96. *See also* kayaking

Sea Life Discovery Tours (Sitka), 94-95

sea otters, 280

seasickness, 16, 37

Seattle, 62-64; activities/attractions, 63-64; air travel to, 62; cruise terminals, 62; cruises departing from, 61-62; driving to, 62; lodging, 62-63, 64; trains to, 62

Seavey's IdidaRide Sled Dog Tours, 281

Second Story Café (Fairbanks), 388

Seldovia, 309-15; activities/attractions, 313-14; calendar of events, 314; ferries to, 310, 312; fishing, 314; hiking, 313; kayaking, 313-14; lodging, 311; resources, 314-15; restaurants, 311-12; transportation in, 310

Seldovia Seaport Cottages, 311

Sgt. Preston's Lodge (Skagway), 126-27

Service, Robert, 210, 211; Robert Service Cabin (Dawson City), 210; Robert Service Show (Dawson City), 211

Seward, 273-84; activities/attractions, 278-83; biking, 279; calendar of events, 284; camping, 277; dog sled riding, 279-81; excursions, 281-83; hiking, 281, 283; horseback riding, 281; lodging, 275-77; museums, 279; resources, 284; restaurants, 277-78; sea kayaking, 281; transportation in, 275; wildlife, 279

Seward Highway (Highway 1/Highway 9), 271, 272-73; Portage to Seward, 272-73

Seward Windsong Lodge, 275-76

Shadow Lake Expeditions (Whitehorse), 188

Sheep Mountain Visitor Reception Centre, 193

Sheldon Jackson Museum (Sitka), 92-93

Sheldon Museum and Cultural Center (Haines), 121

Shuyak Island State Park, 332-33

side trips: Alaska Highway, 219-26; Lake Louise, 262-65

Signpost Forest (Watson Lake), 174

Sikanni Chief, 160

Silver Salmon Derby (Seward), 284

Siska Art Gallery & Museum, 143-44

Sitka, 87-99; activities/attractions, 90-96; biking, 96; bird-watching, 96; bus tours, 91; calendar of events, 97;

camping/cabins, 89-90; flightseeing, 96; hiking, 96; history, 87; lodging, 88-89; museums, 92-93; parks, 91-92; resources, 97-99; restaurants, 90; sea kayaking, 96; swimming, 95; totem poles, 93; transportation in, 88; traveling to, 87-88; wildlife, 94-95

Sitka Fine Arts Camp, 97

Sitka Hotel, The, (Sitka), 89

Sitka National Historical Park (Sitka), 93-94

Sitka Spruce Tree Park (Unalaska/Dutch Harbor), 339

Sitka Summer Music Festival, 97

Sitka Wildlife Quest, 95

Skagway, 124-34; activities/attractions, 129-33; air travel to, 125; calendar of events, 134; camping/cabins, 127-28; driving to, 125; entertainment, 131; excursions, 133; ferries to, 125; flightseeing, 132; gold mining, 131; hiking, 131-32; lodging, 126-27; museums, 129, 131; parks, 130; rafting/float trips, 132; resources, 134; restaurants, 128-29; transportation in, 126; White Pass & Yukon Route Railway, 133; wildlife/fishing, 133

Skagway Fish Company, 128

Skagway Museum and Archives, 131

Skeena, 30-31

skiing: Anchorage, 250; Girdwood, 253-54; Juneau, 109-11; Mount Alyeska, 255; World Extreme Skiing Competition (Valdez), 412

skiing, cross-country: Fairbanks, 396-97; Girdwood, 253-54; Homer, 307; Kenai, 295

Smith, Soapy, 131; "Days of '98 Show with Soapy Smith," 131; grave, 131; Soapy Smith's Wake (Skagway), 134

smoking in Yukon Territory restaurants, 169

snow, Web site, 21

Snow City Café, 238-39

Soapy Smith's Wake (Skagway), 134

softball tournaments, 97, 134

Soldotna, 287-91; activities/attractions, 289-90; camping, 288; fishing, 290; lodging, 288; playgrounds, 290; resources, 290; restaurants, 289

Soldotna Historical Society and Museum, 289

Sourdough Mining Company (Anchorage), 239

South Klondike Highway. *See* Klondike Highway, South

Southeast Alaska State Fair and Bald Eagle Music Festival, 124

Southwest Alaska, 318-46; resources, 318-19

Southwest Alaska Discovery Center (Ketchikan), 80-81

Springhill Suites, 9

Spruce Beetle Interpretive Trail, 192-93

S.S. Keno, 211

S.S. Klondike II National Historic Site (Whitehorse), 184

Stagecoach Inn (Chetwynd), 153

stagecoach tour, Barkerville, 220

state fairs: Alaska State Fair (Palmer), 265-66; Kenai Peninsula State Fair (Ninilchik), 297; Kodiak State Fair and Rodeo, 334; Southeast Alaska State Fair and Bald Eagle Music Festival (Haines), 124; Tanana Valley State Fair, 402

state flag, 339

Steamboat Mountain, 162

Steamers on the Dock (Ketchikan), 78

Sterling Highway (Highway 1), 271; Seward Highway Junction to Soldotna, 284-87; Soldotna to Homer, 296-97

Stewart, 152

Stewart-Cassiar Highway, 151-52, 176

Stop-in Family Hotel (Whitehorse), 181

Stowaway Café (Skagway), 129

Sullivan Roadhouse Historical Museum (Delta Junction), 199

summer: items/clothing, 13-15, 380; visiting in, 12

Summer Music Camp (Whitehorse), 186

Summer Music Conservatory (Anchorage), 248

Summit Lake, 163-64, 406

Summit Lake Lodge, 273

Sun Dog Express (Fairbanks), 397
Sunrise Café, 286
Super 8 Motels, 10; Dawson Creek, 155;
     Fairbanks, 386; Juneau, 101;
     Ketchikan, 76; Sitka, 89; Williams
     Lake, 146
Swan Haven Interpretive Centre, 178
Sweet Tooth (Skagway), 129
Swift River Lodge, 176
swimming: Anchorage, 248; Chetwynd,
     154; Dawson City, 215; Dawson
     Creek, 156; Fairbanks, 398; Fort
     Nelson, 161-62; Fort St. John, 159;
     Haines, 122; Haines Junction, 191;
     Homer, 304; Hudson's Hope, 223;
     Juneau, 107; Kenai, 295; Ketchikan,
     81, 82; Kodiak Island, 328; pools
     along Alaska Highway, 147; Prince
     George, 149-50; Sitka, 95; swimmer's
     itch, 145; Unalaska/Dutch Harbor,
     342; Valdez, 411; Watson Lake, 175;
     Whitehorse, 186; Williams Lake, 147
Swiss-Alaska Inn (Talkeetna), 355

T

Tage Cho Hudän Interpretive Center
     (Carmacks), 202-3
Tails of the Trail with Mary Shields
     (Fairbanks), 397
Takhini Hot Springs, 188
Talisman Café (Whitehorse), 182
Talkeetna, 349, 354-60;
     activities/attractions, 356-59; calendar
     of events, 360; fishing, 359;
     flightseeing, 359; lodging, 355-56;
     map, 348; museums, 357; resources,
     360; restaurants, 356; river trips, 357-
     58
Talkeetna Alaskan Lodge, 355
Talkeetna Historical Society Museum,
     357
Talkeetna River Guides, 358
Talkeetna Roadhouse, 355, 356
Talkeetna Winterfest, 360
Tanana Valley Farmers Market, 390-91
Tanana Valley Model Railway Club, 381
Tanana Valley State Fair, 402
Tangle Lakes, 407

Taylor Highway (Highway 5), 195; side
     trip to Eagle, 224-26; Taylor Highway
     Junction to Tok, 218
Teal House B&B (Kodiak Island), 321
Telegraph Creek, 152
tennis: Fairbanks, 397
Teslin, 176-78; activities/attractions,
     177-78; lodging, 176-77; museums,
     177; restaurants, 177
Tetlin National Wildlife Refuge, 195
Tetsa River Provincial Park, 163
Thai Town (Anchorage), 239
Three Barons Renaissance Fair
     (Anchorage), 250
tidepooling, Ketchikan, 83
Timberline Bar & Grill (Juneau), 102
Tino's Steakhouse (Unalaska/Dutch
     Harbor), 338
Tlingit Heritage Centre (Teslin), 177-78
Toad River Lodge, 164
toaster museum: Toastworks (Stewart),
     152
Tok, 195-97; activities/attractions, 197;
     calendar of events, 199; camping,
     198; lodging, 195-96; resources, 197;
     restaurants, 196-97
Tok Cutoff (Highway 1), 197; Tok to
     Glennallen, 200-1
Tok River State Recreation Site, 196
Tongass Historical Museum (Ketchikan),
     81
Tongass National Forest, 77;
     camping/cabins, 77, 89-90, 101
Tony Knowles Coastal Trail (Anchorage),
     244, 245
Top of the World Highway, Dawson
     City to Taylor Highway Junction,
     217-18
Totem Bight State Historical Park
     (Ketchikan), 85
Totem Heritage Center (Ketchikan), 81
Totem Inn (Valdez), 409
totem poles, 79; Saxman Native Village,
     84-85; Sheldon Jackson Museum, 92-
     93; Sitka National Historical Park,
     93-94; Totem Bight State Historical
     Park, 85; Totem Heritage Center, 81
Tracy Arm, 113, 114
Trail Lake Lodge (Moose Pass), 273

trains: to Alaska, 29; Alaska Railroad, 229-31; Alaska Railroad Museum (Nenana), 381; to Anchorage, 229-31; to Bellingham, 37; to Denali National Park, 350, 362; to Fairbanks, 380; Forget-Me-Not Lodge and Aurora-Express (Fairbanks), 384-85; to Girdwood, 270; Kenai Peninsula, 270-71; Kwinitsa Railway Museum, 40; Northern Alberta Railroad Park, Station Museum and Visitor Info Centre, 156; Prince George Railway and Forestry Museum, 150; to Prince Rupert, 39; to Seattle, 62; *Skeena*, 30-31; sleeping in a caboose (Skagway), 128; Tanana Valley Model Railway Club, 381; to Vancouver, 66; White Pass & Yukon Route Railway, 133; in Yukon Territory, 171

TransCanada Highway, 140; Vancouver to Cache Creek, 143-44

transportation, resources, 31-32. *See also* air travel; buses; driving; ferries; trains

travel planning, 32-33

Travelodge, 10; Fort Nelson, 160; Juneau, 101

Triple J Hotel (Dawson City), 207

Tripod Days, 401

tsunamis: Good Friday 1964, 322-23; Unalaska Island warning system, 335

tunnel, Whittier, 258-59

Tweedsmuir South Provincial Park, 219

Two Sisters Bakery & Espresso, 302

U

Unalaska/Dutch Harbor: activities/attractions, 338-45; berry picking, 343; biking, 342; bird-watching, 341-42; calendar of events, 345; classes/workshops, 342; cruises to, 336; ferries to, 336; ferry from Homer to, 344; flightseeing, 345; hiking, 342; lodging, 337; museums, 339-41; resources, 345-46; restaurants, 337-38; swimming, 342; tours, 345; transportation in, 336; wildlife, 341-42. *See also* Unalaska Island

Unalaska Island, 335-46; air travel to, 335-36; traveling to, 335-36; tsunami warning system, 335. *See also* Unalaska/Dutch Harbor

Unangan Culture Camp, 342

University of Alaska (Fairbanks): Arctic Region Supercomputing Center, 391; Geophysical Institute, 392; Georgeson Botanical Garden Tour, 392; International Arctic Research Center Tour, 392; Large Animal Research Station, 395-96; Poker Flat Research Range, 400; Skarland Trails, 397; University of Alaska Museum, 393; walking tour, 391

V

Vagabond Blues (Palmer), 261

Valdez, 408-12; activities/attractions, 410-11; calendar of events, 412; camping, 409; cruises, 411; flightseeing, 411; hiking, 411; kayaking/river rafting, 411; lodging, 409; museums, 410-11; resources, 412; restaurants, 410; swimming, 411

Valdez Harbor Inn (Best Western), 409

Valdez Museum and Historical Archive, 410

Valley of Ten Thousand Smokes, 343

Vancouver, 65-68; activities/attractions, 67-68; air travel to, 66; cruise terminals, 65, 67; driving to, 65; lodging, 64, 66-67; trains to, 66

Van Gilder Hotel (Seward), 276

Veronica's Coffee House (Kenai), 292

Village Bakery & Deli/The Fish Hook (Haines Junction), 191

volcanoes, 294; Novarupta eruption, 343

Voyager Hotel (Anchorage), 232-34

W

W.A.C. Bennett Dam, 223

Wake-Up Jake (Barkerville), 221

Walker's Continental Divide, 176

Walter Wright Pioneer Village (Dawson Creek), 156

Ward Lake Recreation Area, 77

Wasilla, 351-53; museums, 351-53

Watson Lake, 173-75; activities/attractions, 174-75; camping, 174; lodging, 173; swimming, 175

Watson Lake Hotel, 173

weather, 31, 32; Web site, 21

Web cams, 95

Westchester Lagoon (Anchorage), 244-45

WestCoast Cape Fox Lodge (Ketchikan), 76

West Edmonton Mall, 142

Westmark, 10; Baranof Juneau, 101; Beaver Creek, 193-94; Dawson City, 207; Fairbanks, 386; Fairbanks Hotel and Conference Center, 386; Klondike Inn (Whitehorse), 181; Shee Atiká (Sitka), 89; Skagway Inn, 127; Tok, 195, 196; Whitehorse Hotel & Convention Center, 181

Whalefest: Sitka, 97; Kodiak Island, 333

whales: beluga, 253, 270-71; festivals/events, 97, 333. *See also* whale watching

whale watching: Beluga Point, 252; beluga whales, 270-71; Homer, 308; Juneau, 107

Whitehorse, 178-89; activities/attractions, 183-88; calendar of events, 188-89; camping, 181; children's activities, 186; excursions, 188; flightseeing, 187; hiking, 187; horseback riding, 187; lodging, 179-81; map, 180; museums, 183-86; resources, 189; restaurants, 181-82; swimming, 186; transportation in, 179; wildlife, 186-87

Whitehorse Fishway, 186-87

Whitehorse Rodeo, 188

White Pass & Yukon Route Railway, 171

White Spot (Fort St. John), 158

Whittier, 258-59; tunnel, 258-59

wildlife: Alaska Maritime National Wildlife Refuge, 304; Anchorage Coastal Wildlife Refuge, 245, 251; Anchorage, 245-46; Big Game Alaska (Girdwood), 255; Carl E. Wynn Nature Center (Homer), 307; Denali National Park, 370-71; Fairbanks, 395-96; Haines, 122; Homer, 308; Juneau, 106-7; Kachemak Bay State Park, 308; Kenai Fjords Tours, 282; Kenai National Wildlife Refuge, 287, 290; Kenai Peninsula, 271; Ketchikan, 81; Kodiak Island, 326-28; Kodiak National Wildlife Refuge, 328; Scout Island Nature Center (Williams Lake), 146; Seward, 279; Sitka, 94-95; Skagway, 133; Tetlin National Wildlife Refuge, 195; Unalaska/Dutch Harbor, 341-42; Whitehorse, 186-87; Wolf Song of Alaska (Anchorage), 246. *See also* bears; bird-watching; eagles; moose; salmon; whales

Williams Lake, 146-47; activities/attractions, 146-47; lodging, 146; resources, 147; restaurants, 146

Williams Lake Stampede, 146

Windows to the Universe, Web site, 21

Windsong Lodge (Seward), 276

winter: items/clothing, 14-15, 380; visiting in, 12-13

Winter Solstice Celebration (Fairbanks), 402

Wolf Song of Alaska (Anchorage), 246

Wonowon, 159

World Eskimo-Indian Olympics (Fairbanks), 402

World Extreme Skiing Competition (Valdez), 412

World Record Halibut Derby (Unalaska/Dutch Harbor), 345

World War II: in the Aleutian Islands, 340; Aleutian World War II National Historic Site, 340-41

Worthington Glacier State Recreation Site, 408

Wrangell-St. Elias National Park and Preserve, 200

Wye Lake (Watson Lake), 174

Y

Young's Motel (Tok), 196

Yukon 800 Boat Race, 401

Yukon Arts Centre (Whitehorse), 184

Yukon Beringia Interpretive Centre (Whitehorse), 185

Yukon-Charley Rivers National Preserve Visitor Center, 226

Yukon Game Farm & Wildlife Preserve (Whitehorse), 187

Yukon International Storytelling Festival (Whitehorse), 188

Yukon Motel (Teslin), 176-77

Yukon Queen II (Dawson City), 215-16

Yukon Quest Dog Sled Race: Fairbanks, 401; Whitehorse, 188

Yukon River Bathtub Race (Whitehorse), 188

Yukon River Quest Canoe Race (Whitehorse), 188

Yukon Summer Music Camp (Whitehorse), 186

Yukon Territory, 167-94; air travel to, 26, 170; buses to, 28-29, 170; driving to, 170; history, 168; map, 136; resources, 171-72; road and weather resources, 32; RV rentals, 171; smoking, 169; traveling to, 170-71; Web site, 21

Yukon Transportation Museum (Whitehorse), 186

Yukon Visitor Reception Centre/Alaska Highway Interpretive Centre (Watson Lake), 175

Contributors

Contributors

Author

Nancy Thalia Reynolds

From her first trip up the Inside Passage crewing on her father's sailboat, author Nancy Thalia Reynolds fell in love with Alaska and the Yukon. She has been returning for 25 years by sailboat, cruise ship, ferry, plane, and car, often accompanied by her family. A fifth-generation Pacific Northwesterner, Nancy graduated from Sarah Lawrence College and holds a law degree from York University in Toronto. After living in Canada for 16 years, she returned to the Pacific Northwest. Her articles, stories, and humorous essays on parenting, education, lifestyle, and family travel appear in publications across the U.S. She's the author of *Adopting Your Child* (Self-Counsel Press International, 1993) and coauthor of the fourth edition of *Going Places: Family Getaways in the Pacific Northwest* (Books for Parents, 2000). When she's not writing, Nancy enjoys traveling just about anywhere with her family. She resides in Shoreline, WA, with her husband, son, and daughter.

Our Contributors

Christian Boatsman

Christian Boatsman, a contributor on Alberta, British Columbia, and the Alaska Panhandle, resides in Petaluma, CA. He has traveled with his wife and their two children to Canada, Alaska, Yellowstone, the Rockies, Wyoming, and New England. Christian has a masters degree in film production and has worked as a professional sound editor, news cameraman, video documentary editor, and UNIX Systems Administrator...but he'd much rather travel.

Kevin Cain

Map designer Kevin Cain has been drawing since childhood; after high school he attended the School of Visual Concepts in Seattle. He has been freelancing for about 15 years with many maps to his credit. He lives in Seattle where he shares studio space with his son's Lego collection.

Jan Faull

Contributor Jan Faull, M.Ed., has been a parent educator for more than 25 years. Her weekly "Parenting" column appears in *The Seattle Times*. Jan is the parenting expert for *Ladies Home Journal's* online service and a family advisor to Disney's online service for parents, Family.com and author of books including *Unplugging Parent-Child Power Struggles* (Parenting Press, 2000). The mother of three grown children, she resides in Renton, WA.

Sara Heermans

One of our young contributors on the Kenai Peninsula and the daughter of contributor Rose Williamson, Sara Heermans lives in Seattle, WA, and has traveled to Alaska with her family. She is in the sixth grade and loves to write.

Jay Holtan

Jay Holtan, who writes about the Iditarod with his son Ryan, is a life-long Alaskan who has resided in Anchorage for more than five decades. He works for the local phone company; when he grows up, he wants to be a sporting-goods tester and provide material for Dilbert cartoons.

Ryan Holtan

Ryan Holtan, son of Jay Holtan, is a second-generation Alaskan with a deep love for the back country and the Iditarod. He is a recent graduate of West High School in Anchorage, where he was a member of the varsity cross-country ski team and a three-time participant in the national Junior Olympics.

Liz Kinneberg

Liz Kinneberg, who contributes a grandmother's perspective on northern travel, taught history and economics in the Los Angeles school district for 25 years before retiring. She now lives in Silver City, NM, with her husband, Dave. They enjoy taking trips to Alaska with extended family. Their most recent adventure was a fishing trip to Alaska's Lake Iliamna with their 12-year-old grandson.

Cheryl Loudermilk

Sitka-section contributor Cheryl Loudermilk has resided in Juneau, AK, since 1983. She is a volunteer with the Juneau Convention & Visitor's Bureau greeting visitors to Alaska's state capital. Her son, Elijah, started volunteering with her in 1995 at age 2. Both also volunteer with the Juneau-Douglas City Museum. Cheryl is a medical case manager, enjoys writing and has published poetry.

Bridjette March

Contributor Bridjette March shares tips gleaned from a lifetime in Alaska. Born and raised in Anchorage, she married her childhood sweetheart and, after a stint in Fairbanks, they raised two children in Anchorage. For 21 years, Bridjette owned a travel agency, traveled around the world, and wrote about travel. Alaska is her first love and Mount McKinley is her favorite spot on earth.

Betty Marriott

Our contributor on Kodiak and Unalaska, Betty Marriott moved to Alaska after college graduation with her biologist husband before the 1964 earthquake. Here, Betty raised two daughters and taught elementary school for more than 30 years. Today, she volunteers with the Juneau Convention & Visitor's Bureau, greeting cruise-ship passengers and assisting tourists at the city kiosk. Betty has written for *Alaskan Southeaster* magazine and contributed to books on Alaska.

Rose Williamson

An editor, reviewer, and contributor on southcentral Alaska, Rose Williamson is a Seattle writer and public-relations professional. She enjoys traveling with her husband and two daughters (and, often, her dog). She writes travel books "to point out all the joys—and the occasional pitfalls—of family travel." Rose coauthored *Going Places: Family Getaways in the Pacific Northwest*. She has enjoyed vacationing in southcentral Alaska with her family.

Emily Webb

The author's daughter and one of our younger contributors on cruise travel, Emily Webb lives in Shoreline, WA, with her parents and older brother, where she is now in the eigth grade. Emily has traveled widely and spent three long vacations in Alaska and the Yukon. She loves writing and traveling, especially by cruise ship.

Nicholas Webb

Teen-essay contributor Nicholas, Emily's older brother, also resides in Shoreline, WA, where he is now a senior in high school. He has traveled with his family, to Mexico, England, Wales, and Brazil, as well as destinations throughout the U.S. His biggest regret of a month-long family road trip to the Yukon via the Alaska Highway is that he didn't get to see the aurora borealis.

Kathy Webb

Cruise reviewer and aunt to Nicholas and Emily, Kathy Webb has lived in England and various European countries for many years and traveled extensively. A travel bug at heart, Kathy is stepmother to grown children who also enjoy traveling.

Brooke Whipple

Fairbanks-section contributor Brooke Whipple has fought fires in Montana, taught outdoor skills in Wisconsin, and worked the ski slopes in Colorado. Now residing in the Alaska interior; Brooke has served as a winter caretaker at a remote homestead in the Aleutians, a guide on a floating log raft on the Yukon River, and a recreation director at a resort. Her articles have appeared in *Backpacker* and *Canoe & Kayak* magazines, as well as local newspapers.

Acknowledgments

Acknowledgments

MANY PEOPLE GAVE me their time and expertise, steering me to family-friendly attractions in their communities, offering ideas and tips, and supporting me during the writing process. Providers of accommodation, dining, attractions, cruises, and transportation were unfailingly helpful. Tourist office and chamber of commerce staff throughout Alaska, British Columbia, and Yukon Territory, alerted me to popular hiking trails, parks with playgrounds, and gave tips on where to find free concerts and buy diapers. If they didn't have the answer to a query, they found someone who did. My heartfelt appreciation to all.

Some whose help went far beyond the call of duty or job description deserve special thanks. Carol Scafturon, Director of Visitor Information Services at the Juneau Convention & Visitor's Bureau, recruited excellent parent reviewers. Cruise-line staff at Carnival, Celebrity, Holland America, Norwegian Cruise Lines, Princess, and Royal Caribbean answered detailed queries. Aly Bello-Cabreriza at Carnival, who went out of her way to help me, deserves special mention. The folks at the Alaska Marine Highway System and the Travcon cruise-travel agency also lent their expertise.

The following Alaskans also offered valuable information and insight. In Ketchikan: Maggie Freitag at Parnassus Books, Debra Kinerk at the Southeast Alaska Discovery Center and her son, Vincent Kocinski, and Haida carver Lee Wallace at the Saxman Native Village; in Juneau: Mary Tonkovich at the Mendenhall Glacier Visitor Center and Theresa Walden of Gastineau Guiding; in Haines: Dave Olerud of the American Bald Eagle Foundation and Pam Moore of the Wild Strawberry Restaurant; in Delta Junction: Cheryl Cooper at the Sullivan Roadhouse Museum; in Girdwood: Carol Makar-Gibbs of Bud & Carol's B&B; in Homer: Jenny Stroyeck at The Bookstore; on Lake Louise: Pat Billman of the Point Lodge; in Seward: Leslie Hines of Kenai Fjords Tours; in Kodiak: Pam Foreman of the Kodiak Island Convention & Visitors Bureau; at the Wrangell-St.Elias National Park and Preserve: Thelma Schrank; in Fairbanks: Emma Wilson of the Fairbanks Aspen Hotel.

In British Columbia, thanks to Marianne Schildknecht of the Northern Rockies Lodge. In the Yukon Territory help was provided in Teslin by Tlingit carver Tom Dickson, Jr.; in Whitehorse: Meg O'Shea of the Yukon Arts Centre; in Haines Junction: Hans Nelles of the Raven; in Dawson City: Dick North, Curator of the Jack London Interpretive Centre.

Friends, relations, and acquaintances who lent a hand included Mike and Nancy Hubbard and Trish O'Gorman in Anchorage. Kathy Foster shared travel tips; her aunt, Mardee Roth in Fairbanks, was a goldmine of help and information (and her Fairbanks vegetable garden is awesome). Camille March of Seattle's Elliott Bay Book Company found researchers and regaled me with tales of growing up in Anchorage. Lisa DeGrace, of Oregon Episcopal Schools, helped me locate Alaska family travelers among the school's illustrious alumni. Alice Madsen, Highline Community College's Education Department Coordinator, steered me to parent education resources.

Thanks to many others too numerous to mention in Alaska, British Columbia, and Yukon Territory who patiently answered questions and contributed valuable facts and information by e-mail.

My special and very heartfelt thanks go to the team at Books for Parents: my wonderful editor, Virginia Smyth, sharp-eyed proofreader Irene Calvo, production whiz Emily Johnson, and visionary publisher Ann Bergman, who was willing to take a chance on this new project.

Finally, thanks to my husband, Michael Webb, who not only gave me the benefit of his knowledge of Alaskan port cities but cheerfully shouldered a disproportionate share of parenting and household tasks while I was away researching or holed up writing the book; and to my children, Nicholas and Emily, partners in adventure, who gracefully resigned themselves to extensive northern research trips and were glad, in the end, they did.

FEEDBACK

Going Places: Alaska and the Yukon for Families

WE ARE INTERESTED in your comments on using this guidebook. Did we leave out a wonderful destination? Is there something you'd like other families to know about a destination that we covered? Is there a restaurant that we should have included? A great place to stay that we missed? Or someplace that we included that isn't really worthy of mention? Please give us the details.

_____

_____

_____

_____

_____

_____

_____

_____

_____

_____

_____

_____

_____

_____

_____

_____

_____

Your name: _____

Address: _____

City/State/Zip: _____

Phone: _____

E-mail address: _____

Mail to: Bergman Books
           733 17th Ave. E.
           Seattle, WA 98112